Clinical Neuropsychology: A Practical Guide to Assessment and Management for Clinicians

Edited by

Laura H. Goldstein

*Department of Psychology, Institute of Psychiatry and
The Lishman Unit, Maudsley Hospital, London, UK*

and

Jane E. McNeil

*Department of Psychology, Institute of Psychiatry and
Regional Neurological Rehabilitation Unit, Homerton Hospital, London, UK*

WILEY

This publication is designed to provide accurate and authoritative information in regard to the subject
matter covered. It is sold on the understanding that the Publisher is not engaged in rendering
professional services. If professional advice or other expert assistance is required, the services of a
competent professional should be sought.

Coventry University

Other Wiley Editorial Offices

John Wiley & Sons Inc., 111 River Street, Hoboken, NJ 07030, USA

Jossey-Bass, 989 Market Street, San Francisco, CA 94103-1741, USA

Wiley-VCH Verlag GmbH, Boschstr. 12, D-69469 Weinheim, Germany

John Wiley & Sons Australia Ltd, 33 Park Road, Milton, Queensland 4064, Australia

John Wiley & Sons (Asia) Pte Ltd, 2 Clementi Loop #02-01, Jin Xing Distripark, Singapore 129809

John Wiley & Sons Canada Ltd, 22 Worcester Road, Etobicoke, Ontario, Canada M9W 1L1

Wiley also publishes its books in a variety of electronic formats. Some content that appears in print
may not be available in electronic books.

Library of Congress Cataloging-in-Publication Data

Clinical neuropsychology : a practical guide to assessment and
management for clinicians / edited by Laura H. Goldstein and Jane E. McNeil.
  p. cm.
  Includes bibliographical references and index.
  ISBN 0-470-85401-4 (Cloth) – ISBN 0-470-84391-8 (Paper : alk. paper)
  1. Clinical neuropsychology. I. Goldstein, Laura H. (Laura Hilary), 1960–
II. McNeil, Jane
  RC386.6.N48C52725 2003
  616.89 – dc21   2003007939

British Library Cataloguing in Publication Data

A catalogue record for this book is available from the British Library

ISBN 0-470-85401-4 (hbk)
ISBN 0-470-84391-8 (pbk)

Project management by Originator, Gt Yarmouth, Norfolk (typeset in 10/12pt Times)
Printed and bound in Great Britain by TJ International Ltd, Padstow, Cornwall
This book is printed on acid-free paper responsibly manufactured from sustainable forestry
in which at least two trees are planted for each one used for paper production.

Contents

About the Editors

Dr Laura H. Goldstein is Reader in Neuropsychology at the Institute of Psychiatry and Honorary Consultant Clinical Psychologist at the Maudsley Hospital. Here she has provided the clinical neuropsychology service to the Neuropsychiatry Unit at the Lishman Unit for over 15 years. For some of that time she also either worked in the epilepsy surgery programme at the Maudsley Hospital, or was attached to a regional neurology service. She is actively involved in pre- and post-qualification training of clinical psychologists. She devised and still runs the PG Diploma in Clinical Neuropsychology at the Institute of Psychiatry and has been involved in the developments in post-qualification training in clinical neuropsychology being planned by the British Psychological Society. She is actively involved in neuropsychological and other clinical research and has published widely, in areas including motor neurone disease, epilepsy and dissociative seizures, synaesthesia, bipolar disorder and dyspraxia, holding a number of research grants including from the Medical Research Council and Motor Neurone Disease Association.

After gaining clinical experience with a wide range of psychiatric conditions and receiving a clinical qualification from the Institute of Psychiatry, **Dr Jane E. McNeil** took up a position at the National Hospital for Neurology and Neurosurgery in London, where she specialized in the neuropsychological assessment of a wide range of neurological disorders. Subsequently, Dr McNeil became interested in the practical and treatment applications of theoretical Neuropsychology and moved first to Queen Elizabeth's Military Hospital, during this time publishing studies of confabulation and acquired disorders of calculation, and then to the Homerton University Hospital in London, where she has worked for the last eight years providing a specialist neuropsychological rehabilitation service to patients with single incident neurological disorders. She studied for her PhD on dyscalculia at the University of London under Professors E. K. Warrington and Robin Morris. She also currently works as a clinical lecturer in neuropsychological rehabilitation at the Institute of Psychiatry and teaches on the PG Diploma in Clinical Neuropsychology and the Doctorate in Clinical Psychology. Most recently Dr McNeil has been investigating the efficiency of outcome measures after brain injury and continuing investigations into dyscalculia.

List of Contributors

Dr Nick Alderman, *Consultant Clinical Psychologist, Kemsley National Brain Injury Rehabilitation Centre, St Andrew's Hospital, Northampton NN1 5DG, UK*

Dr Richard Brown, *Reader in Cognitive Neuroscience, Department of Psychology, PO77, The Henry Wellcome Building, Institute of Psychiatry, De Crespigny Park, London SE5 8AF, UK*

Dr Paul W. Burgess, *Reader in Cognitive Neuroscience, UCL Institute of Cognitive Neuroscience, Alexandra House, 17 Queen Square, London WC1N 3AR, UK*

Dr Nigel J. Cairns, *Center for Neurodegenerative Disease Research, University of Pennsylvania School of Medicine, 3600 Spruce Street, Philadelphia, PA 19104-4283, USA*

Professor John R. Crawford, *Department of Psychology, King's College, University of Aberdeen, Aberdeen AB24 2UB, UK*

Dr Jonathan J. Evans, *Associate Director of Research and Consultant Clinical Psychologist, Oliver Zangwill Centre for Neuropsychological Rehabilitation, Princess of Wales Hospital, Lynn Road, Ely, Cambs CB6 1DN, UK*

Dr Laura H. Goldstein, *Reader in Neuropsychology, Department of Psychology, PO77, The Henry Wellcome Building, Institute of Psychiatry, De Crespigny Park, London SE5 8AF, UK*

Dr Camilla Herbert, *Consultant Clinical Psychologist, Brain Injury Rehabilitation Trust, Market Place, Burgess Hill, West Sussex RH15 9NP, UK*

Dr Nigel S. King, *Consultant Clinical Psychologist, Community Head Injury Service, Bedgrove Health Centre, Jansel Square, Aylesbury, Bucks HP21 7ET, UK*

Dr Pat McKenna, *Consultant Neuropsychologist, Department of Clinical Psychology, Rookwood Hospital, Llandaff, Cardiff CF5 2YN*

Dr Jane E. McNeil, *Lecturer in Neuropsychology, Department of Psychology, PO77, The Henry Wellcome Building, Institute of Psychiatry, De Crespigny Park, London SE5 8AF and Regional Neurological Rehabilitation Unit, Homerton Hospital, Homerton Row, London E9 6SR, UK*

Dr Tom Manly, *Clinical Psychologist and Scientist, MRC Cognition and Brain Sciences Unit, Box 58, Addenbrooke's Hospital, Hills Road, Cambridge CB2 2QQ, UK*

Dr Jason B. Mattingley, *Senior Research Fellow, Department of Psychology, School of Behavioural Sciences, University of Melbourne, Victoria 3010, Australia*

Dr John D. C. Mellers, *Consultant Neuropsychiatrist, Department of Neuropsychiatry, Room 32, Outpatients Department, Maudsley Hospital, Denmark Hill, London SE5 8AZ, UK*

Dr Judith A. Middleton, *Consultant Clinical Neuropsychologist, Radcliffe Infirmary, Woodstock Road, Oxford OX2 6HE, UK*

Dr Esme Moniz-Cook, *Clinical Director and Reader in Clinical Psychology, Hull & Holderness Community Health NHS Trust, Coltman Street Day Hospital, Coltman Street, Kingston-upon-Hull HU3 2SG, UK*

Professor Robin G. Morris, *Department of Psychology, PO78, Institute of Psychiatry, De Crespigny Park, London SE5 8AF, UK*

Dr Graham E. Powell, *Consultant Clinical Psychologist, Psychology Service, 9 Devonshire Place, London W1N 1PB, UK*

Professor Jane Powell, *Department of Psychology, Goldsmiths College, Lewisham Way, New Cross, London SE14 6NW, UK*

Dr Jennifer M. Rusted, *Reader in Experimental Psychology, Laboratory of Experimental Psychology, School of Biological Sciences, University of Sussex, Brighton, Sussex BN1 9QG, UK*

Dr Andy D. Tyerman, *Consultant Clinical Neuropsychologist, Community Head Injury Service, Bedgrove Health Centre, Jansel Square, Aylesbury, Bucks HP21 7ET, UK*

Professor Barbara A. Wilson OBE, *Senior Scientist, MRC Cognition and Brain Sciences Unit, Box 58, Addenbrooke's Hospital, Cambridge CB2 2QQ, UK*

Preface

Although often viewed as a specialty within Clinical Psychology, it should be immediately apparent that knowledge of neuropsychology (and its applications) is relevant to all areas of clinical work where people (across the age span) might be showing some change in their cognitive functioning. Thus a working knowledge of neuropsychology and the assessment and management of cognitive impairment may be necessary for the delivery of a competent clinical service by even those practitioners who do not wish to see themselves as experts in the field of clinical neuropsychology and who may well have had little or no experience of clinical neuropsychology during their training as clinical psychologists. While we would argue that neuropsychological assessment should form part of the core skills acquired by all trainee clinical psychologists, our compilation of this volume is based on the more realistic appreciation of the training opportunities available to those who are both pre- and post-qualification, an appreciation gained through many years of being actively involved in both pre- and post-qualification training of clinical psychologists at the Institute of Psychiatry.

There are of course different ways in which to present information on clinical neuropsychological knowledge and practice. One is to focus on specific neurological disorders, and their assessment and management. Within the scope of a relatively short book, however, we feel that this may limit the apparent relevance and generalisability of the skills that we feel it is important for clinicians to possess. Thus for the current volume we have chosen to focus on broad areas of cognitive function (including those such as praxis and number processing and calculation, which are perhaps less well-developed areas of clinical neuropsychology in the UK), which may be relevant to assess across a wide range of neurological and psychiatric disorders. We have also chosen to include chapters that deal with important background information relevant to those being assessed (such as the effects of medication and the interaction between neurological and psychiatric presentations) and, because so much of clinical neuropsychologists' work does involve test interpretation, an overview of key psychometric concepts underpinning neuropsychological assessment.

In addition to addressing specific cognitive functions, it is of course obvious that clinical neuropsychology may be somewhat differently applied at different ends of the age spectrum, where different factors may assume particular importance. For this reason we have chosen to include specific chapters that address the issue of neuropsychological practice with children and older adults. At any point in the age range, neuropsychologists may be required to have an input into the medico-legal system, and for this reason we have included a very practical chapter dealing with the way in which such work should be undertaken.

Clinical neuropsychology is by no means all about assessment, as the chapters on specific cognitive functions will indicate, and the delivery of good rehabilitation services requires every bit as much the generic skills acquired during clinical psychology training as well as neuropsychology-specific ones. However, given the considerable development of neuropsychological rehabilitation, it is important to review the theoretical basis for effective cognitive rehabilitation, in an attempt to maintain an evidence-based approach to clinical practice, as well as to consider how psychotherapeutic interventions designed for use with non-brain-damaged people might be modified and applied to those with acquired brain injury. While most attempts at cognitive rehabilitation have been developed for patients with acquired but non-progressive brain injury, the growing literature on such approaches for adults with dementia, possibly supplemented by the so-called 'anti-dementia' drugs, opens up further areas of work for clinical psychologists. Finally, psychologists should increasingly see themselves as being in a position to inform the process of service planning and should have a good understanding of the service delivery models that may bring about effective care of their patients with neurological impairments.

We believe, however, that clinical neuropsychological practice is most effective when set in the context of more general neuroscientific knowledge and thus feel strongly that clinical neuropsychologists should have at least a basic understanding of neuropathology and the neurological investigations that their patients may well undergo. It is for this reason that two of the early chapters in this book present a relatively concise overview of the central nervous system and some of its common disorders and how these are investigated. While psychologists should never work outside their own area of clinical expertise, an understanding of how medical investigations can inform the design and interpretation of neuropsychological assessments and interventions can only benefit the service psychologists provide to their patients.

We are grateful to the contributors to this volume, many of whom have been actively involved over many years in different aspects of our training of clinical psychologists, for the importance that they, like us, attach to such training and dissemination of good practice. In practical terms we are very grateful to Gail Millard who has, good-humouredly, enabled us to convert very differently prepared manuscripts into a more consistent style and coped with our many revisions. Alex Dionysiou has helped us with the preparation of many of the figures. Finally we express our appreciation to our many colleagues, psychologists and non-psychologists alike, who over the years have set us good examples of how to work effectively as clinicians in our respective clinical settings.

Laura H. Goldstein
Jane E. McNeil

PART I

General Introduction

General Introduction: What Is the Relevance of Neuropsychology for Clinical Psychology Practice?

Laura H. Goldstein and Jane E. McNeil
Institute of Psychiatry, London, UK

WHY STUDY CLINICAL NEUROPSYCHOLOGY?

At this early stage in the 21st century, clinical neuropsychology is rightly finding its feet as a well-delineated and expanding clinical specialty within Clinical Psychology. It has moved away from the purely diagnostic role it acquired after the Second World War, to one in which the characterization of a person's functional strengths and weaknesses and the explanation of their behaviour have become central in extending the range of meaningful questions that can be posed about an individual patient's presentation. Clinical neuropsychology is now very much valued as not simply involving the assessment of cognitive abilities in patients with cerebral pathology, but also as playing a major role in the rehabilitation of such people. It is also contributing to the understanding of the impact on cognitive functioning of disorders hitherto conceptualized as psychiatric or 'functional' (rather than 'organic')—for example, depression or schizophrenia—and is being used to understand and hence possibly conceptualize in neuropsychological terms a variety of antisocial or maladaptive behaviours. Neuropsychology has expanded its area of enquiry beyond the testing room and into the implications of cognitive impairment for everyday life, with a range of tests that are striving to be more ecologically valid (e.g., Wilson et al., 1996) as well as environmentally based (Shallice & Burgess, 1991; Alderman et al., 2003).

It is therefore important that all clinical psychologists, and not just those working in specialist neuropsychological settings, have a basic grounding in neuropsychology. Perhaps the simplest way of illustrating the widespread application of neuropsychological skills comes from the types of questions that clinical psychologists might need to answer about their patients. Thus a clinical psychologist working in a primary care setting, being the first person to undertake a formal assessment of a patient, might need to determine whether their patient's complaint of poor memory represents a condition that merits referral for further investigation

Clinical Neuropsychology: A Practical Guide to Assessment and Management for Clinicians.
Edited by L.H. Goldstein and J.E. McNeil. © 2004 John Wiley & Sons, Ltd.

by a neurologist or is likely to represent the consequences of anxiety or depression. In an adult mental health setting, just as in a neuropsychiatry service, there may be the need to decide whether a newly developed memory disorder is psychogenically determined, perhaps even characteristic of factitious disorder or malingering. A clinical psychologist working with people with learning disabilities might need to be able to assess whether their patient's cognitive profile is indeed characteristic of a particular disorder (e.g., Down's syndrome), whether it represents the likely onset of the dementia that is often found in older adults with Down's syndrome or points to the impact of some additional, acquired neuropathology (e.g., a recent head injury). In a forensic setting the question for the clinical psychologist to address may well take the form of whether the person's offending behaviour could be accounted for by a previous head injury leading to impulsive behaviour characteristic of executive dysfunction. Working with older adults, the clinical psychologist may not only be trying to clarify whether the person's cognitive decline is representative of dementia rather than affective disorder, but may also need to detail the precise nature of any dementia. (e.g., Alzheimer's disease or frontotemporal dementia). In an alcohol abuse service the evaluation of a person's memory and executive dysfunction may have implications for their future treatment or placement. In child psychology settings the need may well be to clarify the impact of developmental as well as acquired neuropathology on educational and social development.

In all of these settings, a good grounding in the principles of neuropsychological assessment and test interpretation (see Chapter 6) will contribute to the delivery of an effective and professional service. This grounding may also, given service constraints, permit the formulation of appropriate interventions designed to ameliorate the cognitive difficulties delineated by means of the assessment, as well as through observations of the patient's everyday behaviour. In all such instances the clinical psychologist should be seeking to act as a scientist–practitioner, using the ever-growing neuropsychological literature on which to base hypotheses for their assessment and gathering information from as wide a range of sources as possible. As Walsh and Darby (1999) indicate, the clinical (neuro)psychologist may be setting out to confirm that certain features of the patient's presentation are consistent with a particular disorder or syndrome, to generate and then test their own hypotheses about the nature of the patient's deficits, or to decide between competing hypotheses about the person's deficits and their causes, often in a medico-legal setting of either a criminal or civil nature.

One of the main reasons that the clinical neuropsychologist's role has moved away from a strictly diagnostic one is the dramatic development in neuroimaging techniques that now offer markedly improved options for identifying structural and functional cerebral abnormalities (see Chapter 3). This has left clinical neuropsychologists free to develop a better understanding of the nature of different disorders and their neuropathological correlates. One example of this development is the careful study of different types of dementia, whereby distinctions have been made between Alzheimer's disease, vascular dementia, and frontotemporal dementias (and their variants), based both on formal neuropsychological test batteries and newly developed behavioural rating scales (e.g., Bathgate et al.,

2001; Grace & Malloy, 2001; Hodges, 2000; Hodges & Patterson, 1996; Hodges et al., 1992, 1999; Kertesz et al., 2000; Snowden et al., 2001; see pp. 12–15 and Chapter 4) as well as between dementias related to other neurodegenerative diseases (e.g., Hodges, 2000; Morris & Worsley, in press). There is now also much better understanding of how to assess psychogenically determined as opposed to organic memory impairment (see, for example, Chapter 7), which has implications both for interventions and medico-legal work, an area where clinical neuropsychologists can assume a very high profile (see Chapter 15).

It is inevitable that clinicians will develop differing approaches to the assessment and documentation of (and also interventions to deal with) their patients' cognitive impairments. This will arise through differing training experiences and both pre- and post-qualification clinical service constraints. In the following section, however, we will outline some of the principles we consider to be essential to the development of personal competence in the delivery of a service that is able to answer neuropsychological questions about patients. We will be focusing in large part on the assessment and interpretation of neuropsychological impairment.

COMMON ISSUES ACROSS DIFFERENT ASSESSMENTS

Irrespective of the specific referral, there are certain types of information that must be collected prior to the assessment in order for clinical psychologists to maximize their opportunity for collecting meaningful data. Here we will expand on, and add to, some of the very helpful suggestions made by Powell and Wilson (1994). Thus information should be collected on:

- *The intended purpose of investigation.* It is important to clarify with the referrer what information is being sought from an assessment, and it may well be necessary to reframe the referrer's question into one that is neuropsychologically meaningful and possible to answer, as neuropsychological assessments are time-intensive and should not be seen as 'trawling' exercises.
- *The patient's demographic variables* (e.g., age, handedness, education/qualifications, current/previous profession, cultural background), in order to set the context for the interpretation of current test performance. Additional information concerning developmental stage reached will be particularly important in the case of children (see Chapter 13).
- *The patient's previous as well as current medical history*, as this may also be relevant to the development of cognitive impairment, and also their history of alcohol and/or substance abuse.
- *The results of previous investigations* (e.g., neurological investigations, EEGs, CT/ MRI or functional brain scans, X-rays, biochemical tests—see Chapter 3 for a description of neurological investigations), and previous (as well as current) psychiatric diagnoses, all of which can assist in the formation of hypotheses about the patient's likely deficits, and so guide the assessment and its interpretation.

- *The results of previous neuropsychological assessments*—these can guide the choice of current tests and permit evaluation of change.
- *The history of the person's lesion/disorder* (e.g., site of trauma, age at and time since injury or onset of illness, history of epilepsy [either predating injury or post-traumatic] if relevant, whether or not anoxic episodes were associated with injury, length of post-traumatic amnesia [PTA] and retrograde amnesia, length of loss of consciousness, Glasgow Coma Scale scores and operation reports), since again these will assist in the formulation of hypotheses about the aetiology, nature and severity of the deficits that may be revealed by the examination.
- *Factors that might affect testing* (e.g., drug types and levels [see Chapter 5], the timing of the assessment in relation to drug ingestion, which may have a direct effect on whether or not the person can be assessed [e.g., in the case of drugs used to treat Parkinson's disease, where 'off' periods at the end of the drug's effectiveness may make assessment extremely difficult or impossible], recent epileptic seizure activity [if relevant], mood and motivation [see Chapter 4], motor/speech/visual problems [which may determine which tests are feasible to administer] and the patient's likely distractibility).
- *Informants' views of the person, their deficits and if/how they have changed*—many patients with acquired brain injury will have little insight into the reason for their referral for assessment/treatment, and the nature and/or extent of their own cognitive deficits. Thus informants may provide important information about the areas to be explored in the neuropsychological assessment (see Chapter 9).
- *The context in which the assessment takes place* (i.e., whether there are relevant compensation or other medico-legal factors that might affect the person's motivation during the assessment).

While not all of the information will be available in every case, it is important to gather as much information as possible prior to seeing the patient since, as indicated with respect to medico-legal work in Chapter 15, this also permits clarification with the patient of inconsistencies in the history and allows what may be a limited time in which to undertake an assessment to be used to cover the most important areas of that person's cognitive function.

The selection of the tests to be administered then needs to be based on:

- predictions of the likely range of deficits to be found, given what is known about the person's history, neurological investigations, presenting complaints and the neuropsychological profile of that particular disorder and other relevant disorders that may form part of a 'differential diagnosis';
- the time available in which to undertake the assessment (e.g., it may be practical to assess an inpatient on more than one occasion, but only one session may be possible, albeit less than desirable, for someone living at a great distance from the clinical setting) and the patient's likely tolerance of testing;
- the suitability of the test in terms of its standardization when compared with the patient (i.e., whether or not the patient is similar to the standardization sample in terms of IQ, age, etc.);
- the potential adaptability of the test to overcome problems posed by the patient's

motor/speech/sensory deficits and how this might affect interpretation of the results that are obtained;

- the need for an interpreter where the patient's first language is not the same as that of the psychologist or that in which the test is published/standardized;

- the tests that have previously been administered (i.e., one may need to use parallel forms of tests if they are available and consider the possibility that practice effects may be present on other measures, serving to mask deterioration);

- whether the patient is part of a research cohort (e.g., evaluating a neurosurgical intervention for epilepsy, deciding upon the suitability of the patient for pharmacological treatment of dementia—see Chapter 19), in which case a fixed protocol may be required for the assessment;

- whether it will be particularly important to use tests that are statistically inter-related (e.g., the Wechsler Test of Adult Reading, the Wechsler Adult Intelligence Scale—3rd edition [WAIS-III] and the Wechsler Memory Scale—3rd edition [WMS-III], see Chapters 6, 7 and 14) or whether this would pose too taxing an assessment load for the patient to yield interpretable data, in which case other tests might be more suitable;

- what is then found during the assessment (i.e., one may wish to follow up on specific findings with further standardized tests or the development of more idiosyncratic measures using a single case design).

It will not be uncommon for a clinician to develop greater familiarity with some tests than with others (see also Chapter 9), but clinicians should remain open to the need to be flexible in their choice of tests when this enables them better to answer the clinical question being posed in an individual case. It is also important to remain up to date with the development of new neuropsychological tests and to be aware of the psychometric implications of changing between older and newer versions of similar tests for the interpretation of between-assessment results. An important example of this is the difference in IQ scores yielded by different versions of the Wechsler Adult Intelligence Scale.

There is also a clear balance to be drawn between undertaking an adequate assessment and over-assessing a patient. It is a frequent mistake for inexperienced clinical neuropsychologists to suppose that the more tests given the better. It is also not uncommon to see reports where patients have been subjected to hours and hours of testing. This is rarely necessary. If after several hours of testing one is still unsure of what to conclude, it will normally be more informative to gather other types of data such as direct behavioural observation or to interview staff or relatives of the patient rather than to reach for yet another standardized test. However, considerable importance also needs to be attached to the overall scope of the assessment in being able to rule out the presence of cognitive impairment. Thus one should always be aware that deficits, for which the patient has not been assessed, cannot be ruled out definitively. Teuber's widely cited view (see, for example, Walsh & Darby, 1999) that 'absence of evidence is not evidence of absence (of impairment)' continues to be an important reminder that generalizations cannot be made from limited assessments. Clinicians should always specify the factors limiting their interpretations, making it clear to the reader exactly what tests were undertaken as part of their assessment of the patient.

We will now address a number of other important issues, which also arise when interpreting and reporting the results of a neuropsychological assessment:

- One should not over-interpret minor discrepancies between test scores. It is common to see in reports that a patient who scores at the 10th percentile on one measure is then felt to be significantly relatively impaired on other measures, on which they score at the 5th or 2nd percentile. The difference in reliability of different tests means that such small differences may not necessarily be interpretable in terms of trying to identify specific deficits (see also Chapter 9). In addition, likely premorbid levels of functioning need to be taken into account when trying to decide whether a currently average level score represents intact performance or evidence of change following acquired neuropathology (see Chapter 6 for a further discussion of important psychometric concepts to consider in test interpretation).
- It is important not to rely on test scores alone when deciding whether an impairment is present. Any clinical neuropsychological report should make some reference to the behaviour of the patient during testing and the manner in which they go about solving the tasks and should give at least some brief details of difficulties the patient is reporting in everyday life. Shallice and Burgess (1991) described three patients with strategy application disorder who performed normally on traditional neuropsychological tests including many measures of executive functions, but nevertheless had profound difficulties in everyday life (see Chapter 9 for further details). These cases illustrated the potential danger in over-reliance on formal test performance in deciding whether the patients did or did not have neuropsychological deficits.
- Similarly, a diagnosis should never be made purely on the basis of neuropsychological test results. There are many different reasons that patients may fail tests, so it is never sufficient to rely purely on test performance. If a patient shows a pattern of performance that would be consistent with a particular disorder, then the most that can be concluded is that their performance is *consistent with* that disorder, not that they *have* the disorder (see also Chapter 9). Similarly, neuropsychological tests results should never be used by a clinical (neuro)psychologist to make a diagnosis for which there is no *a priori* medical basis, as they will be acting outside their area of expertise and place themselves at risk of disciplinary and other action.
- One should not be afraid to conclude that test performance cannot determine what the causal factors are in a patient's current problems. For example, in the case of a patient with a history of psychosis and current cognitive problems or learning difficulties who then has a moderate head injury, it may not be possible to tease out to what extent current problems existed premorbidly or were recently acquired, apart from by relying on the reports of relatives, friends or staff who knew the patient before the head injury. Similarly, medication effects (see Chapter 5) may exaggerate or obscure certain deficits. There is nothing distinctive about

neuropsychological tests that means they are *only* failed by patients with some kind of acquired brain injury.

- It is also important to acknowledge that more than one assessment may be necessary in order to arrive at an accurate interpretation of a patient's difficulties; this is often the case when attempting to distinguish, for example, between a developing dementia and depression. Here a further assessment, once an affective disorder has been treated effectively, may permit clarification of whether the person is demonstrating a progressive, neurodegenerative condition (see Chapters 4 and 14 for further discussion).

- It is not uncommon to see reports that conclude that, because a patient passes tests of malingering, they cannot be faking a bad performance; this is incorrect. If the tests of malingering were developed by asking normal controls to fake a bad performance, then it does not necessarily follow that a patient with a mild injury who is trying to accentuate a deficit on formal testing will perform in the same way.

- A consistently perfect correspondence between CT/MRI scan results and performance on formal neuropsychological tests does not exist (which is not surprising as they are measuring very different things—see Chapter 9—and different types of scan may be more sensitive to particular types of neuropathology than others—see Chapter 3). It is therefore possible to find patients who have normal structural brain scans with significant cognitive deficits, or the converse pattern of a patient with an abnormality on brain scanning but intact performance on formal cognitive tests. Evidence from a brain scan should not be used to confirm or disconfirm the validity of observed cognitive deficits, but rather to offer possible hypotheses as to why the observed deficits may be occurring; test sensitivity and premorbid levels of ability may be factors that need to be considered in interpreting the correspondence or otherwise between different forms of assessment.

- Although many neuropsychological tests are now supposedly ecologically valid, very few provide any formal evidence to support this claim (with the notable exception of some of the Thames Valley Test Company tests such as the Behavioural Assessment of Dysexecutive Syndrome [BADS; Wilson et al., 1996] and the Rivermead Behavioural Memory Test [Wilson et al., 1985]). Great care should therefore be taken before drawing conclusions about how a patient will function in everyday life based on neuropsychological test performance alone. For example, it may be reasonable to expect that perceptual or executive deficits may impact on someone's driving abilities, but a decision as to whether someone is competent to drive should never be taken purely on neuropsychological test performance.

- Remember that a clinical (neuro)psychologist is an independent professional in their own right, with a responsibility to the patients they assess and treat. One should not be afraid to question the appropriateness of referrals. It is always best to take responsibility for providing feedback of one's test results oneself since other professions are far less likely to have the in-depth understanding of neuropsychological tests, although it should be *medical* practitioners who deliver *medical* diagnoses if multi-disciplinary feedback sessions are not possible. Issues relevant to the provision of feedback to people with neuropsychological impairments are discussed by Gass and Brown (1992).

- Interpretation of neuropsychological assessments will be enhanced in certain cases by a good working knowledge of psychiatric disorders, their presentation and diagnosis.

It would be difficult to illustrate the relevance of all the above suggestions for clinical practice in such a short chapter. What follows is a selection of case examples highlighting a number of the points we have made above and demonstrating the diverse issues that assessments may raise.

CASE EXAMPLES

Social Problems or the Consequences of a Previous Head Injury?
The Importance of a Good History

Ms Y, a 32-year-old, right-handed single mother, was referred for a neuropsychological assessment as a preliminary part of care proceedings being undertaken by the local authority in connection with her three children whose behaviour she was having difficulty controlling. Despite considerable social services input she was unable to manage her household affairs. Another clinical psychologist had wondered whether a neuropsychological assessment might be warranted by Ms Y's apparently disorganized behaviour and had heard that Ms Y had sustained a head injury many years previously. Little other information was available about her history, so Ms Y gave consent for her GP records to be obtained. It was these records that provided some of the information indicated in Chapter 3 as being very important in understanding her presentation.

Although Ms Y's GP queried the value of the release of her medical records since 'all her problems were social ones', her records indicated that, at the age of 17 years, she had sustained a significant head injury as a pedestrian and was unconscious for 10 days. Only after a further 10 days or so could she begin to co-operate with instructions and speak short sentences. Her physical progress was good, but she retained some facial asymmetry and slurred speech. At the time an IQ assessment (test unspecified) yielded an IQ of 110, but she was reported to show a marked emotional deficit, lack of drive and initiative, an increased tendency toward immature behaviour and dependence and two years later was still felt to have very little insight into her deficits. She was unable to continue to train as a secretary as she was slow and forgetful and showed insufficient initiative. Her social life was severely curtailed following the accident. There were, therefore, sufficient behavioural descriptions from her medical records to suggest residual, significant deficits resulting from what was an apparently severe head injury.

Although no scanning information was available to demonstrate any long-term neuropathological sequelae of her apparently severe head injury, the requested neuropsychological assessment was undertaken with a view to determining whether deficits could be elicited that would be consistent with a dysexecutive syndrome (see Chapter 9). Her behaviour during testing was rather distractible, and she was unable to pick up on social cues to indicate that she should cease chatting and continue with the tests.

On the WAIS-R, Ms Y obtained a Verbal IQ (VIQ) of 101 and a Performance IQ (PIQ) of 96. Her premorbid estimated WAIS-R IQ on the basis of her reading ability on the National Adult Reading Test was 115 for Verbal IQ and 116 for Performance IQ. There was therefore some slight suggestion of an overall reduction in her general level of intellectual ability.

Given the early descriptions of Ms Y's memory difficulties, and the common association between acquired memory impairment and head injury, a number of memory tests were administered. Ms Y's ability to recall a short story from the Adult Memory and Information Processing Battery (AMIPB) was above average (between the 75th and 90th percentile) for both immediate and delayed recall. However, learning of a list of 15 words revealed no consistent strategy for encoding the words, and overall learning was only at the 10th percentile. Immediate and delayed recall of a complex geometric figure were at the upper end of the average range, but learning of an abstract design fell between the 2nd and 10th percentile and was characterized by frequent errors and perseverations of previously incorrect lines.

In terms of her performance on measures of executive functioning, despite performance on the Controlled Oral Word Association Test (COWAT) consistent with that predicted on the basis of her reading ability (Crawford et al., 1992) and completion of Parts A and B of the Trail Making Test that fell in the 50th to 75th percentile range, completion of the Stroop Test was only at the 4th percentile and performance on a test of cognitive estimates was impaired relative to controls. She also failed several subtests from the BADS, showing poor planning, sequencing and rule-following ability.

Thus despite Ms Y's IQ remaining in the average range, her head injury was likely to have produced lasting impairment, particularly in the domain of executive functioning, whereby she had difficulty in organizing information to be remembered, in undertaking cognitive estimation tasks where checking the plausibility of a response is required when the person has to use everyday information to answer a question (Shallice, 1988), in inhibiting unwanted responses and in planning tasks that require a strategy for their effective completion. She had never received any rehabilitation after her head injury (indeed appropriate cognitive rehabilitation of the sort described in Chapter 9 would not have been available to her at that time), and it was likely that, in an unstructured and less predictable everyday situation, her deficits would have had more marked impact on her everyday functioning, making it more difficult for her to care effectively for her children. Understanding the nature of her head injury and its immediate sequelae had been particularly helpful in this case in terms of trying to identify the likely origin of her everyday difficulties, although, in the absence of neuroimaging data, it was not possible to say with certainty that she had sustained damage specifically to the frontal lobes (see Chapter 9).

Distinguishing between Dementias: Matching Test Results to Disorder Profiles

Mrs A was a 55-year-old, right-handed woman who had obtained a first-class degree in Classics and then a further degree in History at Oxford University. She had gone on to work as a journalist for two major broadsheet newspapers and had subsequently worked in radio broadcasting until the age of 51, when she retired due to stress-related difficulties that took the form of panic attacks. Her history did not permit evaluation of whether these might have been accounted for by incipient cognitive difficulties. Mrs A's husband had retired about two years earlier with physical health difficulties. There was no family history of dementia.

Mrs A was referred for assessment via her local community mental health team who were treating her for depression, as they were concerned that she was developing a semantic dementia. Her husband was reporting that he felt her intellect had become 'rather ordinary' in comparison to the superior level it had been. She had become more socially withdrawn, was apparently less good at conversation than previously and was complaining of word-finding difficulties.

Prior to her referral for a neuropsychological assessment, an MRI scan had shown 'global cerebral atrophy, with more volume loss in the left than the right cerebral hemisphere'. There was no history of procedural, episodic or topographic memory impairment although some episodes of confusion had been reported when playing card games; Mrs A was reported as not knowing which way round the table they were playing or who was to play next.

A particularly significant neuropsychological development in recent years has been the delineation of the cognitive profiles in different types of dementia. This has permitted discriminations between frontotemporal dementias and more posterior dementing processes (notably Alzheimer's disease), and within the frontotemporal dementias there are detailed studies of individuals with semantic dementia and progressive non-fluent aphasia. The main features of these dementia types are described in the literature and summarized briefly in Table 1.1.

Based on the descriptions of these different dementia types, and adopting a hypothesis-testing approach, Mrs A underwent a comprehensive neuropsychological assessment, which aimed to examine the characteristics of semantic dementia and determine the extent to which she was impaired on tests of the relevant functions. Many of the papers that have described these disorders have used experimentally derived test materials (e.g., Hodges & Patterson, 1996; Hodges et al., 1992, 1999), whereas here clinically available tests were used.

During conversation, word-finding difficulties and pauses were apparent, with some semantic circumlocutions. Nonetheless, Mrs A's speech was easily produced and well articulated with appropriate prosody. A number of other findings from the assessment were consistent with a possible diagnosis of semantic dementia. These included worse verbal than visuospatial memory (WMS-R Verbal Index = 59, Visual Memory Index = 110) and impaired naming (13/30 on the Graded Naming Test and 9/15 on Naming from Description; see Chapter 8 for further description of naming tests). In addition, Mrs A was impaired at category fluency to a greater extent than letter-based fluency. She produced disjointed prose when

Table 1.1. Key features of different types of dementia of relevance to Mrs A's diagnosis

	Frontal variant of fronto-temporal dementia	Temporal variant of fronto-temporal dementia (semantic dementia; progressive fluent aphasia)	Progressive non-fluent aphasia	Alzheimer's disease (see also Chapter 14)
Memory	Typically unaffected early in the disease. Early mild impairments likely to be in episodic memory with normal semantic memory	Episodic memory (recall of recent events, recent autobiographical information) relatively well preserved	Relatively well-preserved autobiographical (and day-to-day) episodic memory. Short-term auditory–verbal memory severely disrupted	Impaired or poor anterograde episodic memory often the first feature, semantic memory may be relatively unimpaired early on, but patients ultimately show impairment on tests of semantic memory. Memory for both verbal and visual material impaired in most cases
Language	Language dysfunction is an early, subtle sign. Decreased verbal output, with 'factually empty speech' occurs. Worse letter fluency than category fluency. Mild anomia, but repetition is normal. Comprehension may eventually become impaired. Repetitive speech (spontaneous echolalia). Articulation, phonology and syntax usually preserved	Early word-finding difficulties lead to anomia. Initially, there are mild word-finding difficulties and circumlocutory discourse. As disease progresses, comprehension problems develop and speech becomes stereotyped. Syntax and phonology preserved. Reading irregular words impaired ('surface dyslexia'). Category fluency more impaired than letter fluency	Severe early impairment, with phonological errors, agrammatical sentence structure and disturbed articulation. Phonemic approximations occur when naming. Initially, normal single word comprehension, but there is markedly impaired syntactic comprehension. Letter fluency is more impaired than category fluency	Relatively well-preserved phonology and syntax, but syntax becomes simplified. Conversation initially circumlocutory and later becomes vague and meaningless. Irregular word reading is relatively well preserved until very advanced disease. Category fluency very sensitive to early Alzheimer's disease, while letter fluency is better preserved. Naming to verbal description may yield deficits. Ultimately mutism may occur
Non-verbal skills	Even late in the disease, visuospatial and visual perceptual functions remain normal	Well-preserved constructional, perceptual and visuospatial abilities. Non-verbal semantic knowledge impaired	Non-verbal semantic knowledge well preserved	Visuospatial and visual constructional deficits found

Source: Hodges (2000), Hodges & Patterson (1996), Hodges et al. (1992, 1996, 1999)

asked to describe the Cookie Theft Picture and her auditory comprehension, also assessed using the Boston Diagnostic Aphasia Battery, was impaired.

However, a number of results were not consistent with a diagnosis of semantic dementia. Thus her delayed visuospatial recall (20th percentile) was worse than immediate recall (99th percentile). With respect to IQ measures, there was no difference between PIQ and VIQ scores (PIQ = 95, VIQ = 96, whereas VIQ is thought to show more impairment than PIQ in semantic dementia); in addition, Information and Vocabulary were the best preserved subtests (age scaled scores of 12), while Digit Span and Arithmetic were the least well-preserved verbal subtests (age scaled subtests 6 and 7, respectively), which again is not an expected pattern for semantic dementia. Her PIQ age-scaled subtest scores ranged between 4 and 9. In addition, Mrs A was not impaired at reading the National Adult Reading Test words, making only three errors. Mrs A also passed a measure of non-verbal semantic knowledge, the pictures version of the Pyramids and Palm Trees test (score 51/52) and was able to match written and spoken words and pictures from the Psycholinguistic Assessment of Language Processing in Aphasia test (PALPA) (spoken 40/40; written 40/40). Mrs A was impaired on the Modified Token Test (scoring 11/15) and on the Test for Reception of Grammar (TROG) (passed only 16 blocks), and was poor at reading sentences and paragraphs; she made mistakes on more complex items requiring understanding of more complicated syntax. There was also evidence of executive dysfunction (Trails B was completed in a time that fell below the 10th percentile) and she was classified as 'Impaired' on the Brixton Test, yet was still at the 'Moderate Average' level on the Hayling Sentence Completion Test.

Clearly, the results of this assessment were not clear-cut and demonstrated features that might have been consistent with both semantic dementia and a more typical Alzheimer's disease, and it was therefore felt that at this stage no firm conclusion could be reached. A year later, Mrs A had demonstrated further decline in VIQ but not PIQ, but she had shown further decline in visuospatial memory. Speed of language processing had deteriorated, as had her verbal fluency (letter and category) and naming to description. Single word comprehension remained intact as did her ability to match words to pictures and her access to non-verbal semantic knowledge. Comprehension of verbal material was limited to simpler statements, and oral and written communication was lacking in structure with missing nouns, agrammatic errors and a paucity of content. Thus her profile continued not to fit entirely with any one form of dementia, and, while her anomia, category fluency deficits and diminishing vocabulary and verbal comprehension remained consistent with a semantic dementia diagnosis, it was felt that an atypical form of non-fluent progressive aphasia might have been more descriptive of her difficulties, given her increasing impairment of syntactic comprehension, agrammatism and anomia.

One approach that was not taken in this woman's assessment, but which has received increasing attention, is the use of behavioural profiles in distinguishing between dementia types (e.g., Bathgate et al., 2001; Snowden et al., 2001). These informant-interview-based measures permit discrimination between frontotemporal dementia, Alzheimer's disease and to some extent vascular dementia (Bathgate et al., 2001) and between frontotemporal and semantic dementia (Snowden et al., 2001).

Post-concussional Syndrome or Post-traumatic Stress Disorder after a Mild Head Injury? The Importance of Knowing about Psychiatric as Well as Neurological Diagnoses

Mr P was a 25-year-old, right-handed man who was a passenger involved in a road traffic accident six months earlier. He had sustained a mild head injury with a short loss of consciousness (10–15 minutes) and orthopaedic injuries, which required an eight-week stay in hospital. The driver of the car, who was a close friend of Mr P, was killed in the accident.

Prior to the accident, Mr P was working as an IT consultant. He had been off work for four months after the accident and had recently returned to work, but found he was encountering problems. He had been to see his GP because he was aware of difficulties with his memory and concentration, as well as increased irritability. He was not sleeping, was experiencing headaches and he reported feeling anxious. His GP had referred him for a neurological opinion and a CT scan, which was reported to be normal. The neurologist referred him for a neuropsychological opinion.

In view of the severity of the accident and the death of his close friend, the differential diagnosis was between post-traumatic stress disorder (PTSD) and post-concussional syndrome (PCS). The cardinal features of PTSD (e.g., DSM-IV, American Psychiatric Association, 1994) are intrusive thoughts or nightmares about the event and avoidance of situations related to it, combined with symptoms of heightened arousal. Some authors such as Sbordone and Liter (1995) have claimed that PTSD does not occur following mild traumatic brain injuries since there is usually amnesia for the precipitating event. However, more recent studies have suggested that PTSD can occur even with severe head injuries where there is amnesia for the event (McMillan, 1996; McNeil & Greenwood, 1996) (see also Chapter 3, this volume, p. 83).

PCS is a term used to refer to range of symptoms that may arise after mild traumatic brain injury (where loss of consciousness is less than 20 minutes and PTA less than 1 hour). These include headache, insomnia, sensitivity to noise, poor memory and concentration, irritability and anxiety and depression. For most cases these symptoms will resolve within a few weeks of the injury, but a minority of patients may still show symptoms several months later (e.g., Gronwall & Wrightson, 1980).

On interview, Mr P could not remember the accident itself, but he could remember arriving at his local Accident and Emergency department by ambulance and had reasonable memory for events after this, suggesting a PTA of less than one hour. He reported feeling very distressed about the death of his close friend. He was experiencing some anxiety when travelling as a passenger in a car, and he was more reluctant to travel by car than he had been before the accident. However, he did not report any re-experiencing phenomena such as nightmares, 'flashbacks' or intrusive thoughts about the accident. This lack of any re-experiencing symptoms would preclude a diagnosis of PTSD.

On formal neuropsychological assessment, Mr P performed a little below his estimated premorbid level of functioning on a shortened version of the WAIS-R (VIQ 99, PIQ 83, NART [National Adult Reading Test] IQ equivalent 112). He was found to have particular difficulty with strictly timed tasks, and he performed very poorly in terms of his backwards digit span.

Mr P was found to have mild memory problems on formal testing. He performed poorly on immediate recall of the story and figure from the AMIPB (AMIPB story recall <10th percentile, figure recall <2nd percentile), although he did not show any further loss of information after a 30-minute delay. He also had difficulties with the Doors and Names recognition subtests from the Doors and People test (Doors: between the 5th and 10th percentile; Names: at the 5th percentile).

His visual perceptual and visuospatial skills were satisfactory (Visual Object and Space Perception Battery [VOSP]) Object Decision 18/20, Position Discrimination 19/20), and he did not show any language difficulties in spontaneous speech or on naming to confrontation (Graded Naming Test, 23/30).

His performance on tests of executive functioning was poor. He obtained a poor score on the Brixton Test (error score = 26, scaled score = 2), and he had marked difficulties with the Hayling Sentence Completion Test (overall scaled score = 1). His verbal fluency was a little lower than that predicted by his reading ability (Crawford et al., 1992). He also had problems with tests of speed and concentration and was slow and inaccurate on the AMIPB Information Processing subtest.

Mr P did not rate himself as depressed on the Hospital Anxiety and Depression Scale (HADS), but he did rate himself as mildly anxious (HADS depression score = 5, anxiety score = 10).

Thus Mr P was exhibiting significant cognitive difficulties on formal testing with memory, concentration and executive impairments that confirmed the everyday problems he had reported. This degree of cognitive impairment would not be expected to be observed simply as a result of PTSD. He was exhibiting anxiety symptoms, and he was avoiding some situations related to the accident itself. However, as already indicated, the lack of re-experiencing phenomena such as nightmares, 'flashbacks' or intrusive thoughts would preclude a diagnosis of PTSD. He was therefore felt to be suffering from the residual effects of his mild brain injury combined with additional emotional problems arising from the death of his close friend. Mr P was given education about head injury and strategies for coping with his memory and attentional problems. He was also given advice about attempting a more gradual return to work and offered counselling sessions to address emotional issues. Jones (1974) found that only 1% of patients with mild head injuries showed persistent symptoms at one year. It was therefore recommended that he be reassessed after a further six months to ensure that his symptoms had disappeared.

CLINICAL NEUROPSYCHOLOGY AS A PROFESSIONAL SPECIALTY: WHO IS A CLINICAL NEUROPSYCHOLOGIST?

The discussion so far has dealt with issues relevant to the day-to-day practice of clinical neuropsychology, with respect to how one should go about one's work. However, given the growing specialization of clinical neuropsychology, the issue of professional competence and titles becomes increasingly important.

In the USA there has existed for some time a clear definition of who is a clinical neuropsychologist (American Psychological Association [APA], Division of Clinical Neuropsychology, 1989). This emphasizes the doctoral level of didactic and experiential training that will have been undertaken in both neuropsychology and neuroscience at an accredited university, the acquisition of at least two years of appropriate, supervised training where the person is delivering clinical neuro-psychological services, peer review of their competencies and the compliance with local requirements for licensing and certification in the state in which the person practises. The APA's Division of Clinical Neuropsychology indicates the value placed upon the acquisition of the American Board of Clinical Neuropsychology (ABCN)/American Board of Professional Neuropsychology (ABPN) Diploma in Clinical Neuropsychology as providing the clearest evidence that their criteria have been met.

A number of European countries have developed graduate and postgraduate training programmes (see, for example, Kaschel et al., 1994). In the UK, moves to professionalize clinical neuropsychology as a specialty have only relatively recently become this sophisticated. These have taken the form of the development of formal, post-qualification training for clinical psychologists who are keen, or who need, to be seen as experts within this field. The British Psychological Society's (BPS) Division of Neuropsychology has now developed a Practitioner Full Membership qualification for those who wish to be seen to have achieved a recognized level of competence in the field. A substantial number of people will have acquired this prior to the end of 2003 through 'grandparenting' clauses, which recognizes that they will have:

- been a Fellow, Associate Fellow or Graduate Member of the BPS;
- been eligible to be a Chartered Clinical Psychologist or be a Full Member of one of the BPS's other divisions (but not the Division of Teachers and Researchers in Psychology) with a background relevant to clinical neuropsychology; and have
- been engaged in clinical neuropsychological practice for a period of two years full-time or its equivalent part-time.

People trained overseas may, with a statement of equivalence, have satisfied these criteria if eligible to be a member of one of the BPS's divisions (see BPS Membership and Qualifications Board, 2002a). By the end of 2003, those who have not already met these criteria will have to follow a post-qualification training route leading to an advanced professional qualification in the field of clinical neuropsychology. There will be two forms of this Membership qualification: (i) Adult Clinical Neuropsychology and (ii) Paediatric Clinical Neuropsychology. The full regulations and syllabus for these new Practitioner Full Membership Qualifications have been outlined (BPS Membership and Qualifications Board, 2002b), but essentially those aiming to possess these qualifications will have to:

- have acquired Graduate Basis for registration in the BPS and be registered as a Chartered Clinical Psychologist (in the case of the Adult qualification), or have acquired Graduate Basis for registration in the BPS and be registered as a Chartered Clinical Psychologist or as a Chartered Educational Psychologist (in the case of the Paediatric qualification);
- satisfy the BPS Board of Examiners that he or she can demonstrate possession of underpinning knowledge relevant to clinical neuropsychology usually, but not exclusively, by having completed a part-time, university-based accredited course (MSc or Postgraduate Diploma);
- submit a neuropsychological research portfolio comprising a clinical neuropsychological research report, a research log and supporting evidence in the form of research files (or satisfy the research component by being able to otherwise demonstrate their neuropsychological research skills, in specified ways); and
- submit a portfolio providing evidence of their clinical competence, comprising a case log, including a summary sheet, a clinical supervision log and six detailed case studies.

Obviously anyone seeking to enrol for this qualification should seek to obtain the most up-to-date guidelines available at that time, but it is clear that this qualification is being seen as a means of identifying both competent practitioners and the requirements of competent practice. Ultimately, it may permit regulation of the practice of clinical neuropsychology in the UK (BPS Membership and Qualifications Board, 2002b) and may clearly influence the principles of ethical practice by which clinical neuropsychologists work and against which they may face disciplinary action.

Indeed, the BPS's Division of Neuropsychology (2000) has already set out guidelines for professional practice in the field of clinical neuropsychology. While always subject to development and revision, these guidelines emphasize the importance of the level of competence and experience of the person wishing to offer clinical neuropsychological services and the need to seek supervision from a Practitioner Full Member of the Division of Neuropsychology where such experience might be lacking, both with respect to administration and interpretation of neuropsychological tests. In addition, eligibility for Practitioner Full Membership of the Division of Neuropsychology is seen as justification for the clinician to see himself or herself as competent to act as an expert witness in medico-legal matters (see also Chapter 15).

Of course, not everyone required to demonstrate neuropsychological knowledge in their clinical work in non-neuropsychology settings will wish (or find it possible) to acquire the Practitioner Full Membership qualification. However, this should certainly not dissuade clinical psychologists from acquiring sufficient skills in neuropsychological assessment and test interpretation in order to, within the boundaries of their level of competence, undertake effective pieces of work with their patients and know when to refer on to more specialist services.

CONCLUSIONS

This is a particularly interesting time to be presenting an overview of key areas of clinical neuropsychological practice and its relevance to clinical psychology practice in general. This is because of the enormous development of the neuroscientific context in which neuropsychology is housed, the increasingly sophisticated neuro-psychological assessment techniques available and the considerable strides made in developing evidence-based treatments for patients with neuropsychological impair-ments. It is an area of clinical work in which clinical psychologists can see themselves as uniquely skilled and able to make an important contribution to the overall care of their patients.

REFERENCES

Alderman, N., Burgess, P. W., Knight, C. & Henman, C. (2003) Ecological validity of a simplified version of the multiple errands shopping test. *Journal of the International Neuropsychological Society*, **9**, 31–44.

American Psychiatric Association (1994) *Diagnostic and Statistical Manual of Mental Disorders* (4th edition—DSM-IV). American Psychiatric Association, Washington, DC.

American Psychological Association, Division of Neuropsychology (1989) Definition of a clinical neuropsychologist. *The Clinical Neuropsychologist*, **3**, 22.

Bathgate, D., Snowden, J. S., Varma, A., Blackshaw, A. & Neary, D. (2001) Behaviour in frontotemporal dementia, Alzheimer's disease and vascular dementia. *Acta Neurologica Scandinavica*, **103**, 367–378.

BPS Division of Neuropsychology (2000) *Professional Practice Guidelines*. British Psychological Society, Leicester, UK.

BPS Membership and Qualifications Board (2002a) *Division of Neuropsychology. Guidelines for Interim Provisions Pertaining to the New Practitioner Full Membership Qualification in Clinical Neuropsychology*. British Psychological Society, Leicester, UK.

BPS Membership and Qualifications Board (2002b) *Regulations and Syllabus for the Division of Neuropsychology Practitioner Full Membership Qualification*. British Psychological Society, Leicester, UK.

Crawford, J. R., Moore, J. W. & Cameron, I. M. (1992) Verbal fluency: A NART-based equation for the estimation of premorbid performance. *British Journal of Clinical Psychology*, **31**, 327–329.

Gass, C. G. & Brown, M. C. (1992) Neuropsychological test feedback to patients with brain dysfunction. *Psychological Assessment*, **4**, 272–277.

Grace, J. & Malloy, P. F. (2001) *FrSBe. Frontal Systems Behavior Scale*. Psychological Assessment Resources Inc., Lutz, FL.

Gronwall, D. & Wrightson, P. (1980) Duration of post-traumatic amnesia after mild head injury. *Journal of Clinical Neuropsychology*, **2**, 51–60.

Hodges, J. R. (2000) Memory in the dementias. In: E. Tulving & F. I. M. Craik (eds) *The Oxford Handbook of Memory* (pp. 441–459). Oxford University Press, Oxford, UK.

Hodges, J. R. & Patterson, K. (1996) Nonfluent progressive aphasia and semantic dementia: A comparative neuropsychological study. *Journal of the International Neuropsychological Society*, **2**, 511–524.

Hodges, J. R., Patterson, K., Oxbury, S. & Funnell, E. (1992) Semantic dementia. Progressive fluent aphasia with temporal lobe atrophy. *Brain*, **115**, 1783–1806.

Hodges, J. R., Patterson, K. E., Graham, N. & Dawson, K. (1996) Naming and knowing in dementia of Alzheimer's type. *Brain and Language*, **54**, 302–325.

Hodges, J. R., Patterson, K., Ward, R., Garrard, P., Bak, T., Perry, R. & Gregory, C. (1999) The differentiation of semantic dementia and frontal lobe dementia (temporal and frontal variants of frontotemporal dementia) from early Alzheimer's disease: A comparative neuropsychological study. *Neuropsychology*, **13**, 31–40.

Jones, R. K. (1974) Assessment of minimal head injuries: Indications for hospital care. *Surgical Neurology*, **2**, 101–104.

Kaschel, R., Goldenberg, G., Goldstein, L. H., Risberg, J., Laaksonen, R., Gaillard, F., Perret, E., Tissot, R. & Öktem-Tanör, Ö. (1994) Neuropsychology in Europe: A partial account of history and perspectives. *Approche Neuropsychologique des Apprentissages Chez L'Enfant*, **27**, 114–121.

Kertesz, A., Nadkarni, N., Davidson, W. & Thomas, A. W. (2000) The Frontal Behavioral Inventory in the differential diagnosis of frontal dementia. *Journal of the International Neuropsychological Society*, **6**, 460–468.

McMillan, T. M. (1996) Post-traumatic stress disorder following minor and severe closed head injury: 10 single cases. *Brain Injury*, **10**, 749–758.

McNeil, J. E. & Greenwood, R. J. (1996) Can PTSD occur with amnesia for the precipitating event? *Cognitive Neuropsychiatry*, **1**, 239–246.

Morris, R. G. & Worsley, C. (in press) The neuropsychological presentation of Alzheimer's disease and other neurodegenerative disorders. In: P. Halligan, U. Kischka & J. Marshall (eds) *Handbook of Clinical Neuropsychology*. Oxford University Press, Oxford, UK.

Powell, G. E. & Wilson, B. A. (1994) Introduction to neuropsychology and neuropsychological assessment. In: S. J. E. Lindsay & G. E. Powell (eds) *The Handbook of Clinical Adult Psychology* (2nd edition, pp. 645–687). Routledge, London.

Sbordone, R. J. & Liter, J. C. (1995) Mild traumatic brain injury does not produce post-traumatic stress disorder. *Brain Injury*, **9**, 405–412.

Shallice, T. (1988) *From Neuropsychology to Mental Structure*. Cambridge University Press, Cambridge, UK.

Shallice, T. & Burgess, P. W. (1991) Deficits in strategy application following frontal lobe damage in man. *Brain*, **114**, 727–741.

Snowden, J. S., Bathgate, D., Blackshaw, A., Gibbons, Z. C. & Neary, D. (2001) Distinct behavioural profiles in frontotemporal dementia and semantic dementia. *Journal of Neurology, Neurosurgery and Psychiatry*, **70**, 323–332.

Walsh, K. & Darby, D. (1999) *Neuropsychology. A Clinical Approach* (4th edition). Churchill Livingstone, Edinburgh.

Wilson, B. A., Cockburn, J. & Baddeley, A. D. (1985) *The Rivermead Behavioural Memory Test*. Thames Valley Test Company, Bury St Edmunds, UK.

Wilson, B. A., Alderman, N., Burgess, P., Emslie, H. & Evans, J. J. (1996) *Behavioural Assessment of the Dysexecutive Syndrome*. Thames Valley Test Company, Bury St Edmunds, UK.

PART II

Neuroscience Background

CHAPTER 2

Neuroanatomy and Neuropathology

Nigel J. Cairns

Center for Neurodegenerative Disease Research, University of Pennsylvania School of Medicine, Philadelphia, PA, USA

INTRODUCTION TO NEUROANATOMY

The human brain is a marvel of evolution. In order to appreciate better its complex structure and many functions it is helpful to think of the brain in terms of various layers of organization. At the highest level, one may consider some behaviour that requires an explanation. At the most elementary level there is the activity of nerve cells or neurons. However, neurons do not work in isolation but operate as integral components of pathways and systems of varying degrees of complexity. Although many pathways and circuits have been identified, especially those of the senses such as vision and olfaction, and motor pathways, the connections linking those parts of the brain involved with higher cognitive functions are relatively poorly characterized, but are the subject of continuing investigation. Our understanding of the structure and function of the brain has been facilitated by the application of an ever-widening range of tools including histology, immunohistochemistry, tract tracing methods, methods for structural and functional neuroimaging as well as clinical–pathological studies.

It is important to begin by defining and illustrating a few commonly used terms that are used to describe the relative positions of different brain regions, which will be referred to at different points in this chapter and elsewhere. First, there are three main planes that are relevant when describing sections that have been cut through the brain, either at post mortem or when considering brain images acquired through neuroimaging (see Chapter 3). These are the horizontal, coronal and sagittal planes (see Figure 2.1).

Second, a number of terms are used to describe different directions relative to the long axis of the Central Nervous System (CNS). Figure 2.2 illustrates these directions, with the terms *ventral* and *dorsal* originating in the Latin terms for the stomach-to-back direction, while *rostral* and *caudal* describe the head-to-tail direction (Walsh & Darby, 1999).

Clinical Neuropsychology: A Practical Guide to Assessment and Management for Clinicians.
Edited by L.H. Goldstein and J.E. McNeil. © 2004 John Wiley & Sons, Ltd.

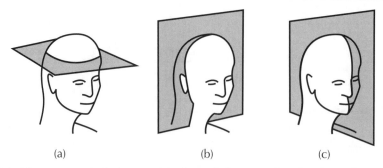

Figure 2.1. Three anatomical planes: (a) horizontal, (b) coronal and (c) sagittal

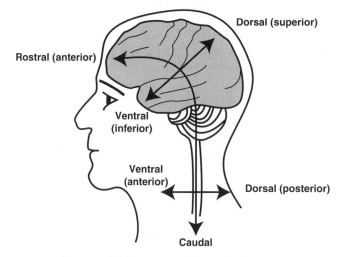

Figure 2.2. Directions relative to the long axis of the central nervous system

Finally, structures can either be described as being *medial* (near the midline) or away from it (*lateral*) (see Walsh & Darby, 1999).

CELLULAR ORGANIZATION

Neurons

If neurons are the building blocks of the CNS, glial cells or neuroglia might be thought of as the mortar holding the structure together. Neurons have four structural features in common. Radiating from the *cell body* are several processes called *dendrites* that make contact with other neurons (Figure 2.3). It is through these dendrites that the neuron receives information in the form of electrical impulses from other neurons. The output of the neuron passes via a specialized process called the *axon*, which may be as much as a metre in length for motor neurons. Information is conveyed along the axon in an all-or-none manner, and the transient

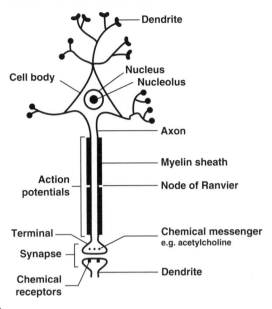

Figure 2.3. A neuron

electrical impulse is called an *action potential*. At the far end of the axon, branches make specialized junctional contacts, called *synapses*, with the dendrites and cell bodies of other neurons. The human brain contains about 10^{11} neurons, each with the potential to contact at least 10,000 other neurons: an immense amount of processing power!

Although neurons come in many shapes and sizes, within the CNS they can be divided functionally into three broad classes. Neurons that convey sensory information from the periphery are called *afferent* or *sensory neurons*. *Motor neurons* convey commands to the muscles and glands. The most abundant neurons are the *interneurons*, and they either process information locally or send information from one centre of specialization to another. However, neurons that have similar functions typically resemble each other structurally.

Most neurons communicate with each other by the release of specific signalling molecules, called neurotransmitters, at synapses. Neurotransmitter substances can be divided into two broad groups: *small signalling molecules* such as acetylcholine, biogenic amines (e.g., dopamine, noradrenaline, serotonin and histamine), the excitatory amino acids (gamma-aminobutyric acid [GABA], glycine and glutamate), and the *neuroactive peptides*, which include hypothalamic-releasing hormones, the neurohypophyseal hormones vasopressin and oxytocin, pituitary peptides, gastrointestinal peptides and others (Cooper et al., 1991). More than 50 neuroactive peptides have been found to be pharmacologically active. In the brain, glutamate is the major excitatory neurotransmitter and GABA the major inhibitory transmitter (Parent, 1996). The molecular dissection of receptor proteins reveals many subtypes, thus offering the possibility of more specific therapeutic compounds to treat those disorders where there are demonstrable neurotransmitter deficits such as the depletion of nicotinic acetylcholine receptors, among others, in Alzheimer's disease.

Neuroglia

Neurons and neuroglia are tightly packed in the CNS with spaces no bigger than 20 nm between cells. There are about 10 neuroglial cells for each neuron in the human brain and they make up about half its volume (Parent, 1996). The neuroglial cells are supporting cells and may be divided into two groups: macroglia comprising astrocytes and oligodendrocytes, and microglial cells that function like the debris-removing macrophages in the periphery. In addition, specialized cells called ependymal cells line the ventricles. However glial cells, like neurons, also have intermediate forms that allow them to respond to changes in their environment (Wilkin et al., 1990).

Astrocytes are the largest and most numerous of the glial cells. They are star-shaped with several processes extending into the surrounding tissue. Astrocytes have an important role in maintaining the stability of the CNS microenvironment. For example, astrocytes maintain adequate concentrations of potassium and glutamate in the extracellular space, and they also play a role in maintaining the blood–brain barrier.

The *oligodendrocyte* has relatively few processes, a smaller rounder nucleus and a smaller cell body than the astrocyte. They are more numerous in the white matter than astrocytes. The oligodendrocytes form and maintain the *myelin sheaths* surrounding axons. The myelin sheath facilitates the passage of the action potential along the axon by having periodic interruptions of the myelin sheath that are called the nodes of Ranvier (see Figure 2.3). Oligodendrocytes are also involved in active remyelination that occurs in response to conditions when there is demyelination such as in multiple sclerosis.

Microglial cells are found both in grey and white matter. They are small in comparison with astrocytes, have elongated nuclei and wavy processes with spine-like projections. Within the cerebral cortex about 10% of glial cells are microglial. Although they are generally inactive in the normal adult brain, they have a role in responding to tissue damage particularly due to inflammation or neurodegeneration.

The *ependymal cells* line the central canal of the spinal cord and the ventricles of the brain. These specialized cells have mobile hair-like structures called microvilli on their ventricular surface. The surface layer of ependymal cells and the under-lying astrocytes make up a functional unit, the brain–cerebrospinal fluid interface. Tight folding of the ependymal membrane into the ventricles form the choroid plexuses, whose major role is to secrete cerebrospinal fluid (CSF).

NEURODEVELOPMENT

The CNS is a segmented structure that becomes increasingly complex as it develops. The nervous system, like other organs, develops according to two basic principles.

Determination refers to a mechanism whereby one group of embryonic cells change into those of the nervous system (neurons and glia) and not any other cell types. The appropriate migration, further specialization and appropriate connections of neurons and glia are referred to as *differentiation*. The mechanisms that cause determination and differentiation are the focus of much work in developmental biology. This section refers to the major developmental events that lead to the formation of the human nervous system.

The Neural Tube

After fertilization, the cells of the embryo soon begin to become specialized. The cells of the nervous system begin from the outer layer of the embryo, called the ectoderm. This sheet of cells, the neural plate, folds into a long hollow tubular structure, the neural tube. The tail part becomes the spinal cord and the head region changes shape so that three swellings emerge from the sides of the tube. These swellings develop into the three major divisions of the brain: the forebrain, which further develops into the cerebral hemispheres, the midbrain and the hindbrain, which develops into the pons and medulla oblongata.

The wall of the developing brain becomes progressively thicker as cells proliferate, migrate to specific positions and mature by forming specific connections. Cells migrate from the inner surface of the neural tube to the outer part, where they aggregate to form the cortical plate, and it is from this layer that the six layers of the cerebral cortex develop. The cortical layers develop in an inverted manner such that cells of the deeper layers (such as layer VI) develop first. Cells in the superficial layers migrate past older cells to reach their appropriate position. Neurons that do not reach their appropriate position, or fail to make the correct connections, will eventually die. The maturing primitive nerve cell, called a neuroblast, does not establish synapses at random, but is influenced in its dendrite and axonal growth by chemical gradients so that synaptic contacts are made only with appropriate post-synaptic neurons. Proteins have been identified that promote the aggregation of neurons in selected areas, and different growth factors, such as nerve growth factor, demonstrate how axons find their way over large distances. Other factors may induce neuroepithelial cells to differentiate into primitive glial cells, called glioblasts, which in turn may form either oligodendrocytes or astrocytes. Glial cells, unlike neurons, may divide and increase in number because of injury or disease.

MENINGES AND CEREBROSPINAL FLUID

The brain and spinal cord are delicate structures that require protection and support. Major protection from physical trauma is provided by the *skull* for the brain and the vertebral column for the spinal cord. In addition, there are three membranes or meninges that surround the brain and spinal cord: the thick fibrous *dura mater* is found on the exterior surface; the fine meshwork of the *arachnoid mater* lines the inner surface of the dura; and the thin *pia mater* follows the contours of the brain and spinal cord. The inner two layers, which both have a delicate structure, are referred to as the *leptomeninges*. The space between the pia mater and the arachnoid mater, the subarachnoid space, is filled with *cerebrospinal fluid* (CSF). The tough dura mater provides the most physical protection and support of the meninges, and the CSF acts as a cushion between the hard skull and delicate brain.

The CSF is normally a clear, colourless fluid that fills the cisterns or ventricles of the brain and the subarachnoid spaces. The bulk (70%) of the CSF is generated by the *choroid plexus* in the walls of the *lateral ventricles* and the remainder (30%) comes largely from the capillaries of the brain. The total volume of CSF in the adult brain is about 140 ml, and 400 ml is generated daily. Hydrostatic pressure drives the CSF through the ventricular system and into the arachnoid spaces surrounding the brain and spinal cord. The CNS contains a number of interconnecting ventricles that derive from the cavity of the neural tube. CSF produced in the lateral ventricles passes into the third ventricle through an interventricular passage, the foramen of Monroe, and then into the fourth ventricle (on the dorsal surface of the brainstem beneath the cerebellum) by way of the cerebral aqueduct (of Sylvius). The CSF then passes through lateral and median apertures in the fourth ventricle into the subarachnoid spaces, where the bulk is passively returned to the venous system via finger-like projections called the arachnoid villi. If the flow of CSF is obstructed in any way by inflammation or a tumour, for example, there will be a rise in the intracranial volume of CSF, resulting in dilatation of the ventricles, a condition called hydrocephalus.

BLOOD SUPPLY OF THE BRAIN

The brain is supplied with blood by two pairs of arterial vessels, the *internal carotid arteries* and the *vertebral arteries*. The two vertebral arteries converge at the junction of the medulla and pons to form the basilar artery. The basilar artery forms the *arterial circle (of Willis)* with the internal carotid arteries at the base of the brain. From this circle, three pairs of arteries radiate to supply blood to the cerebral hemispheres. The *anterior cerebral artery* runs medially above the optic nerve, supplies the medial surface of the frontal and parietal lobes, and includes the motor and sensory cortices for the lower limb. A connecting vessel called the anterior communicating artery joins the two anterior cerebral arteries. The largest of the cerebral arteries is the *middle cerebral artery*, which passes laterally from its origin at the base of the brain to supply a large part of the lateral surface of the frontal, temporal and parietal lobes (see Figures 2.4 and 2.5). This includes the sensory and motor cortices for the whole body except the lower limbs. Branches of the *posterior cerebral artery* supply blood to the lateral surfaces of the inferior temporal gyrus, parts of the occipital lobe and parts of the parietal lobe. Branches of the vertebral and basilar arteries supply the cerebellum and brainstem.

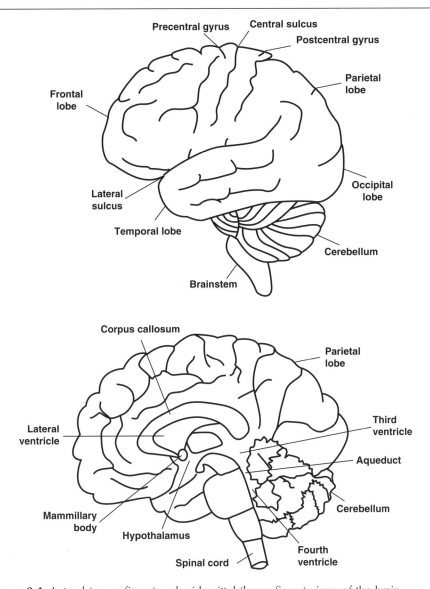

Figure 2.4. Lateral (upper figure) and midsagittal (lower figure) views of the brain

REGIONAL ANATOMY OF THE BRAIN

The adult human brain weighs about 1,400 g and constitutes only about 2% of total body weight. The nervous system is bilateral and essentially symmetrical, and may be divided into two components: the *central nervous system* (CNS) and the *peripheral nervous system* (PNS). The PNS may be divided into somatic and autonomic divisions, while the CNS comprises the brain and spinal cord. The *autonomic*

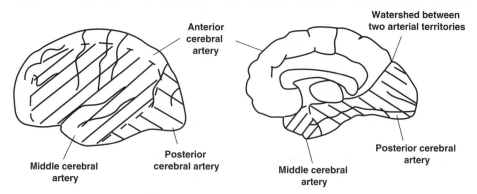

Figure 2.5. Arterial blood supply to the cerebral lobes. Lateral (left figure) and midsagittal (right figure) views of the vascular territories.

nervous system (ANS) can be considered as a separate functional system and has components that are both central and peripheral. The CNS can be further divided into six main parts: the *spinal cord*, the *brainstem* which is divided into three regions (*medulla oblongata*, *pons* and *midbrain*), the *cerebellum*, *basal ganglia*, *diencephalon* and the *cerebral hemispheres* (Figure 2.4).

Spinal Cord

The spinal cord receives incoming or afferent fibres from sensory receptors in the limbs and trunk, controls movement of the limbs and trunk, and provides innervations of the internal organs via the ANS. It has a segmental arrangement, which is preserved along its axis. A slice perpendicular to the axis of the cord reveals a butterfly-shaped central grey matter made up of neurons and their processes and glial cells. Surrounding this central grey matter are bundles of myelinated axons, most of which are either ascending or descending fibres and which constitute the white matter. Afferent fibres enter the spinal cord through dorsal roots and synapses within the grey matter. Motor neurons found in the anterior or ventral horns of the cervical and lumbar enlargements of the cord innervate the upper and lower limbs, respectively. The spinal cord is the anatomical location of several tendon reflexes including the biceps, triceps, quadriceps and Achilles tendon reflexes. The spinal cord also conveys information from pain, heat, tactile, muscle and joint receptors to the brain, where some of it reaches consciousness in the cerebral cortex and some passes to subcortical centres including the cerebellum, where it remains unconscious. The spinal cord merges with the medulla oblongata.

The spinal cord is a common site of injury with an annual incidence of about 5 per 100,000 population. Road traffic accidents account for half of these injuries, about one-quarter is caused by falls and about one-fifth from injuries in sport. The most frequent injury is of the cervical region, followed by thoracic and lumbo-sacral injuries. The level of the lesion can be ascertained by the loss of movement,

Table 2.1. Muscles affected in acute spinal cord lesions

Cord segment	Muscle group affected
C3–C5	Diaphragm
C5–C6	Shoulder abductors and elbow flexors
C7	Wrist flexors
C8	Finger flexors
T1	Hand muscles
T8–T12	Abdominal muscles
L1–L3	Hip muscles
L3–L4	Knee extensors
L4–L5	Ankle flexors
L5–S1	Knee flexors
S2–S4	Anal sphincter

sensation and altered reflexes. Table 2.1 describes the changes associated with lesions to different segmental levels of the spinal cord.

Brainstem

The brainstem receives information from receptors in the skin and muscles of the neck and head, and controls those muscles. It also contains cranial nerve nuclei that receive auditory and vestibular information, and information from special senses (see Table 2.2). It consists of three components: the *medulla oblongata*, the *pons* and *midbrain*. Cranial nerve nuclei located in the medulla oblongata, pons and midbrain are indicated in Table 2.2. The medulla extends from the spinal cord to the caudal border of the pons. The pons consists of a large basal part made up of descending fibres, pontine nuclei and transverse fibres projecting to the cerebellum, and a smaller part called the tegmentum. Ascending and descending pathways and cranial nerve nuclei are located in the tegmentum. A large number of fibres project from the pontine nuclei via the middle cerebellar peduncles to the cerebellum. The smallest part of the brainstem is the midbrain. It consists of a tectum (or roof), a tegmentum (or floor), ventral to the cerebral aqueduct and large white matter tracts. The tegmentum and white matter tracts are separated by an important nucleus containing dopaminergic neurons, the *substantia nigra*.

Cerebellum

The cerebellum is wedge-shaped and consists of a midline structure, the *vermis*, and two *lateral hemispheres*. In section, there is a mantle of grey matter that overlies a core of white matter and intrinsic nuclei, of which the largest is the *dentate nucleus*. The cerebellum is connected to the brainstem by three pairs of *cerebellar peduncles*. The naked eye appearance of the cerebellum is remarkable in that the cortex consists

Table 2.2. The cranial nerves

Number	Name	Function	Dysfunction
I	Olfactory	Smell	Loss of sense of smell
II	Optic	Vision	Visual field defects, loss of visual acuity
III	Oculomotor*	Eye movement	Constriction or dilation of pupils, defective eye movement, drooping of upper lid (ptosis)
IV	Trochlear*	Eye movement	Defective eye movements, squint, double vision
V	Trigeminal*	Sensory and motor fibres of skin, mucous membranes and skeletal muscles of neck and head	Impaired chewing, brisk jaw jerk, swallowing difficulties, facial sensory loss, severe pain (trigeminal neuralgia), abnormal sensory component of corneal reflex
VI	Abducens*	Eye movement	Conjugate gaze palsy, facial weakness
VII	Facial*	Facial movement and reflexes, lacrimation, taste	Loss of lacrimation, facial weakness or paralysis (Bell's palsy), loss of taste in the anterior two-thirds of tongue
VIII	Vestibulocochlear[†‡]	Hearing, balance	Sensation of noise (tinnitus), deafness, vertigo
IX	Glossopharyngeal[‡]	Sensation and movement of tongue and pharynx	Loss of sense of taste (sweet, salt, bitter and acid) in posterior one-third of the tongue. Loss of sensory component of 'gag reflex'. Pain behind the angle of the jaw
X	Vagus[‡]	Sensation and innervation of pharynx, larynx, thoracic and abdominal organs	Paralysis of soft palate, pharynx and larynx, including loss of 'gag reflex'
XI	Accessory[‡]	Movement of neck	Neck muscle wasting. Weakness of sternomastoid (version of the head) and trapezius (elevation and retraction of shoulder) muscles
XII	Hypoglossal[‡]	Tongue muscles	Weakness and wasting of tongue muscles. Speech and swallowing difficulty.

NB. Brainstem location of cranial nerve nuclei: * = midbrain; [†] = pons; [‡] = medulla of a large number of narrow, almost parallel, folds called *folia*, in contrast to the wide foldings of the cerebral cortex. The cerebellum co-ordinates somatic motor function, muscle tone and equilibrium.

Diencephalon

The diencephalon is a paired structure that is continuous with the rostral part of the midbrain. It consists of four structures: the *thalamus, epithalamus, hypothalamus* and *subthalamus*. The epithalamus contains the *pineal gland* that secretes hormones, is involved in the sleep–wake cycle and regulates the onset of puberty. It forms the dorsal part of the diencephalon. The subthalamus lies beneath the thalamus and lateral to the hypothalamus. It contains the subthalamic nucleus that is involved with the integration of motor function. The hypothalamus forms the lateral and inferior walls of the third ventricle. It is continuous with the pituitary, through the pituitary stalk. The nuclei within the hypothalamus contribute to the regulation of endocrine, visceral and metabolic activity, temperature regulation and emotion via connections with the limbic system. The thalamus is an egg-shaped mass at the rostral end of the brainstem. It distributes most of the afferent inputs to the cerebral cortex and receives inputs from most cortical areas. The thalamus controls the electrocortical activity of the cerebral cortex and therefore plays a role in arousal, consciousness and sleep, as well as integrating motor functions through relays from the basal ganglia and cerebellum (Parent, 1996).

Basal Ganglia

The basal ganglia lie within the cerebral hemispheres. They are composed of three anatomically and functionally related structures: the *caudate nucleus*, the *putamen* and the *globus pallidus*. The *amygdala* is anatomically close to the caudate nucleus and has a similar embryological origin to the basal ganglia, but is functionally more closely integrated with structures of the limbic system. The caudate nucleus and putamen constitute the *striatum*, and the putamen and globus pallidus are together referred to as the *lentiform nucleus*. The putamen is the largest and most lateral part of the basal ganglia. The globus pallidus occupies the medial part of the lentiform nucleus and has two divisions, an internal and external segment. The caudate nucleus has an enlarged rostral part, called the head; the body lies near the wall of the lateral ventricle, and a tail follows the curvature of the inferior horn of the lateral ventricle. The major descending motor tracts arise from the cerebral cortex and pass through the brainstem via a prominent structure called the medullary pyramid, the so-called *pyramidal system*. Motor lesions in pathways other than the corticospinal tracts are said to be *extrapyramidal lesions*. The structures of the basal ganglia are primarily concerned with the control of posture and movement. The basal ganglia are often refered to as components of the 'extra-pyramidal motor system', so as to distinguish the symptoms seen in diseases of the basal ganglia and related structures (as in Parkinson's disease) from those seen in strokes where the pyramidal tract is destroyed. However, increased knowledge of the motor system reveals that the pyramidal and extrapyramidal systems are intimately related rather than separate (Crossman & Neary, 2000).

Cerebral Hemispheres

The cerebral hemispheres make up the largest part of the human brain (Figure 2.3). Each hemisphere consists of a highly folded cortex of grey matter that contains neurons, underlying white matter that contains myelinated axons, resulting in a white appearance in fresh tissue, and deep within the hemispheres are the basal ganglia (nuclei of grey matter that contain neurons). The hemispheres are partially separated by the *longitudinal fissure*. Each hemisphere is divided into four lobes: *frontal, temporal, parietal* and *occipital* (mostly named after the bones of the overlying skull). An outfolding of the cortex is called a *gyrus* and an infolding a *sulcus*, or when deep and prominent a *fissure*. About 70% of the cerebral cortex is hidden within the depths of the sulci. On the lateral surface of the brain, the *lateral fissure* separates the temporal lobe below from the frontal and parietal lobes above. Within the depths of the lateral or Sylvian fissure is a cortical area called the *insula*. The *central sulcus*, also called the Rolandic sulcus, separates the frontal and parietal lobes. The frontal lobes are the largest of all the lobes and extend from the *precentral gyrus*. Behind the central gyrus lies the *postcentral gyrus*, the area of the somatosensory cortex (part of the parietal lobe) that has as its boundary with the occipital lobe the parieto-occipital sulcus on the medial surface. The occipital lobe has no landmarks on the lateral surface, but contains the prominent *calcarine sulcus*, the primary visual processing area.

Frontal Lobe

The frontal lobe makes up about one-third of the surface area of the cerebral hemisphere. It extends from the central sulcus to the frontal pole, and its lateral boundary is the lateral sulcus. The four major gyri of the convexity of the frontal lobe are: (a) the precentral gyrus and (b) three roughly horizontal convolutions: the superior, middle and inferior frontal gyri. The precentral gyrus contains the primary motor area, where all parts of the contralateral half of the body are represented in a distorted, inverted, topographical arrangement, often represented as a 'motor homunculus'. Areas rostral to the precentral gyrus are referred to as the premotor and prefrontal areas. The inferior frontal gyrus of the dominant hemisphere contains the motor speech area called *Broca's area*. This region has connections to the temporal, parietal and occipital lobes, and is involved in the motor mechanisms of speech formation. The olfactory tract lies on the ventral surface of the frontal lobe.

Temporal Lobe

The temporal lobe lies ventral to the lateral sulcus. On the lateral convexity, there are three, almost parallel, gyri: the superior, middle and inferior temporal gyri. The depths of the lateral sulcus contain the primary auditory cortex that is found within the transverse temporal gyri, or Heschl's convolutions. Posterior to the primary auditory area is the auditory association cortex, where auditory information is further processed and enters consciousness. In the dominant hemisphere this region is known as *Wernicke's area*, is connected to other language processing areas in the brain and is essential for comprehending speech. On the medial surface of the temporal lobe is the *parahippocampal gyrus* that has projections into the *hippocampus*. The hippocampus is part of the limbic system and plays an important role in memory processing. Anterior to the hippocampus is the *amygdala*, which receives inputs from the olfactory tract and is involved in the conscious perception of smell and emotion.

Parietal Lobe

The boundaries of the parietal lobe include the frontal lobe anteriorly, the temporal lobe inferiorly and the occipital lobe posteriorly. The anterior part is the postcentral gyrus that runs parallel to the central sulcus and contains the primary somatosensory cortex. As with the primary motor cortex, the somatosensory cortex contains an inverted, somatotopic representation of the contralateral half of the body. Posterior to the somatosensory cortex lies the parietal association cortex. Processing of general sensory information and conscious awareness of the contralateral half of the body takes place in the superior parietal lobule. The inferior parietal lobule integrates information from the somatosensory, visual and auditory association cortices, and in the dominant hemisphere it plays a role in language processing.

Occipital Lobe

The occipital lobe is the smallest of the four lobes. It sits above the roof of the cerebellum and behind the parietal and temporal lobes. The boundary with the parietal lobe is the parieto-occipital sulcus on the medial surface of the hemisphere. Additionally on the medial surface is the *calcarine sulcus*, the primary visual processing area. Input to this region comes from the lateral geniculate nuclei of the thalamus by way of the optic nerve and retina. Other parts of the occipital lobe constitute the visual association cortex that is concerned with further processing of the visual image into colour and motion (e.g., conscious awareness and interpretation). Lesions in the primary visual cortex cause blindness, and damage to parts of the visual association cortex cause selective damage to components of the visual scene and its interpretation. Bilateral infarction of the occipital lobes causes *cortical blindness*, the complete loss of all visual sensation. Curiously, not all visual pathways are destroyed in *blindsight*, the phenomenon of non-conscious perception of some visual information.

Summary

The brain is made up of discrete units: neurons and glial cells. A major aim of neuroscience is to explain how these components work together to control behaviour, generate emotions, language, cognition and conscious awareness.

Understanding the nervous system is facilitated by examining the connectivity and functioning of neurons and clusters of neurons (or nuclei), at different levels of organization.

INTRODUCTION TO NEUROPATHOLOGY

Neuropathology is the clinical practice and study of the pathology and pathogenesis of diseases of the nervous system. These may be usefully divided into those that are primary or secondary diseases. Primary diseases, such as Parkinson's disease, develop within the cells and structures of the nervous system. Secondary disorders, such as cerebral metastases, may result from a tumour or other complication outside the nervous system. A neuropathological diagnosis may require a combination of both clinical symptoms and pathological features that meet certain criteria, such as the number and distribution of lesions. Traditionally, the light microscope has been used to examine the structure of tissue in histological sections, and immunohisto-chemistry has added exquisite sensitivity to these approaches. The fine structure of the brain may be further examined with the electron microscope. More recently, molecular genetic and molecular biological methods have been used to supplement structural studies that have been important in elucidating the aetiology of a number of psychiatric and neurological disorders. For the practising neuropsychologist, knowledge of the number, size and location of the lesion within the brain of a particular disorder will facilitate understanding of loss, impairment or alteration in mental function.

Neurodevelopmental and Perinatal Disorders

Disorders that occur during development of the nervous system can be divided into several categories. *Malformations* occur where there is a morphological defect of an organ or part of it, because of an intrinsic cellular process. *Neural tube defects* are characterized by abnormalities in the formation, growth and closure of the anterior and posterior ends of the neural tube. A common neural tube defect is spina bifida, caused by failure of the posterior neural tube to close, while failure of the anterior tube to close is associated with anencephaly. *Disorders of migration* include hetero-topias, where there is failure of neurons to migrate to their appropriate cortical position, which can cause epilepsy. Where there is an absence of sulci, as in lissencephaly, the normal cortical lamination is altered, and commonly only four layers are present instead of the usual six layers. Sporadic and hereditary forms of agenesis of the corpus callosum are other migrational disorders. Intrauterine infections may cause obstruction of the cerebral aqueduct, resulting in congenital hydrocephalus. Displacement of the brainstem to override the spinal cord is a malformation referred to as the Arnold–Chiari malformation and may result in increased intracranial pressure.

Exposure to certain chemicals during critical periods of development may lead to malformations and delayed development. Chemicals that have an adverse effect on development are called *teratogens*. Maternal exposure to tobacco smoke may result in an increase in *neural tube defects*, including *spina bifida* and *anencephaly*, as well as increased mortality. *Fetal alcohol syndrome* is observed in children of mothers who drink heavily during pregnancy. Exposure of the fetus to alcohol is associated with a number of anomalies including: growth retardation, facial and cranial dysmorphias, microcephaly, neuronal migration defects, learning disabilities and neural tube defects (Mattson et al., 2001). Other organ systems are also, but less strikingly, affected.

Two common *chromosomal abnormalities* that cause learning disabilities are *Down's syndrome* and *fragile X syndrome*. Down's syndrome has an incidence of 1 in 600 to 1,000 live births. Trisomy 21 is present in over 90% of cases, and the risk of Down's syndrome increases with maternal age over 35 years. Several abnormalities in the CNS may be present including: flattened occipital lobe, decreased brain weight, narrow superior temporal gyrus, reduced numbers of neurons and abnormalities in neuronal processes (Lubec, 1999). The neuropathology of Alzheimer's disease (see p. 45) is also often present in persons over 30 years of age. There are also multiple defects in other organ systems. The most common hereditary form of learning disability is the chromosomal disorder fragile X syndrome. A fragile site on the long arm of chromosome X has been identified, but the genetic mechanisms resulting in the clinical phenotype are not known. In affected males the brain is small and there are abnormalities in dendrites and synapses, mild dysmorphic features, enlarged testes and learning disabilities (Rudelli et al., 1985). About one-third of affected females may have intellectual impairment.

Injury caused by *mechanical trauma*, *metabolic disturbances* (including hypoxia) and *intoxicating chemicals* may occur at or near birth. *Perinatal brain injuries* include *haemorrhages* and *necrotic lesions*. Both extracranial and intracranial haemorrhages may be encountered at autopsy. Of the intracranial haemorrhages, subdural, subarachnoid, intracerebellar and intraventricular haemorrhages have important clinical sequelae and may be life-threatening in serious cases. Although about 80% of patients with a subdural haemorrhage recover, the remainder have focal neurological deficits and hydrocephalus. Intrauterine asphyxia may cause cardiac output and circulatory insufficiency, resulting in reduced oxygen supply to the brain (ischaemia) or reduced circulatory transport (hypoxaemia). These perinatal injuries are associated with the development of permanent neurological impairment in some, but not all, cases.

Brain Tumours

As in other organs, primary tumours and metastatic tumours may occur in the brain. However, tumours that originate in the brain have some distinct features. Perhaps more than in other organs the anatomical site of the tumour will determine the nature and severity of clinical symptoms. For example, a tumour in the motor cortex will produce prominent signs, whereas a tumour in the white matter of the frontal pole may show modest changes, only detectable by sensitive neuropsychological testing. Tumours in the brain rarely metastasize to other organs, but they may invade adjacent structures including blood vessels and vital nuclei that make their removal difficult. The restricted space occupied by the brain causes additional complications. Tumours are space-occupying structures, and the displacement and damage of normal tissue leads to increased intracranial pressure. Where the normal circulation of the CSF is obstructed, *hydrocephalus* results. In young children, before the closure of the cranial sutures, increased intracranial pressure results in a widening of the sutures and an increase in the size of the head.

Primary brain tumours have an incidence of 12.5 per 100,000 and 11.1 for metastases of the CNS (Percy et al., 1972). About 80% of tumours of the CNS are intracranial and 20% are found in the spinal cord and related structures. The incidence of tumours is not age-related, except that there is a small increase in the first and second decades. In adults, two-thirds of tumours occur within the cerebral hemispheres and about one-third in the brainstem and cerebellum. The most common types in adults are: *glioblastoma multiforme, anaplastic astrocytoma, metastatic tumour, meningioma, pituitary tumour* and *schwannoma*. Other glial tumours include oligodendroglioma, ependymoma, subependymoma and tumours of the choroid plexus. In children, the majority (70%) of tumours are within the cerebellum, brainstem or spinal cord and 30% in the cerebral hemispheres, the reverse of that seen in adults. The aetiology of most primary tumours of the CNS is unknown, although there is an increased risk of lymphoma in patients with immunosuppression, including immunodeficiency syndrome (AIDS), and genetic factors are linked to specific tumours, such as neurofibomatosis and tuberous sclerosis.

Glial tumours are more common in men than women (ratio of 3:2) and are the most commonly occurring brain neoplasm. It is important clinically to distinguish between different types of glial tumour, so that the appropriate intervention can be undertaken. Diffuse astrocytomas are more numerous than circumscribed astrocytomas and are characterized by their invasion of surrounding tissue (Figure 2.6). They also have the ability to progress from a benign form (Grade I as assessed by histology) to a highly malignant form (Grade IV) with a poor prognosis. The circumscribed astrocytoma has a relatively well-demarcated border, is usually of low grade, often cystic and usually treatable by surgical excision. Low-grade (i.e., relatively benign), well-differentiated astrocytomas account for about 20% of all gliomas and are frequently found in the white matter of the frontal lobes of young adults. In contrast to diffuse astrocytomas, the prognosis of the circumscribed astrocytoma is usually good.

Infections Including Acquired Immunodeficiency Syndrome (AIDS)

Infectious organisms include parasites, fungi, bacteria and viruses. Infections of the nervous system are frequently life-threatening and often have important clinical consequences following the acute episode (Nelson et al., 1993). Meningitis, an acute inflammation of the leptomeninges, may be caused by an infectious agent

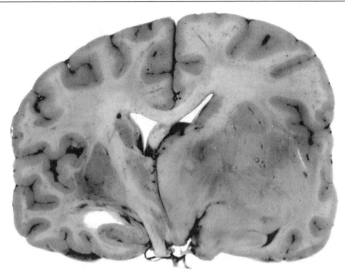

Figure 2.6. A diffuse astrocytoma in the right cerebral hemisphere causing enlargement and distortion of the frontal and temporal lobes and a shift in the midline

entering the skull through a fracture, by direct spread from within (such as from a brain abscess), through the blood stream following bacteraemia as in pneumococcal meningitis, as a complication of encephalitis or as a result of other factors including subarachnoid haemorrhage. Whatever the agent, the pathological changes associated with purulent meningitis are similar. Pus fills the space between the pia and arachnoid mater and may cover the cerebral hemispheres. The resulting oedema and hydrocephalus may be complicated by degeneration of the superficial layers of the cerebral cortex, cerebellum and spinal cord. With early diagnosis, there is a recovery in over 90% of patients. However, where meningitis is treated late or inadequately, there may be permanent damage to the brain, resulting in dementia, deafness, blindness and spastic weakness (Walton, 1993).

Viruses are intracellular parasites that depend on the host cell for energy and the machinery to manufacture proteins. There are two types according to the nucleic acid that they contain: ribonucleic acid (RNA) or deoxyribonucleic acid (DNA), but not both. As they contain no machinery for cellular metabolism they are unaffected by antibiotics. Major RNA viruses include picornavirus and poliomyelitis, paramyxovirus (measles and subacute sclerosing panencephalitis), rhabdovirus (rabies) and retroviruses, such as the human immunodeficiency virus. DNA viruses that migrate to the CNS (neurotrophic viruses) include herpes simplex virus, varicella-zoster virus, cytomegalovirus and papovaviruses, such as the JC virus that causes progressive multifocal leucoencephalopathy. Viruses may cause both meningitis and encephalitis.

Neurological complications, diseases of the PNS and muscle disease occur in patients with *HIV infection*, but are uncommon before the onset of *AIDS*. Both opportunistic infections of the CNS and *HIV-1 associated cognitive–motor disorder* (formerly AIDS dementia complex) occur late in AIDS, as a direct or indirect consequence of immunosuppression. The pathological substrate for this cognitive impairment includes damage to the neurites (Masliah et al., 1997) and neuropsychological impairment in HIV infection has been studied by, among others, Heaton et al. (1995). Before the introduction of combination therapy (highly active antiretroviral therapy [HAART]), HIV encephalitis was found in about one-quarter of the brains of AIDS patients. The characteristic histological stigmata of HIV encephalitis are multinucleated giant cells that contain HIV. Other viruses reported in post mortem brain samples include: cytomegalovirus, JC virus, varicella-zoster and herpes simplex viruses. Parasites include *Toxoplasma gondii* found in about 10% of all AIDS patients at autopsy and the fungi *Cryptococcus* and *Candida*. The most common neoplasm reported in 5% of AIDS patients is lymphoma, mainly of B cell origin (Petito, 1993). Combination antiretroviral therapy appears remarkably effective in delaying the onset of cognitive and motor disturbances in HIV infection, but the long-term effectiveness and toxicity of this treatment remains to be determined.

Demyelinating Diseases

Multiple sclerosis is a common demyelinating disease in young adults of unknown cause. The clinical course may be variable, and 80% of patients who present with episodic neurological symptoms recover at first. Episodes in relapsing/remitting disease occur at random, and in about 10% of patients the disease is progressive from the onset. Magnetic resonance imaging can detect periventricular and white matter lesions, both of which correspond to areas of histological damage (see also Chapter 3). The duration of disease from onset to presentation has been estimated at 25 years or more (Walton, 1993). As many as one-half of patients in a tertiary hospital setting have evidence of impairment of attention, memory, cognition and psychomotor function (O'Brien et al., 2000). The lifetime risk of developing the disease is 1:800. About 15% of patients have an affected relative, indicating a genetic susceptibility.

Multiple sclerosis is characterized macroscopically by *centres of demyelination*, called *plaques*, particularly surrounding the ventricles, veins, optic nerves, brainstem and spinal cord. Microscopically, plaques may be classified into two types: *active* and *inactive*. Active plaques display a loss of myelin and oligodendrocytes, astrocytic and macrophage proliferation, an influx of inflammatory cells (T and B lymphocytes), a variable amount of oedema and relative sparing of axons and remyelination at the edges of the plaque. In contrast, inactive plaques may reflect a period of remission. Few inflammatory cells or macrophages are found. Oligodendrocytes are largely absent, and the plaque boundary is relatively well demarcated. The mechanisms leading to myelin loss in multiple sclerosis remain elusive. However, there is evidence of a genetic factor in some patients, and a number of environmental factors have been implicated including viruses, but these data have not been well corroborated.

Cerebrovascular Diseases

Cerebrovascular disease can be defined as any disease of the cerebral vascular system that results in inadequate blood flow, *ischaemia*, or occlusion causing an area of necrosis or *infarction* of the brain. Clinically, four types of presentation may be distinguished. First, an acute loss of focal cerebral function with symptoms lasting less than 24 hours is referred to as a *transient ischaemic attack* (TIA), resulting from embolic or thrombic vascular disease. Second, a *stroke*, or cerebrovascular accident, describes rapid development of focal or global loss of cerebral function with symptoms lasting more than 24 hours or until death with no cause other than vascular disease. Third, where an ischaemic stroke is less severe with no persisting neurological disability it may be referred to as a *reversible ischaemic attack* (RIA). Fourth, repeated episodes of ischaemia, infarction or haemorrhage may cause *multi-infarct (vascular) dementia.*

Diseases of the cerebral circulation are important causes of mortality, accounting for 1 in 10 of all deaths in England and Wales (Secretary of State for Health, 1992) as well as being important causes of neurological dysfunction. Stroke mortality increases with age (Bonita, 1992) and varies widely between countries with high rates in eastern Europe and Japan and lower rates in North America and western European countries. In the USA and UK, stroke mortality is higher in Black than White populations. In the UK, increased stroke mortality is associated with social deprivation and unemployment (Carstairs & Morris, 1990). There is a seasonal variation in stroke mortality; rates are higher in summer than winter. Age is the strongest risk factor for stroke. There is a small gender difference, with men being at greater risk. Other risk factors for cerebral infarction include: high blood pressure, smoking, diabetes mellitus, obesity and alcohol (Warlow, 1993).

A sudden occlusion or hypoperfusion in an artery may result in a cerebral infarct, a well-demarcated area of cell death, called necrosis. Cerebral infarcts are most commonly caused by disease of the arterial wall, called atherosclerosis. In Western countries, atheroma appears to accompany ageing and may start in childhood, because of damage to the endothelial wall. Atherosclerotic plaques appear first in the large- and medium-sized arteries at places of branching and tortuosity. They spread along and around the artery, resulting in a narrowing of the lumen. Blood components including platelets may adhere to the plaque to form a clot or thrombus, further obstructing the flow of blood. The thrombus may become detached from the vessel wall and travel in the blood as an embolus that may occlude a distal artery, usually at a branching point. Determining the location and extent of the lesion depends on clinicoanatomical correlations and a CT scan.

Other causes of ischaemic stroke are intracranial small-vessel disease, embolism from the heart, cerebral aneurysms and other rare disorders. Atherosclerosis may cause dilatation of an artery called a *saccular aneurysm*. A saccular (berry) aneurysm occurs at the bifurcation of the arteries at the base of the brain. The majority are found in the anterior portion of the arterial circle of Willis. Unless treated, saccular aneurysms may rupture, causing a *subarachnoid haemorrhage*. The accumulation of blood, called a haematoma, in the subarachnoid space may have damaging consequences including vascular compression, brain herniation, hypo-perfusion and acute hydrocephalus, resulting in raised intracranial pressure. The incidence of subarachnoid haemorrhage increases with age and is between 10 and 20 per 100,000 population per year and is slightly more common in women than men (Ingall et al., 1989) (a ruptured saccular aneurysm is the most common cause).

Cerebrovascular disease may also cause dementia (see, for example Starkstein et al., 1996). Atherosclerotic dementia, multi-infarct dementia (MID) or vascular dementia account for about one-third of patients with dementia and increase in prevalence in the elderly, and a majority of individuals dying in their 60s and 70s have some evidence of vascular disease (Esiri & Morris, 1997). Vascular dementia is the deterioration in previously normal cognitive functions by repeated clinical or subclinical episodes of cerebral ischaemia, multiple small infarcts (MID), rarely by a strategic single infarct, and small vessel disease. A difficulty for the neuropathol-ogist is that small and quite large infarcts in the white matter and atherosclerosis may be present without clinical evidence of cognitive impairment. The threshold of pathology required for symptoms is not known, although neuroimaging that allows for the estimation of infarct volumes and their spatial location may allow for more precise clinicopathological correlations. The introduction of standardized diagnos-tic criteria for vascular dementia (Roman et al., 1993) has facilitated the clinical diagnosis of possible and probable vascular dementia with a diagnostic accuracy of about 80% in pathological studies.

In addition, cerebral vascular pathology may be associated with areas of de-myelination in the white matter (Binswanger's disease). The term leukoaraiosis was introduced to describe areas of hypodensity observed on CT and MRI. Although the pathological correlates of leukoaraiosis are not well defined, periventricular hypodensity has been correlated with decreased myelin, a reactive gliosis, increased extracellular fluid and thickening of the walls of small vessels (arteriosclerosis). A number of factors suggest that vascular pathology and ischaemia underlie these white matter changes. For example, leukoaraiosis is more common in patients with cerebrovascular disease and those who have vascular risk factors (arterial hyperten-sion, heart disease and diabetes). Neuropsychological sequelae have been reviewed by Morris (2000).

Trauma

Head injury is a major cause of morbidity and mortality in all age groups. It results in a million patients attending Accident and Emergency departments in the UK, leaving more than 5,000 dead and 1,500 with permanent brain damage each year (Jennet, 1986). Higher rates are found in urban populations. Major causes of trauma include road traffic accidents, falls and assaults, including gunshot wounds. Readers are referred to Ponsford et al. (1995) and Uzzell and Stonnington (1996) for accounts of the neurobehavioural sequelae of traumatic brain injury and their management. The mechanisms that cause brain damage in patients with trauma are multiple and complex. It is helpful, however, to divide brain damage into *primary* and *secondary*

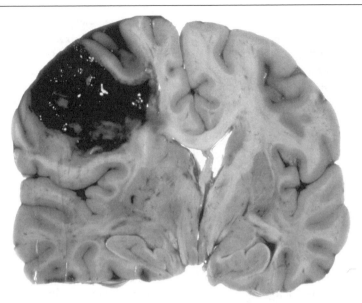

Figure 2.7. Acute head injury. Subarachnoid and intracerebral haemorrhage in the left frontal lobe. Oedema has caused brain swelling, compression of the left lateral ventricle and a shift in the midline. Increased intracranial pressure is the most common cause of death in head injury

forms. *Primary brain damage* includes abrasions, lacerations and contusions, or bruises. A mild form of damage is concussion that has been related to diffuse axonal injury, and this may be detected by histological methods. Primary brain damage typically produces an immediate loss of consciousness, while secondary changes produce later loss of consciousness and focal neurological signs depending on the site and extent of injury.

Secondary brain damage is caused by extra- and intradural haemorrhage, brain oedema (or swelling) and infection (Figure 2.7). Most haemorrhages in, or near, the dura occur in association with skull fracture and constitute 3% of head injuries; the incidence is highest between the ages of 10 and 30 years. They are commonly found over the cerebral convexities. The volume of an epidural haematoma may vary from a few millilitres, which may be significant in a child, to over 100 ml. The volume of an epidural haematoma correlates with the severity of clinical symptoms and influences outcome. There is increased mortality in patients where the clot exceeds 150 ml. Acute subdural haematoma commonly results in death in the majority of patients and a good recovery in only 10%. The timing of surgery for evacuation of the haematoma is a critical factor determining outcome. In shaken infants the amount of subdural blood may be small, but is useful as an indicator of brain acceleration and diffuse axonal injury, a term used to describe diffuse degeneration of the white matter, inner cerebral trauma or shearing injury (Garcia, 1993). Diffuse axonal injuries are most common in victims of road traffic accidents.

Adjacent to the site of any brain injury will be localized swelling. Local alterations in the blood–brain barrier facilitate the passage of plasma proteins and electrolytes into the extracellular space, producing *oedema* and *increased intracranial pressure*, the most common cause of death in head injury. Another complication is *ischaemia* caused by damage to intracranial vessels. Several days following a penetrating injury, further damage may be caused by *infection*, commonly meningitis or a brain abscess.

Epilepsy

An epileptic seizure may be defined as an intermittent, stereotyped disturbance of consciousness, sensation, motor activity, behaviour or emotion that results from cortical neuronal discharge. Epilepsy is thus a condition in which seizures recur, usually spontaneously (Chadwick, 1993). The incidence of epilepsy varies between 20 and 70 per 100,000 per year and is highest at the extremes of life. There are many causes of seizures and epilepsy in adults: head injury, stroke, intracranial infections, vascular disease, tumours, metabolic disorders, antibiotics (particularly penicillin) and drugs, especially alcohol. Neuropsychological deficits associated with focal seizure disorders have been reviewed by, among others, Morris and Cowey (2000) and Oxbury (2000).

Mild epilepsy that is readily controlled by anticonvulsant medication is rarely associated with neuropathology, unless there is a small focal lesion inducing the seizures. Severe and long-standing epilepsy resulting from excessive electrical discharges may be associated with pathology at various sites often within the cerebral cortex, hippocampus and cerebellum. Neuronal loss at the affected site may be so severe and extensive as to produce atrophy visible with the naked eye either at biopsy or with CT. Neuronal loss within the cerebral hemispheres and cerebellum may be present with a reactive astrocytosis. Neurons that fail to migrate to their proper location may form abnormal clusters or heterotopias that are also the focus of abnormal discharges. Brain damage during the seizure is thought to be caused by the excessive release of the neurotransmitter glutamate, which acts on post-synaptic receptors by opening calcium channels, resulting in the entry of excessive and toxic amounts of calcium.

A history of prolonged febrile seizures before the age of four or five years and medial temporal lobe involvement (detected by EEG or electrophysiology) indicates a medial temporal lobe lesion. Fortunately, patients with such lesions have the best results of temporal lobe surgery (Oxbury et al., 1989). Hippocampal scarring or sclerosis is the most common pathological finding in neurosurgically treated patients with complex partial seizures. Experimental evidence suggests that prolonged seizures produce such damage by hypoxic–ischaemic conditions that result in neuronal loss in the hippocampus (Meldrum et al., 1974). These experimental findings are reflected in clinical observations: the frequency of seizures before treatment has an adverse effect on outcome (Reynolds, 1987).

Neurodegenerative Diseases

Alzheimer's Disease

Macroscopically, the naked eye appearance of the Alzheimer's disease (AD) brain varies from unremarkable to grossly abnormal (Graham & Lantos, 1997). Brain weight is quite often reduced, sometimes below 1,000 g. The atrophy is generally diffuse and symmetrical, although the frontoparietal region and the temporal lobes may be more severely affected than the rest of the brain (Figure 2.8). The two hallmark lesions of AD, *neuritic plaques* (NPs) and *neurofibrillary* tangles (NFTs), may be seen in histological preparations with a light microscope. These lesions may be complemented by granulovacuolar degeneration, Hirano bodies, neuronal loss, abnormalities of neuronal processes and synapses, astrocytic and microglial response, as well as vascular and white matter changes (Lantos & Cairns, 2000).

The *senile* or *neuritic plaque* is one of the major lesions found in the AD brain and is present to a lesser extent in the ageing brain. It is an extracellular structure and consists of an amyloid core with a corona of argyrophilic axonal and dendritic processes and microglial cells. The amyloid is a cleavage product of a larger protein called *amyloid precursor protein* (APP). The second histological hallmark of AD is the NFT. These inclusions contain paired helical filaments. NFTs also occur in ageing and other neurodegenerative disorders, including Down's syndrome, progressive supranuclear palsy, postencephalitic parkinsonism, dementia pugilistica and other rare disorders. The NFT is an intraneuronal

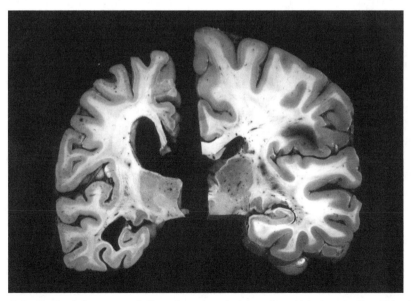

Figure 2.8. On the left, a coronal slice of one hemisphere of an Alzheimer's disease brain of a man aged 65 years. The brain is atrophied and the lateral ventricle is dilated. On the right, a normal aged half-brain for comparison

inclusion composed of abnormal cytoskeletal elements and its shape depends on the neuron in which it forms. A major component of the NFT is the *microtubule-associated protein tau*, which is hyperphosphorylated in AD.

Although AD is primarily a disease of old age, the disease may present at an earlier age, particularly where there is a family history. Familial forms of AD with multiple affected individuals are rare and account for probably fewer than 5% of AD cases. Mutations in the APP gene and two related genes, *presenilin-1 (PS1)* and *presenilin-2 (PS2)*, account for the majority of early-onset, autosomal-dominant cases of familial AD (Goate et al., 1991; Lamb, 1997). Although clinical features may differ between families, the neuropathological features are not markedly different between familial AD and early-onset sporadic cases.

The aetiology and pathogenesis of AD are not fully understood. Although many risk factors have been proposed, the evidence for most of them is weak except for age, family history and *apolipoprotein E genotype* (Jorm, 2000). The discovery of mutations in the APP and PS genes, all of which result in over-production of Aβ, has confirmed the central role of APP and Aβ deposition in the pathogenesis of AD. Despite the fact that the neurohistochemical abnormalities of AD are present, the neuropathological diagnosis is not always straightforward. When there are abundant lesions and a clinical history of dementia the diagnosis is straightforward. However, there are considerable differences from case to case. There may be atypical cases, and AD may be associated with other disease, most commonly vascular disease, and rarely with other neurodegenerative diseases. For these reasons diagnostic criteria have been developed that allow for a semi-quantitative assessment of NPs (Mirra et al., 1991), and the more recent National Institute on Aging and Reagan Institute (NIA-RI) criteria require semi-quantitative measures of both plaque and tangle distribution (Hyman & Trojanowski, 1997).

Parkinson's Disease and Dementia with Lewy Bodies

Parkinson's disease (PD) is characterized clinically by extrapyramidal movement disturbance and neuropathologically by the formation of Lewy bodies. It is a common disorder with a prevalence of between 1 and 2 per 1,000, and the annual incidence in those aged over 50 is 1–2% in the UK. Slightly more males are affected than females, and it has a worldwide distribution (Harding, 1993a). The frequency increases with age, the mean age at onset is around 60 years and the average duration is around 13 years. Rarely, PD may have an onset below the age of 40 years. The onset is gradual and may present with rest tremor of the hand or of the leg, stiffness in the arm or with slowness and difficulty of movement. The hallmark clinical signs are bradykinesia, resting tremor and rigidity. Additional features may develop including dysphagia, autonomic dysfunction and dementia (Harding, 1993a). Cognitive and psychiatric disorders in PD have recently been reviewed by Starkstein and Merello (2002).

Typically, the only macroscopic abnormality is the pallor of the pigmented nuclei of the brainstem, the substantia nigra and locus coeruleus. The hallmark lesion of idiopathic PD is the *Lewy body*. These are spherical, intraneuronal cytoplasmic inclusions. The brainstem Lewy body has a distinct halo. The cortical inclusion is less easy to discern and lacks a distinct halo. Lewy bodies are found in the pigmented nuclei and the cerebral cortex, and may be found in the basal ganglia, hypothalamus, ANS and spinal cord. Lewy bodies contain the protein α-*synuclein* (Spillantini et al., 1997, 1998b). Neuronal loss occurs in the substantia nigra and locus coeruleus. Loss of neurons in the basal ganglia is less severe than those in the pigmented nuclei, but may also contribute to the clinical symptoms. Mutations in the α-*synuclein gene* in rare families cause early-onset PD.

Lewy bodies have also been noted in the cortex, resulting in the definition of *dementia with Lewy bodies*. They usually occur in large numbers in the parahippo-campal gyrus, cingulate and insular cortices and throughout the neocortex, but well in excess of the occasional cortical inclusion in idiopathic PD. This diffuse distribution of Lewy bodies is often associated neuropathologically with Alzheimer-type changes, mainly with plaque formation and clinically with dementia. The incidence of dementia with Lewy bodies varies between 5 and 15% in different series (O'Brien et al., 2000). Clinically, dementia with Lewy bodies is characterized by progressive dementia with fluctuating cognition, visual hallucinations and parkinsonian features including flexed posture, shuffling gait, rigidity and hyperkinesias (McKeith et al., 1996).

Macroscopically, the brain usually shows atrophy that may be diffuse or more severe in the frontotemporal region. The pigmented nuclei of the brainstem show pallor. Microscopically, Lewy bodies, neuronal loss, abnormal neurites, astrocyto-sis and vacuolation of the cortex may be observed. As with PD, the histological hallmark is the Lewy body. The severity of dementia appears to be related to the density of Lewy bodies. In addition, there may be *neuritic plaques* with Aβ deposits that may also contribute to the dementia. NFTs are not a prominent feature, although they may be present. The coexistence of Lewy bodies and Alzheimer's disease pathology in the same brain may present diagnostic problems because it is not always easy to determine the net contribution of each disease to the clinical symptoms.

Frontotemporal Dementias

The frontotemporal dementias (FTDs) constitute a group of clinically and patho-logically heterogeneous dementing disorders with selective degeneration of the frontal and temporal lobes (Kertesz & Munoz, 1998). FTDs may account for between 10 and 20% of all dementing disorders. FTD is primarily a disorder of early onset with a high family incidence. Clinically, it is characterized by changes in personality and social conduct sufficient to render the person incapable of indepen-dent existence, attenuated speech leading to mutism, relative preservation of spatial skills and memory and rarely neurological signs. The usual age at onset is 45–65 years with an average duration of 8 years. Men and women are affected equally and patients are found in all social classes and geographical regions (Neary, 2000). Using the techniques of molecular pathology at least six distinct disease entities can be identified (Lantos & Cairns, 2001):

Tauopathies

- Pick's disease;
- corticobasal degeneration (CBD);
- FTD and parkinsonism linked to chromosome 17.

Neurofilamentopathy

- Dementia with neurofilament inclusions.

Unclassified

- FTD with ubiquitin-positive, tau-negative inclusions;
- dementia lacking distinctive histology.

Pick's disease typically presents with frontal lobe signs. The age at onset varies between 45 and 65 years with an average duration of 5 to 10 years. The *Pick's disease* brain is one of the most dramatic in all neuropathology (see also Chapter 3). Macroscopically, there is striking *focal atrophy* of the *frontal and temporal lobes*. Microscopically, affected areas of cortex show *neuronal loss, astrocytosis* and *vacuolation*, particularly in the outer cortical layers. There may be additional loss of neurons from the basal ganglia. The hallmark lesions of Pick's disease are *swollen achromatic neurons* (so-called 'ballooned' neurons or Pick cells) and generally spherical, neuronal, cytoplasmic inclusions called *Pick bodies*. They contain an abnormal tau protein that is different from that of AD (Delacourte et al., 1998).

The clinical syndrome associated with *corticobasal degeneration* presents in the sixth or seventh decade of life. It is probably not as rare as generally thought. The onset is variable: in some patients the presenting symptom is involuntary and persistent movement of an upper limb (dystonia, myoclonus or the so-called 'alien-limb'), while in other patients dementia is the initial symptom. Most patients develop a supranuclear gaze palsy during the illness and all develop an akinetic-rigid syndrome. The disease is progressive with a duration of four to seven years (Harding, 1993a). At autopsy, there is *frontotemporal atrophy*. Microscopically, this atrophy is associated with *neuronal loss, astrocytosis, vacuolation* and the presence of swollen achromatic neurons. Pick bodies are not seen. Corticobasal *tau-positive inclusions* are seen in superficial cortical neurons and in subcortical nuclei where they have a globose appearance. Tau pathology may also be found in astrocytes in the form of *astrocytic plaques*, and in oligodendrocytes they are called *coiled bodies*. The swollen neurons of CBD can be distinguished from those of Pick's disease (Bell et al., 2000). The tau protein in CBD is different from that of both AD and Pick's disease (Delacourte et al., 1998).

In recent years, a number of families with FTD with and without movement disorder have been identified with mutations in the tau gene on chromosome 17. Although this group of disorders has been referred to as *frontotemporal dementia and parkinsonism linked to chromosome 17* (FTDP-17), not all cases have parkinsonism (Spillantini et al., 1998a). These familial cases typically have atrophy of the frontal and temporal lobes. Microscopically, neuronal loss, astrocytosis, microvacuolation and swollen neurons are found in affected areas together with a spectrum of tau pathology (Lantos et al., 2002). Thus, these familial cases can vary enormously.

Other causes of FTD, which probably account for about half of all cases that lack tau pathology, are: *frontotemporal dementia with ubiquitin inclusions, frontotemporal dementia with neurofilament inclusions* and *frontotemporal dementia lacking distinctive histology*. FTD with ubiquitin inclusions, also called FTD with motor neurone disease (see p. 52), presents with cognitive impairment, and in some, but not all, patients an amyotrophic picture develops with weakness and wasting of limb muscles and bulbar palsy leading to dysarthria, dysphagia and wasting of the tongue (Neary et al., 1998). In addition to frontotemporal atrophy, neuronal loss, astrocytosis and microvacuolation, ubiquitin-positive tau-negative inclusions are observed in the granule cells of the dentate gyrus and occasionally in the surviving neurons of the superficial cortical laminae. There is usually severe neuronal loss in the substantia nigra. These inclusions are indistinguishable from those seen in patients with motor neurone disease who later develop dementia, suggesting that pathogenesis may be similar in disorders with ubiquitin-positive tau-negative inclusions.

Prion Diseases

The prion diseases are characterized by the accumulation of an abnormal, partially protease-resistant glycoprotein known as prion protein (PrP). Human prion diseases include *Creutzfeldt–Jakob disease* (CJD), *Gerstmann–Sträussler–Scheinker disease* (GSS) and *kuru*. Although rare with an incidence of 1 per million people, they are important because of the epidemic of bovine spongiform encephalopathy (BSE) and the evidence that the transmissible agent or BSE prions have infected humans causing the new human prion disease known as *variant CJD*. There is a possibility that an epidemic of BSE-related human prion disease may develop. Prion diseases may be *inherited, sporadic* or *acquired*. Inherited forms such as GSS have great clinical phenotypic variability. The classical symptoms of sporadic CJD are rapidly progressive, multifocal dementia usually with myoclonus. Most have an onset between 45 and 75 years and progress to akinetic mutism and death in less than 6 months. Other symptoms include depression, malaise, extrapyramidal signs, cerebellar ataxia and cortical blindness (Collinge, 2000). Human prion disease may be acquired as a result of cannibalistic practices (kuru), or following accidental inoculation with prions during medical and surgical procedures (iatrogenic CJD).

The neuropathological examination of the brain continues to provide confirmation of the diagnosis in most cases. The exceptions are when a brain biopsy is taken, or when other tissue or blood is taken and from which DNA can be extracted and a molecular genetic analysis undertaken in cases of inherited prion disease. As the clinical course is usually short, the brain appears unremarkable. There may be slight generalized atrophy. Microscopically, CJD is characterized by *spongiform change, neuronal loss, astrocytosis,* microglial cell activation and the presence of *prion plaques.* The prion plaques superficially resemble those seen in AD. *New variant CJD* is characterized by *'florid' plaques* (a central core of prion protein, surrounded by a halo of spongiform vacuoles), more typical of those seen in kuru. These florid prion plaques in new variant CJD are usually much more abundant in the cerebellum and may be present throughout all the lobes, especially the occipital lobe, compared with those seen in sporadic CJD. These cases of new variant CJD also differ from sporadic cases by having an early age at onset (16–39 years), a longer duration of illness (7–22 months), presenting symptoms were behavioural and psychiatric, and electroencephalographic periodic complexes were absent (Will et al., 1996). Kapur et al. (2001) have presented a neuropsychological–neuropathological case study of new variant CJD.

Huntington's Disease

Huntington's disease is an autosomal-dominant neurodegenerative disorder. In 1993 the causative mutation was discovered: an unstable expansion in the length of a cytosine–adenine–guanine (CAG) *triplet repeat* sequence on chromosome 4. The responsible gene encodes the protein *huntingtin.* The huntingtin gene contains a CAG repeat of varying size: in the normal population the mean length is around 19 CAG with a range 9–37. In patients with Huntington's disease, the repeat sequence is expanded to an average repeat length around 46 with a range 37–86. The frequency of Huntington's disease varies in different populations between 4 and 7 per 100,000. The clinical diagnostic criteria of Huntington's disease should include a family history of typical Huntington's chorea, progressive motor disability with chorea or rigidity of no other cause and psychiatric disturbance with gradual dementia of no other cause. The clinical onset is variable and can be divided into juvenile (4–19 years), early (20–34 years), midlife (35–49 years) and late-onset groups (over 50 years). Rigidity is a prominent feature in juvenile cases. Early neuropsychological deficits include impairment of sustained attention and speed of mental processing (Campodonico et al., 1996). Longer CAG repeats are associated with an early onset, cognitive decline and clinically severe disease (Foroud et al., 1995; Jason et al., 1997).

Macroscopically, there is evidence of *severe cerebral atrophy.* The atrophy of the *caudate nucleus* is the principal, naked eye, diagnostic hallmark lesion of the disease. In addition, there may be loss of the cerebral cortex, white matter, putamen and thalamus. The frontal lobes show atrophy in 80% of cases (Vonsattel and DiFiglia, 1998). Microscopically, there is *neuronal loss* and *astrocytosis* in the affected areas of the basal ganglia. *Neuronal intranuclear inclusions* may be detected and may contain the protein huntingtin. These inclusions give support to the possible pathogenic action of the huntingtin protein, which by accumulating may lead to neuronal loss and the symptoms of Huntington's disease. Neuropsychological change in Huntington's disease has recently been evaluated by Bachoud-Levi et al. (2001) and Snowden et al. (2001).

Progressive Supranuclear Palsy

Progressive supranuclear palsy (PSP) was defined as a clinical and neuropathological entity in 1964 by Steele, Richardson and Olszewski. Approximately 4% of parkinsonian patients have PSP or four cases per million per year. The average age at onset is 59 years, the average duration of 6 years and the male : female ratio is 6:4. The clinical features include parkinsonism, a reduction in voluntary downgaze (supranuclear gaze palsy), cognitive impairment (see, for example Savage, 1997), dysarthria and dysphasia. The parkinsonian symptoms include bradykinesia, rigidity, gait disorder, masked fascies, neck dystonia and falls, but there is no tremor and the patient does not respond to levodopa.

Macroscopically, the brain may appear normal or atrophied. The atrophy may include the globus pallidus, thalamus and occasionally the brainstem and cerebellum. The substantia nigra and locus coeruleus often appear pale. Histology reveals NFTs, neuropil threads, glial inclusions, neuronal loss and astrocytosis. The predominant hallmark of PSP is the *neurofibrillary tangle*. These are found in the substantia nigra, globus pallidus, subthalamic nucleus, nucleus basalis of Meynert, pretectal area, tegmentum of the midbrain and pons, locus coeruleus, raphé nuclei and the nuclei of various cranial nerves (Lantos, 1994).

Although PSP is a sporadic disease, familial cases with autosomal-dominant inheritance have been reported. Recently, a polymorphism in the tau gene has been associated with PSP (Conrad et al., 1997). The diagnosis is based on a semi-quantitative assessment of the distribution of NFTs. The criteria also take into account the presence of neuropil threads and tau-positive astrocytes. Based on neuropathological criteria, three types of PSP can be distinguished: *typical*, *atypical* and *combined*. Typical cases show the pathological features as originally described, while atypical cases are variants of the histological changes characteristic of PSP. In combined cases, in addition to PSP there is another disease process such as AD or vascular disease.

Motor Neurone Disease

Motor neurone disease (MND), of which amyotrophic lateral sclerosis is the most common form, is a primary neurodegenerative disease involving the upper and lower motor neurons. Clinically, the disorder is characterized by the progressive wasting of the affected muscles with evidence of corticospinal tract involvement (Harding, 1993b). Respiratory muscle weakness occurs eventually in all patients, but is sometimes an early feature. If the cranial nerve nuclei are involved, the tongue musculature becomes affected early with wasting and fasciculation. Eye movements and continence are usually preserved. MND is usually a disease of late middle life, with onset of symptoms between the ages of 50 and 70 and with a duration of 3–4 years in the limb onset form, but shorter at 2.5 years in the bulbar onset form. In a review of patients with MND, the worldwide incidence ranges between 0.4 and 1.8 per 100,000 and with a prevalence of 5 per 100,000. More men are affected than women, the male : female ratio being 1.5:1. Cognitive aspects of MND have been reviewed by Abrahams and Goldstein (2002).

The naked eye appearance of the brain is generally unremarkable, but in some cases atrophy of the motor (precentral) gyrus is seen. The spinal cord may be atrophied and the anterior nerve roots are generally shrunken and greyish in comparison with the posterior sensory roots. In patients where there is dementia there may be atrophy of the frontal and temporal lobes. Microscopically, there are *loss of motor neurons* and *astrocytosis* in the anterior horns of the spinal cord, in the brainstem and in the motor cortex (Brownell et al., 1970). In addition, *ubiquitin-positive inclusions* are found in upper and lower motor neurons (Chou, 1988). The aetiology and pathogenesis of MND are largely unknown. The discovery of mutations in the superoxide dismutase (SOD1) gene in familial cases of MND suggests that free radical damage may contribute to neuronal loss.

MND may also be found in association with dementia in Western countries and Japan. *Motor neurone disease-associated dementia* has a worldwide distribution (Neary et al., 1998). It is predominantly sporadic, but about 20% may be familial. Onset is between 50 and 60 years and more men are affected than women, the ratio being 2:1. Dementia is usually the presenting symptom with the neurological signs of MND appearing later, or may not even be apparent. Macroscopically, there is atrophy of the frontal and temporal lobes and the substantia nigra may appear pale. Histology reveals neuronal loss, microvacuolation, astrocytosis and ubiquitin-positive inclusions in the cortex and in the dentate gyrus of the hippocampus (Anderson et al., 1995). The substantia nigra shows neuronal loss and the lesions of MND are present in the brainstem nuclei and spinal cord. The relationship between MND-associated dementia and FTD with ubiquitin inclusions (also called motor neurone disease inclusion dementia) is complex and more research is required to properly classify these diseases (Ince et al., 1998).

Summary

The neuropsychology of organic, neurological and psychiatric disorders may be related to macroscopic and microscopic changes within the brain. The anatomic location of an infection, neoplasm or infarct is a main determinant of the resulting neurological signs and symptoms. Brain changes are generally more severe in neurodegenerative diseases with an early onset. The appearance of the brain of these diseases may vary from the unremarkable to the grossly atrophied. In affected areas of the brain, there is neuronal loss and a reactive astrocytosis. In addition, characteristic neuronal and glial inclusions or abnormal aggregates of extracellular protein may be found that define the molecular pathology of neurodegenerative diseases.

REFERENCES

Abrahams, S. & Goldstein, L. H. (2002) Motor neuron disease. In: J. E. Harrison and A. M. Owen (eds) *Cognitive Deficits in Brain Disorders* (pp 341–358). Martin Dunitz, London.

Anderson, V. E. R., Cairns, N. J. & Leigh, P. N. (1995) Involvement of the amygdala, dentate and hippocampus in motor neuron disease. *Journal of the Neurological Sciences*, **129**, 75–78.

Bachoud-Levi, A. C., Maison, P., Bartolomeo, P., Boisse, M. F., Dalla-Barba, G., Ergis, A. M. et al. (2001) Retest effects and cognitive decline in longitudinal follow-up of patients with early HD. *Neurology*, **56**, 1052–1058.

Bell, K., Cairns, N. J., Lantos, P. L. & Rossor, M. N. (2000) Immunohistochemistry distinguishes between Pick's disease and corticobasal degeneration. *Journal of Neurology, Neurosurgery, and Psychiatry*, **69**, 835–836.

Bonita, R. (1992) Epidemiology of stroke. *Lancet*, **339**, 342–344.

Brownell, B., Oppenheimer, D. R. & Hughes, J. T. (1970) The central nervous system in motor neurone disease. *Journal of Neurology, Neurosurgery and Psychiatry*, **33**, 338–357.

Campodonico, J. R., Codori, A. M. & Brandt, J. (1996) Neuropsychological stability over two years in asymptomatic carriers of the Huntington's disease mutation. *Journal of Neurology, Neurosurgery and Psychiatry*, **61**, 621–624.

Carstairs, V. & Morris, R. (1990) Deprivation and health in Scotland. *Health Bulletin*, **48**, 162–175.

Chadwick, D. (1993) Seizures, epilepsy, and other episodic disorders. In: J. Walton (ed.) *Brain's Diseases of the Nervous System* (pp. 697–739). Oxford University Press, Oxford, UK.

Chou, S. M. (1988) Motor neuron inclusions in ALS are heavily ubiquitinated. *Journal of Neuropathology and Experimental Neurology*, **47**, 334.

Collinge, J. (2000) Creutzfeldt–Jakob disease and other prion diseases. In: J. O. O'Brien, D. Ames & A. Burns (eds) *Dementia* (pp. 863–875). Arnold, London.

Conrad, C., Andreadis, A., Trojanowski, J. Q., Dickson, D. W., Kang, D., Cheng, X. et al. (1997) Genetic evidence for the involvement of tau in progressive supranuclear palsy. *Annals of Neurology*, **4**, 277–281.

Cooper, J. R., Bloom, R. E. & Roth, R. H. (eds) (1991) *The Biochemical Basis of Neuropharmacology*. Oxford University Press, New York.

Crossman, A. R. & Neary D. (2000) *Neuroanatomy: An Illustrated Colour Text*. Churchill Livingstone, Edinburgh.

Delacourte, A., Sergeant, N., Wattez, A., Gauvreau, D. & Robitaille, Y. (1998) Vulnerable neuronal subsets in Alzheimer's and Pick's disease are distinguished by their tau isoform distribution and phosphorylation. *Annals of Neurology*, **43**, 193–204.

Esiri, M. M. & Morris, J. H. (eds) (1997) *The Neuropathology of Dementia*. Cambridge University Press, Cambridge, UK.

Foroud, T., Siemers, E., Kleindorfer, D., Bill, D. J., Hodes, M. E., Norton, J. A. et al. (1995) Cognitive scores in carriers of Huntington's disease gene compared to noncarriers. *Annals of Neurology*, **37**, 657–664.

Garcia, J. H. (1993) Pathophysiology of ischaemic injury to the brain. In: J. S. Nelson, J. E. Parisi & S. S. Schochet (eds) *Principles and Practice of Neuropathology* (pp. 459–504). Mosby, London.

Goate, A., Chartier-Harlin, M. C., Mullan, M., Brown, J., Crawford, F., Fidani, L. et al. (1991) Segregation of a missense mutation in the amyloid precursor protein gene with familial Alzheimer's disease. *Nature*, **349**, 704–706.

Graham, D. I. & Lantos, P. L. (eds) (1997) *Greenfield's Neuropathology*. Arnold, London.

Harding, A. E. (1993a) Movement disorders. In: J. Walton (ed.) *Brain's Diseases of the Nervous System* (pp. 393–425). Oxford University Press, Oxford, UK.

Harding, A. E. (1993b) Neurocutaneous disorders and degenerative diseases of the spinal cord and cerebellum. In: J. Walton (ed.) *Brain's Diseases of the Nervous System* (pp. 426–452). Oxford University Press, Oxford, UK.

Heaton, R. K., Grant, I., Butters, N., White, D. A., Kirson, D., Atkinson, J. H. et al. (1995) The HNRC-500 neuropsychology of HIV infection at different stages. *Journal of the International Neuropsychological Society*, **1**, 231–251.

Hyman, B. T. & Trojanowski, J. Q. (1997) Editorial on consensus recommendations for the postmortem diagnosis of Alzheimer's disease from the National Institute on Aging and the Reagan Institute Working Group on diagnostic criteria for the neuropathological assessment of Alzheimer's disease. *Journal of Neuropathology and Experimental Neurology*, **56**, 1095–1097.

Ince, P. G., Lowe, J. & Shaw, P. J. (1998) Amyotrophic lateral sclerosis: Current issues in classification, pathogenesis and molecular pathology. *Neuropathology and Applied Neurobiology*, **24**, 104–117.

Ingall, T. J., Whisnant, J. P., Wiebers, D. O. & O'Fallon, W. M. (1989) Has there been a decline in subarachnoid haemorrhage mortality? *Stroke*, **20**, 718–724.

Jason, G. W., Suchowersky, O., Pajurkova, E. M., Graham, L., Klimek, M. L., Garber, A. T. et al. (1997) Cognitive manifestations of Huntington disease in relation to genetic structure and clinical onset. *Annals of Neurology*, **54**, 1081–1088.

Jennet, B. (1986) *High Technology Medicine: Costs and Benefits*. Oxford University Press, Oxford, UK.

Jorm, A. (2000) Risk factors for Alzheimer's disease. In: J. O. O'Brien, D. Ames & A. Burns (eds) *Dementia* (pp. 383–390). Arnold, London.

Kapur, N., Ironside, J., Abbott, P., Warner, G. & Turner, A. (2001) A neuropsychological–neuropathological case study of variant Creutzfeldt–Jakob disease. *Neurocase*, **7**, 261–267.

Kertesz, A. & Munoz, D. G. (1998) *Pick's Disease and Pick Complex*. Wiley-Liss, Chichester, UK.

Lamb, B. T. (1997) Presenilins, amyloid-β and Alzheimer's disease. *Nature Medicine*, **3**, 28–29.

Lantos, P. L. (1994) The neuropathology of progressive supranuclear palsy. *Journal of Neural Transmission*, **42**, 127–152.

Lantos, P. L. & Cairns, N. J. (2000) The neuropathology of Alzheimer's disease. In: J. O. O'Brien, D. Ames & A. Burns (eds) *Dementia* (pp. 443–459). Arnold, London.

Lantos, P. L. & Cairns, N. J. (2001) Neuropathology. In: J. R. Hodges (ed.) *Early-onset Dementia: A Multidisciplinary Approach* (pp. 227–262). Oxford University Press, Oxford, UK.

Lantos, P. L., Cairns, N. J., Khan, M. N., King, A., Revesz, T., Janssen, J. C. et al. (2002) Neuropathologic variation in frontotemporal dementia due to the intronic *tau* 10^{+16} mutation. *Neurology*, **58**, 1169–1175.

Lubec, G. (ed.) (1999) *The Molecular Biology of Down Syndrome*. Springer-Verlag, Vienna.

Masliah, E., Heaton, R. K., Marcotte, T. D., Ellis, R. J., Wiley, C. A., Mallory, M. et al. (1997) Dendritic injury is a pathological substrate for human immunodeficiency virus-related cognitive disorders. HNRC Group. The HIV Neurobehavioral Research Center. *Annals of Neurology*, **42**, 963–972.

Mattson, S. N., Schoenfeld, A. M. & Riley, E. P. (2001) Teratogenic effects of alcohol on brain and behavior. *Alcohol Research and Health*, **25**, 185–191.

McKeith, I. G., Galasko, G., Kosaka, K., Perry, E. K. & Dickson, D. W. (1996) Consensus guidelines for the clinical and pathologic diagnosis of dementia with Lewy bodies (DLB): Report of the consortium on DLB international workshop. *Neurology*, **47**, 1113–1124.

Meldrum, B. S., Horton, R. W. & Brierley, J. B. (1974) Epileptic brain damage in adolescent baboons following seizures induced by allyglycine. *Brain*, **97**, 407–418.

Mirra, S. S., Heyman, A. & McKeel, D. (1991) The consortium to establish a registry for Alzheimer's disease (CERAD). Part II. Standardization of the neuropathologic assessment of Alzheimer's disease. *Neurology*, **41**, 479–486.

Morris, R. G. (2000) Neuropsychological sequelae of leukoaraiosis. *Clinical Neuropsychological Assessment*, **1**, 231–246.

Morris, R. G. & Cowey, C. M. (2000) Neuropsychological deficits in frontal lobe epilepsy. In: J. M. Oxbury, C. E. Polkey & M. Duchowny (eds) *Intractable Focal Epilepsy* (pp. 393–403). W. B. Saunders, London.

Neary, D. (2000) Frontotemporal dementia. In: J. O. O'Brien, D. Ames & A. Burns (eds) *Dementia* (pp. 737–746). Arnold, London.

Neary, D., Mann, D. M. A. & Snowden, J. S. (1998) Frontotemporal dementia with motor neuron disease. In: A. Kertesz & D. G. Munoz (eds) *Pick's Disease and Pick Complex* (pp. 145–158). Wiley-Liss, Chichester, UK.

Nelson, J. S., Parisi, J. E. & Schochet, S. S. (1993) *Principles and Practice of Neuropathology*. Mosby, London.

O'Brien, J. O., Ames, D. & Burns, A. (eds) (2000) *Dementia*. Arnold, London.

Oxbury, S. M. (2000) Neuropsychological deficits in temporal lobe epilepsy. In: J. M. Oxbury, C. E. Polkey & M. Duchowny (eds) *Intractable Focal Epilepsy* (pp. 377–391). W. B. Saunders, London.

Oxbury, J. M. and Adams, C. B. T. (1989) Neurosurgery for epilepsy. *British Journal of Hospital Medicine*, **41**, 372–377.

Parent A. (1996) *Carpenter's Human Neuroanatomy*. Williams & Wilkins, Baltimore.

Percy, A. K., Elveback, L. R., Okazaki, H. & Kurland, L. T. (1972) Neoplasms of the central nervous system: Epidemiologic considerations. *Neurology*, **22**, 40–48.

Petito, C. K. (1993) Neuropathology of Acquired Immunodeficiency Syndrome. In: J. S. Nelson, J. E. Parisi & S. S. Schochet (eds) *Principles and Practice of Neuropathology* (pp. 88–108). Mosby, London.

Ponsford, J., Sloan, S. & Snow, P. (eds) (1995) *Traumatic Brain Injury: Rehabilitation for Everyday Adaptive Living*. Lawrence Erlbaum, Hove, UK.

Reynolds, E. H. (1987) Early treatment and prognosis of epilepsy. *Epilepsia*, **28**, 97–106.

Roman, G. C., Tatemichi, T. K., Erkinjuntti, T., Cummings, J. L., Masdeu, J. C., Garcia, J. H. et al. (1993) Vascular dementia: Diagnostic criteria for research studies. Report of the NINDS-AIREN International Workshop. *Neurology*, **43**, 250–260.

Rudelli, R. D., Brown, W. T., Wisniewski, K., Jenkins, E. C., Laure-Kamionowska, M., Connell, F. et al. (1985) Adult fragile X syndrome: Cliniconeuropathologic findings. *Acta Neuropathologica*, **67**, 289–295.

Savage, C. R. (1997) Neuropsychology of subcortical dementias. *Psychiatric Clinics of North America*, **201**, 911–931.

Secretary of State for Health (1992) *The Health of the Nation*. Her Majesty's Stationery Office, London.

Snowden, J., Craufurd, D., Griffiths, H., Thompson, J. & Neary, D. (2001) Longitudinal evaluation of cognitive disorder in Huntington's Disease. *Journal of the International Neuropsychological Society*, **7**, 33–44.

Spillantini, M. G., Schmidt, M. L., Lee, V. M.-Y., Trojanowski, J. Q., Jakes, R. & Goedert, M. (1997) α-Synuclein in Lewy bodies. *Nature*, **388**, 839–840.

Spillantini, M. G., Bird, T. D. & Ghetti, B. (1998a) Frontotemporal dementia and Parkinsonism linked to chromosome 17: A new group of tauopathies. *Brain Pathology*, **8**, 387–402.

Spillantini, M. G., Crowther, R. A., Jakes, R., Cairns, N. J., Lantos, P. L. & Goedert, M. (1998b) Filamentous α-synuclein inclusions link multiple system atrophy with Parkinson's disease and dementia with Lewy bodies. *Neuroscience Letters*, **251**, 205–208.

Starkstein, S. E. and Merello, M. (2002) *Psychiatric and Cognitive Disorders in Parkinson's Disease*. Cambridge University Press, Cambridge, UK.

Starkstein, S. E., Sabe, L., Vazquez, S., Teson, A., Petracca, G., Chemerinski, E. et al. (1996) Neuropsychological, psychiatric, and cerebral blood flow findings in vascular dementia and Alzheimer's disease. *Stroke*, **27**, 408–414.

Steele, J. C., Richardson, C. & Olszewski, J. (1964) Progressive supranuclear palsy. *Archives of Neurology*, **10**, 333–359.

Uzzell, B. P. & Stonnington, H. H. (eds) (1996) *Recovery after Traumatic Brain Injury*. Lawrence Erlbaum, Mahwah, NJ.

Vonsattel, J. P. G. & DiFiglia, M. (1998) Huntington's disease. *Journal of Neuropathology and Experimental Neurology*, **57**, 369–384.

Walsh, K. & Darby, D. (1999) *Neuropsychology. A Clinical Approach* (4th edition). Churchill Livingstone, Edinburgh.

Walton, J. (ed.) (1993) *Brain's Diseases of the Nervous System*. Oxford University Press, Oxford, UK.

Warlow, C. (1993) Disorders of the cerebral circulation. In: J. Walton (ed.) *Brain's Diseases of the Nervous System* (pp. 197–268). Oxford University Press, Oxford, UK.

Wilkin, G. P., Marriott, D. R. & Cholewinski, A. J. (1990) Astrocytes heterogeneity. *Trends in Neurosciences*, **13**, 43–46.

Will, R. G., Ironside, J. W., Zeidler, M., Cousens, S. N., Estibeiro, K., Alperovitch, A. et al. (1996) A new variant of Creutzfeldt–Jakob disease in the UK. *Lancet*, **347**, 921–925.

CHAPTER 3

Neurological Investigations

John D. C. Mellers

Department of Neuropsychiatry, Maudsley Hospital, London, UK

INTRODUCTION

This chapter will review the techniques that are currently available to investigate the nervous system. The investigations described are those routinely used by clinicians working in neurology, neurosurgery and psychiatry. As with any branch of medicine, assessment in these fields begins with taking a history and conducting an examination. We will therefore briefly cover these routine clinical methods before considering specialist investigations.

An understanding of the investigations that may be undertaken in patients with neurological problems, together with the information they yield, will enable the clinical neuropsychologist to then undertake a hypothesis-driven assessment of their patients' cognitive state and make more informed contributions to their patients' management, in the manner already described in Chapter 1.

The importance of a careful clinical assessment cannot be overemphasized. The time-honoured method of taking a history and conducting a physical examination leading to a differential diagnosis which then guides the choice of investigations remains as relevant today as ever, and it seems particularly important to emphasize this principle in the introduction to a chapter devoted to the range of sophisticated investigations now available. No matter how impressive the means at our disposal become, for example, to produce images of the brain, results of such tests only contribute to an assessment when they are interpreted in the light of a skilfully elicited history. The standard schema for a clinical neurological/psychiatric assessment is shown in Table 3.1 (Lishman, 1998; Marsden & Fowler, 1998).

The mode of onset of symptoms, their course over time, aggravating and relieving factors and the precise temporal relationship between physical and mental symptoms merit particularly close attention. A history from someone close to the patient is always valuable and often critical. This is most obviously the case where the presenting problem is one of paroxysmal attacks during which the patient has no awareness, or in neurodegenerative disorders where the patient lacks insight or cannot remember details of their own history. In somatoform presentations an informant may reveal significant psychological or social events that are self-evidently important, but which the patient has omitted from their own

Clinical Neuropsychology: A Practical Guide to Assessment and Management for Clinicians.
Edited by L.H. Goldstein and J.E. McNeil. © 2004 John Wiley & Sons, Ltd.

Table 3.1. Format for clinical assessment in neuropsychiatry

History
    Presenting complaint and its history
    Past medical and psychiatric history
    Family history
    Developmental history
    Educational achievement
    Employment history
    Significant relationships
    Use of drugs/alcohol
    Forensic history
    Premorbid personality
    Social circumstances

Mental state examination
    Appearance and behaviour
    Speech
    Mood
    Thought
    Perception
    Cognition
    Insight

Physical (including neurological) examination

account, coloured as it often is by their pursuit of a physical/medical explanation of their symptoms. A family and developmental history should be obtained together with an outline of the patient's educational and occupational achievements. An account of the individual's habitual emotional state, temperament and their characteristic ways of dealing with others before they became unwell—their premorbid personality—is important. A clear description of a patient's former level of functioning will allow a judgement to be made concerning the extent of any deterioration. On occasions it may be helpful to contact the patient's employer or school (with the patient's consent, of course). The history is followed by a description of the patient's current mental state and by cognitive testing and neurological examination. With respect to cognitive testing, it has become common practice to use simple, standardized tests such as the Mini Mental State Examination (MMSE; Folstein et al., 1975). Although this is relatively quick and produces a numerical score that can be compared on consecutive assessments, a more extensive assessment is appropriate in specialist practice (Nestor & Hodges, 2001). In particular, the MMSE incorporates only a very simple test of language function and lacks tests of executive function. The Addenbrooke's Cognitive Examination incorporates items from the MMSE, but has additional tests of language, memory and executive function. It can be conducted in around 10 minutes and has superior sensitivity with equivalent specificity compared with the MMSE (Mathuranath et al., 2000).

From the history a clinician aims to establish the nature and time course of a particular presenting complaint. As the story unfolds the clinician clarifies the information in order to compare the critical features of the history with recognized symptom patterns (syndromes), which point in turn toward the most likely underlying pathological process (e.g., vascular, infection, malignancy, epilepsy, etc.). Guided by the history, the aim of a neurological examination is then to establish whether neurological deficits are present and to determine where in the nervous system a lesion is likely to be found. Thus, with each aspect of the neurological examination the neurologist asks two important questions: (1) Is there an abnormality? and (2) Where is the abnormality?

A full description of the neurological examination is beyond the scope of this chapter. What follows is an outline intended to convey something of the principles of clinical neurological examination and to help the non-neurologist to understand findings on neurological examination as they are presented in clinical discussions. In any particular clinical situation, the examination will focus on areas raised by the history as likely to be abnormal. By convention, the cranial nerves are examined first. The limbs and periphery are then examined, and attention is focused on the motor system, followed by the sensory system. The main aspects of cranial nerve function were outlined in Chapter 2. A simple screen of motor functions should also be undertaken. This might typically involve (1) observing the person's gait and noting the presence of any involuntary movements; (2) observing the person's posture and balance; (3) asking the person to hold their arms outstretched in a supine position with their eyes closed; and (4) asking them to perform rapid finger movements. Where motor symptoms have emerged in the history, or where this simple screen of motor function suggests an abnormality, a more extensive examination is required. For each limb, muscular tone, power, reflexes ('tendon jerks') and co-ordination are examined in turn. In the leg the plantar reflex is a particularly important aspect of the examination. This is elicited by firmly stroking the sole of the foot, along the instep, from the heel toward the toes. The normal ('flexor') response is for the toes to curl downward. An 'extensor' plantar reflex, in which the toes extend upward and may splay apart, is hard evidence of an abnormality in the central motor system. The pattern of abnormalities elicited in the motor system allows the neurologist to determine whether an underlying lesion is to be expected in the central nervous system (CNS), a so-called 'upper motor neuron' lesion, or in the periphery, a 'lower motor neuron' lesion. Examination findings with an upper motor neuron lesion are of a 'spastic paresis' and include increased tone (spasticity), abnormally brisk reflexes and a characteristic pattern of weakness in the arm (weakness greatest in extensor muscle groups) and the leg (flexors weaker than extensors). With lower motor neuron lesions there is a 'flaccid paralysis' with loss of tone, diminished or absent reflexes and a pattern of weakness reflecting the site of the peripheral nervous system (PNS) lesion.

While all aspects of the neurological examination are guided by what has emerged during the history, this is especially pertinent with respect to the sensory examination, which can be time-consuming and is liable to produce spurious findings (e.g., subtle asymmetries in sensitivity to light touch) of dubious significance. Sensory examination is therefore focused on areas of specific concern raised by the history or motor examination. An important concept in interpreting findings on neurological examination concerns the distinction between 'hard' and 'soft' neurological signs. 'Hard' signs are those that are undoubtedly present and do not require a significant component of volition or subjective interpretation from the patient and are therefore unequivocal evidence of an abnormality. Examples include findings such as definite, localized muscle wasting, asymmetrical pupillary response to light and an extensor plantar response. Less objective 'soft signs', on the other hand, include subtle sensory changes and mild weakness. It is the overall pattern of signs that is important. As the examination unfolds the clinician is engaged in a continuous deductive process, seeking to match findings with recognized neuroanatomical templates. In this process hard signs are of primary importance; soft signs may add weight to the emerging conclusions, but inconsistent findings will be checked and may be dismissed. A general physical examination will be conducted, its extent and focus being determined by what, if any, systemic disease is suspected. Thus, where cerebrovascular disease is likely, an examination of the cardiovascular system is important to look for evidence of general vascular disease or sources of arterial emboli (cardiac arrhythmia, valvular or carotid artery flow abnormalities). Malignancy may be suspected, in which case examination will search for evidence of a primary tumour with, for example, a careful examination of the chest, abdomen and lymph nodes.

Having taken a history and conducted an examination the clinician will have a firm idea of whether an abnormality is present, where in the nervous system the abnormality is likely to be and what sort of disease processes may underlie the problem. Investigations will then be chosen to test these clinical hypotheses.

INVESTIGATIONS FOR SYSTEMIC MEDICAL DISORDERS

Many systemic medical disorders may affect the nervous system and are screened for using relatively inexpensive and routine investigations. A list of the most commonly ordered tests and the conditions they are used to screen for in neuropsychiatric practice is listed in Table 3.2. The precise tests chosen will of course be dictated by the presenting clinical problem and the differential diagnosis under consideration.

LUMBAR PUNCTURE

The brain and spinal cord are surrounded by fluid known as cerebrospinal fluid (CSF), which fills the ventricular system and the subarachnoid space. Two-thirds of this fluid is generated by a specialized vascular fringe within the lateral and 4th ventricles known as the choroid plexus, the remainder being accounted for by diffusion at a microvascular level throughout the cerebrum (Thompson, 1995). The CSF flows through the ventricular system and over the cerebral hemispheres, draining out through specialized structures in the cerebral venous sinuses. A variety of pathological processes affecting the CNS may produce changes in the cellular or biochemical content of the CSF, analysis of which may thus provide important

Table 3.2. Tests used in neurological and neuropsychiatric practice to screen for systemic disorders

Test	Disorder screened for/Purpose of test
Haematology and biochemistry	
Full blood count (FBC)	Anaemia, evidence of infection, blood dyscrasia
Erythrocyte sedimentation rate (ESR)	Inflammatory disorders
C reactive protein	Inflammatory disorders
Urea and electrolytes (U&E)	Renal disorder, metabolic abnormalities
Liver function tests (LFT)	Liver disorder
Random blood glucose	Diabetes mellitus, hypoglycaemia
Thyroid function tests	Thyroid disorder
B12/Folate	Vitamin B12 and folate deficiency
Urinary drug screen*	Suspected illicit drug use
Autoantibodies*	Autoimune/Inflammatory disorders
Red cell transketolase*	Thiamine deficiency
Serum prolactin*	Used to verify a seizure as epileptic
Serum copper/Caeruloplasmin*	Wilson's disease
White cell enzymes*	Storage disorder degenerative conditions
24-hour urine collection*	Phaeochromatocytoma, porphyria
Faecal analysis*	Porphyria
Serum drug assays*	Monitoring of certain drug treatments (e.g., some antiepileptic drugs, lithium, antidepressant and antipsychotic treatment in special circumstances)
Microbiology	
Syphilis serology (VDRL/FTA)	Syphilis
HIV test*	HIV infection
Midstream urine*	Urinary tract infection
Genetics	
Karyotype analysis genetic testing	Screening for specific chromosomal and genetic disorders
Other	
Chest X-ray	Malignancy, inflammatory disorders (e.g., sarcoidosis)

* Non-routine tests, only required in specific clinical circumstances

diagnostic information (see Thompson, 1995). A sample of CSF can be obtained by the procedure known as lumbar puncture. With the patient lying on their side a lumbar puncture needle is inserted between the 3rd and 4th lumbar vertebrae (below the caudal extent of the spinal cord, which usually terminates at L1) using a sterile technique and local anaesthetic. Lumbar puncture is contraindicated in the presence of an intracranial or intraspinal mass lesion as there is a danger of shifts and herniation of the intracranial or intraspinal contents with potentially fatal consequences. If a mass lesion is suspected (by evidence of raised intracranial pressure or the presence of focal neurological signs) prior investigation with a CT scan is mandatory. With practice the procedure can be performed quickly and without pain. The most common complication is a transient headache, which may be minimized by ensuring the patient remains recumbent for an hour or two after the procedure.

Lumbar puncture is essential in the diagnosis of subarachnoid haemorrhage, meningitis and encephalitis and is an important investigation for inflammatory and, in some circumstances, malignant processes. CSF pressure is measured during lumbar puncture, and this remains the diagnostic test for benign intracranial hypertension. The important finding in subarachnoid haemorrhage is the presence of red blood cells in the CSF. Bleeding from a subarachnoid haemorrhage may be distinguished from trauma to blood vessels at the time of the lumbar puncture by the presence of uniform concentrations of red blood cells in the three tubes of CSF that are routinely obtained during the procedure and by the presence of xanthochromia, a yellowish stain in the sample after centrifugation due to the presence of haemolysed blood (blood cells that have burst and released degraded haemoglobin). In infective conditions there will be a raised white cell count in the CSF and a low glucose level. The type of white cells in most abundance gives an indication of whether the causative agent is likely to be viral (lymphocytes predominate) or bacterial (polymorphs). Microscopy of the CSF may be used to identify bacteria and other infective micro-organisms, but immunochemical detection of specific antimicrobial antibodies is a more reliable and increasingly important means of determining the causative infectious agent. Among inflammatory conditions suspected multiple sclerosis (MS) is the most common indication for lumbar puncture. The important finding is evidence of synthesis of gamma globulin within the CNS detected by biochemical analysis (electrophoresis) of the CSF sample and referred to as oligoclonal bands. Comparison with the concentration of gamma globulin in the blood serum is necessary to verify that oligoclonal bands are due to CNS pathology. Oligoclonal bands in the CSF are not, however, specific to MS and are found in other infective and inflammatory conditions. Occasionally, carcinoma may involve the meninges, in which case there may be inflammatory changes within the CSF and malignant cells may be identified with microscopy.

ELECTROENCEPHALOGRAPHY (EEG)

The development of methods to measure the electrical activity of the brain provided clinicians with the first means of directly investigating brain function. The EEG is commonly recorded from 16 (less often 8) electrodes placed over the scalp in standard configurations (known as montages). Voltage differences between electrodes are displayed as a continuous trace after amplification and filtering. By convention the voltage fluctuations are classified according to their frequency: beta (13–40 Hz), alpha (7.5–13 Hz), theta (3.5–7.5 Hz) and delta (<3.5 Hz). The normal EEG is dominated by an alpha rhythm that is symmetrical and most prominent posteriorly. It is most conspicuous when the eyes are closed and attenuates with eye opening. In childhood, slower rhythms in the theta range, especially prominent in the posterior temporal regions, are a feature, but these disappear with maturation.

Abnormalities in the EEG fall into two broad categories: (1) abnormalities of the background rhythm; (2) paroxysmal abnormal electrical discharges (Binnie & Prior, 1994). In both cases the EEG also conveys important information about whether the abnormality is diffuse or focal. Abnormally fast background rhythm may be seen as a drug-induced effect (benzodiazepines in particular) and in the early stages of some drug-withdrawal states (alcohol and barbiturate withdrawal). However, the most important abnormality of background rhythm consists of slowing. Diffuse slowing of the EEG is found in acute encephalopathic states (corresponding to the clinical picture of delirium) and in chronic degenerative disorders. In a patient with acute or chronically progressive cognitive impairment the EEG is thus extremely useful in distinguishing between functional psychiatric causes (e.g., conversion disorder, catatonic stupor, depressive 'pseudodementia'), in which the EEG is normal, and organic causes. As a rule of thumb, in chronic neurodegenerative disorders the extent of slowing in the EEG reflects the rate of progression of the underlying disorder. Thus, the EEG is commonly normal until very late in the course of a frontotemporal dementia, which may have a natural history stretching over 10 years or more, but is abnormal early on in rapidly progressive dementias (e.g., Creutzfeldt–Jakob disease [CJD]). A decrease in the amplitude of the EEG trace (voltage attenuation) is also seen in degenerative disorders and may be particularly prominent in Huntington's disease, giving the appearance of a 'flat trace'. With a few exceptions, the slowing seen in delirium and dementia is non-specific and does not convey information about the underlying cause. Some notable exceptions include periodic triphasic slow waves, seen in metabolic encephalopathies—in particular, hepatic encephalopathy, subacute sclerosing panencephalitis (SSPE) and in CJD (though not in the new variant of the disorder). Localized slowing may be seen as an interictal abnormality in patients with epilepsy, but may also reflect an underlying tumour or other space-occupying lesion and always requires further investigation with neuroimaging.

The EEG finds its greatest clinical application in the investigation of patients with suspected epilepsy. It is used to add weight to the diagnosis, to assist in the classification of the type of epilepsy and, where surgery for medically intractable epilepsy is being considered, to establish the site of epileptic discharges. As an aid to the diagnosis of epilepsy the usefulness of the EEG rests on the fact that patients with epilepsy may show abnormal electrical activity between clinical seizures. The 'spike', a high voltage brief discharge, is the EEG hallmark of epilepsy. Other epileptiform changes (abnormal discharges not actually accompanied by an overt clinical seizure) include sharp waves and brief runs of sharp and slow waves. Focal slowing of the background rhythm, as mentioned above, may also be seen for variable lengths of time after seizures of focal onset (partial seizures). Epileptiform abnormalities will be found in a single routine EEG in between 50 and 60% of patients with epilepsy. Repeated routine EEG will improve the yield of positive findings to 70% or so. Photic stimulation (exposing the person to a stroboscopic flashing light) may be used during the EEG in patients with generalized seizures to increase the chance of positive findings, and hyperventilation may similarly be used if petit mal, classical Absence seizures are suspected. A sleep EEG (sleep being induced with thiopentone) and, less commonly, sleep deprivation are further means of enhancing the test. A combination of routine plus sleep EEG will detect abnormalities in approximately 80% of patients with epilepsy. There remain, however, a small proportion of patients with epilepsy who have repeatedly normal EEG findings. Perhaps a greater problem, however, concerns the frequency of false positive results with EEG. Up to 10% of healthy adults may have an 'abnormality' on EEG, although this figure varies depending on how tightly abnormality is defined. The prevalence of more strictly defined 'epileptiform' abnormalities is much less, probably in the region of 3 in 1,000 (Gregory et al., 1993). To a large extent the reported conclusions from an EEG examination depend on the skill and experience of the neurophysiologist interpreting the EEG and the problem of 'over-reading' EEG results, falsely interpreting normal variants or even artefacts as being 'supportive of a diagnosis' of epilepsy is well recognized. Indeed, this problem prompted one leading expert in the field to write 'the EEG is unquestionably responsible for more human suffering than any other clinical investigation' (Chadwick, 1994).

The development of longer term EEG monitoring has been of great importance in the field of epilepsy; the aim is to obtain a recording during a seizure that allows, in most circumstances, a definitive diagnosis to be made and provides information about seizure type and anatomical localization of onset. Without question the most valuable technique is video-EEG telemetry, in which simultaneous video and EEG recordings are obtained. The duration over which telemetry is carried out is not only limited principally by cost but also by practical considerations (e.g., patients' tolerance of the procedure), and in most cases monitoring is conducted over seven days or less. The cost of the procedure and the expertise required to maintain the service and interpret results mean that this technique remains limited to specialist centres. Ambulatory EEG monitoring that uses portable EEG recorders is another option, but has the obvious disadvantage of not including a video recording of seizures. The principal indications for video-EEG telemetry are for clarification of diagnosis and for establishing the anatomical site of origin of medically intractable partial seizures, where surgery is being considered. In the latter situation, telemetry may be performed with surgically implanted 'depth electrodes' (e.g., foramen ovale electrodes or subdural electrode 'mats'), when scalp EEG recordings are inconclusive. When telemetry is being considered for diagnostic purposes the most obvious requirement is that the patient has seizures that are frequent enough to make it likely they will have an episode during the recording period. For this reason, most centres would exclude patients with a seizure frequency of less than one per week. When seizures are found not to be epileptic, the most common diagnosis is dissociative seizures ('pseudoseizures', 'hysterical seizures'), which account for up to 1 in 5 patients in most telemetry series (Meierkord et al., 1991). The diagnosis of dissociative seizures is essentially one of exclusion, the important features being the absence of epileptiform discharge during the seizure and the presence of alpha rhythm during a period of apparently impaired consciousness. However, some 60% of focal seizures without impairment of consciousness (simple partial seizures) are accompanied by no abnormality in the scalp EEG, and so telemetry is of less value in differentiating between such seizures and non-epileptic events mimicking them.

EVOKED POTENTIALS

The EEG may be used to measure brain activity following a sensory stimulus. The most widely used technique of this type involves the measurement of cortical response to a standard visual stimulus, a black and white chequerboard that is moved in front of the eyes. Each movement of the chequerboard triggers a recording, and this process is repeated hundreds of times enabling an average response to be derived with computerized techniques. Such visual evoked potentials (VEPs) may detect lesions in the optic nerve, which are clinically silent and invisible to neuro-imaging. Thus VEPs find their greatest application in the investigation of patients with suspected MS. In the auditory domain, averaged recordings are obtained following a standard click stimulus. The resultant waveform has a number of components that reflect the functional integrity of specific points along the auditory pathway from the cochlear through the brainstem to the cortex. Brainstem auditory evoked responses (BSAERs), as they are known, are used to detect lesions in this pathway (e.g., acoustic neuromas) as well as to evaluate brainstem function in patients who are in a prolonged comatose state. Somatosensory evoked potentials (SSEPs) involve recordings from the cortex and at selected points over the spinal cord to give a measure of central nervous conduction following a somatosensory (electrical) stimulus in the periphery.

ELECTROMYOGRAPHY (EMG) AND NERVE CONDUCTION STUDIES (NCS)

EMG involves recording electrical activity in muscles using superficial or needle electrodes. Recordings are obtained at rest, with voluntary muscular activity and following electrical stimulation. The EMG is used to distinguish between possible causes of muscular weakness. Characteristic abnormal spontaneous contractions at rest are seen in motor neurone disease (MND), denervation and with certain primary muscle diseases. The electrical activity accompanying voluntary movement allows distinctions to be made between central and peripheral neurological deficits and shows characteristic patterns in muscle disorders. NCSs involve administering an electrical impulse to a peripheral nerve and measuring the waveform and velocity with which it is conducted along the nerve. In this way focal lesions of peripheral nerves may be localized and pathological processes affecting peripheral nerves may be identified.

NEUROIMAGING

In many clinical situations neuroimaging plays the most decisive role among investigations (Moseley, 1995). From the patient's point of view, a 'brain scan' is the most easily understood investigation, and undoubtedly the test most frequently requested by patients. The decision as to whether imaging is required and what sort of imaging may be helpful ultimately rests in the hands of the specialist radiologist. In the following section the basic principles underlying the most important clinical imaging methods are outlined, followed by a review of how imaging may contribute to the management of specific clinical problems.

Structural Neuroimaging

X-ray Computer Tomography

X-ray computer tomography (CT) first came into widespread clinical practice some 30 years ago. X-rays (radiation) are emitted from an X-ray tube, which is moved radially around the part of the patient being imaged, in this case the head. After the X-rays have passed through the patient, their intensity is measured by an array of detectors located in a ring, or gantry, surrounding the patient. The intensity of the emergent X-ray beam is compared with the known intensity of the incident beam to give a measure of the attenuation of X-rays along the path that beam has travelled through the patient. Using many such overlapping measurements, a computer constructs a two-dimensional image of the head that effectively represents a cross-sectional 'slice' of the brain.

From this brief description of the technique many of the key features and drawbacks of CT can be understood. First, the contrast in a CT image depends on the extent to which different tissues absorb X-rays, the so-called 'attenuation coefficients'. This is very high for bone and low for water. Unfortunately, the difference in X-ray attenuation between different compartments of brain tissue is negligible, and thus CT is unable to provide sharp images of grey and white matter. It is also relatively insensitive to many important pathologies (e.g., MS, small cerebral infarcts). On the other hand, it is a sensitive method for detecting haemorrhage, as blood is highly absorbant of X-rays (see Figure 3.1). The high attenuation of X-rays by bone means that certain areas in the brain are not well visualized, because the bone essentially casts an obscuring shadow. This particularly applies to the posterior cranial fossa and parts of the temporal lobes. The physical limitations imposed by the necessarily radial arrangement of X-ray generators and detectors impose limits on the plane in which images may be taken, although the relatively recent development of spiral (or helical) CT scanning facilitates image reconstruction in additional planes (coronal and sagittal) and allows patients to be scanned quickly, a study of the head taking as little as two minutes. Finally, CT scanning relies on X-ray technology, with the attendant risks of exposure to ionizing radiation. To put this in some context, a single head CT involves a radiation dose of

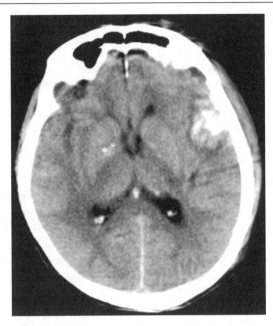

Figure 3.1. CT scan: axial image of a patient with an acute intracerebral haemorrhage. The haemorrhage is clearly demonstrated as high density in the left frontotemporal region (on the right side of the image)

approximately 2.3 mSv, comparable with 100 chest X-rays and equivalent to approximately one year of natural background environmental radiation (Royal College of Radiologists, 1998). The National Radiological Protection Board (1992) have calculated that a single abdominal CT (10 mSv) confers a risk of cancer of approximately 1 in 2,000 (the risk of cancer in the general population is approximately 1 in 3).

Despite these drawbacks, CT remains the investigation of first choice in a number of areas. These particularly include clinical situations in which the detection of CNS haemorrhage early in the course of the presentation is important: for example, acute head trauma, suspected subarachnoid haemorrhage and following acute cerebrovascular accident ('stroke'), in which situation management decisions involving administering antithrombotic treatment hinge critically on being able to distinguish between haemorrhagic lesions and infarction. In other instances, CT may be required when magnetic resonance imaging (MRI) (see p. 68) is contra-indicated (e.g., in a patient with intracranial, metallic vascular clips) or practically difficult to conduct (e.g., in ITU settings). The gantry design in CT is less constricting than for MRI, and patients with claustrophobia may sometimes better tolerate a CT scan. However, with these exceptions, where CT and MRI are both available, the superior sensitivity and anatomical definition of the latter technique mean that MRI is in most instances the preferred imaging investigation. As CT involves exposure to radiation, the practice of 'screening' with a CT scan is to be avoided if a negative result will call for an MRI.

Magnetic Resonance Imaging

In MRI the patient is placed within a strong magnetic field. Under the influence of this magnetic field, protons that have magnetic fields of their own and hence a polarity (they can be thought of as behaving like miniature bar magnets) 'line up' so that they are oriented in accordance with the forces of the field. Under the influence of the field the protons also precess, a movement that may be likened to the wobbling motion of a spinning top. During scanning the patient is stimulated with a brief 'pulse' of radiofrequency electromagnetic energy. This pulse deflects protons from their uniform orientation and causes them to precess in a more synchronized fashion. As the pulse is switched off, the nuclei return to their lined-up state, and in doing so emit radiation in the same frequency. Two types of signal are emitted, one corresponding to the protons realigning with the magnetic field (known as T1 signal) and the other corresponding to protons returning to a state of less synchronized precessing (known as T2). In general terms, T1 contrast provides optimal anatomical definition, while T2 images are especially sensitive to certain types of pathology—in particular, inflammatory lesions. Additional types of contrast can be generated by refinements to the scanning technique, including adjustments to the magnetic field and delivering multiple radiofrequency pulses. By imposing gradients on the magnetic field and giving the field strength a different value at each point in space, the signals emitted by protons can effectively be labelled with information about where in the body they are coming from. Using computer technology similar to the methods used in CT, an image of the brain can then be reconstructed.

The principal advantages of MRI compared with CT is its superior anatomical definition and superior sensitivity to certain types of pathology. MRI images may be reconstructed in multiple planes, which offers advantages when images of specific areas are required for diagnosis or planning surgical approaches to treatment (e.g., coronal images for visualization of medial temporal lobe structures). Since MRI involves exposing patients to high-strength magnetic fields, certain metal objects within the patient such as vascular surgical clips, cochlear implants or pacemakers are a contraindication to the technique. Orthopaedic prostheses and certain non-ferrous surgical clips may not pose a risk, but specialist advice will be necessary before proceeding to MRI. Examples of the different pathologies that can be detected by MRI are shown in Figures 3.2, 3.3 and 3.4.

Intravenous Contrast Agents

Water-soluble injectable compounds are available for both CT and MRI that greatly enhance contrast within blood vessels and in pathological lesions where there is disruption of the normal blood–brain barrier. These agents are associated with a significant risk of severe allergic reactions and, as in most clinical situations they provide little additional sensitivity or diagnostic information, they are not used routinely.

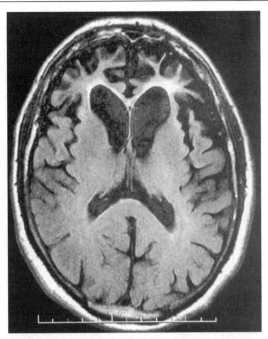

Figure 3.2. MRI: T1 – weighted axial image of a patient with advanced Pick's disease. There is marked bilateral, symmetrical cortical atrophy of the frontal and temporal lobes

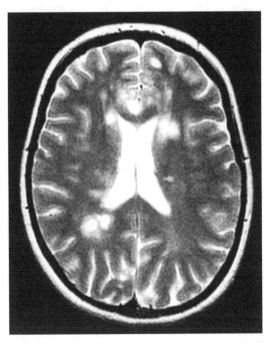

Figure 3.3. MRI: T2 – weighted axial image of a patient with multiple sclerosis. There are multiple areas of T2 signal hyperintensity in a periventricular distribution

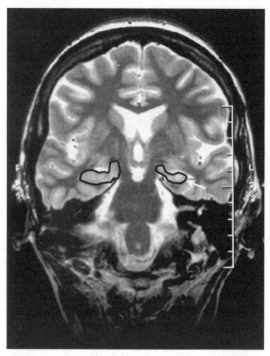

Figure 3.4. MRI: T2-weighted coronal image of a patient with temporal lobe epilepsy and left-sided hippocampal sclerosis. The hippocampi are outlined with a black trace. The hippocampus on the left (arrow) is smaller and demonstrates hyperintensity of the T2-weighted signal compared with the right side

Angiography

The cerebral vasculature may be imaged using conventional radiographic techniques with intra-arterial or intravenous contrast agents. These techniques are however associated with significant risks, and angiographic techniques developed using magnetic resonance angiography (MRA) are now the investigation of choice, when images of the cerebral arterial or venous system are required. MRA relies on the fact that nuclei that are moving within the brain have different magnetic resonance (MR) characteristics compared with those that are macroscopically static. High-resolution images can be achieved using MRA without the need for contrast agents.

Other MR-based Techniques

A number of other applications of MRI that have not yet found widespread use in clinical settings should be mentioned.

Diffusion tensor imaging (DTI) produces images of the brain that reflect the structural integrity of white matter tracts. Multiple images are obtained of each 'slice' of brain during scan acquisition, scanning parameters having been designed to be sensitive to the direction and rate of water movement (Taber et al., 2002). As water moves more freely along axons than across them or within grey matter, so the resulting images portray white matter tracts. DTI has the potential for revealing subtle white matter pathology in traumatic brain injury, vascular lesions, inflammatory disorders and in neurodevelopmental anomalies that escape detection with conventional MR techniques.

Magnetic resonance spectroscopy (MRS) is an older technique, but differs from the MR-based methods already described in that structural anatomical images are not produced. MRS is a method of analysing the chemical composition of a circumscribed volume of brain *in vivo*. The technique relies on the fact that the resonant frequency of nuclei vary depending on the compound that contains them. MRS produces data in the form of 'spectra' that show the intensity of resonance across a range of frequencies, each peak corresponding to a particular compound, with the height (or intensity) of each peak being proportional to the concentration of that compound in the volume of tissue being studied. Such spectra may be obtained using hydrogen or phosphate nuclei providing information on the concentration of biologically important compounds, which in turn reflect specific cellular physiological processes; examples include (from hydrogen spectra) glutamate, glutamine and n-acetyl aspartate (considered a marker of neuronal number or volume) and (from phosphate spectra) a variety of phosphate-containing compounds conveying information about neuronal membranes and metabolism (Stanley et al., 2000). With the availability of higher magnetic field strengths and other advances in MR hardware, the sensitivity of MRS is improving and spectra may be obtained from ever smaller volumes of interest (now less than $1\,cm^3$). As yet, however, the potential of MRS has not been realized in clinical practice (Vion-Dury et al., 1994).

Finally, *functional magnetic resonance imaging* (fMRI) is a relatively recent technique, still largely confined to research applications, in which MR is used to obtain images displaying brain function rather than structure. fMRI relies on the fact that oxygenated and deoxygenated forms of haemoglobin have different resonance properties and images may be produced in which the contrast depicts differences in the relative concentrations of these two forms of haemoglobin (blood oxygenation-level dependent [BOLD] contrast). BOLD contrast in turn reflects metabolism and therefore functional activity in the surrounding brain tissue.

Functional Imaging

An important principle underlying all functional imaging techniques is that cerebral function is closely related to cerebral metabolism, which in turn is tightly coupled to blood flow (Sawle, 1995). When considering activation studies, in which changes in brain function associated with some prescribed task or sensory stimulation are being investigated, an important principle is that when the brain is engaged in such activity there will be a focal, or regional, increase in blood flow in that part of the brain specifically engaged in the task that is disproportionately large compared with any associated general or global increase in cerebral blood flow. For clinical purposes the most commonly used functional imaging method is single photon emission computer tomography (SPECT). Other methods, including fMRI described in the preceding section, may be available in specialist centres, but they find their main application in research.

Positron Emission Tomography

In positron emission tomography (PET), nuclei radiochemically labelled with a positron are incorporated within molecules of biological relevance and administered to the patient most commonly by intravenous injection. Such labelled nuclei are unstable and the positron leaves the nucleus with sufficient kinetic energy to travel up to 2 mm through surrounding tissue before colliding with an electron. In the process of this collision both electron and positron are annihilated and two gamma rays (photons) are emitted travelling at $180°$ to one another. The patient's head is surrounded by a camera, which is designed to register the impact of photons striking opposite parts of the array of detectors simultaneously. In this way the site of origin of the gamma rays and hence the positron can be inferred within an area of $2\,mm^3$, the theoretical limit of PET resolution. In practice a resolution of somewhat less than this (5 mm) may be achieved with current technology. Quantitative techniques are possible with PET by acquiring pre-scan transmission data and arterial blood sampling of tracer concentration during the scan. Commonly used labelled compounds include water (H_2O) for blood flow studies, glucose for studies of cerebral glucose metabolism and dopa for studies of dopamine metabolism. The principal factor limiting the availability of PET is the necessity of having an extremely expensive on-site cyclotron unit for generating the positron-labelled compounds. As radioactivity is involved, the potential for repeated studies is limited.

Single Photon Emission Computer Tomography

The radioisotopes used in SPECT (e.g., technetium-99 or iodine-123) emit single gamma rays. The advantages of coincident detection offered by PET therefore do not apply and spatial information in SPECT is derived from the arrangement of detectors (collimation) and computerized tomography alone. This means that the resolution of SPECT is necessarily less than that of PET. However, SPECT has the advantage of using the less expensive radioisotopes with longer half-lives that, most importantly, are available in general nuclear medicine departments. In practice, therefore, SPECT is much more widely available for clinical use than PET. Blood flow studies are performed using technetium-99-labelled hexamethylpropyleneamine ($[Tc^{99m}]$ HMPAO). After intravenous injection $[Tc^{99m}]$ HMPAO crosses the blood–brain barrier over a period of approximately 10 minutes and then becomes trapped after chemical decomposition to a compound that cannot travel back through the blood–brain barrier. It remains stable for two hours or so, during which time the SPECT images are obtained (see, for example, Figure 3.5 at the end of this chapter [colour plate]). Thus this technique produces what is effectively a snapshot of cerebral blood flow over the 10 minutes after [Tc^{99m}] HMPAO is injected. Other compounds have been developed to image neurotransmitter systems. For example, the dopamine D2 receptor ligand I^{123}-iodobenzamide that binds specifically to D2 receptors over a period of 40 minutes after intravenous injection and then remains stable for up to two hours.

Clinical Applications of Functional Imaging

The advent of functional neuroimaging has created a new research discipline that holds great promise for our understanding of brain function in health and disease. As yet, however, there have been few important clinical applications (Sawle, 1995). Brain disorders in which profound functional impairment is accompanied by relatively little in the way of structural abnormality are the areas in which functional imaging is most likely to have an impact in clinical practice. Thus there is a growing interest in these techniques for investigating neurodegenerative disorders and epilepsy. Among degenerative conditions, PET and SPECT may have a role in distinguishing between different causes of dementia by demonstrating the distribution of hypometabolic areas. In epilepsy, both techniques have been evaluated as methods for localizing the seizure focus, relying on the fact that the epileptogenic focus is characteristically hypometabolic between seizures. The principal problem with these techniques is their lack of sensitivity. Quantitative techniques (with PET) and semi-quantitative methods in which an individual scan is compared with a normal data bank of images obtained in healthy individuals are as yet largely theoretical proposals.

Application of Neuroimaging to Specific Clinical Situations

Cerebrovascular Disease

CT scanning retains an important place in the investigation of acute cerebrovascular events (stroke). Approximately 10 per cent of strokes are due to intracerebral haemorrhage, and these cannot be distinguished reliably from cerebral infarction on clinical grounds alone. Antiplatelet, anticoagulant and thrombolytic treatment, which may be indicated for infarction, are contraindicated following cerebral haemorrhage and so an early distinction between these two diagnoses is important. CT is more sensitive to acute cerebral haemorrhage than MRI. Approximately two weeks after the haemorrhage, however, MRI becomes the more sensitive technique, being able to detect evidence of past haemorrhage months or years after the event.

CT also remains the imaging investigation of first choice when subarachnoid haemorrhage is suspected. Blood in the basal CSF spaces will be detectable with CT in 80% of cases within three days, though this falls to 40% after five days. MRI will detect only 50% of subarachnoid haemorrhages in the first three days. Once the diagnosis has been confirmed, investigation of the cerebral vasculature with MR angiography is employed to identify the underlying abnormality, which in 80% of cases will be an aneurysm in the arteries of the Circle of Willis, 10%

being accounted for by arteriovenous malformations (AVMs). Aneurysms greater than 5 mm in diameter will be detectable with MRI, or with CT using intravenous contrast. Other abnormalities of the cerebrovascular system, including AVMs, thrombosis or dissection of the internal carotid arteries and thrombosis of the cerebral venous sinuses are investigated with MRI.

Head Injury

CT remains the investigation of first choice after acute head injury because it is widely available, quick and can be undertaken relatively simply in patients who are comatose receiving ventilatory support. Most importantly, CT is of equal or superior sensitivitity compared with MRI in the detection of the acute complications of head injury that may require urgent surgical intervention, namely extradural and subdural haemorrhage and obstructive hydrocephalus. MRI is more sensitive than CT to cerebral infarction and diffuse axonal injury, although the detection of these pathological processes does not at present influence management. Claims that functional imaging techniques are of superior sensitivity to structural imaging in detecting abnormalities after head injury have been made, but have not found widespread clinical application as the findings have no impact on management, and their value in predicting outcome remains uncertain.

Inflammatory Conditions

MRI has replaced CT in the investigation of inflammatory processes in the CNS. This situation is exemplified by multiple sclerosis. All but the very largest of de-myelinating plaques in this disorder are invisible to CT, but are readily detected with T2-weighted MRI images (see Figure 3.3). Although multiple sclerosis remains a clinical diagnosis, the appearances on MRI may be sufficiently suggestive as to remove the need for further investigations. Systemic inflammatory conditions such as sarcoidosis and systemic lupus erythematosis may produce lesions in the CNS that are readily detected with MRI and may occasionally closely resemble the appearances of multiple sclerosis. Of infective processes, cerebral abscesses are usually easily identified with either CT or MRI. Encephalitis may produce little in the way of structural change, though herpes encephalitis may produce oedematous or haemorrhagic lesions, especially in the temporal lobe, for which MRI is the more sensitive imaging modality.

Cerebral Mass Lesions

Where MRI is available, it is the preferred investigation if a cerebral mass lesion is suspected. This is especially the case where a tumour in the posterior cranial fossa or adjacent to the sphenoidal ridge is concerned, as these areas are poorly visualized with CT because of shadowing from adjacent bone. MRI will detect smaller tumours than CT and, together with angiography, will enable more precise definition of anatomical boundaries and vascular relations for neurosurgical planning. Intravenous contrast with both CT and MRI has been advocated in the past, but for diagnostic purposes these techniques probably add little in the way of sensitivity.

Epilepsy

Among patients with epilepsy, structural neuroimaging is most strongly indicated in patients with recent onset of partial (focal) seizures after the age of 20. In practice, the majority of patients these days will have a CT scan at the very least, and this will detect most significant underlying mass lesions. However, MRI is sensitive to certain epileptogenic pathologies that are invisible to CT, the most important examples being hippocampal sclerosis (mesial temporal sclerosis, see Figure 3.4), cortical dysplasia and other developmental abnormalities. These pathologies are non-progressive, but may be amenable to surgical treatment where medication fails to control seizures. Thus, some authorities have suggested that MRI should be reserved for the evaluation of patients with medically intractable seizures in whom surgical treatment is being considered. However, where MR scanning is available, it is often performed as a first-line investigation. Both PET and SPECT have been evaluated as methods for localizing seizure focus, relying on the fact that the epileptogenic focus is characteristically hypometabolic (and hypoperfused) between seizures.

Degenerative Conditions

The primary role of neuroimaging in the investigation of a possible degenerative disorder is as a means of excluding other potentially treatable causes of progressive dementia, such as space-occupying lesions, hydrocephalus and inflammatory disorders. As a means of establishing a diagnosis of a primary degenerative condition, especially in the early clinical stages, imaging remains relatively insensitive. The problem is one of false negatives in the context of a wide range of normal variation, especially in the elderly. Methods of obtaining planimetric measurements with CT and hippocampal volume measurements from coronal images with MRI have been described. However, some of these methods are time-consuming, and they require a databank of measurements obtained in normal individuals for comparison. For these practical reasons and because there has as yet been no convincing demonstration that quantitative methods offer any advantage over an experienced radiologist simply inspecting the scan, such methods have had little impact in routine clinical practice. In Alzheimer's disease, the earliest change seen is loss of hippocampal volume. This is accompanied by a reduction of cerebral volume, manifest as an enlargement of cortical sulci and of the ventricular spaces. Focal lobar atrophy strongly suggests a diagnosis of frontotemporal dementia. Multiple infarcts and white matter hyperintensities on MRI scan are suggestive of vascular dementia, but white matter imaging abnormalities are also common both in Alzheimer's disease and in normal ageing. If absent, they make a diagnosis of vascular dementia unlikely. However, it is worth re-emphasizing that in the early stages of the disease the scan may be reported as 'normal for age'.

Other Neuropsychiatric Disorders

Over the last 20 years there have been countless neuroimaging studies of schizophrenia. As each new technique is developed, so it seems a fresh wave of studies is spawned. In group studies comparing patients with schizophrenia to normal controls, a consensus has undoubtedly emerged that schizophrenia is associated with a reduced whole brain volume. This is probably present at the onset of the disorder and is non-progressive. More specific regional structural abnormalities involving the temporal lobe (especially the medial temporal lobe structures), the frontal lobe, corpus callosum and abnormal assymetries have been less consistently replicated. None of these findings, however, can be identified with sufficient sensitivity or specificity in an individual patient to be of any relevance in clinical practice. The fact remains that the majority of patients with this profoundly disabling disorder have brains that, structurally at least, fall well within the normal range. Bipolar affective disorder and obsessional compulsive disorder have been the subject of fewer studies, and again, apart from showing a reduction in whole brain volume in the former condition, there is little in the way of a consensus. Functional imaging appears to offer great promise as a means of investigating the pathophysiology of neuropsychiatric disorders. This is perhaps particularly true of study designs combining brain activation procedures with neurochemical manipulations. However, a place for these sophisticated techniques in clinical practice still seems a long way off.

SUMMARY AND CONCLUSIONS

This chapter has reviewed the special investigations that are used in the assessment of patients with neurological problems. The process of history taking and physical examination was outlined, emphasizing the importance of basic clinical assessment in formulating a differential diagnosis and in guiding the choice of investigations. Methodological considerations underlying specific investigations were outlined and the clinical situations in which each technique might be helpful were described. The problems of misinterpretation that may arise with the EEG were highlighted. Current methods of structural and functional imaging were reviewed and appropriate imaging techniques for investigating specific categories of neurological problems were identified. The field of neuroimaging is rapidly evolving, and several developments in MRI and in functional imaging are likely to have an important impact on clinical practice in the next five to ten years.

Acknowledgements

I am grateful to Dr Ginny Ng, Consultant Neuroradiologist, for kindly providing the structural CT and MRI images for inclusion in this chapter.

REFERENCES

Binnie, C. D. & Prior, P. F. (1994) Electroencephalography. *Journal of Neurology, Neurosurgery and Psychiatry*, **57**, 1308–1319.

Chadwick, D. (1994) Epilepsy. *Journal of Neurology, Neurosurgery and Psychiatry*, **57**, 264–277.

Folstein, M. F., Folstein, S. E. & McHugh, P. R. (1975). 'Mini-mental state.' A practical method for grading the mental state of patients for the clinician. *Journal of Psychiatric Research*, **12**, 189–198.

Gregory, R. P., Oates, T. & Merry, R. T. G. (1993) Electroencephalogram epileptiform abnormalities in candidates for aircrew training. *Electroencephalography and Clinical Neurophysiology*, **86**, 75–77.

Lishman, W. A. (1998) *Organic Psychiatry* (3rd edition). Blackwell, Oxford, UK.

Marsden, C. D. & Fowler, T. J. (1998) *Clinical Neurology* (2nd edition). Arnold, London.

Mathuranath, P. S., Nestor, P. J., Berrios, G. E., Rakowicz, W. & Hodges, J. R. (2000) A brief cognitive test battery to differentiate Alzheimer's disease and frontotemporal dementia. *Neurology*, **55**, 1613–1620.

Meierkord, H., Will, B., Fish, D. & Shorvon, S. (1991) The clinical features and prognosis of pseudoseizures diagnosed using video-EEG telemetry. *Neurology*, **41**, 1643–1646.

Moseley, I. (1995) Imaging the adult brain. *Journal of Neurology, Neurosurgery and Psychiatry*, **58**, 7–21.

National Radiological Protection Board (1992) *Protection of the Patient in X-ray Computed Tomography*. Her Majesty's Stationery Office, London.

Nestor, P. & Hodges, J. R. (2001) The clinical approach to assessing patients with early onset dementia. In: J. R. Hodges (ed.) *Early-onset Dementia: A Multidisciplinary Approach* (pp. 23–46). Oxford University Press, Oxford, UK.

Royal College of Radiologists (1998) *Making the Best Use of a Department of Clinical Radiology. Guidelines for Doctors* (4th edition). Royal College of Radiologists, London.

Sawle, G. V. (1995) Imaging the head: Functional imaging. *Journal of Neurology, Neurosurgery and Psychiatry*, **58**, 132–144.

Stanley, J. A., Pettegrew, J. W. & Keshavan, M. S. (2000) Magnetic resonance spectroscopy in schizophrenia: Methodological issues and findings—Part 1. *Biological Psychiatry*, **48**, 357–368.

Taber, K. H., Pierpaoli, C., Rose, S. E., Rugg-Gunn, F. J., Chalk, J. B., Jones, D. K. et al. (2002) The future for diffusion tensor imaging in neuropsychiatry. *Journal of Neuropsychiatry and Clinical Neuroscience*, **14**, 1–5.

Thompson, E. J. (1995) Cerebrospinal fluid. *Journal of Neurology, Neurosurgery and Psychiatry*, **59**, 349–357.

Vion-Dury, J., Meyerhoff, J., Cozzone, P. L. & Weiner, M. W. (1994) What might be the impact on neurology of the analysis of brain metabolism by in-vivo magnetic resonance spectroscopy? *Journal of Neurology*, **241**, 354–371.

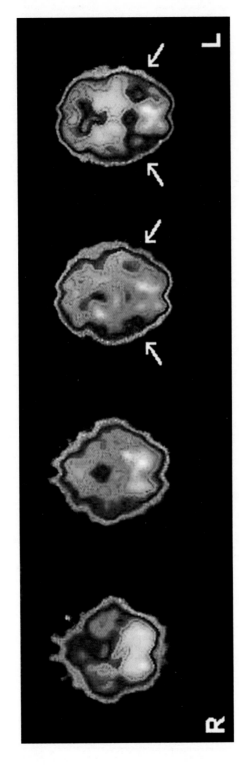

Figure 3.5. [Tc^{99m}] HMPAO SPECT (a limited series of axial images is shown) of a patient with Alzheimer's disease. There is reduced tracer uptake bilaterally in temporo-parietal regions (see arrows), greater on the right side than the left. Consistent with the scan appearances, neuropsychological testing revealed visuospatial deficits that were significantly greater than verbal deficits

PART III

Neuropsychological Assessment—General Issues

Psychological and Psychiatric Aspects of Brain Disorder: Nature, Assessment and Implications for Clinical Neuropsychology

Richard Brown

Institute of Psychiatry, London, UK

INTRODUCTION

This chapter deals with the broad range of psychological and psychiatric problems associated with neurological damage or disease and their significance for assessment. It focuses on traumatic brain injury (TBI), stroke, epilepsy and neurodegenerative disease—particularly Alzheimer's disease (AD) and Parkinson's disease (PD). The first part of the chapter will present a brief overview of psychiatric disorder in these conditions, specifically depression, anxiety, euphoria, apathy, mania and psychosis. The latter sections will focus on the assessment of these conditions in the presence of neurological disease and the implications for cognition and neuropsychological assessment.

PSYCHOLOGICAL AND PSYCHIATRIC PROBLEMS IN PATIENTS WITH NEUROLOGICAL DISORDER

This section will mainly consider studies that have sought to apply formal methods of diagnosis using standardized interviews and criteria. While it will consider the major classes of psychiatric disorder in isolation, co-morbidity is frequent. For example, in TBI, Hibbard et al. (1998) found that more patients were diagnosed with two or more Axis-I disorders (44%) than were diagnosed with a single psychiatric disorder (36%). Similarly, in a study of patients with PD (Menza et al., 1993), almost all patients with a formal anxiety disorder diagnosis had a co-morbid depressive disorder diagnosis.

Clinical Neuropsychology: A Practical Guide to Assessment and Management for Clinicians.
Edited by L.H. Goldstein and J.E. McNeil. © 2004 John Wiley & Sons, Ltd.

Depression

Depression is one of the most commonly identified psychological problems in patients with brain disorders. Jorge et al. (1993) found major depression (MD) in 26% of a sample of patients one month post brain injury, while 42% had depression at some point in the following year. Longer term, Varney et al. (1987) found MD in 77% of their sample three years after injury, while Hibbard et al. (1998) quote rates of 61% in a community sample an average of 7.6 years post trauma. Robinson (1998) provides one of the best reviews and discussions of depression (and other psychiatric sequelae) following stroke. Across a range of studies, 34% of patients were identified as having post-stroke depression. As with TBI, depression may occur either acutely or later in the course. It is frequently suggested that depression is more common following left hemisphere and frontal damage. However, a recent systematic review failed to find any relationship between lesion location and post-stroke depression (Carson et al., 1994).

Depression is commonly reported in patients with degenerative neurological disease including AD and PD. However, there are wide variations depending on the methods of sampling and assessment. Depressive symptoms are typically reported in the region of 30–40% in these patient groups, but MD may not be elevated in community samples. Weiner et al. (2002) examined the prevalence of MD in AD from two prospective databases of almost 1,000 patients and found a prevalence of only 1–5%. In PD also, the population prevalence of MD (3–5%) is less than that suggested by outpatient samples, although the figure appears higher in patients with dementia (Hantz et al., 1994; Tandberg et al., 1996).

In epilepsy, depressive symptoms as well as anxiety and fear may be found as part of the ictal or peri-ictal phenomena. In the inter-ictal phase depression is common, although the prevalence is unclear with the most typical presentation being chronic dysthymic disorder with intermittent course. As in other conditions, the presence of co-morbid depression can exacerbate cognitive deficits revealed by neuropsychological assessment (Paradiso et al., 2001). The study of depression (and other psychiatric disorders) in epilepsy is further complicated by the interaction between symptoms and medication. Drugs used in the treatment of psychiatric disorder can lead to seizures (Alldredge, 1999), while anti-epileptic drugs can cause or exacerbate psychiatric problems in some patients (Ketter et al., 1999).

Pathological crying is sometimes observed in patients with neurological disorder, often in conjunction with pathological laughing. Such pathological behaviour is reported in patients with amyotrophic lateral sclerosis (ALS), multiple sclerosis, stroke and AD. While it can accompany a congruent mood disorder, the extreme emotional response can often be found in absence of abnormal affect.

Anxiety

Major classes of anxiety disorder include generalized anxiety disorder (GAD), obsessive compulsive disorder (OCD), phobic disorder and post-traumatic stress disorder (PTSD).

GAD is the most common anxiety disorder in patients with neurological conditions. It has been reported in 9–25% of patients following TBI (Fann et al., 1995; Hibbard et al., 1998) and almost 30% following stroke (Astrom, 1996). Figures closer to the population base rate of 4% have been reported for PD (Menza et al., 1993), although a 10-fold increase was noted in the small clinic sample of Starkstein et al. (1992).

Although some authors suggest that post-traumatic amnesia may protect against PTSD (Bryant, 2001), prevalence rates of 19% (Hibbard et al., 1998) to 26% (Bryant et al., 2000) have been reported. Interestingly, however, in patients with severe brain injury, PTSD is only rarely accompanied by intrusive memories of the trauma (Bryant et al., 2000). A preliminary study also suggests the occurrence of PTSD-like symptoms in a group of patients suffering first stroke (Sembi et al., 1998), while in the elderly where PTSD is generally rare combat-related PTSD symptoms may emerge or worsen with the onset of a dementing disorder (van Achterberg et al., 2001; Verma et al., 2001). Finally, in epilepsy, symptoms of PTSD-like anxiety disorder have been reported in patients with apparent psychogenic non-epileptic seizures (Rosenberg et al., 2000).

Panic disorder is complexly associated with epilepsy, presenting problems for diagnosis. Some patients with primary panic disorder experience non-epileptic seizures (Bowman, 1998), while in other cases a seizure disorder may present in a way that is misdiagnosed as a psychiatric condition (Tisher et al., 1993). A sense of panic sometimes accompanies a more general fear aura. Panic disorder has received little attention in other conditions. There is little useful epidemiological or even good clinical data, although there is some evidence of increased rates following traumatic brain injury (Hibbard et al., 1998) and in PD (Menza et al., 1993; Vazquez et al., 1993).

Research evidence on phobic disorder is even more scarce and seems to reflect the low prevalence of such problems in patients with neurological disorder, although one community-based study suggests that agoraphobia may be common following stroke (Burvill et al., 1995).

Apathy

Apathy refers to a constellation of behavioural, emotional and motivational features, including: reduced interest and participation in normal purposeful behaviour; lack of initiative with problems in initiation or sustaining an activity to completion; lack of concern or indifference; and a flattening of affect. Only recently has the term 'apathy' been used to define an independent clinical entity (Marin, 1991) or specific diagnostic criteria and assessment instruments developed (see p. 89).

Recent studies point to the widespread occurrence of apathy in neurological disorders (see Brown & Pluck, 2000 for a review). Andersson et al. (1999) found apathy following TBI (46%), stroke (57%) and hypoxic brain damage (79%) and noted higher rates in patients with right hemisphere damage or subcortical involvement, this latter observation supported by other studies (Galynker et al., 1995; Starkstein et al., 1993). Consistent with these findings, apathy is one of the defining features of subcortical dementia (Cummings, 1986), and correspondingly high rates are reported in PD (17–42%; Aarsland et al., 1999; Starkstein et al., 1992), Huntington's disease and particularly progressive supranuclear palsy (PSP) (80–90%; Levy et al., 1998; Litvan et al., 1998). However, apathy is also a common feature of AD (Kuzis et al., 1999; Mega et al., 1996), with a recent study that applied strict diagnostic reporting a rate of 37% (Starkstein et al., 2001).

In contrast, the literature reveals an absence of reports of apathy in epilepsy other than as a sedative-related side-effect of some anticonvulsant medication.

As already noted, depression and apathy often coexist, although each can present in isolation. When co-morbid the severities of the two conditions are typically only weakly associated. They also differ in their relationship to other clinical features and symptoms (Levy et al., 1998). In particular, cognitive impairment shows a strong association with the severity of apathy, but not with depressive symptoms (Pluck & Brown, 2002; Starkstein et al., 1992). Other phenomenological differences include an absence of subjective distress in apathy, an absence of negative thoughts about self, present and future, and a general flattening of affect.

Psychosis

Robinson (1998) reports a number of cases of psychosis following stroke, but emphasizes the rarity of the phenomena. Although isolated hallucinatory or delusional symptoms can occur following focal lesions, psychosis is more common in combination with more global deterioration in patients with diffuse cerebrovascular disease where the symptoms may follow an episodic, stepwise occurrence, or in patients with degenerative white matter disease. Misidentification syndromes, such as Capras or Fregoli, are other examples of complex delusional perceptions following brain injury.

Delusions and hallucinations are more frequent in PD, although cases are often related to the adverse impact of dopaminergic medication. Aarsland et al. (1999) found delusions in 16% of a community sample and hallucinations in 27%. Most hallucinations are visual and occur with insight. However, even if clearly related to medication side-effects, the presence of psychotic symptoms is an important risk factor for dementia, and the presence of hallucinations with fluctuating cognition are key features of dementia with Lewy bodies. In AD, the prevalence of psychotic symptoms is similar to that found in PD (Ballard et al., 1995). Although delusions and hallucinations only rarely occur as a presenting symptom, they become more frequent with disease progression and accompany other behavioural symptoms, such as anxiety and agitation.

Although psychotic symptoms can be found in the disorders considered above, they are rarely confusable with schizophrenia. However, among patients with epilepsy, particularly those with partial seizures arising from mesial temporal structures, a chronic schizophrenia-like psychosis has been found in 3–7% of cases (Toone, 2000), while more acute post-ictal symptoms can be observed in other cases (Lancman, 1999).

Euphoria, Hypomania and Mania

Abnormal levels of positive mood, particularly in the presence of a disabling neuro-logical condition, are seen as a symptom of dysregulation of the normal mechanisms of affect and a direct result of the brain disorder. Abnormal positive affect appears to be rare following stroke or brain injury. Hibbard et al. (1998) found mania in 2% of her sample of TBI patients, while Starkstein et al. (1987) found mania in only 1% of acute stroke patients, more commonly in older patients and those with a positive family history of mood disorder. Similar low figures are reported in PD (even in the presence of dementia), AD (Aarsland et al., 2001) and in epilepsy. Conditions with stronger association with mania or euphoric mood include Huntington's disease, multiple sclerosis, Creuzfeldt–Jakob disease and frontotemporal dementia (see Mendez, 2000 for a review).

THE ASSESSMENT OF PSYCHOLOGICAL PROBLEMS IN PATIENTS WITH NEUROLOGICAL DISORDER

Where the goal of assessment is diagnosis, there is no alternative to the formal psychiatric interview and application of standard diagnostic criteria. Assessment may have implications for differential diagnosis (e.g., depression vs. dementia in an elderly patient), or to identify a psychiatric condition that requires direct treat-ment. Assessment and diagnosis are enhanced by the use of a structured interview such as the Structured Clinical Interview for DSM-IV (SCID; First et al., 1997) or Schedules of Clinical Assessment in Neuropsychiatry (SCAN; World Health Organ-ization, 1994), although such instruments are time-consuming to employ and require formal training.

More commonly, psychologists will wish to investigate the nature and severity of psychological symptoms as part of a wider assessment. However, this can be complicated by overlap between the signs and symptoms of the psychiatric state and those of the brain disorder itself. Additionally, the presence of dementia, impaired insight, denial of illness or aphasia can all pose problems for the choice of assessment methods and instruments.

Clinical Interview and Observation

Together with information from the referral letter or case notes, the clinical interview and history taking is the ideal place to start assessing the presence, nature and severity of psychological problems. The opportunity should be taken to undertake a brief assessment of the patient's psychiatric history and current state, as well as their current and recent medication history. This process can be aided by a checklist of signs and symptoms that may indicate the presence of psychological disorder, either as a diagnosable condition, or of a type that may influence the neuropsycho-logical assessment. Such a checklist may serve as an *aide mémoire*, encouraging the clinician to evaluate the range of problems commonly encountered in patients with neurological disorder. Where appropriate, further assessment may be required, just as in the investigation of cognitive problems. The Brief Psychiatric Rating Scale (Lukoff et al., 1986) can be useful where a more detailed interview is required.

However, although interview and observation are important tools for the clinician, caution is required. The test situation is highly artificial and can be threatening or a cause of great concern to patients. While all clinicians will seek to provide reassurance, a patient may remain anxious, suspicious or even hostile without it necessarily indicating their normal state. Further information from a third-party informant should be obtained to test whether the observed signs reflect a more general pattern of emotional response or behaviour. This is particularly important where the patient appears to lack insight, or where there is an apparent denial of illness.

In some patient groups, physical symptoms can mimic emotional disorders. Patients with extrapyramidal disorders, such as PD, can present with many of the symptoms of depression, such as hunched posture, slowness and lack of expression in the voice, face and gesture. It is particularly important in such patients to check their level of affect directly to determine whether their mood state is congruent with their physical presentation.

Self-report Instruments

Self-report instruments can provide an economical means of assessing specific psychological problems. The challenge is choosing ones that are valid and reliable for that clinical group, typically without empirical research to guide the decision. Psychologists must also decide on the appropriateness of standard cut-off scores, typically developed for use in non-neurological populations. Given such problems, a number of instruments have been developed for specific patient populations. However, all should be used with caution unless their reliability and validity have been demonstrated.

As noted above, patients with dementia and/or aphasia can be particularly difficult to assess. The Visual Analogue Mood Scales (VAMS; Stern, 1996) attempts to tackle this problem by using simple, symbolic representations of facial expressions to assess a variety of emotions. There is some evidence that the instruments provide a valid assessment of mood in stroke patients and are sensitive to change (Arruda et al., 1996).

Informant Reports

An alternative or supplement to self-report is information from another individual who knows the patient well, typically another family member or professional carer. This may be the only method available for patients with significant dementia or where there are cognitive deficits, such as aphasia or lack of insight, that preclude other assessment methods. Logsdon and Teri (1995) adapted the Beck Depression

Inventory (BDI; Beck & Beamesderfer, 1974), Geriatric Depression Scale (GDS; Sheikh & Yesavage 1986) and the Centre for Epidemiological Studies-Depression Scale (CES-D; Radloff, 1977) for completion by the carers of patients with AD. The results suggested good agreement between the carer's completion of the scales and the findings from standard diagnostic interviews. Although a promising approach, it remains unproven with other scales for different problems or clinical populations.

More commonly a standardized interview with the caregiver is used to assess the presence and severity of psychological problems in the patient. Perhaps the most widely used in research is the Neuropsychiatric Inventory (NPI; Cummings et al., 1994). This semi-structured interview enables the clinician to rate both the frequency and severity of a range of psychopathologies associated with dementia and other neurological conditions: delusions, hallucinations, agitation, depression, anxiety, euphoria, apathy, disinhibition, irritability and aberrant motor behaviour. The instrument can also be used to assess the degree to which those symptoms that are present are a cause of distress to the family caregiver (Kaufer et al., 1998) or disruption in a nursing home context (Wood et al., 2000).

A number of instruments have been developed to assess 'non-cognitive' symptoms in patients with AD including the Manchester and Oxford Universities Scale for the Psychopathological Assessment of Dementia MOUSEPAD; Allen et al., 1996) and Behavioural Pathology in AD (BEHAVE-AD; Reisberg et al., 1996). All assess a slightly different set of symptoms, while none appear to provide a complete assessment of known psychopathology (e.g., while the MOUSEPAD includes wandering and provides a more detailed evaluation of hallucinatory and delusional behaviour than the NPI, it neglects affective disturbance and apathy).

Other instruments have been developed for the informant-based assessment of psychopathology associated with frontal lobe dysfunction where lack of insight can be a problem. The 20-item Dysexecutive Questionnaire (DEX; Wilson et al., 1996) assesses a range of emotional, personality, behaviour and cognitive symptoms, while the 46-item Frontal Lobe Personality Scale (FLOPS; Grace et al., 1999) assesses apathy, disinhibition and problems with self-monitoring and appears to have good reliability and validity (Grace et al., 1999; Norton et al., 2001; Paulsen et al. 1995). Bozeat et al. (2000) reported a new carer-rated questionnaire aimed at distinguishing patients with AD and frontotemporal dementia, assessing stereotypic and eating behaviour, executive dysfunction and self-care, mood changes and social awareness. Similarly the 24-item Frontal Behavioural Inventory (Kertesz et al., 1997), a scale with good internal consistency and inter-rater reliability, distinguishes between frontal lobe dementia and AD.

Choosing a Suitable Instrument

This section seeks to guide the clinician in choosing the most appropriate assessment methods and instruments. There is no space to consider the properties of all popular instruments for each clinical condition. Instead, the more commonly used measures will be discussed along with any disease-specific instruments that have been developed. All of the problems are tapped by the NPI which can provide a convenient screening instrument to be supplemented by more detailed evaluation where necessary.

Depression and Anxiety

Many clinicians will employ instruments to assess depression and anxiety as part of their routine practice, with the BDI (Beck & Beamesderfer, 1974), Hospital Anxiety and Depression Scale (HADS; Zigmond & Snaith, 1983) and Wakefield Self-Assessment Depression Scale (Snaith et al., 1971) among the most widely used, while in the elderly the GDS (Sheikh & Yesavage, 1986) is popular. The Hamilton Depression Rating Scale (HDRS; Hamilton, 1960) can also be valuable for the clinical rating of depressive symptomatology based on information obtained from clinical or semi-structured interview.

Although popular, the BDI may be highly susceptible to interference from other non-affective aspects of brain injury and neurological disorder relating to fatigue, cognitive impairment and poor decision-making, psychomotor slowing, anhedonia and loss of interest, as well as behavioural disturbances such as agitation and irritability. All of these symptoms can occur in patients without them indicating a depressive disorder. Raw scores and standard cut-offs should be used with caution and certainly not without a careful examination of which items are being endorsed by the patient.

The HADS places less emphasis on physical and behavioural aspects of depression, but in doing so focuses more on loss of interest and enjoyment. Although these are important aspects of depressive symptomatology, there is the potential for detecting patients with apathy rather than a primary depressive disorder. Ultimately, the validity of such scales and their sensitivity and specificity can only be judged against formal psychiatric diagnoses. Unfortunately, there have been relatively few such studies in patients with brain disorders.

There are problems in using the BDI in patients with motor disorders, such as PD, if the clinician seeks both reasonable levels of sensitivity and specificity, although there is support for the use of the Montgomery Asberg Depression Rating Scale (MADRS; Montgomery & Asberg, 1979) as both a screening and diagnostic instrument (Leentjens et al., 2000). Similar problems are found in the assessment of post-stroke depression. O'Rourke et al. (1998) supported the use of the HADS in stroke patients, although the recommended cut-offs were found to be suboptimal, with a value of 6/7 providing greater utility. However, Johnson et al. (1995) found little support for the use of the HADS in screening for depression following stroke, recommending instead the GDS or General Health Questionnaire (GHQ-28; Goldberg, 1978). Other investigators have developed stroke-specific instruments for screening or assessment (Gainotti et al., 1997; Sutcliffe & Lincoln, 1998; Watkins et al., 2001), although little is known yet about their formal properties of clinical utility.

Assessing depression in dementia patients is particularly problematic. The BDI performs poorly in AD (Wagle et al., 2000), and even the GDS has been shown to be unsuitable for patients with mild–moderate dementia (Montorio & Izal, 1996). Disease-specific instruments include the Cornell Scale for Depression in Dementia (CSDD; Alexopoulos et al., 1988) and the dementia Mood Assessment Scale (Sunderland & Minichiello, 1996).

In contrast to the assessment of depression, the assessment of anxiety appears less complicated, in part because of less confusion between symptoms of anxiety and brain disorder and the narrower choice of available instruments. In terms of self-report measures the HADS has already been mentioned above, although with the same caveats in patients with significant cognitive impairment. It provides a useful combined screening instrument with depression where co-morbidity is suspected, as does the GHQ.

Apathy

Apathy is typically accompanied by a lack of concern and possibly insight into the nature and severity of the condition. Although self-report instruments are available, informant report and clinician ratings are preferable. The NPI includes an assessment of apathy and provides a quick and convenient screening. For more detailed investigation the Apathy Evaluation Scale (AES; Marin et al., 1991) provides an interview-based clinician-rated scale, although carer- and patient-rated versions are also available. The instrument has excellent intra-test, inter-rater and test–retest reliability and good discriminative and predictive validity. The AES has been adapted for use with the elderly (Resnick et al., 1998) and in PD (Starkstein et al., 1992). Recently, Starkstein et al. (2001) suggested a set of criteria for translating caregiver-derived AES data into a formal 'diagnosis' of apathy. The Scale for the Assessment of Negative Symptoms in Alzheimer's Disease (SANS-AD) (Reichman et al., 1996) measures the symptoms of avolition–apathy, affective blunting and social–emotional withdrawal in patients with AD, although few data are available to date.

Finally, because apathy can be formulated as a disorder of motivation, direct behavioural assessment may provide a useful adjunct to clinical ratings. The Card Arrangement Reward Responsivity Objective Test (CARROT; Al-Adawi et al., 1998) assesses the degree to which individuals can improve their performance on a simple card arrangement task in response to small financial incentives. Although only used experimentally to date, the test is sensitive to the impact of brain injury, and its validity has been shown through association with independent rating of motivation in a rehabilitation programme.

Psychosis, Mania and Disorders of Positive Affect

Psychotic behaviour and mania are likely to lead to a formal psychiatric referral and assessment. Where a neuropsychologist wishes to screen for such symptoms, assessment is best achieved through clinical examination and informant report. The NPI permits a brief assessment, although the MOUSEPAD offers a more thorough evaluation. Designed for use in dementia, these instruments may nevertheless have a role in other brain-disordered groups that share similar clinical phenomenology. For mania, a number of self-report instruments for mania exist where the patient is cognitively intact (Altman et al., 2001), while a clinician-rated instrument may be useful where a detailed objective assessment is required (Altman et al., 1994). Euphoria tends to be assessed through clinical observation and informant report, and some of the frontal lobe instruments described above will tap this dimension. Finally, specific measures exist to assess pathological laughing and crying (Newsom-Davis et al., 1999; Robinson et al., 1993).

IMPLICATIONS FOR COGNITIVE FUNCTION AND NEUROPSYCHOLOGICAL ASSESSMENT

The neuropsychological assessment is a structured situation designed to provide a sample of the patient's behaviour for clinical decision-making. Even if the purpose of assessment is to measure cognitive change, patients will be bringing with them possible psychological and psychiatric problems that may have an impact on their performance. The relationships between psychological disorder, cognitive function and performance in the assessment situation are complex. For the neuropsychologist, planning, conducting and interpreting an assessment there are three main sets of issues:

1 Does the patient present with a psychological or psychiatric problem and how might this be assessed?
2 How might such a problem interact with, and impact on, cognitive function and test performance?
3 What are the consequences of any such changes for the accurate assessment of cognitive dysfunction resulting from the known or suspected brain disorder?

The first of these issues concerns assessment that has already been dealt with. The final sections will consider the remaining questions, focusing on three major problem areas: apathy, depression and anxiety. Similar issues will apply for other conditions, such as bipolar disorder (Zubieta et al., 2001) and schizophrenia (Kuperberg & Heckers, 2000), where cognitive dysfunction is also commonly found.

Apathy

Apathy needs to be distinguished from an isolated indifference or ambivalence to the test situation or its outcome. As noted, apathy is a feature of the primary brain disorder and will be a pervasive feature of the patient's life. The apparent lack of motivation in apathetic patients is one of the most obvious factors likely to influence test performance. When present, this should be seen as a core part of the clinical presentation of the organic disorder and not as a confound to assessment. However, unless apathy is formally assessed and identified, there is a danger that the neuropsychologist may misattribute such lack of motivation as a functional symptom and de-emphasize any performance deficits observed on formal cognitive assessment.

With apathy the patient may have a reduced hedonic response to positive events, such as success, and an emotional indifference to the practical or social consequences of failure. As a result of this we cannot rely upon self-motivation in the test situation, while the usual approaches to encourage patients during assessment may have little impact.

The degree to which apathy impacts on test performance may depend upon the nature and demands of the test being used. Where the tasks tap more automatic processes, such as those involved in perception or the familiarity involved in recognition memory, performance may be unaffected. The majority of tests, however, depend on the exercise of effort—either physical or mental—and so will be sensitive to a patient's willingness and ability to allocate more resources on difficult tasks or as demands increase.

Behaviourally, apathetic patients may appear relatively normal when performing routine tasks or when responding to external cues or triggers, but will show a marked deficit in conditions of novelty or when required to self-initiate behaviour. In these situations they tend to show an absence of spontaneous emotion, cognition and overt behaviour (avolition).

In some respects the test situation is a poor one to tap this deficit, as neuropsychological tests tend to be administered in a highly structured way, often providing explicit instruction and prompts. Deficits associated with apathy are more likely to emerge in testing as the degree of structure decreases or where patients are freer to self-select a strategy for performing the task. Consequently, apathetic patients will often show significant deficits on tests of executive function or tests in other domains with a significant executive component (Kuzis et al., 1999; Starkstein et al., 1992). Such a pattern fits well with the clinicopathological association between apathy and dysfunction to frontostriatal circuits.

While there is no 'apathy test', verbal fluency is probably one of the most useful measures sensitive to the disorder. From a minimal task instruction, patients have to initiate and sustain an extended cognitive operation of search and retrieval of information from semantic memory. Apathetic patients will typically have very diminished output on such tasks. They may produce no words at all after the first few responses, paralleling the subjective experience that their mind is empty of spontaneous thought.

Depression

Whereas apathy is 'part and parcel' of the patient's brain disorder and therefore inseparable from the other cognitive and behavioural deficits, depression presents the neuropsychologist with a more challenging problem. In some patients the cognitive impairment may be the direct result of the psychiatric condition. In others, co-morbid neurological illness and depression may each contribute to the cognitive profile. Finally, the presence of depression may lead to secondary problems with testing that do not necessarily reflect an underlying cognitive impairment.

In a meta-analysis of cognitive impairment in MD, Zakzanis et al. (1998) was unable to find any measure that reliably distinguished between depressed and healthy non-depressed samples. However, among the most sensitive measures were tests of long-term verbal learning and memory (particularly free recall), complex psychomotor tests, measures of attention and timed executive tests. A similar profile was revealed in the study of Veiel (1997), although a more general deficit in executive function was suggested. Such a pattern of impairment is also widely found in patients with organic brain disorder, particularly when it is relatively diffuse or involves frontosubcortical regions.

In older adults depression may present as a dementing disorder, and even in younger patients up to a third may score within the range of clinically significant cognitive impairment (Brown et al., 1994). While the severity of impairment is typically unrelated to the severity of the mood disorder (unlike the association between cognitive decline and apathy), there is evidence that certain classes of depressive illness may be more strongly associated with cognitive impairment than others. Specifically, evidence suggests a link between cognitive deficits and the presence of 'melancholic' symptoms of depression (Austin et al., 1999). Melancholic depression, with a later age of onset and greater association with psychotic symptoms, is characterized by psychomotor retardation, agitation and decreased attentiveness, responsivity and spontaneity. It is of note that some of these features overlap with the core features of apathy and may well share a common neurological substrate.

Separating depression from dementia is one of the main problems faced by neuropsychologists working with older adults. Despite years of efforts, there is still no definitive way to distinguish the two groups on a single occasion. DesRosiers et al. (1995) assessed the sensitivity and specificity of a range of common measures in patients presenting at a memory clinic. Based on a two to four-year follow-up, the Kendrick Object Learning Test (Kendrick et al., 1979), percentage delayed recall on the Wechsler Logical Memory and Visual Reproductions Test (Wechsler, 1987) correctly classified all dementing patients, although there was a significant misdiagnosis rate for patients with a primary depressive disorder. Thus longitudinal assessment remains important, although evidence suggests that longer term even these depressed patients may be at increased risk of developing a degenerative condition (Reding et al., 1985).

Outside of the context of the elderly and dementia, depression is still an important factor in assessment. Where a patient has a suspected brain injury or neurological disorder, the presence of depression may be sufficient explanation for any cognitive impairment observed, particularly where this fits the pattern typically observed with MD. Alternatively, a relatively mild 'organic' impairment may be exacerbated by co-morbid depression, thus complicating the clinical decision-making process. In patients with primarily frontal or frontostriatal disorders, depression may lead to accentuation of the normal pattern of impairment. Even in patients with temporal lobe damage, evidence suggests that the profile of cognitive impairment is exacerbated by co-morbid depression, particularly in patients with left-hemisphere foci (Paradiso et al., 2001).

Finally, we need to be aware of the impact that testing itself may have on the patients. Performance on cognitive tests can lead to a significant deterioration in subjective mood even in healthy subjects (Holdwick & Wingenfield, 1999). One might expect that demanding tests associated with significant rates of failure would exacerbate the mood state of currently depressed patients, further impacting on their cognitive performance. Depressed patients may also be liable to give up after real or perceived task failure (Elliott et al., 1996) or suffer interference from off-task thoughts or ruminations (Watkins & Brown, 2002).

Anxiety

It has long been recognized, and reflected in the Yerkes–Dodson Law, that increasing arousal leads to improving performance to a point at which it starts to deteriorate. Moderate levels of anxiety may therefore be beneficial to maintain optimum performance, but the over-arousal found in some anxious patients may be detrimental (Darke, 1988a, b). While there is little evidence of an impact of anxiety on episodic memory (Waldstein et al., 1997), it may exacerbate the memory impairment in patients with co-morbid depression (Kizilbash et al., 2002). In addition, as in depression, anxious individuals may indulge in off-task ruminations about their performance, the perceptions of others, etc. or just indulge in more general worry, also associated with poor test performance (Pratt et al., 1997). This would be consistent with the idea that anxiety leads to reduced attentional capacity, tending to impairment on more demanding tasks (Eysenck & Calvo, 1992).

Finally, patients with an anxiety disorder may well be receiving pharmacological treatment for the condition. The impact of benzodiazepines on memory and psychomotor function are well documented, with both acute and chronic administration (Allen et al., 1991; Curran, 1991) and even weeks after discontinuation of treatment (Curran et al., 1994).

CONCLUSIONS

Patients with brain damage or disorder can show a variety of psychological symptoms and psychiatric illnesses, and these can have a direct impact on their cognitive profile. The accurate assessment of these neurobehavioural, emotional and psychiatric symptoms are as important in neuropsychology as the assessment of cognition itself. Far more research is required to evaluate existing instruments and methods of assessment for their reliability and validity in the context of neurological disorder and in the development of new instruments. More research is also required into the interaction between neurological and psychiatric symptoms on cognition. Finally, although the focus of this chapter has been on neuropsychological assessment, similar issues arise when considering broader issues of psychological practice, such as the planning, implementation and evaluation of rehabilitation programmes (Wilson, 1997) and the measurement of progression and outcome.

REFERENCES

Aarsland, D., Larsen, J. P., Geok Lim, N., Janvin, C., Kaarlsen, K., Tandberg, E. et al. (1999) Range of neuropsychiatric disturbances in patients with Parkinsons's disease. *Journal of Neurology, Neurosurgery and Psychiatry*, **67**, 492–496.

Aarsland, D., Cummings, J. L. & Larsen, J. P. (2001) Neuropsychiatric differences between Parkinson's disease with dementia and Alzheimer's disease. *International Journal of Geriatric Psychiatry*, **16**, 184–191.

Al-Adawi, S., Powell, J. H. & Greenwood, R. J. (1998) Motivational deficits after brain injury: A neuropsychological approach using new assessment techniques. *Neuropsychology*, **12**, 115–124.

Alexopoulos, G. S., Abrams, R. C., Young, R. C. & Shamoian, C. A. (1988) Cornell Scale for Depression in Dementia. *Biological Psychiatry*, **23**, 271–284.

Alldredge, B. K. (1999) Seizure risk associated with psychotropic drugs: Clinical and pharmacokinetic considerations. *Neurology*, **53**, S68–S75.

Allen, D., Curran, H. V. & Lader, M. (1991) The effects of repeated doses of clomipramine and alprazolam on physiological, psychomotor and cognitive functions in normal subjects. *European Journal of Clinical Pharmacology*, **40**, 355–362.

Allen, N. H., Gordon, S., Hope, T. & Burns, A. (1996) Manchester and Oxford Universities Scale for the Psychopathological Assessment of Dementia (MOUSEPAD). *British Journal of Psychiatry*, **169**, 293–307.

Altman, E. G., Hedeker, D. R., Janicak, P. G., Peterson, J. L. & Davis, J. M. (1994) The Clinician-Administered Rating Scale for Mania (CARS-M): Development, reliability, and validity. *Biological Psychiatry*, **36**, 124–134.

Altman, E., Hedeker, D., Peterson, J. L. & Davis, J. M. (2001) A comparative evaluation of three self-rating scales for acute mania. *Biological Psychiatry*, **50**, 468–471.

Andersson, S., Krogstad, J. M. & Finest, A. (1999) Apathy and depressed mood in acquired brain damage: Relationship to lesion localization and psychophysiological reactivity. *Psychological Medicine*, **29**, 447–456.

Arruda, J. E., Stern, R. A. & Legendre, S. A. (1996) Assessment of mood state in patients undergoing electroconvulsive therapy: The utility of visual analog mood scales developed for cognitively impaired patients. *Convulsive Therapy*, **12**, 207–212.

Astrom, M. (1996) Generalized anxiety disorder in stroke patients. A 3-year longitudinal study. *Stroke*, **27**, 270–275.

Austin, M.-P., Mitchell, P., Wilhelm, K., Parker, G., Hickie, I., Brodaty, H. et al. (1999) Cognitive function in depression: A distinct pattern of frontal impairment in melancholia? *Psychological Medicine*, **29**, 73–85.

Ballard, C. G., Saad, K., Patel, A., Gahir, M., Solis, M., Coope, B. et al. (1995) The prevalence and phenomenology of psychotic symptoms in dementia sufferers. *International Journal of Geriatric Psychiatry*, **10**, 477–485.

Beck, A. T. & Beamesderfer, A. (1974) Assessment of depression: The depression inventory. In: P. Pichot (ed.) *Psychological Measurements in Psychopharmacology*. Karger-Basel, Paris.

Bowman, E. S. (1998) Pseudoseizures. *Psychiatric Clinics of North America*, **21**, 649–657.

Bozeat, S., Gregory, C. A., Ralph, M. A. & Hodges, J. R. (2000) Which neuropsychiatric and behavioural features distinguish frontal and temporal variants of frontotemporal dementia from Alzheimer's disease? *Journal of Neurology, Neurosurgery and Psychiatry*, **69**, 178–186.

Brown, R. G. & Pluck, G. (2000) Negative symptoms: The 'pathology' of motivation and goal-direct behaviour. *Trends in Neurosciences*, **23**, 412–417.

Brown, R. G., Scott, L. C., Bench, C. J. & Dolan, R. J. (1994) Cognitive function in depression: Its relationship to the presence and severity of intellectual decline. *Psychological Medicine*, **24**, 829–847.

Bryant, R. A. (2001) Posttraumatic stress disorder and traumatic brain injury: Can they co-exist? *Clinical Psychology Review*, **21**, 931–948.

Bryant, R. A., Marosszeky, J. E., Crooks, J. & Gurka, J. A. (2000) Posttraumatic stress disorder after severe traumatic brain injury. *American Journal of Psychiatry*, **157**, 629–631.

Burvill, P. W., Johnson, G. A., Jamrozik, K. D., Anderson, C. S., Stewart-Wynne, E. G. & Chakera, T. M. (1995) Anxiety disorders after stroke: Results from the Perth Community Stroke Study. *British Journal of Psychiatry*, **166**, 328–332.

Carson, R. G., Byblow, W. D. & Goodman, D. (1994) The dynamical substructure of bimanual coordination. In: S. P. Swinnen, H. Heuer, J. Massion & P. Casaer (eds) *Interlimb Coordination: Neural, Dynamical, and Cognitive Constraints* (pp. 319–337). Academic Press, San Diego, CA.

Cummings, J. L. (1986) Subcortical dementia. Neuropsychology, neuropsychiatry, and pathophysiology. *British Journal of Psychiatry*, **149**, 682–697.

Cummings, J. L., Mega, M., Gray, K., Rosenberg-Thompson, S., Carusi, D. A. & Gornbein, J. (1994) The Neuropsychiatric Inventory: Comprehensive assessment of psychopathology in dementia. *Neurology*, **44**, 2308–2314.

Curran, H. V. (1991) Benzodiazepines, memory and mood: A review. *Psychopharmacology (Berlin)*, **105**, 1–8.

Curran, H. V., Bond, A., O'Sullivan, G., Bruce, M., Marks, I., Lelliot, P. et al. (1994) Memory functions, alprazolam and exposure therapy: A controlled longitudinal study of agoraphobia with panic disorder. *Psychological Medicine*, **24**, 969–976.

Darke, S. (1988a) Anxiety and working memory capacity. *Cognition and Emotion*, **2**, 145–154.

Darke, S. (1988b) Effects of anxiety on inferential reasoning task performance. *Journal of Personality and Social Psychology*, **55**, 499–505.

desRosiers, G., Hodges, J. R. & Berrios, G. (1995) The neuropsychological differentiation of patients with very mild Alzheimer's disease and/or major depression. *Journal of the American Geriatric Society*, **43**, 1256–1263.

Elliott, R., Sahakian, B. J., McKay, A. P., Herrod, J. J., Robbins, T. W. & Paykel, E. S. (1996) Neuropsychological impairments in unipolar depression: The influence of perceived failure on subsequent performance. *Psychological Medicine*, **26**, 975–989.

Eysenck, M. W. & Calvo, M. G. (1992) Anxiety and performance: The processing efficiency theory. *Cognition and Emotion*, **6**, 409–434.

Fann, J. R., Katon, W. J., Uomoto, J. M. & Esselman, P. C. (1995) Psychiatric disorders and functional disability in outpatients with traumatic brain injuries. *American Journal of Psychiatry*, **152**, 1493–1499.

First, M. B., Spitzer, R. L., Gibbon, M. & Williams, J. B. W. (1997) User's Guide for the Structured Clinical Interview for DSM-IV Axis I Disorders—Clinician Version (SCID-I). American Psychiatric Press, Washington, DC.

Gainotti, G., Azzoni, A., Razzano, C., Lanzillotta, M., Marra, C. & Gasparini, F. (1997) The Post-Stroke Depression Rating Scale: A test specifically devised to investigate affective disorders of stroke patients. *Journal of Clinical and Experimental Neuropsychology*, **19**, 340–356.

Galynker, I. I., Levinson, I., Miner, C. & Rosenthal, R. N. (1995) Negative symptoms in patients with basal ganglia strokes. *Neuropsychiatry, Neuropsychology and Behavioral Neurology*, **8**, 113–117.

Goldberg, D. (1978) *General Health Questionnaire*. NFER-Nelson, Windsor, UK.

Grace, J., Stout, J. C. & Malloy, P. F. (1999) Assessing frontal lobe behavioral syndromes with the frontal lobe personality scale. *Assessment*, **6**, 269–284.

Hamilton, M. (1960) A rating scale for depression. *Journal of Neurology, Neurosurgery and Psychiatry*, **23**, 56–62.

Hantz, P., Caradoc-Davies, G., Caradoc-Davies, T., Weatherall, M. & Dixon, G. (1994) Depression in Parkinson's disease. *American Journal of Psychiatry*, **151**, 1010–1014.

Hibbard, M. R., Uysal, S., Kepler, K., Bogdany, J. & Silver, J. (1998) Axis I psychopathology in individuals with traumatic brain injury. *Journal of Head Trauma and Rehabilitation*, **13**, 24–39.

Holdwick, D. C. & Wingenfield, S. A. (1999) The subjective experience of the PASAT [Paced Auditory Serial Addition Test]: Does the PASAT induce negative mood? *Archives of Clinical Neuropsychology*, **14**, 273–284.

Johnson, G., Burvill, P. W., Anderson, C. S., Jamrozik, K., Stewart-Wynne, E. G. & Chakera, T. M. (1995) Screening instruments for depression and anxiety following stroke: Experience in the Perth Community Stroke Study. *Acta Psychiatrica Scandinavica*, **91**, 252–257.

Jorge, R. E., Robinson, R. G., Arndt, S. V., Starkstein, S. E., Forrester, A. W. & Geisler, F. (1993) Depression following traumatic brain injury: A 1 year longitudinal study. *Journal of Affective Disorders*, **27**, 233–243.

Kaufer, D. I., Cummings, J. L., Christine, D., Bray, T., Castellon, S., Masterman, D. et al. (1998) Assessing the impact of neuropsychiatric symptoms in Alzheimer's disease: The Neuropsychiatric Inventory Caregiver Distress Scale. *Journal of the American Geriatric Society*, **46**, 210–215.

Kendrick, D. C., Gibson, A. J. & Moyes, I. C. (1979) The Revised Kendrick Battery: Clinical studies. *British Journal of Social and Clinical Psychology*, **18**, 329–340.

Kertesz, A., Davidson, W. & Fox, H. (1997) Frontal behavioral inventory: Diagnostic criteria for frontal lobe dementia. *Canadian Journal of Neurological Science*, **24**, 29–36.

Ketter, T. A., Post, R. M. & Theodore, W. H. (1999) Positive and negative psychiatric effects of antiepileptic drugs in patients with seizure disorders. *Neurology*, **53**, S53–S67.

Kizilbash, A. H., Vanderploeg, R. D. & Curtiss, G. (2002) The effects of depression and anxiety on memory performance. *Archives of Clinical Neuropsychology*, **17**, 57–67.

Kuperberg, G. & Heckers, S. (2000) Schizophrenia and cognitive function. *Current Opinion in Neurobiology*, **10**, 205–210.

Kuzis, G., Sabe, L., Tiberti, C., Dorrengo, F. & Starkstein, S. E. (1999) Neuropsychological correlates of apathy and depression in patients with dementia. *Neurology*, **52**, 1403–1407.

Lancman, M. (1999) Psychosis and peri-ictal confusional states. *Neurology*, **53**, S33–S38.

Leentjens, A. F., Verhey, F. R., Lousberg, R., Spitsbergen, H. & Wilmink, F. W. (2000) The validity of the Hamilton and Montgomery–Asberg depression rating scales as screening and diagnostic tools for depression in Parkinson's disease. *International Journal of Geriatric Psychiatry*, **15**, 644–649.

Levy, M. L., Cummings, J. L., Fairbanks, L. A., Masterman, D., Miller, B. L., Craig, A. H. et al. (1998) Apathy is not depression. *Journal of Neuropsychiatry and Clinical Neurosciences*, **10**, 314–319.

Litvan, I., Paulsen, J. S., Mega, M. S. & Cummings, J. L. (1998) Neuropsychiatric assessment of patients with hyperkinetic and hypokinetic movement disorders. *Archives of Neurology*, **55**, 1313–1319.

Logsdon, R. G. & Teri, L. (1995) Depression in Alzheimer's disease patients: Caregivers as surrogate reporters. *Journal of the American Geriatric Society*, **43**, 150–155.

Lukoff, D., Neuchterlein, K. H. & Ventura, J. (1986) Manual for expanded brief psychiatric rating scale (BPRS). *Schizophrenia Bulletin*, **12**, 594–602.

Marin, R. S. (1991) Apathy: A neuropsychiatric syndrome. *Journal of Neuropsychiatry and Clinical Neurosciences*, **3**, 243–254.

Marin, R. S., Biedrzycki, R. C. & Firinciogullari, S. (1991) Reliability and validity of the Apathy Evaluation Scale. *Psychiatry Research*, **38**, 143–162.

Mega, M. S., Cummings, J. L., Fiorello, T. & Gornbein, J. (1996) The spectrum of behavioral changes in Alzheimer's disease. *Neurology*, **46**, 130–135.

Mendez, M. F. (2000) Mania in neurologic disorders. *Current Psychiatry Report*, **2**, 440–445.

Menza, M. A., Robertson, H. D. & Bonapace, A. S. (1993) Parkinson's disease and anxiety: Comorbidity with depression. *Biological Psychiatry*, **34**, 465–470.

Montgomery, S. A. & Asberg, M. (1979) A new depression scale designed to be sensitive to change. *British Journal of Psychiatry*, **134**, 382–389.

Montorio, I. & Izal, M. (1996) The Geriatric Depression Scale: A review of its development and utility. *International Psychogeriatrics*, **8**, 103–112.

Newsom-Davis, I. C., Abrahams, S., Goldstein, L. H. & Leigh, P. N. (1999) The emotional lability questionnaire: A new measure of emotional lability in amyotrophic lateral sclerosis. *Journal of Neurological Science*, **169**, 22–25.

Norton, L. E., Malloy, P. F. & Salloway, S. (2001) The impact of behavioral symptoms on activities of daily living in patients with dementia. *American Journal of Geriatric Psychiatry*, **9**, 41–48.

O'Rourke, S., MacHale, S., Signorini, D. & Dennis, M. (1998) Detecting psychiatric morbidity after stroke: Comparison of the GHQ and the HAD Scale. *Stroke*, **29**, 980–985.

Paradiso, S., Hermann, B. P., Blumer, D., Davies, K. & Robinson, R. G. (2001) Impact of depressed mood on neuropsychological status in temporal lobe epilepsy. *Journal of Neurology, Neurosurgery and Psychiatry*, **70**, 180–185.

Paulsen, J. S., Butters, N., Sadek, J. R., Johnson, S. A., Salmon, D. P., Swerdlow, N. R. et al. (1995) Distinct cognitive profiles of cortical and subcortical dementia in advanced illness. *Neurology*, **45**, 951–956.

Pluck, G. E. & Brown, R. G. (2002) Apathy in Parkinson's disease. *Journal of Neurology, Neurosurgery and Psychiatry*, **73**, 636–642.

Pratt, P., Tallis, F. & Eysenck, M. (1997) Information-processing, storage characteristics and worry. *Behaviour Research and Therapy*, **35**, 1015–1023.

Radloff, L. S. (1977) The CES-D Scale: A self-report depression scale for research in the general population. *Applied Psychological Measurement*, **1**, 385–401.

Reding, M., Haycox, J. & Blass, J. (1985) Depression in patients referred to a dementia clinic. A three-year prospective study. *Archives of Neurology*, **42**, 894–896.

Reichman, W. E., Coyne, A. C., Amirneni, S., Molino, J. B. & Egan, S. (1996) Negative symptoms in Alzheimer's disease. *American Journal of Psychiatry*, **153**, 424–426.

Reisberg, B., Auer, S. R. & Monteiro, I. M. (1996) Behavioral pathology in Alzheimer's disease (BEHAVE-AD) rating scale. *International Psychogeriatrics*, **8**(Suppl. 3), 301–308.

Resnick, B., Zimmerman, S. I., Magaziner, J. & Adelman, A. (1998) Use of the apathy evaluation scale as a measure of motivation in elderly people. *Rehabilitation Nursing*, **23**, 141–147.

Robinson, R. G. (1998) *The Clinical Neuropsychiatry of Stroke*. Cambridge University Press, Cambridge, UK.

Robinson, R. G., Parikh, R. M., Lipsey, J. R., Starkstein, S. E. & Price, T. R. (1993) Pathological laughing and crying following stroke: Validation of a measurement scale and a double-blind treatment study. *American Journal of Psychiatry*, **150**, 286–293.

Rosenberg, H. J., Rosenberg, S. D., Williamson, P. D. & Wolford, G. L. (2000) A comparative study of trauma and posttraumatic stress disorder prevalence in epilepsy patients and psychogenic nonepileptic seizure patients. *Epilepsia*, **41**, 447–452.

Sembi, S., Tarrier, N., O'Neill, P., Burns, A. & Faragher, B. (1998) Does post-traumatic stress disorder occur after stroke: A preliminary study. *International Journal of Geriatric Psychiatry*, **13**, 315–322.

Sheikh, J. A. & Yesavage, J. A. (1986) Geriatric Depression Scale (GDS): Recent findings and development of a shorter version. In: T. L. Brink (ed.) *Clinical Gerontology: A Guide to Assessment and Intervention*. Howarth Press, New York.

Snaith, R. P., Ahmed, S. N., Mehta, S. & Hamilton, M. (1971) Assessment of the severity of primary depressive illness. Wakefield Self-Assessment Depression Inventory. *Psychological Medicine*, **1**, 143–149.

Starkstein, S. E., Pearlson, G. D., Boston, J. & Robinson, R. G. (1987) Mania after brain injury. A controlled study of causative factors. *Archives of Neurology*, **44**, 1069–1073.

Starkstein, S. E., Mayberg, H. S., Preziosi, T. J., Andrezejewski, P., Leiguarda, R. & Robinson, R. G. (1992) Reliability, validity, and clinical correlates of apathy in Parkinson's disease. *Journal of Neuropsychiatry and Clinical Neurosciences*, **4**, 134–139.

Starkstein, S. E., Fedoroff, J. P., Price, T. R., Leiguarda, R. & Robinson, R. G. (1993) Apathy following cerebrovascular lesions. *Stroke*, **24**, 1625–1630.

Starkstein, S. E., Petracca, G., Chemerinski, E. & Kremer, J. (2001) Syndromic validity of apathy in Alzheimer's disease. *American Journal of Psychiatry*, **158**, 872–877.

Stern, R. A. (1996) *Visual Analogue Mood Scales. Professional Manual*. Psychological Assessment Resources, Inc., Odessa, FL.

Sunderland, T. & Minichiello, M. (1996) Dementia Mood Assessment Scale. *International Psychogeriatrics*, **8**(Suppl. 3), 329–331.

Sutcliffe, L. M. & Lincoln, N. B. (1998) The assessment of depression in aphasic stroke patients: The development of the Stroke Aphasic Depression Questionnaire. *Clinical Rehabilitation*, **12**, 506–513.

Tandberg, E., Larsen, J. P., Aarsland, D. & Cummings, J. L. (1996) The occurrence of depression in Parkinson's disease. A community-based study. *Archives of Neurology*, **53**, 175–179.

Tisher, P. W., Holzer, J. C., Greenberg, M., Benjamin, S., Devinsky, O. & Bear, D. M. (1993) Psychiatric presentations of epilepsy. *Harvard Review of Psychiatry*, **1**, 219–228.

Toone, B. K. (2000) The psychoses of epilepsy. *Journal of Neurology, Neurosurgery and Psychiatry*, **69**, 1–3.

van Achterberg, M. E., Rohrbaugh, R. M. & Southwick, S. M. (2001) Emergence of PTSD in trauma survivors with dementia. *Journal of Clinical Psychiatry*, **62**, 206–207.

Varney, N. R., Martzke, J. S. & Roberts, R. J. (1987) Major depression in patients with closed head injury. *Neuropsychology*, **1**, 7–8.

Vazquez, A., Jimenez-Jimenez, F. J., Garcia-Ruiz, P. & Garcia-Urra, D. (1993). 'Panic attacks' in Parkinson's disease. A long-term complication of levodopa therapy. *Acta Neurologica Scandinavica*, **87**, 14–18.

Veiel, H. O. F. (1997) A preliminary profile of neuropsychological deficits associated with major depression. *Journal of Clinical and Experimental Neuropsychology*, **19**, 587–603.

Verma, S., Orengo, C. A., Maxwell, R., Kunik, M. E., Molinari, V. A., Vasterling, J. J. et al. (2001) Contribution of PTSD/POW history to behavioral disturbances in dementia. *International Journal of Geriatric Psychiatry*, **16**, 356–360.

Wagle, A. C., Ho, L. W., Wagle, S. A. & Berrios, G. E. (2000) Psychometric behaviour of BDI in Alzheimer's disease patients with depression. *International Journal of Geriatric Psychiatry*, **15**, 63–69.

Waldstein, S. R., Ryan, C. M., Jennings, J. R., Muldoon, M. F. & Manuck, S. B. (1997) Self-reported levels of anxiety do not predict neuropsychological performance in healthy men. *Archives of Clinical Neuropsychology*, **12**, 567–574.

Watkins, C., Daniels, L., Jack, C., Dickinson, H. and van Den, B. M. (2001) Accuracy of a single question in screening for depression in a cohort of patients after stroke: Comparative study. *British Medical Journal*, **323**, 1159.

Watkins, E. & Brown, R. G. (2002) Rumination and executive function in depression: An experimental study. *Journal of Neurology, Neurosurgery and Psychiatry*, **72**, 400–402.

Wechsler, D. (1987) Wechsler Memory Scale—Revised. The Psychological Corporation, San Antonio, TX.

Weiner, M. F., Doody, R. S., Sairam, R., Foster, B. & Liao, T. Y. (2002) Prevalence and incidence of major depressive disorder in Alzheimer's disease: Findings from two databases. *Dementia and Geriatric Cognitive Disorders*, **13**, 8–12.

Wilson, B. A. (1997) Cognitive rehabilitation: How it is and how it might be. *Journal of the International Neuropsychological Society*, **3**, 487–496.

Wilson, B. A., Alderman, N., Burgess, P. W., Emslie, H. & Evans, J. J. (1996) *Behavioural Assessment of the Dysexecutive Syndrome* (BADS). Thames Valley Test Company, Bury St Edmunds, UK.

Wood, S., Cummings, J. L., Hsu, M. A., Barclay, T., Wheatley, M. V., Yarema, K. T. et al. (2000) The use of the neuropsychiatric inventory in nursing home residents. Characterization and measurement. *American Journal of Geriatric Psychiatry*, **8**, 75–83.

World Health Organization (1994) *Schedules for Clinical Assessment in Neuropsychiatry (SCAN, v2.0)*. World Health Organization, Geneva.

Zakzanis, K. K., Leach, L. & Kaplan, E. (1998) On the nature and pattern of neurocognitive function in major depressive disorder. *Neuropsychiatry, Neuropsychology and Behavioral Neurology*, **11**, 111–119.

Zigmond, A. S. & Snaith, R. P. (1983) The Hospital Anxiety and Depression Scale. *Acta Psychiatrica Scandinavica*, **67**, 361–370.

Zubieta, J. K., Huguelet, P., O'Neil, R. L. & Giordani, B. J. (2001) Cognitive function in euthymic bipolar I disorder. *Psychiatry Research*, **102**, 9–20.

CHAPTER 5

The Effects of Medication and Other Substances on Cognitive Functioning

Jane Powell

Goldsmiths College, London, UK

INTRODUCTION

The most meticulous neuropsychological investigation attempting to relate an index event, such as brain injury, to a carefully delineated profile of cognitive functioning is often laid open to interpretative guesswork when the examinee has a history of past or current use of psychoactive drugs. It seems, a priori, probable that this will have had an effect on cognition, yet it is frequently difficult to ascertain either the form or severity of such effects. Neuropsychological reports all too often give a general acknowledgement that drug use may have influenced test performance and then largely disregard it for lack of hard information. Alternatively, observed impairments may be construed as resulting from substance use on the basis of assumption rather than a critical evaluation of the evidence. Both of these strategies can result in inaccurate conclusions, sometimes with serious practical implications: for example, financial compensation for cognitive impairments after a traumatic brain injury could easily be under- or overestimated depending on the neuropsychologist's opinion about the extent to which the plaintiff's heavy social drinking, occasional cannabis use or antidepressant medication may have contributed to the observed problems. However, the sheer range of psychoactive drugs that are used either medicinally or recreationally within contemporary society, and the inconsistency with which their cognitive effects have been researched, make it difficult for most practising clinicians to maintain the level of detailed knowledge that is necessary for an evidence-based approach to these issues.

The latter approach involves ascertaining the type and degree of cognitive disturbance associated with the drug(s) used by the person being assessed and then determining the degree to which the observed pattern of performance corresponds to the drug-related profile. Significantly greater impairments than those attributable to drug use can then be more confidently attributed to other factors, and treatment plans can take appropriate account of drug/medication-induced

Clinical Neuropsychology: A Practical Guide to Assessment and Management for Clinicians.
Edited by L.H. Goldstein and J.E. McNeil. © 2004 John Wiley & Sons, Ltd.

problems. Of course, though, it is not so simple in practice. Although the pharmacological literature is vast, much of the research is preclinical and thus cannot be generalized directly to human performance. Relatedly, many of the studies that do test human participants use esoteric or experimental measures rather than 'noisier' standard clinical assessment procedures; rarely can findings be straightforwardly extrapolated from the one to the other. Studies that do present data for commonly used drugs on widely used neuropsychological measures, such as the Wechsler scales, are relatively rare. Moreover, many of those that do exist have methodological shortcomings or apply to a specific population.

Is the case then hopeless? This chapter will first consider some of the general mechanisms by which psychoactive substances can affect cognitive functioning; second, it will identify important methodological issues that should influence our interpretation of such studies as do exist; third, it will briefly review the current literature in relation to selected drugs that are commonly either prescribed or used recreationally and will direct the reader to more substantial reviews of the literature; and, finally, it will draw out some implications of this literature both for clinical neuropsychological practice and for future clinical research questions. To pre-empt the answer to the question at the start of this paragraph, and to hearten the reader before he or she embarks on the factual account that follows, the answer is a definitive NO: though much remains to be done, the existing literature contains much of great value to thoughtful neuropsychological evaluation.

Mechanisms for Cognitive Effects

Psychoactive substances that are used either recreationally to achieve changes in mood state or conscious experience, or are prescribed medicinally to modify maladaptive psychological or neurological states, are almost certain by their very nature to have an acute impact on cognitive functioning. The magnitude and duration of the acute effect may vary immensely depending on characteristics both of the substance itself (e.g., its neurochemical properties, half-life, dose) and of the person using it (e.g., weight, age, gender, prior level of functioning, concurrent drug use, mood). In addition to predictable and desired effects, there will also be 'side-effects', which may either be positive though unintended, or adverse but tolerated. There may also be indirect effects on cognition where drugs partially or fully reverse pre-existing deficiencies or symptoms (e.g., epileptic discharges, agitation, low mood) which themselves interfere with cognitive functioning.

Complex as these issues are, acute effects represent only part of the story to be considered when evaluating the contribution of drug use to a patient's pattern of performance. Some substances, when used repeatedly or chronically, produce alterations in brain structure or function that may give rise to more persistent changes in the way information is processed; these physiological sequelae may be to varying degrees reversible, over often uncertain timescales, or irreversible. The addiction literature suggests that some neuroadaptations develop as homeostatic responses to counteract acute and potentially toxic or even lethal drug effects. For example, if damagingly high levels of a particular neurotransmitter are triggered by drug consumption, then protective neuroadaptations could include reductions in endogenous production of that neurotransmitter, increases in production of the enzymes that metabolize it or alterations in the properties of its receptor sites. This may have no overt consequence for the individual's functioning as long as he or she continues to consume the same level of the drug; however, during early abstinence the underlying down-regulated system will be exposed and the person may experience *withdrawal symptoms*. These are widely perceived as being somatic in nature, the prototype being the runny eyes, shaky hands and 'flu-like symptoms that accompany withdrawal from opiates, or *delirium tremens* in alcoholics. However, more subtle symptoms can include dysregulation of mood and, potentially, cognitive disturbances that are dissociable from somatic signs. Abstinence may also produce cognitive impairment indirectly (e.g., through a general physical and psychological malaise which adversely affects concentration and motivation).

Another consequence of neuroadaptation is *drug tolerance*, whereby in order to achieve a desired effect the drug user has to progressively increase the dose. This is an important factor in assessing the likely cognitive effect of a particular dose of a particular drug: if the person using it has become tolerant to some or all of its effects, the prescribed dose may be having a much less powerful effect on test performance than reported for a similar dose in drug-naive individuals.

Methodological Considerations in the Empirical Literature in Humans

For medically prescribed drugs, the clinical trials required by law to evaluate their safety and efficacy frequently fail to include detailed assessment of their cognitive effects. There are occasional exceptions to this, particularly where there is little difference between the clinical effectiveness of several different brands and where it is in the interests of the pharmaceutical company to demonstrate cognitive benefits (or less cognitive disadvantage) from their own brand. In the absence of well-controlled, large-scale randomized trials, there are a number of other approaches that give some useful but more limited data. Single case studies or case series can highlight the possibility of cognitive impairments in some patients, but randomization is usually necessary if drug-induced effects are to be clearly distinguishable from symptoms of the condition being treated or from other presenting characteristics of the patients. Good placebo control conditions are especially important in the evaluation of cognitive or psychological effects, since these variables are more likely than 'objective' physiological markers to be susceptible to expectancy or demand characteristics. Opportunistic cross-sectional comparisons of groups of well-matched patients on different drugs or no drug, and prospective evaluations of cognitive functioning in patients before, during and after drug treatment, can add weight to a hypothesis concerning possible drug effects, but as noted above other factors are likely to inflate any 'real' effects.

Although clinical neuropsychologists may decide to use the findings of single case or uncontrolled studies as a guide for interpreting findings in the individual case, it is generally wise to assume that the magnitude of apparent drug-related impairments (or in some cases benefits) may have been inflated by methodological factors such as expectancy effects. In cases where the reported effects on cognitive functioning are small (e.g., within the known measurement error for a particular scale) and methodological limitations are significant, it may be appropriate to adopt a conservative approach and assume that any effects are negligible. An exception to this, however, would be when the nature of the methodological problem might have biased findings *away* from detecting a real decline in functioning (e.g., if the same version of a test is used on consecutive occasions). In this eventuality, virtually nothing can be concluded from failure to detect an effect, while even a small but statistically significant effect (a drug-related impairment) takes on greater clinical significance.

If the problems with evaluating the effects of clinically prescribed drugs are great, they pale by comparison with the pitfalls that beset evaluation of recreational or illicit drug use. The researcher rarely has much control over, or even much ability to monitor/verify, participants' patterns of drug use, but has to rely on their own accounts. Physiological indicators, such as urine or hair analysis, may be available but logistically difficult to gather or alienating to participants, and are hence impractical. Illicit drugs cannot generally be given under controlled conditions, so the purity or quantity of drugs ingested is largely unknown. Many users of one substance are either currently using other substances as well or have done so in the recent or longer term past, which makes it difficult if not impossible to disentangle the effects of a particular substance from the effects of polysubstance use or from other lifestyle factors. Randomized studies of the development of addiction are almost never possible in humans, and it is difficult to conduct well-controlled cross-sectional studies because the backgrounds of drug users both shape and are shaped by their addictions. Thus it is rare to find control groups adequately matched with drug users for socio-economic, family, medical and educational background. The secondary problems associated with addiction (e.g., poor health, criminality, unemployment) are often also debilitating in their own right, making it yet more difficult to isolate the effect of drug use *per se* from other influences. Many studies have indicated that polysubstance users perform below average on diverse cognitive tests, but since clinical neuropsychologists routinely make adjustments for premorbid social factors in their assessments they should resist the conclusion that recent or past drug use is likely to depress scores still further, unless the evidence is compelling.

SPECIFIC DRUGS

The following discussions of specific drug classes are necessarily brief and selective. For a comprehensible and wide-ranging account of the psychopharmacological mechanisms implicated in the effects of different drugs and in the emotional and psychiatric disturbances that they can be used to treat, the reader is referred to Stahl (2000).

Drugs that are most commonly prescribed for medical or psychiatric conditions are considered first, and those most often used recreationally or illicitly second. However, there is no clear dividing line between these two broad classes of drug use, with many substances that are used medically having a strong illicit take-up by individuals for either self-medication or recreational purposes. Likewise, there is frequently an implicit presumption in neuropsychological assessments that 'social' use of legal drugs, such as alcohol and nicotine, is less noteworthy than use of Class A drugs, such as opiates or cocaine. As the following sections will demonstrate, this is often far from the case.

Prescribed Drugs

Antidepressants

The three main classes of antidepressant are the tricyclics (e.g., amitryptiline, imipramine); the monoamine oxidase inhibitors (MAOIs, e.g., moclobemide, isocarboxazid); and the selective serotonergic reuptake inhibitors (SSRIs, e.g., fluoxetine, bupropion, paroxetine). Of these three groups, it is primarily the tricyclics that have been associated with mild cognitive impairments, probably either because of their sedative effects or the fact that, unlike the other two groups, they impact on cholinergic mechanisms that are implicated in aspects of memory function. Amado-Boccara et al. (1995) provide useful explanations of the biochemical effects of the drugs and the methodologies used to investigate their cognitive effects. Although the effects of acute and sustained treatment have been reasonably well explored, there has been very little investigation of withdrawal-related changes.

One of the most studied tricyclics is amitryptiline, and since it exerts more powerful sedative and anticholinergic effects than many of the others in this class it is used here as a prime example (see Amado-Boccara et al., 1995, for comparisons with other compounds). When administered in a single dose to drug-naive participants, amitryptiline has been found, fairly consistently, to impair attention, working memory, verbal learning and psychomotor functions. These effects manifest not only on a range of formal psychometric tests but also on more functional measures (e.g., car driving). Effects typically emerge about 30 minutes after drug administration, reaching maximum between two and four hours after a 10-mg dose. The drug's sedative properties are likely to be a key factor in these impairments, since several tricyclics that have less powerful sedative effects (e.g. nomifensine) produce fewer performance impairments (see Curran, 1992).

Where healthy volunteers continue to take the drug over a more extended period, the general trend is for impairments to be evident over the first 7 to 14 days and then to reverse over the following week or 2 (e.g., Seppala et al., 1975). Depressed patients who are prescribed amitryptiline likewise show performance improvement on most measures by about the fourth week of treatment: for instance, Lamping et al. (1984) found no persisting impairments on prose or word recall at this stage, despite some indication of an implicit memory deficit. However, this study did not include a placebo-treated control group, and it is thus possible that improvements might have reflected increasing familiarity with the test material or procedures.

It is also possible that some drug-related impairments do persist, but are offset by the effects of mood enhancement. Depression itself may have an adverse impact on aspects of episodic memory, memory for unstructured information and psycho-motor functions (Curran, 1992), though these effects tend to be mild (within 0.5 standard deviations of non-depressed subjects) or confined to cases of severe depression (e.g., Burt et al., 1995). Since some of these impairments are similar to those that can be produced by tricyclic antidepressants, observations that im-provements in cognitive functioning over a period of treatment correlate with the therapeutic response (e.g., Sternberg & Jarvik, 1976) suggest that the observed gains partly reflect indirect benefits associated with mood enhancement.

MAOIs are now less likely to be prescribed because of the dietary constraints they impose. Consequently, they have received relatively little formal evaluation. However, moclobemide appears from the existing evidence to produce little or no measurable impairment when administered to healthy individuals either as a single dose (e.g., Hindmarch & Kerr, 1992; Tiller, 1990) or when given over several days (Ramaekers et al., 1992). Few studies have investigated medium- to long-term effects in depressed patients, but Allain et al. (1992) compared it with two other antidepressants (viloxazine and maprotiline) and found no impairment on tests of attention/alertness or memory after two, four or six weeks of treatment.

The SSRIs, which tend to be stimulating rather than sedating, have generally shown few adverse effects on any aspect of cognitive functioning when given acutely to healthy volunteers (e.g., Hindmarch, 1988; Peck et al., 1979) and may even enhance alertness (see Amado-Boccara et al., 1995). Few studies have evaluated effects over more extended periods in either healthy or depressed partici-pants; however, Siegfried and O'Connolly (1986) found that depressed patients treated with the SSRI nomifensine showed more rapid normalization of cognitive functioning than those treated with two other non-SSRI antidepressants. Hindmarch et al. (2000) evaluated the effects of abruptly discontinuing treatment with four SSRIs and found that cessation of only one (paroxetine) was associated with a subsequent increase in 'cognitive failures'. This effect was reversed when the drug was restarted.

With respect to the implications for neuropsychological assessment, then, it would appear that untreated depression is more likely to produce mild adverse effects on cognitive functioning than is antidepressant medication. However, it is generally wise to avoid assessing patients during the first three weeks that tricyclic medication is being prescribed, since the combined effects of low mood and pharmacological disturbance over this period could be additive and give rise to significant under-functioning. Although non-tricyclics appear relatively benign, it is nevertheless preferable to defer assessment until any therapeutic effect has had a chance to emerge, so that the patient is tested when he or she is most likely to perform at optimum levels. There may also be important sources of individual differences in susceptibility to adverse effects of antidepressant medications. Linnoila et al. (1983), for example, found the effects of sedative medication to be amplified by recent alcohol consumption. Similarly, Curran (1992) notes that the elderly metabolize drugs more slowly and often have lower baseline levels of performance, potentially making them more sensitive to drug-induced deficits. Organic brain injury may also increase susceptibility, and the neuropsychologist should therefore be cautious in extrapolating findings from the healthy, or depressed but otherwise healthy, populations to those with neurological conditions.

Anxiolytics

Benzodiazepines (BDZs: e.g., diazepam, nitrazepam, lorazepam) are the most commonly prescribed class of anxiolytic medication; although barbiturates also fall into this category, they are heavier duty drugs with more grossly detrimental effects and are now rarely prescribed in general practice (see Stahl, 2000). BDZs have anticholinergic actions and stimulate γ-aminobutyric acid (GABA) receptors in brain regions, such as the amygdala and hippocampus, that are strongly implicated in memory functioning. They vary in terms of their half-life (e.g., 2.5 hours for triazolam, 80 or more hours for fluorazepam). Consequently, to properly take into account the effects of recent BDZ use on cognitive test performance, the psychologist should know which drug was taken, in what dose and how long previously.

The literature on cognitive effects of BDZs indicates that, while single doses in healthy adults typically do not affect tests of attention span, executive function, retrograde memory for events preceding drug administration, semantic memory or procedural learning, they *do* tend to slow information processing and can produce temporary anterograde amnesia (i.e., impaired episodic and source memory for events occurring in the immediate aftermath of drug administration; Curran, 1999, 2000). There is persuasive evidence that the effects on memory are direct rather than secondary to generalized sedation: for example, Smirne et al. (1989) found BDZs to impair memory at low doses but attention only at higher doses, while Curran et al. (1998) found that antihistamines with similar sedative effects to BDZs did not affect episodic memory.

The effects of chronic BDZ use by patients with anxiety disorders are less clear. Morton and Lader (1990) reported that patients with generalized anxiety disorder showed no subjective or motor sedation from either lorazepam or alpidem after four weeks of treatment, though lorazepam was associated with verbal recall deficits. Tata et al. (1994) studied 21 patients who withdrew from BDZs after having used them for an average of 13 years and found impairments of verbal memory up to six months later. If the observed impairments were directly related to use of the BDZs, this would seem to suggest persistent structural or functional changes resulting from prolonged use, though imaging studies have produced conflicting findings in this regard (e.g., Busto et al., 2000). Alternatively, impairments might have preceded the use of medication or have been secondary to anxiety-related symptoms. Interestingly, when Curran et al. (1994) reassessed agoraphobics after withdrawal from alprazolam, impairments of word list recall, which were apparent at eight weeks, had disappeared by $3\frac{1}{2}$ years.

The evidence of anterograde amnesia after acute treatment with BDZs is potentially very important to neuropsychological interpretation, since in many cases of traumatic brain injury (TBI) the duration of anterograde amnesia, which often follows the insult and which is referred to as post-traumatic amnesia (PTA), is often used as the best available indicator of the severity of brain trauma. It has been empirically shown to predict long-term outcome (e.g., Wilson et al., 1993) and is consequently often used to guide compensation claims (see Chapter 15) and to substantiate a hypothesis that ongoing cognitive problems reflect residual brain injury. However, TBI is often incurred in the context of other painful injuries or stressful circumstances for which sedative medication (often heavy doses of a BDZ) may be prescribed. In these circumstances, patients may have little or patchy memory for the hours or days following an accident because of their medication rather than because of brain injury. It is therefore crucial to ascertain whether, when and for how long the patient was sedated before concluding that absence of memory implies cerebral trauma.

Anti-epileptic drugs

Disentangling adverse effects of medication from impairments attributable to under-lying neurological dysfunction or to the psychological reactions to living with epilepsy is obviously problematic, especially when the choice of anti-epileptic drug in clinical practice is often dictated in part by the type or severity of the presenting condition. Evaluation of the cognitive effects of patients' anti-epileptic medication is profoundly complicated by the fact that most studies have been compromised by selection biases, non-equivalence of groups on critical clinical variables (e.g., type/severity of epilepsy, dose levels), insensitivity or inappropriateness of neuropsycho-logical testing protocols and low power or inappropriate statistical analysis (Kwan & Brodie, 2001). Single dose studies in healthy volunteers or patients are of limited help in elucidating the effects of these drugs in clinical populations, where initial impairments have been found to disappear over several weeks of continuous use, presumably reflecting the development of tolerance (e.g., Larkin et al., 1992).

Where randomized trials have demonstrated differences between drugs, subse-quent research has sometimes suggested that the observed differences are attribut-able to particularly adverse effects in only some rather than all participants (e.g., Dodrill & Troupin 1977, 1991), possibly due to toxic blood plasma concentrations in those showing impairment. Elsewhere it has been found that concurrent use of two or more anti-epileptic drugs can be associated with more severe impairment, possibly due either to cumulative neurotoxicity or to interactions between the drugs. Such findings highlight not only the need to treat group findings with caution but also the importance of being aware that some individual patients may suffer adverse cognitive effects of a medication even when this is not the general finding.

Bearing such methodological limitations in mind, Kwan and Brodie (2001) conclude from the existing literature that there is reasonably robust evidence that the older, 'established', anti-epileptic drugs (including phenobarbitol, pheny-toin, carbamazepine and sodium valproate) do have mild to marked dose-related effects on cognition, with phenobarbitol being most consistently found to have pronounced and widespread adverse effects on cognitive and behavioural function-ing. Among the other drugs in this category, cognitive effects are typically de-scribed as 'subtle' and are similar between drugs (e.g., Duncan et al., 1990). Vigabatrin, lamotrigine and gabapentin, three newer anti-epileptic drugs, have generally been found remarkably free of adverse effects on extensive neuropsycho-logical batteries, though there is some individual susceptibility to behavioural or affective disturbances in reaction to vigabatrin and gabapentin. Another 'new' drug, topiramate, has been associated with impairments of language, attention and concentration persisting over at least a month of its use by healthy adults (e.g., Martin et al., 1999) and, prescribed clinically, severe psychiatric side-effects have been reported.

For practical purposes, the relative subtlety and diffuseness of the cognitive effects that have been reported to arise from anti-epileptic drug use mean that in general, while they might slightly inflate deficits attributable to the epilepsy itself or to associated neurological damage, they are unlikely on their own to account for any severe or specific cognitive impairments. However, as noted above, there are some cases in which anti-epileptic drugs produce atypically large effects, possibly because of variations in individual susceptibility or in aspects of the treatment regime (dose, duration, etc.) that may result in toxicity. The neuropsychologist should therefore be alert to any clinical or behavioural evidence of unusual adverse reactions.

Recreational/Addictive Drugs

Most of the drugs used recreationally, including both socially sanctioned substances such as alcohol and nicotine, and illicit substances, such as opiates, cocaine, cannabis and ecstasy (methylenedioxymethamphetamine—MDMA), are now recognized to have physically and/or psychologically addictive properties. Although these drugs have complex and varied biochemical effects, contemporary neurobiological models of addiction strongly implicate the common involvement of the mesocorticolimbic brain system, which comprises dopaminergic projections from the ventral tegmental area (VTA) to structures including the nucleus accumbens, amygdala, anterior cingulate (AC) and prefrontal cortex (PFC). Functionally, this circuitry corresponds to the so-called 'reward pathways' of the brain since its activation is associated with appetitive behaviours directed at obtaining a wide range of reinforcers including brain electro-stimulation, food and sex (e.g., Wise, 1998). Drugs that increase activa-tion of this system are associated both with the subjective experience of pleasure and, when used chronically, with neuroadaptations that may sensitize the individual to their effects in the future (Robinson & Berridge, 1993, 2000) and that manifest in withdrawal symptoms during abstinence. Wise and Munn (1995) have suggested that dysfunction of brain reward pathways during withdrawal might underlie reports of anhedonia and dysphoria, which are likely indirectly to produce temporary cognitive interference. In addition, the fact that cortical projection sites of these pathways include the AC and PFC suggests that addictive drug use may be associated with alterations of 'executive' cognitive functions.

Some recreational drugs, including alcohol, nicotine and cannabis, are used relatively widely and often without associated use of other substances; this is also increasingly true of ecstasy as it has become increasingly available on the party scene and perceived to be largely harmless. As a result, it has been possible to investigate the cognitive effects of these drugs separately from the effects of other substances. By contrast, drugs that are perceived as 'harder' and are less widely used—heroin, cocaine, amphetamines—tend to be taken as part of a more broad-ranging pattern of 'polysubstance use'. Thus it is much harder to disentangle their effects in naturalistic studies, since users of one substance either also use or have used several others. Experimental laboratory studies in drug-naive individuals face legal and ethical problems and so are rare. In the following sections, therefore, the effects of drugs used primarily as part of a polysubstance pattern will be addressed first, with the substances that it has been possible to investigate separately considered subsequently.

Polysubstance Use (Including Opiates, Cocaine, Amphetamines)

Until fairly recently the evidence suggested remarkably little adverse effect of even chronic polysubstance use on cognitive functioning, with few gross impairments seen consistently in adequately controlled studies of long-term cocaine or heroin users. Horner (1999) reviewed 17 studies conducted between 1988 and 1998 investigating attentional processes in cocaine users and noted that despite the fact that methodological problems (e.g., inclusion of polydrug users, failure to exclude participants with neurological or psychiatric problems, poor matching of control subjects) tended to inflate the occurrence of apparent drug-related impairments, few studies found many deficits. Although cocaine users sometimes showed reduced information-processing speed, this was inconsistent across tests and was often likely to be attributable to recent or past use of alcohol. Indeed, none of the 'best' seven studies showed clear impairments of focused, sustained or divided attention. Selby and Azrin (1998) compared 138 male prisoners with no history of substance use disorder with those with histories of alcohol dependence only, cocaine abuse only and polysubstance abuse that included use of alcohol equivalent to that in the alcohol-dependent group. Anyone with past or present neurological or psychiatric conditions, head injuries or learning difficulties was excluded. Cocaine users were not impaired, relative to non-drug users, on any of 15 separate cognitive indices. Although polysubstance users showed deficits on most tests, they did not differ from those with a history of alcohol dependence only. This pattern suggests that the cognitive problems of polysubstance users might be attributable to their alcohol use. However, findings are somewhat inconsistent: for example, Robinson et al. (1999) found codependent alcohol and cocaine users to show few differences from demographically well-matched non-users, while cocaine-only users were mildly impaired especially on psychomotor tasks.

Despite the lack of convincing evidence for measurable impairments on widely used neuropsychological tests, heroin and cocaine use may be associated with subtle impairments of specific executive functions, such as decision-making and judgement (e.g., Bechara et al., 2001; Grant et al., 2000). These findings are complemented by neuroimaging studies showing abnormalities of the structure and function of frontal cortex in drug users (e.g., Liu et al., 1998; London et al., 2000). Different drugs may however produce subtly different effects depending on how they impact neurochemically on the pathways innervating different regions of the PFC. For instance, Ornstein et al. (2000) compared addicts whose primary drug was either heroin or amphetamine with matched non-drug-using controls on a variety of neuropsychological tests sensitive to frontostriatal and temporal damage. Addicts showed selective and partially drug-specific patterns of impairment, the heavy stimulant users showing more difficulty than the heavy opiate users on some frontostriatal indices and the pattern reversing on others. Rogers and Robbins (2001) provide a useful synopsis of some of these recent investigations.

There are few studies of the acute cognitive effects of opiates or cocaine in regular drug users, though recently Curran et al. (2001) found that the opiate methadone, when administered at the full daily dose to addicts during a detoxification programme, produced significant impairments in delayed prose recall. When the dose was split over the day, this adverse effect was not apparent.

As a general rule in neuropsychological assessment, if a patient is known to be a regular user of drugs that have powerful sedative or stimulating effects, the examiner should at the very least ascertain how long has elapsed since their last use. If he or she is not physically dependent, then test results will be more reliably interpretable if assessment is deferred until at least 24 and preferably 48 hours after last use. However, if he or she is using very regularly and shows signs of addiction, with withdrawal symptoms manifesting during abstinent periods, there is no phase in the daily routine when test results will be uncontaminated by the effects of either acute drug use or acute abstinence. Under these circumstances it is probably best to assess as long as possible after a dose, but before the individual becomes aware of withdrawal symptoms and/or begins to experience drug craving. Logistically, of course, this may not be feasible; in any event it is advisable to assess subjective mood and physical state as well as to document at what point in their drug use cycle they have been tested so that the possible impact of these factors can be explicitly acknowledged.

MDMA (3,4-Methylenedioxymethamphetamine, or 'Ecstasy')

MDMA (or 'ecstasy') use tends to be situationally specific (e.g., at parties and 'raves') rather than daily or continuous and is widely perceived by users as non-addictive and relatively harmless. However, there is growing evidence that MDMA has enduring neurotoxic effects, including long-term depletions of serotonin levels and degenerative changes to serotonergic structures, in both animals (e.g., Frederick & Paule, 1997) and in humans (see McCann et al., 2000). The last few years have seen the publication of a series of independent investigations of cognitive functioning in relation to MDMA use, reporting a strikingly uniform pattern of small but significant impairments of immediate and delayed verbal memory in users of the substance relative to well-matched non-using controls.

In many cases these deficits have been apparent in people who have used on only a few occasions as well as in heavier users (e.g., Parrott et al., 1998), while abstinence has usually *not* been associated with recovery of function (e.g., Parrott and Lasky, 1998). Bolla et al. (1998) found verbal memory impairments in abstinent ecstasy users and reported an inverse correlation between average monthly consumption and severity of cognitive impairment. Bhattachary and Powell (2001) took concurrent use of cannabis into account when comparing novice, regular and abstaining MDMA users with non-MDMA users and again demonstrated impairments of prose recall in all three user groups. None had taken any drugs within the 24 hours prior to testing. Verbal fluency was also impaired in the regular and abstaining users; within the three MDMA groups, scores on both this task and on immediate and delayed recall were highly correlated with estimated lifetime consumption. Gouzoulis-Mayfrank et al. (2000) have also reported ecstasy users to be impaired on verbal learning, working memory and reaction time tasks, and poorer performance on several of these tests was again found to be associated with heavier past use.

There is less consistency concerning observed relationships between ecstasy use and visuospatial test performance. Thus, while Bhattachary and Powell (2001) found no abnormalities of functioning on the Rey–Osterreith test in any of the user groups, there was a trend toward an association with lifetime consumption in the abstainers. Likewise, Bolla et al. (1998) reported that within a group of abstinent users those who had used most heavily showed impairments of delayed memory for visual material.

MDMA use has also been associated with disturbances of mood that persist for several days after it has been consumed (e.g., Curran & Travill, 1997). These typically pass within a week (Parrott & Lasky, 1998), and it is therefore unlikely that the cognitive impairments found at least in abstinent users are secondary to low mood. Nevertheless, when testing someone who does take MDMA recreationally, time since last dose and current mood state should be noted as potentially transient influences on cognitive performance.

Cannabis/Marijuana

The active component of cannabis (or marijuana), tetrahydrocannabinol, has a half-life of up to 60 hours; the acute effects can last for several hours after it has been ingested, and chronic users may show cannabinoids in their urine after weeks or even months of abstinence, suggesting that a residue is also left in the central nervous system (CNS). Cannabinoids increase dopaminergic activity in the mesolimbic system; their biological properties and actions are well described by Ameri (1999). Withdrawal can be characterized by restlessness and insomnia, and in vulnerable individuals cannabis ingestion may interact with an existing predisposition to trigger or exacerbate psychosis. Possible mechanisms by which cannabis might induce cognitive impairment therefore include acute intoxication, the effects of any residue in the CNS, withdrawal-related effects, mood disorders induced by cannabis and, conceivably, long-term structural damage.

Despite all these potential sources of impairment, the empirical data are conflicting, and many studies have found no impairments in cannabis/marijuana users relative to carefully matched controls. Pope et al. (1995) reviewed 15 studies in which cognitive functions were measured after experimentally controlled drug administration and found no clear evidence of measurable deficits persisting for more than 48 hours after the last drug dose. Their review also identified 29 naturalistic studies assessing cognitive function in long-term users. No cognitive impairment was found in 11 studies. Although this might have reflected light-to-moderate rather than heavy drug consumption or the use of insensitive tests, they noted that most of the studies finding some impairment were also compromised by serious methodological shortcomings. More recently, Gouzoulis-Mayfrank et al. (2000) compared 28 cannabis users with 28 ecstasy + cannabis users and 28 non-drug users, well matched for educational attainment, on 15 tests of attention, memory, working memory, executive and general intellectual functions. The cannabis users were not significantly impaired relative to non-users on any of the 27 indices yielded by these tests.

Pope and Yurgelun-Todd (1996) found that, after 19 hours of supervised abstinence, heavy cannabis users (close to daily use in previous month) performed slightly more poorly than light users (median of one use in previous month) on a number of tests; however, the differences were small and often confined to particular subgroups or to single indices from tests that yield several scores. For example, immediate (but not delayed) recall of the Rey Figure and Stroop scores were impaired in male but not female heavy users and verbal fluency differed between the heavy and light users, but only for those with low verbal IQ. Such patchy results do not permit clear conclusions about either the severity or mechanism of impairments; interestingly, however, there was no association between test scores and total lifetime consumption of the drug, which argues against the observed impairments being a direct manifestation of drug-induced structural damage. Residual effects of recent consumption are a more plausible explanation of the observed impairments.

At the single case level, Solowij et al. (1995) reported abnormalities of evoked potential indices of selective attention throughout six weeks of abstinence by a heavy long-term cannabis user; responses normalized during acute intoxication. In a group study, Solowij et al. (1995) found evoked potential impairments to correlate with duration (years) of use. Together, these findings may suggest long-lasting neuroadaptations developing as a response to chronic cannabis ingestion. However, in the absence of clear associated cognitive impairments in chronic users, the functional significance of these changes is uncertain.

In conclusion then, for pragmatic assessment purposes it would be wise to take recent cannabis use (within the last 48 hours) into account in interpreting subtle indications of impairment (e.g., where scores are slightly below expected levels, but still within the range of measurement error). Neither recent nor chronic cannabis use, however, are likely to explain any gross cognitive impairments except possibly in vulnerable individuals (e.g., those with a prior neurological or psychiatric history) who may be at greater risk of amplified emotional/psychotic reactions to psychoactive drug use.

Alcohol

The literature on the cognitive effects of alcohol, the most widely used drug in contemporary society, is immense, and it is beyond the scope of the present chapter to do more than summarize some of the key issues. The reader is referred to Lezak (1995) for a detailed though still succinct discussion of patterns of cognitive impairment associated with different patterns, severities and phases of alcohol consumption.

In addition to increasing levels of dopamine and serotonin, alcohol exerts non-specific inhibitory effects on the flow of sodium across cell membranes, alters the functioning of $GABA_A$ receptors (probably accounting for its ability to decrease anxiety), inhibits glutamate receptors and interacts either directly or indirectly with opioid receptors. As it is a CNS depressant, its general sedating effects are likely to affect cognitive test performance in a broad and non-specific manner. Consequently, if the examinee is still acutely intoxicated he or she is likely to underperform on tests that require alertness, and any deficits that he or she has for any other reason are likely to be amplified. Alcohol can affect different people in different ways and the same person in different ways on different occasions; Kerr and Hindmarch (1998) note that many other drugs interact with alcohol, some (e.g., nicotine and caffeine) offsetting its cognitive effects and others (particularly sedatives) amplifying them. On the whole, therefore, testing within a couple of hours of a single drink or within 24 hours of a heavy drinking session is to be avoided.

Chronic alcohol use can damage nerve cells, particularly in the frontal cortex, hypothalamus and cerebellum, with conflicting findings for the amygdala, hippo-campus and locus coeruleus (see Harper, 1998). However, some of these anatomical changes have been found to reverse over a period of abstinence in both rats (Dlugos & Pentney, 1997) and humans, where short-term abstinence is associated with an increase in the volume of cortical grey matter (Pfefferbaum et al., 1995).

Moderate social drinking is rarely found to have more than very subtle cognitive effects. While there have been some reports of a correlation between level of consumption and mild impairments of short-term verbal recall and/or executive functions, others have found no such associations. Parsons and Nixon (1998) reviewed 19 studies conducted after 1986 and concluded that deficits were unlikely to be found in people drinking up to four 'standard drinks' per day over extended time periods, but that 'cognitive inefficiencies' were often evident at five or six drinks per day, 'mild cognitive deficits' at between seven and nine drinks per day and 'moderate cognitive deficits equivalent to those found in diagnosed alcoholics' at 10 or more drinks per day.

Current alcoholics show impairments of short-term learning and memory that are typically subtle, but become more pronounced as task difficulty increases. In some studies they have been more in evidence on visual than on verbal tasks, and impairments in visual search and scanning and in executive functions have also been noted (e.g., Ryan & Butters, 1986). However, many of the observed abnorm-alities of functioning appear to show good recovery over periods of days to years of abstinence, probably reflecting a combination of receding acute withdrawal-related deficits and neural recovery. For example, Horner et al. (1999) found that after a few days of abstinence 69 mild to moderately dependent alcoholics being treated as outpatients showed circumscribed deficits in reaction time and verbal memory; amount of recent consumption, but not estimated lifetime consumption, correlated with impairments across a range of tests. Elsewhere, only 4 out of 101 young alcoholics, assessed on an extensive range of neuropsychological tests after several weeks of abstinence, showed mild cognitive dysfunction (Eckardt et al., 1995). Total lifetime consumption was associated with worse performance, while increasing duration of abstinence was associated with improvements in perform- ance. This is consistent with findings from a classic study by Brandt et al. (1983), who found that the longer the period of abstinence the better the scores on tests of verbal and non-verbal short-term memory and two coding tasks, and that in the group abstinent for longest (>5 years) most of these scores were at normal levels.

In addition to ascertaining duration since last drink, then, the neuropsychologist needs to determine whether the examinee is or has ever been dependent on alcohol and the duration of abstinence. Alcohol dependence is indicated: if the person has received treatment for alcohol problems; if he or she has had a period of drinking daily and/or feeling out of control such that drinking has impinged adversely on important aspects of social and occupational lifestyle; if he or she has had black- outs, overpowering cravings or other withdrawal symptoms during periods of abstinence. If this is the case, the neuropsychologist should also ascertain whether there is any evidence of Korsakoff's syndrome (KS), an alcohol-related condition characterized by brain lesions resulting from thiamine deficiencies and by gross memory impairment.

Ryan and Butters (1986) note that KS patients show significant loss of grey matter in the orbitofrontal and mesiotemporal cortex, and in diencephalic struc- tures. They perform essentially normally on tests of general intellectual ability that are structured and untimed, but are impaired on tests that involve speed, visuo- perceptual processes and spatial organization. They may do well on tests of focused attention, though show deficits on tests where they are required to divide or shift attention and on tests of executive function. The most pronounced difficulties relate to defective coding of new information and impaired retrieval processes, which manifest in severe anterograde and retrograde amnesia (e.g., Janowsky et al., 1989).

To summarize, then, despite the complex neurochemical effects of alcohol, a past history of heavy use or dependence is unlikely to be responsible for gross current cognitive deficits, unless it has only recently ended or the person has developed KS. Subtle cognitive impairments might be found in patients who have been severely dependent at some time in the past, but moderately dependent alcoholics are likely to show more or less complete cognitive recovery after a few years, or possibly even shorter periods, of abstinence. Social drinkers consuming fewer than about six drinks a day are unlikely to show significant cognitive impairments except when intoxicated, though individuals drinking more heavily than this are likely to be bordering on dependence and to show mild impairments on a range of tests until they maintain abstinence for at least a few days or weeks.

Nicotine

Nicotine is generally believed to be the critical (though not the only) psychoactive ingredient of tobacco and cigarettes. It is a cholinergic agonist that also increases release of dopamine in the mesocorticolimbic circuitry affected by other addictive drugs (Gamberino & Gold, 1999). Blood nicotine concentration reaches its peak within approximately 15 minutes of smoking a cigarette and then decreases by about half over the next hour, returning to close to baseline level by two hours. The time course of these effects suggests that habitual smokers, who commonly inhale the drug 20–40 times in the course of each day and so keep their nicotine levels elevated, are likely to show disturbances associated with nicotine abstinence if they are tested more than an hour or two after smoking. This, of course, is the norm in most neuropsychological assessments, unless the examiner permits smoking during the assessment or stops periodically to allow the examinee a cigarette break.

Consistent with an impact of nicotine on executive functions, there is robust evidence that when given to smokers via cigarettes or through some other delivery method (e.g., gum, patches), it enhances sustained, divided and focused attention (Kassel, 1997) and decreases response speed and some other aspects of cognitive performance (e.g., Parrott & Craig, 1992). Conversely, abstinence has been associated with impaired working memory (e.g., Blake & Smith, 1997). Dependent smokers, like addicts of other substances, have been found to show impairments of inhibitory response control (e.g., Hatsukami et al., 1989) and poor decision-making on gambling tasks (e.g., Grant et al., 2000). Al-Adawi and Powell (1997) found that heavy smokers (ca 20 cigarettes per day) who had abstained for a few hours showed reductions in incentive motivation, verbal fluency and digit span relative both to non-smokers and to their own performance immediately after smoking. The impairments of incentive motivation, though not of the other cognitive indices, were confirmed in a subsequent study (Powell et al., 2002) with lighter smokers (median 10 cigarettes per day). It remains unclear to what extent improvements in performance seen after smoking compared with during abstinence reflect a direct enhancement (i.e., elevation of alertness or efficiency of information-processing to supra-normal levels) rather than a reversal of the debilitating effects of withdrawal, which in chronic smokers is characterized by symptoms such as dysphoria, restlessness and poor concentration. However, a number of studies have also shown positive effects of subcutaneous nicotine in non-smokers on tests of attention and reaction time (e.g., Foulds et al., 1992), suggesting that there are some real enhancements.

By contrast, a few studies have shown adverse acute effects of smoking on some tasks. For example, Park et al. (1999) found that recent nicotine consumption by smokers was associated with a *decline* in performance on a test of spatial working memory, although spatial selective attention was unaffected. Although these findings await replication, they highlight the complexity of the cognitive effects of smoking and abstinence.

These data suggest that when testing a smoker who normally smokes at intervals shorter than the anticipated duration of the assessment session, it would be advisable if possible to allow them a cigarette break at an appropriate interval in order to avoid abstinence-related declines in test performance. Although this is often a practical inconvenience, the results of the assessment are likely to have more ecological validity if normal levels of nicotine intake are maintained. Where this is not feasible, the assessor could consider suggesting to heavy smokers that they might use some other form of nicotine delivery, such as a patch, gum or lozenge, that will help to prevent the onset of withdrawal symptoms.

NO CONCLUSIONS, BUT SOME HELPFUL QUESTIONS . . .

Enormous variation in the neurochemical and functional effects of different psycho-active drugs, as well as in their patterns of use, precludes many generalizations about either their cognitive effects or indeed about factors the neuropsychologist needs to take into account in conducting an assessment. However, issues that should be thought through, ideally prior to the assessment but otherwise at the stage of interpretation, include the following:

- Time since last use. Are either acute intoxication or acute withdrawal likely to compromise performance?
- Lifetime use. If there has ever been a period of heavy use, how long ago was it? Are any abstinence-related effects likely to have abated? Are enduring deficits likely?
- Duration of prescribed drug use. Has it started to exert therapeutic effects? Is the examinee likely to have developed tolerance to initial adverse cognitive effects?
- Associated drug use. Is adjunctive medication being taken to suppress adverse side effects? Is it being taken in conjunction with alcohol, which may amplify normally small effects? If the drug is illicit, is it part of a pattern of polydrug and alcohol use?
- The condition being treated. Are the symptoms of any underlying condition that is rectified or partly rectified by the medication likely to affect performance on cognitive tests? Are unwanted (e.g., motor, sedative) effects of the medication likely to counteract improvements related to therapeutic efficacy?
- Individual vulnerability factors. Does the examinee have any characteristics (e.g., being elderly; having a prior psychiatric or neurological condition) that may result in abnormal sensitivity to cognitive effects of drugs?

The implications of these questions vary between classes of drugs and even between different drugs within a class. The answers do not yet exist for all questions for all drugs, and the information available is constantly being updated. However, it is hoped that reference to the preceding synopses for some common drug groups will at least provide a framework for identifying relevant issues in each case and will direct the reader who needs more detail to pertinent and recent review articles.

REFERENCES

Al-Adawi, S. & Powell, J. (1997) The influence of smoking on reward responsiveness and cognitive functions: A natural experiment. *Addiction*, **92**, 1773–1782.

Allain, H., Lieury, A., Brunetbourgin, F., Mirabaud, C., Trebon, P., Lecoz, F. et al. (1992) Antidepressants and cognition—Comparative effects of moclobemide, viloxazine and maprotiline. *Psychopharmacology*, **106**, S56–S61.

Amado-Boccara, I., Gougoulis, N., Poirier Littre, M. F., Galinowski, A. & Lôo, H. (1995) Effects of antidepressants on cognitive functions: A review. *Neuroscience and Biobehavioural Reviews*, **19**, 479–493.

Ameri, A. (1999) The effects of cannabinoids on the brain. *Progress in Neurobiology*, **58**, 315–348.

Bechara, A., Dolan, S., Denburg, N., Hindes, A., Anderson, S. W. & Nathan. P. E. (2001) Decision-making deficits, linked to a dysfunctional ventromedial prefrontal cortex, revealed in alcohol and stimulant abusers. *Neuropsychologia*, **39**, 376–389.

Bhattachary, S. & Powell, J. H. (2001) Recreational use of 3,4-methylenedioxymethamphetamine (MDMA) or 'ecstasy': Evidence for cognitive impairment. *Psychological Medicine*, **31**, 647–658.

Blake, J. & Smith, A. (1997) Effects of smoking and smoking deprivation on the articulatory loop of human memory. *Human Psychopharmacology—Clinical and Experimental*, **12**, 259–264.

Bolla, K. L., McCann, U. D. & Ricaurte, G. A. (1998) Memory impairment in abstinent MDMA ('Ecstasy') users. *Neurology*, **51**, 1532–1537.

Brandt, J., Butters, N., Ryan, C. & Bayog, R. (1983) Cognitive loss and recovery in long-term alcohol abusers. *Archives of General Psychiatry*, **40**, 435–442.

Burt, D. B., Zembar, M. J. & Niederehe, G. (1995) Depression and memory impairment: A meta-analysis of the association, its pattern, and specificity. *Psychological Bulletin*, **117**, 285–305.

Busto, U. E., Bremner, K. E., Knight, K., terBrugge, K. & Sellers, E. M. (2000) Long-term benzodiazepine therapy does not result in brain abnormalities. *Journal of Clinical Psychopharmacology*, **20**, 2–6.

Curran, H. V. (1992) Antidepressant drugs, cognitive function and human performance. *Handbook of Human Performance* (Vol. 2, pp. 319–336). Academic Press, New York.

Curran, H. V. (1999) Effects of anxiolytics on memory. *Human Psychopharmacology*, **14**, S72–S79.

Curran, H. V. (2000) Psychopharmacological perspectives on memory. In: E. Tulving and F. I. M. Craik (eds) *The Oxford Handbook of Memory* (pp. 539–554). Oxford University Press, Oxford, UK.

Curran, H. V. & Travill, R. A. (1997) Mood and cognitive effects of 3,4-methylenedioxymethamphetamine (MDMA; 'ecstasy'): Weekend 'high' followed by mid-week low. *Addiction*, **92**, 821–831.

Curran, H. V., Bond, A., O'Sullivan, G., Bruce, M., Marks, I., Lelliot, P. et al. (1994) Memory functions, alpraxolam and exposure therapy: A controlled longitudinal study of patients with agoraphobia and panic disorder. *Psychological Medicine*, **24**, 969–976.

Curran, H. V., Poovibunsuk, P., Dalton, J. & Lader, M. H. (1998) Differentiating the effects of centrally acting drugs on arousal and memory: An event-related potential study of scopolamine, lorazepam and diphenhydramine. *Psychopharmacology*, **95**, 520–527.

Curran, H. V., Kleckham, J., Bearn, J., Strang, J. & Wanigaratne, S. (2001) Effects of methadone on cognition, mood and craving in detoxifying opiate addicts: A dose-response study. *Psychopharmacology*, **154**, 153–160.

Dlugos, C. & Pentney, R. (1997) Morphometric evidence that the total number of synapses on purkinje neurons of old f344 rats is reduced after long-term ethanol treatment and restored to control levels after recovery. *Alcohol and Alcoholism*, **32**, 161–172.

Dodrill, C. B. & Troupin, A. S. (1977) Psychotropic effects of carbamazepine in epilepsy: A double-blind comparison with phenytoin. *Neurology*, **27**, 1023–1028.

Dodrill, C. B. & Troupin, A. S. (1991) Neuropsychological effects of carbamazepine and phenytoin: A reanalysis. *Neurology*, **41**, 141–143.

Duncan, J. S., Shorvon, S. D. & Trimble, M. R. (1990) Effects of removal of phenytoin, carbamazepine and valproate on cognitive function. *Epilepsia*, **31**, 584–591.

Eckardt, M. J., Stapleton, J. M., Rawlings, R. R., Davis, E. Z. & Grodin, D. M. (1995) Neuropsychological functioning in detoxified alcoholics between 18 and 35 years of age. *American Journal of Psychiatry*, **152**, 53–59.

Foulds, J., Stapleton, J., Feyerabend, C., Vesey, C., Jarvis, M. & Russell, M. A. H. (1992) Effect of transdermal nicotine patches on cigarette smoking: A double blind crossover study. *Psychopharmacology*, **106**, 421–427.

Frederick, D. L. & Paule, M. G. (1997) Effects of MDMA on complex brain function in laboratory animals. *Neuroscience Behavioural Reviews*, **21**, 67–78.

Gamberino, W. C. & Gold, M. S. (1999) Neurobiology of tobacco smoking and other addictive disorders. *Psychiatric Clinics of North America*, **22**, 301–312.

Gouzoulis-Mayfrank, E., Daumann, J., Tuchtenhagen, F., Pelz, S., Becker, S., Kunert, H.-J. et al. (2000) Impaired cognitive performance in drug free users of recreational ecstasy (MDMA). *Journal of Neurology, Neurosurgery and Psychiatry*, **68**, 719–725.

Grant, S., Contoreggi, C. & London, E. D. (2000) Drug abusers show impaired performance in a laboratory test of decision-making. *Neuropsychologia*, **38**, 1180–1187.

Harper, C. (1998) The neuropathology of alcohol-specific brain damage, or does alcohol damage the brain? *Journal of Neuropathology and Experimental Neurology*, **57**, 101–110.

Hatsukami, D., Fletcher, L., Morgan, S., Keenan, R. & Amble, P. (1989) The effects of varying cigarette deprivation duration on cognitive and performance tasks. *Journal of Substance Abuse*, **1**, 407–416.

Hindmarch, I. (1988) A pharmacological profile of fluoxetine and other antidepressants on aspects of skilled performance and car handling ability. *British Journal of Psychiatry*, **153**, 99–104.

Hindmarch, I. & Kerr, J. (1992) Behavioural toxicity of antidepressants with particular reference to moclobemide. *Psychopharmacology*, **106**(Suppl.), S49–S55.

Hindmarch, I., Kimber, S. & Cockle, S. M. (2000) Abrupt and brief discontinuation of antidepressant treatment: Effects on cognitive function and psychomotor performance. *International Clinical Psychopharmacology*, **15**, 305–318.

Horner, M. D. (1999) Attentional functioning in abstinent cocaine users. *Drug and Alcohol Dependence*, **54**, 19–33.

Horner, M. D., Waid, L. R., Johnson, D. E., Latham, P. K. & Anton, R. F. (1999) The relationship of cognitive functioning to amount of recent and lifetime alcohol consumption in outpatient alcoholics. *Addictive Behaviours*, **24**, 449–453.

Janowsky, J. S., Shimamura, A. P., Kritchevsky, M. & Squire, L. R. (1989) Cognitive impairment following frontal lobe damage and its relevance to human amnesia. *Behavioural Neuroscience*, **103**, 548–560.

Kassel, J. D. (1997) Smoking and attention: A review and reformulation of the stimulus-filter hypothesis. *Clinical Psychology Review*, **17**, 451–478.

Kerr, J. S. & Hindmarch, I. (1998) The effects of alcohol alone or in combination with other drugs on information-processing, task performance and subjective responses. *Human Psychopharmacology—Clinical and Experimental*, **13**, 1–9.

Kwan, P. & Brodie, M. J. (2001) Neuropsychological effects of epilepsy and antiepileptic drugs. *The Lancet*, **357**, 216–222.

Lamping, D. L., Spring, B. & Gelenberg, A. J. (1984) Effects of two antidepressants on memory performance in depressed outpatients: A double-blind study. *Psychopharmacology*, **84**, 254–261.

Larkin, J. G., Mckee, P. J. W. & Brodie, M. J. (1992) Rapid tolerance to acute psychomotor impairment with carbamazepine in epileptic patients. *British Journal of Clinical Pharmacology*, **33**, 111–114.

Lezak, M. D. (1995) *Neuropsychological Assessment* (3rd edn). Oxford University Press, New York.

Linnoila, M., Johnson, J., Dubyoski, T., Ross, R., Buchsbaum, M., Potter, W. Z. et al. (1983) Effects of amitryptiline, desipramine and zimeldine alone and in combination with ethanol, in information processing and memory in healthy volunteers. *Acta Psychiatrica Scandinavica*, **68**(Suppl. 308), 175–181.

Liu, X., Matochik, J. A., Cadet, J. L. & London, E. D. (1998) Smaller volume of prefrontal lobe in polysubstance abusers: A magnetic resonance imaging study. *Neuropsychopharmacology*, **18**, 243–252.

London, E. D., Ernst, M., Grant, S., Bonson, K. & Weinstein, A. (2000) Orbitofrontal cortex and human drug abuse: Functional imaging. *Cerebral Cortex*, **10**, 334–342.

Martin, R., Kuzniecky, R., Ho, S., Hetherington, H., Pan, J., Sinclair, K. et al. (1999) Cognitive effects of topiramate, gabapentin, and lamotrogine in healthy young adults. *Neurology*, **52**, 321–327.

McCann, U. D., Eligulashvili, V. & Ricaurte, G. A. (2000) (±)3,4-methylenedioxymethamphetamine ('ecstasy')-induced serotonin neurotoxicity: Clinical studies. *Neuropsychobiology*, **42**, 11–16.

Morton, S. & Lader, M. (1990) Studies with alpidem in normal volunteers and anxious patients. *Pharmacopsychiatry*, **23**(Suppl. 3), 120–123.

Ornstein, T. J., Iddon, J. L., Baldacchino, A. M., Sahakian, B. J., London, M., Everitt, B. J. et al. (2000) Profiles of cognitive dysfunction in chronic amphetamine and heroin abusers. *Neuropsychopharmacology*, **23**, 113–126.

Park, S., Knopick, C., McGurk, S. & Meltzer, H. (1999) Nicotine impairs spatial working memory while leaving spatial attention intact. *Neuropsychopharmacology*, **22**, 200–209.

Parrott, A. C. & Craig, D. (1992) Cigarette smoking and nicotine gum (0, 2, and 4 mg): Effects upon four visual attention tasks. *Neuropsychobiology*, **25**, 34–43.

Parrott, A. C. & Lasky, J. (1998) Ecstasy (MDMA) effects upon mood and cognition: Before, during and after a Saturday night dance. *Psychopharmacology*, **139**, 261–268.

Parrott, A. C., Lees, A., Garnham, N. J., Jones, M. & Wesnes, K. (1998) Cognitive performance in recreational users of MDMA or 'ecstasy': Evidence for memory deficits. *Journal of Psychopharmacology*, **12**, 79–83.

Parsons, O. A. & Nixon, S. J. (1998) Cognitive functioning in sober social drinkers: A review of the research since 1986. *Journal of Studies on Alcohol*, **59**, 180–190.

Peck, A. W., Bye, C. E., Clubley, M., Henson, T. & Riddington, C. (1979) A comparison of bupropion hydrochloride with dexamphetamine and amitryptiline in healthy subjects. *British Journal of Clinical Pharmacology*, **7**, 469–478.

Pfefferbaum, A., Sullivan, E. V., Mathalon, D. H., Shear, P. K., Rosenbaum, M. J. & Lim, K. O. (1995) Longitudinal changes in magnetic resonance imaging brain volumes in abstinent and relapsed alcoholics. *Alcoholism: Clinical and Experimental Research*, **19**, 1177–1191.

Pope, H. G. Jr & Yurgelun-Todd, D. (1996) The residual cognitive effects of heavy marijuana use in college students. *Journal of the American Medical Association*, **275**, 521–527.

Pope, H. G., Gruber, A. J. & Yurgelun-Todd, D. (1995) The residual neuropsychological effects of cannabis: The current status of research. *Drug and Alcohol Dependence*, **38**, 25–34.

Powell, J., Dawkins, L. & Davis, R. (2002) Smoking, desire, and planfulness: Tests of an incentive motivational model. *Biological Psychiatry*, **51**, 151–163.

Ramaekers, S. G., Swijgman, H. F. & O'Hanlon, J. F. (1992) Effects of moclobemide and mianserin on highway driving, psychometric performance and subjective parameters relative to placebo. *Psychopharmacology*, **106**(Suppl.), S62–S67.

Robinson, T. E. & Berridge, K. C. (1993) The neural basis of drug craving: An incentive-sensitisation theory of addiction. *Brain Research Review*, **18**, 247–291.

Robinson, T. E. & Berridge, K. C. (2000) The psychobiology and neurobiology of addiction: An incentive-sensitization view. *Addiction*, **95**, S91–S117.

Robinson, J. E., Heaton, R. K. & O'Malley, S. S. (1999) Neuropsychological functioning in cocaine abusers with and without alcohol dependence. *Journal of the International Neuropsychological Society*, **5**, 10–19.

Rogers, R. D. & Robbins, T. W. (2001) Investigating the neurocognitive deficits associated with chronic drug misuse. *Current Opinion in Neurobiology*, **11**, 250–257.

Ryan, C. & Butters, N. (1986) Neuropsychology of alcoholism. In: D. Wedding, A. M. Horton Jr & J. S. Webster (eds) *The Neuropsychology Handbook*. Springer Verlag, New York.

Selby, M. J. & Azrin, R. L. (1998) Neuropsychological functioning in drug abusers. *Drug and Alcohol Dependence*, **50**, 39–45.

Seppala, T., Linnoila, M., Elonan, F., Mattila, M. J. & Maki, M. (1975) Effect of tricyclic antidepressants and alcohol in psychomotor skills related to car driving. *Clinical Pharmacological Therapeutics*, **17**, 515–522.

Siegfried, K. & O'Connolly, M. (1986) Cognitive and psychomotor effects of different antidepressants in the treatment of old age depression. *International Clinical Psychopharmacology*, **1**, 231–243.

Smirne, S., Ferini-Strambi, L., Pirola, R., Tancredi, O., Franceschi, M., Pinto, P. et al. (1989) Effects of flunitrazepam on cognitive functions. *Psychopharmacology*, **108**, 371–379.

Solowij, N., Michie, P. T. & Fox, A. M. (1995) Differential impairments of selective attention due to frequency and duration of cannabis use. *Biological Psychiatry*, **37**, 731–739.

Stahl, S. M. (2002) *Essential Psychopharmacology: Neuroscientific Basis and Practical Applications*. Cambridge University Press, Cambridge, UK.

Sternberg, D. E. & Jarvik, M. E. (1976) Memory functions in depression. *Archives of General Psychiatry*, **33**, 219–224.

Tata, P. R., Rollings, J., Collins, M., Pickering, A. & Jacobson, R. R. (1994) Lack of cognitive recovery following withdrawal from long-term benzodiazepine use. *Psychological Medicine*, **24**, 203–213.

Tiller, J. W. (1990) Antidepressants, alcohol and psychomotor performance. *Acta Psychologica Scandivica*, **82**(Suppl. 360), 13–17.

Wilson, J. T. L., Teasdale, G. M., Hadley, D. M., Wiedmann, K. D. & Lang, D. (1993) Post-traumatic amnesia; still a valuable yardstick. *Journal of Neurology, Neurosurgery and Psychiatry*, **56**, 198–201.

Wise, R. A. (1998) Drug-activation of brain reward pathways. *Drug and Alcohol Dependence*, **51**, 13–22.

Wise, R. A. & Munn, E. (1995) Withdrawal from chronic amphetamine elevates baseline intracranial self-stimulation thresholds. *Psychopharmacology*, **117**, 130–136.

CHAPTER 6

Psychometric Foundations of Neuropsychological Assessment

John R. Crawford

University of Aberdeen, Aberdeen, UK

INTRODUCTION

Clinical neuropsychologists make a unique contribution to the assessment of clients with neurological or psychiatric disorders. First, they can call on their specialized knowledge of sophisticated models of the human cognitive architecture when arriving at a formulation. Second, they have expertise in quantitative methods for both the measurement of cognitive and behavioural functioning and for the interpretation of resultant findings. This chapter will set out the basics of these quantitative methods.

Among the topics covered will be the advantages and disadvantages of the various metrics for expressing test scores, the use of reliability information in assessment, the distinction between the reliability and the abnormality of test scores and test score differences, and the measurement of change in the individual case. And, then, finally, the role of measures of intelligence in neuropsychological assessment will be considered, in addition to methods for estimating premorbid intelligence.

METRICS FOR EXPRESSING TEST SCORES

In constructing a neuropsychological profile of a client's strengths and weaknesses most clinicians use instruments drawn from diverse sources. These instruments will differ from each other in the metric used to express test scores (in extreme cases no formal metric will have been applied, so that clinicians will be working from the means and standard deviations [SDs] of the raw scores from normative samples). The process of assimilating the information from these tests is greatly eased if the scores are all converted to a common metric (Crawford et al., 1998c; Lezak, 1995).

Clinical Neuropsychology: A Practical Guide to Assessment and Management for Clinicians.
Edited by L.H. Goldstein and J.E. McNeil. © 2004 John Wiley & Sons, Ltd.

Converting all scores to percentiles has the important advantage that percentiles directly express the rarity or abnormality of an individual's score. In addition, percentiles are easily comprehended by other health workers. However, because such a conversion involves an area (i.e., non-linear) transformation, they are not ideally suited for the rapid and accurate assimilation of information from a client's profile. For example, as scores on most standardized tests are normally distributed, the difference between a percentile score of 10 and 20 does not reflect the same underlying raw score (or standard score) difference as that between 40 and 50. In addition, percentiles are not a suitable metric for use with most inferential statistical methods. Expressing scores as percentiles can however be a useful fallback option when raw scores depart markedly from a normal distribution and a normalizing transformation cannot be found (such as when skew is acute and there is a limited number of scale points).

A simple method of expressing scores that does not suffer from the limitations outlined above is the usage of z scores. However, they have the disadvantage of including negative values and decimal places, which make them awkward to work with and can cause problems in communication. It is also important to be aware that simply converting raw scores to standard or z scores has no effect on the shape of the distribution. If the raw scores are normally distributed (as will normally be the case with standardized tests), then so will the resultant z scores. However, if raw scores are skewed (i.e., the distribution is asymmetric), as may be the case when working with raw scores from a non-standardized measure, then the z scores will be equally skewed. In contrast, *normalized z* scores, as the term suggests, *are* normally distributed. There are a number of methods employed to normalize distributions: a common one is to convert raw scores to percentiles, then convert the percentiles to normalized z scores by referring to a table of the areas under the normal curve (or using a computer package to the same effect). For example, if a raw score corresponds to the 5th percentile then the corresponding normalized z score is -1.64.

McKinlay (1992) suggested converting all scores to have a mean of 100 and an SD of 15, as tests commonly forming a part of the neuropsychologist's armamentarium are already expressed on this metric. For example, IQs and Indexes on the Wechsler Adult Intelligence Scale—3rd edition (WAIS-III; Wechsler, 1997a), memory Indexes from the Wechsler Memory Scale—3rd edition (WMS-III; Wechsler, 1997b) and estimates of premorbid ability such as the National Adult Reading Test (NART; Nelson & Willison, 1991). A common alternative is to use T scores (mean = 50, SD = 10), which have much to recommend them. The gradation between T scores is neither too coarse, so that potentially meaningful differences between raw scores are obscured (such as would commonly be the case with sten scores in which a difference of one unit corresponds to 0.5 of an SD), nor too finely graded, so as to lend a spurious air of precision (for T scores, a difference of one unit corresponds to 0.1 of an SD). The meaning of T scores is also easy to communicate and is free of the conceptual baggage associated with IQs (Lezak, 1995).

With the exception of percentiles (which, as noted, involve a non-linear transformation) conversion of scores expressed on any of these different metrics can be achieved using a simple formula (the formula is generic in that it can be used to convert scores having *any* particular mean and SD to scores having any other desired mean and SD):

$$X_{new} = \frac{S_{new}}{S_{old}}(X_{old} - \bar{X}_{old}) + \bar{X}_{new} \qquad (6.1)$$

where X_{new} = the transformed score, X_{old} = the original score, S_{old} = the SD of the original scale, S_{new} = the SD of the metric you wish to convert to, $\bar{X}_{old}$ = the mean of the original scale and $\bar{X}_{new}$ = the mean of the metric you wish to convert to. Much of the time this formula is superfluous as the mapping of one metric on to another is straightforward (e.g., no thought is required to transform an IQ of 115 to a T score of 60). However, if a clinician is regularly converting large numbers of test scores, then entering the formula into a spreadsheet can save time and reduce the chance of clerical errors.

Regardless of which method is used to express the score on a common metric, the clinician must be aware that the validity of any inferences regarding relative strengths and weaknesses in the resultant profile of scores is heavily dependent on the degree of equivalence of the normative samples involved. Although the quality of normative data for neuropsychological tests has improved markedly, there are still tests used in clinical practice that are normed on small samples of convenience. Thus, discrepancies in an individual's profile may in some cases be more a reflection of differences between normative samples than differences in the individual's relative level of functioning in the domains covered by the tests.

RELIABILITY

Adequate reliability is a fundamental requirement for any instrument used in neuropsychology, regardless of purpose. However, when the concern is with assessing the cognitive status of an *individual*, its importance is magnified, particularly as clinicians frequently need to arrive at a formulation based on information from single administrations of each instrument (Crawford et al., 1998c).

The reliability coefficient represents the proportion of variance in test scores that is true variance. Thus, if a test has a reliability of 0.90, 90% of the variance reflects real differences between individuals and 10% reflects measurement error. Information on test reliability is used to quantify the degree of confidence that can be placed in test scores, for example, when comparing an individual's scores with appropriate normative data, or assessing whether discrepancies between scores on different tests represent genuine differences in the functioning of the underlying components of the cognitive system, as opposed to simply reflecting measurement error in the tests employed to measure the functioning of these components. In the latter case (i.e., where evidence for a dissociation or differential deficit is being evaluated), it is important to consider the extent to which the tests are matched for reliability; an apparent deficit in function A with relative sparing of function B may simply reflect the fact that the measure of function B is less reliable.

This point was well made in a classic paper by Chapman and Chapman (1973) in which the performance of a schizophrenic sample on two *parallel* reasoning tests was examined. By manipulating the number of test items, and hence the reliability of the tests, the schizophrenic sample could be made to appear to have a large differential deficit on either of the tests. Particular care should be taken in comparing test scores when one of the measures is not a simple score, but a difference (or ratio score). Such measures will typically have modest reliability (the measurement error in the individual components that are used to form the difference score is additive).

The standard error of measurement (SEM) is the vehicle used to convert a test's reliability coefficient into information that is directly relevant to the assessment of individuals. The SEM can be conceived of as the SD of obtained scores around an individual's hypothetical true score that would result from administering an infinite number of parallel tests. The formula for the SEM is:

$$\text{SEM} = s_X \sqrt{1 - r_{xx}} \qquad (6.2)$$

where s_x = the SD of scores on test X and r_{xx} is the test's reliability coefficient. As noted, the reliability coefficient is the proportion of variance that is true variance; therefore, subtracting this from unity gives us the proportion of variance that is error variance (i.e., measurement error). However, we want to obtain the SD of errors (rather than the variance) on the metric used to express the obtained scores. Therefore, we take the square root of this quantity and multiply it by the SD of obtained scores.

The SEM allows us to form a confidence interval (CI) on a score. Most authorities on psychological measurement stress the use of these intervals (e.g., Nunnally & Bernstein, 1994); they serve the general purpose of reminding us that all test scores are fallible and serve the specific purpose of allowing us to quantify the effects of this fallibility. CIs are formed by multiplying the SEM by the standard normal deviate corresponding to the desired level of confidence. Therefore, for a 95% CI, the SEM is multiplied by 1.96. To illustrate, if an individual obtained a score of 80 on a test and the SEM was 5.0, then the (rounded) CI would be 80 ± 10 (i.e., the interval would range from 70 to 90).

There is however a slight complication: many authorities on measurement have argued that the CI should be centred round the individual's estimated true score rather than their obtained score (e.g., Nunnally & Bernstein, 1994; Stanley, 1971). The estimated true score is obtained by multiplying the obtained score, in deviation form, by the reliability of the test:

$$\text{Estimated true score} = r_{xx}(X - \bar{X}) + \bar{X} \qquad (6.3)$$

where X is the obtained score and $\bar{X}$ is the mean for the test. The estimated true score represents a compromise between plumping for an individual being at the mean (which is our best guess if we had no information) and plumping for them being as extreme as the score they obtained on the particular version of the test on the particular occasion on which they were tested. The more reliable the test, the more we can trust the score and therefore the less the estimated true score is regressed to the mean.

To extend the previous example, suppose that the mean of the test in question was 100 and the reliability coefficient was 0.7. Therefore, the estimated true score is 84, and, using this to centre the CI, we find that it ranges from 74 to 94. Before leaving this topic, it can be noted that this CI does not encompass the mean of the test; therefore, it can be concluded that the individual's level of ability on the test is reliably below the mean level of ability.

As noted, a central aim in neuropsychological assessment is to identify relative strengths and weaknesses in a client's cognitive profile; as a result clinicians will commonly be concerned with evaluating test score *differences*. One question that can be asked of any difference is whether it is reliable (i.e., whether it is unlikely to simply reflect measurement error). To answer this question requires the SEM of the difference. When we are only concerned with comparing a pair of test scores, then one formula for this quantity is as follows:

$$\text{SEM}_{X-Y} = \sqrt{\text{SEM}_X^2 + \text{SEM}_Y^2} \tag{6.4}$$

To use this formula the two scores must already be expressed on the same metric or transformed so that they are. The SEM_{X-Y} can be multiplied by a standard normal deviate corresponding to the required level of significance to obtain a critical value (i.e., multiplying by 1.96 gives the critical value for a reliable difference at the 0.05 level, two-tailed). If the difference between a client's scores exceeds this critical value, it can be concluded that the scores are reliably different. This is the method usually employed in test manuals. Alternatively, the difference between the client's scores can be divided by the SEM_{X-Y} to yield a standard normal deviate, and the precise probability determined using a table of areas under the normal curve. To illustrate both methods, suppose that the SEM for tests X and Y are 3.0 and 4.0, respectively; therefore, the SEM_{X-Y} is 5.0 and the critical value is 9.8. Further, suppose that a client's scores on tests X and Y were 104 and 92, respectively. The difference (12) exceeds the critical value; therefore, the scores are reliably different ($p < 0.05$). Alternatively, dividing the difference by the SEM_{X-Y} yields a z of 2.4, and reference to a table of the normal curve reveals that the precise (two-tailed) probability that this difference occurred by chance is 0.016.

The method outlined is concerned with testing for a difference between a client's obtained scores. An alternative (but less common) method is to test for a reliable difference between estimated true scores; see Crawford et al. (2003b) and Silverstein (1989) for examples of this latter approach.

Formula (6.4) is for comparing a client's scores on a single pair of tests. However, in a typical neuropsychological assessment many tests will have been administered. This leads to a large number of potential pairwise comparisons. For example, if 12 tests have been administered, then there are 66 potential pairwise comparisons. Even with a relatively modest number of tests, the process of assimilating this information on differences is formidable (particularly when it has to be integrated with all the other data available to the clinician). It can also be readily appreciated that, when a large number of comparisons are involved, there will be an increase in the probability of making type I errors (in this context a type I error would occur if we concluded that there was a difference between a client's scores when there is not). Limiting the number of pairwise comparisons does not get round this problem, unless the decision as to which tests will be compared is made *prior* to obtaining the test results; if the clinician selects the comparisons to be made *post hoc* on the basis of the magnitude of the observed differences, then this is equivalent to having conducted all possible comparisons.

A useful solution to these problems was proposed independently by Knight and Godfrey (1984) and Silverstein (1982). In their approach a patient's score on each of *k* individual tests is compared with the patient's mean score on the *k* tests (just as is the case when comparing a pair of tests, all the tests must be expressed on the same metric or transformed so that they are). It can be seen that with 12 tests, there are 12 comparisons rather than the 66 involved in a full pairwise comparison. Another feature of this approach is that a Bonferroni correction is applied to maintain the overall type I error rate at the desired level. This approach has been applied to the analysis of strengths and weaknesses on the subtests of the Wechsler intelligence scales, including the WAIS-III (see table B.3 of the WAIS-III manual). It has also been applied to various other tests; for example, Crawford et al. (1997b) have applied it to the Test of Everyday Attention (Robertson et al., 1994).

RELIABILITY VERSUS ABNORMALITY OF TEST SCORES AND TEST SCORE DIFFERENCES

The distinction between the reliability and the abnormality of test scores and test score differences is an important one in clinical neuropsychology. As noted, if the CI on a client's score does not encompass the mean of the test, then we can consider it to be reliably different from the mean (i.e., a difference of this magnitude is unlikely to have arisen from measurement error). However, it does not follow from this that the score is necessarily unusually low (i.e., rare or abnormal), nor that the score reflects an acquired impairment.

Provided that the normative sample for a test is large (see next section), estimating the *abnormality* of a test score is straightforward. If scores are expressed as percentiles then we immediately have the required information (e.g., if a client's score is at the 5th percentile, then we know that 5% of the population would be expected to obtain lower scores). If scores are expressed on other metrics, we need only refer to a table of the normal curve. For example, a *T* score of 30 or an IQ score of 70 are exactly 2 SDs below the mean (i.e., $z = -2.0$) and therefore only 2.3% of the population would be expected to obtain lower scores.

Most of the confusion around the distinction between the reliability and abnormality of test scores seems to arise when the focus is on differences between an individual's scores. Methods of testing for reliable differences between test scores were covered in the previous section. However, establishing if a difference is reliable is only the first step in neuropsychological profile analysis. There is considerable *intra*-individual variability in cognitive abilities in the general population such that reliable differences between tests of different abilities are common; indeed, if the reliabilities of the tests involved are very high, then such differences may be very common. Therefore, when evaluating the possibility that a difference between scores reflects acquired impairment, evidence on the reliability of the difference should be supplemented with information on the abnormality or rarity of the difference. That is, we need to ask the question 'what percentage of the healthy population would be expected to exhibit a discrepancy larger than that exhibited by my client?'

To highlight the distinction between the reliability and abnormality of a difference, take the example of a discrepancy between the Verbal and Perceptual Organization Indexes of the WAIS-III. Consulting table B.1 of the WAIS-III manual, it can be seen that a discrepancy of 10 points would be necessary for a reliable difference ($p < 0.5$). However, such a discrepancy is by no means unusual; from table B.2 we can see that 42% of the general population would be expected to exhibit a discrepancy of this magnitude. If we define an abnormal discrepancy as one that would occur in less than 5% of the general population, then a 26-point discrepancy would be required to fulfil this criterion.

Base rate data on differences between test scores such as that contained in table B.2 of the WAIS-III manual are available for a number of tests used in neuropsychology. An alternative to this empirical approach is to estimate the degree of abnormality of a discrepancy using a formula provided by Payne and Jones (1957). This formula will be described briefly below so that clinicians understand it when they encounter it in the literature and can use it themselves when the necessary summary statistics are available for a healthy sample. The method can be employed when it is reasonable to assume that the scores are normally distributed and requires only the means and SDs of the two tests plus their intercorrelation (r_{xy}). The first step is to convert the individual's scores on the two tasks to z scores and then enter them into the formula:

$$z_D = \frac{z_X - z_Y}{\sqrt{2 - 2r_{xy}}} \tag{6.5}$$

This formula is very straightforward. The denominator is the SD of the difference between scores when the scores are expressed as z scores. The numerator instructs us to subtract the individual's z score on test X from their z score on test Y. In the numerator the difference between the individual's z scores are subtracted from the mean difference in controls. However, the mean difference between z scores in the controls is necessarily zero and therefore need not appear. In summary, the difference between z scores is divided by the SD of the difference to obtain a z score *for the difference*.

This z score (z_D) can then be referred to a table of the areas under the normal curve to provide an estimate of the proportion or percentage of the population that would exhibit a difference more extreme than the patient. For example, suppose scores on tests of verbal and spatial short-term memory were expressed as T scores, and further suppose that the correlation between the tasks is 0.6 and that a patient obtained scores of 55 and 36, respectively. Therefore, the patient's z scores on the tasks are 0.50 and -1.40, the difference is 1.90, the SD for the difference is 0.894, and so $z_D = 2.13$. Referring to a table of the normal curve reveals that only 3.32% of the population would be expected to exhibit a difference larger than that exhibited by the patient (1.66% if we concern ourselves only with a difference in the same direction as the patient's).

It is also possible to assess the abnormality of discrepancies between a client's mean score on k tests and his or her scores on each of the tests contributing to that mean (Silverstein, 1984). This method complements the method discussed in the previous section that was concerned with the *reliability* of such discrepancies; it has the same advantage of reducing the comparisons to a manageable proportion. Silverstein's formula estimates the degree of abnormality from the statistics of a normative sample, an alternative is to generate the base rate data empirically (this latter approach is used for the WAIS-III).

The importance of evaluating the abnormality of discrepancies through the use of base rate data or methods such as the Payne and Jones formula cannot be overstressed. Most clinical neuropsychologists have not had the opportunity to administer neuropsychological measures to significant numbers of individuals drawn from the general population. It is possible therefore to form a distorted impression of the degree of intra-individual variability found in the general population; the indications are that clinicians commonly underestimate the degree of normal variability, leading to a danger of over-inference when working with clinical populations (Crawford et al., 1998c).

ASSESSING THE ABNORMALITY OF TEST SCORES AND TEST SCORE DIFFERENCES WHEN NORMATIVE OR CONTROL SAMPLES ARE SMALL

In the procedures just described for assessing the abnormality of scores and score differences, the normative sample against which a patient is compared is treated as if it were a population (i.e., the means and SDs are used as if they were population parameters rather than sample statistics). When the normative sample is large (e.g., such as when a patient's score or score difference is compared against normative data from the WAIS-III or WMS-III), this is not a problem as the sample provides very good estimates of these parameters.

However, there are a number of reasons why neuropsychologists may wish to compare the test scores of an individual with norms derived from a small sample. For example, although the quality of normative data has improved in recent years, there are still many useful neuropsychological instruments that have modest normative data. This is not surprising: advances in neuropsychological theory occur at a rapid rate whereas the process of devising practical measures of new constructs and obtaining norms from a large and representative sample is a time-consuming and arduous process. Furthermore, even when the overall N for a normative sample is reasonably large, the size of the actual sample (n) against which an individual's score is compared can be small, if the normative data have been broken down by demographic characteristics (e.g., age and/or gender).

Therefore, there is a need for methods that are suitable for use with small normative samples. This need is perhaps most apparent when one considers single case research in neuropsychology. The resurgence of interest in single case studies has led to significant advances in our understanding of normal and pathological cognitive function (e.g., see Ellis & Young, 1996). However, in the typical single case study the sample size of the control or normative sample recruited for comparison purposes is often < 10 or even < 5; it is inadvisable to treat samples of this size as though they were a population, yet this is what is commonly done (Crawford & Howell, 1998a). The most common method of comparing a patient against such samples is to convert the patient's score to a z score and refer it to a table of the normal curve. This not only gives an estimate of the abnormality of the score but is also used as an inferential statistical method (i.e., if the z score exceeds a specified critical value, then the patient's score is considered to be significantly different from controls). However, because this approach treats the control sample statistics as parameters, it overestimates the abnormality of the score and increases type I errors.

The solution is to use a modified t-test to conduct such comparisons, as this method treats the control sample *as* a sample (Crawford & Howell, 1998a). Crawford et al. (1998a) extended this approach to allow neuropsychologists to estimate the abnormality of the difference between a patient's scores on a pair of tests and to test whether the patient's difference is significantly different from the differences observed in a control or normative sample (this method is the equivalent of the Payne and Jones method, but is not constrained by the need for a large normative sample). A fuller discussion of these issues can be found in Crawford et al. (2003a); this paper proposes formal criteria for dissociations and evaluates them using Monte Carlo simulations.

This test can be used to provide an operational definition of a dissociation. The typical existing definitions of a classical dissociation are not stringent as they require only that a patient is 'impaired' on task X and 'normal' or 'within normal limits' on task Y. One half of this typical definition requires us to prove the null hypothesis (we must demonstrate that a patient is not different from the controls), whereas, as is well known, we can only fail to reject it. Further, a patient's score on the impaired task could lie just below the critical value for defining impairment and the performance on the other test lie just above it. That is, the difference between the patient's relative standing on the two tasks of interest could be very trivial. A test on the difference between scores overcomes both these problems.

Crawford and Garthwaite (2002) have further extended these methods by providing a means of establishing CIs on the abnormality of a score or score difference. These intervals quantify the uncertainty arising from using sample statistics to estimate population parameters and, in combination with the methods discussed above, provide clinicians or researchers with information of the form 'the estimated percentage of the healthy population that would obtain a score (or score difference) lower than the patient is 2.1% and the 95% CI on the percentage is from 0.2% to 6.7%'. Computer programs that implement all of the methods covered in this section are available (see Crawford & Garthwaite, 2002 for details).

DETECTING CHANGE IN NEUROPSYCHOLOGICAL FUNCTIONING IN THE INDIVIDUAL CASE

There are many situations in which the neuropsychologist needs to measure potential changes in cognitive functioning. Common examples would be to determine whether cognitive decline has occurred in an individual in whom a degenerative neurological process is suspected, or to determine the extent of recovery of function following a stroke or traumatic brain injury. In both these cases neuropsychological assessment will provide useful information to assist clients, relatives and other health professionals to plan for the future. Monitoring the cognitive effects of surgical, pharmacological or cognitive interventions in the individual case is also an important role for the neuropsychologist. Although the aim here is most commonly to determine if there has been any improvement, the possibility of detrimental effects can also often be an issue. For example, many drugs can potentially impair cognitive functioning, particularly in the elderly.

In assessing the effectiveness of a rehabilitation effort it is often possible to obtain *multiple* repeated measures of an individual's performance before, during and after intervention (see Wilson, 1987). A number of inferential statistical techniques can be used in this situation because there are multiple data points for the different phases. However, in general clinical practice the neuropsychologist often must come to conclusions about change from only a *single* retesting. This situation will also arise in rehabilitation settings; although multiple measures may have been obtained on the training task(s), the issue of the generalizability of any improvement is often addressed by comparing single before-and-after scores on related but separate tests.

Monitoring change on the basis of a single retesting is a formidable task, except in cases where the level of change has been dramatic. It is rendered more formidable by the fact that many of the standard instruments currently used in clinical neuropsychology do not have parallel or analogue versions. This is a particular problem for tests of executive function, which often depend on novelty for their effectiveness.

The clinician must differentiate changes resulting from systematic practice effects and random measurement error from change reflecting genuine improvement or deterioration. Among other complications are the fact that (1) the magnitude of practice effects vary with the nature of the task (e.g., tasks with a psychomotor component tend to have larger practice effects than tasks that do not), (2) the length of time that has elapsed between test and retest is liable to influence the magnitude of effects and (3) a diminution of practice effects is to be expected in neurological populations (given the high prevalence of memory and learning deficits), but the expected diminution is difficult to estimate for individuals.

One approach to dealing with some, although not all, of these considerable interpretive problems is to use regression to predict scores at retest from scores on initial testing. An individual's predicted score is compared with the retest score actually obtained to assess whether the observed gain or decline significantly exceeds that expected by chance. This can be achieved by dividing the difference between predicted and obtained scores by the equation's standard error of estimate to obtain a z for the difference.[1]

The utility of this approach is determined by the extent and nature of retest studies available for a particular test. For example, the test–retest scores on memory tasks for an elderly client with suspected dementia could be compared with estimated retest scores derived from a healthy, elderly sample retested after a similar period to gauge how atypical any decline may be. For some questions, equations derived from a clinical sample may be used. For example, a head-injured client's scores on measures of attention or speed of processing could be compared with estimated retest scores from a head-injured sample, if the clinician suspects that the extent of recovery is atypical.

An excellent example of the regression-based approach is provided by Temkin et al. (1999). Using a healthy sample ($N = 384$), these authors built regression equations to predict performance at retest for a large number of tests commonly used in clinical neuropsychology. The regression-based approach compared favourably with alternative approaches (e.g., Jacobson & Traux, 1991). This study also serves to illustrate a further point: if other variables (e.g., age or years of education) moderate the relationship between initial performance and performance at retest, these variables can simply be incorporated into the equations to improve the accuracy of prediction.

It is not necessary for the clinician to have access to existing equations to make use of regression to assess change. If basic summary data are available from a sample retested on a neuropsychological measure, then an equation can be built with relative ease; all that is required is the correlation between scores at test and retest and the means and SDs of these scores. The relevant formulae for obtaining a regression equation and its associated standard error of estimate can be found in most statistics textbooks (e.g., Howell, 2002).

THE ROLE OF MEASURES OF INTELLIGENCE IN NEUROPSYCHOLOGICAL ASSESSMENT

Lezak (1988) has described the Wechsler intelligence scales as the 'the workhorse of neuropsychological assessment' and noted that it is 'the single most utilized component of the neuropsychological repertory' (p. 53). In the UK, the British Psychological Society proposed that Wechsler IQ cut-off scores should be used as the sole formal criteria for the legal definition of mental impairment (Alves et al., 1991).

The most recent incarnation of these scales is the WAIS-III and its UK edition (WAIS-III[UK]; Wechsler et al., 1998). The WAIS-III has many of the strengths of its predecessors, including a large and highly representative standardization sample

---

[1] This method is used widely in clinical neuropsychology, but provides only an approximation to the technically correct method. However, in practice, the approximation is adequate unless the sample used to generate the equation is very small (see Crawford & Howell, 1998b for details).

and very impressive levels of reliability. For example, the reliability of the WAIS-III Full Scale IQ (FSIQ) is 0.98 (therefore, only 2% of the variance in scores is error variance); this compares very favourably with the reliability of most medical testing procedures.

The WAIS-III also has a number of advantages over earlier editions. These include an upward extension of the age range (norms are available to cover ages 16 to 89) and an increased ability to differentiate at the lower end of ability (i.e., there has been a downward extension of measurable IQ to 54). In addition, the inclusion of the Matrix Reasoning subtest has bolstered the measurement of fluid ability and contributes to the lesser emphasis on timed performance in determining scores (there are also lesser time bonuses on some existing subtests). A minor but welcome change is that subtest scaled scores are age-corrected (previously, the clinician had to convert to scaled scores to derive IQs and age-graded scaled scores if they wanted to examine strengths and weaknesses at the subtest level).

Perhaps the most significant improvement is the inclusion of factor-based composite measures (i.e., the Indexes) as alternatives to IQs. Two of these Indexes also represent attempts to measure constructs that are of great theoretical importance in neuropsychology and cognitive psychology, namely working memory (Baddeley & Hitch, 1994) and speed of processing (e.g., Salthouse, 1991).

One limitation of earlier versions of the Wechsler scales was that they did not have parallel versions. Although a full parallel version is still not available for the WAIS-III, the development of the Wechsler Abbreviated Scale of Intelligence (WASI; Wechsler, 1999) means that there are now parallel versions for four of the subtests (Vocabulary, Similarities, Block Design and Matrix Reasoning). The WASI is also useful in its own right as a short form when clinical considerations rule out use of a full WAIS-III.

Given that the WAIS-III performance can be analysed at the level of IQs, Indexes and subtests, it is appropriate to consider what the *primary* level of analysis should be. Lezak (1988) argued that IQs obscure clinically important strengths and weaknesses and suggested that the solution was to focus on the subtest profile. Few clinical neuropsychologists would disagree with the first half of this position, but issue could be taken with the proposed solution. A number of authors have argued that the primary level of analysis should be at the level of factorially derived Indexes (e.g., Atkinson, 1991; Crawford et al., 1997a).

In the present author's view the arguments in favour of Indexes are compelling. The Indexes are empirically derived, whereas the subtests comprising the Verbal IQs (VIQ) and Performance IQs (PIQ) were allocated to these scales on intuitive grounds. Factor analysis of the WAIS-III and its predecessors have consistently found that the ability dimensions underlying the Wechsler fail to map on to the VIQ and PIQ scales. Three factors emerge on the WAIS-R (subtests from both the VIQ and PIQ scales load on the third factor). Four factors emerge on the WAIS-III, reflecting the addition of an additional speeded measure (Symbol Search) to accompany Digit Symbol. Furthermore, the factor structure has proven itself to be surprisingly robust: the same factors emerge across cultures and across healthy versus clinical populations (Atkinson, 1991).

Evidence of the superior clinical utility of factor-based Indexes over IQs is provided by Crawford et al.'s (1997a) study of WAIS-R performance following head injury. Their head-injured (HI) sample ($N = 233$) exhibited highly significant and broadly equivalent deficits on VIQ and PIQ. In contrast to this uninformative pattern, examination of the indexes revealed that the HI sample did not differ significantly from controls on the Verbal Index (despite high statistical power), but exhibited a very substantial deficit on the attention/concentration index (now termed Working Memory in the WAIS-III). This pattern of spared and severely compromised abilities was hidden within the VIQ scale because it represents an amalgam of variance reflecting well-consolidated verbal abilities (as indexed by the Verbal index) and attention/concentration or working memory (Arithmetic and Digit Span contribute strongly to this Index). Furthermore, discriminant function analysis revealed that VIQ and PIQ did not improve differentiation of the HI sample from healthy controls ($N = 356$) over that achieved by FSIQ alone (i.e., the VIQ/PIQ discrepancy was not useful). In contrast, the factor-based Indexes achieved significantly better discrimination than the IQ scales.

The primary advantage of the Indexes over individual subtests is that they have superior reliability. The reliability of a composite will normally substantially exceed that of its individual components (i.e., the subtests), if these components are correlated with each other. Substantial difference among individual subtests is not uncommon in the healthy, unimpaired population because of measurement error and because each subtest has a proportion of unique (but not necessarily clinically important) variance associated with it, in addition to variance that reflects the common underlying factor. Such extreme differences in normals are less likely at the level of Indexes (because they are composites); therefore, when large differences are observed, they are more likely to be of clinical significance. Empirical evidence of this was provided by Crawford et al.'s (1997a) study of HI: the factor-based Indexes achieved vastly superior discrimination between healthy and HI cases than indexes of subtest scatter (these latter indexes quantified the overall level of intra-individual variability in subtest scores). Indeed, counter to expectations, the HI sample exhibited no more subtest scatter than healthy controls.

The arguments and evidence reviewed above suggest that clinical interpretation of strengths and weaknesses on the WAIS-III should primarily be conducted at the level of the indexes. As previously noted, table B.1. of the manual allows clinicians to examine the reliability of differences between indexes, and table B.2 allows them to assess the abnormality of the differences. In addition, a fundamental role for the WAIS-III in neuropsychological assessment is to provide context for interpretation of *other* test results. As Crawford et al. (1997a) note, the Wechsler provides 'broad indicators of current functioning against which more specific neuropsychological measures are compared' (p. 352). The evidence and arguments reviewed above also suggest that Indexes, rather than the IQs, should fulfil this role.

METHODS FOR ESTIMATING PREMORBID ABILITY

The detection and quantification of cognitive impairment in the individual case is problematic because of the wide variability in cognitive abilities in the general adult population. Scores on cognitive measures that are average, or even above average, can still represent a significant impairment for an individual of high premorbid ability. Conversely, for individuals with modest premorbid resources, test scores that fall well below the mean may be entirely consistent with their prior level of functioning. Consequently, simple normative comparison standards are of limited utility in the detection of impairment and are supplemented with *individual* comparison standards when attempting to assess acquired deficits (Crawford et al., 1998c; Lezak, 1995; O'Carroll, 1995). Ideally, these individual standards would be obtained from cognitive test scores obtained in the premorbid period. However, this is rarely a viable option as few individuals have had prior formal testing and, even where they have, it is difficult or impossible to obtain the results. Thus clinicians and researchers usually have to settle for some other means of estimating an individual's premorbid ability.

The most common means of obtaining such an estimate is to use a measure of present ability that is relatively unaffected by neurological or psychiatric disorder. Currently, the test most widely used for this purpose is the NART (Nelson & Willison, 1991). The NART is a 50-item single word reading test of graded difficulty. It is argued that the NART makes minimal demands on current cognitive capacity because it requires only oral reading of short, single words (Nelson & O'Connell, 1978). In addition, all the words are irregular: that is, they violate grapheme–phoneme correspondence rules (e.g., *ache*, *thyme*, *topiary*). The supposition is that, as a result, the test depends on prior or premorbid ability, because a testee must have prior knowledge of a word's pronunciation; deployment of *current* cognitive resources (e.g., the intelligent application of grapheme–phoneme correspondence rules) will not result in a correct pronunciation.

To be considered valid, any putative measure of premorbid intelligence must fulfil three criteria (Crawford, 1992). First, like any psychological test, it must possess adequate reliability. Second, it must have adequate criterion validity (i.e., it must correlate highly with measures of psychometric intelligence). Third, performance on the measure must be largely impervious to the effects of neurological or psychiatric disorder. The NART fulfils the first criterion in that it possesses high internal consistency, test–retest reliability and inter-rater reliability (Crawford, 1992; O'Carroll, 1995).

The results from studies that have addressed the criterion validity of the NART have also been generally positive. For example, in UK studies the NART predicted between 55% and 72% of the variance in FSIQ as measured by the WAIS and WAIS-R (see Crawford, 1992; O'Carroll, 1995). The NART also predicts a substantial proportion of the variance in most of the IQs and Indexes of the WAIS-III (Crawford et al., submitted).

A feature of all these studies is that, although the NART is intended to measure *prior* or *premorbid* intelligence, the criterion validity information they provide is based solely on *concurrent* administration of the NART and an IQ measure. Therefore, it is important to know whether the criterion validity of the NART is equally impressive when it is compared against a criterion that genuinely represents prior ability. Crawford et al. (2001a) administered the NART to a sample of 77-year-olds ($N = 197$) and reported that it retrospectively accounted for 53% of the variance in the IQ scores obtained by this sample at age 11 (i.e., 66 years previously). Furthermore, the NART's correlation with prior IQ was higher than its correlation with IQ measured concurrently and was higher than the correlation between the two IQ tests. This remarkable pattern of results lends support to the validity of the notion that the NART primarily indexes prior rather than current ability.

Using a North American variant of the NART, Smith et al. (1997) conducted an important longitudinal study that simultaneously assessed the issue of criterion validity and the question of the robustness of NART performance (further evidence on this latter issue is reviewed below). Smith et al. reported that, in a sample of participants with cognitive impairment, the NART provided accurate predictions of VIQs obtained five years earlier, when the sample had been cognitively normal.

The final criterion for a putative measure of premorbid ability is that test performance be resistant to neurological or psychiatric disorder. NART performance appears to be largely resistant to the effects of many neurological and psychiatric disorders (e.g., depression, acute schizophrenia, alcoholic dementia and Parkinson's disease (see Crawford, 1992; Franzen et al., 1997; and O'Carroll, 1995, for reviews). The results for head injury have generally been positive (e.g., Watt & O'Carroll, 1999), although there are indications of impaired performance in a minority of cases (Freeman et al., 2001); the available evidence also suggests that the NART 'holds' following focal frontal lesions (Bright et al., 2002; Crawford & Warrington, 2002).

The findings from early studies have been most mixed in the case of dementia of the Alzheimer type (DAT) (see aforementioned reviews). Subsequent studies have continued to produce conflicting results in DAT, some reporting clear evidence of impairment (e.g., Cockburn et al., 2000; Patterson et al., 1994), others finding that NART performance 'held' (Bright et al., 2002; Sharpe & O'Carroll, 1991). However, it has become increasingly clear that NART performance is impaired in many cases of severe and even moderate dementia.

Any findings of impaired NART performance threaten the validity of this approach. However, the practical implications of impaired performance in cases of *severe* neurological disorder are not as serious as they may appear; in such cases the presence of deficits is unfortunately only too obvious, thereby largely obviating the need for the NART or similar instrument to assist in its detection and quantification (Crawford et al., 1998c). Nevertheless, given the accumulating evidence that NART performance can be impaired in some conditions, it would be useful to have a means of evaluating the likely validity of the premorbid estimate provided by the NART in the individual case.

To address this need, Crawford et al. (1990a) built a regression equation in a healthy sample ($N = 659$) to predict NART scores from demographic variables (e.g., years of education and occupational classification); an obtained NART score that was significantly lower than the demographically predicted NART score would indicate that the NART is unlikely to provide a valid estimate of premorbid ability for the individual concerned.

It has been suggested (Crawford et al., 1990b) that the NART should fulfil a fourth criterion that is more concerned with its clinical utility than its validity. It could be that, contrary to the assumptions underlying the use of the NART, simply using obtained scores alone, rather than the discrepancy between NART estimates of premorbid scores and obtained scores, would be just as effective a means of detecting impairment.

This basic issue has received little empirical scrutiny. Crawford et al. (1990b) used hierarchical discriminant function analysis to examine the ability of the NART in combination with WAIS IQ to correctly classify a sample consisting of healthy participants and patients with Alzheimer's disease (AD). The inclusion of the NART significantly improved the accuracy of classification over that achieved by WAIS IQs alone; 85% of cases were correctly classified by IQ scores and this rose to 96% for the combination of IQs and NART scores. An analogous result was obtained by Crawford and Warrington (2002), who reported that the use of the NART significantly improved the ability of a verbal fluency task (homophone-meaning generation) to discriminate between the performance of healthy participants and patients with focal anterior lesions.

Most research on the NART's ability to estimate premorbid ability has used scores on IQ tests as the criterion variable. Although this is in keeping with the notion of obtaining an estimate of an individual's general level of premorbid functioning, the NART also has the potential to provide estimates of premorbid functioning for more specific neuropsychological tests. For example, Crawford et al. (1992) built a regression equation that can be used to estimate premorbid performance on the FAS verbal fluency test; an equation is also available for the Homophone Meaning Generation Test (Crawford & Warrington, 2002). Similarly, Crawford et al. (1998b) have provided an equation that uses NART and age to estimate premorbid scores on the PASAT (Paced Auditory Serial Addition Test; Gronwall, 1977), a measure that is sensitive to the presence of attentional dysfunction following head injury (McMillan & Glucksman, 1987).

A proposed modification to the NART is the Cambridge Contextual Reading Test (Beardsall & Huppert, 1994). As its name suggests, the NART words are embedded in sentences to provide context for the examinee. Another reading test is the Spot-The-Word Test (STW; Baddeley et al., 1993). STW is a lexical decision task in which the examinee has to identify the legitimate words from a series of word/pseudo-word pairs (e.g., stamen/floxid); see Law & O'Carroll (1998) for an evaluation. Finally, the Wechsler Test of Adult Reading (WTAR; Holdnack, 2001) is based on the same rationale as the NART (it requires the reading of single, irregular words). All of these tests have considerable potential as alternatives to the NART, but have a relatively modest research base at present. Space limitations means that they cannot be considered in any further detail in the present work.

An entirely different approach uses regression equations to estimate premorbid ability from demographic variables (e.g., years of education, occupational classification, etc.). This approach can be seen as a formalization of clinical 'guesstimates' based on the same information, but one that is more accurate and free from demonstrable clinical biases (Crawford et al., 2001b). The advantage of the demographic approach over the use of tests such as the NART is that the estimate it provides is entirely independent of a client's current level of functioning. As evidence of impaired NART performance in various clinical conditions accumulates, the demographic approach offers an alternative method in cases where use of the NART would be inappropriate. However, the obvious disadvantage of the demographic approach is its modest criterion validity.

Where Wechsler IQs have been used as the criterion variables, regression equations based solely on demographic variables account for between only 36% and 54% of FSIQ variance (e.g., Barona et al., 1984; Crawford & Allan, 1997). This compares unfavourably with the corresponding figures for the NART and its variants. Finally, regression equations have been developed that use both the NART *and* demographic variables as predictors (see O'Carroll, 1995, for an evaluation).

CONCLUSION

This chapter has covered the basic quantitative methods for analysing test scores. A solid grounding in these methods and associated issues (i.e., the distinction between the reliability and abnormality of differences) is fundamental to the practice of clinical neuropsychology and, as noted, is an important part of what makes the clinical neuropsychologist unique among health professionals.

REFERENCES

Alves, E., Williams, C., Stephen, I. & Prosser, G. (1991) *Mental Impairment and Severe Mental Impairment*. British Psychological Society, Leicester, UK.

Atkinson, L. (1991) Some tables for statistically based interpretation of WAIS-R factor scores. *Psychological Assessment*, **3**, 288–291.

Baddeley, A., Emslie, H. & Nimmo-Smith, I. (1993) The Spot-the-Word Test: A robust estimate of verbal intelligence based on lexical decision. *British Journal of Clinical Psychology*, **32**, 55–65.

Baddeley, A. D. & Hitch, G. J. (1994) Developments in the concept of working memory. *Neuropsychology*, **8**, 485–493.

Barona, A., Reynolds, C. R. & Chastain, R. (1984) A demographically based index of premorbid intelligence for the WAIS-R. *Journal of Consulting and Clinical Psychology*, **52**, 885–887.

Beardsall, L. & Huppert, F. A. (1994) Improvement in NART word reading in demented and normal older persons using the Cambridge Contextual Reading Test. *Journal of Clinical and Experimental Neuropsychology*, **16**, 232–242.

Bright, P., Jaldow, E. & Kopelman, M. D. (2002) The National Adult Reading Test as a measure of premorbid intelligence: A comparison with estimates derived from demographic variables. *Journal of the International Neuropsychological Society*, **8**, 847–854.

Chapman, L. J. & Chapman, J. P. (1973) Problems in the measurement of cognitive deficit. *Psychological Bulletin*, **79**, 380–385.

Cockburn, J., Keene, J., Hope, T. & Smith, P. (2000) Progressive decline in NART score with increasing dementia severity. *Journal of the International Neuropsychological Society*, **22**, 508–517.

Crawford, J. R. (1992) Current and premorbid intelligence measures in neuropsychological assessment. In: J. R. Crawford, D. M. Parker & W. W. McKinlay (eds) *A Handbook of Neuropsychological Assessment* (pp. 21–49). Lawrence Erlbaum, London.

Crawford, J. R. & Allan, K. M. (1997) Estimating premorbid IQ with demographic variables: Regression equations derived from a U.K. sample. *The Clinical Neuropsychologist*, **11**, 192–197.

Crawford, J. R. & Garthwaite, P. H. (2002) Investigation of the single case in neuropsychology: Confidence limits on the abnormality of test scores and test score differences. *Neuropsychologia*, **40**, 1196–1208.

Crawford, J. R. & Howell, D. C. (1998a) Comparing an individual's test score against norms derived from small samples. *The Clinical Neuropsychologist*, **12**, 482–486.

Crawford, J. R. & Howell, D. C. (1998b) Regression equations in clinical neuropsychology: An evaluation of statistical methods for comparing predicted and obtained scores. *Journal of Clinical and Experimental Neuropsychology*, **20**, 755–762.

Crawford, J. R. & Warrington, E. K. (2002) The Homophone Meaning Generation Test: Psychometric properties and a method for estimating premorbid performance. *Journal of the International Neuropsychological Society*, **8**, 547–554.

Crawford, J. R., Allan, K. M., Cochrane, R. H. B. & Parker, D. M. (1990a) Assessing the validity of NART estimated premorbid IQs in the individual case. *British Journal of Clinical Psychology*, **29**, 435–436.

Crawford, J. R., Hart, S. & Nelson, H. E. (1990b) Improved detection of cognitive impairment with the NART: An investigation employing hierarchical discriminant function analysis. *British Journal of Clinical Psychology*, **29**, 239–241.

Crawford, J. R., Moore, J. W. & Cameron, I. M. (1992) Verbal fluency: A NART-based equation for the estimation of premorbid performance. *British Journal of Clinical Psychology*, **31**, 327–329.

Crawford, J. R., Johnson, D. A., Mychalkiw, B. & Moore, J. W. (1997a) WAIS-R performance following closed head injury: A comparison of the clinical utility of summary IQs, factor scores and subtest scatter indices. *The Clinical Neuropsychologist*, **11**, 345–355.

Crawford, J. R., Sommerville, J. & Robertson, I. H. (1997b) Assessing the reliability and abnormality of subtest differences on the Test of Everyday Attention. *British Journal of Clinical Psychology*, **36**, 609–617.

Crawford, J. R., Howell, D. C. & Garthwaite, P. H. (1998a) Payne and Jones revisited: Estimating the abnormality of test score differences using a modified paired samples *t*-test. *Journal of Clinical and Experimental Neuropsychology*, **20**, 898–905.

Crawford, J. R., Obonsawin, M. C. & Allan, K. M. (1998b) PASAT and components of WAIS-R performance: Convergent and discriminant validity. *Neuropsychological Rehabilitation*, **8**, 255–272.

Crawford, J. R., Venneri, A. & O'Carroll, R. E. (1998c) Neuropsychological assessment of the elderly. In: A. S. Bellack & M. Hersen (eds), *Comprehensive Clinical Psychology, Vol. 7: Clinical Geropsychology* (pp. 133–169). Pergamon, Oxford, UK.

Crawford, J. R., Deary, I. J., Starr, J. M. & Whalley, L. J. (2001a) The NART as an index of prior intellectual functioning: A retrospective validity study covering a 66 year interval. *Psychological Medicine*, **31**, 451–458.

Crawford, J. R., Miller, J. & Milne, A. B. (2001b) Estimating premorbid IQ from demographic variables: A comparison of a regression equation versus clinical judgement. *British Journal of Clinical Psychology*, **40**, 97–105.

Crawford, J. R., Garthwaite, P. H. & Gray, C. D. (2003a) Wanted: Fully operational definitions of dissociations in single-case studies. *Cortex*, **39**, 357–370.

Crawford, J. R., Smith, G. V., Maylor, E. A. M., Della Sala, S. & Logie, R. H. (2003b) The Prospective and Retrospective Memory Questionnaire (PRMQ): Normative data and latent structure in a large non-clinical sample. *Memory*, **11**, 261–275.

Crawford, J. R., Martin, D., Mockler, D., Allner, K. & Cipolotti, L. (submitted) Estimation of premorbid performance on WAIS-III IQs and indexes using the National Adult Reading Test (NART).

Ellis, A. W. & Young, A. W. (1996) *Human Cognitive Neuropsychology: A Textbook with Readings.* Psychology Press, Hove, UK.

Franzen, M. D., Burgess, E. J. & Smith-Seemiller, L. (1997) Methods of estimating premorbid functioning. *Archives of Clinical Neuropsychology,* **12,** 711–738.

Freeman, J., Godfrey, H. P. D., Harris, K. J. H. & Partridge, F. M. (2001) Utility of a demographic equation in detecting impaired NART performance. *British Journal of Clinical Psychology,* **40,** 221–224.

Gronwall, D. (1977) Paced Auditory Serial Addition Task: A measure of recovery from concussion. *Perceptual and Motor Skills,* **44,** 367–373.

Holdnack, J. A. (2001) *WTAR. Wechsler Test of Adult Reading Manual.* Psychological Corporation, San Antonio, TX.

Howell, D. C. (2002) *Statistical Methods for Psychology* (5th edn). Duxbury Press, Belmont, CA.

Jacobson, N. S. & Traux, P. (1991) Clinical significance: A statistical approach to defining meaningful change in psychotherapy research. *Journal of Consulting and Clinical Psychology,* **59,** 12–19.

Knight, R. G. & Godfrey, H. P. D. (1984) Assessing the significance of differences between subtests on the Wechsler Adult Intelligence Scale—Revised. *Journal of Clinical Psychology,* **40,** 808–810.

Law, R. & O'Carroll, R. E. (1998) A comparison of three measures of estimating premorbid intellectual level in dementia of the Alzheimer type. *International Journal of Geriatric Psychiatry,* **13,** 727–730.

Lezak, M. D. (1988). IQ: R.I.P. *Journal of Clinical and Experimental Neuropsychology,* **10,** 351–361.

Lezak, M. D. (1995) *Neuropsychological Assessment* (3rd edn). Oxford University Press, New York.

McKinlay, W. W. (1992) Assessment of the head-injured for compensation. In: J. R. Crawford, D. M. Parker & W. W. McKinlay (eds) *A Handbook of Neuropsychological Assessment* (pp. 381–392). Lawrence Erlbaum, Hove, UK.

McMillan, T. M. & Glucksman, E. E. (1987) The neuropsychology of moderate head injury. *Journal of Neurology, Neurosurgery and Psychiatry,* **50,** 393–397.

Nelson, H. E. & O'Connell, A. (1978) Dementia: The estimation of premorbid intelligence levels using the new adult reading test. *Cortex,* **14,** 234–244.

Nelson, H. E. & Willison, J. (1991) *National Adult Reading Test Manual* (2nd edn). NFER-Nelson, Windsor, UK.

Nunnally, J. C. & Bernstein, I. H. (1994) *Psychometric Theory* (3rd edn). McGraw-Hill, New York.

O'Carroll, R. (1995) The assessment of premorbid ability: A critical review. *Neurocase,* **1,** 83–89.

Patterson, K., Graham, N. & Hodges, J. R. (1994) Reading in dementia: A preserved ability? *Neuropsychology,* **8,** 395–407.

Payne, R. W. & Jones, G. (1957) Statistics for the investigation of individual cases. *Journal of Clinical Psychology,* **13,** 115–121.

Robertson, I. H., Ward, T., Ridgeway, V. & Nimmo-Smith, I. (1994) *The Test of Everyday Attention.* Thames Valley Test Company, Bury St Edmunds, UK.

Salthouse, T. A. (1991) *Theoretical Perspectives on Cognitive Aging.* Lawrence Erlbaum, Hillsdale, NJ.

Sharpe, K. & O'Carroll, R. (1991) Estimating premorbid intellectual level in dementia using the National Adult Reading Test: A Canadian study. *British Journal of Clinical Psychology,* **30,** 381–384.

Silverstein, A. B. (1982) Pattern analysis as simultaneous statistical inference. *Journal of Consulting and Clinical Psychology,* **50,** 234–240.

Silverstein, A. B. (1984) Pattern analysis: The question of abnormality. *Journal of Consulting and Clinical Psychology,* **52,** 936–939.

Silverstein, A. B. (1989) Confidence intervals for test scores and significance tests for test score differences: A comparison of methods. *Journal of Clinical Psychology*, **45**, 828–832.

Smith, G. E., Bohac, D. L., Ivnik, R. J. & Malec, J. F. (1997) Using word recognition scores to predict premorbid IQ in dementia patients. *Journal of the International Neuropsychological Society*, **3**, 528–533.

Stanley, J. C. (1971) Reliability. In: R. L. Thorndike (ed.) *Educational Measurement* (2nd edn, pp. 356–442). American Council on Education, Washington, DC.

Temkin, N. R., Heaton, R. K., Grant, I. & Dikmen, S. S. (1999) Detecting significant change in neuropsychological test performance: A comparison of four models. *Journal of the International Neuropsychological Society*, **5**, 357–369.

Watt, K. J. & O'Carroll, R. E. (1999) Evaluating methods for estimating premorbid intellectual ability in closed head injury. *Journal of Neurology, Neurosurgery and Psychiatry*, **66**, 474–479.

Wechsler, D. (1997a) *Manual for the Wechsler Adult Intelligence Scale* (3rd edn). Psychological Corporation, San Antonio, TX.

Wechsler, D. (1997b) *Manual for the Wechsler Memory Scale* (3rd edn). Psychological Corporation, San Antonio, TX.

Wechsler, D. (1999) *Wechsler Abbreviated Scale of Intelligence Manual*. Psychological Corporation, San Antonio, TX.

Wechsler, D., Wycherley, R. J., Benjamin, L., Crawford, J. R. & Mockler, D. (1998) *Manual for the Wechsler Adult Intelligence Scale* (3rd edn, UK). Psychological Corporation, London.

Wilson, B. (1987) Single-case experimental designs in neuropsychological rehabilitation. *Journal of Clinical and Experimental Neuropsychology*, **9**, 527–544.

PART IV

Adult Neuropsychology

CHAPTER 7

Disorders of Memory

Jonathan J. Evans

Oliver Zangwill Centre, Princess of Wales Hospital, Ely, UK

INTRODUCTION

Memory impairment is one of the most common sequelae of brain injury or disease. The fact that many different patterns of impairment may arise from damage to the brain reflects the now well-established fact that 'memory' is not a unitary concept or process, at either a psychological or anatomical level of explanation. This chapter will begin with a description of the most clinically useful theories of memory. Methods for assessing memory are then described, with a focus on tests that are useful for identifying the presence and nature of any memory impairment, as well as enabling the clinician to make predictions about the likely practical consequences of a memory deficit. The final section discusses the rehabilitation of memory, focusing on interventions aimed at reducing the disability associated with memory impairment.

MEMORY THEORY

One of the most important conceptual divisions in memory is that between short-term or working memory and long-term memory. Working memory is considered to be used to store temporarily information for a matter of seconds, while long-term memory is the permanent repository of memory for knowledge and events that may have been acquired or occurred anything from a few minutes to a few decades ago. Working memory is thought to involve three components (Baddeley, 1986): the phonological loop holds verbal information for as long as it is rehearsed, but without rehearsal only for a few seconds; the visuospatial sketchpad has the same function for non-verbal material; and the central executive is the attentional controller that modulates the functioning of the two slave systems.

Within the domain of long-term memory, conceptual divisions have been made at the level of (i) stimulus material, (ii) accessibility to conscious recollection and (iii) type of information. Each of these divisions will be discussed briefly.

Clinical Neuropsychology: A Practical Guide to Assessment and Management for Clinicians.
Edited by L.H. Goldstein and J.E. McNeil. © 2004 John Wiley & Sons, Ltd.

Stimulus Material

The main division within stimulus types is between verbal and non-verbal material. This division appears to result from the hemispheric asymmetry within the brain, with the left hemisphere being more concerned with verbal information processing and the right hemisphere for non-verbal information. Until recently evidence for this division was based primarily on the patterns of selective memory impairment found in some patients with unilateral lesions (e.g., Morris et al., 1995). Latterly, the same distinction has been shown in callosotomy ('split-brain') patients (Funnell et al., 2001) and in normal adults using functional magnetic resonance imaging (fMRI) studies (e.g., Golby et al., 2001).

Accessibility to Conscious Recollection

Squire (1992) has distinguished declarative (explicit) from non-declarative (implicit) memory systems. Non-declarative or implicit memory refers to learning that can be demonstrated to have occurred without the need for conscious recollection of the learned information or the episode of learning. The different forms of implicit learning include procedural learning (acquiring motor skills or habits), priming and classical conditioning. Declarative memory refers to the learning of information that is consciously recollected (such as facts or events).

Type of Information

The distinction between facts and events is reflected in Tulving's (1972) division of memory into *semantic* and *episodic* systems. Semantic memory is a store of factual knowledge of the world, knowledge that is context-independent and acquired through multiple exposure to, or rehearsal of, the material. It includes knowledge of word meanings, objects, people and encyclopaedic information. Episodic memory refers to context-dependent information, such as personally experienced events, or information linked to a particular time and spatial location (e.g., remembering what you did last weekend). Episodic memory is what most people would think of as memory and is the main focus of neuropsychological assessment of memory. Verfaellie et al. (2000) noted that, for a period of time, amnesia was represented as a selective deficit of episodic memory with sparing of semantic memory. However, this conclusion was not valid because of a confound between the way in which these two types of memory were evaluated. Episodic memory was evaluated using standard tests of anterograde memory (new learning), while semantic memory was evaluated using tests of old (premorbid) knowledge (e.g., object-naming tests or tests of famous person knowledge). The most recent studies (Verfaellie et al., 2000) suggest that the acquisition of new semantic information is likely to be compromised when an episodic memory impairment is present, but the severity of the impairment is likely to relate the extent of damage to temporal lobe structures. Although it can be useful to think of episodic and semantic memory as distinctive forms of memory, the reality is that these forms of memory arise in the normal brain from the integrated working of several subsystems.

Recall and Recognition

Another important aspect of memory theory concerns the mode of recollection, with the distinction between recall and recognition. Some situations require material to be recognized (i.e., matched with a memory of a previous exposure to the material). Recognizing a friend's face, a place you have been to or a film you have seen are all common examples of situations where you may not be able to bring to mind (recall) the thing you are trying to remember, but instantly remember it (recognize it) when you see or read it. By contrast, recall involves the recollection of something in the absence of the thing to be remembered. It is likely that the cognitive processes required for recognition are also involved in recall, but for recall additional retrieval or strategic search processes are required.

Prospective Memory

One of the most practically important uses for memory is remembering to do things in the future. Remembering to buy milk on the way home from work, remembering to post a birthday card in good time and remembering to pass on a telephone message are all examples of tasks of this type. The term 'prospective memory' is often used for this function, though use of the term should not be taken to imply the existence of a separate memory system. Ellis (1996) uses the term 'realizing delayed intentions', to describe these tasks. Realizing delayed intentions requires the co-ordinated integration of planning skills (setting up the intention to do something), attention and memory (recognizing that it is time to carry out the intended action, remembering what the intended action is and then remembering that it has been carried out).

Neuroanatomy of Memory

The process of encoding, storing over time and later retrieving information is dependent upon a number of different structures in the brain. Since Scoville and Milner's (1957) description of patient HM's severe amnesia following bilateral medial temporal lobe ablation as a treatment for epilepsy, much of the focus of the search for the anatomical architecture of memory has been on the limbic–diencephalic system. Contemporary models of memory, discussed later, emphasize the importance of integrated, modular systems within the brain working together. One of the critical modules in this integrated system is the hippocampus, which forms part of the medial temporal lobe. The hippocampus is seen as critical for remembering episodes or events. More lateral temporal lobe structures, along with other areas of the wider neocortex, are generally viewed as necessary for the long-term storage of memories.

The frontal lobes are also important for memory, with evidence of modularity of function. In line with the idea that they are the primary site for executive functions, the frontal lobes have been attributed a role in the more strategic aspects of remembering. More specifically, it is argued that the left frontal lobe makes an important contribution to the encoding of information, while the right frontal lobe is important for retrieval of information, particularly in situations where some form of strategic search for information is required. This theory has been referred to as the hemispheric encoding/retrieval asymmetry (HERA) model (Tulving et al., 1994).

Models of Memory

In recent years, several models of memory have attempted to incorporate evidence from neuropsychological, neuroanatomical and computational modelling studies (e.g., Alvarez & Squire, 1995; Damasio, 1989; Mesulam, 2000; Murre, 1996; Nadel & Moscovitch, 1997). Each model tries to account for the relationship between the wider neocortex and the medial temporal lobe structures (in particular the hippocampus). The models of Damasio (1989) and Mesulam (2000) are perhaps the most comprehensive. Both models argue that the brain can be thought of as a series of hierarchically organized functional zones. At the bottom of the hierarchy are regions that undertake the most basic level of sensory motor processing and code for feature fragments. Next come convergence zones that receive input from the sensory motor regions and code for 'coherent entities' (e.g., objects) and finally there are zones that code for the co-occurrence of entities that constitutes an event. This latter zone is considered to include the hippocampus and related medial temporal lobe structures. Memory of an event involves the reactivation of the hippocampal–neocortical network initially established during initial encoding of the event. Some of the models (e.g., Alvarez & Squire, 1995; Murre, 1996; Damasio, 1989) suggest that through repeated recollection (and hence reactivation) over time, event memories become established at the neocortical level, while in other models (Mesulam, 2000; Nadel & Moscovitch, 1997), the hippocampus is seen as always being involved in the recollection of events. However, all of the models agree that semantic or factual knowledge is acquired by the gradual formation of associations at the lower levels of the hierarchy, which can take place without the involvement of the higher levels, but under normal circumstances the process is facilitated by the higher levels. Thus people with a damaged or dysfunctional medial temporal lobe system can still learn new semantic or factual information, but much more slowly than individuals with an intact hippocampus.

Memory Impairments Arising from Brain Injury or Disease

One further distinction in memory that is relevant in the context of brain injury or disease is that between anterograde and retrograde memory. Anterograde memory refers to the acquisition of new information following the onset of injury or disease. Retrograde memory refers to memory for facts that were acquired or events that took place before the onset of injury or disease (see Kapur, 1999 for a review of various forms of retrograde amnesia).

The classic memory disorder is the amnesic syndrome. This involves (i) intact working memory, (ii) intact general intellectual and semantic memory functioning, (iii) anterograde amnesia (impaired ability to recall or recognize new facts or personal episodes), (iv) a variable degree of retrograde amnesia (difficulty remembering information that has previously been available) and (v) intact implicit memory. This pattern of impairment tends to follow from selective bilateral medial temporal lobe damage. Cases of pure amnesia are relatively uncommon as most people with brain injury or disease have more extensive damage. The viral infection herpes simplex encephalitis may sometimes lead to severe destruction of medial temporal lobe structures, but may also damage more lateral regions of temporal lobes and cause more extensive retrograde and semantic memory deficits (see Wilson et al., 1995). People with traumatic brain injury tend to have less complete destruction of medial temporal lobe structures and thus may have slightly milder memory impairment, but are also likely to have damage to frontal lobe structures and so have associated attentional and executive impairments, which will also impact on memory performance. People with dementia of the Alzheimer's type (DAT) may present initially with a significant episodic memory impairment, but rapidly develop problems in attention and executive skills, semantic and remote memory, language, perception and praxis (see Chapter 14 of this book).

Although anterograde memory deficits sometimes occur with little in the way of retrograde impairment (e.g., Zola Morgan et al.'s, 1986 patient RB), the question of whether retrograde memory impairments can arise in the absence of anterograde memory deficits has proved more controversial (Kapur, 2000; Kopelman, 2000). One of the reasons for the controversy is that a pattern of severe (and sometimes total) retrograde amnesia, accompanied by a normal ability to acquire new information, is associated with psychogenic forms of amnesia, or fugue states. However, a number of cases of focal retrograde amnesia arising from organic impairment have been described (Evans et al., 1996; see also Kapur, 1999).

Selective disorders of short-term or working memory are very rare, but have been reported (see Mayes, 2000). Patients with selective phonological loop deficits are unable to hold in mind more than two or three digits, words or letters, compared with the normal seven or so. Despite this they show normal language processing (Vallar & Papagno, 1995; Warrington & Shallice, 1969). These patients show normal learning of some information (which has led to the conclusion that working memory and long-term memory work in parallel), but Mayes (2000, p. 428) notes that there is evidence that long-term memory is impaired when it taps the same information that is impaired in short-term memory. For example, Baddeley et al. (1988) showed that patient PV, who has very impaired phonological short-term memory, was completely unable to learn new vocabulary (Russian words). An impairment in phonological working memory has been found in some children with specific problems learning vocabulary (Gathercole &

Baddeley, 1989). Phonological loop deficits have tended to be associated with left parietal lesions, though working memory impairments may also arise from dorso-lateral frontal lobe damage.

Selective deficits in semantic memory are also relatively uncommon, but can occur following damage to lateral temporal lobes, following head injury, infection or as a result of a focal dementia process referred to as semantic dementia or frontotemporal dementia (Hodges et al., 1992; Snowden et al., 1989). In semantic dementia, anterograde memory is often impaired on formal testing, but there is usually evidence of a degree of intact autobiographical episodic memory, particularly for more recent time periods. Within semantic memory, there is evidence that semantic memories for different categories break down in a dissociable manner. The most commonly reported dissociation is between living and non-living items (Warrington & Shallice, 1984). Controversy continues about whether this dissociation reflects uncontrolled differences between the categories, like frequency, familiarity and age of acquisition (Mayes, 2000), but nevertheless has been demonstrated in a number of cases of differing aetiology (Wilson, 1997a).

ASSESSMENT OF MEMORY

There are no pure tests of any single cognitive function, and any test designed to assess memory is likely to also make demands on other cognitive skills such as attention, perception and language. For this reason it is important that memory assessment is undertaken within the context of a more comprehensive neuropsycho-logical assessment. This is critical, as the interpretation of the results from memory tests will need to take into account performance on other cognitive tests. Impair-ments in executive functioning, attention/concentration, language and perception will all affect performance on tests of memory. It is also necessary to take into account the possible impact of mood and motivational factors when interpreting memory test results.

A comprehensive assessment of memory will utilize information from clinical interview with the patient and an informant (relative, carer, etc.). Sunderland et al. (1983) demonstrated that there was a much stronger correlation between reports of everyday memory slips and performance on standardized tests when the reports were from relatives of head-injured patients, rather than the patients themselves. To support the clinical interview, checklists of common memory problems can sometimes be useful in helping patients and relatives to identify the most trouble-some everyday consequences of memory impairment. Wilson (1999) discusses several of these behavioural memory assessments in more detail. It is also useful in an initial clinical interview to ask the patient and relative about how the patient is currently coping with the problems caused by the memory impairment. The opportunity to set specific tasks for a patient and observe his or her performance is also useful in the assessment of the functional impact of memory impairment.

Memory Tests–Batteries versus Individual Tests

The selection of tests for the assessment of memory will partly depend on the main question being addressed in the assessment. Ideally, any assessment of memory should cover all of the main forms of memory and Table 7.1 provides a summary with examples of the tests used most commonly to examine each of the key memory functions. There is an ever-increasing number of memory tests available, and it is therefore only possible to mention some of the more commonly used tests here. In practice, most clinicians will use a memory test battery and then follow up with further assessment on individual tests, if more detailed information is required.

The most commonly used battery of tests is the Wechsler Memory Scales, now in its third edition (WMS-III; Wechsler, 1997). A useful discussion of the WMS-III is provided by Franzen & Iverson (2000). Perhaps the greatest asset of the WMS-III is the large normative sample (1,250 individuals between the ages of 16 and 89) and the fact that it was co-normed with half of the normative sample of the Wechsler Adult Intelligence Scale—Third Edition (WAIS-III). This means that determining whether an IQ memory discrepancy is abnormal is more accurate.

The WMS-III, like, and perhaps better than, its predecessor, should prove to be a useful instrument for the detection of organic memory impairment. The extent to which it is useful for making specific predictions about the everyday consequences of memory impairment remains to be determined. One obvious limitation of WMS-III is the lack of parallel versions. Repeated assessment of memory is a common requirement in clinical practice for monitoring decline in progressive conditions and for monitoring improvement during recovery from injury or illness. One memory test battery that is useful in predicting the everyday consequences of memory impairment (Evans et al., in press; Wilson & Watson, 1996) and has parallel versions is the Rivermead Behavioural Memory Test (RBMT; Wilson et al., 1985) and its more recent revised version, the Rivermead Behavioural Memory Test—Extended Version (Wilson et al., 1998), devised to overcome criticisms of the lack of sensitivity of the RBMT to subtle levels of impairment. Summary screening and profile scores are calculated.

Two other memory test batteries are also relatively commonly used, at least in the UK. The Adult Memory and Information Processing Battery (Coughlan & Hollows, 1985) consists of a number of verbal and visual memory tests. It is less widely available, but can be obtained from the senior author (see p. 150). The Doors and People Test (Baddeley et al., 1994) is a test of visual and verbal recall and recognition. This battery of four tests provides the opportunity to examine learning (of names and shapes) over a series of repeated trials. Furthermore, the recognition tasks use the forced choice technique (choose target from three distractors), which eliminates problems with response bias that can affect tests that use a yes–no format. The Doors test is a useful test of visual recognition as the stimuli have been designed to minimize the contribution of verbal mediation, as the distractor items have been selected to be similar in most of the gross characteristics of the target.

As noted, Table 7.1 includes reference to a range of other memory tests that can be used for assessing specific aspects of memory. Verbal working memory can be

Table 7.1. A summary of key aspects of memory that should be assessed as part of a comprehensive neuropsychological assessment and examples of some of the tests commonly used to assess each form of memory

Forms of memory examined during memory assessment			Examples of tests commonly used to assess each memory function
1. Short-term/Working memory	(A) Verbal		Digit Span[1]; Letter Number Sequencing[1]
	(B) Visuospatial		Spatial Span[1]; Visual Patterns Test[6]
2. Long-term memory	(A) Anterograde	(i) Verbal — (a) Recall	Logical Memory I & II[1]; Verbal Paired Associates[1]; Story Recall[2/3]; People[5]; Word List[1/3]; RAVLT[7]; CVLT[8]
		(b) Recognition	RMT-Words[4]; Names[5]
		(ii) Non-verbal — (a) Recall	Family Pictures[1]; Visual Reproduction[1]; Shapes[5]; Complex Figure Recall[3/9]; Design Learning[3]; Route[2]
		(b) Recognition	RMT-Faces[4]; Faces I & II[1]; Doors[5]; RBMT Faces[2]; Camden Pictures[10]; Picture Recognition[2]
	(B) Retrograde	(i) General semantics	Pyramids and Palm Trees[11]; PALPA[12] Vocabulary[13]; Verbal Fluency[14]; PALPA, Pyramids and Palm Trees[9]
		(ii) Autobiographical events	Autobiographical Memory Interview[15]
		(iii) Personal semantics	Autobiographical Memory Interview[15]
3. Prospective memory			Appointment[2]; Belonging[2]; Message[2]
4. Procedural/Implicit memory			Standardized tests not available. Tests such as Stem Completion and Fragmented Pictures sometimes used

1 = Wechsler, D. (1997a) *Wechsler Memory Scales—Third Edition.* San Antonio, TX: Psychological Corporation.
2 = Wilson, B. A., Cockburn, J., Baddeley, A. D. (1985) *The Rivermead Behavioural Memory Test.* Bury St Edmunds, UK: Thames Valley Test Company.
3 = Coughlan, A. K., Hollows, S. E. (1985) *The Adult Memory and Information Processing Battery.* St James Hospital, Leeds, UK: A. K. Coughlan.
4 = Warrington, E. K. (1984) *Recognition Memory Test.* Windsor, UK: NFER-Nelson.
5 = Baddeley, A. D., Emslie, H., Nimmo-Smith, I. (1994) *Doors and People Test.* Bury St Edmunds, UK: Thames Valley Test Company.
6 = Della Sala, S., Gray, C., Baddeley, A. D., Wilson, L. (1997) *Visual Patterns Test.* Bury St Edmunds, UK: Thames Valley Test Company.
7 = Schmidt, M. (1996) *Rey Auditory Verbal Learning Test: A Handbook.* Los Angeles: Western Psychological Services.
8 = Delis, D. C., Kramer, J. H., Kaplan, E., Ober, B. A. (1987) *California Verbal Learning Test.* San Antonio, TX: Psychological Corporation.
9 = Meyers, J. E., Meyers, K. R. (1995) *Rey Complex Figure Test and Recognition Trial.* Odessa, FL: Psychological Assessment Resources.
10 = Warrington, E. K. (1996) *The Camden Memory Tests.* Hove, UK: Psychology Press.
11 = Howard, D., Patterson, K. (1992) *Pyramids and Palm Trees.* Bury St Edmunds, UK: Thames Valley Test Company.
12 = Kay, J., Lesser, R., Coltheart, M. (1992) *Psycholinguistic Assessments of Language Processing in Aphasia.* Hove, UK: Lawrence Erlbaum.
13 = Wechsler, D. (1997b) *Wechsler Adult Intelligence Scales—Third Edition.* San Antonio, TX: Psychological Corporation.
14 = Benton, A. L. (1968) Differential behavioural effects in frontal lobe disease. *Neuropsychologia,* **6**, 53–60.
15 = Kopelman, M., Wilson, B. A., Baddeley, A. D. (1989) *Autobiographical Memory Interview.* Bury St Edmunds, UK: Thames Valley Test Company.

assessed with Digit Span or Letter–Number Sequencing tasks from the WMS-III, though it is likely that both of these tests also make demands on visuospatial working memory (for manipulating information in the mind) and so, strictly speaking, may not be pure measures of verbal working memory. The Spatial Span test in the WMS-III uses a Corsi-blocks format in which blocks are tapped in a sequence by the examiner, which must be copied by the examinee. The Visual Patterns Test (Della Sala et al., 1997) involves the testee being shown a matrix of squares, some of which are blank and some are shaded. The testee must then, from memory, shade in the same squares on a blank template.

Additional tests of verbal learning include the word list learning tests, such as the Rey Auditory Verbal Learning Test (RAVLT) and the California Verbal Learning Test (CVLT). The RAVLT consists of a set of 15 words learned over five trials. Alternative word lists are available for repeated testing (see Helmes, 2000). The CVLT has a list of 16 words in the form of a shopping list. The words can be clustered into four semantic categories, which provides evidence concerning the extent to which subjects use strategies to support their remembering. These tests can be particularly useful in examining people who aim to return to education or work that involves the learning of large amounts of verbal information and can provide a useful starting point for discussion of memory strategies in a rehabilitation context.

The Recognition Memory Test (Warrington, 1984) continues to provide an additional, useful tool for examining verbal and non-verbal recognition memory. The verbal version involves the presentation of words, followed by presentation of pairs of words from which the testee must select the previously presented target word. The non-verbal version uses the same format, with black and white photographs of faces as stimuli. There has been some criticism that the faces version is open to considerable verbal coding (Kapur, 1987). The more recently developed Camden Memory Tests (Warrington, 1996) provides further tests of non-verbal recognition skills.

The assessment of semantic memory tends to be carried out in the context of the examination of language skills and is likely to be carried out by a speech and language therapist (speech pathologist). However, two tests are useful in this domain: the Pyramids and Palm Trees (Howard & Patterson, 1992) tests of visual and verbal semantics. The main format of the test is that two objects are presented (as pictures or object names) along with a third object. The third object must be matched to one of the other two objects, selecting the one with which it has the closest association. One example, from which the name of the test is derived, is where a pyramid must be matched with either a fir tree or a palm tree. The Psycholinguistic Assessment of Language Processing in Aphasia (PALPA) (Kay et al., 1992) involves a series of tasks designed to assess a range of language functions and involves tests of object naming, picture–picture matching and word–picture matching.

Retrograde or remote memory for personal semantic information (e.g., knowledge of old friends, schools, places lived, work history, etc.) and autobiographical events is frequently not assessed in detail in most clinical neuropsychological assessments. This is because there are few standardized tests available. It is not as sensitive to brain injury as other memory functions, and deficits in this area may have less practical, everyday consequences. However, for some individuals loss of memory for premorbid knowledge or life experiences may be very significant and can have a major impact on relationships (e.g., when a spouse cannot remember his or her wedding, honeymoon and other shared experiences). The Autobiographical Memory Interview (Kopelman et al., 1989) therefore is a useful tool. It is divided into three time periods (childhood, early adult and recent life), and in each period there is an examination of personal semantic knowledge (e.g., name of friends/teachers, schools, places lived, etc.) and of auto-biographical events (an event at a wedding, meeting someone new). It should be noted that for most patients the recent life section (which asks about hospital attendance) is post injury/illness and therefore is a test of anterograde, rather than retrograde memory. It is common for people to have relatively intact personal semantic knowledge (which can sometimes create the impression that they have no retrograde memory impairment), but impairment on their recollection of events. All information should be corroborated with a relative where possible. Kapur's Dead-or-Alive Test (Kapur et al., 1989) is a useful test of public semantic knowledge (famous people), though clinical use is currently limited by lack of normative data.

Finally in this section, a note on the assessment of prospective memory. Despite the obvious importance of this domain of memory functioning in everyday life, there is a dearth of tools available for assessing it. The only memory battery that includes prospective memory tasks is the RBMT, with items involving remember-ing to ask for a belonging at the end of the test and remembering to ask about an appointment when an alarm sounds. Another item, delivering the message, is sometimes thought of as a prospective memory task, but is essentially a task embedded within a route-learning task. Sohlberg et al. (1985) devised a test called the Prospective Memory Screening Test (PROMS), which samples prospec-tive responding to both time and event cues. However, little clinical or experi-mental data have been published on this test.

Assessment of Psychogenic Amnesia and Malingering

The classic 'fugue' state, sometimes referred to as hysterical amnesia, involves a complete or near complete loss of personal history from prior to the onset of the state. Kopelman et al. (1994) describes a woman who presented to a police station in London, apparently having completely lost her memory of who she was, where she was from and her entire life history. She continued to show a virtually complete loss of autobiographical memory for well over a year. Subsequent evidence revealed that she had been at least partially simulating her amnesia for part of this prolonged period. On tests of anterograde memory, including several designed to detect mal-ingering, she performed normally. On some retrograde tests, Kopelman et al. argued that she could be distinguished from people with organic amnesia on the basis of her extreme loss of autobiographical memory in comparison to memory for news events. She also failed to show any priming effect on word stem completion tasks involving pre-onset autobiographical material. However, following a sodium amytal abreaction procedure she showed some recovery of memories and an improvement on the word stem completion task. Kopelman et al. interpreted these results in terms of a hierarchy of awareness, with the implication that, although not 'organic' in origin, patients in this state may genuinely fail to have access to some memories. The similarity between the clinical presentation associated with the fugue state and that in cases described as having a focal retrograde amnesia is very similar and has indeed led to considerable scepticism as to whether focal retrograde amnesia can have an organic origin (Kopelman, 2000). Kapur (2000) is less sceptical about its existence *per se*, but presents a set of criteria that may help to exclude a psychogenic origin to retrograde amnesia. Kapur lists 22 features in favour of a psychological basis to retrograde amnesia, divided into five background features (e.g., history of pre-injury psychiatric symptoms or general difficulty in coping with stress), eight clinical features (e.g., delayed occurrence of severe retrograde amnesia some months after onset of brain pathology) and nine neuropsychological features (e.g., loss of personal identity, no significant anterograde amnesia in acute stages of illness).

Psychogenic retrograde amnesia is extremely rare and most clinicians are unlikely to encounter this condition. What is more common is the situation where someone is motivated to exaggerate memory impairment for some form of secondary gain such as financial compensation. In this situation the exaggeration is likely to be in the anterograde memory domain. Detecting motivated forgetting (or malingering) is relatively easy in the unsophisticated faker, but much harder in someone who is simply exaggerating the presence of a genuine impairment. Sweet (1999) suggests a range of strategies that may help detect motivated forgetting. The main strategy is probably the use of tests specifically designed for the purpose, which are based on the principle that someone attempting to exaggerate a deficit will perform badly even on simple tests that would ordinarily be performed satisfactorily by someone with a genuine impairment. Perhaps the best known is the Rey-15 Item Test (see Lezak, 1995, p. 802). The 15 items are simple combinations of letters, numbers and shapes that are easy to remember. A cut-off score of 8/15 has been suggested, though other cut-offs have also been discussed. Kapur (1994) describes another simple test, called the Coin-in-the-Hand test, which involves the patient having to recall, after 10 seconds of counting backwards from 10, in which hand the examiner is holding a coin. This exercise is repeated 10 times, with five left- and five right-hand locations of the coin. Hanley et al. (1999) showed that this test was effective at detecting 19/20 simulators, with no false positives among 20 patients with amnesia. Other strategies that can be useful include (i) evaluation of insufficient effort on common measures (such as below chance performance on tests of recognition memory), (ii) examination of excessive inconsistency on tests (though one must be cautious not to interpret inconsistency arising from fatigue problems, emotional state, medications and practice effects) and (iii) examination of inconsistency between test results and day-to-day levels of functioning. The difficulty in detecting conclusively that an individual is exaggerating a memory deficit highlights that interpretation of memory test performance is a complex process. Several issues, discussed in the following section, need to be considered.

Key Issues in the Interpretation of Memory Test Results

Perhaps the most important point to make about interpretation of memory test results is that an impaired performance on a single test should not be taken as definitive evidence for an organic impairment of memory. As discussed earlier, there are many factors that will affect performance on any cognitive test and the formulation of a patient's pattern of cognitive strengths and weaknesses is a complex task involving the assimilation of information from a wide range of different sources. The fact that a variety of memory tests is available means that a number of tests that make demands on similar skills can be used to provide converging evidence of impairment.

A further point, which applies to any cognitive test, is that a performance in the average range is not necessarily normal for the patient being assessed. Among the normal population, memory performance varies widely, even among people of a similar age. Hence the possibility always exists that an individual who was pre-viously functioning at a superior level suffers a significant deterioration in perform-ance, but to a level that is still within the 'normal' range. Hence, as with the assessment of general intellectual skills, comparison of current performance with estimates of premorbid levels is useful. The comparison of index scores on the WMS-III with IQ scores on the WAIS-III can be useful, though WAIS-III scores may also be reduced. However, normal individual variability means that one should be cautious about interpreting a normal memory score as impaired in the context of superior IQ performance. Equally, it is important not to over-interpret a poor memory test score in someone for whom there may be evidence of premorbid weakness. For example, individuals with a history of dyslexia may have had a premorbid weakness in verbal working memory and hence a poor score on Digit Span may need to be interpreted cautiously in this case.

REHABILITATION OF MEMORY

In the rehabilitation of memory the emphasis is typically on alleviating the impact of the memory impairment and as a consequence improving day-to-day functioning. Following brain injury, through head injury, stroke or infection, there is usually some improvement in cognitive functioning, including memory functioning over a period of weeks and months, and possibly years. The extent of the recovery of function is very variable. A range of mechanisms are responsible for this recovery of function, from very acute changes in brain swelling after head injury to dendritic sprouting (Kolb, 1995), though we have little knowledge of how to influence most of these mechanisms. In the future, stem cell treatment and other similar interventions may provide much greater scope for us to influence the biological process of recovery (Virley et al., 1999). At the present time, however, this process largely proceeds regardless of any rehabilitation effort. Within the field of cognitive rehabilitation there is a tradition of cognitive retraining, which typically involves repeated exercise on tasks that make demands on the cognitive functioning being retrained. Memory is

Table 7.2. Compensatory approaches to the rehabilitation of memory

Enhanced learning	Mnemonics	External aids	Environmental modification
Attention	Mental retracing	Notebook/Diary	Signposts
Encoding/Elaboration	Numbers to words	Filofax	Labels
Repetition	Visual imagery	Lists	Orientation board
Expanding/Rehearsal	First letter cues	Wall calendars	Coloured doors
Vanishing cues	Method of loci	Memo boards	Coloured lines
Errorless learning	Rhyming peg	Electronic organizers	Routine
PQRST	Rhymes	NeuroPage	
Mind Maps		Watch	
		Alarms/Timers	
		DataBank	
		Watches	
		Voice organizer	
		Dictaphone	
		Pill reminders	

one of a range of cognitive processes for which attempts at retraining have been made in this way. Wilson (1997b), Glisky et al. (1986) and Robertson (1999) note that the main problem with this approach is a distinct lack of evidence of its effectiveness. Despite these rather disappointing conclusions, with respect to restitutive approaches, there is nevertheless a number of compensatory approaches that have been shown to be helpful for people with memory impairment. Four different types of approach can be identified: (i) enhanced learning (making more effective use of residual memory skills); (ii) mnemonic strategies; (iii) external aids; (iv) environmental modification. Table 7.2 provides a list of examples of specific strategies within each of these intervention categories, which are discussed in the following sections.

Enhanced Learning

Most people with memory impairment retain some residual learning capacity, and it is therefore important that this capacity is used to maximum effect. Berg et al. (1991) describe a group intervention in which they provide participants with a set of 'memory rules'. These include:

- *Attention*: Pay more attention to the information to be remembered. Make sure that you are not distracted by your environment and that you consciously focus on whatever you have to remember.
- *Time*: Spend more time on encoding. Generally, the more time you spend on encoding the more you will remember. But spend your time economically—not too long without a pause, but frequently and little by little.
- *Repetition*: Whatever you have to remember will sink in more easily if you repeat it. There are several forms of repetition—simple repetition, spaced repetition (with increasing time intervals) and varied repetition (in several ways and situations).

The spaced repetition or retrieval technique is also known as expanded rehearsal. This is based on a general learning principle that spaced practice is a more effective learning technique than massed practice (i.e., little and often is better than cramming!). The technique involves information being presented and tested for recall immediately, then again after a few seconds interval, then a few minutes and so on gradually increasing the time gap before recall is tested. Camp et al. (1996) describe the use of spaced retrieval in training people with mild to moderate Alzheimer's disease to perform prospective memory tasks relevant to their day-to-day life (see also Chapter 19).

The vanishing cues and errorless learning techniques were both derived from behavioural and cognitive psychology. The vanishing cues technique (Glisky et al., 1986) is essentially a 'backward chaining' method, similar to the chaining approaches to teach multi-step tasks (such as dressing) to people with severe learning disability. Glisky et al. demonstrated that people with amnesia could learn new computer-related vocabulary using the technique, which involves pre-senting the individual with the whole of the information they must learn to begin with and then gradually withdrawing letters. For example, if the individual is learning how to print a document, the sentence, 'to make a paper copy of a document, press PRINT', would be presented. Then over successive trials, letters would be successively removed (i.e., PRIN, PRI, PR, P) until no letters are present. One theoretical influence on this work is the literature on implicit memory and priming and, in particular, the finding that people with amnesia often are able to show word stem completion priming. One potential limitation of this technique is that the benefit of the technique may only be present when there is at least one letter of the target word left, acting as a perceptual prime.

One hypothesis as to why the vanishing cues technique is effective is that it is less likely that people will make mistakes during the learning process. The old adage that we learn from our mistakes only applies if we can remember our mistakes. While learning something new, the person with amnesia who makes a mistake on one occasion (e.g., calling somebody by the wrong name) will forget the error, but in addition may be 'primed' to make the same mistake again, so reinforcing the error. This implies that if the person with memory impairment can be prevented from making errors during the learning process, then that learning ought to be more rapid. Errorless learning has been used for many years to teach new skills to teach people with learning disabilities (Jones & Earys, 1992), and more recently this technique has been used with people with acquired neurological impairment. Since Baddeley and Wilson (1994) published the first study in which a stem completion task was used to teach a list of words, demonstrating that people with amnesia learn better when prevented from making mistakes during the learning process, several single case studies have shown the benefit of errorless learning methods in teaching more practical, everyday information (Clare et al., 1999; Hunkin et al., 1998; Squires et al., 1996; Wilson et al., 1994).

For people whose aim is to return to some form of formal education, study techniques such as PQRST and Mind Maps are useful. They are not specifically designed for people with memory impairments, but can be useful nevertheless. Both are means of enhancing the meaningfulness and memorability of information to be learned. PQRST is an acronym for Preview, Question, Read, State and Test (Robinson, 1970) and is described in Chapter 19 of this book. Mind Mapping is another means of enhancing the multimodality encoding of information (Buzan & Buzan, 2000). The technique involves producing a one-page visual summary of whatever is being learned, with the use of drawings, coloured text, boxes and arrows to link ideas and information. Mind Maps may also be useful in any context where a significant amount of information is required to be retained and used (e.g., preparing for a presentation).

Mnemonics

Mnemonics are the techniques favoured by the stage performers who demonstrate 'great feats of memory', such as remembering the order of a shuffled pack of cards with only brief exposure to each card. The most commonly used technique is a form of the method of loci—a route around a familiar place or a journey with many specific locations is pre-learned. Then each item to be remembered is associated with locations on the route (using visual imagery). These techniques require considerable practice and are best when learning lists. Most people with memory impairment find such techniques difficult to use or unnecessary, and few people use them (Evans et al., in press). One 'internal' technique that people do use more often is 'mental retracing'. This is the simple idea of retracing your steps in order to remember what you have done, or perhaps where you have left an item that is lost. Given that many people with memory impairments, particularly arising from head injury, may also be impulsive (as a result of frontal lobe deficits), teaching a simple 'stop–think–retrace your steps' approach can be helpful.

One further mnemonic strategy that can also be helpful, particularly in a world full of PIN codes, is one where numbers are converted to words. For example, WB, who was severely amnesic as a result of carbon monoxide poisoning, had a horse that she kept at a livery yard. The owner of the yard decided to use combination locks on each of the field gates, and so WB needed to learn a four-digit combination code (1534). She learned this by learning a more meaningful sentence (A Field Has Mice), in which the number of letters in each word corresponded to the numbers in the code. She was taught the sentence using a vanishing cues technique. She was progressing to learn two other sentences for the other fields she used, when the yard owner went back to using keys and padlocks as several other people had complained that they could not remember the combinations!

External Aids

The most commonly used strategies for supporting memory are external aids. Evans et al. (in press) found that nearly 70% of people with a memory impairment used a wall calendar or notebook or diary. External memory aids need to form the core 'memory system' for most people with significant memory impairment. Indeed, most people without memory impairment use some form of external memory aid. However, for the person with a memory impairment, the process of learning to use such aids is not straightforward and may require considerable support. Despite this need, memory rehabilitation is still not often provided for patients with severe disorders of memory (Tate, 1997). However, studies have shown that comprehensive training approaches can lead to effective use of memory journals, even in people with severe amnesia (Donaghy & Williams, 1998; Kime et al., 1996).

Several issues make it difficult for many people with memory impairments to learn to use external aids. One is the fact that, as a result of their impairment, individuals are given very few responsibilities for remembering things. Until they have something to remember there is little need for a memory aid, but until they can use an aid they are unlikely to remember and so few demands on memory tend to be made. In the rehabilitation context, therefore, there needs to be a gradual increasing of memory demands and a gradual introduction of memory aids, which might change as demands increase. For those people who are perhaps later post injury and do have greater remembering responsibilities, but who may be failing to do things effectively, a careful process of matching an external aid to the needs of the patient should be undertaken, taking into account (a) the nature and severity of cognitive impairment, (b) premorbid experience of memory aids usage, (c) personal preference for type of aid. With regard to the latter issue, one of the major choices is between paper-based systems (e.g., filofax) and electronic-based systems (e.g., palmtop computers, electronic organizers). Electronic systems offer the major advantage of having the facility to prompt an action using alarms. However, some people have a strong preference for paper-based systems, while others are keen to use technology. Furthermore, the problem with many of the electronic systems is that they are quite complicated to learn how to use and offer many functions that are not needed. Nonetheless, Wright et al. (2001) have shown that it is possible to simplify palmtop computer interfaces for use by people with brain injury. A new memory aid that uses palmtop technology with a simple interface is currently being evaluated (Inglis et al., 2002).

One of the simplest-to-use technological external aids is NeuroPage, a pager-based system (Hersh & Treadgold, 1994). The person with the memory impairment wears an ordinary alphanumeric pager. Reminders are entered onto a remote computer, and, at the correct time, the computer sends the message, via a modem and paging company, to the individual's pager. He or she then simply presses one button to cancel the alert and reads the message. This system has now been evaluated extensively in clinical trials, has been shown to be very effective at increasing day-to-day performance (Wilson et al., 1997a, 2001) and is available nationally in the UK.

Other useful aids include databank watches (such as the Timex DataBank), which can be programmed to deliver reminders at specified times, and the Voice Organiser (on which dictated messages are replayed at specified times). Electronic dictaphones can be used to record a number of spoken notes during the day, with the option of transferring information to a diary, electronic organizer, etc. at a later date. Dosset boxes, which have multiple sections for storing daily medication doses, can be obtained through pharmacies and are particularly helpful for people who have complicated medication regimes. They can be prepared in advance. Clare and Wilson (1997) and Kapur (1995) provide good summaries of a range of memory aids. Clare and Wilson (1997) also provide a basic introduction to memory problems and how to cope with them for people with memory impairments, their relatives, friends and carers. Wilson et al. (1997b) also provide a fascinating discussion of the development of a comprehensive compensatory memory system by one man (JC), who became amnesic following a subarachnoid haemorrhage.

Environmental Modification

The final approach is the method of choice when an individual is unable to use other aids or strategies independently. The idea is simply to reduce the memory demands placed upon the person. The use of signposts, labels or colour-coding (e.g., toilet doors always being a particular colour) can aid orientation to the environment. Orientation boards help maintain knowledge of time and place. Reducing clutter and always keeping particular things in particular places (e.g., keys on a key ring) may be helpful. 'Smart houses' contain a range of technology that may help people with disabilities, including memory impairment, live more independently (Wilson & Evans, 2000).

One form of environmental modification is to provide a highly structured environment, involving a great deal of routine. People with severe memory impairment are usually still able to learn routines through repetition. Daily routines provide a way for an individual to maintain a sense of independently completing activities, with minimal demands on memory.

CONCLUSIONS

Theories of memory continue to develop apace with the gradual integration of cognitive and neuroanatomical models. As theories develop further, so assessment tools will need to be adapted. At the present time a huge variety of memory assessment tools are available to the clinician, whose task is to select those tests suitable to address the key questions being posed. Although the future is bright, as far as the development of restorative treatment techniques is concerned, for the time being evidence suggests that compensatory strategies are the treatment of choice for most organic memory disorders. External memory aids remain the most practical and widely used tools. Emerging technologies in the form of Internet-ready personal digital assistants may prove useful, though the application of techniques such as errorless learning methods may prove essential in giving the person with a memory impairment the best chance of acquiring the knowledge and skills required to cope with day-to-day, personal, social or vocational demands.

REFERENCES

Alvarez, P. & Squire, L. R. (1995) Memory consolidation and the medial temporal lobe: A simple network model. *Proceedings of the National Academy of Science, USA*, **91**, 7041–7045.

Baddeley, A. D. (1986) *Working Memory*. Oxford University Press, Oxford, UK.

Baddeley, A. D. and Wilson, B. A. (1994) When implicit learning fails: Amnesia and the problem of error elimination. *Neuropsychologia*, **32**, 53–68.

Baddeley, A. D., Papagno, C. & Vallar, G. (1988) When long-term learning depends on short-term storage. *Journal of Memory and Language*, **27**, 586–595.

Baddeley, A. D., Emslie, H. & Nimmo-Smith, I. (1994) *Doors and People Test*. Thames Valley Test Company, Bury St Edmunds, UK.

Berg, I. J., Koning-Haanstra, M. & Deelman, B. G. (1991) Long term effects of memory rehabilitation: A controlled study. *Neuropsychological Rehabilitation*, **1**, 91–111.

Buzan, T. & Buzan, B. (2000) *The Mind Map Book*. BBC Worldwide, London.

Camp, C. J., Foss, J. W., Stevens, A. B. & O'Hanlon, A. M. (1996) Improving prospective memory task performance in persons with Alzheimer's disease. In: M. Brandimonte, G. O. Einstein & M. A. McDaniel (eds) *Prospective Memory: Theory and Applications* (pp. 351–367). Lawrence Erlbaum, Mahwah, NJ.

Clare, L. & Wilson, B. A. (1997) *Coping with Memory Problems: A Practical Guide for People with Memory Impairments, Their Relatives, Friends and Carers*. Thames Valley Test Company, Bury St Edmunds, UK.

Clare, L., Wilson, B. A., Breen, E. K. & Hodges, J. R. (1999) Errorless learning of face–name associations in early Alzheimer's disease. *Neurocase*, **5**, 37–46.

Coughlan, A. K. & Hollows, S. E. (1985) *The Adult Memory and Information Processing Battery*. A. K. Coughlan, St James Hospital, Leeds, UK.

Damasio, A. R. (1989) Time-locked multiregional retroactivation: A systems level proposal for the neural substrates of recall and recognition. *Cognition*, **33**, 25–62.

Della Sala, S., Gray, C., Baddeley, A. D. & Wilson, L. (1997) *Visual Patterns Test*. Thames Valley Test Company, Bury St Edmunds, UK.

Donaghy, S. & Williams, W. (1998) A new protocol for training severely impaired patients in the usage of memory journals. *Brain Injury*, **12**, 1061–1077.

Ellis, J. (1996) Prospective memory or the realization of delayed intentions: A conceptual framework for research. In: M. Brandimonte, G. O. Einstein & M. A. McDaniel (eds) *Prospective Memory: Theory and Applications* (pp. 1–22). Lawrence Erlbaum, Mahwah, NJ.

Evans, J. J., Breen, E. K., Antoun, N. & Hodges, J. R. (1996) Focal retrograde amnesia for autobiographical events following cerebral vasculitis: A connectionist account. *Neurocase*, **2**, 1–11.

Evans, J. J., Needham, P., Wilson, B. A. & Brentnall, S. (in press) Who makes good use of memory aids? Results of a survey of people with acquired brain injury. *Journal of the International Neuropsychological Society*.

Franzen, A. D. & Iverson, G. L. (2000) The Wechsler memory scales. In: G. Groth-Marnat (ed.) *Neuropsychological Assessment in Clinical Practice: A Guide to Test Interpretation and Integration* (pp. 195–222). John Wiley & Sons, New York.

Funnell, M. G., Corballis, P. M. & Gazzaniga, M. S. (2001) Hemispheric processing asymmetries: Implications for memory. *Brain and Cognition*, **46**, 135–139.

Gathercole, S. & Baddeley, A. D. (1989) Evaluation of the role of phonological STM in the development of vocabulary in children: A longitudinal study. *Journal of Memory and Language*, **28**, 200–213.

Glisky, E. L., Schacter, D. L. & Tulving, E. (1986) Computer learning by memory impaired patients: Acquisition and retention of complex knowledge. *Neuropsychologia*, **24**(3), 313–328.

Golby, A. J., Poldracj, R. A., Brewer, J. B., Spencer, D., Desmond, J. E., Aron, A. P. et al. (2001) Material-specific lateralization in the medial temporal lobe and pre-frontal cortex during memory encoding. *Brain*, **124**, 1841–1854.

Hanley, J. R., Baker, G. A. & Ledson, S. (1999) Detecting the faking of amnesia: A comparison of the effectiveness of three different techniques for distinguishing simulators from patients with amnesia. *Journal of Clinical and Experimental Neuropsychology*, **21**, 59–69.

Helmes, E. (2000) Learning and memory. In: G. Groth-Marnat (ed.) *Neuropsychological Assessment in Clinical Practice: A Guide to Test Interpretation and Integration* (pp. 293–334). John Wiley & Sons, New York.

Hersh, N. & Treadgold, L. (1994) NeuroPage: The rehabilitation of memory dysfunction by prosthetic memory and cueing. *Neurorehabilitation*, **4**, 187–197.

Hodges, J. R., Patterson, K., Oxbury, S. & Funnell, E. (1992) Semantic dementia: Progressive fluent aphasia with temporal lobe atrophy. *Brain*, **115**, 1783–1806.

Howard, D. & Patterson, K. (1992) *Pyramids and Palm Trees*. Thames Valley Test Company, Bury St Edmunds, UK.

Hunkin, N. M., Squires, E. J., Aldrich, F. K. & Parkin, A. J. (1998) Errorless learning and the acquisition of work processing skills. *Neuropsychological Rehabilitation*, **8**, 433–449.

Inglis, E. A., Szymkowiak, A., Gregor, P., Newell, A. F., Hine, N., Wilson, B. A. et al. (2002) Issues surrounding the user centered development of a new interactive memory aid. In: S. Keates, P. Langdon, P. J. Clarkson & P. Robinson (eds) *Universal Access and Assistive Technology: Proceedings of Cambridge Workshop 2002* (pp. 171–178). Springer-Verlag, London.

Jones, R. S. & Earys, C. B. (1992) The use of errorless learning procedures in teaching people with a learning disability: A critical review. *Mental Handicap Research*, **5**, 204–212.

Kapur, N. (1987) Some comments on the technical acceptability of Warrington's Recognition Memory Test. *British Journal of Clinical Psychology*, **26**, 144–146.

Kapur, N. (1994) The coin-in-the-hand test: A new 'bedside' test for the detection of malingering in patients with suspected memory disorder. *Journal of Neurology, Neurosurgery and Psychiatry*, **57**, 385–386.

Kapur, N. (1995) Memory aids in rehabilitation of memory disordered patients. In: A. D. Baddeley, B. A. Wilson & F. Watts (eds) *Handbook of Memory Disorders* (pp. 533–556). John Wiley & Sons, Chichester, UK.

Kapur, N. (1999) Syndromes of retrograde amnesia: A conceptual and empirical synthesis. *Psychological Bulletin*, **125**, 800–825.

Kapur, N. (2000) Focal retrograde amnesia and the attribution of causality—an exceptionally benign commentary. *Cognitive Neuropsychology*, **17**, 623–637.

Kapur, N., Young, A., Bateman, D. & Kennedy, P. (1989) Focal retrograde amnesia: A long term clinical and neuropsychological follow-up. *Cortex*, **25**, 387–402.

Kay, J., Lesser, R. & Coltheart, M. (1992) *Psycholinguistic Assessments of Language Processing in Aphasia*. Lawrence Erlbaum, Hove, UK.

Kime, S. K., Lamb, D. G. & Wilson, B. A. (1996) Use of a comprehensive programme of external cueing to enhance procedural memory in a patient with dense amnesia. *Brain Injury*, **10**, 17–25.

Kolb, B. (1995) *Brain Plasticity and Behavior*. Lawrence Erlbaum, Mahwah, NJ.

Kopelman, M. D. (2000) Focal retrograde amnesia and the attribution of causality—an exceptionally critical review. *Cognitive Neuropsychology*, **17**, 585–621.

Kopelman, M., Wilson, B. A. & Baddeley, A. D. (1989) *Autobiographical Memory Interview*. Thames Valley Test Company, Bury St Edmunds, UK.

Kopelman, M. D, Christensen, H., Puffett, A. & Stanhope, N. (1994) The great escape: A neuropsychological study of psychogenic amnesia. *Neuropsychologia*, **32**, 675–691.

Lezak, M. D. (1995) *Neuropsychological Assessment* (3rd edn). Oxford University Press, Oxford, UK.

Mayes, A. R. (2000) Selective memory disorders. In: E. Tulving & F. I. M. Craik (eds) *The Oxford Handbook of Memory Disorders* (pp. 427–440). Oxford University Press, Oxford, UK.

Mesulam, M. M. (2000) Behavioural neuroanatomy: Large-scale networks, associations cortex, frontal syndromes, the limbic system and hemispheric specialisations. In: M. M. Mesulam (ed.) *Principles of Behavioral and Cognitive Neurology* (2nd edn, pp. 1–120). Oxford University Press, Oxford, UK.

Morris, R. G., Abrahams, S. & Polkey, C. E. (1995) Recognition memory for words and faces following unilateral temporal lobectomy. *British Journal of Clinical Psychology*, **34**, 571–576.

Murre, J. M. J. (1996) A model of amnesia and consolidation of memory. *Hippocampus*, **6**, 675–684.

Nadel, L. & Moscovitch, M. (1997) Memory consolidation, retrograde amnesia and the hippo-campal complex. *Current Opinion in Neurobiology*, **7**, 217–227.

Robertson, I. R. (1999) Setting goals for rehabilitation. *Current Opinion in Neurology*, **12**, 703–708.

Robinson, F. B. (1970) *Effective Study*. Harper, New York.

Scoville, W. B. & Milner, B. (1957) Loss of recent memory after bilateral hippocampal lesions. *Journal of Neurology, Neurosurgery and Psychiatry*, **20**, 11–21.

Sohlberg, M. M., Mateer, C. A. & Geyer, S. (1985) *Prospective Memory Screening (PROMS) and Prospective Memory Process Training (PROMPT)*. Association for Neuropsychological Research and Development, Puyallup, WA.

Snowden, J. S., Goulding, H. & Neary, D. (1989) Semantic dementia: A form of circumscribed cerebral atrophy. *Behavioural Neurology*, **2**, 167–182.

Squire, L. R. (1992) Declarative and non-declarative memory: Multiple brain systems supporting learning and memory. *Journal of Cognitive Neuroscience*, **4**, 232–243.

Squires, E., Hunkin, N. M. & Parkin, A. J. (1996) Memory notebook training in a case of severe amnesia: Generalising from paired associate learning to real life. *Neuropsychological Rehabilitation*, **6**, 55–65.

Sunderland, A., Harris, J. E. & Baddeley, A. D. (1983) Do laboratory tests predict everyday memory? A neuropsychological study. *Journal of Verbal Learning and Behaviour*, **22**, 341–357.

Sweet, J. J. (1999) Malingering: Differential diagnosis. In: J. J. Sweet (ed.) *Forensic Neuropsychology: Fundamentals and Practice* (pp. 255–285). Swets & Zeitlinger, Lisse, The Netherlands.

Tate, R. L. (1997) Beyond one-bun, two-shoe: Recent advances in the psychological rehabilitation of memory disorders after acquired brain injury. *Brain Injury*, **11**, 907–918.

Tulving, E. (1972) Episodic and semantic memory. In: E. Tulving & W. Donaldson (eds) *Organization of Memory* (pp. 381–403). Academic Press, New York.

Tulving, E., Kapur, S., Craik, F. I., Moscovitch, M. & Houle, S. (1994) Hemispheric encoding/retrieval asymmetry in episodic memory: Positron emission tomography findings. *Proceedings of the National Academy of Science, USA*, **91**, 2016–2020.

Vallar, G. & Papagno, C. (1995) Neuropsychological impairments of short-term memory. In: A. D. Baddeley, B. A. Wilson & F. Watts (eds) *Handbook of Memory Disorders* (pp. 135–165). John Wiley & Sons, Chichester, UK.

Verfaellie, M., Koseff, P. & Alexander, M. P. (2000) Acquisition of novel semantic information in amnesia: Effects of lesion location. *Neuropsychologia*, **38**, 484–492.

Virley, D., Ridley, R. M., Sinden, J. D., Kershaw, T. R., Harland, S., Rashid, T. et al. (1999) Primary CA1 and conditionally immortal MHP36 cell grafts restore conditional discrimination learning and recall in marmosets after excitotoxic lesions of the hippocampal CA1 field. *Brain*, **122**, 2321–2335.

Warrington, E. K. (1984) *Recognition Memory Test*. NFER, Windsor, UK.

Warrington, E. K. (1996) *The Camden Memory Tests*. Psychology Press, Hove, UK.

Warrington, E. K. and Shallice, T. (1969) The selective impairment of auditory verbal short term memory. *Brain*, **92**, 885–896.

Warrington, E. K. & Shallice, T. (1984) Category specific semantic impairments. *Brain*, **107**, 829–854.

Wechsler, D. (1997a) *Wechsler Memory Scales—Third Edition*. Psychological Corporation, San Antonio, TX.

Wechsler, D. (1997b) *Wechsler Adult Intelligence Scales—Third Edition*. Psychological Corporation, San Antonio, TX.

Wilson, B. A. (1997a) Semantic memory impairments following non-progressive brain damage: A study of four cases. *Brain Injury*, **11**, 259–269.

Wilson, B. A. (1997b) Cognitive rehabilitation: How it is and how it should be. *Journal of the International Neuropsychological Society*, **3**, 487–496.

Wilson, B. A. (1999) *Case Studies in Neuropsychological Rehabilitation*. Oxford University Press, New York.

Wilson, B. A. & Evans, J. J. (2000) Practical management of memory problems. In: G. E. Berrios & J. R. Hodges (eds) *Memory Disorders in Psychiatric Practice* (pp. 291–310). Cambridge University Press, Cambridge, UK.

Wilson, B. A. & Watson, P. C. (1996) A practical framework for understanding compensatory behaviour in people with organic memory impairment. *Memory*, **4**, 465–486.

Wilson, B. A., Cockburn, J. & Baddeley, A. D. (1985) *The Rivermead Behavioural Memory Test*. Thames Valley Test Company, Bury St Edmunds, UK.

Wilson, B. A., Baddeley, A. D., Evans, J. J. & Shiel, A. (1994) Errorless learning in the rehabilitation of memory impaired people. *Neuropsychological Rehabilitation*, **4**, 307–326.

Wilson, B. A., Baddeley, A. D. & Kapur, N. (1995) Dense amnesia in a professional musician following herpes simplex virus encephalitis. *Journal of Clinical and Experimental Neuropsychology*, **17**, 668–681.

Wilson, B. A., Evans, J. J., Emslie, H. & Malinek, V. (1997a) Evaluation of NeuroPage: A new memory aid. *Journal of Neurosurgery, Neurology and Psychiatry*, **63**, 113–115.

Wilson, B. A., J. C. & Hughes, E. (1997b) Coping with amnesia: The natural history of a compensatory memory system. *Neuropsychological Rehabilitation*, **7**, 43–56.

Wilson, B. A., Clare, L., Baddeley, A. D., Cockburn, J., Watson, P. & Tate, R. (1998) *The Rivermead Behavioural Memory Test—Extended Version*. Thames Valley Test Company, Bury St Edmunds, UK.

Wilson, B. A., Emslie, H., Quirk, K. & Evans, J. J. (2001) Reducing everyday memory and planning problems by means of a paging system: A randomised control crossover study. *Journal of Neurosurgery, Neurology and Psychiatry*, **70**, 477–482.

Wright, P., Rogers, N., Hall, C., Wilson, B. A., Evans, J. J., Emslie, H. et al. (2001) Comparison of pocket-computer memory aids for people with brain injury. *Brain Injury*, **15**, 787–800.

Zola Morgan, S. M., Squire, L. R. & Amaral, D. G. (1986) Human amnesia and the medial temporal region: Enduring memory impairment following a bilateral lesion limited to field CA1 of the hippocampus. *Journal of Neuroscience*, **6**, 2950–2967.

CHAPTER 8

Disorders of Language and Communication

Pat McKenna

Rookwood Hospital, Cardiff and
School of Psychology, Cardiff University, Cardiff, UK

INTRODUCTION

As with all areas of cerebral functioning, those underlying language and communication are still very far from being understood. However, it has proved fruitful to use as a working model stages of processing information that are organized serially and hierarchically (e.g., see Goodglass & Wingfield, 1997, pp. 15–18). This principled approach also fits our evolutionary and ontogenetic development, so that those operations subserving comprehension of the world occur long before our ability to express that comprehension in words. Even in adulthood, we can see these differential weightings in our behaviours. For example, we practically never fail to understand a word that is well within our vocabulary store when we hear it, but not infrequently experience the tip-of-the-tongue phenomenon when we fail to utter it. In short, expressive language is much harder for us than language comprehension. This differential level of difficulty is also apparent when language breaks down either slowly as in dementia, or after acute damage as in stroke. Thus aphasiologists, neuroscientists and cognitive psychologists all adopt a serial stage model, though their models are not interchangeable. For the clinician, working at the interface of this multilayered knowledge base and practice, this approach also provides the best framework for mapping, analysing and treating cognitive deficits in the clinical population and especially so for the very complex, sometimes bewildering, deficits of language and communication.

Most clinical and research attention has been given to spoken and written language but, and this is the proviso to the serial framework, there is a distinct and parallel form of non-verbal communication that occurs simultaneously in our discourse and social interactions—and undoubtedly has a much longer evolutionary history.

Clinical Neuropsychology: A Practical Guide to Assessment and Management for Clinicians.
Edited by L.H. Goldstein and J.E. McNeil. © 2004 John Wiley & Sons, Ltd.

NON-VERBAL COMMUNICATION

The commonplace assumption that it is the words that count in language and communication has not really been challenged in the field of cognitive neuropsychology. This bias is also reflected in the burgeoning literature on language, linguistics and aphasiology, and in state-of-the-art test batteries such as the Psycholinguistic Assessment of Language Performance in Aphasia (PALPA; Kay et al., 1992). A rare exception is the Right Hemisphere Language Battery (Bryan, 1995) which looks at non-literal use of language (metaphor, prosody, humour) and inferences (but still as conveyed in words and sentences, apart from a final section on discourse analysis). Traditionally, the analysis and treatment of the non-verbal components of communication have been restricted to the prosodic aspects of spoken language (i.e., the stress, inflection, rhythm and intonation of words and sentences) and the music and cadence of auditory prose, which appears to depend critically on the right hemisphere and the temporal lobe in particular (e.g., Scott et al., 2000).

Beyond these auditory characteristics of words, the non-verbal aspects of communication have no neuropsychological taxonomy and, until recently, have only attracted sporadic and occasional interest as a secondary or subsidiary component of language. Yet, without the gestures, body stance, facial expressions, eye contact and the cadence, prosody, tone and rhythm of speech, much of the communication is lost. So highly developed and automatic are these behaviours that they do not require the online, conscious processing afforded to the verbal content of communication and can allow one to appear engrossed in one conversation while tuned in to another that is occurring within earshot at a gathering. Though of increasing psychological interest (see Bull, 2001 for a state-of-the-art account), there is no neuropsychological theory of what must be a very complex set of modular operations underpinning non-verbal aspects of communication. The devastating consequences of poor non-verbal communication are revealed in our emerging understanding of some developmental syndromes. For instance, the many right hemisphere deficits found in people with Asperger's syndrome include impairment in prosody and the ability to read facial expressions (e.g., Ellis, Ellis et al., 1994), deficits that contribute to their inability to develop an empathetic understanding of others. Thus, in assessing an individual's language and communication, the clinician needs to be attentive equally to non-verbal and to verbal aspects of language and communication.

Some patients with right hemisphere pathology in a rehabilitation unit at first appear to have intact communication, but gradually provoke a feeling of disquiet in therapists. There is an ambiguity in the sense of rapport, which can be traced to the patient's lack of facial expression and body language, reduced smiling, paucity of gesture and a flat monotonous quality to speech in conversation. These subtle characteristics are often attributed to the physical immobility of hemiplegia, reduced energy, a general depletion in cognitive functioning or depression. This reduction in expression is usually accompanied by a decreased ability to decode these non-verbal aspects of communication in others. Only after this has persisted for some weeks and there is little generalization in learning do the nurses and therapists begin to feel that something is amiss. Questioning family and friends can confirm that the person is not behaving 'in character', and a spouse will often report more difficulties understanding what their partner is feeling or thinking in their discussions or plans for the future.

Following a severe brain injury, most patients spend a protracted period in intensive care with a very gradual return of consciousness. Staff and family interact in their usual fashion with the patient and unwittingly reinforce a state of facial impassivity, which they would never have tolerated under normal circumstances. Patients recovering from severe head injury will almost inevitably have executive difficulties, which will also underlie altered social behaviour at higher levels of cognitive processing. Here, however, we are talking about the immediate aspects of non-verbal communication that signal sympathetic connection automatically in the simplest of exchanges—when we smile. Facial exercises, reminders to smile when greeting people and practice in meaningful expressions, such as frowning, grimacing and raising an eyebrow, can help revive overt expression of the person's affective state.

Research to map the detailed structure of these functions has yet to be undertaken. However, Perry et al. (2001), contrasting left and right hemisphere cases of frontotemporal dementia, found that individuals with predominantly left temporal lobe involvement had severe impairment of semantic operations, but normal performance on emotional tasks, whereas individuals with right temporal lobe atrophy could not recognize emotion from faces and voices, had a fixed, expressionless face and lacked empathy. Emerging evidence from some single case reports from the clinical population, the animal literature and electrophysiological and radiological evidence from normal participants implicates the right temporal lobe in decoding facial expressions and environmental sounds (e.g., Ojemann et al., 1992).

Although auditory agnosia usually results from bilateral lesions (e.g., Habib et al., 1995) and generally affects all domains of sounds, Fujii et al. (1990) reported a deficit in recognizing environmental sounds, other than speech, in one individual with right temporal pathology. However, there has only been sporadic interest in our processing of non-verbal noises whether from other humans, the natural world or the man-made world.

One area of non-verbal functioning that has a more respectable research base is the use of gesture and skilled action, known as praxis (see Chapter 10). Praxis skills refer to culturally skilled or symbolic movements that are voluntarily controlled as opposed to instinctive, automatic body movements. These praxis skills are for the most part subserved by the left parietal lobe. Dysphasia and apraxia often co-occur, although they can dissociate, and the attention this area of functioning has received is mostly due to its close relationship to verbal communication (e.g., Bavelas & Chovil, 2000).

VERBAL COMMUNICATION

This section follows the serial model of verbal communication, which begins with the detection and coding of the units of speech sounds or *phonemes*, their combinations

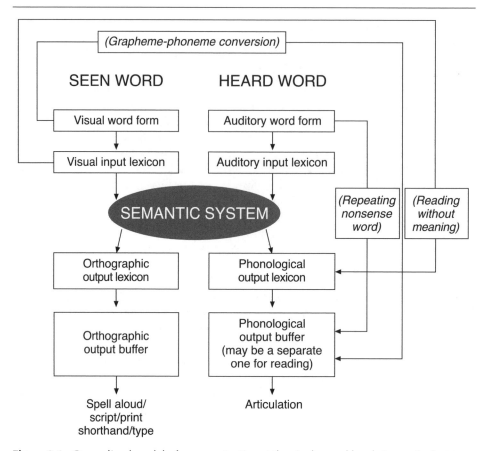

Figure 8.1. Generalized model of communication at the single word level. An equivalent term for 'lexicon' is 'logogen' (Morton & Patterson, 1980). The semantic system is sometimes called the cognitive system, which allows a black box explanation to include complex sentence processing and thinking and avoids tackling visual as opposed to verbal representation

at the level of word units (called *lexicons*), the decoding and encoding of the symbolic meaning of these words (*semantics*) and sentences (*syntax*) and finally the creative generation of these words and sentences for self-expression in spoken and written form (see Figure 8.1 for a generalized model).

PROCESSING AUDITORY INPUT

When considering pre-semantic stages of processing auditory input, there is a growing and cohesive literature on disturbances in complex sound processing (Griffiths et al., 1999). When this only occurs for words and other sounds are recognized normally, with no other language impairment, the condition is traditionally termed *pure word deafness* (Ellis, Franklin & Crerar, 1994), with a further dissociation between *word sound deafness* where the sound appears distorted and *word form deafness* where the ability to discriminate phonemes is intact, but the individual cannot tell if a spoken word is a real word or not. Screening for word deafness is easily carried out informally by using a devised set of real and nonsense words contrasted in spoken and written form, taking care to prevent lip-reading. The use of a taped series of environmental sounds can also be used to screen for auditory agnosia.

Word meaning deafness refers to a subsequent processing stage—when the individual can identify the spoken word as a real word, but no longer knows its meaning unless written down. This latter stage is to all intents and purposes equivalent to a verbal agnosia for the spoken word, whether occurring at the point of access to the semantic system or within the semantic system, a phenomenon that is discussed in the following section.

CENTRAL PROCESSES—WORDS AND SENTENCES

Assuming there is no difficulty in processing a word in terms of its sound and form, the next stage of processing is for meaning. It is helpful to use a developmental model to distinguish a semantic memory store or thesaurus comprising the representations of things in the natural and man-made world separately from those words that denote propositional speech and comprise syntax (including articles, auxiliary verbs, inflections, etc.). This is more than just a heuristic device, and there is much evidence to warrant this approach.

Developmentally, the ability to name things is acquired first and may well be the source of our language evolution (Terrace, 1985). This formulation of semantics before syntax and comprehension before production has some harmony with our understanding of neuronal organization within the cortex. Difficulties with semantics arise from lesions in the dominant temporal lobe surrounding the auditory cortex, while difficulties with syntax arise from lesions in the dominant frontal lobe close to the motor speech area. This dichotomy has been known since the turn of the century and formed the basis for the classic syndromes of Wernicke's and Broca's aphasias, respectively. Broca's aphasia is characterized by short utterances devoid of syntax and heavily dependent on semantically loaded words, while Wernicke's aphasia has fluent, grammatically correct speech, but with damaged semantics, and speech is consequently characterized as empty with no meaning (also termed jargon aphasia). Comprehension difficulties are associated with lesions predominantly in Wernicke's area and expressive difficulties with Broca's area. The arcuate fasciculus is a tract connecting the two regions; a simplistic serial model of processing suggests auditory input arrives at the primary auditory cortex ensconced within the upper sulcus of the temporal lobe, then cascades to the adjacent secondary auditory cortex (Wernicke's area and beyond), where the input is semantically processed and can be relayed forward via the arcuate fasciculus to the syntactical and speech production centre (Broca's area and beyond) for articulation. This is of course far too simplistic, but has proved very useful as a clinical aid, and formed the basis of the traditional taxonomy of aphasia used by speech and language therapists to classify patients for assessment and treatment (e.g., using the Boston Diagnostic Aphasia Examination; Goodglass et al., 2002). It is also important to see this pathway as the main highway in an extensive topographical language area that radiates over most of the dominant hemisphere, with the exception of much of the occipital lobe and the prefrontal cortex. The interaction of these systems with prefrontal areas of executive function will of course be hugely important for the cognitive processes involved in thinking in verbal form, but how this occurs is almost completely unknown. Furthermore, a non-dysphasic individual with executive difficulties is often described as having high-level language difficulties because they are unable to monitor, verify or initiate their thought processes and behaviour. It is useful at this stage of our understanding of cerebral functions to differentiate between the linguistic and executive systems to minimize executive difficulties masquerading as dysphasia or vice versa in clinical formulations.

A further important differentiation is between the *short-term memory store* and language comprehension. The short-term memory store refers to an acoustic buffer store, which allows us to hold an incoming stream of auditory input altogether in order to process it linguistically. It is better conceptualized as a measure of the present, not the past, and is measured by tests such as the Digit Span subtest of the Wechsler Adult Intelligence Scale—3rd edition (WAIS-III). Individuals who have a reduced short-term memory (and this can often be reduced to two or three digits or 'bits' of information following acquired brain pathology) may not be able to process some long sentences that they hear, even with intact comprehension of semantics and syntax.

In language disintegration, name retrieval is extremely sensitive to pathology compared with name comprehension; thus anomia is consequently far more common following brain insult than is difficulty with name comprehension. In both normal and clinical populations, this facility in comprehending names of objects compared with producing them implies that comprehension is a more robust skill and relies on a different set of cerebral processes from those involved in name production. It is possible that this even extends to different central representations for comprehension and production of a name (see, e.g., Kremin, 1986). Thus the very mildest form of aphasia is an increase in this word-finding difficulty, often an early symptom of an incipient lesion or a degenerative process, including normal ageing.

The Word as a Name

A 'name' can be heard, spoken, read or written. Each of these four forms can be selectively impaired or preserved following cerebral pathology. A 'name' then is not a unitary phenomenon, but has different context-specific representations. The traditional assumption that the semantic representation of a name and its underlying concept is one and the same is being seriously questioned by contemporary findings. It is becoming evident that any explanation of naming behaviour requires an appreciation of how a name, and its underlying concept, is represented within the semantic system or systems as well as the processes that allow access to and output from this central representation.

For diagnostic purposes a simple naming test will suffice to detect *anomia*—a difficulty in retrieving names of objects at will. However, if the problem is subtle, then a test that is graded in difficulty is needed. Commonly used tests, devised for this purpose and using simple black and white drawings, are the Boston Naming Test (part of the Boston Diagnostic Aphasia Battery—3rd Edition; Goodglass et al., 2002) and the Graded Naming Test (McKenna & Warrington, 1983). A significant degree of anomia will nearly always accompany more global difficulties of aphasia, but can occur in a severe and circumscribed form with no other disruption to speech production or comprehension. Naming ability should be practically examined by use of picture naming and from a verbal description such as Naming from Description (Coughlan & Warrington, 1978). When the effect is predominantly confined to visual confrontation naming—to a picture, a photograph or the actual object—the phenomenon is termed *optic aphasia* (Beauvois, 1982) and refers to a difficulty at the stage of accessing the name and not in the visual analysis nor in the recognition of the object. Less often, the effect can be restricted to touch (*tactile anomia*) or auditory input (there is no generally accepted clinical term, but it has been called *acoustic anomia*). These various tests of naming to confrontation are artificial indices for measuring the individual's ability to spontaneously produce a name at will. Some individuals may have more extensive difficulties within the semantic system, when it is not just the name that is elusive, but the concept itself.

The Semantic Memory System

There is strong evidence to suggest that the dominant temporal lobe is the repository for a store of concepts of those things that make up our world, termed the semantic memory system. These concepts include both concrete things in the physical world and abstract ideas. The concrete things can be either generic (e.g., 'dog', 'mountain', 'book') or item-specific (e.g. 'Eiffel Tower', 'Tony Blair', 'Spain'). Some patients will have lost some of this knowledge base, or their access to it, so they not only fail to name an object but cannot recognize its name or say much about it other than give the superordinate category to which it belongs (i.e., they know a sheep is an animal of some sort, but nothing more). Research over the past three decades has produced much evidence to show that different categories of semantic concepts can be differentially damaged by brain pathology, and increasingly sophisticated radiological techniques are beginning to map the cerebral correlates of these phenomena.

Categorical Features in Semantic Processing

One striking characteristic to emerge in contemporary studies of both the retrieval and comprehension of names is category-specificity, when the difficulties are restricted to particular semantic categories, or when isolated categories are spared in

an otherwise global comprehension or retrieval deficit. This remarkable characteristic of categorical breakdown in naming ability has provided some insight not only
into the access and retrieval processes of lexical representation but also into the
organization of these semantic representations.

Goodglass et al. (1966) produced the first systematic study of category effects in
name retrieval and name comprehension in the aphasic population. The six
categories examined—colours, numbers, letters, body parts, actions and objects—
were those traditionally recognized as sometimes being impaired or spared in
isolation, and the authors found that selective category preservation or impairment
was a common feature in the disturbed retrieval and comprehension of names in
their population. This theme was carefully examined and expanded by Warrington
and her colleagues. Further fractionations of category naming and comprehension
in patients have been reported, not only confirming the independence of these
traditional categories but also revealing clear dissociations between and within
the categories of proper names, abstract names, names of natural kinds (e.g.,
animals, fruits and vegetables) and names of man-made artefacts. The category-
specific reports not only concern name retrieval and name comprehension difficulties but also the recognition of objects or pictures of objects. Sometimes the
problem appears to be one of unreliable access to intact semantic representations
of specific categories of concepts, more often a loss or disturbance of the central
representations of those categories, termed *agnosia*.

Warrington and Shallice (1984) first provided quantitative evidence of specific
sparing of abstract words and selective difficulty in identifying living things and
foods as compared with man-made objects in their report of four patients with
herpes simplex encephalitis. For instance, in defining the spoken word 'briefcase',
one patient JBR described it as 'a small case held by students to carry papers', but
to 'parrot' replied 'don't know'. Similarly, a second patient SBY to 'whistle'
replied, 'thing you blow to make a piping sound', whereas to 'kangaroo' replied
'animal that swims'. Less often the category of man-made objects is degraded
compared with the realm of natural kinds (e.g., Warrington & McCarthy, 1983).
Reports of a category-specific difficulty for natural kinds or man-made objects in
individuals following brain pathology have been documented ever since (see
McKenna & Warrington, 2000 for a chronological list of case reports from 1975
to 1998).

The selective impairment of proper names as a clinical phenomenon has only
recently been given the academic attention it deserves (Valentine et al., 1996).
Published clinical reports are sparse, but an overview is provided by Semenza
(1997). Within the wider category of proper names, dissociations between names
of people and countries have been reported, but in terms of the needs of the
clinical population, the inability to access names of family, friends and acquain-
tances is of immediate concern, and the inability to retrieve names of contemporary celebrities a mere irritant.

Testing for Category Effects

Contemporary aphasia batteries may screen for naming and comprehension of colour, number, body parts and actions, but do not distinguish between natural kinds and man-made artefacts and do not include proper names. Category effects, especially in those patients with moderate to severe aphasia, are not obvious in the hospital setting. One picture test of category-specific naming and comprehension, the Category Specific Names Test (McKenna, 1998) incorporates two category sets of natural kinds (animals, fruits and vegetables) and two sets of man-made objects (with and without a specific skilled action attached to their use). A category-specific concrete and abstract word comprehension test is provided by Warrington et al. (1998), but in-depth testing for other categories requires improvised material.

Modality Features of Semantic Processing

When examining the semantic system, it is essential to consider modality as well as category. The intimate connections between vision and language in semantic processes are readily demonstrated by a comparison of our effortless ability to identify foodstuffs from sight, as compared with our effortful ability to recognize them from smell (e.g., Cain, 1982).

There is still some debate as to whether visually based and verbally based representations of concepts can dissociate, but there are clear individual cases where they appear to. For instance, Hart et al. (1985) reported a patient MD who could not name nor classify fruits and vegetables from sight, but once given the names, whether in spoken or written form, could classify them correctly and could match the name to its picture without error. The converse pattern occurred in patient TOB (McCarthy & Warrington, 1988). He could recognize a living thing from its picture (a rhinoceros—'enormous, weighs over one ton, lives in Africa'), but not from its spoken name ('animal—can't give you any functions'). However, when he was presented with spoken names he gave excellent descriptions of man-made objects, but very poor responses to living things (e.g., 'wheelbarrow'—'the item we have here in the gardens for carrying bits and pieces, wheelbarrows are used by people doing maintenance here on your buildings. They can put their cement and all sorts of things in it to carry around', but for 'peacock' his response was 'common name, can't place it'). He therefore appeared to be able to access knowledge about animals visually, but not verbally.

Testing for Modality Effects

Most tests of name comprehension and object recognition employ a mixed modality paradigm of name–picture matching, so it is difficult to tell if it is the name or the picture that is the problem. A very useful exception is the Pyramids and Palm Trees Test (Howard & Patterson, 1992), whereby a target item has to be matched to one of an adjacent pair. The test has both a picture form and a written form, so a comparison of competence in visual and verbal representations can be made. The test does not explicitly incorporate a category dimension, but uses an eclectic assortment of items and matches mostly by association (e.g., a pair of spectacles to be matched to an eye or a nose).

Syntax and Sentences

Clearly, the initiation, formulation and monitoring of ideas is heavily dependent on the executive system, but this chapter is concerned only with the linguistic processes that allow verbal expression of those ideas. Syntax incorporates all those rules of grammar that give rise to a sentence and allow the expression of a complex idea composed of the interaction of things (semantics) to be conveyed in spoken or written form. The interaction of 'girl–horse–park' can be conveyed by 'I saw the girl ride her horse in the park', to describe the dynamic relations between these things over time and space.

These differences are mirrored in Broca's and Wernicke's aphasias. When these syndromes present in pure form (very rarely), the Broca's aphasic, with content words intact, is more intelligible with an actual message to convey compared with the Wernicke's aphasic who is describing relationships between no things! This expression without meaning is not uncommon in the dysphasic population, and most therapists can report the experience of a most exhaustive exploration of a dysphasic's seemingly intense efforts to communicate a concern coming to nothing. The same can be true of people in advanced stages of dementia. Although the intent to communicate looks real enough, an experienced therapist can bring closure to the episode and reassurance to the client working purely on affective prosody. Much of normal sentence production is semi-automatic with redundant phrases appearing to fill in thinking time—'know what I mean?' Quite often we mutter to ourselves (when we would rather not) in a way that is beyond our control, and in aphasia this even extends to profanities. This *non-propositional* speech also extends to clichés, lyrics, serial speech learnt by heart (such as counting or days of the weeks), greetings and an individual's idiosyncratic phrase patterns. Even in severe aphasia, patients can usually access these automatic patterns of recitation and sing well-known lyrics. Like much of our non-verbal communication, it is thought, at least in part, to be subserved by the non-dominant hemisphere (e.g., see Yamadori et al., 1977).

Even for propositional speech that is under our voluntary control, we do not consciously choose each word in the sentence nor even have more than an intention to do so—the words for this operation just emerge for us. The status of verbs or action words has attracted some interest when considering syntax. Further evidence for verb processing being associated with Broca's area continues to emerge (e.g., Bak et al., 2001), but the holistic processing of action concepts appears to be dependent on posterior as well as frontal regions of the left hemisphere. Shapiro et al. (2001) argue for the left prefrontal cortex being selectively engaged in processing verbs as 'grammatical' objects, while other aspects of representation are subserved elsewhere. This formula allows for the dual role of action words in semantics and syntax. Beyond this, the neuropsychology of syntax is undeveloped as yet and is uninformative on the status of other semantically and syntactically significant parts of speech, such as adjectives and adverbs.

The cognitive model and neurological framework for comprehension and expression of both areas of language is more complex than this simple model allows and is far from understood. Indeed, syntax needs to be decoded as well as encoded, and semantics need to be expressed as well as understood. More recently, Warrington (2000) produced the first documented case of a patient who had a selective and very profound deficit for sentence comprehension that could not be accounted for by a deficit in auditory span and whose expressive language function for sentences was intact. This is a very rare finding, as comprehension is usually more robust than expressive language function in dysphasia. It does however add weight to the idea that, even at central stages of language, processes for comprehension and expression may be different.

Testing Syntax

Tests examining syntax are necessarily limited to comprehension and incorporate increasing sentence length and grammatical complexity. One of the most popular of such tests is the Test for Reception of Grammar (TROG; Bishop, 1989). Detailed analysis of the grammatical characteristic of dysphasia are best left to speech and language therapists, but a neuropsychological assessment can incorporate a shortened form of the Token Test of comprehension (Coughlan & Warrington, 1978). This requires 12 coloured shapes using four colours (red, blue, green and yellow) and three shapes (triangle, square and circle) that need to be cast in easily manipulable form, such as plastic or wood.

PROCESSING VERBAL OUTPUT

The speed at which an idea is translated into a sentence using all the complex rules of syntax and accessing the exact semantics is staggering, and generating language is far more difficult to achieve than processing heard speech—an observation already made at the level of a single name. Equally impressive are the complexities of the phonological and articulatory rules needed to convey all this as sound. This section will examine further characteristics of dysphasic patients as they attempt to speak and communicate and in so doing will highlight the complexities of the dynamic interactions between the different stages of information processing and the limitations in our knowledge base.

Phonology

Some of the complexities of phonology have already been introduced in the section on comprehension, when the ability to understand what is heard breaks down at the level of sound or phonological processing. The *phonological output system* has not only to select but also order the correct phonemes. That this occurs is evident from the type of errors dysphasics make and which result in *phonemic paraphasias*, often resulting in nonsense words or *neologisms* (e.g., 'odange' and 'orjan' for 'orange' for errors in selection and ordering, respectively), though a response could as easily bear no resemblance to the target word. For purposes of clinical practice, the first phoneme or letter of a name seems critical (e.g., Papagno & Capitani, 2001). Some patients are able to access only this, while others, more rarely, can access everything except this. More commonly, patients can retrieve names once given the first phoneme. Sometimes, an individual can access the first phoneme and total numbers of syllables—perhaps calling on written representation of phonology (as in the example given by Kay & Ellis, 1987, where their patient EST could say 'it begins with "t" and has five letters' for 'table'). In milder forms of word-finding difficulties, individuals often spontaneously, if slowly, produce the name, probably using a medley of these strategies, as if to boost the activity of a refractory speech output lexicon or its pathways to the phonological output systems. This 'refractoriness' is thought to explain why some dysphasics sometimes do, and sometimes do not, have access to the name of an object. Having an extended gap between presentation of items also aids some patients in retrieving a name (e.g., McCarthy & Kartsounis, 2000). The facilitatory use of a spoken sentence can often be demonstrated as an aid to retrieval (e.g., Breen & Warrington, 1994) and, even in very severe dysphasia, individuals are often able to complete well-versed expressions, such as 'black and . . .', 'bread and . . .' 'cat and . . .' , 'cup of . . .'.

There is disagreement on the question of whether there are separate phono-logical systems for speech input versus speech output, but recent studies suggest functional overlap in the left posterior superior temporal gyrus (e.g., Wise et al., 2001). Certainly, there appears to be a direct connection from the phonological input system to the phonological output system, and a recent study by McCarthy and Warrington (2001) found the phonological representation of words to be functionally independent of the semantic system in patient MNA, who had a near total semantic dementia, but who could repeat lists and sentences. More recent single case studies have provided convincing evidence to indicate separate phonological output processes for reading and speaking (e.g., Crutch & Warrington, 2001).

Articulation

Articulation refers to the orchestration of the vocal and breathing apparatus to transform speech operations into sound. A difficulty at this level of speech output can arise from two distinct output stages: the first involves the central blueprints for co-ordinating and orchestrating the vocal apparatus, and the second is the motor nervous system directly controlling the musculature. Difficulties at the first stage can be determined by the presence of a *bucco-facial apraxia*, also called a *kinetic speech production impairment* (see McCarthy & Warrington, 1990), and is usually referred to simply as *dyspraxia* by speech therapists. The second, more peripheral, stage gives rise to the *dysarthrias*.

Individuals with bucco-facial apraxia are usually unable to copy facial movements, produce facial gesture or mime the use of objects (such as blowing out candles). The difficulty may be restricted to words and is thought to underlie the 'foreign accent syndrome', a variation whereby a native speaker, though fluent, sounds foreign (Graff-Radford et al., 1986). This inability to activate a blueprint for co-ordinating the muscles results from damage in the anterior dominant hemisphere, close to Broca's area. A further but much rarer syndrome resulting from a lesion in this region is *mutism*, in which an individual makes no attempt to try to speak at all, although there is no dysphasia and the inertia is not volitional.

While dysphasia is not particularly associated with severe head injury, dysarthria is (Murdoch & Theodoros, 1999). It can result from damage to widespread areas of the brain, including the bulbar nerve nuclei in the brainstem, the basal ganglia or the cerebellum, and affects a third of people following a severe head injury. While semantic, syntactic and phonological systems can be intact, difficulties at this end stage of motor output can sabotage effective communication. Even when intelligible, the prosodic distortion can significantly detract from the intended message. This is a major area of expertise for speech and language therapists who are specialists in assessment and rehabilitation not only of articulation but also of swallowing and breathing, which are all intimately connected at this level of processing.

LITERACY

Unlike the deep and universal structure of language proposed by Chomsky (or those processes underlying analysis of the visual world), literacy is a cultural invention, a comparatively recent result of human creative endeavour and cannot have an innate cerebral system pre-programmed for it. It nonetheless appears to be subserved by the dominant parietal lobe alongside areas associated with constructional and praxis skills for voluntary action. Though dysphasia often extends to written as well as spoken language, an acquired inability to read (dyslexia) or write (dysgraphia) can occur in isolation without dysphasia.

Reading—Peripheral Stages

A peripheral stage in reading, subserved by occipital areas of the brain, allows the acquisition of a *visual word form* (Warrington & Shallice, 1980), which refers to the ability to register the pattern of the word as an entire and stable visual unit before it is identified as a stimulus-specific pattern (*visual input lexicon*). This first stage became apparent because of the nature of deficits at this level. Many individuals with visual neglect resulting from right hemisphere pathology will miss clumps of words on the left when reading prose and may read individual words incorrectly by changing the beginning of the word. Furthermore, a visual neglect dyslexia may occur in isolation without any other form of neglect.

Other patients are unable to see a word as a whole and can only read laboriously letter by letter. They cannot read handwriting, because it is impossible to see where one letter ends and the next begins in joined-up script. Nor can they read a word from brief exposure, as this precludes the painstaking identification of each letter. This difficulty is usually called *letter-by-letter reading* (e.g., Patterson & Kay, 1982; Shallice & Saffron, 1986).

Attentional dyslexia, a rare syndrome, can be viewed as the opposite syndrome, when the word can only be processed as a unitary form, but not the individual letters comprising it. Shallice and Warrington's (1977) two patients, who showed this deficit, transposed letters when identifying them, selecting adjacent letters on the page. All these deficits occur at the level of perceptual grouping specific to the class of written words.

Reading—Central Stages

Once the visual input lexicon is secured, there appears to be a direct route—from it to the phonological output lexicon—capable of bypassing the semantic system altogether (the *print-to-sound route*). This permits reading aloud when one's concentration is elsewhere and is not uncommon in dementia, when even irregularly pronounced words can be read correctly by an individual who is no longer aware of their meaning (Schwartz et al., 1980). However, as the disease progresses the individual becomes increasingly reliant on residual knowledge of the rules of print-to-sound conversion (a grapheme is the written equivalent of a phoneme).

Thus there are two distinct ways to read a word: by converting it to sound (using the phonological route) and then processing it for meaning as an auditory unit, or by processing it directly as a visual unit for meaning (the direct route).

The phonological route to reading is the only way we can read new words, but if this is damaged then we have no idea how to pronounce the set of letters composing the word. So long as the direct route into the semantic system is intact, a difficulty may not be apparent unless a new, or nonsense, word is presented. Patients with this difficulty cannot read nonsense words such as 'slue' or 'bleash'. It is this difficulty that characterizes phonological dyslexia. In the testing situation, therefore, a ready-made set of printed nonsense words can be very useful.

If, however, an individual has no phonological route and a partially impaired direct route, *deep dyslexia* results. These patients are reading by 'sight vocabulary' (McCarthy & Warrington, 1990, p. 237), but they make semantic errors and might read 'chapel' for 'church', 'pain' for 'ache', etc. These semantic errors are the core feature of this syndrome and indicate that the error is arising within the semantic system. The correct semantic concept is accessed (e.g., a church), but the wrong phonological output lexicon (e.g., 'chapel')—as if the back-up support from the phonological route is needed to fine-tune accuracy in accessing the exact semantic

Table 8.1. Central dyslexias

Phonological dyslexia	Intact direct route, no phonological route
Deep dyslexia	Partially impaired direct route, no phonological route
Surface dyslexia	No direct route, intact phonological route

concept and/or the phonological output lexicon. Why this happens is still not understood, but frequent features, in addition to their inability to read nonsense words and to make semantic errors, are visual errors (e.g., 'shack' for 'stack'), impairments in reading grammatical words and having more difficulty reading abstract words than concrete words. This syndrome is one of the most intensely investigated, with several consequent theoretical interpretations (for a collection of papers on deep dyslexia see Coltheart et al., 1980).

The converse syndrome *surface dyslexia* occurs when the direct route is impaired and the individual resorts to using the phonological route. These patients can read regular words, but not irregular ones. When these individuals are presented with words, such as 'yacht', 'rhyme', they cannot recognize them using sight vocabulary and read them incorrectly because the words break the rules of grapheme-to-sound conversion.

A summary of these central dyslexias is presented in Table 8.1.

Writing

Writing appears to mirror the complexity of reading and can break down in similar ways. This is obvious in a common form of developmental dyslexia when the difficulty is only in spelling, not reading. In acquired dyslexia, a similar spelling-specific breakdown may be seen, or the difficulty may be restricted to writing, leaving intact the ability to spell aloud. There appears to be a parallel set of routes to spelling, corresponding to the phonological and direct routes in reading. The ability to spell by using sound-to-letter correspondences may be faulty, while sight spelling is intact (*phonological dysgraphia*) and only apparent when the individual is asked to spell a nonsense word for which of course there is no entry in their output lexicon (e.g., patient PR; Shallice, 1981). An analogous pattern to deep dyslexia can also be seen in written output, with semantic errors, visual errors and more difficulty in spelling abstract than concrete words occurring when the direct output route is partially faulty and there is no functioning phonological route available. This has been described in patient JC (Bub & Kertesz, 1982) and given the name *deep dysgraphia*. The opposite syndrome, where a spelling is produced from sounds in the absence of the direct route, is termed *surface dysgraphia* and is described in patient RG (Beauvois & Derousne, 1981). These findings necessitate the presence of a *graphemic* or *orthographic output lexicon*, similar to the phonological output lexicon. This is connected to an output system that allows for recoding in several forms (e.g., handwriting in script or print, typing, lower case, upper case. shorthand, etc.). Further elaboration of theory and research for models of literacy can be found in Ellis and Young (1996), with a clinical perspective in McCarthy and Warrington (1990).

Category-specific Effects in Reading and Writing

Further support for the categorical organization of semantic memory can be seen in the patterns of intact and impaired comprehension of the written word seen in some patients (e.g., McKenna & Parry, 1994). There are various competing interpretations about whether written semantics represent an independent system to spoken semantics, which is favoured by clinical practitioners (and, particularly, Warrington and colleagues), or whether the dissociations reflect disconnections (a view more favoured by academics). In clinical practice, however, an exploration of both spoken and written comprehension of different categories is important for those patients who have severe comprehension deficits. Category-specific dissociations in the ability to write names have now also been reported (e.g., Cipolotti et al., 1993).

REMEDIATION AND REHABILITATION

Increased understanding of the complexities of cognitive processes has been central to advances in rehabilitation techniques, which are becoming more sophisticated not only in the narrow sense of remediation but also in the wider sense of rehabilitation to address the individual's psychosocial status and holistic needs.

Developments in impairment-based therapy include the use of patient-specific creative techniques that reflect this more fine-grained understanding of cognitive functioning. They also include the need for tighter structure and monitoring of the intervention to check its efficacy in the pursuit of evidence-based practice. For example, Byng (1988) reported the remediation of a circumscribed difficulty in a patient with a Broca-type aphasia, who had specific difficulty with reversible locative sentences (e.g., 'the box is in the bag'/'the bag is in the box'), where the relationship is specified by syntactic rules and cannot be deduced from the meaning of the nouns. Though his understanding of the grammatical operations and semantics was intact, he could not map one onto the other (a process referred to as thematic mapping). Their technique of aiding his thematic mapping included the imaginative use of drawings and colour-coding for him to self-monitor his relearning, with the result that his ability to decode and produce these sentences was permanently restored, while other non-treated impairments remained unchanged. Best and Nickels (2000) in a series of studies using self-cueing, with first letter and sound as the intervention, highlight the unique pattern of deficits across superficially similar anomic clients and the unique way each individual uses the therapy, resulting in differential outcomes—all of which becomes predictable once these complexities have been submitted to a microanalysis. Other approaches to the management of acquired language impairments have been described by Code and Miller (1995) and Murdoch and Theodoros (2001).

Similar advances have occurred in the social model of rehabilitation to empower the individual in his or her relationships with significant others and the community in his or her altered communication status. These developments address the reality that most aphasic individuals will need to rebuild confidence and skill in living with communication difficulties in the long term. The delivery of these 1 : 1 programmes and group work requires intensive preparation, structure and systematic application over time and are reflected in the practice of specialist speech and language therapists, such as those based at the City University in London and described in their book *Beyond Aphasia* (Pound et al., 2000). Their methods include therapists modelling new communication strategies in real-life situations in the community, promoting self-run groups and developing skill in communication by drawings, among many others. The work is targeted at educating society as well as empowering individuals and freeing them from the social and cultural barriers and even the power relation intrinsic in the therapist–client alliance.

CONCLUSIONS

Though far from complete, our understanding of the macroscopic organization and logic of cognitive systems including language and communication has led to breakthroughs in assessment and rehabilitation of individuals with communication difficulties. In attempting a neuropsychological assessment, the clinical psychologist needs to be particularly sensitive and skilled in mapping the interface of language functions with other cognitive functions (i.e., perceptual, executive and episodic memory functions). Test procedures should follow the information processing model of language outlined here in trying to specify the individual's difficulties to inform the rehabilitation process—though the depth of analysis will vary depending on whether a specialist speech and language therapist is involved. In this analysis several pitfalls for the less experienced have emerged, which are summarized in Table 8.2.

Finally, good rehabilitation relies on good assessment not only of the hardware of linguistic and communication skill but also of the individual's psychosocial needs.

Table 8.2. Things to be aware of

Do	Distinguish between verbal and non-verbal communication
	Distinguish between semantics and syntax
	Distinguish between visual and verbal modalities
	Check for the possibility of dissociations between and within language functions
Don't	Mistake a shape perception problem for anomia in picture naming
	Mistake a short-term memory deficit for a comprehension deficit
	Mistake an executive deficit for a linguistic one

REFERENCES

Bak, T. H., O'Donovan, D. G., Xuereb, J. H., Boniface, S. & Hodges, J. R. (2001) Selective impairment of verb processing associated with pathological changes in Brodmann areas 44 and 45 in the motor neurone disease-dementia-aphasia syndrome. *Brain*, **124**, 103–120.

Bavelas, J. B. & Chovil, N. (2000) Visible acts of meaning: An integrated message model of language in face-to-face dialogue. *Journal of Language and Social Psychology*, **19**, 163–194.

Beauvois, M. F. (1982) Optic aphasia: A process of interaction between vision and language. *Philosophical Transactions of the Royal Society of London*, **B298**, 35–48.

Beauvois, M. F. & Derousne, J. (1981) Lexical or orthographic agraphia. *Brain*, **104**, 21–49.

Best, W. & Nickels, L. (2000) From theory to therapy in aphasia: Where are we now and where to next? *Neuropsychological Rehabilitation*, **10**, 231–247.

Bishop, D. V. M. (1983) *The Test for Reception of Grammar*. Published by the author and available from Age and Cognitive Performance Research Centre, University of Manchester, M13 9PL.

Breen, K. & Warrington, E. K. (1994) A study of anomia: Evidence for a distinction between nominal and prepositional language. *Cortex*, **30**, 231–245.

Bryan, K. (1995) *The Right Hemisphere Language Battery (RHLB)* (2nd edn). Whurr, London.

Bub, D. & Kertesz, A. (1982) Deep agraphia. *Brain and Language*, **17**, 146–165.

Bull, P. (2001) Nonverbal communication. *The Psychologist*, **14**, 644–647.

Byng, S. (1988) Sentence processing deficits: Theory and therapy. *Cognitive Neuropsychology*, **5**, 629–676.

Cain, W. S. (1982) Odor identification by males and females: Predictions versus performance. *Chemical Senses*, **7**, 129–142.

Cipolotti, L., McNeil, J. E. & Warrington, E. K. (1993) Spared written naming of proper nouns: A case report. *Memory*, **1**, 289–311.

Code, C. & Miller, D. (1995) *Treatment of Aphasia from Treatment to Practice—Studies in Disorders of Communication*. Whurr, London.

Coltheart, M., Patterson, K. & Marshall, J. (1980) *Deep Dyslexia* (2nd edn). Routledge & Kegan Paul, London.

Coughlan, A. K. & Warrington, E. K. (1978) Word comprehension and word retrieval in patients with localised cerebral lesions. *Brain*, **101**, 163–185.

Crutch, S. J. and Warrington, E. K. (2001) Refractory dyslexia: Evidence of multiple task-specific phonological output stores. *Brain*, **124**, 1533–1543.

Ellis, A. E. & Young, A. W. (1996) *Human Cognitive Neuropsychology*. Lawrence Erlbaum, Hove, UK.

Ellis, A., Franklin, S. & Crerar, A. (1994) Cognitive neuropsychology and the remediation of disorders of spoken language. In: M. J. Riddoch & G. W. Humphreys (eds) *Cognitive Neuropsychology and Cognitive Rehabilitation* (pp. 287–315). Lawrence Erlbaum, Hove, UK.

Ellis, H. D., Ellis, D. M., Fraser, W. & Deb, S. (1994) A preliminary study of right hemisphere cognitive deficits and impaired social judgements among young people with Asperger syndrome. *European Child and Adolescent Psychiatry*, **3**, 255–266.

Fujii, T., Fukatsu, R., Watable, S., Ohnuma, A., Teramura, K., Kimura, I. et al. (1990) Auditory sound agnosia without aphasia following a right temporal lobe lesion. *Cortex*, **26**, 263–268.

Goodglass, H. & Wingfield, A. (1997) Word finding deficits in aphasia: Brain–behaviour relations and clinical symptomatology. In: H. Goodglass & A. Wingfield (eds) *Anomia: Neuroanatomical and Cognitive Correlates* (pp. 3–27). Academic Press, London.

Goodglass, H., Klein, B., Carey, P. & Jones, K. (1966) Specific semantic word categories in aphasia. *Cortex*, **2**, 74–89.

Goodglass, H., Kaplan, E. & Baressi, B. (2002) *Boston Diagnostic Aphasia Examination* (3rd edn, BDAE-3). The Psychological Corporation. Sidcup, UK.

Graaf-Radford, N. R., Cooper, W. E., Colsher, P. L. & Damasio, A. R. (1986) An unlearned foreign 'accent' in a patient with aphasia. *Brain and Language*, **28**, 86–94.

Griffiths, T. D., Rees, A. & Green, G. G. R. (1999) Disorders of human complex sound processing. *Neurocase*, **5**, 365–398.

Habib, M., Daquin, G., Milandre, L., Rey, M., Lanteri, A., Salamon, G. et al. (1995) Mutism and auditory agnosia due to bilateral insular damage—role of the insular in human communication. *Neuropsychologia*, **33**, 327–339.

Hart, J. Jr, Berndt, R. S. & Caramazza, A. (1985) Category specific naming deficit following cerebral infarction. *Nature*, **316**, 439–440.

Howard, D. & Patterson, K. (1992) *The Pyramids and Palm Trees*. Thames Valley Test Co., Bury St Edmunds, UK.

Kay, J. & Ellis, A.W. (1987) A cognitive neuropsychological case study of anomia: Implications for psychological models of word retrieval. *Brain*, **110**, 613–629.

Kay, J., Lesser, R. & Coltheart, M. (1992) *Psycholinguistic Assessment of Language Performance in Aphasia (PALPA)*. Psychology Press, Hove, UK.

Kremin, H. (1986) Spared naming without comprehension. *Journal of Neurolinguistics*, **2**, 131–150.

McCarthy, R. A. & Kartsounis, L. D. (2000) Wobbly words: Refractory anomia with preserved semantics. *Neurocase*, **6**, 487–497.

McCarthy, R. A. & Warrington, E. K. (1988) Evidence for modality-specific meaning systems in the brain. *Nature*, **334**, 428–430.

McCarthy, R. A. & Warrington, E. K. (1990) *Cognitive Neuropsychology: A Clinical Introduction*. Academic Press, San Diego, CA.

McCarthy, R. A. & Warrington, E. K. (2001) Repeating without semantics. Surface dysphasia? *Neurocase*, **7**, 77–78.

McKenna, P. (1998) *Category Specific Names Test*. Psychology Press, Hove, UK.

McKenna, P. & Parry, R. (1994) Category and modality deficits of semantic memory in patients with left hemisphere pathology. *Neuropsychological Rehabilitation*, **4**, 283–305.

McKenna, P. & Warrington, E. K. (1983) *Graded Naming Test*. Cambridge Cognition, Cambridge, UK.

McKenna, P. & Warrington. E. K. (2000) The neuropsychology of semantic memory. In: L. S. Cermak (ed.) *Handbook of Neuropsychology, Vol. 2 Memory and Its Disorders* (2nd edn). Elsevier, Amsterdam.

Morton, J. & Patterson, K. (1980) A new attempt at an interpretation, or, an attempt at a new interpretation. In: M. Coltheart, K. Patterson & J. C. Marshall (eds) *Deep Dyslexia*. Routledge & Kegan Paul, London, UK.

Murdoch, B. E. & Theodoros, D. G. (1999) Dysarthria following traumatic brain injury. In: S. McDonald, L. Togher & C. Code (eds) *Communication Disorders Following Traumatic Brain Injury* (pp. 211–233). Psychology Press, Hove, UK.

Murdoch, B. E. & Theodoros, D. G. (2001) *Traumatic Brain Injury—Associated Speech, Language and Swallowing Disorders*. Singular Publishers, San Diego.

Ojemann, J. G., Ojemann, G. A. & Lettich, E. (1992) Neuronal activity related to faces and matching in human right nondominant temporal cortex. *Brain*, **115**, 1–13.

Papagno, C. & Capitani, E. (2001) Slowly progressive aphasia: A four-year follow-up study. *Neuropsychologia*, **39**, 678–686.

Patterson, K. E. & Kay, J. (1982) Letter-by-letter reading: Psychological descriptions of a neurological syndrome. *Quarterly Journal of Experimental Psychology*, **34A**, 411–441.

Perry, R. J., Rosen, H. R., Kramer, J. H., Beer, J. S., Levenson, R. L. & Miller, B. L. (2001) Hemispheric dominance for emotions, empathy and social behaviour: Evidence from right and left handers with frontotemporal dementia. *Neurocase*, **7**, 145–160.

Pound, C., Parr, S., Lindsay J. & Woolf, C. (2000) *Beyond Aphasia: Therapies for Living with Communication Disability*. Winslow Press, Bicester, UK.

Schwartz, M. F., Saffran, E. M. & Marin, O. S. M. (1980) Fractionating the reading process in dementia: Evidence for word specific print-to-sound associations In: M. Coltheart, K. E. Patterson & J. C. Marshall (eds) *Deep Dyslexia*. Routledge & Kegan Paul, London.

Scott, S. K., Rosen, S., Blank, C. & Wise, R. J. S. (2000) Subsystems in the human auditory cortex—evidence from functional neuroimaging studies. *Proceedings of BPS 17th Annual Conference, University of Bristol, September.*

Semenza, C. (1997) Proper-name-specific aphasias. In: H. Goodglass & A. Wingfield (eds) *Anomia: Neuroanatomical and Cognitive Correlates* (Foundation of Neuropsychology Series, pp. 115–134). Academic Press, London.

Shallice, T. (1981) Phonological agraphia and the lexical route in writing. *Brain,* **104,** 413–429.

Shallice, T. & Saffron, E.M. (1986) Lexical processing in the absence of explicit word identification. Evidence from a letter by letter reader. *Cognitive Neuropsychology,* **3,** 429–458.

Shallice, T. & Warrington, E. K. (1977) The possible role of selective attention in acquired dyslexia. *Neuropsychologia,* **15,** 31–41.

Shapiro, K. A., Pascual-Leone, A., Mottaghy, F. M., Gangitano, M. & Caramazza, A. (2001) Grammatical distinction in the left frontal cortex. *Journal of Cognitive Neuroscience,* **13,** 713–720.

Terrace, H. S. (1985) In the beginning was the 'name'. *American Psychologist,* **40,** 1011–1028.

Valentine, T., Brennan, T. & Bredart, S. (1996) *The Cognitive Psychology of Proper Names.* Routledge, London.

Warrington, E. K. (2000) The failure of language comprehension at sentence and phrasal levels in a patient who can speak normally. *Cortex,* **36,** 435–444.

Warrington, E. K. & McCarthy, R. (1983) Category specific dysphasia. *Brain,* **106,** 859–878.

Warrington, E. K. & Shallice, T. (1980). Word form dyslexia. *Brain,* **30,** 99–112.

Warrington, E. K. & Shallice, T. (1984) Category specific semantic impairments. *Brain,* **107,** 829–854.

Warrington, E. K., McKenna, P. & Orpwood, L. (1998) Single word comprehension: A concrete and abstract word synonym test. *Neuropsychological Rehabilitation,* **8,** 143–154.

Wise, R. J. S., Scott, S. K., Blank, S. C., Mummery, C. J., Murphy, K. & Warburton, E. A. (2001) Separate neural subsystems within Wernicke's area. *Brain,* **124,** 83–95.

Yamadori, A., Osumi, Y., Masuhara, S. & Okubo, M. (1977) Preservation of singing in Broca's aphasia. *Journal of Neurology, Neurosurgery and Psychiatry,* **40,** 221–224.

CHAPTER 9

Executive Dysfunction

Paul W. Burgess

UCL Institute of Cognitive Neuroscience, London, UK

and

Nick Alderman

St Andrew's Hospital, Northampton, UK

INTRODUCTION

The term 'executive functions' refers to those abilities that enable a person to determine goals, formulate new and useful ways of achieving them, and then follow and adapt this proposed course in the face of competing demands and changing circumstances, often over long periods of time. Crucial aspects of these abilities are thought to be supported by the frontal lobes of the brain, and sometimes the term 'frontal lobe function' is (imprecisely) used as a shorthand to refer to them. Damage to these processes results in a range of symptoms collectively referred to as the *dysexecutive syndrome*. This chapter gives an introduction to how dysexecutive symptoms caused by neurological incident may be measured and how then they might be treated using cognitive rehabilitation techniques.

ASSESSMENT OF EXECUTIVE FUNCTIONS

A number of tools are available for the clinician to determine the presence of the dysexecutive syndrome, its principal characteristics, the functional problems it causes and its severity. These comprise the clinical interview, assessment through questionnaire administration, neuropsychological tests, and behavioural and functional assessment.

The Unstructured Clinical Interview

This method can be highly effective for the very experienced clinician, but it is an unwise choice for the less experienced. The use of open-ended questions, such

Clinical Neuropsychology: A Practical Guide to Assessment and Management for Clinicians.
Edited by L.H. Goldstein and J.E. McNeil. © 2004 John Wiley & Sons, Ltd.

as '... do you have any problems following your accident?' may not be particularly helpful in assessing executive problems. Answering these questions requires considerable insight, verbal initiation ability and abstract reasoning, which may well be damaged in the dysexecutive patient. Such questioning is useful if one is experienced enough to be able to spot these difficulties, but the inexperienced clinician will be left with little useful information. Regardless of experience, the interviewer should then progress to asking more specific questions. Particular emphasis should be placed on asking the interviewee how well they cope in novel situations, encouraging them to compare this with their perception of their behaviour and functioning in routine situations.

Problems with reduced insight are, however, frequently present. It is not uncommon for some individuals with a dysexecutive syndrome to deny a particular difficulty, but then to say that a close relative or friend does acknowledge it and that the interviewer should talk to them about the problem.

In any case it is essential, where at all feasible, that somebody who knows the individual well is also interviewed and asked for their observations. This information is particularly helpful if the person knew the interviewee prior to the event in which neurological damage was acquired (i.e., 'premorbidly'). Comparison of the two sets of information will give some general impression regarding preservation of insight.

The Structured Clinical Interview

While useful qualitative information may be gleaned through an unstructured clinical interview, information regarding specific aspects of executive functioning may be difficult to obtain without more directed questioning.

An additional, and generally easier method for assessing the presence of dysexecutive symptoms is to base the interview around the use of a questionnaire. One of the most readily available questionnaires for such use is the Dysexecutive Questionnaire (DEX; Burgess et al, 1996a). The DEX is a 20-item questionnaire that prompts respondents to rate a variety of potential functional problems using a five-point Likert scale. Each item takes the form of a brief statement. A higher rating indicates that the respondent perceives the problem as more frequent or severe. The items are based on the work of Stuss and Benson (1984) and sample four broad areas of change or difficulty attributable to the dysexecutive syndrome, these being emotional or personality changes, motivational changes, behavioural changes and cognitive changes. The characteristics that each statement attempts to measure are functional problems impacting on everyday life.

A relative or carer should also complete the DEX, giving their ratings of the person they know well. Where possible, it may be helpful to have a number of people who know the individual to rate him or her (e.g., several members of the multidisciplinary team involved in the rehabilitation of that person). The mean rating for each item may then be compared with that made by the person him or herself. Use of questionnaires of this type should not replace an interview, but should be incorporated within it. One can either administer the questionnaire and then base one's interview on the information given, or use the questions used in the DEX as a prompt or 'starting question' for the interviewer, in order to ensure that the interview covers the main areas of likely concern.

Neuropsychological Tests

Administration of neuropsychological tests may also be useful in arriving at a diagnosis of the dysexecutive syndrome and in measuring its severity. When used properly, the data they provide will generally be more objective and precise than that gleaned by interview. In the same way as it would be unwise not to use an interview in one's assessment procedure, it would also for these reasons be unwise to rely upon an interview alone. There are many commercially available neuropsychological tests of executive function. So which tests should one use?

This is a matter that is not as straightforward as it might seem. The ideal assessment would obviously attempt to assess all of the symptoms shown in Table 9.1, as well as the less common signs of executive dysfunction (e.g., utilization behaviour, alien hand sign, subtle attentional changes). However, this is impractical in most clinical settings, and formal assessment measures do not yet exist for many of the symptoms. Moreover, relatively little is known about what

Table 9.1. Frequency of reporting of 20 of the commonest dysexecutive problems in a mixed aetiology neurological group

Adapted from Burgess and Robertson, 2002; data originally from the study of Wilson et al., 1996

Symptom	Carers (%)	Patients (%)
Planning problems	48	16
Distractibility	42	32
Lack of insight	39	27
Poor decision-making	38	26
Social unconcern	38	13
Euphoria	28	14
Restlessness	28	25
Apathy	27	20
Lack of concern for others' feelings	26	26
Perseveration	26	17
Aggression	25	12
Temporal sequencing problems	25	18
Social disinhibition	23	15
Shallow affect	23	14
Impulsivity	22	22
Response inhibition problems	21	11
Poor abstract thought	21	17
Knowing–doing dissociation	21	13
Variable motivation	15	13
Confabulation	5	5

many of the tests shown to be sensitive to frontal lobe lesions are actually measuring in these cases. One is left therefore with five choices of how to proceed:

- Method 1: *Time* Administer the greatest number of tests possible in the available time.
- Method 2: *Psychometrics* Base one's choice of measures on test-based factors such as ease of use and cost, psychometric validity, how widely the tests are used, how often they have been used with a particular client group, etc.
- Method 3: *Expectation* Base assessment on what one expects to find, given knowledge of medical history and/or previous assessments.
- Method 4: *Observation* Base assessment on symptoms already observed by carers or relatives.
- Method 5: *Theory* Adopt a particular theoretical stance and choose the tests that make most sense according to it.

These methods have different strengths, but none is entirely meritless, and in practice most experienced clinicians develop their own assessment procedure based on a personal weighting of them. In principle this is appropriate, although too often this choice has merely evolved haphazardly over time. Instead, the choice should be made deliberately and with good justification. If the same battery of tests is given to all clients, this choice should be reviewed regularly. One should always be able to clearly articulate and defend the reasons behind one's choice of procedures.

Let us consider these approaches in turn.

Method 1: Time

This is not as unjustifiable as might at first seem. Relatively little is known about what many of the traditional tests of executive function (e.g., Wisconsin Card Sorting Test [WCST], Stroop Test) actually measure. Moreover, their ecological validity (i.e., the extent to which they are indicators of real-world impairment) has not yet been clearly established, although the more modern tests, which have been designed to be more like real-life activities, are often—but not always—better in this respect. So, one solution to this problem is just to administer as many tests as one can in the available time, in the hope of covering as many different functions/situations as possible. The disadvantages of this approach are: (a) as the number of tests administered increases, so does the likelihood of obtaining a false positive result (unless one statistically corrects for the number of tests administered, which is uncommon), and (b) unless one has at least some hypothesis about what one is measuring, it is difficult to know what might be usefully concluded from a task failure; clinically, it is rarely sufficient to just baldly state 'this person failed this test', without further interpretation.

Method 2: Psychometrics

All people involved in the administration of psychometric tests should have at least some basic grounding in psychometric theory (see Chapter 6). This allows one to understand the relative merits of the measurement aspects of different tests and to select accordingly. In particular, there may be times when some aspect of the psychometric dynamic of relative tests might strongly influence one's choice. Examples might be where one requires parallel forms, where there is to be repeated testing using the same measure or where various different people may make assessments on the same person.

In general, however, it is harder in the field of executive function to use psychometric values (e.g., test–retest and inter-rater reliability, inter-item consistency, etc.) as a guide to test choice. This is because the tests are often measuring abilities such as response to novelty or strategy formation. These can subvert the theory behind traditional psychometrics and render the values a poor guide to a test's actual clinical utility (see Burgess, 1997 for more detail). Another problem is that the construct validity of a task (i.e., the extent to which the test measures what it is intended to measure) alters with level of performance. Overall, these matters present a highly complex theoretical problem when trying to base one's choice of assessment procedure on psychometric values, especially when they are derived from the performance of a different population (e.g., healthy control subjects) from the clinical one being tested. In summary, *all other things being equal*, one should choose the test with the best psychometric validity. However, all other things are unlikely often to be equal.

Method 3: Expectation

If more was known about what executive tests measure, this would probably be the most frequently appropriate single method. For success it relies upon at least four variables. First, the quality of the information, case history or previous assessment that is available. Second, one's knowledge of the test's performance in different populations. Third, how the test is affected by a variety of background variables (e.g., education, culture, age, etc.). Fourth, the ecological validity of the task (i.e., how strongly one can predict that the test measures the function that was observed to be impaired elsewhere). This method therefore requires a high degree of knowledge and clinical judgement.

Method 4: Observation

Patients should always be asked about the symptoms they notice, since it is important to assess their degree of insight and knowledge about their condition. However, it is unwise to base one's assessment upon this report since, as already noted, self-report of dysexecutive difficulties is notoriously inaccurate (see, e.g., Burgess & Robertson, 2002). However, the reports of carers, relatives or other people who know the patient well can be very useful and should always be sought, if possible.

The best witnesses are usually those who knew the person premorbidly, since *change* in behaviour is usually more instructive than comparisons of current behaviour with some population norm. This is important since the behaviours under examination are often more at the extreme of the range of behaviours than might be observed occasionally in the normal population. This is one of the important ways in which executive function assessment differs from assessment of other functions in neuropsychology. In, say, language assessment or assessment of visuo-spatial skills, pathological symptoms (e.g., jargon aphasia, neglect) are rarely or never seen in the healthy normal population. However, many of the symptoms of executive dysfunction are seen occasionally in the healthy population, albeit perhaps under special circumstances and in a milder form (e.g., confabulation: Burgess & Shallice, 1996; impulsivity; disinhibition). Since, therefore, it is often the *extremeness* (i.e., severity, frequency) of the behavioural sign rather than its *type* that is at issue, it is important if possible to have an observer 'baseline' with which to compare current behaviour.

Having collected the observations, however, one is faced with the challenge of translating them into examination procedure. There is no substitute for experience and knowledge in this respect. The job is however made easier by some of the newer assessment procedures that are more like real-world situations, since one can ask the observer about situations in which one's client experiences problems and then choose the closest test situations. However, for experienced examiners, more experimentally derived procedures also have their merits; often the theory of what they measure is more developed, they may be more specific in what they measure and the link with damage to certain brain regions may be more direct (but see cautionary notes below). These factors can add up to a strong advantage if one has a clear idea what it is that one is looking for and have experience in interpreting the observations of others.

Method 5: Theory

All assessment and treatment has to start with some theory of what it is that is being studied, even if this is very basic. The assessment implications of all theories of executive function cannot be covered here. However, a few of the leading ones will be selected as examples.

Single-process Theories

These maintain that damage to a single process or system is responsible for a number of different dysexecutive symptoms. An example is the theory of Cohen (e.g., Cohen et al., 1990). This holds that the prefrontal cortex is used to represent *context information*, which is the 'information necessary to mediate an appropriate behavioural response' (Cohen et al., 1998, p. 196). Two functions of the prefrontal cortex may be effected by this system: active memory and behavioural inhibition, with both functions reflecting the operation of the context layer under different task conditions. Under the conditions of response competition the context module plays an inhibitory role by supporting the processing of task-relevant information. However, when there is a delay until the execution of a response, the context module plays a role in memory by maintaining that information over time.

Following this theory, one's clinical assessment would include tests of response suppression (e.g., Hayling Test, Burgess & Shallice, 1997; Stroop Test, see Spreen & Strauss, 1998 for details) and tests with a 'working memory' component (e.g., WCST, Milner, 1963, originally invented by Berg, 1948; CANTAB [Cambridge Neuropsychological Test Automated Battery] spatial working memory test, Robbins et al., 1994).

Construct-led Theories

Construct-led theories are those that propose a construct (i.e., a theoretical ability), such as *working memory* or *fluid intelligence*, as a key function of the frontal lobe executive system.

(a) Working memory theories
Two leading theorists in this area are Petrides and Goldman-Rakic. Petrides believes that the mid-dorsolateral prefrontal region (areas 9 and 46) supports a brain system 'in which information can be held on-line for monitoring and manipulation of stimuli' (Petrides, 1998, p. 106). The mid-ventrolateral region, however, is used in explicit encoding and retrieval of information. Obvious suggested tests are therefore the Petrides and Milner's (1982) Self-Ordered Pointing Test, and other memory tests that particularly stress explicit encoding and retrieval (e.g., recall of complex figures, such as the Rey figure, and recall of short stories or word lists).

Goldman-Rakic's position differs in that she believes that various frontal lobe regions all perform a similar role in working memory, but that each processes a different type of information (Goldman-Rakic, 1995). She suggests that dysfunction of this system can cause a variety of deficits on, for example, verbal fluency and Stroop tasks, due to an inability to use working memory to initiate the correct response.

(b) Duncan's theory of 'g' (e.g., Duncan et al., 1995, 2000)
Duncan suggests that the principal purpose of the frontal executive system is to support a single function that is used in many situations, called *fluid intelligence* or Spearman's g. Of the commercially available tests, he believes Cattell's Culture-Fair Test and (by implication from his studies) the Six Element Test of the Behavioural Assessment of the Dysexecutive Syndrome (BADS; Wilson et al., 1996) measure this function.

Multiple-process Theories

These propose that the frontal lobe executive system consists of a number of components that typically work together in everyday actions.

(a) Fuster's temporal integration framework (Fuster, 1997)
This holds that the frontal lobe executive system performs three functions: Working Memory; Set Attainment; Inhibition. Suggested tasks are therefore, for example,

WCST or CANTAB working memory tests; Brixton Test (Burgess & Shallice, 1997); Hayling Test or Stroop Test.

(b) Stuss's anterior attentional functions (e.g., Stuss & Alexander, 2000; Stuss et al., 1995)

The focus of Stuss et al.'s theorizing is attention. They propose seven different attentional functions. The closest clinical test is probably the Test of Everyday Attention (TEA; Robertson et al., 1996).

(c) Shallice's supervisory attentional system (e.g., Burgess et al., 2000; Norman & Shallice, 1986; Shallice, 1988; Shallice, 2002; Shallice & Burgess, 1991a, 1991b, 1996)

This is one of the longest established and best known theories. In this model, the frontal lobes support a cognitive system known as the Supervisory Attentional System (SAS). This plays a part in at least eight different processes, each of which may be impaired in isolation: working memory; monitoring; rejection of schema; spontaneous schema generation; adoption of processing mode; goal setting; delayed intention marker realization; and episodic memory retrieval. On these grounds, and the result of a study that examined the relationship between symptoms in everyday life and executive test performance, Burgess et al. (1998) recommend that *at the very least* an assessment of a dysexecutive patient should include:

1 A general measure of inhibitory abilities (e.g., Hayling Test; however, this function is probably also measured to varying degrees by many other tests, such as verbal fluency, Trail-making Test, see Spreen & Strauss, 1998 for details).
2 Measures of executive memory abilities both in the short term (i.e., working memory tests) and long term (i.e., accuracy of episodic recollection). Suggested tests would be WCST; Brixton Test; story, figure and word list recall tests; and observation of real-life ability to recollect events accurately.
3 A measure of multitasking ability (e.g., Six Element Test from the BADS, Wilson et al., 1996; Multiple Errands Test, Alderman et al., 2003; Burgess et al., 1996b, 2000; Shallice & Burgess, 1991a).

However, Burgess et al. (1998) make two further points. First, neuropsychological tests of executive function do not measure well many of the emotional changes that can be part of the dysexecutive syndrome (e.g., euphoria, apathy). The formal tests need therefore to be supplemented by more general observation, preferably using a structured or semi-structured interview, perhaps based around a symptom checklist or questionnaire such as the DEX (Burgess et al., 1996a) from the BADS test battery (see also Chapter 4). Second, since many impairments can be seen in isolation, a true assessment will be as comprehensive as possible; the list above could be considered only as a basic screening assessment. For instance, one might also wish to supplement it routinely with measures of planning (e.g., Zoo Map Test of the BADS, Wilson et al., 1996); abstract reasoning and judgement (e.g., proverb interpretation; cognitive estimates or similar); initiation (e.g., Hayling Test, section 1); problem-solving and strategy formation (e.g., Action Program and Key Search Tests from the BADS, Wilson et al., 1996); rule attainment and following (e.g., Brixton Test).

Single-symptom Theories

These are theories of specific symptoms, such as confabulation (e.g., Burgess & McNeil, 1999; Burgess & Shallice, 1996) or multitasking deficits (e.g., Burgess et al., 2000). In many instances, however, there are no tests specifically marketed to measure single symptoms (e.g., there is, to our knowledge, currently no standardized commercially available test for measuring confabulation). In these cases, clinicians therefore typically just make observations or copy an experimental procedure reported in a research paper.

Behavioural and Functional Assessment

Many dysexecutive symptoms demonstrate themselves best outside tightly constrained situations, such as being formally assessed in a clinic. Ideally, therefore, the person being assessed should be observed in a naturalistic setting. Typically, this approach involves placing individuals into controlled situations in which specific variables are manipulated and responses noted. However, as Hart and Jacobs (1993) note, functional assessment procedures '… are generally not standardised or normed to populations'.

A useful exception is however the Multiple Errands Test (MET), originally described by Shallice and Burgess (1991a, b), where normative data do now exist (see Alderman et al., 2003). The MET is a shopping test, which is carried out in a real shopping precinct. The participant is given some money, and a list of tasks to carry out, which they have to do while following some simple rules (e.g., 'don't go into a shop unless it is to buy something'). The individual tasks themselves are simple (e.g., 'buy a loaf of bread' or 'find out the film times at the local cinema'), but the rules increase the planning, monitoring and prospective memory demands of the task. Figure 9.1a shows a diagrammatic representation of the performance of a typical control on the MET, and Figure 9.1b shows the performance of an age- and education-matched patient who has suffered frontal lobe damage, taken from the study by Shallice and Burgess (1991a). A key aspect here is that, despite this severely impaired performance in an everyday life-type situation, the patient performed normally or near-normally on an extensive range of neuropsychological tests, including traditional tests of executive function. Thus traditional executive tests may not always measure functions (in this case, multitasking) that can be crucial to effective performance in everyday life. In fact, the MET has been shown to be extremely sensitive to neurological problems: in a recent study, 82% of a mixed aetiology neurological group performed below the 5% level of age and reading IQ-matched controls on a version of this task (Alderman et al., 2003; see Burgess, 2000 for a review of multitasking deficits).

There are of course strengths and weaknesses to functional assessment of this kind. Weaknesses, for instance, are that examiners have to actually leave the cosy examination room and deal with the unforeseeable hitches that can occur in the real world; no two assessments are exactly alike since small changes in the environment will occur (different weather, interactions with the public, etc.), and the

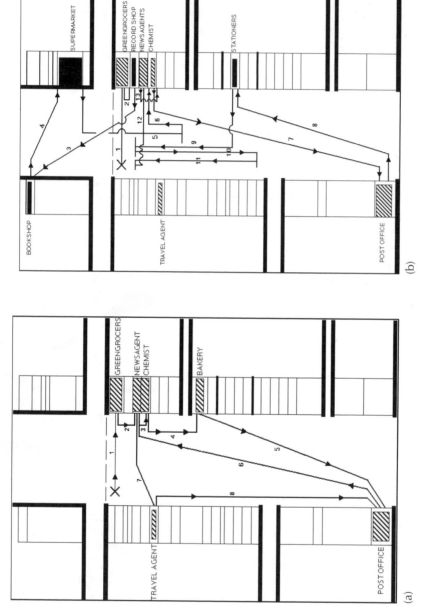

Figure 9.1. Performance on the Multiple Errands Test (Shallice & Burgess, 1991a). (a) Schematic representation of a typical control performance on Shallice and Burgess's (1991a) Multiple Errands Test. (b) (Impaired) performance of a patient with frontal lobe damage who was matched to the control for intellectual functioning, and who also performed well on 10 traditional clinical tests of executive function (see Shallice & Burgess, 1991a for further details). Hatched shading indicates shops that need to be entered in order to complete the test. Solid block shading indicates shops that either do not need to be entered, or are forbidden by the task rules

specificity of the tasks (i.e., the degree to which they measure a specific cognitive ability rather than many) may be less than for some neuropsychological tests. However the strengths are very considerable, given that a structured task with normative information is used. For instance, one can observe social interactions and see how the participant behaves when obvious cues to appropriate behaviour are absent. They can also be good tests of functions, such as prospective memory, planning and multitasking, which are difficult to test well in the laboratory, but are very important to everyday competence. Moreover, the tasks may be very closely related to everyday life, so ecological validity is high. Generally, such procedures yield large amounts of useful information in fairly short time periods and touch upon very important areas (e.g., social interaction) that cannot be easily assessed in the examination room. Moreover, they are not as difficult to arrange as one might think. For instance, Knight et al. (2002) describe the way in which a MET-type procedure can be adapted to any hospital (or similar) environment. Consequently, we recommend the use of these procedures (alongside more formal methods), where at all feasible.

SOME IMPORTANT FINAL WORDS CONCERNING EXECUTIVE FUNCTION ASSESSMENT

Dissociations in Performance Between Executive Tasks are Perfectly Natural and Very Instructive

No theorist these days seriously holds that the entire frontal lobe region (almost a third of the total brain mass) subserves just one function. Although the use of the term 'dysexecutive syndrome' is a convenient label, it is a misnomer: symptoms do not invariably cluster together. It is natural therefore that patients will show various patterns of impairments, and, while it is true that some symptoms seem to co-occur more frequently than others (Burgess et al., 1998), one should not expect failure on one executive test to predict failure on another. To demonstrate this point, Table 9.2 reports performance differences in individual patients who have circumscribed cerebral lesions on a test of response initiation and inhibition (sections 1 and 2, respectively, of the Hayling Test; Burgess & Shallice, 1997) and a test of rule attainment (Brixton Test; Burgess & Shallice, 1997). In the Hayling Test, participants are asked to verbally complete 30 spoken sentences, from which the last word is omitted. In the first half (initiation condition), they complete the sentences with a word that makes sense. In the second half (inhibition condition), they have to supply a word that is unconnected to the context of the sentence (e.g., 'London is a very busy ... *banana*'). For the initiation condition the measure is response latency. For the inhibition condition it is also the degree to which the answer is unconnected to the sentence. Patients often fail by just straightforwardly completing the sentence, although they often make less obvious types of failure, including bizarre and inappropriate responses. For instance, one frontal patient was presented with the

Table 9.2. Brixton–Hayling Test dissociations (percentiles)

Lesion	Age	Brixton	Hayling 1	Hayling 2 errors	Difference[1]
Right frontal	47	62	—	2	60**
Left frontal	28	76	8	—	68**
Left frontal	49	0.1	—	82	>82**
Left frontal	49	0.1	67	—	>66**
Right frontal	31	—	1	76	75**
Left frontal	54	—	66	0.1	>66**

[1] The percentile difference between the two scores.
** Indicates that the difference between the scores is significant at the < 0.01 level after reliability is taken into account.

sentence, 'The whole town came to hear the mayor . . .' and gave the response 'fart through a megaphone'.

With the Brixton Test, the participant is shown a 56-page stimulus book, one page at a time. All pages contain 10 circles in the same basic rectangular array. Only one circle is filled on each page, and patients have to predict where the next filled position will be, based on what they have seen in the previous pages. Deficits in rule attainment, initiation and inhibition are some of the commonest executive impairments. However, as Table 9.2 shows, even these symptoms may be seen independently of each other.

Do Not Overinterpret Differences in Performance on Two Tests

The typically modest reliability of executive function tests does not permit the clinician to make much of differences in performance on two tests. It is not uncommon to see reports that cite as noteworthy that the examinee scored, say, at the 25th percentile on one test and at the 75th percentile on another. This is quite incorrect. Both scores are within the normal range, and, if the variation in performance that occurs quite naturally given the reliability of the tests is taken into account, a performance discrepancy of this size would almost certainly be unremarkable. In general, one should only take note of discrepancies where one score is very low (e.g., 5th percentile or preferably below) and the other is comfortably within the average range (see Table 9.2 for examples).

Failure on an Executive Test Does Not Mean the Patient Has Frontal Lobe Damage

In most circumstances it is not correct to assert that, since someone fails an executive test, they probably have frontal lobe damage (or damage to any part of the brain for that matter).

The probability of the test failure being caused by frontal lobe dysfunction varies considerably with the circumstance. Let us assume that we use a cut-off for 'failure' as the 5th percentile level of healthy age- and premorbid IQ-matched controls. Now let us consider the following fairly typical circumstances:

1 Somebody randomly selected from the general population fails one's chosen executive task. They have no obvious neurological history. What is the probability that they have frontal lobe dysfunction?

The answer is that the probability is considerably greater that this person is absolutely normal from a neurological point of view than it is that they have frontal lobe dysfunction. Five per cent of the population will score at or below the cut-off point chosen here (i.e., 1 in 20 people). That is a lot of people and certainly a very much larger group than the number of people in the population who have frontal lobe dysfunction due to an undetected neurological condition. So it is more likely, by far, that the test participant is neurologically normal.

2 A person is referred for neuropsychological assessment. The patient is complaining of non-specific symptoms that may (or may not) have a neurological origin. CT and MRI scans have shown nothing, and there are no 'hard' neurological signs.

The probability here is extremely difficult (perhaps impossible) to calculate. The person neither belongs to a randomly selected sample of the healthy population nor to the patient sample used in the test development (say, for the Hayling and Brixton Tests, 75% with tumours and the rest mainly vascular events, all with brain damage confirmed by CT or MRI). It seems likely that the probability that their test failure is a result of frontal brain damage lies somewhere between the probabilities in these two groups. However, that gives such a wide range that it is practically useless. It would therefore be safer to conclude nothing at all regarding the likelihood of brain damage in this case. One does not have enough information on which to base a judgement.

3 A person with brain damage confirmed by brain scan (e.g., MRI/CT) fails the executive task.

The situation here is quite different. Table 9.3 shows the cumulative percentiles for four groups on the Hayling Test (i.e., healthy control participants, people with acute lesions [mainly tumours] that involve the frontal lobes, those whose lesions fall outside the frontal lobes and those whose lesions involve the frontal lobes bilaterally). We can quite clearly see that if we take, for instance, a scaled score of 2 as our criterion, then *proportionally* 10 times as many patients with frontal lobe damage performed at this level (41%) than controls (4%).

However, these kinds of statistics need to be understood clearly. They apply where one *already knows* which group the people belong to. If one does not know for sure whether they have a neurological condition or not, then in deciding upon the probability of a poor performance being indicative of frontal lobe dysfunction, one needs to consider the relative sizes of the different populations from which one might be sampling (see point 1). Only in the situation where someone presents with a known lesion, therefore, and fails an executive test is one entitled to say that it is more probable that the brain damage has caused an impairment in the processes tapped by

Table 9.3. Cumulative percentages for Hayling 2 errors[1]

Group	Scaled score							
	1	2	3	4	5	6	7	8
Controls[2]	0	4	7	8	13	34	69	100
Posteriors[3]	0	7	7	7	18	48	85	100
Anteriors[4]	26	41	47	68	87	100		
Bifrontals[5]	53	77	77	77	95	95	100	

[1] This table indicates, for instance, that 4% of controls attained a scaled score of 2 on the Hayling Test (section 2 errors subscale), but 77% of the bifrontal group attained this score or below and 53% of bifrontals were worse than any control (data from the study by Burgess & Shallice, 1996). Please note that, for all patient groups, exclusion criteria included marked aphasia and all patients were able to complete an extensive clinical neuropsychological assessment.
[2] A group of 118 healthy controls with no neurological or psychiatric history; for further details see Burgess and Shallice (1997).
[3] 27 acute neurological patients with circumscribed unilateral lesions outside the frontal lobes confirmed by CT or MRI brain scan.
[4] 47 patients whose lesions involved the frontal lobes unilaterally.
[5] 17 patients with bilateral lesions confined to the frontal lobes.

the test than that the poor performance is reflective of the naturally occurring variation in ability that occurs in the healthy population.

It is *still* however incorrect to conclude that the test scores indicate frontal lobe damage. The test score *indicates a functional impairment that is often associated with* frontal lobe damage (see also Chapter 1). There is no direct necessary link between the test performance and the state of a particular part of the brain. One must at all times remember that an executive test measures function and does *not* directly measure structural integrity, biochemistry, electrophysiology or any other biophysical property of the brain. If one is still not convinced by this logic, consider again the data in Table 9.3. This clearly indicates that some people with frontal lobe damage will not fail the executive test and some people with damage outside the frontal lobes will do so. This may be because the people who were not impaired did not have damage to those particular subregions of the frontal lobes that cause impairment. However, one should also consider that the complexity of the demands made by even the simplest test, together with the highly interconnected nature of the brain, means that it is extremely unlikely that we will ever be able to localize a function entirely to one discrete area of the brain. This is not a failure of the test, but just reflects nature. It is also important to bear in mind that in the sample from which the data in Table 9.3 were taken, the Hayling Test was *much* more specifically associated with frontal lobe damage (contrasted with damage elsewhere) than a number of other executive function tests for which we had data.

What then can be learnt by considering all three situations together? Well, in the case of situation 1 one would be wrong to conclude that the test score suggests brain dysfunction. In the case of situation 2 one would be reckless to do so, since one does not have enough information on which to base such a judgement. In the case of situation 3 the question of whether the test score suggests brain damage is irrelevant, since the brain scans have already provided the answer. There are many other situations that one might consider—space does not permit describing them all—where one would come to similar conclusions. So, to summarize, only under very special circumstances might it be accurate, sensible or useful to suggest that a test score indicates that someone has brain damage. The role of the neuropsychological assessment is to measure *function*, not brain integrity.

REHABILITATION OF THE DYSEXECUTIVE SYNDROME

Many approaches to the rehabilitation of impaired executive functions have been reported in the last decade. However, as the dysexecutive problems one encounters are multidimensional, there can be no single treatment approach that will be useful for them all (see Mateer, 1999; Robertson, 1999, for reviews). Interventions reported in the literature are influenced by a number of variables. Some are clearly driven by cognitive models of executive functioning (see, e.g. Burgess & Alderman, 1990; Sohlberg et al., 1993). Others attempt to alleviate problems through circumventing the underlying executive impairment, often by training people to use external aids that act as cueing systems (e.g., Burke et al., 1991; Zec et al., 1992). Further methods adopt a process-oriented approach to rehabilitation in which the goal is to stimulate recovery of cognitive functioning and promote reorganization of cortical function (see Sohlberg et al., 1993 for a review of this work).

Treatment interventions can also be differentiated by the problem they are attempting to alleviate at the *construct* level (see Burgess & Robertson, 2002 for further explanation). For example, Stuss and Benson (1986) describe many functional problems in terms of difficulties with anticipation, goal selection, planning, organization, initiation, execution and self-regulation of goal-directed activity. Alternatively, problems may be described functionally, perhaps highlighted through use of the DEX questionnaire or similar (see section on structured interviewing on p. 186). We will consider first the different general approaches and then progress to the more individual construct and symptom-based approaches.

The Therapeutic Milieu Approach

This approach attempts to ameliorate dysexecutive problems through involvement in a whole therapeutic milieu, rather than through individual treatments aimed at specific problems that are manipulated in turn. Von Cramon and Matthes-von Cramon (1994) argue that most people with dysexecutive syndrome present with both cognitive and behavioural difficulties and are therefore best treated through 'holistic' rehabilitation that involves both cognitive retraining and psychotherapeutic techniques. Successful outcomes have been reported in response to such multidimensional programmes, most notably from within North America (e.g., Ben-Yishay & Diller, 1978, 1983; Ben-Yishay et al., 1985; Prigatano, 1986; Scherzer, 1986).

All treatment approaches have their strengths and weaknesses. In this case, there are limiting variables that place some restrictions on who is able to participate in such programmes. One of these is the length of time required for treatment. Von Cramon and Matthes-von Cramon (1994) claim that most holistic rehabilitation programmes require the individual's participation for up to two years. It should be noted, however, that these authors designed a problem-solving programme of six weeks' duration and reported good outcome (von Cramon & Matthes-von Cramon, 1992).

Moreover, regardless of the duration of the programme, the criteria for determining which participants may be suitable for these programmes appear to be particularly stringent. For example, in order to be eligible to participate in the programme reported by von Cramon and Matthes-von Cramon (1992), individuals must be able to concentrate for at least 20 minutes, have insight into the nature of their problems, be motivated and free from significant behavioural problems, be able to think in abstract terms, have no significant memory impairment and no visuoperceptual deficits or major language disorders. Unfortunately, these criteria will exclude a significant proportion of potential participants.

Modification of the Environment

This approach attempts to alleviate problems by circumventing the need to use the (damaged) executive system or, by providing external aids, individuals may use it to subsume the function that has become impaired. Some of these strategies may be particularly effective for individuals whose executive dysfunction is very impaired and for whom the ability to initiate routine behaviour has been lost. For example, Sohlberg et al. (1993) describe modifying the environment to include visual prompts (such as labels) and verbal prompts (including audiotaped 'action messages'). Modification of the environment may also include the use of trained facilitators, who can direct the individual's actions, thereby acting as a kind of 'substitute executive system'. In this respect, education of carers is paramount. Another approach is to use such people in conjunction with a programme that aims to return the client to some form of useful, productive employment (i.e., a 'job coach'), since problems with executive functioning are acknowledged to play a significant role in determining outcome (e.g., see Brantner, 1992).

Behavioural Retraining of Specific Action Sequences

Attempts to reteach previously automatic behaviour that has become lost have also been reported and are best pursued using a behaviour modification approach (e.g., Fussey & Giles, 1988; Wood 1987). First, a task analysis is undertaken regarding the behaviour to be retrained; this may most frequently concern activities of daily living, including personal hygiene skills. Next, the behaviour is broken down into a discrete number of steps, or task-parts. The individual is then asked to engage in the behaviour (e.g., to wash and dress). If no action is forthcoming, or when the sequence of the task-parts is deviated from, staff intervene and prompt the individual to engage in the appropriate behaviour. The number of 'independents' (i.e., task-parts carried out without the necessity of staff intervention) and prompts given are recorded. Training sessions should take place frequently and regularly in order to facilitate learning. In the case of hygiene skills this would be daily. When behavioural problems co-exist, it will be necessary to introduce additional strategies to manage these (e.g., Alderman & Knight, 1997). Successful learning is demonstrated by a reduction in the number of prompts and an increase in task-parts carried out independently with the passage of time. With regular repetition, these behaviours become over-learned, habitual and automatic. The ideal conclusion to such training would be that the individual would simply need one prompt to get washed and dressed in order to initiate a routine that was once again automatic. These very structured approaches can be used successfully with patients whose problems are quite severe.

Use of External Aids to Initiate Action Sequences

In the case of people for whom the basic 'units of behaviour' or schemas (see Burgess, 1997) are reasonably intact, higher level executive impairment may be the chief problem. When this is the case, ongoing behaviour may not be modified appropriately in response to changing conditions, or it may be poorly sequenced, or triggered at inappropriate times or places (Sohlberg et al., 1993).

When this is the case, external cueing systems may be used with great effect in order to facilitate appropriate initiation and sequencing of automatic behaviours. A good example of this approach has been reported by Burke et al. (1991), in which improvement in three executive functions was reported and illustrated through presentation of six individual case studies. The executive functions were problem-solving (the ability to develop plans and modify them when appropriate), self-initiation (the ability to carry out plans) and self-monitoring/self-regulation (increased ability to monitor and regulate goal-directed performance). Immediate improvement was brought about through the use of an external aid, in the form of an initiation checklist or through use of a notebook. Additional improvement occurred when a facilitator gave regular feedback about behaviour and when a problem-solving component was introduced following use of the external aids. Data concerning all six case studies reflected significant improvement to those areas of function targeted for treatment and good maintenance of the improvements.

Other examples of the use of external aids to facilitate initiation of behaviour are reported in the literature. For example, Zec et al. (1992) described the use of an 'executive board system', the heart of which consists of 'job cards'. These break down a task into the components of command, analysis and reinforcement analysis. The information on a card acts to cue and reinforce behaviour, by organizing and advertising the tasks that require completion, the steps required and the consequences of task completion. In this way, the method constitutes a self-help system. Another example of this approach has been reported by Sohlberg and Mateer (1989), who described a three-phase behavioural approach that trained notebook use to improve executive and memory problems. The first phase educated the user about how the system worked. Practice in the use of the notebook as an aid to help plan and execute tasks was carried out in the second stage, while generalization of the system was considered in the third.

Recently, the use of a radio paging system developed primarily for use with memory impaired people, NeuroPage (Hersh & Treadgold, 1994), has been explored in relation to treatment of dysexecutive impairment. NeuroPage consists of a simple pager, with a screen, which is attached to the belt of the user (see also Chapters 7, 16 and 19). It is used in conjunction with a micro-computer system that is linked via a modem to a commercial paging company. Reminders are entered into the microcomputer and from there sent out to the paging company for transmission on the designated date and time.

Wilson et al. (1997) reported the effectiveness of NeuroPage in a study that involved 15 neurologically damaged people. All had memory problems, while some had additional impairment of executive functions. Before the trial, only 37.05% of tasks requiring action were completed independently across the patient group. While using NeuroPage, this dramatically improved to 84.46%. During the three-week period immediately following withdrawal of the system, the average number of tasks completed independently across the participants decreased only marginally, to 74.46%. However, the authors noted that there was considerable inter-individual variability in the maintenance of improvement at this stage of the trial. For example, some people's performance did not deteriorate at all, while others returned to baseline levels. The authors argued that a particular impairment of executive function was responsible for the lack of continued improvement in these cases. This hypothesis was explored in detail in a case where memory impairment was itself secondary to the presence of a dysexecutive syndrome: use of NeuroPage was again demonstrated to be helpful (Evans et al., 1998). Two important advantages of the NeuroPage system are its simplicity and relatively low running costs.

Changing Action in Response to Changes in the Environment: 'Metacognitive Strategies'

Despite their efficacy, the use of external aids (perhaps with the exception of other people acting as facilitators) may remain vulnerable to abrupt, unforeseen changes occurring within the environment. Under these conditions, the classic dysexecutive characteristic of failure to modify ongoing action in response to changing circumstances may become apparent.

One method to remediate this difficulty may be to use so-called 'metacognitive' strategies (Sohlberg et al., 1993). These treatment techniques are based around some methods routinely used in cognitive therapy, particularly self-instructional strategies (for examples of this see Cicerone and Giacino, 1992; Cicerone & Wood, 1987; Sohlberg et al., 1988; von Cramon & Matthes-von Cramon, 1990). For the more impaired patient, who lacks the necessary cognitive skills to engage successfully in such training, similar results may be attained by using combinations of more overt behaviour modification methods (Alderman & Ward, 1991), although this is likely to take longer.

Attentional Retraining

We move now to the 'construct-based' treatments. These aim to rehabilitate a specific set of hypothetical cognitive processes. The most prevalent of these is probably attentional retraining. Deficits in attentional processes are hypothesized to drive many of the functional problems that characterize the dysexecutive syndrome. In particular, impairment in the central executive component of working memory may lead to inefficiency in the allocation of attentional resources (Baddeley, 1986; Baddeley & Wilson, 1988). Difficulties with attending to two or more sets of stimuli simultaneously may show itself as problems with monitoring one's own performance, or in noticing changes in the environment, and can result in problems in utilizing feedback. It is this reduced perception of feedback that has been hypothesized to result in failure to modify behaviour in response to changing circumstances (Alderman, 1996; Alderman et al., 1995). Individuals with these problems may benefit from attentional retraining (e.g., see Burke et al., 1991; Freeman et al., 1992; Lawson & Rice, 1989; Sohlberg et al., 1988, 1993; von Cramon & Matthes von-Cramon, 1994; Zec et al., 1992).

The distinction between attentional retraining and improving self-monitoring skills (which is described below) may in fact just reflect the context in which the therapeutic activity takes place, since the aim in both cases is to improve the efficacy of the central executive component of working memory. Attentional retraining is typically undertaken using computer-mediated exercises, with the assumption that improvements evident on these tasks will generalize to other contexts. On the other hand, attempts to improve self-monitoring are usually made directly in the functional situation itself.

Investigations into the effectiveness of attentional retraining have reported mixed success (see also Chapter 11). However, Gray et al. (1992) have argued that this apparent inconsistency is at least in part the result of some investigators conceptualizing attention as a unitary phenomena. They highlight instead its multidimensional nature, including a component that deals with control and resource allocation, and argue that functional problems arise when attentional resources are not allocated appropriately in complex situations, leading in particular to distractibility and difficulties in dealing with multiple tasks.

As a consequence of this, Gray et al. (1992) described a programme in which microcomputer-delivered attentional training tasks were used with a group of 17 brain-injured people. These tasks were selected because they made demands on a number of attentional processes, including increased alerting, manipulating material in working memory, alternating attention and dividing attention. Training took place over 14 sessions of 75 minutes each, over 3–9 weeks. A matched control group of 14 brain-injured people were also exposed to a range of recreational computing activities over a comparable time period, and a battery of psychometric tests was administered before and after training to both groups.

The group that received the attentional retraining achieved significantly better scores on measures relating to auditory verbal working memory at follow-up. This was not attributable to factors such as IQ, motivation, general stimulation or spontaneous recovery; most improvement was evident on tests involving storage and manipulation of numerical material in working memory. Furthermore, improvement continued after training stopped. The authors argued that this was attributable to the attentional strategies acquired during training becoming increasingly automated and integrated into a wider range of behaviours and that the improvements made represented real-life gains, reflecting improvement in working memory.

Improving Self-monitoring Skills

As mentioned above, one manifestation of attentional problems is a deficit in self-monitoring (i.e., being aware of one's effect upon the environment and others, and picking up on cues and environmental changes in order to modulate one's own behaviour). Changes in the attentional processes that permit the switching of the focus of one's attention, or the dividing of attention between many sources, can cause problems with self-monitoring. Self-monitoring training differs from attentional training in that it is usually undertaken *in situ*. Alderman et al. (1995) described a programme of self-monitoring training (SMT) that had two specific aims: first, to improve the ability of the individual to attend to multiple events and, second, once this has been established, to reduce the behaviour of concern using an appropriate operant strategy. They argued that the latter would only be effective when the ability to attend to multiple events, and in particular to monitor one's own behaviour and modify it in response to change in the environment, is possible. The training involved the following five stages:

- *Stage 1—baseline.* The therapist first obtained a baseline of the target behaviour.
- *Stage 2—spontaneous self-monitoring.* In the second stage, the participant was instructed to monitor the target behaviour while conducting some background task over a discrete time period. The participant was given an external counting device to enable them to achieve this (a mechanical 'clicker', whereby each time a button is pressed a number display is advanced by one digit). At the same time, the therapist discretely monitored the behaviour using a similar device. At the end of the trial, the therapist compared their recording with that of the participant.
- *Stage 3—prompted self-monitoring.* Stage 2 was repeated with one modification: each time the participant engaged in the target behaviour, but did not record it, the therapist gave a verbal prompt that they should do so. The purpose of this stage of the training was to encourage the participant to monitor their own behaviour more accurately and get into the habit of routinely making a recording whenever it occurred.
- *Stage 4—independent self-monitoring and accuracy reward.* The purpose of this stage was to withdraw external structure and facilitate self-monitoring by reinforcing accuracy within gross limits. This involved explaining to the participant

that they would receive a reward at the end of the trial, providing the recording they made was accurate to within 50% of that made by the therapist. During the trial itself, prompts to record would not be given to the participant.

• *Stage 5—independent self-monitoring and reduction of the target behaviour.* The aim of the final stage of training was to encourage inhibition of the target behaviour using an appropriate operant strategy. To this aim, the patient was rewarded at the end of a trial, providing they had met a specified criterion (e.g., a certain number of occasions of the target behaviour). During the training period, they continued to use the external counter to monitor behaviour in an effort to keep within the limit that had been set. With success, this target was gradually reduced until the target behaviour was eliminated, or occurred infrequently. Of course, the point is that successful participation in the operant stage of the training is only possible because it has been preceded by improvement in the accuracy of multiple-monitoring skills.

In the original case described by Alderman et al. (1995), considerable reduction in a very frequent, disruptive target behaviour was achieved using SMT. It had not been possible to develop inhibitory control over this behaviour previously using other operant approaches due to a gross impairment in monitoring skills. Furthermore, this improvement was still evident when reassessed some months after the training had been completed (see also an example of SMT to treat confabulation: Dayus & van den Broek, 2000).

Executive Strategy Training to Generalize Other Cognitive Skills

Finally, it should be noted that the rehabilitation of other cognitive functions should not only include training to improve that domain but executive strategy training to enable those skills to be used outside the training context. For example, Lawson and Rice (1989) argued that the lack of generalization noted in some studies that had attempted to improve memory function could be attributed to the absence of the therapist, who had previously acted as the external executive system for the individual. Use of self-instructional approaches, such as those described by Lawson and Rice, attempts to facilitate the use of skills taught in rehabilitation so that individuals may use them in a spontaneous manner when they are required.

Single Symptom Rehabilitation Methods

These are methods that are specifically aimed at one particular dysexecutive symptom, rather than a class of them. An example would be, for instance, Burgess and McNeil's (1999) use of a diary method to treat a case of confabulation. The limiting factor for the development of these treatment methods is our under-standing of these extraordinary symptoms and their inter-individual variability. However, this certainly does not mean that they will not in time become highly influential, as our basic scientific knowledge of the rarer disorders increases.

CONCLUSIONS

'Executive function' is one of the newest fields of human neuropsychology. Remarkable advances in our understanding have been made in the last 30 years or so, and we now have a range of assessment and treatment techniques that are specialized to this area and have been shown repeatedly to be effective. However, we still lack much basic information about how the brain supports executive functions, and this limits our understanding of how best to treat some of the problems that result from impairment. Fortunately, the speed at which new discoveries are being made, and techniques and procedures developed, is increasing and one can be optimistic about the future. This does mean, however, that the clinician must try to keep up with the latest developments and not be afraid to try new techniques and reject old ones as fresh evidence becomes available. In the meantime one would be wise, when assessing and treating executive function impairments, to be both open-minded and cautious in equal measure. Having acknowledged these limitations, however, one should note that we do not have the luxury of waiting until we have perfect knowledge before applying the best techniques currently available. Deficits of executive function that appear quite mild in the examination room can nevertheless have a devastating effect on everyday life functioning. Moreover, they can interfere with treatment progress in other areas. For this reason, assessment and treatment of executive deficits should be a priority for neurorehabilitation.

Acknowledgements

Paul Burgess is supported by Wellcome Trust grant number 061171/MW. We would like to thank Laure Coates for her help with the preparation of this chapter.

REFERENCES

Alderman, N. (1996) Central executive deficit and response to operant conditioning methods. *Neuropsychological Rehabilitation*, **6**, 161–186.

Alderman, N. & Knight, C. (1997) The effectiveness of DRL in the management and treatment of severe behaviour disorders following brain injury. *Brain Injury*, **11**, 79–101.

Alderman, N. & Ward, A. (1991) Behavioural treatment of the dysexecutive syndrome: Reduction of repetitive speech using response cost and cognitive overlearning. *Neuropsychological Rehabilitation*, **1**, 65–80.

Alderman, N., Fry, R. K. & Youngson, H. A. (1995) Improvement of self-monitoring skills, reduction of behaviour disturbance and the dysexecutive syndrome: Comparison of response cost and a new programme of self-monitoring training. *Neuropsychological Rehabilitation*, **5**, 193–221.

Alderman, N., Burgess, P. W., Knight, C. & Henman, C. (2003) Ecological validity of a simplified version of the multiple errands shopping test. *Journal of the International Neuropsychological Society*, **9**, 31–44.

Baddeley, A. D. (1986) *Working Memory*. Clarendon Press, Oxford, UK.

Baddeley, A. D. & Wilson, B. (1988) Frontal amnesia and the dysexecutive syndrome. *Brain and Cognition*, **7**, 212–230.

Ben-Yishay, Y. & Diller, L. (1978) *Working Approaches to Remediation of Cognitive Deficits in Brain Damaged Persons* (Rehabilitation Monographs No. 60). New York University Medical Center, New York.

Ben-Yishay, Y. & Diller, L. (1983) Cognitive deficits. In: M. Rosenthal (ed.) *Rehabilitation of the Head Injured Adult*. F.A. Davis, Philadelphia.

Ben-Yishay, Y., Rattock, J. & Lakin, P. (1985) Neuropsychological rehabilitation: Quest for a holistic approach. *Seminars in Neurology*, **5**, 252–259.

Berg, E. A. (1948) A simple objective technique for measuring flexibility in thinking. *The Journal of General Psychology*, **39**, 15–22.

Brantner, C. L. (1992) Job coaching for persons with traumatic brain injuries employed in professional and technical occupations. *Journal of Applied Rehabilitation Counselling*, **23**, 3–14.

Burgess, P. W. (1997) Theory and methodology in executive function research. In: P. Rabbitt (ed.) *Methodology of Frontal and Executive Function* (pp. 81–111). Psychology Press, Hove, UK.

Burgess, P. W. (2002) Strategy application disorder: The role of the frontal lobes in human multitasking. *Psychological Research*, **63**, 279–288.

Burgess, P. W. & Alderman, N. (1990) Rehabilitation of dyscontrol syndromes following frontal lobe damage: A cognitive neuropsychological approach. In: R. Ll. Wood & I. Fussey (eds) *Cognitive Rehabilitation in Perspective*. Taylor & Francis, Basingstoke, UK.

Burgess, P. W. & McNeil, J. E. (1999) Content-specific confabulation. *Cortex*, **35**, 163–182.

Burgess, P. W. & Robertson, I. H. (2002) Principles of the rehabilitation of frontal lobe function. In: D. T. Stuss & R. T. Knight (eds) *Principles of Frontal Lobe Function* (pp. 557–572). Oxford University Press, New York.

Burgess, P. W. & Shallice, T. (1996) Confabulation and the control of recollection. *Memory*, **4**, 359–411.

Burgess, P. W. & Shallice, T. (1997) *The Hayling and Brixton Tests*. Thames Valley Test Company, Bury St Edmunds, UK.

Burgess, P. W., Alderman, N., Emslie, H., Evans, J. J. & Wilson, B. A. (1996a) The Dysexecutive Questionnaire. In: B. A. Wilson, N. Alderman, P. W. Burgess, H. Emslie & J. J. Evans (eds) *Behavioural Assessment of the Dysexecutive Syndrome*. Thames Valley Test Company, Bury St Edmunds, UK.

Burgess, P. W., Alderman, N., Emslie, H., Evans, J. J., Wilson, B. A. & Shallice, T. (1996b) The simplified six element test. In: B. A. Wilson, N. Alderman, P. W. Burgess, H. Emslie & J. J. Evans (eds) *Behavioural Assessment of the Dysexecutive Syndrome*. Thames Valley Test Company, Bury St Edmunds, UK.

Burgess, P. W., Alderman, N., Evans, J., Emslie, H. & Wilson, B. A. (1998) The ecological validity of tests of executive function. *Journal of the International Neuropsychological Society*, **4**, 547–558.

Burgess, P. W., Veitch, E., de Lacy Costello, A. & Shallice, T. (2000) The cognitive and neuro-anatomical correlates of multitasking. *Neuropsychologia*, **38**, 848–863.

Burke, W. H., Zencius, A. H., Weslowski, M. D. & Doubleday, F. (1991) Improving executive function disorders in brain-injured clients. *Brain Injury*, **5**, 241–252.

Cicerone, K. D. & Giacino, J. T. (1992) Remediation of executive function deficits after traumatic brain injury. *Neuropsychological Rehabilitation*, **2**, 12–22.

Cicerone, K. D. & Wood, J. C. (1987) Planning disorder after closed head injury: A case study. *Archives of Physical Medicine Rehabilitation*, **68**, 111–115.

Cohen, J. D., Dunbar, K. & McClelland, J. L. (1990) On the control of automatic processes: A parallel distributed processing account of the Stroop effect. *Psychological Review*, **97**, 332–361.

Cohen, L. D., Braver, T. S. & O'Reilly, R. C. (1998) A computational approach to prefrontal cortex, cognitive control, and schizophrenia: Recent developments and current challenges. In: A. C. Roberts, T. W. Robbins & L. Weiskrantz (eds) *The Prefrontal Cortex: Executive and Cognitive Functions*. Oxford University Press, Oxford, UK.

Dayus, B. & van den Broek, M. D. (2000) Treatment of stable delusional confabulations using self-monitoring training. *Neuropsychological Rehabilitation*, **10**, 415–427.

Duncan, J., Burgess, P. W. & Emslie, H. (1995) Fluid intelligence after frontal lobe lesions. *Neuropsychologia*, **33**, 261–268.

Duncan, J., Seitz, R. J., Kolodny, J., Bor, D., Herzog, H., Ahmed, A. et al. (2000) A neural basis for intelligence. *Science*, **289**(5478), 457–460.

Evans, J. J, Emslie, H. & Wilson, B. A. (1998) External cueing systems in the rehabilitation of executive impairments of action. *Journal of the International Neuropsychological Society*, **4**, 399–408.

Freeman, M. R., Mittenberg, W., Dicowden, M. & Bat-Ami, M. (1992) Executive and compensatory memory retraining in traumatic brain injury. *Brain Injury*, **6**, 65–70.

Fussey, I. & Giles, G. M. (eds) (1988) *Rehabilitation of the Severely Brain Injured Adult: A Practical Approach*. Croom Helm, London.

Fuster, J. M. (1997) *The Prefrontal Cortex: Anatomy, Physiology and Neuropsychology of the Frontal Lobe* (3rd edn). Lippincott-Raven, Philadelphia.

Goldman-Rakic, P. S. (1995) Architecture of the prefrontal cortex and the central executive. *Annals of the New York Academy of Science*, **769**, 212–220.

Gray, J. M., Robertson, I., Pentland, B. & Anderson, S. (1992) Microcomputer-based attentional retraining after brain damage: A randomised group controlled study. *Neuropsychological Rehabilitation*, **2**, 97–115.

Hart, T. & Jacobs, H. E. (1993) Rehabilitation and management of behavioural disturbances following frontal lobe damage. *Journal of Head Trauma Rehabilitation*, **8**, 1–12.

Hersh, N. & Treadgold, L. (1994) NeuroPage: The rehabilitation of memory dysfunction by prosthetic memory and cueing. *Neurorehabilitation*, **4**, 187–197.

Knight, C., Alderman, N. & Burgess, P. W. (2002) Development of a simplified version of the multiple errands test for use in hospital settings. *Neuropsychological Rehabilitation*, **12**, 231–255.

Lawson, M. & Rice, D. (1989) Effects of training in use of executive strategies on a verbal memory problem resulting from closed head injury. *Journal of Clinical and Experimental Neuropsychology*, **11**, 842–854.

Mateer, C. A. (1999) The rehabilitation of executive disorders. In: D. T. Stuss, G. Winocur & I. H. Robertson (eds) *Cognitive Neurorehabilitation* (pp. 314–332). Cambridge University Press, Cambridge, UK.

Milner, B. (1963) Effects of different brain lesions on card-sorting. *Archives of Neurology*, **9**, 90–100.

Norman, D. & Shallice, T. (1986) Attention to action. In: R. J. Davidson, G. E. Schwartz & D. Shapiro (eds) *Consciousness and Self-Regulation* (pp. 1–18). Plenum Press, New York.

Petrides, M. (1998) Specialized systems for the processing of mnemonic information within the primate frontal cortex. In: A. C. Roberts, T. W. Robbins & L. Weiskrantz (eds) *The Prefrontal Cortex: Executive and Cognitive Functions* (pp. 103–116). Oxford University Press, Oxford, UK.

Petrides, M. & Milner, B. (1982) Deficits on subject-ordered tasks after frontal- and temporal-lobe lesions in man. *Neuropsychologia*, **20**, 249–262.

Prigatano, G. P. (1986) *Neuropsychological Rehabilitation after Brain Injury*. Johns Hopkins University Press, Baltimore.

Robertson, I. H. (1999) The rehabilitation of attention. In: D. T. Stuss, G. Winocur & I. H. Robertson (eds) *Cognitive Neurorehabilitation* (pp. 302–313). Cambridge University Press, Cambridge, UK.

Robertson, I. H., Ward, T., Ridgeway, V. & Nimmo-Smith, I. (1996) The structure of normal human attention: The Test of Everyday Attention. *Journal of the International Neuropsychological Society*, **2**, 525–534.

Robbins, T. W., James, M., Owen, A. M., Sahakian, B. J., McInnes, L. & Rabbit, P. (1994) Cambridge Neuropsychological Test Automated Battery (CANTAB): A factor analytic study of a large sample of normal elderly volunteers. *Dementia*, **5**, 266–281.

Scherzer, B. P. (1986) Rehabilitation following severe head trauma: Results of a three year program. *Archives of Physical Medicine and Rehabilitation*, **67**, 366–373.

Shallice, T. (1988) *From Neuropsychology to Mental Structure*. Cambridge University Press, New York.

Shallice, T. (2002) Fractionation of the Supervisory System. In: D. T. Stuss & R. T. Knight (eds) *Principles of Frontal Lobe Function* (pp. 261–277). Oxford University Press, New York.

Shallice, T. & Burgess, P. W. (1991a) Deficits in strategy application following frontal lobe damage in man. *Brain*, **114**, 727–741.

Shallice, T. & Burgess, P. W. (1991b) Higher-order cognitive impairments and frontal lobe lesions in man. In: H. S. Levin, H. M. Eisenberg & A. L. Benton (eds) *Frontal Lobe Function and Dysfunction* (pp. 125–138). Oxford University Press, New York.

Shallice, T. & Burgess, P. W. (1996) The domain of supervisory processes and the temporal organisation of behaviour. *Philosophical Transactions of the Royal Society of London, Series B*, **351**, 1405–1412.

Sohlberg, M. M. & Mateer, C. A. (1989) Training use of compensatory memory books: A three stage behavioural approach. *Journal of Clinical and Experimental Neuropsychology*, **11**, 871–891.

Sohlberg, M. M., Sprunk, H. & Metelaar, K. (1988) Efficacy of an external cueing system in an individual with severe frontal lobe damage. *Cognitive Rehabilitation*, **6**, 36–41.

Sohlberg, M. M., Mateer, C. A. & Stuss, D. T. (1993) Contemporary approaches to the management of executive control dysfunction. *Journal of Head Trauma Rehabilitation*, **8**, 45–58.

Spreen, O. & Strauss, E. (1998) *A Compendium of Neuropsychological Tests* (2nd edn). Oxford University Press, Oxford, UK.

Stuss, D. T. & Alexander, M. P. (2000) Executive functions and the frontal lobes: A conceptual view. *Psychological Research*, **63**, 289–298.

Stuss, D. T. & Benson, D. F. (1984) Neuropsychological studies of the frontal lobes. *Psychological Bulletin*, **95**, 3–28.

Stuss, D. T. & Benson, D. F. (1986) *The Frontal Lobes*. Raven Press, New York.

Stuss, D. T., Shallice, T., Alexander, M. P. & Picton, T. W. (1995) A multidisciplinary approach to anterior attentional functions. *Annals of the New York Academy of Sciences*, **769**, 191–211.

von Cramon, D. Y. & Matthes-von Cramon, G. (1990) Frontal lobe dysfunction in patients: Therapeutical approaches. In: R. Ll. Wood & I. Fussey (eds) *Cognitive Rehabilitation in Perspective*. Taylor & Francis, London.

von Cramon, D. Y. & Matthes-von Cramon, G. (1992) Reflections on the treatment of brain-injured patients suffering from problem-solving disorders. *Neuropsychological Rehabilitation*, **2**, 207–229.

von Cramon, D. Y & Matthes-von Cramon, G. (1994) Back to work with a chronic dysexecutive syndrome? *Neuropsychological Rehabilitation*, **4**, 399–417.

Wilson, B. A., Alderman, N., Burgess, P. W., Emslie, H. & Evans, J. J. (1996) *Behavioural Assessment of the Dysexecutive Syndrome*. Thames Valley Test Company, Bury St Edmunds, UK.

Wilson, B. A., Evans, J. J., Emslie, H. & Malinek, V. (1997) Evaluation of NeuroPage: A new memory aid. *Journal of Neurology, Neurosurgery and Psychiatry*, **6**, 113–115.

Wood, R. Ll. (1987) *Brain Injury Rehabilitation: A Neurobehavioural Approach*. Croom Helm, London.

Zec, R. F., Parks, R. W., Gambach, J. & Vicari, S. (1992) The executive board system: An innovative approach to cognitive-behavioural rehabilitation in patients with traumatic brain injury. In: C. J. Long & L. K. Ross (eds) *Handbook of Head Trauma: Acute Care to Recovery*. Plenum Press, New York.

CHAPTER 10

Disorders of Voluntary Movement

Laura H. Goldstein

Institute of Psychiatry, London, UK

INTRODUCTION

Apraxia, a disorder of voluntary movement, is commonly defined as an impairment in the ability to carry out learned or, in other definitions, purposeful voluntary movements, by an individual who has normal primary motor skills (strength, reflexes, co-ordination) and normal comprehension of the acts (and their constituent elements) to be carried out. In everyday life dyspraxia might manifest itself as a person being unable to spread butter on toast, squeeze toothpaste onto their toothbrush and clean their teeth or lay the table for a meal. In practice, as Tate and McDonald (1995) have pointed out, the above definition of apraxia is problematic since it becomes one of exclusion and is made more difficult by the presence of a neurodegenerative disorder where the damage is more widespread than would be due to a focal lesion. Even in the case of a cerebrovascular accident (CVA), sensory and motor deficits may coexist. However, Leiguarda and Marsden (2000) indicate that, since dyspraxic errors can be well defined, it is not inconsistent for them to exist in addition to weakness, rigidity, tremor, ataxia and dystonia.

Interest has long existed in the association between apraxia and aphasia. That both should occur in the same person who has sustained a left hemisphere injury is unsurprising, given the key role ascribed to left hemisphere damage in the development of apraxia. Indeed, the two disorders may coexist (Ajuriaguerra et al., 1960); while aphasia is commonly found without apraxia, it has been less common for apraxia to be found without aphasia (Papagno et al., 1993). However, examples of apraxia presenting without aphasia have been reported in left-hemisphere brain-damaged patients (e.g., De Renzi et al., 1980; Heilman et al., 1974; Selnes et al., 1991), and Papagno et al. (1993) have demonstrated a double dissociation between aphasia and apraxia. The same dissociation is also found in Alzheimer's disease, where apraxia is less common and less severe than aphasia (Della Sala et al., 1987; Spinnler & Della Sala, 1988). Tate and McDonald (1995) have pointed out that the relationship between aphasia and apraxia is not causal, but depends on the contiguity of the lesions in both conditions.

As Lezak (1995) indicates, given the potential complexity of voluntary movements, it is not surprising that apraxia can occur with disruption of brain systems

Clinical Neuropsychology: A Practical Guide to Assessment and Management for Clinicians.
Edited by L.H. Goldstein and J.E. McNeil. © 2004 John Wiley & Sons, Ltd.

that affect movements in different ways. Indeed, Luria (1973) used apraxia as an example of a *complex functional system* within the brain that defies a simple, unique localization. Thus while apraxia can be a sign of a focal brain lesion, the specific characteristics of the apraxia will be affected by where in the functional system that lesion has occurred.

Two very different approaches exist in the discussion of apraxia with respect to clinical issues. The first is pragmatic, recognizing inconsistencies in the terminology and in definitions of different types of apraxia. Lezak (1995), for example, does not distinguish between traditional categories of apraxia (see next paragraph), but adopts Kimura and Archibald's (1974) view that these relate to 'disturbances at different points in a hypothetical sequence of cognitive events involved in making a movement'. Lezak (1995), therefore, simply refers to 'apraxias', recommending Dee et al.'s (1970) use of functional labels (e.g., 'apraxia of symbolic actions', 'apraxia of utilisation of objects'). McCarthy and Warrington (1990) also note the inconsistency of terminology for disorders of voluntary action and the absence of a universally agreed classification scheme. They, to some extent like Lezak (1995) after them, adopt a functional, empirical task-oriented scheme in their description of such disorders.

The second approach, based on Liepmann's original model of apraxia, is to subdivide apraxias into at least three main categories: *ideomotor, ideokinetic* and *ideational* apraxia. Other disorders, often considered to be related, are *constructional apraxia* and *dressing apraxia*; however, controversy exists as to whether these latter disorders should truly be considered apraxias, or, rather, for example, a consequence of visuospatial disorders, disorientation or left-sided neglect (Heilman & Rothi, 1997), a 'disorder of construction' or 'constructional impairment' (see Lezak, 1995; Poeck, 1986; Tate & McDonald, 1995); these will not be considered in the current chapter. Tate and McDonald (1995) also note the absence of a single accepted taxonomy for apraxia and query the existence of ideokinetic (also called limb-kinetic) apraxia as a separate entity. Tate and McDonald (1995) conclude that there remain two classical forms of apraxia— ideomotor and ideational—and that despite problems in their definition, these terms remain difficult to avoid.

Thus although for clinical purposes it may be more important to note that a person has difficulty in the generation and execution of voluntary movements rather than in categorizing the deficits as ideomotor or ideational, it would seem necessary to discuss these categories and the extent to which they may overlap (e.g., Hanna-Pladdy & Rothi, 2001), if only to enable the clinician to feel at least somewhat familiar with the terminology used in this large and complex literature.

There are four testing conditions in which apraxia is typically described in clinical situations (Geschwind & Damasio, 1985). Thus apraxia may be observed when people fail to produce a correct movement in response to a verbal instruction, when they fail to imitate correctly a movement made by the examiner, to perform a movement correctly in response to a real, seen object or to handle an object correctly. However, the nature of a 'failure' has never been clearly defined (Tate & McDonald, 1995).

CLASSIFICATION OF APRAXIA

As noted above, the major forms of apraxia that are discussed in the literature are: (a) ideomotor apraxia and (b) ideational apraxia, although for current purposes it would seem sensible to at least describe briefly the third (mentioned above) ideo-kinetic (limb-kinetic) apraxia.

Ideomotor Apraxia

Ideomotor apraxia has been defined in different ways. Geschwind and Damasio (1985) indicate that it is the failure to carry out a requested movement properly. Rothi et al. (1991), however, have defined it as a disturbance 'in programming the timing, sequencing and spatial organisation of gestural movements.' Poeck (1986) considered the incorrect selection of movements and the incorrect sequencing of their elements to be paramount in ideomotor apraxia.

Ideomotor apraxia occurs in about 80% of patients who have a CVA in the middle cerebral artery of the dominant (usually left) hemisphere. Most of the reports of ideomotor apraxia concern dyspraxic movements originating in the upper limbs. Upper limb apraxia can be bilateral or unilateral. It can also occur in the lower limbs as well as in the orofacial musculature, although this is less commonly focused on. Some (Howes, 1988; Poeck et al., 1982) have also discussed the existence of dyspraxia involving the axial or midline body structures. This latter type of apraxia remains somewhat controversial (Tate & McDonald, 1995).

In principle, ideomotor apraxia is limited to single, simple gestures while the level of ideation needed for complex gestures is preserved. Thus complex acts can be executed, but their constituent elements are disturbed. Therefore, the overall goal of the action can be identified, but the movements required to attain it are incorrectly produced. The movements that are executed are generally of irregular speed and there are sequencing errors. In addition: there are characteristic spatial errors whereby movements are of the wrong amplitude; there is incorrect spatial orientation of objects and of movements in relation to these; abnormal hand and limb configurations are seen; and there is 'use of body-part-as-object' (see p. 222; Leiguarda & Marsden, 2000).

Ideomotor apraxia is traditionally thought to affect differentially the inten-tionality of movement, with automatic movements being spared. As a result it is thought that patients do not complain about the disorder, as it is not obvious in everyday activities, but only becomes apparent when the person is asked to perform the action in the clinical setting. More recently, however, this voluntary–automatic dissociation has been challenged by evidence suggesting that patients with ideomotor apraxia may nonetheless show difficulties in interact-ing with their everyday environment, where clumsy and awkward behaviour may be observed (Cubelli & Della Sala, 1996; De Renzi & Lucchelli, 1988). In addition, measures of ideomotor apraxia have predictive value with respect to everyday activities in a group of patients who had sustained left-hemisphere CVAs (Sundet et al., 1988).

Ideomotor apraxia is tested using response to verbal command and to imitation. Response to imitation may be better than to verbal command, but even on imitation the person's performance may remain partly impaired; this is important in distinguishing this defect from aphasia.

As a complaint, ideomotor apraxia may quickly resolve post-brain insult (usually a stroke), but Basso et al. (1987) found that 50% of their series remained apraxic five or more months post onset and 20% at one year or more. In most patients recovery from apraxia takes place in the first few months after its development and then reaches a plateau (Basso et al., 2000, 2002). However, its true incidence and time course may be hard to ascertain given the general view that ideomotor apraxia is only elicited on formal testing and not in everyday activities.

Ideokinetic or Limb-kinetic Apraxia

Patients with limb-kinetic apraxia demonstrate a loss of deftness, including fine and precise movements and independent finger movements, and they have difficulty in co-ordinating simultaneous movements (Heilman et al., 2000). The movements in limb-kinetic apraxia are 'coarse and mutilated', and the benefit gained by practice is lost; movements become 'clumsy, awkward and rough' (Leiguarda & Marsden, 2000). They note that imitation of finger postures is often incorrect and extraneous movements may contaminate responses. Everyday actions are affected as much as when tested formally. Limb-kinetic apraxia occurs in the context of neurodegenerative disorders, such as corticobasal degeneration and Pick's disease.

Ideational Apraxia

Ideational apraxia is seen when the person attempts to carry out a complex gesture, such as striking a match to light a candle, or when miming how they would make a cup of tea. Although individual elements of the total act may be executed correctly, there is disruption in the logical sequencing of these elements. Thus the overall act is incorrectly performed because the normal sequence of movements is altered. The disorder is bilateral and general, rather than segmented with respect to body parts.

Within the literature ideational apraxia has been defined in a number of ways (see, e.g., Hanna-Pladdy & Rothi, 2001). Thus it is not uncommon for Liepmann's original concept of ideational apraxia to be used, this being defined as 'a disturbance in the performance of complex actions involving the serial ordering of simple movements, which in isolation could be executed correctly' (see Poeck & Lehmkuhl, 1980). De Renzi and colleagues, however, have adopted Morlaas's early definition whereby ideational apraxia is a disturbance in the use of real objects and in simple as well as complex serial movements (see Poeck & Lehmkuhl, 1980; Tate & McDonald, 1995). Pick (1905; cited in Leiguarda & Marsden, 2000) had considered that ideational apraxia involved the inability to undertake a series of acts involving the use of several objects, whereas others have indicated that it refers to the inability to use single objects correctly. Others refer to conceptual apraxia, whereby patients 'exhibit primarily content errors in the per-formance of transitive movements' (Leiguarda & Marsden, 2000): examples include a person using a toothbrush as if it were a shaver, or selecting an inadequate object to complete a task rather than a more appropriate one, when the best tool is not available. They also note that those with this type of apraxia may fail to describe the function of a tool, even when they are able to name it when it is shown to them. Those with ideational apraxia may be unable to recognize correct and incorrect sequences of actions that are depicted in photographs (Poeck, 1983).

With ideational apraxia, problems are seen in everyday life with familiar actions (e.g., when cooking, eating breakfast or changing a plug) and are not just evident in the testing situation. Leiguarda and Marsden (2000) indicate that this is because the person uses tools or objects incorrectly, mis-selects tools or objects for an intended activity, performs a complex sequence of tasks in the wrong order or does not complete the task at all (Foundas et al., 1995). Thus the person may show patterns of behaviour that stop when the act is only partially completed, or the person may confound the order of steps necessary to complete the task; evidence of perseveration of motor acts is common. It is a rare disorder, seen in patients with dominant hemisphere lesions; it is not however due to poor comprehension of what the person is required to do.

Initially, 'ideational apraxia' was applied to people with both sequencing and conceptual errors. More recently, it has been used to classify those individuals who are unable to perform a series of acts leading to a goal (e.g., making a cup of tea), whereas the term 'conceptual apraxia' describes a loss of knowledge of tool–action and tool–object associations and other forms of mechanical knowledge (Heilman & Rothi, 1997). Thus, according to Roy and Square (1985), while patients with ideomotor apraxia make spatial and timing errors, those with conceptual apraxia make content errors (e.g., using a tube of toothpaste to brush one's teeth: Ochipa et al., 1989). Ochipa et al. (1992) described a range of errors that might be made by those with conceptual apraxia. These occurred in the domains of: *tool–action* associations—knowing the types of movements that are associated with particular objects (e.g., twisting movements associated with a screw cap); *tool–object* associations—knowing the type of object that works with a specific object (e.g., using scissors to cut paper); the *mechanical advantage* afforded by tools/mechanical knowledge (e.g., that if a hammer is not available to hit a nail, then a wrench would be preferable to an ice-pick); and *tool fabrication* or the ability to make a tool (e.g., the ability to make a wire key to open a car door). Raymer and Ochipa (1997) express a preference for the term *conceptual apraxia* over *ideational apraxia*, because of the different ways in which ideational apraxia has been defined.

How Clear Are the Distinctions between Ideomotor and Ideational Apraxia?

In general, ideomotor and ideational apraxia are considered to represent two separate disorders. The inability to pantomime and/or imitate (e.g., salute, make brushing movements as if to brush teeth, copy a movement) is characteristic of ideomotor apraxia, whereas the inability to use multiple objects in a serial order (e.g., place toothpaste on toothbrush and brush teeth) usually defines ideational apraxia. However, the extent to which these two disorders are really distinct is unclear, this confusion relating to the different definitions of the disorders and the possible relationship between single and multiple object use (De Renzi & Lucchelli, 1988; Neiman et al., 2000). Poizner et al. (1990) noted that the movement of spatial and timing errors, which might be characteristic of pantomimed actions in ideomotor apraxia, were observed albeit to a less severe degree even when patients with ideomotor apraxia used real objects or tools. Thus it may not always be possible to separate out patients with each type of disorder since object use *per se* can be impaired, irrespective of the need to undertake a sequence of movements involving object use.

Other Classifications of Apraxia

In addition to the classification of apraxia outlined above, apraxia has been sub-divided on the basis of anatomical considerations. Thus, for example, *callosal apraxia* results from naturally or surgically induced lesions of the genu and/or body of the corpus callosum. This is regarded essentially as a disconnection syndrome, whereby a left-sided apraxia develops as a result of the disconnection of the right motor cortex from the areas controlling movement and language in the left hemisphere. Leiguarda and Marsden (2000), reviewing a number of case studies, indicate the variability in findings dependent upon the type of test given and note that the most consistent deficits involve the requirement to undertake pantomime tasks under motor command.

In *sympathetic apraxia*, there is left-sided apraxia and a right-sided hemiplegia; Leiguarda and Marsden (2000) note that this is due to an anterior lesion located deep beneath Broca's area and in this case performance is poor under verbal command, imitation and object use. It can also be associated with orofacial apraxia (Tate & McDonald, 1995).

Heilman and Rothi (1997) and Leiguarda and Marsden (2000) also review the *modality-specific* or *dissociation apraxias*. Here patterns of errors are displayed only or predominantly under one testing modality (e.g., verbal command, imitation, visual object use).

BRAIN LOCALIZATION OF APRAXIC DEFICITS

It is not possible within the limits of the current chapter to do justice to the numerous attempts to identify the brain regions giving rise to the many types of dyspraxic deficits that can be observed. The left hemisphere has, in a recent positron emission tomography (PET) study, in line with many earlier studies, been demonstrated to play a dominant role in the selection of actions (e.g., Schluter et al., 2001), and Haaland et al. (2000) demonstrated the importance of a network involving the left middle frontal gyrus and intraparietal sulcus region for the control of complex goal-directed movements, such as writing or teeth-brushing. McCarthy and Warrington (1990) have summarized a number of early lesion studies where left hemisphere lesions gave rise to slow rates of stylus tapping (Wyke, 1967) (with disproportionate involvement of the right hemisphere when the required tapping rate was slow; Carmon, 1971) and impaired copying of single hand movements (De Renzi et al., 1983; Kimura, 1982; Pieczuro & Vignolo, 1967). Left-hemisphere lesions (frontal and parietal) produced deficits in the learning of unfamiliar motor sequences (Kimura, 1982) with greater impairment produced by parietal than frontal lesions (McCarthy & Warrington, 1990). The production of meaningful gestures to verbal command is affected by left parietal lesions, in a manner similar to that seen for the production of single hand positions (see McCarthy & Warrington, 1990). However, the role of the left hemisphere has been demonstrated in the copying of hand positions, and the right hemisphere in the copying of finger configurations (Goldenberg, 1996; Goldenberg et al., 2001). McCarthy and Warrington (1990) summarized studies (e.g., Ajuriaguerra et al., 1960) to show that left-hemisphere lesions may be implicated in affecting successful object use. More severe apraxia may be seen after anterior rather than posterior lesions (Basso et al., 2000, 2002). Oral apraxia has been reported most consistently in individuals with lesions in the anterior left hemisphere, although right-hemisphere involvement in the production of upper and lower face movements has recently been confirmed (Bizzozero et al., 2000).

THE ASSESSMENT OF APRAXIA

One of the greatest challenges facing the clinician in the assessment of apraxia is the absence of a widely used and well-standardized assessment tool. Most attempts to develop assessment approaches have focused on limb apraxia, and, as Rothi et al. (1997) indicate, those assessments that do exist are not theoretically related to cognitive neuropsychological models of apraxia. Lezak (1995) comments on the multiplicity of scoring systems that have been developed by different groups of researchers; this, compounded by the differing tasks that are included within each assessment protocol, only serves to complicate matters further.

In general, assessments of limb apraxia involve the examination of transitive movements (requiring the use of objects) and intransitive movements (which do not require object use). Geschwind and Damasio's (1985) different testing conditions under which apraxia may be observed in clinical situations should form the basis of an assessment. Thus movements should be tested in response to verbal instruction, under conditions of imitation of the movement made by the examiner and in response to a real object, where this is appropriate to the task at hand. The importance of testing under conditions of imitation and in the presence of real objects is accentuated when the patient is aphasic, since lack of responding to verbal instructions may otherwise lead to the misattribution of deficits. Similarly, it may be necessary to ensure that poor object use is not the consequence of a visual object agnosia.

Lezak (1995) indicates that the examiner would typically introduce actions to be imitated by saying, 'show me what you see me doing'; actions to be pantomimed would be introduced by saying, 'show me how you would ...'. Rothi et al. (1997) report instructions to the person to pantomime object use in the presence of a real object by saying, 'show me how you would use this' and, when given the object, 'show me how you use this tool I am placing in your hand'. Gesture imitation is tested by saying, 'I will produce a gesture and I want you to do it the same way I do it. Don't name the gesture and don't produce your gesture until I am finished' (Rothi et al. 1997). In general, actions should be tested for both left and right hands. Rothi et al. (1997) recommend that assessments be videotaped for later scoring; for the inexperienced assessor of apraxia, this would seem essential.

Within the general category of limb movements it is usual to assess the person's ability to produce meaningful and meaningless movements, to verbal command and under conditions of imitation. The assessment needs to include tests of meaningful and meaningless movements, for the limbs and for the facial musculature. De Renzi et al. (1980) reported that apraxia was elicited more easily by non-meaningful than by meaningful movements, so imitation tasks should include both types of movement.

In the absence of any widely accepted and standardized clinical assessment batteries, a few examples of approaches to assessment that have been described will be outlined in Table 10.1. Ease of access to one of these approaches is likely to influence their use. Some reports (e.g., De Renzi et al., 1980) provide insufficient detail for the reader to be able to apply a specific battery in a clinical setting, and the extent of the possible assessment may depend on the facilities available for naturalistic as well as formal assessment.

The procedures documented in Table 10.1 all assess apraxia in a formal testing situation. A different approach has however been adopted by Rothi et al. (1997) who, in addition to studying apraxia with a formal assessment battery, described the assessment of dyspraxic behaviour in a real-life setting. Rothi et al. (1997) indicated the problems of standardizing a real-life assessment because of the poor control over extraneous variables. They documented a method of evaluating real-life apraxia in hospital patients, by videotaping their eating of their midday meal in their hospital room (Foundas et al., 1995), once their meal tray had been placed on a bedside table in front of the patient. In addition to the usual items to be found on a lunch tray, distractor items (e.g., a toothbrush, comb and pencil) were mixed up with the standard items. The patient was left for 30 minutes to eat the meal. Their performance was assessed in terms of (i) preparing the meal (e.g., taking the lid off the food, opening the condiment packages); (ii) eating the food (following the second bite, which allows the person to return to the condiments to season the food after the first mouthful) and (iii) cleaning up behaviours (e.g., returning the serviette to the tray, tidying up the plate). Actions within the meal were characterized as 'tool-related' or 'non-tool-related', and using the videotaped record of the meal the middle five-minute section of the tape was assessed for the proportion of correct 'tool' and 'non-tool' actions, the incidence of misuse

Table 10.1. Approaches to the formal assessment of limb and oral apraxia

Type of apraxia/ movements under assessment	Content of assessment and examples	Method of examination	Scoring	Comments
Limb, whole body and facial apraxia (Goodglass & Kaplan, 1983; Goodglass et al., 2001)	Goodglass and Kaplan (1983): five tests each of bucco-facial function (e.g., cough, blow), intransitive limb actions (e.g., wave good-bye, salute), transitive limb actions (e.g., brush teeth, use hammer), whole body movements (e.g., how does a boxer stand? How do you shovel snow?). In addition, three serial actions to be undertaken (e.g., put the paper in the envelope, seal it and stamp it)	Goodglass and Kaplan (1983): single gestures to be performed to verbal command. If failed, then under imitation. If still failed, test in the presence of real objects if appropriate. Serial actions should be tested in the presence of real objects	Goodglass and Kaplan (1983): no normative data, but can be scored as 'normal', 'partially correct' and 'failed'	Borod et al. (1989) expanded Goodglass and Kaplan's (1983) scale to a four-point scale
	Goodglass et al. (2001): four items of limb/hand praxis involving natural gestures, four involving conventional gestures, eight involving the pretended use of objects and four assessing bucco-facial/respiratory praxis	Goodglass et al. (2001): single gestures to be performed to verbal command and, if not perfect, then under imitation	Goodglass et al. (2001): 0 = unrecognizable/no response; 1 = unsuccessful attempt; 2 = recognizable; 3 = normal. Performance under imitation rated as improved, unchanged or poorer than performance to verbal request	

continued

Table 10.1. (cont.)

Type of apraxia/ movements under assessment	Content of assessment and examples	Method of examination	Scoring	Comments
Ideomotor and ideational apraxia (Poeck, 1986)	Ideomotor apraxia: 10 items for orofacial apraxia (e.g., wiggle nose, stick out tongue); 20 items for upper limb movements to include meaningful gestures (e.g., comb their hair, smoke a cigarette) and meaningless gestures (e.g., place hand on opposite shoulder, place fist on chest) Ideational apraxia: serial actions (e.g., opening a tin, making a cup of coffee)	Verbal command and imitation. Recommends that for limb-based tasks the left arm and hand should be used to avoid effects of paresis and to assess sympathetic dypraxia of left arm/hand For tests of ideational apraxia, use real objects and explain to person that they are to be used in action. Need to test several actions and they should be familiar to the person	For clinical purpose Poeck (1986) suggests that pass/ fail is adequate; for research may need more qualitative analysis. For ideational apraxia inter-individuality may make quantitative scoring system difficult	Poeck (1986) emphasized the importance of clinical experience; he suggested that lower limb movement should only be assessed if person had a CVA in territory of anterior cerebral artery
Limb praxis (Rothi et al., 1992). Florida Apraxia Screening Test-Revised (FAST-R)	Details of FAST-R given by Rothi et al. (1997); 30-item test with 20 items involving transitive gestures to be pantomimed	Gestures are performed to verbal command. Patient uses dominant hand/arm to produce the gestures, unless motor symptoms prevent use of the limb. They recommend pre-test practice for patients in pantomiming	Rothi et al. (1997) recommend videotaping patients' responses and using two judges to rate performance. For clinical use they encourage judges to reach a single consensus score	FAST-R is a research tool that may be of use clinically. Need to consider generalizability of test performance across different patient populations; need to develop local norms

		gestures to overcome embarrassment	Foundas et al. (1993) reported a bimodal distribution of scores for left-hemisphere damaged patients
Florida Apraxia Battery (FAB; Rothi et al., 1992)	FAB subtests use same body of stimuli employed for the FAST-R; experimental test not for clinical use and may need local variations to match characteristics of local population		
Face apraxia (Bizzozero et al., 2000).	Two components. Upper face apraxia (UFA): 29 items (e.g., close your eyes, look up at ceiling). Lower face apraxia (LFA): 9 items (e.g., open your mouth, bite the inside of your left cheek)	Items demonstrated by examiner for imitation by patient	Items scored 'pass' or 'fail'. Failed if movements random or amorphous, if preceded by long pauses, if person made incomplete movement or made no movement. Items ranked for ease/difficulty. Can correct scores for difference in age and educational level	Items allocated to tests on basis of innervatory territory of cranial nerves involved. Age found to affect performance on UFA and LFA tests; education only affected LFA test. Test–retest reliability of both tests >0.9 after 5–7 days

or mis-selection of tools and sequencing or timing errors during the total mealtime, the length of which was also measured. Foundas et al. (1995) described eating patterns in dyspraxic adults as disorganized and inconsistent. Rothi et al. (1997) noted that because Foundas et al. (1995) had found that in all cases meals were eaten, irrespective of the manner in which this was achieved by the apraxic patients, without such an assessment impairments in the organization and execution of meal consumption would not otherwise be detected.

Types of Apraxic Errors

It quickly becomes apparent that much of the theoretical interest in the assessment of apraxia arises from a consideration of the types of errors that the patient makes during testing. Attempts have been made to formalize definitions of these errors (e.g., Goodglass & Kaplan, 1983; Mozaz, 1992; Poeck, 1986; Rothi et al., 1997). Identifying the type of error made is obviously very different from simply rating the accuracy or otherwise of a movement, and different emphasis has been placed on the types of errors that may be made. In addition, whether a spatial error is made in terms of hand positions or finger positions may have implications for the localization of brain damage underlying the person's dyspraxia (Goldenberg, 1996).

It is not possible to provide detailed definitions of all error types within this chapter (but see Goodglass & Kaplan, 1983; Mozaz, 1992; Rothi et al., 1997 for good descriptions of error types). Briefly, however, according to Rothi et al. (1997) the types of errors that one may observe may, in general terms, be subdivided in the following manner: errors in the *spatial* aspects of the movement (e.g., augmentation phenomena whereby the movement may be made more exaggerated than it should be, incorrect amplitude of the movement, incorrect orientation of the hand/limb in relation to the object and the use of body part as object/tool); errors in the *temporal* aspects of the movement (sequencing and timing errors and the incorrect performance of number/cycles of movements needed to complete the task); and errors in the *content* of the movement (e.g., the presence of related and non-related movements; perseveration of all or part of a previously performed movement or the performance of the task in the absence of the real or imagined tool). In addition, Rothi et al. (1997) indicate that the person may make no response, an unrecognizable response or a very concrete response.

Goodglass and Kaplan (1983) and Poeck (1986) place some emphasis on the error known as *body-part-as-object*. Thus, for example, when a person is told to demonstrate how they would use a hammer, they make the hammering movement with a closed fist rather than miming holding a hammer; when asked to demonstrate how they would clean their teeth they move their finger across their teeth rather than pantomiming holding a toothbrush. This type of error is common in young children, but has been thought to be rare in adults. If it occurs in brain-damaged patients, it is often considered highly suggestive of ideomotor apraxia (Poeck, 1986). However, it may be a sign of brain damage only if it occurs when real objects are presented for use, as otherwise (on imitation or verbal command) it may also be seen in normal people (Mozaz et al., 1993).

Goodglass and Kaplan (1983) also comment on verbalizations of the required action, which may be seen in people with orofacial apraxia when instructed to perform a task involving activation of the oral–respiratory system. Perseveration, where a previous response is repeated when a new response is required, has also attracted attention (Mozaz, 1992).

MANAGEMENT AND TREATMENT OF APRAXIA

Relatively little has been written about the management and treatment of limb apraxia. Maher and Ochipa (1997) attribute this in part to the lack of awareness by people with apraxia concerning their own deficits or to their tendency to consider their difficulties as being due to having to use their non-dominant hand; in addition, where aphasia and apraxia co-exist, people may find it hard to express their difficulties. It has also been widely believed that apraxia will recover spontaneously. Finally, Maher and Ochipa (1997) suggest that, as apraxia is often most clearly demonstrated under conditions of pantomime or tool use outside their natural context, it is unlikely that individuals will be greatly inconvenienced on a daily basis. However, they cite a number of studies (e.g., Heilman & Rothi, 1993; McDonald et al., 1994; Poizner et al., 1989) indicating that people with apraxia may be impaired with actual tool use in natural settings (Mayer et al., 1990; Ochipa et al., 1989; Schwartz et al., 1991). As already described, Foundas et al. (1995) observed mealtime difficulties in hospitalized patients with apraxia.

Maher and Ochipa (1997) have interpreted management of apraxia as involving the modification of the person's environment to try to reduce problems in tool use. They suggested that if tool use cannot be avoided, then patients and their families must be aware that access to certain tools might be dangerous. Thus it might be appropriate to try to replace tasks requiring tools with others that can be undertaken without tools, to restrict the range of tools available for use or to require the person to perform only familiar tasks, making use of cues wherever possible. In addition, the use of proximal rather than distal movements should be employed, and the required movements should be made as simple as possible.

Treatment, as opposed to management, involves improving the deficient movements (Maher & Ochipa, 1997). This might either involve preventing the person from persisting with movement strategies that are no longer effective, or teaching new, more effective movements. They suggested that approaches to rehabilitation are to some extent governed by one's philosophy in this area and can, as with other areas of deficit, either be *restitutive* or *substitutive* (Rothi, 1995). Rothi (1995) suggested that initially both approaches should be adopted for people with apraxia, with restitutive approaches being directed at those behaviours most likely to recover and substitutive strategies being employed for those behaviours that are most likely to remain impaired beyond the initial recovery phase. However, as Maher and Ochipa (1997) note, this is somewhat controversial since relatively little is known about the natural time course of apraxia or which aspects of apraxia are most amenable to treatment.

A number of studies suggest that treatment effects for apraxia are item-specific. Maher et al. (1991) reported a single case whereby a two-week period of treatment was undertaken for 10/20 gestures requiring the use of common tools and household items. Treatment involved presenting the patient with multiple cues (tool, object, visual model and feedback) and withdrawing cues gradually until he achieved 90% accuracy of gestures made in response to the visual presentations of the cues. Feedback of errors was immediate, and erroneous responses were immediately corrected. Improvement was observed in both treated and untreated movements, but was maintained to a higher level for the treated items. Initially, a sequence of 'probe' items consisting of meaningless gestures showed no improvement, indicating that generalized improvement in movements was not occurring; the meaningless gestures only showed an improvement when the person later practised them.

Maher and Ochipa (1997) describe in some detail work by Ochipa et al. (1995), who attempted to determine the effects of treating specific error types in two individuals in whom gesture recognition was largely preserved. Interventions were designed to treat the dominant pattern of errors made by each person under pantomime-to-command testing conditions. Thus, for example, where the person made errors characterized as external configuration errors (whereby hand movements were incorrectly directed), the person was trained to direct his hand to the object that had to be acted upon. Similarly, for a 'movement error' where the incorrect joint movements were used to produce a movement (such as failing to rotate the fingers to turn a can opener while keeping the wrist fixed), the person was given verbal prompts to tell the person which joints to use and how, during the pantomime. In general, treatment of one error type did not lead to a reduction of other error types, and improvement was specific to the gestures undergoing treatment.

Goldenberg and Hagmann (1998) undertook a study of 15 adults with aphasia and right-sided hemiplegia after left-hemisphere CVA and who were impaired on a specific activity of daily living (e.g., brushing teeth, spreading margarine on a slice of bread, putting on a pullover or tee shirt). Training was undertaken of one activity each week, with a different one being trained on subsequent weeks. Two treatment approaches were combined, these involving errorless completion of the whole activity (with support being given at all critical stages of the activity) and training of specific details, by directing the person's attention to the functional significance of perceptual aspects and to critical features of the associated actions. Treatment was found to reduce the number of so-called 'fatal errors' (i.e., those stopping the task from being completed) rather than the so-called 'reparable errors' (i.e., those that would not completely prevent the task from being completed). However, the benefits of treatment were lost in people who were subsequently unable to practise the activities independently when discharged home, and there was no generalization of training benefits to non-trained activities.

Relatively short-term benefits of specific treatment were also demonstrated by Donkervort et al. (2001), who, in a rare, randomized clinical trial with apraxic individuals, compared the effects of strategy training integrated into standard occupational therapy (OT) with standard OT alone, following left-hemisphere stroke. Strategy training involved the development of strategies to compensate for the apraxic impairment and consisted, for example, of self-verbalization to support performance or the use of pictures to show the correct sequence of activities. Treatment was based on the assumption that the apraxic deficit is often permanent. Following eight weeks of treatment, those who had received strategy training demonstrated greater improvement on a measure of activities of daily living than the standard OT group, but no benefits of strategy training were found at a five-month follow-up period.

Maher and Ochipa (1997), noting the lack of generalization of treatment effects, suggested that this may in part be due to the application of treatments to people with chronic apraxia; they suggested that in the acute phase, generalization might occur more readily. They have also suggested that the selection of people with coexisting aphasia might contribute to the specific nature of the effects found. Finally, a substitutive approach might achieve better results than the restitutive approach that has been used in these studies, and to this end they cited a study by Pilgrim and Humphreys (1994), which adopted a form of 'conductive education' and included the use of verbalization of the task in hand as well as an analysis of the movements involved in the task. Treatment gains were again specific to the items trained, and the patient involved required frequent prompting to use the strategy.

Thus, as a result of the lack of generalization of treatment effects, it would seem important to select tasks on the basis of their functional significance for the person and train the person to complete these in their everyday environment rather than in a laboratory setting (Maher and Ochipa, 1997).

CONCLUSIONS

As can be seen from this chapter, the clinical investigation and treatment of apraxia poses a number of challenges, resulting from the proliferation of conceptualizations of the disorder and the absence of a widely accepted and well-validated assessment tool. A clinician new to this area would thus be wise to select one of the assessment approaches described earlier, gain a prior appreciation of the variability in the performance by healthy adults on any specific selection of movements to be used for assessment and undertake a videotaped assessment of their patient in order to have time to reflect on the nature of the disorder that they observe. However, further understanding of the different cognitive models of apraxia will be important in order to devise appropriate interventions, since those currently reported may be considered only to have relatively limited effect.

REFERENCES

Ajuriaguerra de, J., Hécaen, H. & Angelergues, R. (1960) Les Apraxies: Variétés cliniques et latéralisation lésionelle. *Revue Neurologique*, **102**, 566–594 [in French].

Basso, A., Capitani, E., Della Sala, S., Laiacona, M. & Spinnler, H. (1987) Recovery from ideomotor apraxia: A study of acute stroke patients. *Brain*, **110**, 740–760.

Basso, A., Burgio, F., Paulin, M. & Prandoni, P. (2000) Long-term follow-up of ideomotor apraxia. *Neuropsychological Rehabilitation*, **10**, 1–13.

Basso, A., Burgio, F. & Faglioni, P. (2002) Long-term follow-up of ideomotor apraxia: A response to Cauraugh. *Neuropsychological Rehabilitation*, **12**, 111–115.

Bizzozero, I., Costato, D., Della Salla, S., Papagno, C., Spinnler, H. & Venneri, A. (2000) Upper and lower face apraxia: Role of the right hemisphere. *Brain*, **123**, 2213–2230.

Borod, J. C., Fitzpatrick, P. M., Helm-Estabrooks, N. & Goodglass, H. (1989) The relationship between the spontaneous use of communicative gesture in aphasia. *Brain and Cognition*, **10**, 121–131.

Carmon, A. (1971) Disturbance in tactile sensitivity in patients with cerebral lesions. *Cortex*, **7**, 83–97.

Cubelli, R. & Della Sala, S. (1996) The legacy of automatic/voluntary dissociation in apraxia. *Neurocase*, **2**, 449–454.

Dee, H. L., Benton, A. L. & Van Allen, M. W. (1970) Apraxia in relation to hemisphere locus of lesion and aphasia. *Transactions of the American Neurological Association*, **95**, 147–148.

Della Sala, S., Lucchelli, F. & Spinnler, H. (1987) Ideomotor apraxia in patients with dementia of Alzheimer type. *Journal of Neurology*, **234**, 91–93.

De Renzi, E. & Lucchelli, F. (1988) Ideational apraxia. *Brain*, **111**, 1173–1185.

De Renzi, E., Motti, F. & Nichelli, P. (1980) Imitating gestures: A quantitative approach to ideomotor apraxia. *Archives of Neurology*, **37**, 6–10.

De Renzi, E., Faglioni, P., Lodesani, M. & Vecchi, A. (1983) Performance of left brain damaged patients on imitation of single movements and motor sequences. Frontal and parietal-injured patients compared. *Cortex*, **19**, 333–343.

Donkervoort, M., Dekker, J., Stehmann-Saris, F. C. & Deelman, B. G. (2001) Efficacy of strategy training in left hemisphere stroke patients with apraxia: A randomised clinical trial. *Neuropsychological Rehabilitation*, **11**, 549–566.

Foundas, A. L., Raymer, A., Maher, L. M., Rothi, L. J. G. & Heilman, K. M. (1993) Recovery in ideomotor apraxia. *Journal of Clinical and Experimental Neuropsychology*, **15**, 44.

Foundas, A., Macauley, B. L., Raymer, A. M., Maher, L. M., Heilman, K. M. & Rothi, L. J. (1995) Ecological implications of limb apraxia: Evidence from mealtime behaviour. *Journal of the International Neuropsychological Society*, **1**, 62–66.

Geschwind, N. & Damasio, A. R. (1985) Apraxia. In: P. J. Vinken, G. W. Bruyn & H. L. Klawans (eds) *Handbook of Clinical Neurology* (Vol 45, pp. 423–432). Elsevier, Amsterdam.

Goldenberg, G. (1996) Defective imitation of gestures in patients with damage in the left or right hemispheres. *Journal of Neurology, Neurosurgery and Psychiatry*, **61**, 176–180.

Goldenberg, G. & Hagmann, S. (1998) Therapy of activities of daily living in patients with apraxia. *Neuropsychological Rehabilitation*, **8**, 123–141.

Goldenberg, G., Laimgruber, K. & Hermsdörfer, J. (2001) Imitation of gestures by disconnected hemispheres. *Neuropsychological Rehabilitation*, **39**, 1432–1443.

Goodglass, H. & Kaplan, E. (1983) *The Assessment of Aphasia and Related Disorders* (2nd edn). Lea & Febiger, Philadelphia.

Goodglass, H., Kaplan, E. & Barresi, B. (2001) *The Assessment of Aphasia and Related Disorders* (3rd edn). Lippincott Williams & Wilkins, Philadelphia.

Haaland, K. Y., Harrington, D. L. & Knight, R. T. (2000) Neural representations of skilled movement. *Brain*, **123**, 2306–2313.

Hanna-Pladdy, B. & Rothi, L. J. G. (2001) Ideational apraxia: Confusion that began with Liepmann. *Neuropsychological Rehabilitation*, **11**, 539–547.

Heilman, K. M. & Rothi, L. J. G. (1993) Limb apraxia. In: K. M. Heilman & E. Valenstein (eds) *Clinical Neuropsychology* (3rd edn). Oxford University Press, New York.

Heilman, K. M. & Rothi, L. J. G. (1997) Limb apraxia: A look back. In: L. J. G Rothi & K. M. Heilman (eds) *Apraxia. The Neuropsychology of Action* (pp. 7–18). Psychology Press, Hove, UK.

Heilman, K. M., Goneya, E. F. & Geschwind, N. (1974) Apraxia and aphasia in a right hander. *Cortex*, **10**, 284–288.

Heilman, K. M., Meador, K. J. & Loring, D. W. (2000) Hemispheric asymmetries of limb-kinetic apraxia. A loss of deftness. *Neurology*, **55**, 523–526.

Howes, D. H. (1988) Ideomotor apraxia: Evidence for the preservation of axial commands. *Journal of Neurology, Neurosurgery and Psychiatry*, **51**, 593–596.

Kimura, D. (1982) Left hemisphere control of oral and brachial movements and their relationship to communication. *Philosophical Transactions of the Royal Society of London, Series B*, **298**, 135–149.

Kimura, D. & Archibald, Y. (1974) Motor functions of the left hemisphere, *Brain*, **97**, 337–350.

Leiguarda, R. C. & Marsden, C. D. (2000) Limb apraxias. Higher-order disorders of sensorimotor integration. *Brain*, **123**, 860–879.

Lezak, M. D. (1995) *Neuropsychological Assessment* (3rd edn). Oxford University Press, New York.

Luria, A. R. (1973) *The Working Brain. An Introduction to Neuropsychology*. Penguin, Harmondsworth, UK.

Maher, L. M. & Ochipa, C. (1997) Management and treatment of limb apraxia. In: L. J. G. Rothi & K. M. Heilman (eds) *Apraxia. The Neuropsychology of Action* (pp 75–91) Psychology Press, Hove, UK.

Maher, L. M., Rothi, L. J. G. & Greenwald, M. L. (1991) Treatment of gesture impairment: A single case. *ASHA*, **33**, 195.

Mayer, N. H., Reed, E., Schwartz, M. F., Montgomery, M. & Palmer, C. (1990) Buttering a hot cup of coffee: An approach to the study of errors of actions in patients with brain damage. In: D. E. Tupper & K. D. Cicerone (eds) *The Neuropsychology of Everyday Life. Vol. 2: Assessment and Basic Competencies*. Kluwer Academic, Norwell, MA.

McCarthy, R. A. & Warrington, E. K. (1990) *Cognitive Neuropsychology. A Clinical Introduction*. Academic Press, San Diego.

McDonald, S., Tate, R. C. & Rigby, J. (1994) Error types in ideomotor apraxia: A qualitative analysis. *Brain and Cognition*, **25**, 250–270.

Mozaz, M. J. (1992) Ideational and ideomotor apraxia: A qualitative analysis. *Behavioural Neurology*, **5**, 11–17.

Mozaz, M. J., Peña, J., Barraquer, L. L., Martí, J. & Goldstein, L. H. (1993) Use of body part as object in brain-damaged subjects. *The Clinical Neuropsychologist*, **7**, 39–47.

Neiman, M. R., Duffy, R. J., Belanger, S. A. & Coelho, C. A. (2000) The assessment of limb apraxia: Relationship between performances on single- and multiple-object tasks by left hemisphere damaged aphasic subjects. *Neuropsychological Rehabilitation*, **10**, 429–448.

Ochipa, C., Rothi, L. J. G. & Heilman, K. M. (1989) Ideational apraxia: A deficit in tool selection and use. *Annals of Neurology*, **25**, 190–193.

Ochipa, C., Rothi, L. J. G. and Heilman, K. M. (1992) Conceptual apraxia in Alzheimer's Disease. *Brain*, **115**, 1061–1071.

Ochipa, C., Maher, L. M. & Rothi, L. J. G. (1995) Treatment of ideomotor apraxia. *Journal of the International Neuropsychological Society*, **1**, 149.

Papagno, C., Della Sala, S. & Basso, A. (1993) Ideomotor apraxia without aphasia and aphasia without apraxia: The anatomical support for a double dissociation. *Journal of Neurology, Neurosurgery and Psychiatry*, **56**, 286–289.

Pieczuro, A. C. & Vignolo, L. A. (1967) Studio sperimentale sulla aprassia ideomotoria. *Sistema Nervoso*, **19**, 131–143 [in Italian].

Pilgrim, E. & Humphreys, G. W. (1994) Rehabilitation of a case of ideomotor apraxia. In: M. J. Riddoch & G. W. Humphreys (eds) *Cognitive Neuropsychology and Cognitive Rehabilitation* (pp. 271–285). Lawrence Erlbaum, Hove, UK.

Poeck, K. (1983) Ideational apraxia. *Journal of Neurology*, **230**, 1–5.

Poeck, K. (1986) The clinical examination for motor apraxia. *Neuropsychologia*, **24**, 129–134.

Poeck, K. & Lehmkuhl, G. (1980) Ideatory apraxia in a left handed patient with right sided brain lesion. *Cortex*, **16**, 273–284.

Poeck, K., Lehmkuhl, G. & Willmes, K. (1982) Axial movements in ideomotor apraxia. *Journal of Neurology, Neurosurgery and Psychiatry*, **45**, 1125–1129.

Poizner, H., Soechting, J. F., Bracewell, M., Rothi, L. J. G. & Heilman, K. M. (1989) Disruption of joint and hand kinematics in limb apraxia. *Society for Neuroscience*, **15**, 481.

Poizner, H., Mack, L., Verfaellie, M., Rothi, L. J. & Heilman, K. M. (1990) Three-dimensional computergraphic analysis of apraxia. *Brain*, **118**, 227–242.

Raymer, A. M. & Ochipa, C. (1997) Conceptual praxis. In: L. J. G. Rothi & K. M. Heilman (eds) *Apraxia. The Neuropsychology of Action* (pp. 51–60). Psychology Press, Hove, UK.

Rothi, L. J. G. (1995) Behavioural compensation in the case of treatment of acquired language disorders resulting from brain damage. In: R. A. Dixon & L. Baeckman (eds) *Psychological Compensation: Managing Losses and Promoting Gains* (pp. 219–230). Lawrence Erlbaum, Hove, UK.

Rothi, L. J. G., Ochipa, C. & Heilman, K. M. N. (1991) A cognitive neuropsychological model of limb praxis. *Cognitive Neuropsychology*, **8**, 443–458.

Rothi, L. J. G., Raymer, A. M., Ochipa, C., Maher, L. M., Greenwald, M. L. and Heilman, K. M. (1992) *Florida Apraxia Battery* (unpublished experimental edition).

Rothi, L. J. G., Raymer, A. M. & Heilman, K. M. (1997) Limb praxis assessment. In: L. J. G. Rothi & K. M. Heilman (eds) *Apraxia. The Neuropsychology of Action* (pp. 61–73). Psychology Press, Hove, UK.

Roy, E. A. & Square, P. A. (1985) Common considerations in the study of limb, verbal and oral apraxia. In: E. A. Roy (ed.) *Advances in Psychology. Vol. 23: Neuropsychological Studies of Apraxia and Related Disorders* (pp. 111–162). North Holland, Amsterdam.

Schluter, N. D., Krams, M., Rushworth, M. F. S. & Passingham, R. E. (2001) Cerebral dominance for action in the human brain: The selection of actions. *Neuropsychologia*, **39**, 105–113.

Schwartz, M. F., Reed, E. S., Montgomery, M., Palmer, C. & Mayer, N. H. (1991) The quantitative description of action disorganisation after brain damage. A case study. *Cognitive Neuropsychology*, **8**, 381–414.

Selnes, O. A., Pestronk, A., Hart, J. & Gordon, B. (1991) Limb apraxia without aphasia from a left-sided lesion in a right-handed patient. *Journal of Neurology, Neurosurgery and Psychiatry*, **54**, 734–737.

Spinnler, H. & Della Sala, S. (1988) The role of clinical neuropsychology in the neurological diagnosis of Alzheimer's Disease. *Journal of Neurology*, **235**, 258–271.

Sundet, K., Finset, A. & Reinvang, I. (1988) Neuropsychological predictors in stroke rehabilitation. *Journal of Clinical and Experimental Neuropsychology*, **10**, 363–379.

Tate, R. L. & McDonald, S. (1995) What is apraxia? The clinician's dilemma. *Neuropsychological Rehabilitation*, **5**, 273–297.

Wyke, M. (1967) The effect of brain lesions on the rapidity of arm movement. *Neurology*, **17**, 1113–1130.

CHAPTER 11

Visuospatial and Attentional Disorders

Tom Manly

Addenbrooke's Hospital, Cambridge, UK

and

Jason B. Mattingley

University of Melbourne, Australia

This chapter will consider some common problems that can arise in visuospatial and attentional function as the result of brain damage, focusing on practical assessment and rehabilitation techniques. We begin with a brief overview of the structure and function of the visual system and a discussion of non-attentional visual field disorders that often co-occur with, and exacerbate, attention deficits. After introducing the separable systems that contribute to higher level visual processing (in particular, the 'what' and 'where' pathways), the main discussion will focus on unilateral spatial neglect—a difficulty in detecting, acting on or even thinking about information arising from the side of space opposite the damaged hemisphere. Neglect is emphasized for three reasons. First, neglect is a surprisingly common consequence of stroke, especially when the right cerebral hemisphere is affected; second, neglect is associated with poor recovery and return to independence; third, in contrast with many neuropsychological disorders, there are a number of simple, effective and well-validated techniques that can be used in the rehabilitation of the disorder. The final section of the chapter discusses non-spatial disorders of attention and considers how commonly reported complaints of 'poor concentration', 'difficulty staying on task' and 'distractibility' are currently operationalized. Recent rehabilitative interventions will be discussed.

EARLY VISUAL PROCESSING AND VISUAL FIELD DISORDERS

Light falling on the retina of each eye is transmitted from the optic nerves, via the optic chiasm, to the lateral geniculate nucleus of the thalamus and then onward to the primary visual cortex in the occipital lobe (the geniculostriate pathway). As

Clinical Neuropsychology: A Practical Guide to Assessment and Management for Clinicians.
Edited by L.H. Goldstein and J.E. McNeil. © 2004 John Wiley & Sons, Ltd.

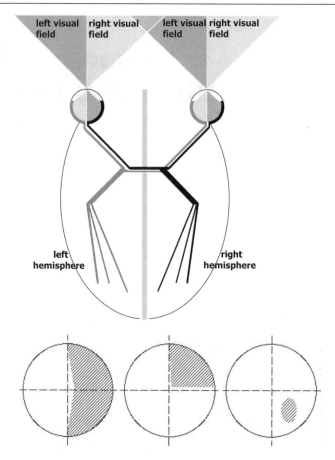

Figure 11.1 Upper: schematic of visual fields showing the crossing of the optic tracts and the projection of information from the contralateral field into each hemisphere. Lower: patterns of field loss—(left to right) hemianopia, quadrantanopia and a patchy scotoma

shown in Figure 11.1, each eye is sensitive to light arising from both the left and right visual fields. Thereafter, a broad division occurs with signals from the two left visual fields combining to project to the contralateral (right) hemisphere, while signals from the two right visual fields combine and project to the left. Due to this anatomical arrangement, complete damage to an optic nerve *before* the optic chiasm causes blindness in the affected eye, but leaves all but the most peripheral region of contralesional space visible in the unaffected eye. Conversely, unilateral damage to the geniculostriate pathway (*after* the optic chiasm) can impair visual sensitivity for an entire hemifield or quadrant.

Stroke is the most common cause of visual field disorders, affecting between 20 and 40% of patients to some degree (Hier et al., 1983). The location and extent of damage produces different patterns of impairment, both in terms of the region of space affected and the type of visual information compromised. Complete unilateral damage to the optic tract (from the optic chiasm to its destination in primary visual cortex) deprives the brain of input from the majority of one hemifield (hemianopia or 'homonymous hemianopia'). Quadrantanopia (loss of information from the upper or lower section of a hemifield), scotoma (small islands of blindness within a field) or selective impairment of a specific aspect of visual sensitivity (e.g. colour) are also possible (see Figure 11.1). Bilateral hemispheric damage typically produces impairments in both visual fields and in severe cases can cause 'tunnel vision' (blindness for all but the central region of space).

Assessment of Visual Field Disorders

Visual field disorders are formally assessed using perimetry—in which the patient is asked to fixate (maintain gaze) at the centre of a uniformly illuminated hemisphere and report the detection of a light stimulus brought from the periphery toward the centre of the display. Through the repetition of this procedure, a map of the patient's sensitivity is created. A crude assessment can be performed without special equipment using the confrontation technique. Here the patient is asked to maintain fixation on the examiner's nose while attempting to detect small movements of the examiner's fingers made to the left or the right, or in upper and lower fields.

Recovery and Adaptation of Visual Field Disorders

Some spontaneous recovery of visual sensitivity within a hemianopic field occurs in 12–30% of patients, assessed between three and eight months post lesion (Hier et al., 1983). Further improvements may continue for up to two years in some cases. Complete recovery appears to be relatively rare, however, and even within areas that have regained some sensitivity to light, colour and form detection may remain impaired (Zihl, 2000).

Visual field disorders are strictly retinotopic (i.e., the affected region of visual space moves with the eyes). Consequently, all parts of space can be perceived visually through compensatory movements of the eyes, head or body. Thus patients may be able to compensate behaviourally for their disorder to a considerable degree. For some patients, however, there may be little or no sense that the visual world is incomplete—just as we are normally unaware of our own physiological blind spot—and therefore have no immediate imperative to search for the 'missing' information. Awareness may emerge from noticing one's own errors or from being told about the problem—but remembering to compensate in everyday situations may be difficult, particularly if there are other cognitive deficits. Zihl and colleagues (see Zihl, 2000) analysed spontaneous eye movement compensation for visual field disorders in 166 patients (none of whom showed visual neglect). They found that approximately 70% made eye movements of insufficient angle or speed to compensate for their loss, and this in turn was related to reported difficulties in everyday life (e.g., seeing things 'too late').

Rehabilitation of Visual Field Disorders

Systematic training in detecting stimuli presented toward the edge of the 'blind field' may promote some recovery of the underlying pathway (Zihl & von Cramon, 1979). Such improvements are typically modest and may be of limited functional benefit to the patient (Zihl, 2000). As compensatory eye movements remain the principal route for functional adaptation, it is important to determine whether specific training can facilitate this process. Zihl (2000) attempted to increase patients' capacity to 'take in' the whole scene by encouraging them to make single eye movements of large amplitude rather than a large number of small, inefficient saccades when searching for targets. Significant improvements in target detection and, crucially, reductions in everyday life problems were reported in a group of 77 patients (without unilateral neglect) given this training over approximately a week. In summary, while some recovery from visual field cuts may take place, the major improvements in function usually arise from awareness of the deficit and the use of compensatory scanning.

DISORDERS OF HIGHER VISUAL PROCESSING

Visual Recognition and Action

The brain constructs several different visual representations of the world in parallel. Thus different functional modules of the visual system specialize in extracting specific aspects of a visual scene relatively independently of one another. Damage to one area can therefore affect some aspects of vision, while leaving others intact. Such dissociations have been noted between perception of colour and form (Wechsler, 1933) and between perception of form and motion (Zihl et al., 1983). A further distinction has been drawn between visual mechanisms subserving object recognition and those involved in spatial perception and action. Ungerleider and Mishkin (1982) argued for two distinct cortical streams of information processing; a *ventral* ('what') stream that projects from the occipital cortex to the inferotemporal cortex—responsible for object recognition; and a *dorsal* ('where') stream that projects from the occipital region to the posterior parietal cortex—responsible for determining the spatial location of an object. In a reformulation of this basic dichotomy, Milner and Goodale (1993) proposed that the dorsal stream might be better conceptualized as subserving visually guided action (the 'how' stream). In support of the what/how distinction, patients with inferotemporal cortex lesions may suffer *visual form agnosia*, an inability to visually recognize otherwise familiar objects. Despite their profound recognition problems, some patients can perform visually guided movements toward objects with remarkable accuracy (e.g., Farah, 1990). In contrast, following superior parietal cortex damage, patients may exhibit *optic ataxia*, an impairment of reaching under visual guidance while retaining the ability to recognize objects (Perenin & Vighetto, 1988).

UNILATERAL SPATIAL NEGLECT

Unilateral spatial neglect (also called 'hemispatial neglect' or 'hemispatial inattention') refers to a difficulty in detecting, acting on or—in some cases—even imagining information from one side of space that is not due to primary sensory or motor deficit. In some cases, patients may exhibit the phenomenon of *extinction*. Here patients are able to report brief, isolated events on their affected side, but fail to do so when these appear concurrently with—or in 'competition' with—a stimulus on the ipsilesional (unaffected) side.

Although it can result from other forms of brain injury, by far the main cause of unilateral neglect is cerebrovascular disease. Aspects of neglect have been observed in up to 82% of right-hemisphere (RH) and 65% of left-hemisphere (LH) patients, assessed within the first three days following a stroke (Stone et al., 1993). Although most closely associated with lesions to the parietal cortex (Vallar & Perani, 1986), neglect can occur following damage to a variety of other structures, including the temporal (Karnath et al., 2001) and frontal cortices (Mesulam, 1981) and to subcortical structures (e.g., Samuelsson et al., 1997).

As discussed, neglect is observed with almost equal frequency following LH or RH damage in the very early post-stroke period. Most patients, however, appear to recover spontaneously, often within days or weeks. This process appears to disproportionately favour patients with LH lesions, so that chronic forms of neglect are overwhelmingly associated with RH damage. Persistent signs of neglect have been reported in approximately one-third of RH patients at three months post stroke and, in some studies, a spatial bias has been detectable up to 12 years after the initial damage (Zarit & Kahn, 1974).

Chronic unilateral neglect is a severe clinical problem. The presence of neglect is associated with poor recovery, poor response to rehabilitation and increased dependence (e.g., Paolucci et al., 2001a, b). Detecting whether neglect is present—and where possible intervening to reduce its effects—is therefore an important clinical goal.

The Assessment of Unilateral Spatial Neglect

A key issue in the assessment of neuropsychological status is judging how well a patient can perform in relation to a representative normative sample. This can be a rather complex activity with a wide margin for error. In assessing unilateral neglect there is a considerable advantage—a perfect 'control' who is exactly matched on all relevant variables—namely, the patient's own performance on their ipsilesional ('intact') side. Provided that sensory or motor loss can be ruled out as a primary cause of difficulty, almost any task in which it is possible to demonstrate a significant performance discrepancy between ipsi- and contralesional space may be considered diagnostic of neglect. An important point to note, however, is that neglect is a heterogeneous syndrome that includes several underlying functional impairments (Halligan & Marshall, 1994). This means that, although spatially biased performance on one task may suggest neglect, the absence of such performance on any particular task cannot *rule out* neglect. Similarly, the severity and manifestations of neglect are notoriously unstable, changing in apparent severity depending on the task, context, time of day, practice, fatigue and so forth. Therefore, a patient may not show clear neglect on a test administered in the hospital (perhaps particularly one that has been administered on repeated occasions), but may nevertheless show signs of the disorder in activities of daily living. With these cautions in mind, in the following sections a number of clinical observations and simple behavioural tests will be outlined that are commonly used to determine the presence of spatial neglect.

Observation

Although standardized tests for neglect often have some resemblance to common activities, clinical observation of the patient in a naturalistic setting can provide the clearest guide of everyday difficulties. Patients may, for example, fail to wash or dress their left side, ignore their left limbs, eat food from only the right side of their plate, collide with objects, have difficulty in finding items that are in 'clear view' and ignore people who approach from their left side.

A further important feature of neglect that may become apparent through informal observation is the patient's characteristic loss of insight into the nature of his or her deficits. By definition, patients with neglect show a *behavioural* lack of awareness, in the sense that they do not spontaneously search for information on the left. In addition, for some patients there seems to be a curious inability or reluctance to cognitively accept that the deficit is present (anosognosia), which may have implications for their active engagement in rehabilitative activity.

Cancellation Tasks

Active spatial exploration of the visual world is a fundamental component of adaptive perceptual and motor behaviour. Cancellation tasks, perhaps the most commonly used and straightforward measures of neglect, are designed to assess this capacity. Typically, the patient is presented with a paper sheet and is asked to find and cross out (cancel) specified visual targets (e.g., stars, letters). The typical pattern is to miss some or many of the targets, with omissions predominating on the contralesional side. Most cancellation measures do not impose any time limit on the patient, who is simply asked to indicate when the task has been completed to their satisfaction.

Line Bisection

Line bisection tasks are another quick and easy measure. Patients are presented with plain horizontal lines and asked to make a pencil mark at the midpoint. Healthy individuals are typically quite accurate in the task, though they tend to exhibit a slight leftward error (Bradshaw et al., 1985). In contrast, neglect patients will tend to make bisections significantly to the *right* of the midpoint, as if they have ignored the full leftward extent of the line. Normed and standardized cancellation and line bisection measures form part of the Behavioural Inattention Test (BIT) battery (Wilson et al., 1987).

In interpreting performance on tests such as cancellation and line bisection—and many other measures of neglect—several important issues should be considered. The first is whether biased performance results from primary sensory loss (e.g., hemianopia) or from neglect. The second is whether impairment is attributable to a perceptual difficulty in 'seeing' the materials or to a motoric difficulty in acting upon them. The third stems from the many dissociations between different forms of spatial neglect: To what extent is one measure predictive of functional difficulties in another activity or domain?

Neglect or Basic Sensory Loss?

The effects of visual field deficits and unilateral neglect can be difficult to disentangle, because the two disorders frequently co-occur. While it is possible to use scalp electrodes to record visual evoked potentials (and therefore show that the brain is receiving *some* visual information despite the patient's inability to report it), this technique is rarely available to most clinicians and, in any case, does not provide a clear index of the potential of the input for subsequent processing. A number of simple behavioural principles that may be applied to help distinguish between visual field defects and spatial neglect include the following:

1 As discussed, visual field loss due to geniculostriate lesions is retinotopic. Manifestations of spatial neglect, on the other hand, are often modulated by extra-retinal information. In other words, rather than detection relying on where the light is hitting the retina, it will depend on where the information is located in relation to the head or body, or where it is in relation to other objects, or the scene as a whole (e.g., Karnath, 1994)

2 The phenomenon of extinction provides a straightforward means of distinguishing primary sensory deficits from spatial biases of attention. In confrontation testing (described earlier in relation to visual field assessment), patients with extinction can report *single* contralesional stimuli—clearly indicating relatively preserved sensation in that region. If they fail to reliably detect the same stimulus when it is presented in competition with an ipsilesional competitor, an attentional account is suggested. Extinction can be assessed in all three major sensory modalities (vision, hearing and touch). Extinction between stimuli in different modalities (e.g., an ipsilesional visual stimulus extinguishing a contralateral tactile stimulus) has also been observed (Mattingley et al., 1997).

3 Patients with neglect can often improve their detection of contralesional stimuli following a cue that directs focal attention toward the affected side (Halligan & Marshall, 1989b), even when eye movements are not permitted (Posner, 1980).

Whenever such cueing improves contralesional performance, the presence of neglect is likely.

4 Neglect and extinction can occur in different sensory modalities. Ambiguities in distinguishing primary sensory loss from neglect can potentially be resolved by testing perceptual and attentional abilities in vision, hearing and touch, and looking for consistent patterns across the modalities. The presence of a spatial bias in the recall of remembered scenes (see pp. 237–238) is also compelling evidence in favour of a more 'central' deficit.

5 There is evidence that, at least in some patients, neglected information may be processed implicitly (i.e., unconsciously), through to a semantic level of representation (e.g., Berti & Rizzolatti, 1992). Patients with primary visual field cuts generally will not exhibit such residual processing (McGlinchey-Berroth et al., 1993, but see also Weiskrantz, 1986).

Perceptual or Motor Neglect?

Separable perceptual and motoric aspects of neglect have been reported (Mattingley & Driver, 1997), and, although sophisticated techniques are required to distinguish unequivocally between the two, some estimate of the relative contributions of each can be made. The picture description subtests of the BIT, for example, requires patients to name objects presented in photographs of everyday scenes and does not require a manual response. Impaired performance here (leaving aside the issue of eye movements) would be consistent with a 'perceptual' neglect.

Forced choice visual tasks have been used to separate perceptual from motoric asymmetries. In the 'greyscales' test (Mattingley et al., 1994) patients must decide which of two vertically aligned rectangles, each shaded incrementally from black on one side to white on the other, is darker overall (see Figure 11.2). Although the overall brightness of the two stimuli is identical, in contrast to normal individuals and in line with a rightward attentional bias, neglect patients tend to select the rectangle with the darker end to the right. In the Wundt-Jastrow illusion test (Massironi et al., 1987) patients must judge which of two arcs is the larger. In the example shown in Figure 11.2, although the arcs are identical in size, healthy individuals will typically select the lower. However, as the illusion is largely generated by the misalignment of the two arcs on the left, patients with neglect are generally less vulnerable to the illusion in this orientation. A purely perceptual version of the line bisection task, in which patients are asked to make judgements about pre-bisected lines, has also been developed (Milner et al., 1993).

Personal, Peripersonal and Extrapersonal Neglect

Evidence from neglect patients suggests that we have access to at least three rather different spatial/action representations. The first (personal space) refers to our awareness of the location of the sensations from our own body and the relative location of our limbs. The second (peripersonal space), concerns the area in the

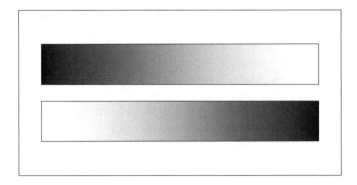

Figure 11.2. Tests of perceptual neglect. Upper: greyscales test. Lower: the Wundt–Jastrow illusion

Source: Greyscales test from Mattingley et al. (1994) and Wundt–Jastrow illusion from Massironi et al. (1987)

immediate vicinity of our body in which most of our actions on the world (e.g., reaching for a cup) will occur. The third (extrapersonal space) refers to the wider visual world that generally lies outside of our immediate ability to act physically on the objects (e.g., Rizzolatti & Gallese, 1988). Given the possible dissociations between these different reference frames, the clinical/predictive value of assessment is undermined if, as often occurs, it is restricted to visuomotor table-top activities performed in peripersonal space.

Beschin and Robertson (1997) developed a simple, standardized and normed procedure designed to assess personal neglect. Patients were asked to comb their hair and pantomime shaving or applying make-up, with the relative number of actions on each side of the body being the crucial measure. Although motoric factors may clearly influence performance, its predictive value for important self-care activities may be greater than for many existing peripersonal tests.

Neglect in Imagery

Bisiach and Luzzatti (1978) demonstrated that neglect could occur for purely imagined visual scenes. Two Milanese patients were asked to imagine themselves in a famous square in the city. When asked to describe the scene from one perspective, they omitted important details from the (remembered) left. When, however, they were asked to imagine the scene as if from the opposite end of the square, these details (now to the right) were recalled—while the previously reported landmarks (now to the left) were more likely to be omitted. Although it is difficult to formalize, similar techniques can be employed, for example, in comparing a patient's description of their own house from imagined positions in front and behind the property.

Grossi et al. (1993) developed a more standardized procedure by exploiting an almost universally familiar spatial array: a clock face. Here patients are asked to imagine the angle made by the hour and minute hands, as specified by a verbal cue (e.g., 'imagine twenty to eleven'). Left neglect patients were worse at judging the angle made by the hands when they appeared on the left of the clock face than when they appeared on the right.

Although drawing from memory is often used to assess distortions in underlying imagery, it is extremely difficult to convincingly separate imaginal from perceptual or motoric factors on the basis of such tests.

Reading and Writing

Reading and writing both involve spatially directed cognitive activity, and it is not surprising that many patients with neglect have difficulties with these tasks. In reading, patients may omit the beginnings of words, particularly if the remaining section of the word forms a meaningful group (e.g., /Train/ as 'rain), or omit entire words from the beginning of a line (Young et al., 1991). In writing, patients will often crowd their words into the right side of the page. In practice almost any task that requires reading aloud or writing can be used to assess this problem, although standardized reading and copying tasks are available (Wilson et al., 1987).

Spontaneous Recovery from Neglect?

As mentioned earlier, most patients who show neglect immediately following a stroke, even those with RH lesions, apparently recover from any striking spatial bias quite rapidly. Many of the rapid improvements may be related to a re-emergence of underlying function, for example, through the reperfusion of hypoperfused but otherwise relatively intact tissue (Hillis et al., 2000). This is an area where early medical interventions could play an increasing role. For other patients, however, improvements may stem less from a recovery in underlying spatial bias than from compensation that serves to mask the bias in everyday activities.

This compensatory process is suggested, for example, in the results of Goodale et al. (1990). Careful analysis of the visually guided reaches of 'recovered' patients showed that they continued to show an ipsilesional distortion in their arm movements, which was corrected 'in flight'—leading to accurate reaches to targets. Further evidence comes from dual task studies. Recently, Bartolomeo (2000) found that, under single task conditions, 'recovered' neglect patients showed no particular lateralized bias on a spatial task. When, however, they were asked to simultaneously tackle a second attentionally demanding activity, their neglect reappeared. This result, taken together with similar findings by other investigators (e.g., Lazar et al., 2002) suggests that patients who appear to have recovered when tested on conventional neuropsychological tests (invariably single tasks) may continue to show problems in complex and demanding real-world settings. It also suggests that behavioural recovery may rely, to an extent, on the availability of more general, limited-capacity, 'top–down' resources. If it is the case that patients who have chronic neglect find it difficult to mobilize attentional resources to overcome their spatial bias, can they be assisted by interventions that make compensation less demanding? This is the central question that has been addressed in a number of very different approaches to neglect rehabilitation, to which we now turn.

REHABILITATION OF UNILATERAL NEGLECT

Scanning Training

Despite a preserved ability to explore left space (e.g., if cued to do so), patients with neglect generally fail to do this spontaneously. Encouraging and reinforcing this behaviour is therefore an obvious place to begin rehabilitation.

Early attempts at evaluating such training showed positive results. Lawson (1962), for example, worked with a patient who tended to miss words to the left of the page. She was trained in a very simple strategy of finding the left side of the page before attempting to read each line. As a consequence, her rate of omissions declined. However, the benefits were remarkably task-specific, not even generalizing to a different book. This difficulty in generalizing improvements in leftward scanning from trained to untrained activities has been reported elsewhere (e.g., Lincoln, 1991; Robertson, 1990; Ross, 1992).

More recently, however, Pizzamiglio et al. (1992) have considered whether scanning training might generalize if carried out over a longer period of time on a *variety* of tasks. Using initially rather simple tasks with strong reinforcement for any leftward scanning, patients were offered over 40 hours of training, the difficulty of the activities increasing as progress occurred. Tasks included naming objects in spatially distributed arrays and visually tracking a leftward-moving light. The results, replicated in a fully randomized controlled study (Antonucci et al., 1995), showed that improvements occurred on untrained tasks and, importantly, in activities of everyday living.

The current evidence suggests, therefore, that scanning training can produce generalized benefits, but that this probably requires rather long periods of intensive and highly structured programmes that may not be easy to provide in all settings. Nonetheless, generalization is not always an essential goal for effective rehabilitation. A clear implication from the earlier studies is that, where scanning training is used, it is best directed toward activities that are of maximal relevance for the patient's life rather than toward abstract tasks.

Prism Lens Adaptation and Hemifield-patching Techniques

The light-distorting effects of wedge-shaped prism lenses, if worn as spectacles, can be used to shift the visual world to the left or right, up or down, or even invert the entire scene. If people wear such lenses, their initial attempts to interact with the world by pointing or gripping objects will tend to be difficult and error-prone, as they are reaching to where the object appears to be rather than where it is. Given more experience, the visuomotor system will adapt to the new reality, and accuracy will be restored. When such glasses are removed, there is again a period of recalibration or adaptation in which reaches are now temporarily inaccurate in the opposite direction.

In a pioneering study, Rossetti et al. (1998) gave patients with left-sided neglect brief exposure (less than five minutes) to prism lenses that distorted space 10 degrees to the *right*. Following a period of adaptation, in which the patients made reaches to targets presented to their left and right, the prisms were removed. The patients not only demonstrated the negative after-effect (reaching 'straight ahead' being significantly further to the left than a pre-exposure baseline), but also showed improvements on a number of neglect tests (line bisection, line cancellation, drawing and reading). These improvements were still apparent two hours later.

Subsequent studies have confirmed the apparently generalized nature of these effects, including on postural control (Tilikete et al., 2001), wheelchair navigation (Rossetti et al., 1998), mental imagery (Rode et al., 1999) and purely tactile spatial exploration (McIntosh et al., 2002). In the largest clinical trial so far reported, Frassinetti et al. (2002) examined the effects of a two-week programme of prism exposure (20 minutes per day, 5 days per week). Compared with a well-matched control group, the prism exposed group showed significant improvements across a range of tasks. Interestingly, although the effects appear to be dependent on the negative after-effect of prisms, the gains on the neglect measures were of much greater longevity than the after-effect—and were still present, even strengthened, five weeks after the end of the training period. Although the mechanisms under-pinning these dramatic effects remain unclear, if the promise of these initial studies is maintained, prism lens adaptation is likely to be a key and easily applied treatment for patients with unilateral neglect.

As a potential method for encouraging the frequency of leftward visual scans, Beis et al. (1999) asked patients to wear glasses with patches over the right half of each lens, significantly reducing stimulation to the right hemifield. The patients wore the adapted glasses for approximately 12 hours a day for 3 months. In a fully randomized study, when compared with patients who had worn patches that completely occluded their right eye, patients with the hemifield patches showed significantly more spontaneous eye movements into left space and significant im-provements in activities of daily living. The fact that the patients were effectively encouraged to scan to the left over many hours, while performing normal everyday activities, may account for these apparently generalized effects in comparison with many scanning training studies. Clearly, however, the use of this technique requires some care if there is an extensive left hemianopia.

Limb Activation Training

Following observations that neglect patients may show less spatial bias when using their left hand to perform a task (Halligan & Marshall, 1989a; Joanette & Brouchon, 1984), Robertson and North (1992, 1993, 1994) systematically investigated this ameliorative effect. To summarize the results: movements of the patients' left hands within left space (relative to the body) reduced omissions on a spatial task, relative to no movement, right-hand movements or bimanual movement conditions, whether or not the movement was visible to the patient. If patients crossed the midline to make movements with their left hand within right space, the improvements were greatly attenuated. Movement of the right hand within left space also produced far less dramatic improvements.

Although this curious interaction between the moving hand, the location of that movement relative to the body midline and visual awareness raises interesting theoretical questions, the results clearly suggest that encouraging left limb movements may have rehabilitative value. It is notable that many neglect patients who can exert adequate power when asked to move their left arm/hand make little spontaneous use of that limb in everyday activity. Robertson et al. (1998a) therefore developed an automated cueing device that involved a patient carrying, and remembering to periodically press, a switch held in the left hand. If no movement occurred within a given period, the buzzer would sound as a reminder. Robertson et al. demonstrated significant improvements in everyday tasks, such as cooking and mobility. Encouragingly, it seems that the training can lead to greater spontaneous use of the left hand for a number of patients. Thus cueing may have a role in motor as well as neglect rehabilitation and provides one explanation of why reductions in neglect were well maintained after the end of formal training in a number of cases.

There are a number of advantages to limb activation training, including its relative conceptual simplicity and its potential to generalize across many tasks. Clearly, however, many neglect patients have severely limited function in their contralesional hand, and there are some patients in whom the effect is apparently absent (Brunila et al., 2002).

Modulating Alertness—Behavioural and Pharmacological Approaches

Damage to the RH is associated with disproportionate deficits in a range of non-spatial attention functions variously termed 'alerting', 'general arousal' and 'vigilance/sustained attention'. As RH lesions are also associated with chronic unilateral neglect, it would be expected that many patients might experience deficits in both spatial and non-spatial attentional functions.

The clinical impression that neglect patients are often under-aroused and appear to have difficulty in maintaining their focus on tasks has received experimental support. Robertson et al. (1997) found that, within a RH patient group, patients showing neglect were disproportionately impaired in a non-spatial sustained attention task (see also Samuelsson et al., 1988). More compellingly, Robertson et al. (1998b) showed that exposing patients to rather unexpected and loud alerting tones abolished or even reversed neglect for brief periods, suggesting a more direct modulatory relationship. If as discussed earlier a lack of more general attentional/executive resources may serve to prevent spontaneous recovery and compensation in the disorder, can inducing a more alert state have lasting benefits for patients with neglect?

Robertson et al. (1995) adapted a procedure first described by Meichenbaum and Goodman (1971) as a means to enable patients to self-maintain a more alert state. In the training (conducted over one week) neglect patients were initially exposed to an inherently alerting stimulus (the therapist slapping the desk). When this occurred, the patients were instructed to say 'Attend!', the idea being to associate this self-instruction with the alert state. As the training progressed, the patients were first asked to take over the table-slapping duties and then to simply say, 'Attend!', while trying to induce the alert state internally. Finally, the patients were asked to conduct this exercise in imagination. The training was associated with improvements in a non-spatial sustained attention measure. Importantly, although the patients had not been trained on spatial tests, significant reductions in neglect were noted.

Given the modulating effects of alertness on neglect (and indeed the re-emergence of neglect in apparently recovered patients who were given medication that reduces alertness: Lazar et al., 2002), a second approach has been to explore the use of stimulant medication. Fleet et al. (1987) administered bromocriptine (a dopamine agonist) to two patients. This stimulant was associated with improvements in some but not all neglect measures, improvements that tended to reverse when the medication was withdrawn. More recently, Hurford et al. (1998) compared the effects of methylphenidate with bromocriptine. They report that, although methylphenidate produced benefits compared with the no treatment condition, bromocriptine produced the stronger results. These preliminary studies suggest that stimulant medication may indeed have a role within rehabilitation for neglect, although larger, fully controlled trials are required.

NON-SPATIAL FORMS OF ATTENTION

Problems that come under the general headings of 'poor concentration', 'difficulty staying on task', 'distractibility' and 'absent-mindedness' are among the most commonly reported complaints of brain-injured patients and their carers. They are also among the most difficult impairments to operationalize and assess.

Although attention has a compelling subjective reality, it is notoriously difficult to define and still harder to measure. It makes little sense, for example, to consider attention as a passive resource, waiting to be engaged on a task. The only way that we can measure attention is by asking people to do *something*—and anything that we ask them to do will make demands on many different abilities, which may themselves be impaired by a brain lesion. Unlike spatial neglect, we cannot easily control for these extraneous factors by comparing performance on one side of space with the other.

To get around these problems, experimental psychology has often operationalized non-spatial forms of attention as the difference between two *levels* of attentional difficulty in the same task. The colour–word Stroop Test is a good example. In the baseline conditions, participants are asked to name colour patches or read colour words as quickly as possible. In the attentionally demanding condition, they are asked to name the colour of the ink in which a colour word is written, with the two being in conflict (e.g., the word RED written in blue ink). The additional time required in this demanding condition relative to the baseline conditions provides an index of the 'attention' needed to suppress the automatic reading response. To take another example, if people are asked to perform a rather dull activity over a long period of time, their performance can deteriorate. Since the basic demands of the task are constant across time, this *change* in performance can be taken as a measure of the efficiency with which attention is sustained (Mackworth, 1948).

Such operational definitions led to a strong resurgence of scientific interest in attention in the second half of the 20th century, including in recent years the use of functional brain-imaging techniques to examine the neural correlates of these capacities. Reviewing this area, Posner and Petersen (1990) proposed two key principles of attention. First, they suggested that brain systems specialized for attention are separable from underlying perceptual processes, so that in principle a given patient may have impaired perception but intact attention, or intact perception and impaired attention. Second, they suggested that within the attention system, different networks perform distinct functions (again implying the potential for dissociation). Their taxonomy includes *alertness* or *vigilance* (an ability to develop and maintain a general responsivity to events occurring in the world); *target selection* or *focused attention* (the ability to select task-relevant information and suppress task-irrelevant information, regardless of its spatial source); and *orienting* or *spatial attention* (the ability to orient toward and prioritize information from a particular region of space). Other investigators have suggested somewhat different taxonomies (see Leclerk & Zimmermann, 2002; Parasuraman et al., 1998).

The Assessment of Non-spatial Forms of Attention

Observation, Self-report and Informant Report

Although it can be difficult to operationalize precisely what we are detecting, it seems clear that in many ways we are acutely sensitive to the direction, intensity and limitations in another's attention. Observing patients during lengthy testing or therapy sessions or, ideally, in the busy noisy context of their everyday lives can be invaluable in helping to interpret their difficulties. Another route is to use questionnaires and checklists that can, in principle, distil this sensitivity across a range of different tasks and over time into a reliable index.

Performance-based Inferences from General Measures

Components of widely used batteries, such as the Wechsler Adult Intelligence Scales (WAIS; Wechsler, 1981) are considered to make greater demands on attention than others. In three-factor solutions of the WAIS-R, the Digit Span and Arithmetic subtests diverge somewhat from the other verbal subtests and have been used as an index of 'Attention/Freedom from distractibility' (Leckliter et al., 1986). Factor-analytic studies of the WAIS-III (both exploratory and confirmatory) support a four-factor model with Arithmetic, Digit Span and Letter–Number–Sequencing contributing to, what has now been termed, the Working Memory Index (Tulsky & Ledbetter, 1997). Although this is economic in the sense that the tests have often already been performed for other reasons, it remains rather unspecific and some caution is required before attributing poor performance to poor attention, working memory, or any other inferred underlying construct.

Specific Measures

Alertness and Sustained Attention

Alertness, the capacity to maintain a readiness to respond, has generally been measured using reaction time tasks. In a typical test, patients are asked to press a key in response to a target light or sound. On occasional trials, a cue is given warning that the target is imminent. Comparison of reaction times between warned and unwarned trials gives an index of the patient's capacity to *self*-maintain a 'ready-to-respond' state. Although such tests have previously required special equipment, normed, standardized programs for personal computers are increasingly available (e.g., the English language version of the computerized Test of Attentional Performance (TAP) battery; Zimmermann & Fimm, 1993).

The two key concepts in the assessment of sustained attention are time and tedium. Often measures use an essentially simple task (e.g., waiting for a particular visual target to appear or keeping a count of the number of tones presented) and, through increasing either the interval between relevant events or the total duration of the test, render the main challenge one of trying to keep one's mind actively engaged in the process. While examining *decrements* in performance is a conceptually tidy measure (comparison of the first and second half of the test effectively controlling for non-attentive aspects of task difficulty), in practice overall levels of performance on these tasks may be more sensitive to short-scale lapses in attention. Various forms of computerized continuous performance tests are available. An auditory vigilance task and slow tone counting measure form part of the Test of Everyday Attention (TEA) battery (Robertson et al., 1994).

Selective Attention

Clinically, selective attention is almost always assessed in the visual domain with, to our knowledge, no well-normed or standardized tasks being available for the auditory or tactile modalities. The Stroop task, described earlier, is perhaps most closely associated with this ability, and normed versions are available (Trenerry et al., 1989). As with neglect, varieties of visual search task are also employed, the Trail Making Test (Part A) (Reitan, 1958) remaining a popular example. It should be remembered, however, that a number of non-attentive factors (poor vision, motor slowness) can contribute to poor performance on such tasks.

Dual Tasks

Activities in which participants are required to divide their attention between two tasks simultaneously, or to switch repeatedly between one task and another, can be very sensitive markers of cognitive deficits (Baddeley et al., 1991). Although these types of measure are often considered under the heading of 'executive function', clear distinctions between these categories, and indeed aspects of working memory, are frequently more a matter of terminological preference than conceptual difference. A normed dual task measure is presented as part of the TEA.

Rehabilitation of Non-spatial Attention

Behavioural Shaping of Attentive Behaviour

While impairments in cognitive domains such as working memory or attention may play a clear role in preventing the achievement of real-life goals, it is by no means certain that retraining these capacities in a highly specific way (e.g., by using the types of tasks that have been developed to assess them) will necessarily produce improvements. Consequently, in rehabilitation it is often more effective to target *functional goals* than to focus on particular impairments. An illustration of this approach in the context of an attentional difficulty is provided by Wilson and Robertson (1992). Their head-injured patient, despite relatively well-preserved IQ and memory, found it very difficult to keep his mind on what he was reading. In a behavioural training programme he was initially asked to read for only brief periods (during which, according to baseline data, a self-reported slip in attention was unlikely to occur). If this was achieved without slip, the period was increased at the next session by 10%. In this manner, the man's experience of error-free reading (and possibly his confidence) was systematically increased until, after 160 sessions, his goal of reading without a slip for five minutes was achieved. Clearly, as such lapses are not generally observable by others, this form of approach relies on self-report, and this may be modulated by factors such as an urge to please one's therapist. The results nevertheless provide an optimistic pointer that forms of poor attention may be amenable to systematic shaping within the context of particular useful activities.

Computerized Approaches to Retraining Attention

The exponential rise in the availability, sophistication and decreasing price of personal computers has encouraged the consideration of their potential value in cognitive rehabilitation. Computers offer a number of clear advantages. They can deliver highly structured, standardized (i.e., replicable) training packages involving attractive graphics/sound and instant feedback on performance. Such packages can be delivered economically, at times that are most convenient for patients, and may be easily transferred from the hospital to the patient's home. There are potential disadvantages, of course, including whether patients feel at ease with the technology, whether a 'one size fits all' approach is merited for patients with potentially quite different difficulties and, in particular, whether benefits generalize from the computer to everyday life.

Gray et al. (1992) developed a computer package that was designed to train attentional function in a rather general way. The training regime was broadly derived from neuropsychological measures and included a reaction time task, a digit–symbol translation task and the colour–word Stroop Test. In a randomized, controlled study, 15 hours of training were compared with 15 hours of recreational computing, with any change being evaluated on a range of standardized measures. Gains on the Paced Auditory Serial Addition Test and the WAIS Picture Completion subtest seen immediately following treatment were followed by more generalized test improvements relative to the control group at six months follow-up. The results suggest that attentive functions may be amenable, repetitive, progressive ('mental muscle') training. Unfortunately, however, generalization to activities of everyday life was not examined in this study.

More recently, Sturm et al. (1997) developed a computerized training package (AIXTENT) designed specifically to target hypothetically separable attention functions (alertness, sustained attention, selective attention and divided attention). This modularity also allowed the researchers to evaluate the package in a particularly elegant manner. Rather than leave some participants untreated, the 38 patients reported in the initial study (mainly stroke patients with documented attentional problems) were allocated to a different *order* of training. The hypothesis was that if the training was successful, the order of improvement would follow the order of modules completed. Following approximately 56 hours of training, the hypothesis was broadly supported. As measured on an untrained computer task, the detection rate for targets in a vigilance task was significantly improved only after vigilance training, but not following training in selective or divided attention. Similarly, reaction times in the selective attention test were improved following selective attention training, but not after training of sustained attention. Due to the difficulty in assessing attentional function in complex real-world activities, however, the generalization of these improvements away from the computer context requires further evaluation (though see Sturm et al., 2002). An English language version of the training program is currently being developed.

Enhancing Attention through Changing the Environment

In thinking about rehabilitation the emphasis is often on producing change within the individual (e.g., reducing the impairment or teaching strategies to get around a problem). An alternative that has been explored successfully in a number of domains, particularly memory, is to change the environment to make a particular functional outcome easier to achieve. In terms of attention, many of us make such adjustments everyday (e.g., turning off the radio if we want to study, or taking a break before beginning an exacting task). Such environmental management is likely to be even more crucial in the context of attentional deficits through brain injury. However, therapists and carers need to be aware that the lack of insight and difficulty in flexibly adapting behaviour that can accompany such injuries may undermine a patient's ability to spontaneously adopt these apparently simple strategies.

Manly et al. (2002) recently examined whether more specific environmental cues can be useful. Head injured patients were asked to perform the Hotel Test (a modification of Shallice & Burgess's, 1991 Six Elements task), in which they were presented with five activities that might plausibly be associated with the trade (e.g., calculating bills, sorting conference labels into alphabetical order). The task was to 'sample' each of the jobs over a 15-minute period, with the explicit instruction that this time would be insufficient to finish even one of the tasks completely. As with the Six Elements task, therefore, the test emphasized patients' ability to maintain attention to the main goal of trying each of the tasks and to shift flexibly between the components at reasonable intervals. A key error in the standard version of the task was for patients to get 'caught up' in one of the tasks and to neglect the main goal, despite being able to recall this goal both before and after the test.

In an 'environmentally cued' version of the task, a tone was presented at random intervals. Before beginning, the patients were trained to use the tone as a cue to think about what they were doing. Under this condition the patients not only showed significant improvements, but their performance was now also indistinguishable from that of healthy, IQ matched controls. This technique is useful in isolating the cause of problems on complex tasks (e.g., a simple failure to remember the goal can be ruled out). It also suggests portable devices can be used to cue particular cognitive operations. A good example of this approach applied to real-life goals can be found in Evans et al. (1998).

CONCLUSIONS

The scientific and clinical analysis of disorders of attention, not to mention the rehabilitation of those disorders, are at a relatively early stage. Many questions remain about the precise functional mechanisms of attention and their relationship to underlying neural systems. There is, however, growing evidence that these capacities, however crudely assessed, are very important in determining functional outcome from brain injury and patients' abilities to maximally benefit from rehabilitation.

Unilateral neglect remains perhaps the clearest and most striking example of an attentional disorder and is the area where rehabilitation is most advanced. The recent findings on prism adaptation together with previous work on limb activation, hemifield patching, scanning training and enhancing patients' ability to maintain an alert state offer a range of techniques for the clinician to explore. To date, few if any studies have directly contrasted one treatment approach with another in the same patient group, or specifically examined the additive effects of combining treatments. As we have also stressed in the section on assessment, 'neglect' is a rather heterogeneous disorder, and, as yet, the applicability of different approaches to the quite varied manifestations of the condition remain largely unknown.

In comparison with neglect, there is currently less convergence on how non-spatial forms of attention are best operationalized or divided into functionally or anatomically important subgroups. Inferences on attentional dysfunction are still often drawn from observation, interviews with relatives or from interpretation of measures, such as the WAIS-III, that make demands on many capacities. Although rehabilitation should always ultimately be directed at improving performance in complex everyday activities, this lack of specificity has implications for the development of clear and theoretically driven interventions in this area. This situation is improving, however, and an increasing number of more specific tests are now becoming available. This, in turn, should facilitate a clearer analysis of whether and how interventions are effective and of the relationship between particular therapeutic gains and overall outcome. The existing evidence gives some grounds for optimism in this respect. The results of behaviourally shaping attentive behaviour and of providing long periods of systematic computerized practice both suggest the potential for improving underlying function. In addition to controlling distractions in the environment, the use of portable devices to cue patients to make better use of residual function is another area warranting further exploration.

REFERENCES

Antonucci, G., Guariglia, C., Judica, A., Magnotti, L., Paoloucci, S., Pizzamiglio, L. et al. (1995) Effectiveness of neglect rehabilitation in a randomised group-study. *Journal of Clinical and Experimental Neuropsychology*, **17**, 383–389.

Baddeley, A. D., Bressi, S., Salla, S. D., Logie, R. & Spinnler, H. (1991) The decline of working memory in Alzheimer's Disease. *Brain*, **114**, 2521–2542.

Bartolomeo, P. (2000) Inhibitory processes and spatial bias after right hemisphere damage. *Neuropsychological Rehabilitation*, **10**, 511–526.

Beis, J. M., Andre, J. M., Baumgarten, A. & Challier, B. (1999) Eye patching in unilateral spatial neglect: Efficacy of two methods. *Archives of Physical Medicine and Rehabilitation*, **80**, 71–76.

Berti, A. & Rizzolatti, G. (1992) Visual processing without awareness: Evidence from unilateral neglect. *Journal of Cognitive Neuroscience*, **4**, 345–351.

Beschin, N. & Robertson, I. H. (1997) Personal versus extrapersonal neglect: A group study of their dissociation using a reliable clinical test. *Cortex*, **33**, 379–384.

Bisiach, E. & Luzzatti, C. (1978) Unilateral neglect of representational space. *Cortex*, **14**, 129–133.

Bradshaw, J. L., Nettleton, N. C., Nathan, G. & Wilson, L. (1985) Bisecting rods and lines: Effects of horizontal and vertical posture on left-side underestimation by normal subjects. *Neuropsychologia*, **23**, 421–425.

Brunila, T., Lincoln, N., Lindell, A., Tenovuo, O. & Hämäläinen, H. (2002) Experiences of combined visual training and arm activation in the rehabilitation of unilateral visual neglect: A clinical study. *Neuropsychological Rehabilitation*, **12**, 27–40.

Evans, J. J., Emslie, H. & Wilson, B. A. (1998) External cueing systems in the rehabilitation of executive impairments of action. *Journal of the International Neuropsychological Society*, **4**, 399–408.

Farah, M. J. (1990) *Visual Agnosia: Disorders of Object Recognition and What They Tell Us about Normal Vision*. MIT Press, Cambridge, MA.

Fleet, W. S., Valenstein, E., Watson, R. T. & Heilman, K. M. (1987) Dopamine agonist therapy for neglect in humans. *Neurology*, **37**, 1765–1771.

Frassinetti, F., Angeli, V., Meneghello, F., Avanzi, S. & Ladavas, E. (2002) Long-lasting amelioration of visuospatial neglect by prism adaptation. *Brain*, **125**, 608–623.

Goodale, M. A., Milner, A. D., Jakobson, L. S. & Carey, D. P. (1990) Kinematic analysis of limb movements in neuropsychological research: Subtle deficits and recovery of function. *Canadian Journal of Psychology*, **44**, 180–195.

Gray, J. M., Robertson, I. H., Pentland, B. & Anderson, S. I. (1992) Microcomputer based cognitive rehabilitation for brain damage: A randomised group controlled trial. *Neuropsychological Rehabilitation*, **2**, 97–116.

Grossi, D., Angelini, R., Pecchinenda, A. & Pizzamiglio, L. (1993) Left imaginal neglect in hemi-inattention: Experimental study with the clock test. *Behavioural Neurology*, **6**, 155–158.

Halligan, P. W. & Marshall, J. C. (1989a) Laterality of motor response in visuo-spatial neglect: A case study. *Neuropsychologia*, **27**, 1301–1307.

Halligan, P. W. & Marshall, J. C. (1989b) Perceptual cueing and perceptuo-motor compatibility in visuospatial neglect: A single case study. *Cognitive Neuropsychology*, **6**, 423–435.

Halligan, P. W. & Marshall, J. C. (1994) Spatial neglect: Position papers on theory and practice. *Neuropsychological Rehabilitation*: Special Issue, 4(2).

Hier, D. B., Mondlock, J. & Caplan, L. R. (1983) Recovery of behavioural abnormalities after right hemisphere stroke. *Neurology*, **33**, 345–350.

Hillis, A. E., Barker, P. B., Beauchamp, N. J., Gordon, B. & Wityk, R. J. (2000) MR perfusion imaging reveals regions of hypoperfusion associated with aphasia and neglect. *Neurology*, **55**, 782–788.

Hurford, P., Stringer, A. & Jann, B. (1998) Neuropharmacologic treatment of hemineglect: A case report comparing bromocriptine and methylphenidate. *Archives of Physical Medicine and Rehabilitation*, **79**, 346–349.

Joanette, Y. & Brouchon, M. (1984) Visual allesthesia in manual pointing: Some evidence for a sensori-motor cerebral organisation. *Brain and Cognition*, **3**, 152–165.

Karnath, H. O. (1994) Subjective body orientation in neglect and the interactive contribution of neck muscle proprioception and vestibular stimulation. *Brain*, **117**, 1001–1012.

Karnath, H. O., Ferber, S. & Himmelbach, M. (2001) Spatial awareness is a function of the temporal not the posterior parietal lobe. *Nature*, **411**, 950–953.

Lawson, I. R. (1962) Visual-spatial neglect in lesions of the right cerebral hemisphere: A study in recovery. *Neurology*, **12**, 23–33.

Lazar, R., Fitzsimmons, B., Marshall, R., Berman, M., Bustillo, M., Young, W. et al. (2002) Re-emergence of stroke deficits with midazolam challenge. *Stroke*, **33**, 283–285.

Leckliter, I. N., Silverstein, A. B. & Matarazzo, J. D. (1986) A literature review of factor analytic studies of the WAIS-R. *Journal of Clinical Psychology*, **42**, 332–342.

Leclerk, M. & Zimmermann, P. (2002) *Applied Neuropsychology of Attention*. Psychology Press, Hove, UK.

Lincoln, N. B. (1991) The recognition and treatment of visual perceptual disorders. *Topics in Geriatric Rehabilitation*, **7**, 25–34.

Mackworth, N. H. (1948) The breakdown of vigilance during prolonged visual search. *The Quarterly Journal of Experimental Psychology*, **1**, 6–21.

Manly, T., Hawkins, K., Evans, J. J., Woldt, K. & Robertson, I. H. (2002) Rehabilitation of executive function: Facilitation of effective goal management on complex tasks using periodic auditory alerts. *Neuropsychologia*, **40**, 271–281.

Massironi, M., Antonucci, G., Pizzamiglio, L., Vitale, M. & Zoccolotti, P. (1987) The Wundt–Jastrow area illusion as a measure of hemineglect disturbances. *Journal of Clinical and Experimental Neuropsychology*, **9**, 258–258.

Mattingley, J. B. & Driver, J. (1997) Distinguishing sensory and motor deficits after parietal damage: An evaluation of response selection biases in unilateral neglect. In: P. Thier & H. O. Karnath (eds), *Parietal Lobe Contributions to Orientation in 3D Space* (pp. 309–338). Springer-Verlag, Heidelberg.

Mattingley, J. B., Driver, J., Beschin, N. & Robertson, I. H. (1997) Attentional competition between modalities: Extinction between touch and vision after right hemisphere damage. *Neuropsychologia*, **35**, 867–880.

McGlinchey-Berroth, R., Milberg, W. P., Verfaellie, M., Alexander, M. & Kilduff, P. T. (1993) Semantic processing in the neglected visual field: Evidence from a lexical decision task. *Clinical Neuropsychologist*, **10**, 79–108.

McIntosh, R. D., Rossetti, Y. & Milner, A. D. (2002) Prism adaptation improves chronic visual and haptic neglect: A single case study. *Cortex*, **38**, 309–320.

Meichenbaum, D. & Goodman, J. (1971) Training impulsive children to talk to themselves: A means of developing self-control. *Journal of Abnormal Psychology*, **77**, 115–126.

Mesulam, M. M. (1981) A cortical network for directed attention and unilateral neglect. *Annals of Neurology*, **10**, 309–325.

Milner, A. D. & Goodale, M. A. (1993) Visual pathways to perception and action. In: T. P. Hicks, S. Molotchnikoff & T. Ono (eds), *Progress in Brain Research* (Vol. 95, pp. 317–337). Elsevier, Amsterdam.

Milner, A. D., Brechmann, M., Roberts, R. C. & Forster, S. V. (1993) Line bisection errors in visual neglect: Misguided action or size distortion? *Neuropsychologia*, **31**, 39–49.

Paolucci, S., Antonucci, G., Grasso, M. & Pizzamiglio, L. (2001a) The role of unilateral spatial neglect in rehabilitation of right brain-damaged ischemic stroke patients: A matched comparison. *Archives of Physical Medicine and Rehabilitation*, **82**, 743–749.

Paolucci, S., Grasso, M. G., Antonucci, G., Bragoni, M., Troisi, E., Morelli, D. et al. (2001b) Mobility status after inpatient stroke rehabilitation: 1-year follow-up and prognostic factors. *Archives of Physical Medicine and Rehabilitation*, **82**, 2–8.

Parasuraman, R., Warm, J. S. & See, J. E. (1998) Brain systems of vigilance. In: R. Parasuraman (ed.) *The Attentive Brain* (pp. 221–256). MIT Press, Cambridge, MA.

Perenin, M. & Vighetto, A. (1988) Optic ataxia: A specific disruption of visuomotor representations. *Brain*, **111**, 643–674.

Pizzamiglio, L., Antonucci, G., Judica, A., Montenero, P., Prazzano, C. & Zoccolotti, P. (1992) Cognitive rehabilitation of the hemineglect disorder in chronic-patients with unilateral right brain-damage. *Journal of Clinical and Experimental Neuropsychology*, **14**, 901–923.

Posner, M. I. (1980) Orientating of attention. *Quarterly Journal of Experimental Psychology*, **32**, 3–25.

Posner, M. I. & Petersen, S. E. (1990) The attention system of the human brain. *Annual Review of Neuroscience*, **13**, 25–42.

Reitan, R. M. (1958) The validity of the Trail Making Test as an indicator of organic brain damage. *Perceptual and Motor Skills*, **9**, 127–130.

Rizzolatti, G. & Gallese, V. (1988) Mechanisms and theories of spatial neglect. In: F. Boller & J. Grafman (eds), *Handbook of Neuropsychology* (Vol. 1, pp. 223–246). Elsevier, Amsterdam.

Robertson, I. (1990) Does computerized cognitive rehabilitation work? A review. *Aphasiology*, **4**, 381–405.

Robertson, I. H. & North, N. (1992) Spatio-motor cueing in unilateral neglect: The role of hemispace, hand and motor activation. *Neuropsychologia*, **30**, 553–563.

Robertson, I. H. & North, N. (1993) Active and passive activation of left limbs: Influence on visual and sensory neglect. *Neuropsychologia*, **31**, 293–300.

Robertson, I. H. & North, N. (1994) One hand is better than two: Motor extinction of left hand advantage in unilateral neglect. *Neuropsychologia*, **32**, 1–11.

Robertson, I. H., Ward, A., Ridgeway, V. & Nimmo-Smith, I. (1994) *Test of Everyday Attention*. Thames Valley Test Company, Bury St Edmunds, UK.

Robertson, I. H., Tegnér, R., Tham, K., Lo, A. & Nimmo-Smith, I. (1995) Sustained attention training for unilateral neglect: Theoretical and rehabilitation implications. *Journal of Clinical and Experimental Neuropsychology*, **17**, 416–430.

Robertson, I. H., Manly, T., Beschin, N., Haeske-Dewick, H., Hömberg, V., Jehkonen, M. et al. (1997) Auditory sustained attention is a marker of unilateral spatial neglect. *Neuropsychologia*, **35**, 1527–1532.

Robertson, I. H., Hogg, K. & McMillan, T. M. (1998a) Rehabilitation of unilateral neglect: Improving function by contralesional limb activation. *Neuropsychological Rehabilitation*, **8**, 19–29.

Robertson, I. H., Mattingley, J. M., Rorden, C. & Driver, J. (1998b) Phasic alerting of neglect patients overcomes their spatial deficit in visual awareness. *Nature*, **395**, 169–172.

Rode, G., Rossetti, Y. & Boisson, D. (1999) Improvement of mental imagery after prism exposure in neglect: A case study. *Behavioural Neurology*, **11**, 251–258.

Ross, F. L. (1992) The use of computers in occupational therapy in visual scanning training. *American Journal of Occupational Therapy*, **46**, 314–322.

Rossetti, Y., Rode, G., Pisella, L., Farne, A., Li, L., Boisson, D. & Perenin, M. T. (1998) Prism adaptation to a rightward optical deviation rehabilitates left hemispatial neglect. *Nature*, **395**, 166–169.

Samuelsson, H., Hjelmquist, E., Jensen, C., Ekholm, S. & Blomstrand, C. (1988) Nonlateralized attentional deficits: An important component behind persisting visuospatial neglect? *Journal of Clinical and Experimental Psychology*, **20**, 73–88.

Samuelsson, H., Jensen, C., Ekholm, S., Naver, H. & Blomstrand, C. (1997) Anatomical and neurological correlates of acute and chronic visuospatial neglect following right hemisphere stroke. *Cortex*, **33**, 271–285.

Shallice, T. & Burgess, P. (1991) Deficit in strategy application following frontal lobe damage in man. *Brain*, **114**, 727–741.

Stone, S. P., Halligan, P. W. & Greenwood, R. J. (1993) The incidence of neglect phenomena and related disorders in patients with an acute right or left-hemisphere stroke. *Age and Ageing*, **22**, 46–52.

Sturm, W., Willmes, K., Orgass, B. & Hartje, W. (1997) Do specific attention deficits need specific training? *Neuropsychological Rehabilitation*, **7**, 81–103.

Sturm, W., Fimm, B., Cantagallo, A., Cremel, N., North, P., Passadori, A. et al. (2002) Computerised training of specific attention deficits in stroke and traumatic brain injured patients: A multicentric efficacy study. In: M. Leclecq & P. Zimmermann (eds) *Applied Neuropsychology of Attention* (pp. 365–380). Psychology Press, Hove, UK.

Tilikete, C., Rode, G., Rossetti, Y., Pichon, J., Li, L. & Boisson, D. (2001) Prism adaptation to rightward optical deviation improves postural imbalance in left-hemiparetic patients. *Current Biology*, **11**, 524–528.

Trenerry, M. R., Crosson, B., DeBoe, J. & Leber, W. R. (1989) *Stroop Neuropsychological Screening Test*. Psychological Assessment Resources, Odessa, FL.

Tulsky, D. & Ledbetter, M. F. (1997) *WAIS-III: Technical Manual*. Psychological Corporation, London.

Ungerleider, L. & Mishkin, M. (1982) Two cortical visual systems. In: D. Ingle, R. Mansfield and M. Goodale (eds) *The Analysis of Visual Behaviour*. MIT Press, Cambridge, MA.

Vallar, G. & Perani, D. (1986) The anatomy of unilateral neglect after right-hemisphere stroke lesions: A clinical/CT scan correlation study in man. *Neuropsychologia*, **24**, 609–622.

Wechsler, D. (1981) *Wechsler Adult Intelligence Scale—Revised*. Psychological Corporation, New York.

Wechsler, I. S. (1933) Partial cortical blindness with preservation of colour vision. *Archives of Ophthalmology*, **9**, 957–965.

Weiskrantz, L. (1986) *Blindsight: A Case Study and Implications*. Oxford University Press, Oxford, UK.

Wilson, B., Cockburn, J. & Halligan, P. (1987) *The Behavioural Inattention Test*. Thames Valley Test Co., Bury St Edmunds, UK.

Wilson, C. & Robertson, I. H. (1992) A home-based intervention for attentional slips during reading following head injury: A single case study. *Neuropsychological Rehabilitation*, **2**, 193–205.

Young, A. W., Newcombe, F. & Ellis, A. W. (1991) Different impairments contribute to neglect dyslexia. *Cognitive Neuropsychology*, **8**, 177–191.

Zarit, S. & Kahn, R. (1974) Impairment and adaptation in chronic disabilities. *Journal of Nervous and Mental Diseases*, **159**, 63–72.

Zihl, J. (2000) *Rehabilitation of Visual Disorders Following Brain Injury*. Psychology Press, Hove, UK.

Zihl, J. & von Cramon, D. (1979) Restitution of visual function in patients with cerebral blindness. *Journal of Neurology, Neurosurgery and Psychiatry*, **42**, 312–322.

Zihl, J., von Cramon, D. & Mai, N. (1983) Selective disturbance of movement vision after bilateral brain damage. *Brain*, **106**, 313–340.

Zimmermann, P. & Fimm, B. (1993) *Testbatterie zur Erfassung von Aufmerksamkeitsstörungen* (Version 1.02). Psytest, Freiburg, Germany.

CHAPTER 12

Disorders of Number Processing and Calculation

Jane E. McNeil

Institute of Psychiatry, London, UK

INTRODUCTION

An acquired disorder of number processing or calculation can have an enormous impact on a patient's ability to cope in everyday life. We need to be able to understand and manipulate numbers to manage money and financial affairs, understand dates and times and to be able to use telephones or public transport. Neurological patients with the acquired inability to carry out these fundamental mental operations, which most of us take for granted, can therefore be severely handicapped. The study of the devastating deficits these patients experience can however provide strong evidence about how the normal brain processes and transforms numerical information. An understanding of the models proposed to explain number processing and calculation can assist in the appropriate assessment of patients' selective difficulties and inform rehabilitation strategies. This chapter will therefore deal in particular detail with the cognitive neuropsychological aspects of number processing and calculation.

Until early in the 20th century, disorders of number processing and calculation had received little interest as they had been seen as arising from more general language disorders. However, in 1919 Henschen concluded that it was possible to have an impairment of calculation without necessarily having a language or reading disorder. He used the term 'acalculia' to refer to a specific difficulty with arithmetic that could be said to be independent of general intelligence. The concept of acalculia was further developed by Berger (1926), who distinguished between primary and secondary acalculia. He defined a *secondary acalculia* as a disturbance of calculation arising from an underlying language, reading or attentional deficit. A *primary acalculia* occurred when no such deficit was present and the acalculia could be said to be a pure deficit of calculation or *anarithmetria*. Berger's distinction between primary and secondary acalculia was further expanded by Hécaen et al. (1961). They proposed three types of acalculia: *anarithmetria* (a relatively pure disorder in carrying out the operations involved in calculation), *alexic* or *agraphic acalculia* (where the deficits were secondary to difficulties reading or

Clinical Neuropsychology: A Practical Guide to Assessment and Management for Clinicians.
Edited by L.H. Goldstein and J.E. McNeil. © 2004 John Wiley & Sons, Ltd.

writing numbers) and *spatial acalculia* (where the calculation disorder was due to spatial problems [e.g., putting columns down incorrectly for written calculations]).

The following, more recent, studies have attempted to look in more detail at the relative contributions of other background cognitive processes to number processing and calculation by investigating patients with the selective preservation of numerical processing or mathematical skills despite evidence of severe cognitive deficits in other areas.

THE SELECTIVE PRESERVATION OF NUMBER PROCESSING OR CALCULATION

Studies of aphasic patients have commonly found that number processing can remain unimpaired despite severe language problems. For example, Gardner (1973) compared naming abilities across different categories and found that number naming was the most frequently preserved category when compared with animals, colours and letters. Anderson et al. (1990) described a patient with a left frontal lesion and a selective dyslexia and dysgraphia. In contrast to her problems reading and writing letters and words, her number processing (with Arabic numerals[1]) was excellent. She was able to read and write multi-digit numbers without error and her written addition, subtraction, multiplication and division were all good. Warrington (1982) also reported a patient with impaired single word comprehension and dyslexia and dysgraphia following a left posterior tumour. She was unable to comprehend spoken numbers, but her comprehension of Arabic numerals was good.

A case with the selective preservation of calculation skills was reported by Rossor et al. (1995). This man with probable Pick's disease had very severely impaired language skills. By contrast, his number processing skills were only mildly impaired. He could repeat single digits, match spoken numbers to Arabic numerals, read single digit Arabic numerals and passed a written cardinality judgement task deciding which of two numbers is the largest using two and three digit Arabic numerals. His calculation skills were also fairly well preserved when sums were presented visually, and he could write an Arabic numeral as a response. He performed simple single digit addition and subtraction sums well, although he had difficulties with multiplication sums and appeared to have lost many of his multiplication facts[2] and instead solved many of the sums by the use of serial addition.

McNeil's (1999) patient with severely impaired language skills but well-preserved numerical abilities had received a diagnosis of primary progressive aphasia and had no functional use of language, being unable to comprehend simple high-frequency

---

[1] The term 'Arabic numeral' will be used to refer to numbers written as Arabic digits (e.g., '43') and the terms 'written verbal numbers' and 'spoken verbal numbers' to refer to verbal numbers (e.g., 'forty three') in written or spoken format, respectively.

[2] Models of calculation have proposed a semantic network of arithmetic facts that can be retrieved directly without having to work out the solution each time it is encountered (e.g., Groen & Parkman, 1972).

words, such as *shoe* or *key*. In contrast, he could read, write and understand Arabic numerals and had no difficulties with simple addition and subtraction sums with spoken or written presentation. However, as with Rossor et al.'s (1995) case, he had also lost most of his multiplication facts and had to resort to serial addition to solve multiplication sums, which may suggest that multiplication facts are more reliant on language processes.

There has also been some evidence that calculation skills can be preserved despite severely reduced auditory verbal working memory. It had been argued by several authors (e.g., Baddeley & Hitch, 1974) that auditory verbal working memory is required for the temporary storage of information to be used in problem-solving tasks, such as complex mental arithmetic. However, a case by Butterworth et al. (1996) has suggested that this may not be the case. Their patient, MRF, who had a left-hemisphere infarct and severely compromised auditory short-term memory, had remarkably well-preserved calculation skills. He was only able to reliably repeat two digits forwards, but could perform orally presented addition and subtraction sums consisting of two and three digit numbers.

THE SELECTIVE IMPAIRMENT OF NUMBER PROCESSING

Investigations of disorders of number processing have considered both comprehension and production of written and spoken number names and Arabic numerals, although there have been rather more reports of patients with selective difficulties of production than comprehension. There have been cases reported with selective difficulty comprehending spoken number names (Warrington, 1982) or written number names (McCloskey et al., 1985) with preserved Arabic numeral comprehension. However, neither of these cases addressed whether comprehension of spoken number names and written number names could dissociate from each other.

A considerable amount of research has investigated the ability to read Arabic numerals aloud. McCloskey and colleagues have built on pioneering earlier work (Deloche & Seron, 1982; Seron & Deloche, 1983) to show that, as with word reading, our reading of Arabic numerals appears to involve both a lexical and syntactic component. For example, McCloskey et al.'s (1986) patient, HY, made primarily lexical substitution errors (where the incorrect number name is accessed, but the number is the correct order of magnitude [e.g., reading '4,014' as 'four thousand and nineteen']). In contrast, patient JG (McCloskey et al., 1990) made syntactic errors (where the number name is correct, but the order of magnitude is incorrect [e.g., reading '312' as 'three hundred and twenty' and '50,300' as 'five thousand, three hundred']). These cases led McCloskey and colleagues to conclude that the number processing system must involve lexical and syntactic processing mechanisms that may be impaired independently of each other.

THE SELECTIVE IMPAIRMENT OF CALCULATION

There have been fewer published studies of specific calculation impairments than there have been of number processing impairments, but studies can be broadly divided into those looking at arithmetical facts and those looking at procedures.

Arithmetic Facts

Models of calculation have proposed a semantic network of arithmetic facts that can be retrieved directly (e.g., Groen & Parkman, 1972). Neuropsychological support for this hypothesis came from a patient who was unable to solve simple sums (such as '6 + 4'), but who could apply the correct arithmetical procedures and could still solve complex calculations if given unlimited time and allowed to use a laborious counting process (Warrington, 1982). Warrington interpreted these findings as reflecting a selective deficit accessing arithmetical facts, with arithmetical operations and number processing relatively well preserved. This distinction has been incorporated into many current models of calculation.

Further cases with a selective impairment of facts have confirmed Warrington's distinction between facts and procedures. For instance, McCloskey et al. (1985) reported a case with impaired multiplication facts but intact arithmetical procedures, as was shown by his ability to work out the answer to multiplication sums when he was unable to access the answer directly. For example, he could not remember the answer to '7 × 7', but used procedures and his residual preserved facts to arrive at the correct answer $(70(7 \times 10) - 21(7 \times 3)$, answer 49). Hittmair-Delazer et al.'s (1994) case had lost his simple knowledge of facts, such as '2 + 3', but nevertheless showed excellent conceptual understanding of mathematical concepts and could work out the answer to simple sums using this preserved knowledge.

The following papers have attempted to use single cases to investigate the extent to which arithmetical facts for different arithmetical operations are independent of each other.

Operation-specific Calculation Deficits

It has been assumed from the developmental and cognitive literature that each arithmetical operation (i.e., addition, multiplication, subtraction) has its own memory representation (e.g., Miller et al., 1984) and some supporting evidence is emerging from neuropsychological single cases (see Table 12.1).

For instance, Singer and Low (1933) first reported a patient with the selective impairment of subtraction and division, after suffering encephalitis due to carbon monoxide poisoning. These difficulties were the same with spoken or written presentation.

Benson and Weir's (1972) case had a specific difficulty with multiplication and

Table 12.1. A summary of reported cases with operation-specific calculation impairments

		Addition	Subtraction	Multiplication	Division
Singer & Low (1933)		✓	✗	✓	✗
Benson & Weir (1972)		✓	✓	✗	✗
Dagenbach & McCloskey (1992)		✗	✓	NT	NT
McNeil & Warrington (1994)		✗	✓	✗	NT
Presenti et al. (1994)		✗	✓	✗	NT
Lampl et al. (1994)		✗	✓	✗	✗
Cipolotti & Costello (1995)		✓	✓	✓	✗
Delazer & Benke (1997)		✗	✗	✓	✗
Van Harskamp & Cipolotti (2001)	FS	✗	✓	✓	NT
	DT	✓	✗	✓	NT
	VP	✓	✓	✗	NT

NT = Not tested

division, but addition and subtraction were well preserved. The few examples given in the text suggest that he not only had problems with multiplication sums involving numbers larger than two, but also some problems applying the correct procedures with multi-digit multiplication sums.

Dagenbach and McCloskey's (1992) patient RG had severe language problems. His number processing skills were also impaired, and he was found to be significantly better at solving subtraction sums than addition sums. The authors interpreted their results as indicating that arithmetical facts are segregated in memory according to operation.

Further evidence for the segregation of arithmetic facts in memory includes Lampl et al.'s (1994) case with the selective preservation of subtraction. Simple and complex subtraction sums were performed quickly and without error. However, he had severe problems with equivalent addition and multiplication sums. His multiplication and addition sums were impaired with both oral and written presentation. McNeil and Warrington's (1994) case also showed the selective preservation of subtraction when sums were presented visually.

Presenti et al. (1994) reported the case of BB with a 'precocious evolving dementia'. She had marked memory and language problems, but her number processing skills were relatively well preserved. Her arithmetic was impaired for single digit addition and multiplication sums, but she only made occasional errors with subtraction tasks.

Delazer and Benke's (1997) patient, JG, had severe calculation problems including difficulties with arithmetical procedures and impaired conceptual knowledge. He showed the selective preservation of multiplication facts and the impairment of addition, subtraction and division. The authors felt that this operation-specific preservation could be consistent with the idea of operation-specific stored representations as suggested by previous authors (e.g., Dagenbach & McCloskey, 1992). However, they also felt that it could be explained by Noel and Seron's (1993, 1995) preferred entry hypothesis, which suggests that different arithmetical and numerical tasks have a preferred entry code (such as phonological, visual, graphemic, etc.). The preferred code may vary between people as well as tasks, so that certain individuals prefer a verbal entry code whereas others prefer a visual code. The authors emphasized that, in Austria, multiplication facts are taught verbally (by reciting tables out loud), but addition and subtraction are not (this being similar to the English educational system). It might therefore be expected that multiplication would use a preferred verbal entry code as this was how these facts were learnt. However, if addition and subtraction were learnt using more visually based strategies, then it might be plausible to expect them to have a preferred visual code.

One of the only studies to investigate division in any detail is that by Cipolotti and Costello (1995). CB was severely impaired on simple division problems, but simple and complex addition, subtraction and multiplication were all well preserved. He was also unable to solve problems in the format $N \times ? = M$ (e.g., 'five times what equals fifteen?'). The authors proposed two possible explanations for their data: first, that division problems require access to their own table of division facts, which are completely separate from the table of multiplication facts, or, second, that division problems do not require access to specific 'division facts', but rather rely on the manipulation of problems in the format $N \times ? = M$. If this is the case, then it should not be possible to find a case who has preserved division and impaired multiplication.

Van Harskamp and Cipolotti (2001) have more recently documented three patients with selective difficulties with different arithmetical operations. The first patient showed impaired addition with preserved subtraction and multiplication. The second had a selective impairment in subtraction. The last had a selective impairment in multiplication. The authors argued for separate addition, subtraction and multiplication facts.

These cases have shown that it is possible to find patients with specific difficulties with certain arithmetical operations. One possible interpretation is obviously that the semantic store for calculation facts is segregated according to operation, so neurological damage can affect one or more operations according to which areas are damaged (in an analogous way to category specificity in aphasia). However, although this may be the most obvious explanation of the results, it is not the only interpretation: it is implausible that internal cognitive structures necessarily conform to psychological distinctions. Pertinent to this point is that if these dissociations do indeed reflect an operation-specific semantic organization for arithmetic facts, then it should be possible to find a selective impairment of any arithmetical operation that leaves the others intact. It is worth emphasizing therefore that no cases have yet been described with an impairment of subtraction and multiplication with the preservation of addition.

Arithmetical Procedures

The evidence for the selective impairment of arithmetical procedures is presently rather more tentative than for arithmetical facts. McCloskey et al. (1985) give very brief descriptions of three patients who had particular difficulty with, for example, carrying processes in addition or aligning the intermediate products correctly in multi-digit multiplication sums.

There is some evidence from the developmental literature suggesting a double dissociation between facts and procedures. Temple (1991) reported two single cases. The first of these, SW, was a 17-year-old boy who had well-preserved arithmetical facts, but a marked impairment of arithmetical procedures. The second case, HM, was a 19-year-old girl with a developmental dyslexia. She had normal number processing skills and could perform a number of different arithmetical procedures normally, but she was impaired on tests of multiplication table knowledge. Temple interpreted these results as suggesting that these two components of the calculation system can develop independently of each other.

Semenza et al. (1997) reported a further developmental case who had suffered from severe neurological problems since early childhood. His language and number processing skills were good, but he had memory and visuospatial problems and was apraxic. He could access multiplication facts flawlessly and perform two digit addition and subtraction sums orally. When presented with multi-digit sums in written format he was again able to perform addition and subtraction sums, but he had severe problems with multiplication sums. He had greater difficulty with sums with more digits, and his performance deteriorated with each successive step in the sum. The authors interpreted his deficit as a specific difficulty monitoring his performance. However, it is also possible that his results reflect some task difficulty artefact, particularly as one of the main findings was that he made more errors with sums with more digits.

McNeil and Burgess's (2002) case with a diagnosis of probable Alzheimer's disease (AD) showed some mild deterioration in his verbal intellectual abilities, and his verbal memory, praxis and spelling and writing skills were all impaired. He passed addition, subtraction, multiplication and division sums when they involved single digits as operands (or as the answer, in the case of division). However, he had severe problems with a range of different arithmetical procedures including multi-digit sums, fractions and decimals. The authors suggested that arithmetical procedures can be impaired independently of arithmetical fact knowledge, but appear to be more affected by general resource deficits, particularly executive functions. Further evidence for this comes from the finding that AD patients commonly have more difficulty with arithmetic procedures and relatively better fact retrieval (Mantovan et al., 1999).

These studies suggest that different arithmetical operations and numerical processes can be impaired independently of each other and are related in varying degrees to various background processes. There seems to be some evidence that Arabic numeral reading and comprehension can be selectively impaired independently of other non-numerical categories. This is perhaps not surprising as Arabic numerals share little in common with other stimuli. However, the same does not seem to hold for written number words. When patients have difficulties reading non-numerical words this appears to extend to written number words and patients who can read non-numerical words appear to be able to use the same reading system to read number words. As regards calculation processes, there are patients

with selective problems with calculation, but none of the patients with the preservation of calculation skills in the light of severe language difficulties have been
able to access multiplication facts directly, without resorting to the use of other
strategies. Therefore, different aspects of calculation appear to differ in the extent
to which they share resources with other non-numerical processes.

CURRENT THEORETICAL MODELS

McCloskey et al.'s (1985) Model

There are two main, competing theoretical models of number processing and calculation. The first and possibly most influential is the one described by McCloskey et al.
(1985) that drew primarily on data from cognitive neuropsychological single cases.
The basic tenets of the model are that there are separate number comprehension and
number production systems that are dedicated to Arabic numerals or verbal
numbers. It proposes that any numerical input must be converted into an abstract
internal representation before it is processed any further either to perform a calculation or to read or write the number. In other words, calculation is carried out using
modality-independent semantic representations. The calculation system itself is
divided into two stores: arithmetical facts and arithmetical procedures. Arithmetical
facts are those rote learnt facts that can be retrieved directly, while procedures are
required to perform more complex calculations, such as '29 + 42'. This model makes
a number of predictions that can be empirically tested. The most obvious of these are
that impairments in number comprehension can be restricted to one modality (e.g.,
verbal spoken numbers impaired in the context of unimpaired verbal written
numbers) and that deficits can selectively affect either production or comprehension
mechanisms. It also suggests that arithmetical computations are carried out independently of the format of input or output.

These hypotheses are generally well supported by neuropsychological evidence.
There is some support for the hypothesis that number comprehension impairments
can be restricted to one modality of input (e.g., case STH, reported by Warrington,
1982, with a selective difficulty understanding spoken number names). There is also
evidence that number processing deficits can selectively affect production or comprehension, such as a case reported by Benson and Denckla (1969) with intact
number comprehension, but severely impaired production of numbers.

However, the prediction that arithmetical computations can be carried out independently of the surface form in which a number is presented or produced has
been the most problematic and has provoked the most criticism in the literature.
Limited support has come from studies by McCloskey and colleagues reporting
cases with similar error rates in particular types of calculation across modality of
input or output (e.g., Macaruso et al., 1993). These data give some credence to the
idea of a unitary semantic store that is accessed irrespective of the surface form in
which numbers are presented. However, other cases are difficult to interpret in
these terms. For example, McNeil and Warrington (1994) reported a patient

with difficulties with calculation that were dependent on the surface form in which the numbers were presented. He had some number processing problems, but his comprehension and writing of Arabic numerals was good. When given simple spoken addition, subtraction and multiplication sums, his performance was good for all three operations. However, when given the same sums in written format, he could perform the subtraction sums, but not the addition and multiplication sums. His deficit with written calculation could not be explained as being secondary to his number processing impairment as he was near perfect with one arithmetical operation. It was suggested that addition and multiplication may use a verbal/spoken route as this is how these facts are learnt and rehearsed, whereas subtraction sums may be able to be performed equally well using a visual/Arabic route. It was also suggested that transcoding numbers may not require activation of the semantic system, so there may be a direct 'asemantic' transcoding route for reading and writing numbers and a different semantic route for calculation.

Deloche and Seron (1987) have also suggested that the activation of a semantic representation is not necessary for many number processing tasks. They propose that some number transcoding tasks can be carried out using asemantic transcoding mechanisms. Cipolotti (1995) has come to a similar conclusion in accounting for the results found with patient SF, whose pattern of performance reading Arabic numerals was problematic for McCloskey et al.'s model as it neither obviously indicated an Arabic numeral comprehension difficulty nor a verbal number production problem. On the basis of this evidence, Cipolotti proposed that there is an asemantic transcoding route and SF's deficit was with the syntactic component of this asemantic route. It was also suggested that he did not utilize the semantic route because of the particular task demands. Thus the instructions to read the numbers aloud would activate asemantic transcoding and inhibit the semantic route. A second case reported by Cipolotti and Butterworth (1995) with number processing problems but well-preserved calculation poses similar difficulties for the McCloskey model. The authors interpreted their results as further evidence for the existence of asemantic transcoding routes.

However, the postulation of an additional asemantic transcoding route has its own problems. Noel and Seron (1995) have claimed that, although the contrast between deep dyslexia and surface dyslexia (see Chapter 8, this book) is good evidence to show that the semantic and asemantic reading routes are independent, this kind of analysis is problematic when applied to numbers. First, every Arabic numeral can theoretically be transcoded through a non-lexical route (i.e., there are no numerical equivalents of irregular words). Second, a semantic representation can easily be generated for new numbers that have not been experienced before. So in the case of a lesion of the asemantic route the semantic route would allow the reading of every numeral (i.e., while there is no equivalent to an unknown [novel] word, even if you have not seen a specific number before, e.g., '5,348,237', you can still compute a meaning for it).

In summary, there are difficulties with the McCloskey model in its current form, although the addition of asemantic transcoding routes would go some way to answering these criticisms. However, these proposals for such modifications are not without their own problems. A consideration of the other main current model will evaluate whether it can provide a more parsimonious account for such data.

Dehaene and Cohen (1995) Triple-code Model

First proposed by Dehaene (1992) and expanded by Dehaene and Cohen (1995, 1997), the triple-code model proposes three types of mental representations in which numbers can be manipulated by the brain. The first type of representation is the *visual Arabic number form*, which consists of numbers represented as 'strings of digits on an internal visuospatial scratchpad' (Dehaene & Cohen, 1995, p. 85). So, for example, the number 'fifty-two' will be represented as the Arabic numeral '52' in the visual Arabic number form. The second type is the *analogical magnitude representation*, which contains the meanings of numbers (i.e., the quantity associated with the number). The third form is the *verbal word frame*, and this contains numbers as 'syntactically organized sequences of words'. The first and second forms—the visual Arabic number form and the analogical magnitude representation—are available to both hemispheres. However, the third type of representation—the verbal word frame—underlies arithmetical fact retrieval and is only available to the left hemisphere. The model also proposes that the Arabic number form and the verbal word frame do not contain any semantic information. The analogue magnitude representation contains information about the size of a number on an oriented number line.

Dehaene and Cohen's triple-code model is the only model that attempts to formulate a functional–anatomical model of number processing. They incorporate both scanning and lesion data into their model and the claim that the retrieval of rote verbal arithmetic facts is performed by a corticostriatal route through the left basal ganglia. By contrast, the semantic elaboration and recoding of problems is carried out in the parieto-occipitotemporal areas of the left hemisphere. The planning, sequencing and controlling of successive operations required by more complex arithmetic problems is controlled by dorsolateral prefrontal circuits. The crucial differences with previous models are that Dehaene and Cohen propose three separate internal representations rather than a unitary semantic representation. Which internal code is accessed depends on which task is being carried out. For example, by this account subjects can read or write Arabic numerals without having to access a semantic representation.

Evidence for this model comes from studies on normal participants and single case studies of neurological patients. The concept of an internal-oriented number line extending horizontally from left to right comes from a series of experiments investigating the SNARC effect (spatial–numerical association of response codes) where smaller numbers are responded to more quickly with the left hand (Dehaene et al., 1993). Dehaene and Cohen (1991) also report neuropsychological evidence for this concept of magnitude representation with a patient whose number reading and calculation were severely impaired. However, he showed some knowledge of approximate answers to questions to which he could not give the correct answer (e.g., he said an hour was about 50 minutes). He could verify whether sums were correct or not if he was presented with an erroneous answer that was some distance from the correct answer (e.g., '1 + 3 = 9'), but not if the incorrect answer was close to the correct answer 'e.g., '1 + 3 = 5'). The authors interpreted these results as evidence for an intact magnitude representation in the right hemisphere that can perform approximate arithmetic by comparing quantities.

Cohen and Dehaene (1995) reported two further patients as evidence for this model. They both had severe alexia without agraphia, resulting from left posterior lesions. On Arabic numeral reading tasks they made significantly more errors per digit on multi-digit numbers than single digit numbers. This could not be explained in terms of visual complexity of the multi-digit numbers as a significant discrepancy was also found between pairs of numerals that either had to be read as a two-digit number or as two, one digit numbers (e.g., '24' read as 'twenty-four' or 'two, four'). The patients made more errors reading the numerals as a two digit number. In addition it could not be interpreted as a number comprehension problem as both patients had good comprehension of the multi-digit numerals. Both patients also made more errors reading Arabic numerals when they were presented as a sum they had to read aloud then calculate than when they had to read both numbers aloud and then say which was larger. Their accuracy reading the digits was dependent on the task, suggesting that they were not using the same digit identification procedure for the two tasks. The patients' deficits were interpreted by the authors in terms of the triple code model. Their deficits could be seen as arising from a disconnection between the visual number form and the auditory verbal code, but leaving the visual Arabic to magnitude representation route intact.

Dehaene and Cohen (1997) reported two further cases providing evidence for the triple code model. Both patients could read and write Arabic numerals, but had difficulties with simple calculation. MAR made errors with all four arithmetical operations, but had more difficulty with subtraction and division than with addition and multiplication. In contrast, BOO made more errors with multiplication than with addition, subtraction or division. BOO also performed normally on a wide variety of tasks tapping quantitative number knowledge, such as number comparison tasks, while MAR was severely impaired. The authors argue for a double dissociation in the pattern of performance between the two patients. MAR had a left parietal lesion and was primarily impaired on tasks requiring quantity-based strategies (i.e., those that cannot be solved by the retrieval of rote verbal knowledge—subtraction and division), whereas BOO had a left basal ganglia lesion and had impaired retrieval of rote arithmetic tables (multiplication), but well-preserved quantity-based strategies. The authors also emphasize the fact that many of the operation-specific cases reported to date have the selective preservation of subtraction (e.g., McNeil & Warrington, 1994). They interpret this as illustrating the different contributions of rote verbal knowledge and quantity knowledge to the different operations, with multiplication and, possibly to a lesser extent, addition dependent on the retrieval of rote learnt facts, and subtraction and division probably more dependent on quantity knowledge.

In summary, therefore, the Dehaene and Cohen model addresses some of the criticisms levelled at the McCloskey model. It can also give a reasonable account of some of the problematic cases (e.g., McNeil & Warrington, 1994), and it makes a number of experimentally testable predictions. However, the evidence for the model is not yet entirely convincing and so must at this stage remain rather tentative.

Current theoretical models make very few specific predictions about higher level arithmetic problem-solving that are obviously going to place greater demands on other cognitive systems. It is worth therefore giving brief consideration to some of the research looking at these processes.

ARITHMETICAL WORD PROBLEM-SOLVING

There are certain patients who may have particular difficulties solving arithmetical word problems without any underlying disorder of number processing or calculation. The classic example is given by Luria (1973), who reported that patients with frontal lobe lesions commonly fail simple problems of the form: 'If you have nine books and you want to put twice as many books on the top shelf as on the bottom shelf, how many will you put on each shelf?' This kind of problem cannot be solved by the direct retrieval of a fact from memory, but rather requires more general reasoning and problem-solving skills, as the information contained in the problem has to be analysed, the correct mathematical operations have to be identified, selected, then carried out in a logical stepwise solution and finally the answer must be verified. Patients with frontal lobe lesions commonly give impulsive answers missing out one or more of the stages and give some answer such as 'four and a half books on each shelf'. However, these same patients may still be able to pass the easier problem, such as 'Jack has four apples, Jill has three apples, how many do they have in total?', even though the level of numerical operation required for each problem is similar. It is claimed that these patients have difficulties with problems that have items that need to be recoded, as in the bookshelf example above. Fasotti (1992) found that patients with frontal lesions had problems with arithmetic word problem-solving because they responded to fragments of the problem and simplified the information they had been given.

Clinicians commonly report that patients with frontal lesions have similar difficulties with some items from the Wechsler-Adult Intelligence Scale (WAIS-III) arithmetic subtest. However, the only systematic study investigating patients with unilateral lesions on the WAIS showed that patients with left parietal lesions performed most poorly on the arithmetic subtest (Warrington et al., 1986). The potential impairments on tasks of this type may therefore be twofold: one of basic calculation and another of problem-solving or recoding.

LOCALIZATION ISSUES

It has long since been established from lesion studies that the posterior areas of the left hemisphere play a crucial role in arithmetic. The classic work by Hécaen et al. (1961) reported a high incidence of dyscalculia in patients with posterior lesions of the left hemisphere. Many other studies came to similar conclusions.

More recently, brain-imaging studies have also contributed to our understanding of the localization of numerical processes. The area of number processing and calculation again remains a relatively neglected area when compared with the amount of functional imaging research investigating speech or reading processes. However, there are a few studies that are generally consistent with the lesion group studies.

Roland and Frieberg (1985) used xenon[133] to investigate blood flow while performing the serial subtraction of 7 from 100 and contrasted this with resting blood flow. They observed activations of the left and right angular gyri as well as prefrontal cortex. More recently, Appolonio et al. (1994) used the same task with functional magnetic resonance imaging (fMRI) and contrasted this with 'automatic number production' (presumably counting). For the calculation tasks both studies found activation in both inferior parietal regions, although this was more marked on the left than the right. They also found extensive activation of the prefrontal, premotor and motor cortex. Perhaps this is not surprising given that their task was complex, involving many other cognitive skills, such as working memory, and self-monitoring and sequencing skills.

Dehaene et al. (1996) used position emission tomography (PET) scanning to contrast a number comparison task and a simple multiplication task and contrasted both of these with a control condition (resting with eyes closed). MRI was used to define anatomical regions of interest for each participant rather than normalization to a fixed standard. A number of different brain regions were activated by both the multiplication and comparison tasks. Statistical analysis therefore compared each task with the resting state as well as with each other. For both the multiplication and comparison tasks, blood flow was significantly increased in the left and right occipital regions, the left precentral gyrus and the supplementary motor area. The authors proposed that these were the areas involved in both tasks (such as visual recognition of numbers, attention and covert speech production). The additional areas, which were only activated by the multiplication task relative to rest, were the left fusiform and lingual gyri, the left and right internal parietal areas and the right cuneus. They therefore suggested that the left fusiform/lingual area is involved in multiplication, particularly in converting numerical input into the appropriate format to retrieve rote verbal multiplication facts. For multiplication relative to the comparison task, there was also activation of the left lenticular nucleus, Brodmann's area 8 and the right calcarine cortex. Their interpretation of the activation of the calcarine cortex during multiplication is that it was due to the left-to-right scanning required, leading to activation of right visual pathways. They did not identify any specific area for the number comparison task apart from small activations in left and right inferior parietal regions (which were also found with the multiplication task). However, although this work is in good accord with the lesion data and current theoretical models, the authors themselves acknowledge that this work is very tentative and open to criticism.

More recently, Rickard et al. (2000) used fMRI to compare multiplication with a magnitude judgement task. Verification of simple multiplication led to bilateral activation of Brodmann's area 44, dorsolateral prefrontal cortex (areas 9 and 10) and inferior and superior parietal areas. The angular and supramarginal gyri were deactivated.

Further work is obviously needed to tease out the areas involved in different aspects of number processing and calculation.

ASSESSMENT OF NUMBER PROCESSING AND CALCULATION

Numbers are unique in being able to express the same information in many different ways, such as written or spoken verbal numbers or Arabic numerals. There are also the less frequently used dots, or even Roman numerals. To fully assess all aspects of the numerical system, all possible transcoding combinations would have to be tested, as in several of the more theoretically driven batteries. This would obviously be very time-consuming and is of questionable clinical utility. A number processing assessment should therefore concentrate on those aspects of numbers that are most important for daily life (see Table 12.2).

A thorough assessment of number processing abilities is useful not only in indicating any impairments but also in highlighting any areas of selective preservation. For example, a patient who can no longer understand spoken numbers, but who can still read Arabic numerals, can use this information very effectively in everyday life (e.g., in shops to look at the numbers on the till or by asking the assistant to write down the cost of goods rather than trying to listen to what is said to them).

There are very few available standardized assessments of calculation skills. The measure that clinicians will most commonly use is the WAIS-III arithmetic subtest, but, as already mentioned above, this is not a pure measure of calculation skills, as it is also dependent on problem-solving and working memory processes. Therefore, if a patient has difficulties on this task further assessment is required.

Hitch (1978) developed a series of tests tapping a range of arithmetical procedures including percentages, ratios and fractions. They were standardized on a group of trainee industrial apprentices. However, these tests are no longer widely in use.

Table 12.2. The assessment of number processing skills

Numerical input	Numerical output	Real-life analogue
Arabic numerals (9)	Spoken number name	Reading numbers aloud (e.g., bus numbers)
Spoken number name ('nine')	Arabic numeral	Writing down a dictated telephone number
Arabic numeral (9)	Written number name	Writing amount on a cheque
Written number name ('four')	Spoken number name	Reading written numbers aloud from text

Jackson and Warrington's (1986) Graded Difficulty Arithmetic Test consists of simple two and three digit addition and subtraction sums, which are presented orally and require a spoken answer within a 10-second cut-off time. The easier items from this test will consist of addition and subtraction facts, but the more difficult items consist of two and three digit numbers (e.g., '173 + 68') that will require more complex arithmetical procedures and working memory processes.

McCloskey et al. (1991) report a theory-based assessment that includes several tests of number transcoding, magnitude comparison and single and multi-digit calculation. It only includes one test of number comprehension, as it is based on McCloskey et al.'s (1985) model, which assumes that there is only one semantic representation for numerical information. The battery was developed for use theoretically rather than clinically, so minimal normative data are available.

Deloche et al. (1994) developed a comprehensive assessment battery (EC301 battery) that comprises 31 different tests assessing production and comprehension of numbers in different notational formats (Arabic numerals, spoken number names and written number names) as well as calculation. There are seven transcoding tasks, tests of written and 'mental' calculation, numerical knowledge, magnitude judgements, counting and arithmetical sign identification. It was standardized on 180 normal participants, but it is worth noting that the controls had a high error rate with only 12% of the sample making no errors (the highest error rate was for written calculation with a 46% error rate). One disadvantage of such a comprehensive battery is that there are so few items included for each operation. For example, there are only two written addition sums and two spoken addition sums, which would make it difficult to detect an operation-specific deficit. It also takes approximately one hour to administer, which is probably too detailed to be used routinely in clinical assessment. Carlomagno et al. (1999) used a shortened version of this battery (EC301-R) that consists of number processing and calculation tests to assess patients with AD.

The Wechsler Objective Numerical Dimensions (WOND; Wechsler 1996) is a test developed for use with children (aged 6–16 years) and assesses a range of different numerical skills. It is divided into two components: *mathematics reasoning*, which consists mainly of arithmetic word problems, but also includes graphs, averages and simple geometry, and *numerical operations*, which includes tests of addition, subtraction, multiplication and division, fractions, decimals and simple algebra. It has the advantage of a large normative sample (4,252 children in the US standardization, 418 additional children for the UK version) and can generate percentiles and age-equivalent scores. It is also possible to predict WOND scores from Wechsler Intelligence Scale for Children (WISC-III) full-scale IQ scores and calculate the discrepancy between the predicted and actual scores.

REHABILITATION

There have been very few studies attempting to rehabilitate dyscalculic problems. Those that have been published have taken a very traditional cognitive rehabilitation approach and focused on some very specific aspect of number processing or calculation. There are no published studies that have attempted to remediate the ability to use numbers in a real-life context.

Hittmair-Delazer et al. (1994) used a theoretically driven rehabilitation study with a patient with impaired multiplication facts. BE had difficulty recalling one digit multiplication or division facts. He was still able to retrieve some multiplication products quickly and automatically, and there was consistency between the items he could access directly and those he had to work out using his intact conceptual knowledge. Interestingly, he showed a high correlation between problems and their complements and the corresponding division sum. Thus, for example, he could access '5 × 3' and '3 × 5' and '15 divided by 3' directly, but he had to work out '5 × 7' and '7 × 5' and '35 divided by 5' using alternative strategies. Rehabilitation consisted of teaching him the answers he could not access directly using rote learning techniques and utilizing a multiple baseline design. He demonstrated a significant improvement in his ability to retrieve the correct answers to the treated items compared with untreated items, and his reaction times improved. The use of the newly acquired fact knowledge also generalized to new contexts (e.g., the use of the facts in multi-digit multiplication sums that had not been specifically trained).

Interestingly, the authors found that teaching one sum of a complement, such as '3 × 7', had little benefit on the sum '7 × 3', which led them to conclude that the storage format of each fact is independent of that for other facts.

Girelli et al. (1996) reported the rehabilitation of two patients who had sustained left-hemisphere strokes and had selective difficulty retrieving multiplication facts. Number processing skills for both patients were good. Multiplication problems were divided into two sets. The first set of sums was presented in written form and the patient gave a spoken answer. Any errors were corrected immediately, and the patient then had to repeat the whole sums correctly twice. Performance on the trained set improved from 9% correct to 90% correct over the training period. There was also some generalization of the improvement to division sums. The second patient did not relearn the answers to the sums as labels, but rather worked them out by serial addition, which became automized during the course of training (improving from 18% correct to 93% correct). This also led to some improvement in addition. The authors noted some generalization of improvements to other calculation tasks, such as solving easy text problems, which they felt may have been due to improved motivation.

Whetstone (1998) retaught multiplication facts to a 42-year-old man with a left parietal tumour. He was presented with facts in one of three formats: Arabic numerals, written verbal or spoken verbal numbers (all answers were spoken). Training consisted of a pre-test without feedback, then all the problems were presented with answers for five seconds each. The sums were then presented a second time in a different order, and finally a post-test without feedback. Training consisted of 12, one-hour sessions. After training his performance was virtually perfect, although his reaction times were fastest when the testing format was the same as the training format. This obviously has implications for single versus multiple code theoretical models.

Deloche et al. (1992) contrasted two treatments for relearning the syntactic component of number processing. The first treatment consisted of presenting written number words that were either grammatically correct (e.g., 'cent trente deux', '132') or incorrect ('cent treize deux'). The patient received immediate feedback on his answers. The second therapy involved explicit instruction in the syntactic rules. The patient showed improvements with both types of training. Unfortunately, the experimental design meant that the relative improvement for each type of training could not be determined.

Fasotti et al. (1992) rehabilitated arithmetical word problem-solving. They showed that patients with frontal lesions make a variety of common errors, such as simplifying the information they have been given and only responding to a fragment of the problem. They used a rehabilitation strategy with the patients with frontal lesions and patients with left posterior lesions with the aim of facilitating the patients' translation of the problem into the correct series of operations and appreciation of the underlying nature of the problem (i.e., what was actually being asked). Using a series of cues, which drew attention to various aspects of the problem one by one, Fasotti et al. found that the patients with frontal lesions (but not those with left posterior lesions) benefited significantly from the cueing process as measured by accuracy, although the time they took to reach a solution increased as they were now processing the sentences fully rather than responding impulsively to some small fragment of it. However, for the left posterior patients, the cueing procedure only increased their confusion and misunderstanding.

These studies show that treatments are beginning to be developed for specific difficulties with number processing or calculation. There has been most focus on patients with selective difficulties retrieving multiplication facts, which is surprising as this is likely to be the least problematic deficit in everyday life (as in most situations where one needs to multiply numbers, it is easy to use a calculator). There appear to be several methods that have been shown to result in significant gains, although it should be acknowledged that treatments often involve nothing more sophisticated than rote learning. Most interventions also require fairly intensive training, usually consisting of many hours' input, which must be weighed up against how disabling the deficit is likely to be for the individual in everyday life.

CONCLUSION

Number processing and calculation have received much less interest than other areas of cognitive functioning. This is reflected not only in theoretical studies but also in the relative scarcity of assessment batteries and rehabilitation techniques. However, numerical processing remains an extremely important function for everyday life, and dyscalculic difficulties can be profoundly disabling. Clinicians should therefore start to include the routine assessment of number processing and calculation skills in their clinical assessments.

REFERENCES

Anderson, S. W., Damasio, A. R. & Damasio, H. (1990) Troubled letters but not numbers: Domain specific cognitive impairments following focal damage in frontal cortex. *Brain*, **113**, 749–766.

Appolonio, L., Rueckert, L., Partiot, A., Litvan, L., Sorenson, J., Le Bihan, D. et al. (1994) Functional magnetic resonance imaging (f-MRI) of calculation ability in normal volunteers. *Neurology*, **44**(Suppl. 2), 262.

Baddeley, A. D. & Hitch, G. (1974) Working memory. In: G. H. Bower (ed.) *The Psychology of Learning and Motivation* (Vol. 8, pp. 47–89). Lawrence Erlbaum, Hillsdale, NJ.

Benson, D. F. & Denckla, M. B. (1969) Verbal paraphasia as a source of calculation disturbance. *Archives of Neurology (Chicago)*, **21**, 96–102.

Benson, F. & Weir, W. S. (1972) Acalculia: Acquired anarithmetria. *Cortex*, **8**, 465–472.

Berger, H. (1926) Über Rechenstörungen bei Herderkränkungen des Grosshirns. *Archiv für Psychiatrie und Nervenkrankheiten*, **78**, 238–263 [in German].

Butterworth, B., Cipolotti, L. & Warrington, E. K. (1996) Short-term memory impairment and arithmetical ability. *The Quarterly Journal of Experimental Psychology*, **49**(A), 251–262.

Carlomagno, S., Iavarone, A., Nolfe, G., Bourene, G., Martin, C. & Deloche, G. (1999) Dyscalculia in the early stages of Alzheimer's disease. *Acta Neurologica Scandinavica*, **99**, 166–174.

Cipolotti, L. (1995) Multiple routes for reading words, why not numbers? Evidence from a case of dense acalculia. *Cognitive Neuropsychology*, **12**, 313–342.

Cipolotti, L. & Butterworth, B. (1995) Towards a multiroute model of number processing: Impaired number transcoding with preserved calculation skills. *Journal of Experimental Psychology: General*, **124**, 375–390.

Cipolotti, L. & Costello, A. de L. (1995) Selective impairment for simple division. *Cortex*, **31**, 433–449.

Dagenbach, D. & McCloskey, M. (1992) The organization of arithmetic facts in memory: Evidence from a brain-damaged patient. *Brain and Cognition*, **20**, 345–366.

Dehaene, S. (1992) Varieties of numerical abilities. *Cognition*, **44**, 1–42.

Dehaene, S. & Cohen, L. (1991) Two mental calculation systems: A case study of severe calculia with preserved approximation. *Neuropsychologia*, **29**, 1045–1074.

Dehaene, S. & Cohen, L. (1995) Towards an anatomical and functional model of number processing. *Mathematical Cognition*, **1**, 83–120.

Dehaene, S. & Cohen, L. (1997) Cerebral pathways for calculation: Double dissociation between rote verbal and quantitative knowledge of arithmetic. *Cortex*, **33**, 219–250.

Dehaene, S., Bossini, S. & Giraux, P. (1993) The mental representation of parity and numerical magnitude. *Journal of Experimental Psychology: General*, **122**, 371–396.

Dehaene, S., Tzourio, N., Frak, V., Raynaud, L., Cohen, L., Mehler, J. et al. (1996) Cerebral activations during number multiplication and comparison: A PET study. *Neuropsychologia*, **34**, 1097–1106.

Delazer, M. & Benke, Th. (1997) Arithmetic facts without meaning. *Cortex*, **33**, 697–710.

Deloche, G. & Seron, X. (1982) From one to 1: An analysis of a transcoding process by means of neuropsychological data. *Cognition*, **12**, 119–149.

Deloche, G. & Seron, X. (1987) Numerical transcoding: A general production model. In: G. Deloche & X. Seron (eds) *Mathematical Disabilities: A Cognitive Neuropsychological Perspective* (pp. 137–170). Lawrence Erlbaum, Hillsdale, NJ.

Deloche, G., Ferrand, I., Naud, E., Baeta, E., Vendrell, J. & Claros-Salinas, D. (1992) Differential effects of covert and overt training of the syntactical component of verbal number processing and generalisations to other tasks: A single case study. *Neuropsychological Rehabilitation*, **2**, 257–281.

Deloche, G., Seron, W., Larroque, C., Magnien, C., Metz-Lutz, M. N., Noel, M. N. et al. (1994) Calculation and number processing assessment battery: Role of demographic factors. *Journal of Clinical and Experimental Neuropsychology*, **16**, 195–208.

Fasotti, L. (1992) *Arithmetical Word Problem Solving after Frontal Lobe Damage*. Swets & Zeitlinger, Amsterdam.

Fasotti, L., Bremner, J. J. C. B. & Eling, P. A. T. M. (1992) Influence of improved text encoding on arithmetical word problem-solving after frontal lobe damage. *Neuropsychological Rehabilitation*, **2**, 3–20.

Gardner, H. (1973) The contribution of operativity to naming capacity in aphasic patients. *Neuropsychologia*, **11**, 213–220.

Girelli, L., Delazer, M., Semenza, C. & Denes, G. (1996) The representation of arithmetic facts: Evidence from two rehabilitation studies. *Cortex*, **32**, 49–66.

Groen, G. J. & Parkman, J. M. (1972) A chronometric analysis of simple addition. *Psychological Review*, **79**, 329–343.

Hécaen, H., Angelergues, R. & Houillier, S. (1961) Les variétés cliniques des acalculias au cours des lésions rétrolandiques: Approche statistique du problème. *Revue Neurologique*, **2**, 85–103 [in French].

Henschen, S. E. (1919) Über Sprach-, Musik- und Rechenmechanismen und ihre Lokalisationen im Gehirn. *Zeitschrift für die Gesamte Neurologie und Psychiatrie*, **52**, 273–298 [in German].

Hitch, G. J. (1978) The numerical abilities of industrial trainee apprentices. *Journal of Occupational Psychology*, **51**, 163–176.

Hittmair-Delazer, M., Semenza, C. & Denes, G. (1994) Concepts and facts in calculation. *Brain*, **117**, 715–728.

Jackson, M. & Warrington, E. K. (1986) Arithmetic skills in patients with unilateral cerebral lesions. *Cortex*, **22**, 611–620.

Lampl, Y., Eshel, Y., Gilad, R. & Sarova-Pinhas, I. (1994) Selective acalculia with sparing of the subtraction process in a patient with left parietotemporal haemorrhage. *Neurology*, **44**, 1759–1761.

Luria, A. R. (1973) *The Working Brain. An Introduction to Neuropsychology*. Basic Books, New York.

Macaruso, P., McCloskey, M. & Aliminosa, D. (1993) The functional architecture of the cognitive numerical-processing system: Evidence from a patient with multiple impairments. *Cognitive Neuropsychology*, **10**, 341–376.

Mantovan, M. C., Delazer, M., Ermani, M. & Denes, G. (1999) The breakdown of calculation procedures in Alzheimer's disease. *Cortex*, **35**, 21–38.

McCloskey, M., Caramazza, A. & Basili, A. (1985) Cognitive mechanisms in number processing and calculation: Evidence from dyscalculia. *Brain and Cognition*, **4**, 171–196.

McCloskey, M., Sokol, S. M. and Goodman, R. A. (1986) Cognitive processes in verbal-number production: Inferences from the performance of brain-damaged subjects. *Journal of Experimental Psychology: General*, **115**, 307–330.

McCloskey, M., Sokol, S. M., Goodman-Schulman, R. A. & Caramazza, A. (1990) Cognitive representations and processes in number production: Evidence from cases of acquired dyscalculia. In: A. Caramazza (ed.) *Advances in Cognitive Neuropsychology and Neurolinguistics* (pp. 1–32). Lawrence Erlbaum, Hillsdale, NJ.

McCloskey, M., Aliminosa, D. & Macaruso, P. (1991) Theory-based assessment of acquired dyscalculia. *Brain and Cognition*, **17**, 285–308.

McNeil, J. E (1999) Acquired disorders of number processing and calculation in neurological patients. Unpublished PhD thesis, University of London.

McNeil, J. E. & Burgess, P. W. (2002) The selective impairment of arithmetical procedures. *Cortex*, **38**, 569–587.

McNeil, J. E. & Warrington, E. K. (1994) A dissociation between addition and subtraction with written calculation. *Neuropsychologia*, **32**, 717–728.

Miller, K., Perlmutter, M. & Keating, D. (1984) Cognitive arithmetic: Comparison of operation. *Journal of Experimental Psychology: Learning, Memory and Cognition*, **10**, 46–60.

Noel, M.-P. & Seron, X. (1993) Arabic number reading deficit: A single-case study of when 236 is read (2306) and judged superior to 1258. *Cognitive Neuropsychology*, **10**, 317–339.

Noel, M.-P. & Seron, X. (1995) Lexicalisation errors in writing Arabic numerals. *Brain and Cognition*, **29**, 151–179.

Presenti, M., Seron, X. & Van Der Linden, M (1994) Selective impairment as evidence for mental organisation of arithmetical facts: BB, a case of preserved subtraction? *Cortex*, **30**, 661–671.

Rickard, T. C., Romero, S. G., Basso, G., Wharton, C., Flitman, S. & Grafman, I. (2000) The calculating brain: An fMRI study. *Neuropsychologia*, **38**, 325–335.

Roland, P. E. & Frieberg, L. (1985) Localisation of cortical areas activated by thinking. *Journal of Neurophysiology*, **53**, 1219–1243.

Rossor, M. N., Warrington, E. K. & Cipolotti, L. (1995) The isolation of calculation skills. *Journal of Neurology*, **242**, 78–81.

Semenza, C., Miceli, L. & Girelli, L. (1997) A deficit for arithmetical procedures: Lack of knowledge or lack of monitoring? *Cortex*, **33**, 483–498.

Seron, X. & Deloche, G. (1983) From 4 to 'four': A supplement to 'from three to 3'. *Brain*, **106**, 735–744.

Singer, H. D. & Low, A. A. (1933) Acalculia: A clinical study. *Archives of Neurology and Psychiatry*, **29**, 467–498.

Temple, C. M. (1991) Procedural dyscalculia and number fact dyscalculia: Double dissociation in developmental dyscalculia. *Cognitive Neuropsychology*, **8**, 155–176.

Van Harskamp, N. J. & Cipolotti, L. (2001) Selective impairment for addition, subtraction and multiplication. Implications for the organisation of arithmetical facts. *Cortex*, **37**, 363–388.

Warrington, E. K. (1982) The fractionation of arithmetical skills: A single case study. *Quarterly Journal of Experimental Psychology*, **34A**, 31–51.

Warrington, E. K., James, M. & Maciejewski, C. (1986) The WAIS as a lateralising and localising instrument: A study of 656 patients with unilateral cerebral lesions. *Neuropsychologia*, **24**, 223–239.

Wechsler, D. (1996) *Wechsler Objective Numerical Dimensions (WOND)* Psychological Corporation, London.

Whetstone, T. (1998) The representation of arithmetic facts in memory: Results from retraining a brain-damaged patient. *Brain and Cognition*, **36**, 290–309.

PART V

Neuropsychology:
Specialist Areas of Work

CHAPTER 13

Clinical Neuropsychological Assessment of Children

Judith A. Middleton
Radcliffe Infirmary, Oxford, UK

INTRODUCTION

Child neuropsychology is not adult neuropsychology writ small and deserves the same status as work in the adult field. Consequently, any clinician considering working in child neuropsychology has to come from a background informed by developmental models and have an understanding of the crucial influence of the child's family and social environment and their educational history on their neuropsychological functioning. This chapter is addressed to clinicians who might consider assessing children or who wish to understand how neurodevelopmental issues may affect their adult clients.

Within this context, the present chapter can only highlight basic principles and attempt to give a broad overview of some of the issues that need to be considered when carrying out a neuropsychological assessment of children and young people. It suggests some fundamental practical procedures, but anyone contemplating working in child neuropsychology is referred to more detailed texts (Anderson et al., 2001; Fennell, 2000a; Holmes-Bernstein, 2000; Temple, 1997; Ylvisaker, 1998).

HOW CHILD NEUROPSYCHOLOGY DIFFERS FROM ADULT NEUROPSYCHOLOGY

Age and Developmental Factors

Children are expected to, and do, change and develop, at times very rapidly. Clinical assessment of children needs to take account of the child's age and developmental level, and the timing of any index event. Neurological damage may lead to different problems at different ages. While adult brains are relatively static, the child's brain is rapidly maturing. Damage at a time of rapid change is likely to cause more functional damage than when development is slow.

Clinical Neuropsychology: A Practical Guide to Assessment and Management for Clinicians.
Edited by L.H. Goldstein and J.E. McNeil. © 2004 John Wiley & Sons, Ltd.

In addition, not only will appropriate tests differ radically depending on the age of the child, but the child's age at testing and age at index event will also affect their performance on assessments and outcomes in a way that is dynamically different from those of adults.

In children the brain is going through dynamic developmental changes from the earliest days of conception until adult life.

Prenatal Development

The structural development of the brain takes place during the early prenatal period. Monk et al. (2000) provide a concise summary of prenatal neurobiological development highlighting both molecular mechanisms and anatomical change. Developmental mechanisms transform undifferentiated tissue to a complex neurological network that is capable of both processing information about the outside world and regulating and initiating behaviour, emotions and thought.

Divergence from this inexorable process, caused by even subtle changes in the neurochemistry of the embryonic or foetal environment, can have specific, devastating results, although more subtle aberrations might not be apparent until relatively later in development (Monk et al., 2000). For instance, very early interference in the developmental process may lead to complete failure of brain development (anencephaly). An event occurring during the stage of neural proliferation can lead to microcephaly; migrational abnormalities can give rise, for instance, to heterotopias (an extra layer of grey matter) or lissencephaly (a smooth cerebral cortex with no gyri) (see also Chapter 2). All can lead to varying degrees of developmental or cognitive problems.

Post-natal Development

Elaboration of the central nervous system occurs at the latter end of pregnancy and post-natally. Processes include axonal and dendritic development, synaptogenesis and myelination, the latter continuing well into the second decade. Children will, of course, be concurrently continuing to develop their skills and capacity to process information.

An understanding of when major developmental milestones should be achieved is a prerequisite of any assessment. Many behaviours that might be considered to reflect neurological impairment in adults are developmentally appropriate at some stage in development. Consequently, it is crucial to understand whether an observation of a particular behaviour is developmentally appropriate, delayed or deviant. This changes with age. While motor and language skills are more commonly understood, the development of attention and concentration, memory and learning, visuoperceptual skills, reasoning and executive skills also need to be appreciated as well as the emergence of metacognitive skills.

Damage to the adult brain is likely to be shown by loss in skills or capacity, or in changes in personality, rate of processing and judgement. In children the impact of brain damage, once the initial recovery phase has occurred, is often less obvious than it is with adults. This may be due to neurological or functional plasticity.

Potential for Plasticity of Function

There is a potential for some plasticity of function when early brain damage occurs. Children, who lose language through left-hemisphere damage prior to their sixth birthday, may well recover language skills (Smith & Sugar, 1975), although both expressive and receptive language may show residual deficits depending on the site and age at injury. Relevant to this is Lenneberg's (1967) proposal of a critical period for the acquisition of language. Stiles (2001), looking at children with focal lesions, has shown that language deficits and recovery are dependent on an interaction between age at lesion and site of damage. The earlier the damage or disease process to areas affecting language acquisition the more likely there is to be reasonable recovery of language skills, although subtle deficits may continue. One exception to this is children with Landau–Kleffner syndrome (or acquired childhood aphasia). Here, the earlier the symptoms and losses occur the worse the prognosis (Bishop, 1985).

Vargha-Khadem et al. (1997), investigating children with hippocampal sclerosis, found that the relatively positive outcome from early damage in terms of language acquisition and skills does not hold for some aspects of memory functioning. Their work suggests that children who suffer unilateral hippocampal damage in very early life will continue to have severe episodic memory problems, while semantic memory is relatively spared.

With general brain damage, such as that following closed head injury (Middleton, 2001) or treatment effects from radiation (Mulhern et al., 1992), recovery can be poor, especially in young children, and there is rarely evidence of plasticity. As Goodman (1989) points out, for any potential plasticity to occur in the other hemisphere that hemisphere must itself be intact. Following head injuries, it is likely that there will be bilateral shearing of fibres causing axonal damage and cerebral oedema, which will have pervasive effects. Thus evidence of just focal bleeding or damage on MRI with no other obvious pervasive effects should not be used as the basis predicting the potential for plasticity.

Returning to the earlier argument about the importance of age and development at injury and how the effects of brain damage at different ages can give rise to different problems, Kolb and Whishaw (1987) have shown that damage to the developing brain (in this case lesioned rats) had lasting effects on brain development. Indeed, damage at one site (frontal lobe) led to abnormal development throughout the whole of the hemisphere ipsilateral to the damage.

Goodman (1989) also argues that new, anomalous connections can enhance recovery in some instances, but if they do not follow previous neural pathways, there may be misconnections between regions of the brain not normally connected. This might lead to what he describes as 'neural noise'. It is this, among other things, that could give rise to problems with attention and concentration.

Anderson et al. (2001) review the complexity of evidence in considering the issue of plasticity. They conclude that neither the theories of plasticity nor vulnerability can fully explain recovery. They argue for the possibility of these two models being 'extremes along a recovery continuum'. Against this, a number of different factors may interact, which can be grouped as: (1) pathology (the type, size and timing of the lesion); (2) child's developmental stage and gender—there is tentative evidence that the female brain may be more capable of adapting following early injury (Anderson et al., 2001); and (3) the psychosocial environment.

In summary, there is evidence that plasticity of function occurs in specific areas, such as language, if damage is discrete and occurs early enough. Recovery may be less good when both pervasive and focal damage are present, compared with when there is just focal damage. Indeed, much of the debate about the effect of plasticity may well relate to whether the damage is focal or diffuse. In the former, there may be recovery due to a number of factors, including functional and biological restitution or substitution (see Anderson et al., 2001, for further discussion). The general belief that young children make a better recovery after a generalized injury to the brain than older children or adults does not hold, whether for head injury (Levin et al., 1995) or treatment effects, such as leukaemia (Said et al., 1989).

Family, Social Factors, Education, Cultural and Ethnic Context and Related Issues

The clinical neuropsychological assessment of children differs in many ways from the assessment of adults. It also differs from the normal assessment procedure of children brought to child mental health services, not by ignoring family, social factors, cultural and ethnic context and related issues, but by adding another dimension to the procedure, which explicitly explores the effects of organic brain damage and how all these factors interact.

Depending where clinicians work, they may see children from a wide range of social, cultural and ethnic backgrounds. Families may come from very different backgrounds from the dominant social group of the examiner and have experienced different child-rearing practices, educational systems and goals and possibly may have lived through war, famine and refugee status. It is self-evident that these will affect psychological functioning.

Children from different cultures may not have had the same experience of play, or education, that is generally accepted as the norm in Western society (see Gopaul-McNicol & Armour-Thomas, 2002 for a detailed discussion on the effect of cultural issues). For instance, children who have been to schools where memory and organizational strategies have been integrated into normal classroom instruction may be at an advantage in assessments compared with those who have not (Bjorklund & Douglas, 1998). Boys from a strong Islamic heritage, for example, may have spent time being taught to read and learn religious texts by rote. This early training may well affect their memory capacity or their strategy to carry out certain tests. Not only may this affect their test performance but failure may also have specific connotations in some cultures but not in others.

It is also important to consider the language to which children are exposed at home. While they may speak English fluently in school or in the clinic, if the dominant language at home is different, this will affect their performance where subtle nuances in understanding and performing tests are important. In addition, parents may not be fluent in English themselves, making it difficult to obtain a detailed history about pregnancy, birth and early development unless through an interpreter. Children may also be brought up by the extended family, so that the carers who bring a child to an assessment may not have all the relevant information.

Such issues are, of course, true in all clinical settings, but in child neuropsychology, when subtle aspects of cognitive functioning are being considered, these social and cultural issues are particularly important.

Change and Predicting Future Functioning

A common issue raised when assessing children is the extent to which acquired brain damage can account for a child's behaviour and cognitive functioning some time, even years, after an index event. In adults, early loss of skills and subsequent partial recovery can be assessed, measured and compared with pre-injury functioning. In children, the use of this model is confounded by the fact that, while there may be little change after the early recovery period compared with premorbid functioning, this does not mean there has been no effect. The expectation is that children will change and develop over time. Thus the mere lack of developmental progress after recovery can indicate that there has been a serious effect. Another way of looking at these issues is to consider that prediction in adult neuropsychology is about which skills the individual will recover, while in child neuropsychology predicting the *future* development of skills and functional independence is also important.

Since children continue to develop for many years, not only will neurological damage cause different problems depending on the age at injury but also some problems will not become evident for a number of years, and their impact may only gradually become more noticeable. This is for a number of reasons, both direct and indirect:

- Slower speed of processing—this can have an enormous impact on education, where the required pace of learning increases as children progress through school. Slow assimilation of information and responding may be better accommodated in small primary schools, but after transition to secondary school the effect of slow learning can be profound.
- Attention and concentration—these are invariably affected following neurological damage and the impact of impairments here on learning can be considerable.
- Memory and learning—if new learning is affected, there can be an accumulated effect of failing to keep up over a few years, so an initially minor problem slowly develops into a major difficulty.
- Executive functioning—since the frontal lobes only fully mature later than the rest of the brain, early damage may be almost completely silent until adolescence

begins. Thus as a child enters the second decade problems can emerge at some considerable time from the index event. At this age, it can also often be difficult to differentiate between some 'frontal' problems and normal teenage behaviour.

Furthermore, there will be concern over how well children will subsequently develop in the adult world where they do not have the protection of caring and supportive adults. It may be only at the points of transition from one social situation into another environment, such as moving from primary to secondary school or secondary school to further education, that the effects of damage become apparent. In addition, children and young people will have increasingly more work to complete and the pace of work will also gather, leading to greater pressure. Academic work is likely to become more abstract and verbally (rather than practically) based, and children will need to become able to work individually, structuring their own work and monitoring their own progress. These are all tasks that children with neuropsychological problems are likely to find far more difficult than normal children. Thus it is crucial to continue to monitor children for many years as these problems may emerge over time.

Premorbid Functioning

Some children sustaining head injuries are a self-selecting group. Early work by Chadwick et al. (1981) and Max et al. (1997) found that those children with mild as opposed to severe head injuries had pre-existing problems, and Bijur and Haslum (1995) found that children with mild head injuries were more likely to have had pre-existing problems than controls. Children who have poor attention, are impulsive or hyperactive are more likely to be at risk. Thus while an issue in assessing children with acquired brain damage is the existence of and extent to which an injury has led to appreciable and measurable functional problems, this is particularly problematic if there have been pre-existing problems, although there is also evidence that pre-existing problems will be exacerbated (Donders & Strom, 1997). Fletcher and Taylor (1984) argue that what is important to look for is the subsequent change in how a child functions. It is the trajectory of a child's development that is crucial, whether they are learning at the same rate as before or whether any premorbid problematic behaviour has become more intense, more frequent or longer lasting than before the index event.

In addition, the child's post-injury management will influence their performance. If new behaviour problems or difficulties in learning emerge, then the index neurological event may be seen as the direct cause for change. However, there may also be indirect psychosocial reasons why children's performance in school or their behaviour generally changes, these including time away from school due to hospitalizations, or parents' changed attitudes, expectations and child-rearing practices. Unfortunately, these latter reasons are sometimes used to explain everything, especially in mainstream education, where few teachers will have experience of children with acquired brain damage. This can mean that after time there is an expectation of recovery and normal development when the environmental factors are no longer considered important. If the neurological damage is not understood as being a significant factor in the child's difficulties, then problems are compounded. It is also possible that neurological reasons can be held solely responsible for change when this is not the case.

THE NEUROPSYCHOLOGICAL ASSESSMENT OF CHILDREN

While there are many principles common to assessing children and adults (e.g., the psychometric properties of tests used, issues of reliability and validity and general testing procedures), the assessment of children is in some respects very different from that of adults, in that, in addition to considering the underlying neuropathology (where known), the child's family and cultural background, their general level of cognitive ability and any co-morbid difficulties, it is of particular importance to consider the child's age and developmental level. A thorough assessment will also depend on functional information gleaned from careful clinical interviewing, observations of how the child performs and finally the results of psychometric tests.

Major errors can occur when inferences and conclusions are made from partial information, particularly when knowledge about neuropathology and the results of psychometric testing are used in isolation. In other words, incorrect assumptions can be made about direct brain–behaviour links when the child's age and development, cultural context, clinical history and careful observations of how they perform tasks are omitted when forming hypotheses. In addition, with respect to the underlying neuropathology of the child's disorders, as with adults problems may be acute or chronic and of recent or long-term origin. Prior knowledge of the neuropathology (whether arising congenitally, from trauma, iatrogenic reasons, disease or from metabolic causes) is not always known.

Key Aspects of Development to Be Focused on When Taking Developmental Histories

In all assessments of children, the initial clinical interview with the child's primary carer is a crucial foundation. Parents have a wealth of information about their children, and, although they may interpret behaviour differently from professionals and have their own agendas and theories of what is wrong, they almost always have a greater in-depth knowledge of their children than anyone else. In addition, older children may also have views about what it is that is different for them or what it is that they cannot do.

Pregnancy

Careful histories of problems and events in pregnancy, the mother's health and health-related behaviour (i.e., diet, smoking and alcohol or drug abuse) can give vital information about possible problems. Maternal trauma or illnesses, such as phenylketonuria (PKU) or epilepsy and the associated medication and treatment, need to be explored. For instance, foetal anticonvulsant syndrome can be associated with language and developmental problems (Rovet, 1995b).

Birth Events

The human brain is relatively small and vulnerable at birth, so a careful birth history is needed, which where possible should include Apgar scores (a measure of neonatal status of colour, tone and breathing) if these are known, length of gestation and any difficulties during the birth process. Neurological damage can arise from a number of reasons at birth, including mechanical causes (see Anderson et al., 2001) and hypoxia. An infant with a prenatal problem may have a difficult birth, and a difficult birth may give rise to later problems. There is also good evidence that very low birth weight children or infants born before 32 weeks' gestation have a higher incidence of developmental problems than full-term infants (Pharoah et al., 1994).

Developmental History

With a sound knowledge of developmental milestones (see Harris & Butterworth, 2002; Small, 1990), a history of the child's early development may provide clues when forming initial hypotheses, which can be pursued later. Thus, within a hypothesis testing model, evidence of late gross motor control development, problems with fine motor skills, concerns about difficulties feeding and delayed language emergence, and a history of a failure to develop normal, personal social skills can form the basis for more detailed interviewing and finally guide testing.

Medical History

Within the interview, questions relating to hearing, vision, a history of systemic or neurological illness, previous head injuries, epilepsy (seizures, febrile convulsions or infantile spasms) and associated medication can be pursued. Younger children will often not be aware that they have problems with hearing and vision, unlike adults who may be aware of sensory impairments. Consequently, it is important to ask whether the child has had regular check-ups and about parental concerns. In addition, if the referral has arisen in the absence of a specific index event, enquiry about previous injuries, seizures or major systemic illnesses is important.

Family Background

As some problems have a genetic cause, and because of different child-rearing practices, enquiring about the family background, education of parents and other siblings and a history of neurological problems or learning difficulties in the extended family is important. As already mentioned, it is crucial to understand the ethnic and cultural influences on development and the impact of a neurological problem on the family's self-perception.

Educational History

Neuropsychological problems will often first become apparent in school. It is therefore essential to obtain a good history of a child's education, and past and present concerns about learning from teachers. This may also include information about styles of teaching to which a child has been exposed. A history of the child's psychosocial functioning in the school is also necessary. Ideally, a school visit with observations of the child in the classroom may be appropriate, but this is often not practical. With the permission of parents, telephone calls to a key teacher at school can be helpful. A telephone pro forma or interview schedule can be useful in priming teachers with key questions about how children perform in terms of cognitive processing (i.e., attention, planning and memory) rather than concentrating on details of the results from reading tests, SATS, etc., although this is still helpful.

Sibling and Peer Relationships

Early signs of the functional impact of problems may come from information about a child's social relationships with peers, either in the home or in school. Comments from parents, such as 'the other children are very kind to her and make sure she's always got her books' or 'he is always by himself in the playground as he can never remember the rules of football, or can never kick the ball', are an indication of the kind of functional problems that arise from neuropsychological difficulties.

Hypothetical case

To illustrate these points:

A child was referred for reading problems at nine years following a mild head injury at six-and-a-half years. A developmental history revealed a difficult birth, with Apgar scores still low at five minutes. He then had a normal perinatal period. Concerns about delayed speech development at three-and-a-half years led to a referral to speech and language therapy, but no major problems were found apart from the comment the child had poor attention. He was seen intermittently for a year before discharge. The family history revealed that there were a number of members of the extended family who had dyslexia. A history of the head injury revealed the boy had not lost consciousness for more than a few minutes. There were no neurological sequelae 48 hours after the event, although he did not say anything for 48 hours.

This kind of history, which is not uncommon, suggests a number of factors likely to affect the presenting problem. These are the family history of dyslexia, which suggests a possible genetic loading, and the less than optimal birth may also suggest a further negative factor, particularly given the concerns about early language development. A short period of aphasia following the injury might also indicate cerebral contusions in the left hemisphere. With problems reported in language and attention, one hypothesis to pursue might be to look specifically at those areas that can be co-morbid with reading difficulties (i.e., language development and poor attention).

If the history stopped at this point, however, other important factors would be overlooked:

> This same family had moved on two occasions in the last three years, as the father worked in the armed forces. Thus the child's education had twice been interrupted, and in the space of three years he had attended three different schools where he had had to settle into new classes in the middle of the school year. In addition, his parents had had another child when he was eight-and-a-half years.

This case shows how a child with a potential biological vulnerability had to face additional stresses at the very time when his reading skills were developing. The aetiology of his problem was complex, involving not only possible neuropathological involvement but also genetic factors and important events occurring in his family context at crucial times in his development.

Choosing Assessment Tools

There are many discussions about the advantages and disadvantages of using fixed batteries to screen all children, specific protocols for different conditions or whether to be led by the functional problems of individual children on a hypothesis-testing basis. The decision may depend on the availability of assessments in a particular setting and whether or not clinical work is also part of a clinical research project where specific protocols need to be followed.

In addition to appreciating the possibly complex background diversity of any child that is assessed, the relevance of any assessment tool needs to be considered. Tests are rarely culture-free, so that some tests may be inappropriate for some children coming from some cultures. Many neuropsychology studies do not allude to the cultural bias of tests, which may mean that findings are only pertinent to a specific social/cultural group or that in a group of mixed ethnic background cultural differences are lost. In the standardization of many major tests, the cultural mix is usually representative of the population of the United States. The ethnic/cultural mix in the United Kingdom is different to that of the USA, so one has to consider the appropriateness of the tests in use. Where a service is being delivered in a multicultural setting with considerable local ethnic, social and cultural diversity, it is crucial to take into account this very significant information, which can influence test results (Gopaul-McNicol & Armour-Thomas 2002).

Research-based clinical work may begin with fixed protocols for particular problems (e.g., in epilepsy surgery or neuro-oncology). Such protocols may focus on an assumed cluster of problems based on the underlying neuropathology. In addition, questions about the neuropsychological effects of surgery may be relevant. However, in many cases of neurodevelopmental disorders and children with more diffuse problems, such as closed head injury, the referral focuses on the functional problems: how these can be explained and what strengths may be used in education and rehabilitation. Here, hypotheses may relate to the behavioural and emotional difficulties or cognitive problems and only later track back to the actual or possible neuropathology.

Whatever the focus, a hypothesis-based approach to assessment is advocated here and followed by many clinical neuropsychologists working with children (Fletcher & Taylor, 1984; Anderson et al., 2001). It is both scientifically rigorous and frequently more useful than the use of fixed protocols and *ad hoc* decisions about testing. Nonetheless, some basic principles are needed in the stepwise progression through the assessment.

Establishing a Baseline

The importance of establishing the general level of cognitive functioning prior to more sophisticated neuropsychological assessment is as important with children as it is with adults. It is simply not possible to comment on specific impairment without a full basic assessment, and shortened forms of some of the major tests (e.g., the Wechsler Abbreviated Scales of Intelligence; WASI) only give an incomplete picture. Compared with assessing adults where the WAIS-III is now almost universally used, there is a wider range of assessments to choose from when working with children, and as children develop different assessment tools become appropriate. This can also create problems in comparing general cognitive development over time as different tests assess differently acquired and emerging skills at different times. Because of the expected development, it may be useful to look at both scaled scores as well as raw scores on different occasions, provided the same test is used. A fall in scaled scores may mean: (1) a change in the trajectory of progress although development is still taking place; (2) a plateau in development has occurred; or (3) a real loss of skills has taken place. Referrals may mention a loss of skills, but mean that a child is simply not making progress.

Given the limited space, the reader is referred to four websites for details of child neuropsychological tests:

- www.psychcorp.com/catalogs/paicpc/paic_toc.htm
  (The Psychological Corporation);
- www.parinc.com (Psychological Assessment Resources Inc.);
- www.tvtc.com:8080/tvtc/tvtcpage/children.html
  (Thames Valley Test Corporation); and
- http//frontier-s.unl.edu/cgi-bin/BUROS/trolpage1a.html
  (this site has hundreds of online tests with full reviews).

Table 13.1. Selected assessments of infant development

Test	Age range (months)	Functions assessed/Subscales
Griffiths Mental Developmental Scale—2nd edn (Griffiths [Huntley Revision], 1996)	1–24	Locomotor; personal social; hearing and speech; eye–hand co-ordination; performance
Bayley Scales of Infant Development—2nd edn (Bayley, 1993)	1–42	Motor scale: body control, co-ordination, fine manipulation, dynamic movement, postural imitation, stereognosis Mental scale: sensory/perceptual acuities, discriminations, object constancy, memory, learning/problem-solving, volcalization, early verbal communication, abstract thinking, habituation, mental mapping, complex language, mathematical concept formation Behavioural rating scale: attention, arousal, orientation and engagement, emotional regulation, motor quality
Bayley Infant Neurodevelopmental Screener (Aylward, 1995)	3–24	Neurological functions; auditory and visual receptive functions; verbal and motor expressive functions; cognitive processes

Assessing Infants

Assessing specific cognitive skills of infants under the age of 24–30 months is particularly problematic. Many of the early measures are heavily loaded on infants' skills, and these developmental measures are poor predictors of future cognitive functioning (see Anderson et al., 2001). A selection of widely used tests is shown in Table 13.1.

Assessing Younger Children, Older Children and Adolescents

At around the age of two to three years it becomes easier to carry out a variety of verbal and performance tasks, which may begin to give some indication of a child's strengths and weaknesses over a range of cognitive skills (see Table 13.2 for a selection of available measures).

When considering the assessment of older children and adolescents, it is not possible within this chapter to explore the merits and disadvantages of individual assessments (see Table 13.2), and few departments will have a sufficient range of

Table 13.2. General assessments for children and adolescents

Test	Age range (years)	Functions assessed/Subscales
Wechsler Pre-School and Primary Scale of Intelligence—Revised (Wechsler, 1993)*	3.0–6.11	Verbal scale; Performance scale
British Ability Scales—2nd edn: Early Years (Elliott, 1996)	2.6–3.5 (extended to 7.11)	Lower level: general cognitive ability, special non-verbal composite Upper level clusters: verbal; pictoral reasoning; spatial; general cognitive ability; special non-verbal composite
	6–17.11 (extended down to 5–5.11)	Verbal cluster; non-verbal cluster; spatial cluster; general cognitive ability: special non-verbal composite; diagnostic scales; achievement scales
Kaufman Assessment Battery for Children (Kaufman & Kaufman, 1983)	2.6–12.11	Sequential processing scale; simultaneous processing scale; achievement scale
McCarthy Scales of Children's Abilities (McCarthy, 1972)	3.6–8.6	Verbal scale; perceptual performance scale; quantitative scale; general cognitive scale; memory scale; motor scale
NEPSY—A Developmental Neuropsychological Assessment (Korkman et al., 1998)	3–4	Attention/Executive; language; sensorimotor; visuospatial; memory
	5–12.11	Attention/Executive; language; sensorimotor; visuospatial; memory
Wechsler Intelligence Scales for Children—3rd edn (Wechsler, 1991)	6–16.11	Verbal scale; Performance scale; Full Scale; Verbal Comprehension Index; Perceptual Organization Index; Freedom from Distractibility Index
WISC-III (Process Instrument) (Kaplan, 1999)		Speed of Processing Index

*WPPSI-III due in Autumn 2002

different tests for children in any one age range for there to be choice. In view of the internationally wide use of Wechsler tests (WPPSI-R, Wechsler, 1993; WISC-III, Wechsler, 1991) and because the most comprehensive neuropsychological assessments are undertaken on children over the age of six years, the following discussion concentrates on use of the WISC-III and the relatively new WISC-III as a process instrument (WISC-III PI, Kaplan, 1999). However, this process could be applied to other tests (see Kaufman & Lichtenberger, 2000 for similar coverage of the WPPSI-R and Kaufman, 2000 for the Bayley Scales).

Kaufman's (1995) invaluable analysis of the use of the WISC-III is based on an information processing model of understanding profiles in test scores that do not necessarily conform to the two traditional IQ scale scores or four indices. Kaufman's model involves four basic processes: (1) input (verbal or visual); (2) storage (short or long term); (3) integration (memory or reasoning); and (4) output (motor or verbal). His discussion on how to approach the analysis of the WISC-III is detailed and thorough and provides insight into how more refined hypotheses may be generated. The psychologist assessing children is strongly recommended to refer to this text.

The WISC-III PI (Kaplan, 1999), used in conjunction with the WISC-III, is described as a process-oriented approach, incorporating multiple-choice versions of some subtests (e.g., Information and Vocabulary) and an analogue test—Sentence Arrangement—which is meant to parallel Picture Arrangement; expansions of some tests, such as Coding and Block Design; and a new test—the Elithorne Mazes—which is supposedly more sensitive to some executive functions.

Qualitative Assessment

The assessment procedure itself also allows for close and detailed observation of how children respond to the testing process, both generally and specifically across the whole range of subtests. Although the manner by which children undertake particular tests is not standardized, careful observation can lead to hypothesis generation as the assessment progresses, and such hypotheses can be tested out within the session. Talking to children between subtests not only increases rapport and often relaxes them but also allows the opportunity to ask them how they carried out a particular test, etc. and why they think one task appeared to be easier to do than another. Thus failing to do the testing oneself can lead to the loss of invaluable qualitative information. In addition to the total raw and scaled scores, a child's performance in a particular subtest and the scatter of their scores can also be informative. The WISC-III PI provides an opportunity to make systematic qualitative observations of how children go about some of the subtests. This is a useful adjunct in refining where to go next.

Following Hypotheses

With a baseline it is possible to follow hypotheses, also based on reported functional problems. The following sections on attention, memory and learning, language skills, visuospatial skills and executive skills will attempt to integrate the kinds of difficulties parents or teachers are concerned about and the qualitative observations obtained when carrying out the basic assessment and will give a selection of test materials to be used in each area.

Attention

Presenting Problems

One of the most common causes for concern for parents and schools is a child's lack of attention. This may include concerns about a child being unable to stay on task for a few minutes, the need for constant refocusing on tasks in the classroom, being easily distracted, flitting from one play activity to another or only being able to focus on tasks of their choosing. There may also be worries about road and other safety issues, general forgetfulness and such comments as 'she often seems to be in a world of her own', this latter remark being in the absence of epileptic activity.

Observations

Very inattentive children are obvious from the moment they enter the clinic room, and assessment of these children demands great skill and stamina from the clinician in engaging them in the assessment and in helping them attend and focus on specific tasks. However, the problems in many children with attentional impairments may be less obvious and may only become apparent from observations of them during the clinical interview of the parents and the manner in which they complete early basic assessments.

As well as looking at differences between the Freedom from Distractibility index and other indices in the WISC-III, qualitatively these children may show a pattern of failing early items in subtests, but passing more complex ones, slowing down halfway through timed tasks and needing to be refocused. Requests for repeating instructions and questions (where appropriate) and partial understanding of questions can be indicators of poor attention (as well as other problems). Poor visual attention may be apparent when children fail to attend to visual information and need gesture and verbal direction to look, or if they scan poorly perhaps dreamily looking at the page without taking very much in.

Attentional functions can be evaluated using subtests from a number of standardized measures. These include the Freedom from Distractibility index from the WISC-III and the attentional subtests from the NEPSY (see Table 13.2). In addition, the Test of Everyday Attention for Children (Manly et al., 1998), suitable for children between 6 and 16 years, assesses selective, divided and sustained attention. An Attention Index can be derived from the Children's Memory Scale (suitable for children between 5 and 16.11 years of age) using the Numbers and Sequences tests. The Test of Memory and Learning (Reynolds & Bigler, 1994), which can be used for children between the ages of 5 and 19.11 years, also contains an Attention Index.

Memory and Learning

Presenting Problems

Problems with memory and learning in children may first present with concerns being expressed by parents and teachers that a child is not learning in the classroom and is slowly falling behind their peers. Complaints about absent-mindedness or forgetfulness may also occur. In addition there can be reports of the children failing to recall instructions properly, or not being able to remember more than one thing at a time. They may forget they have homework or what they have to do. Their parents may report that they can never remember where their things are, what they are meant to take to school or that they forget and lose their belongings both at home and at school.

More subtle problems of verbal memory may present with children having difficulty remembering what they have read, needing to reread their books or own work in order to remember what they have read or written. Learning tables and spellings may take longer than with other children, and retention may be poor.

Observations

During assessment, children who forget will often ask for questions to be repeated. In addition, if they find a question difficult and need to think about it for some time, they then may need to ask for it to be repeated, just as if they have forgotten what they are meant to be doing or what they have to answer.

Failure to remember which room they were in after a break and frequently asking about how long the session is going to last should be noted. The latter, of course, may be because a child is anxious, but some children seem to forget where they are and have no idea of time. Qualitative examination of how stories, lists or items are recalled can reveal evidence of primary or recency problems and whether they use strategies to remember and learn (see Middleton, 2003 for more detailed discussion of memory tests and Table 13.3 for a list of memory tests).

Language

Presenting Problems

Some children will already have had a speech and language therapy assessment. More frequently, this is not the case, but parents will complain that their child has delayed language development. This can include problems in expressing themselves and/or in understanding what is said to them. There may be concerns about a difficulty in naming, verbal fluency or mispronunciation. At other times teachers and parents feel that the child does not seem to understand instructions or stories that are read to them. These problems can be quite obvious, but parents may also complain that on a one-to-one basis the child seems to have good language skills, but in the classroom or in a group has difficulty following the general conversation. The child may generally be fairly quiet socially and only respond when spoken to. Most subtle of all are difficulties in making inference or abstraction, in understanding double meanings or in grasping verbal jokes. There may also be concerns about comprehension of the written word in children who are fluent readers but do not seem to understand anything that they have read.

Table 13.3. Assessments of memory and learning

Test	Age range (years)	Functions assessed/Subscales
Wide Range Assessment of Memory and Learning (Sheslow & Adams, 1990)	5.0–16.11	Verbal memory; visual memory; learning; delayed memory
Test of Memory and Learning (Reynolds & Bigler, 1994)	5.0–19.11	Verbal memory; visual memory; general memory; delayed memory
Children's Memory Scale (Cohen, 1997)	5.0–16.11	Verbal memory; visual memory; learning; attention; delayed recognition
California Verbal Learning Test—Children's Version (Dean et al., 1994)	5–16	List Learning
Rivermead Behavioural Memory Test for Children (Wilson et al., 1991)	5.0–10.0	Screening score; profile score; assesses recall, learning, recognition, prospective memory and orientation
NEPSY—subtests (Korkman et al., 1998)	3.0–12.11	Names and faces; narrative; sentences; list learning
Rey–Osterreith Complex Figure and Recognition Trial (Meyers & Meyers, 1995)	6.0–16.11	Copy; immediate and delayed visuospatial recall; delayed visuospatial recognition
British Ability Scales—II subtests (Elliot, 1996)	2.6–17.11	Object memory; spatial memory; visual recognition

Observations

In a one-to-one assessment session it is not always obvious initially that children may have quite profound language and communication difficulties. It is possible to observe whether or not they initiate conversation during the assessment session or merely respond to questions and instructions. Issues about clarity of speech, articulation and grammatical structure may be observed and recorded. Word-finding difficulties or a tendency to point to answers (e.g., in Picture Completion) may be noted. Scoring better in those subtests where only single word answers as opposed to explanations are required may indicate problems with the ability to expand ideas.

Alternatively, circumlocution in describing word meaning or giving unnecessarily long explanations will also give an indication of language problems. Children who are unable to answer more complex questions or who provide tangential answers may indicate poor receptive language or a failure to track their own conversation. They may be quite fluent and loquacious when leading the conversation, but once the examiner tries to take over the subject matter then difficulties arise. Observing

Table 13.4. Assessments of language functioning

Test	Age range (years)	Functions assessed/Subscales
Test of Reception of Grammar (Bishop, 1989)	4–13	Understanding of grammatical contrasts
Clinical Evaluation of Language Fundamentals—Pre-school Language Scales (Zimmerman et al., 1992)	3–6	Receptive language score; expressive language score; total language score
Clinical Evaluation of Language Fundamentals—3rd edn (Semel et al., 1995)	6–21	Receptive language score; expressive language score; total language score; supplementary tests
Wechsler Objective Language Dimensions (Rust, 1996)	6–16.11	Listening comprehension; oral expression; written expression
The British Picture Vocabulary Scale—2nd edn (Dunn et al., 1997)	3–15.8	Receptive vocabulary
NEPSY—language subscale (Korkman et al., 1998)	3.0–12.11	Phonological processing; speeded naming; repetition of non-words; comprehension of instructions

the effects of slowing down or speeding up questions or simplifying language can be ways of testing out hypotheses.

In addition the pragmatic use of language can be observed within the assessment session. A child's style of communication may be inappropriate, or he or she may generally try to lead the conversation by concentrating on his or her own particular interests, without noticing that the subject matter is not suitable in the session. Poor eye contact when in conversation and failing to grasp communicative intent may also be observed. Tests of language functioning are presented in Table 13.4.

Visuoperceptual Skills

Presenting Problems

Among some of the issues that are often raised by parents and teachers is that the child has difficulty in writing. It is untidy and the size of writing is too small, too large or uneven. Drawings may be immature and the child is reported not to like puzzles or is not at all artistically creative. In addition, parents may also talk about the child having difficulty in sport and ball games, bumping into things and tripping over, and having poor appreciation of other people's space.

Table 13.5. Assessments of visual perceptual/motor skills

Test	Age range (years)	Functions assessed/Subscales
Wide Range Assessment of Visual Motor Abilities (Adams & Sheslow, 1995)	3–17	Visual motor skills; visual spatial skills; fine motor skills
Benton Visual Retention Test—5th edn (Benton-Sivan, 1992)	8–adult	Visual memory; visual perception; visuoconstructive abilities
Rey Complex Figure Test and Recognition Trial (Meyers & Meyers, 1995)	6–adult	Visuospatial constructional ability
Movement Ability Battery for Children (Henderson & Sugden, 1992)	4–12	Manual dexterity; static and dynamic balance; ball skills; behaviour checklist
Developmental Test of Visual-Motor Integration (Beery, 1997)	5–16	Visuomotor integration; visual perception; motor co-ordination
NEPSY—subtests (Korkman et al., 1998)	3–12.11	Design copy; arrows; route finding; visuomotor precision

Observations

Children who have visuoperceptual difficulties may automatically adapt their approach to tasks to compensate for their difficulties. It is always worth recording if children tend to occlude one eye when they are drawing, writing or reading by their hair or a hand, in case they are having double vision and are unconsciously adapting to this. Observations may reveal that they miss information on one side of the page or ignore parts of puzzles at the edge of the visual field. They seem to scan information poorly and fail to check their work inadequately. Relative slowness in completing visuospatial tasks compared with giving verbal answers may also indicate problems with these skills. Observations of subtests such as Block Design, Picture Completion or Object Assembly may indicate whether it is abstract or meaningful material that causes the most problems, whether they see partially correct solutions or whether they fail to see the 'whole' and rather concentrate on the parts. Assessments of visuoperceptual and motor skills are listed in Table 13.5.

Executive Functioning

Presenting Problems

Children with executive problems may present with a variety of difficulties. Parents may complain that they are always untidy, can never plan their homework or other activities, have difficulty initiating activity or when they start work they never complete it and tend to go off at tangents. Schools are likely to complain that children never get their homework in on time, that it is poorly organized and they have very little thought in the planning and preparing of work or are so over-whelmed by what they have to do that they cannot begin to plan where to start. Other issues may relate to parents and teachers being worried about children's ability to evaluate or judge their own work, which is seen as more than anxiety over failing. There may also be concerns expressed about disinhibited behaviour, poor or unusual affect, or undue lack of initiation.

Observations

Children with executive problems are likely to be very poor at planning to carry out tasks. For instance, older children may approach tasks such as the Rey Figure in a disorganized way, and throughout the assessment there will be little evidence of planning responses systematically. There may be an attempt to restart a test because they have realized that they have not begun it properly—such as in Mazes or the Tower of London—or some of the constructional tasks—such as Block Design and Object Assembly. Examples of perseveration in tasks, such as giving the same answer to a number of verbal questions or failure to change their tactics in completing constructional tasks when their response is clearly wrong, may also indicate executive skill difficulties (see Pennington & Ozonoff, 1996 for further discussion about assessment of executive functioning). Measures used to assess executive functioning are listed in Table 13.6.

APPLICATIONS OF CHILD NEUROPSYCHOLOGY

Types of Disorders Seen

Children with epilepsy, central nervous system tumours, head injuries, such infec-tions as meningitis and encephalitis, hypoxia from drowning and such evaluating treatment effects as radiation in leukaemia have long been the major areas of focus for paediatric neuropsychology. However, the range of diagnostic groups being referred is growing.

Systemic Illness

Neuropsychological deficits are being picked up in an increasing number of systemic illnesses and include a whole range of problems. For example, some children with severe cardiac defects who may have to undergo long and complex surgery are found to have neuropsychological sequelae (Oates et al., 1995; Uzark et al., 1998). There is evidence that children with early onset diabetes (prior to the age of five years) do not do so well as those with late onset insulin-dependent diabetes (Ryan et al., 1990). The effects of poor control of the disease by insulin resulting in a series of hypo- or

Table 13.6. Assessments of executive functioning

Test	Age range (years)	Functions assessed/Subscales
Wisconsin Card Sorting Task (Grant & Berg, 1993)	6–adult	Strategic planning; organized search; shifting set; modulating impulsive responding; learning from feedback
Children's Category Test (Boll, 1993)	5–8 and 9–16	Non-verbal learning; memory concept formation
Tower of London (Anderson et al., 1996; Shallice, 1988)	7–13	Planning; working memory
NEPSY—subtests (Korkman et al., 1998)	5–12.11	Tower; verbal fluency; design fluency; statue; knock tap
Behavior Rating Inventory of Executive Functioning (Gioia et al., 1996)	5–18	Behaviour regulation; metacognition; global executive composite
Stroop Colour and Word Test (Golden, 1992)	7–16	Inhibition
Mazes—WISC-III (Wechsler, 1991)	6–16.11	Planning; modulating impulsive responding
Trail Making Test (Reitan, 1958) and *Child Norms* (Spreen & Strauss,1998)	5–15	Motor speed; shifting set
Behavioural Assessment of the Dysexecutive Syndrome in Children—BADS-C (Emslie et al., 2003)	8–15.11	Response inhibition; planning; strategy formation; rule following

hyperglycaemic attacks may have subtle deleterious effects (lower Verbal IQ and poor attention) (Rovet, 2002). Serious, prolonged, hypoglycaemic or hyperglycaemic attacks leading to coma can have devasting neuropsychological consequences. Children with renal failure and the need for dialysis are another group where a wide range of neuropsychological problems have arisen (Fennell, 2000b).

Metabolic Illness

PKU and infantile hypothyroidism are examples of medical conditions that if managed well can lead to a normal life. However, there is evidence that late diagnosis of PKU and late onset or poor dietary control throughout childhood can give rise to immediate difficulties as well as long-term consequences (Smith et al., 1990a, b; Welsh & Pennington, 2000). Even if hypothyroidism is well controlled from birth, it is possible that there may be adverse effects prenatally affecting brain development that later give rise to visuospatial, attentional, psychomotor and concept formation problems (Rovet, 1995a).

Syndromes and Congenital Problems

Children with congenital problems and with rare syndromes have usually been seen by child development centres. Although there are inherent difficulties in assessing infants and very young children from a neuropsychological perspective, it may be possible to look at early weaknesses and, more importantly, follow these children for a number of years as their difficulties become more obvious. Children with different syndromes do have specific cognitive profiles (see O'Brien & Yule, 1995 for a more detailed discussion), and it is important to assess children for predicted cognitive and behavioural profiles if they are known to have a specific syndrome in order to advise on education.

Learning Difficulties

Traditionally, children with moderate and severe learning difficulties have rarely been assessed in detail. There are inherent problems looking at the neuropsychological profiles of children who are globally impaired, as the majority of neuropsychological tests are standardized on children within the normal range. Children with severe and profound cognitive difficulties may be unable to carry out specific memory tasks, for example, and score badly because of their underlying low level of cognitive functioning rather than because of a specific difficulty. On the other hand, it may be possible to look at their individual profiles, particularly their strengths, in order to build on these to create individual educational packages for them.

Neurodevelopmental Problems and Neuropsychiatry

Children with a range of problems frequently referred to child and adolescent mental health teams include those with autistic spectrum disorders, attention deficit hyperactivity disorder, dyspraxia or developmental motor delay, dyslexia, Tourette's syndrome and obsessive compulsive disorder and may well benefit from a thorough investigation of their difficulties. Pennington and Ozonoff (1996) have summarized the neuropsychological findings of this group of children and list those assessments they have found most useful. Work with children with pervasive and disintegrative developmental disorders including childhood schizophrenia may also be appropriate.

Clinical Neuropsychology Services for Children

Traditionally, neuropsychologists seeing adult clients have worked alongside colleagues in neurosurgery and neurology and in rehabilitation settings. In the past this pattern has transferred to those working with children. However, as the focus and application of child neuropsychology widens, child neuropsychologists are likely to work in more varied settings than they have done in the past and in collaboration with new colleagues. Away from the neuroscience centre or acute general hospital, there have been small initiatives in setting up primary care settings (O'Neil & Griffiths, 2001), where a variety of children with acquired and neurodevelopmental problems will be seen.

Those working in child clinical neuropsychology will, by the very nature of their work, liaise with schools and the education system. The detailed assessments prepared for medical colleagues also contain extremely useful information about how and why children may perform and, more particularly, fail in school. The rehabilitation and re-education of children following brain damage takes place in schools almost exclusively, except in extremely severe cases. Reports from child clinical neuropsychologists can make a valuable contribution to understanding problems in schools, are used in preparing individual educational plans and add to the statement of special educational needs.

CONCLUSIONS

An appreciation of the implications of child neuropsychology is not only crucial for those working with children but may also be fundamental in understanding a whole variety of problems that present in adulthood. In recent years child neuropsychology has been seen to become increasingly important in working with children, making a value contribution to defining and understanding problems.

REFERENCES

Adams, W. & Sheslow, D. (1995) *Wide Range Assessment of Visual Motor Abilities*. Wide Range Inc., Wilmington, DE.

Anderson, P., Anderson, V. & Lajoie (1996) The Tower of London test: Validation and standardization for paediatric populations. *The Clinical Neuropsychologist*, **10**, 54–65.

Anderson, V., Northam, E., Hendy, J. & Wrennall, J. (2001) *Developmental Neuropsychology: A Clinical Approach*. Psychological Press, Hove, UK.

Aylward, G. P. (1995) *Bayley Infant Neurodevelopmental Screener*. Psychological Corporation, San Antonio, TX.

Bayley, N. (1993) *Bayley Scales of Infant Development* (2nd edn). Psychological Corporation, San Antonio, TX.

Beery, K. E. (1997) *Developmental Test of Visual-Motor Integration* (4th edn). Modern Curriculum Press, Parsippany, NJ.

Benton-Sivan, A. (1992) *Benton Visual Retention Test* (5th edn). Psychological Corporation, San Antonio, TX.

Bijur, P. E. & Haslum, M. (1995) Cognitive, behavioural, and motoric sequelae of mild head injury in a National Cohort Study. In: S. H. Broman & M. E. Michel (eds) *Traumatic Brain Injury in Children* (pp. 147–164). Oxford University Press, Oxford, UK.

Bishop, D. (1985) Age of onset and outcome in acquired aphasia with convlusive disorder. *Developmental Medicine and Child Neurology*, **27**, 705–712

Bishop, D. (1989) *Test of Reception of Grammar* (2nd edn). Chapel Press, Abingdon, UK.

Bjorklund, D. G. & Douglas, R. N. (1998) The development of memory strategies. In: N. Cowan (ed.) *The Development of Memory in Childhood* (pp. 201–246). Psychology Press, Hove, UK.

Boll, T. (1993) *Children's Category Test*. Psychological Corporation, San Antonio, TX.

Chadwick, O., Rutter, M., Brown, G., Schaffer, D. & Traub, M. (1981) A prospective study of children with head injury: II. Cognitive sequelae. *Psychological Medicine*, **11**, 49–61.

Cohen, M. (1997) *Children's Memory Scale*. Psychological Corporation, San Antonio, TX.

Dean, C. D., Kramer, J. H., Kaplan, E. & Ober, B. A. (1994) *California Verbal Learning Test— Children's Version*. Psychological Corporation, San Antonio, TX.

Donders, J. & Strom, D. (1997) The effect of traumatic brain injury on children with learning disability. *Pediatric Rehabilitation*, **1**, 179–184.

Dunn, L. M., Whetton, C. & Burley, J. (1997) *British Picture Vocabulary Scale* (2nd edn). NFER-Nelson, Windsor, UK.

Elliott, C. D. (1996) *British Ability Scales* (2nd edn). NFER-Nelson, Windsor, UK.

Emslie, H., Wilson, C., Burden, V., Nimmo-Smith, I. & Wilson, B. A. (2003) *Behavioural Assessment of the Dysexecutive Syndrome in Children (BADS-C)*. Thames Valley Test Co., Bury St Edmunds, UK.

Fennell, E. B. (2000a) Issues in child neuropsychological assessment. In: R. D. Vanderploeg (ed.) *Clincian's Guide to Neuropsychological Assessment* (2nd edn, pp. 357–382). Lawrence Erlbaum, London.

Fennell, E. B. (2000b) End-stage renal disease. In: K. O. Yeates, M. D. Ris & H. G. Taylor (eds) *Pediatric Neuropsychology: Research, Theory and Practice* (pp. 366–380). Guilford Press, New York.

Fletcher, J. M. & Taylor, H. G. (1984) Neuropsychological approaches to childen: Towards a developmental neuropsychology. *Journal of Clinical Neuropsychology*, **6**, 39–56.

Gioia, G. A., Isquith, P. K., Guy, S. C. & Kenworthy, L. (1996) *Behavior Rating Inventory of Executive Functioning*. Psychological Assessment Resources Inc., Odessa, FL.

Golden, C. J. (1992) *Stroop Colour and Word Test: A Manual for Clinical and Experimental Uses*. Stoelting Co., Chicago.

Goodman, R. (1989) Limits of cerebral plasticity. In: D. Johnson, D. Uttley & M. Wyke (eds) *Children's Head Injury: Who Cares?* (pp. 12–22). Falmer Press, Brighton, UK.

Gopaul-McNicol, S. & Armour-Thomas, E. (2002) *Assessment and Culture: Psychological Tests with Minority Populations*. Academic Press, San Diego.

Grant, D. A. & Berg, E. A. (1993) *Wisconsin Card Sorting Test*. Psychological Assessment Resources Inc., Odessa, FL.

Griffiths, R. (1996) *The Griffiths Mental Development Scales*. The Test Agency Ltd, Henley-on-Thames, UK [revised by M. Huntley].

Harris, M. & Butterworth, G. (2002) *Developmental Psychology*. Psychology Press and Taylor & Francis, Andover, UK.

Henderson, S. E. & Sugden, D. A. (1992) *Movement Assessment Battery for Children*. Psychological Corporation, San Antonio, TX.

Holmes-Bernstein, J. (2000) Developmental neuropsychological assessment. In: K. O. Yeates, M. D. Ris & H. G. Taylor (eds) *Pediatric Neuropsychology: Research, Theory and Practice* (pp. 405–438). Guilford Press, New York.

Kaplan, E. (1999) *WISC-III as a Processing Instrument*. Psychological Corporation, San Antonio, TX.

Kaufman, A. S. (1995) *Intelligent Testing with the WISC-III*. John Wiley & Sons, New York.

Kaufman, A. S. (2000) *Bayley Scales of Infant Development Assessment*. John Wiley & Sons, New York.

Kaufman, A. S. & Kaufman, N. L. (1983) *The Kaufman Assessment Battery for Children (K-ABC)*. American Guild Service, Circles Pines, MN.

Kaufman, A. S. & Lichtenberger, E. O. (2000) *Essentials of WISC-III and WPPSI-R Assessment*. John Wiley & Sons, New York.

Kolb, B. & Whishaw, I. Q. (1987) Recovery from early cortical damage in rats. I. Differential behavioural and anatomical effects of frontal lesions at different ages of neural maturation. *Behavioral Brain Research*, **25**, 205–220.

Korkman, M., Kirk, U. & Kemp, S. (1998) *NEPSY: A Developmental Neuropsychological Assessment*. Psychological Corporation, San Antonio, TX.

Lenneberg, E. (1967) *Biological Foundations of Language*. Wiley, New York.

Levin, H. S., Ewing-Cobbs, L. & Eisenberg, H. M. (1995) Neurobehavioural outcome of pediatric closed head injury. In: S. H. Broman & M. E. Michel (eds) *Traumatic Brain Injury in Children* (pp. 70–94). Oxford University Press, Oxford, UK.

Manly, T., Robertson, I. H., Anderson, V. & Nimmo-Smith, I. (1998) *Test of Everyday Attention for Children*. Thames Valley Test Co., Bury St Edmunds, UK.

Max, J. E., Robin, D. A., Lindgren, S. D., Smith, W. L., Sato, Y., Mattheis, P. J. et al. (1997) Traumatic brain injury in children and adolescents: Psychiatric disorder at two years. *Journal of the American Academy of Child and Adolescent Psychiatry*, **36**, 1278–1285.

McCarthy, D. (1972) *McCarthy Scales of Children's Abilities*. Psychological Corporation, New York.

Meyers, J. E. & Meyers, K. R. (1995) *Rey Complex Figure Test and Recognition Trial: Professional Manual*. Psychological Assessment Resources Inc., Odessa, FL.

Middleton, J. A. (2001) Practitioner review: Psychological sequelae of head injury in children and adolescents. *Journal of Child Psychology and Psychiatry*, **42**, 165–180.

Middleton, J. A. (2003) Assessment and management of memory problems in children. In: A. D. Baddeley, M. D. Kopelman & B. A. Wilson (eds) *Handbook of Memory Disorders*. John Wiley & Sons, Chichester, UK.

Monk, C. S., Webb, S. J. & Nelson, C. A. (2000) Prenatal neurobiological development: Molecular mechanisms and anatomical change. *Developmental Neuropsychology*, **19**, 211–236.

Mulhern, R. K., Hancock, J., Fairclough, D. & Kun, L. (1992) Neuropsychological status of children treated for brain tumors: A critical review and integrative analysis. *Medical and Paediatric Oncology*, **20**, 181–191.

Oates, R. K., Simpson, J. M., Cartmill, T. B. & Turnbull, J. A. B. (1995) Intellectual function and age of repair in cyanotic congenital heart disease. *Archives of Disease in Childhood*, **72**, 298–301.

O'Brien, G. & Yule, W. (1995) *Behavioural Phenotypes*. Cambridge University Press, Cambridge, UK.

O'Neil, J. & Griffiths, P. (2001) Paediatric neuropsychology in primary care: A one-year overview of a new service. *Clinical Psychology*, **8**, December, 15–18.

Pennington, B. F. & Ozonoff, S. (1996) Executive functions and developmental psychopathology. *Journal of Child Psychology and Psychiatry*, **37**, 51–87.

Pharoah, P. O. D., Stevenson, C. J., Cooke, R. W. I. & Stevenson, R. C. (1994) Clinical and subclinical deficits at 8 years in a geographically defined cohort of low birthweight infants. *Archives of Disease in Childhood*, **70**, 264–270.

Reitan, R. M. (1958) Validity of the Trail Making Test as an indicator of organic brain damage. *Perceptual and Motor Skills*, **8**, 271–276.

Reynolds, C. R. & Bigler, E. D. (1994) *Test of Memory and Learning*. Pro-Ed, Austin, TX.

Rovet, J. F. (1995a) Congenital hypothyroidism. In: B. P. Rourke (ed.) *Syndrome of Nonverbal Learning Disabilities* (pp. 255–281). Guilford Press, New York.

Rovet, J. F. (1995b) Effects of maternal epilepsy on children's neurodevelopment. *Child Neuropsychology*, **1**, 1–8.

Rovet, J. F. (2002) Diabetes. In: K. O. Yeates, M. D. Ris & H. G. Taylor (eds) *Pediatric Neuropsychology: Research, Theory and Practice* (pp. 336–365). Guilford Press, New York.

Rust, J. (1996) *Wechsler Objective Language Dimensions*. Psychological Corporation, San Antonio, TX.

Ryan, C., Atchison, J., Puczynski, M., Arslanian, S. & Becker, D. (1990) Mild hypoglycemia associated with deterioration of mental efficiency in children with insulin-dependent diabetes mellitus. *The Journal of Pediatrics*, **117**, 32–38.

Said, J. A., Waters, B. G. H., Cousens, P. & Stevens, M. M. (1989) Neuropsychological sequelae of central nervous system prophylaxis in survivors of childhood acute lymphoblastic leukaemia. *Journal of Consulting and Clinical Psychology*, **57**, 251–256.

Semel, E., Wiig, E. H. & Secord, W. A. (1995) *Clinical Evaluation of Language Fundamentals* (3rd edn). Psychological Corporation, San Antonio, TX.

Shallice T. (1988) *From Neuropsychology to Mental Structure*. Cambridge University Press, Cambridge, UK.

Sheslow, D. & Adams, W. (1990) *Wide Range Assessment of Memory and Learning*. Jastak Associates, Inc., Wilmington, DE.

Small, M. Y. (1990) *Cognitive Development*. Harcourt Brace Jovanovich, New York.

Smith, A. & Sugar, O. (1975) Development of above normal language and intelligence 21 years after left hemispherectomy. *Neurology*, **25**, 813–818.

Smith, I., Beasley, M. G. & Ades, A. E. (1990a) Effect on intelligence of relaxing the low phenylalanine diet in phenylketonuria. *Archives of Disease in Childhood*, **65**, 311–316.

Smith, I., Beasley, M. G. & Ades, A. E. (1990b) Intelligence and quality of dietary treatment in phenylketonuria. *Archives of Disease in Childhood*, **65**, 472–478.

Spreen, O. & Strauss, E. (1998) *A Compendium of Neuropsychological Tests: Administration, Norms and Commentary* (3rd edn). Oxford University Press, Oxford, UK.

Stiles, J. (2001) Neural plasticity and cognitive development. *Developmental Neuropsychology*, **18**, 237–272.

Temple, C. (1997) *Developmental Cognitive Neuropsychology*. Psychology Press, Hove, UK.

Uzark, K., Lincoln, A., Lamberti, J. J., Mainwaring, R. D., Spicer, R. L. & Moore, J.W. (1998) Neurodevelopmental outcomes in children with fontan repair of functional single ventricle. *Pediatrics*, **101**, 630–633.

Vargha-Khadem, F., Gadian, D. G., Watkins, K. E., Connelly, A., Van Paesschen, W. & Mishkin, M. (1997) Differential effects of early hippocampal pathology on episodic and semantic memory. *Science*, **277**, 18 July, 376–380.

Wechsler, D. (1991) *Wechsler Intelligence Scale for Children* (3rd edn). Psychological Corporation, San Antonio, TX.

Wechsler, D. (1993) *Wechsler Pre-School and Primary Scale of Intelligence—Revised*. The Psychological Corporation, San Antonio, TX.

Welsh, M. & Pennington, B. (2000) Phenylketonuria. In: K. O. Yeates, M. D. Ris & H. G. Taylor (eds) *Pediatric Neuropsychology: Research, Theory and Practice* (pp. 275–299). Guilford Press, New York.

Wilson, B. A., Ivani-Chalian, R. & Aldrich, B. (1991) *Rivermead Behaviour Memory Test for Children*. Thames Valley Test Co., Bury St Edmunds, UK.

Ylvisaker, M. (1998) *Traumatic Brain Injury Rehabilitation: Children and Adolescents* (2nd edn). Butterworth-Heinemann, Boston.

Zimmerman, I. L., Steiner, V. G. & Pond, R. E. (1992) *Preschool Language Scale—3*. Psychological Corporation, San Antonio, TX.

CHAPTER 14

Neuropsychology of Older Adults

Robin G. Morris
Institute of Psychiatry, London, UK

INTRODUCTION

Neuropsychological assessment is commonplace in clinical practice with older adults, not least because of the various neurodegenerative illnesses that are associated with ageing (Morris & Worsley, in press). In a broad sense, neuropsychological assessments are widely used in the form of mental status examinations, with more specialist and in-depth assessments provided by a clinical psychologist or clinical neuropsychologist. If used appropriately, this type of assessment can provide a useful role in the management and rehabilitation of older adults. This chapter provides an overview of the assessment techniques being used and some of the recent developments in procedures. The focus is on the assessment methods, with the neuropsychological features of the various neurological disorders associated with old age covered elsewhere (cf. Morris & Worsley, 2002; in press).

As with other assessments, it is important to keep in mind the overall goal and the type of information needed, tailoring the procedures toward a particular patient. As a result of the time taken for full neuropsychological assessment, the purpose should be considered carefully and balanced against the available resources. These purposes can be divided into three main areas:

1. *Detecting neuropsychological impairment.* This applies particularly at the early stages of dementia, where there is uncertainty as to whether neuropsychological impairment exists. Beyond simple rating scales and the patient's own report, a more extensive neuropsychological assessment can be used to provide a sensitive indicator of impairment, which in turn can be followed up with a more detailed medical investigation if necessary. At this point, there may be a number of scenarios. For example, a person may have mild cognitive impairment or be presenting prodromally, but not diagnosable as having Alzheimer's disease, in which case following up the patient can further aid with diagnosis. This can also help to rule out impairment in cases of people who perceive cognitive decline, but in fact fall in the category 'worried well'. Early detection and diagnosis can also be used to aid the early implementation of pharmacological interventions that may prove beneficial if started early (see Chapter 19). A general point is that

Clinical Neuropsychology: A Practical Guide to Assessment and Management for Clinicians.
Edited by L.H. Goldstein and J.E. McNeil. © 2004 John Wiley & Sons, Ltd.

neuropsychological procedures tend to have relatively high sensitivity in detecting impairment, but less specificity in relation to determining causation, so the results of a neuropsychological assessment should be interpreted in the context of a psychiatric or neurological examination.

2. *Ascertaining change*. Multiple assessments are not uncommon with older adults, and these can be used to monitor the rate of decline or, in more research mode, to determine the efficacy of treatment effects. The approach is also useful in differential diagnosis, for example, between dementia and depression. Here, the manner in which depression may complicate establishing whether a patient has dementia can be disambiguated by tracking the change in these two disorders over time. Specifically, if the level of depression remits and cognitive function decreases, then this may be indicative of neurodegenerative disease. As a caveat to this, although there is usually an improvement in cognitive function when depression lifts, there is evidence for some persistence of cognitive dysfunction in some cases (cf. Stoudemire et al., 1993). Neuropsychological assessments have also been used in monitoring the effects of rehabilitation outcome (Woods, 1979). Here, the use may be more limited because of the manner in which neurorehabilitation is targeted, particularly toward activity or behavioural goals that can be measured more directly.

3. *Determining types of impairments*. There are a variety of neurological disorders, principally of old age, each having their own pattern of cognitive impairment. Consequently, it is necessary to orientate the types of procedures used to suit the particular aetiology of the patient (Morris & Worsley, 2002). For example, early Alzheimer's disease is associated with a pattern of impairment principally causing loss of intellectual function, memory and executive function with difficulties in naming as an early feature of language disturbance. While the pattern of Alzheimer's can vary substantially, this is even more the case with cerebrovascular disorders (e.g., multi-infarct dementia). Here the aim of the assessment may be to identify the strengths and weaknesses of a patient with a view to understanding the cognitive presentation and behaviour. The information can then be used to improve the overall management of the patient and explain to caregivers the nature of their disabilities. The assessment can be used to tackle a wide range of issues. This includes, for example, confidence to drive, ward orientation and the effects of visuospatial disturbances and executive dysfunction on the ability of the patient to perform certain everyday tasks.

WORKING WITH AN OLDER ADULT

Approaches to the assessment of individual older adults can vary quite widely according to the needs of the assessment and the level of neuropsychological impairment. Hence there is the need for the neuropsychologist to tailor their procedures accordingly in each case (Morris & McKiernan, 1994; Morris et al., 2000). There are, however, a number of general principles that concern the assessment of an older adult as considered below.

One consideration is that older adults may less readily 'engage' with the purpose of the assessment, and more time may be needed to ensure a mutual understanding about the session and procedures. Despite this, loss of insight or comprehension may make this process more difficult, and it may be necessary to use more concrete and simpler explanations of the purpose of the assessment. Additional to this, a lack of understanding can be ameliorated to some extent by a pleasant, unhurried approach in which the examiner takes care to establish good rapport with the patient before and during the assessment. In certain instances it can also be the case that the patient is unable to communicate verbally their feelings and thoughts about the assessment, and it is important to attend to non-verbal signs of frustration or impatience and to respond to these accordingly. This, for example, may involve adjusting the procedures used during the assessment in order to shorten those sessions where patients reach the limits of their attention. If possible, stressing the patient with unpleasant procedures should be avoided, with the protocol designed for each patient determined with this limitation in mind.

A further factor is the greater likelihood of sensory impairment in older adults, either visual or auditory, since such impairments are known to correlate with performance on neuropsychological tests (O'Neill & Calhoun, 1975). Therefore, it is important to try and compensate for a sensory loss as much as possible. For example, in relation to vision, where this is uncorrected, it may be possible to use enlarged stimuli. When a patient has a hearing disability, various steps can be taken. To assist communication, it may be necessary to speak more loudly, but without raising the pitch of the voice. In addition, increasing volume should take into account that this may exceed the threshold of the patient and lead to discomfort or distortions. The person should be seen in a quiet room, free from distraction, and, if a hearing aid is used, then it may be necessary to ensure that it is working properly. These are obvious procedures, but can easily be forgotten about if the examiner is focusing on other aspects of the neuropsychological assessment.

A final consideration is the conduct of the examination with respect to speed. Cognitive slowing is a feature with both the cognitive ageing process and also different neurodegenerative disorders. To compensate for this, assessments should not be hurried and the number of tests used adjusted to take into account what can realistically be achieved in a session. Similarly, tests that pace the subjects and apply time pressure in certain instances should be avoided. An example of this is the difficulty some older adults may have in keeping to the three seconds that are provided for making a judgement about the stimulus material in Warrington's (1984) Recognition Memory Test battery.

In summary, skilled assessment of older adults means tailoring the approach carefully to the individual with additional effort made to establish good rapport with the patient, compensate for sensory loss and be able to adapt to the changing circumstances of the session.

ASSESSMENT PROCEDURES

As indicated above, a tailored approach to the choice of neuropsychological test is especially important when working with older adults. This usually entails using a basic set of tests that can be supplemented in order to follow up a particular type of deficit. In older adults, tailoring is important for a number of reasons:

1. *To avoid exposure to failure.* Inflexible use of a standard battery can result in many of the items being too difficult for an older adult, particularly if the neuropsychological dysfunction is severe. Older adults may become demotivated more easily when exposed to failure, particularly if they are not in tune with the reasons for the assessment. This is exacerbated in patients with neurodegenerative disorders, such as Alzheimer's disease (AD), where there be may be poor insight into their level of impairment and hence greater need for assessment. To get round this, tests can be selected that tap into the ability levels of the patient, while still being sensitive to impairment.

2. *To reduce fatigue effects.* Generally, older adults are less able to complete extensive test batteries in one sitting because of fatigue effects. However, there is considerable variability in this respect, and each patient should be considered in relation to how much can be realistically achieved with a testing session. Additionally, splitting assessments into shorter ones can reduce fatigue, although multiple sessions may not sustain motivation in certain patients.

3. *To match aetiology.* There is considerable variation in neuropsychological dysfunction according to different types of neurological disorder, and time can be saved by selecting tests that are appropriate for the patient. For example, extensive testing of memory might not be necessary in a patient with a confident diagnosis of AD, but may be useful to determine whether there is significant memory disorder in patients with mild cognitive impairment.

In general, it may be useful to start with the notion of a test battery that covers the main areas of cognition and background intellectual function, and modify this according to the patient's type. For patients with more severe impairment, a more specialized approach may be needed as outlined below.

Screening Assessments

If patients cannot tolerate a more extensive assessment, simple screening procedures can be used to obtain a reasonable amount of information about their cognitive function. At the most straightforward level, this includes using a mental status examination, with many different versions available, perhaps the most commonly used one being the Mini-Mental State Examination (MMSE; Folstein & Folstein, 1988). These are designed to provide a crude indication of level of dementia and contain items that are usually very acceptable to a wide range of patients, such that they have been adopted as neuropsychiatric or neurological screening devices.

Beyond this are brief batteries that have been developed specifically for older adults and are used by neuropsychologists. An example is the Cambridge Cognitive Examination (CAMCOG), developed as part of the larger assessment instrument for dementia—the Cambridge Mental Disorders of the Elderly Examination (CAMDEX: Roth et al., 1988) and now in revised form (Roth et al., 1999). Based on the idea of dividing cognition into different neuropsychological functions, it comprises very short subtests that cover orientation, language, memory, praxis, attention, abstract-thinking and perception. Studies by Huppert et al. (1996) have shown the CAMCOG to be highly reliable, with factor-analytical analysis of data suggesting two main points: one concerning intellectual functioning and the other related to memory. It has also been validated on different patient groups, including those with AD, vascular dementia, depression and delirium. A near equivalent to the CAMCOG is the Middlesex Elderly Assessment of Mental State (MEAMS; Golding, 1989). This assesses similar neuropsychological functions and includes, for example, tests of orientation, name learning, verbal comprehension, arithmetic and perception. It has the added advantage of having two parallel forms for repeated testing. The design of the test is such that, regardless of intellectual ability, all items should be passed to establish normality. This may make it less sensitive to mild impairments. Nevertheless, in a patient with moderate cognitive impairment, it is useful as a screening instrument for exploring the overall profile of impairment across a range of functions.

An alternative to these two batteries is the Consortium to Establish a Registry for AD (CERAD) neuropsychological battery, which is used extensively and has been investigated in a number of different nationalities (see Unverzagt et al., 1999). It includes tests of fluency, naming, constructional praxis, free recall and recognition and has been found to discriminate well between normal older adults and those with dementia (Morris et al., 1989). A more specialist, but more widely used test, is the Kendrick Cognitive Test for the Elderly (Kendrick, 1985). This contains two tests: an object recall test, which involves being presented with arrays of line drawings of objects and having to recall their names; and a digit copying test, which requires the patient to copy a series of visually presented digits. A feature of this battery is that it has parallel forms, and there are normative data relating to retesting after a six-week interval, useful for serial testing. This test has been revised into the Kendrick Assessment Scales of Cognitive Ageing (*KASCA*; Kendrick & Watts, 1999). It is intended for testing people without neuropsychological–neuropsychiatric impairments, as an expansion of the old version. The test includes measures of object recall, digit copying, reasoning and visuospatial abilities.

In summary, most of these instruments have the advantage of brevity and can either be used as screening instruments for dementia or to provide an accrued measure of severity and to detect specific deficits. However, care must be taken in terms of overinterpreting individual items in the tests due to their brevity. This includes being cautious about interpreting deficits on a specific test as being due to an impairment only in the function it purports to measure.

Intellectual Assessment

An intellectual assessment of older adults can have several purposes. The main one is
that the overall level of functioning provides a way of gauging the severity of
impairment in specific areas of function. For example, if it is established that there
is a high level of intellectual functioning, then average or low average range memory
may represent a clinically significant deficit (see also Chapter 6). The current level
intellectual function can also give an indication of deterioration, either by comparison with an estimate of premorbid ability or by using longitudinal testing with the
intelligence test scores acting as the original baseline. In general, intellectual assessment is used when the patient has a reasonable level of function and provides the
starting point for testing other functions. Determining this level of function can be a
matter of clinical judgement in each case, but the general principle is that the patient
should be able to attempt the various subtests and achieve some success beyond the
very preliminary items.

A number of issues arise in testing intelligence, including establishing the
person's premorbid level of function, tailoring the procedure so as to keep a
reasonable length and deciding what the profile of intellectual dysfunction may
indicate diagnostically.

Premorbid Intelligence

Since many older adults with neuropsychological impairment have neurodegenerative diseases, there is very frequently the need to ascertain the presence and extent of
cognitive decline. A crude method of doing this is to establish the educational and
occupational success of the patient. This can be very useful in the case of high-
achieving patients, where, for example, success in these areas gives a good indication
of premorbid ability. On the other hand, if a person has not been successful, for
obvious reasons this does not rule out high premorbid ability.

Another technique is to make inferences from cognitive tests that are known to
be resistant to decline, depending upon the patient population studied. In neurodegenerative disorders like AD this tends to apply to cognitive functions that rely
on over-learned material or procedures from the past that minimize processing of
information or problem-solving. An example of this is the Vocabulary subtest of
the Wechsler Adult Intelligence Scale (WAIS) series (see p. 308), where it has been
established that decline is slow (e.g., Miller, 1977). Nevertheless, this test still
requires a range of cognitive processes and is subject to the effects of perseveration.

An alternative method is the oral reading of single words. The resilience to
dementia was first reported by Nelson and McKenna (1975) using the Schonell
Graded Word Reading Test (SGWRT), where no difference was observed between
people with dementia and control subjects, despite intellectual deficits. The
SGWRT is still useful for people who are like to have premorbidly low ability
because it covers the low end range more fully. Nevertheless, using oral reading of
words with irregular spellings has been found to be more resilient. This is because
(e.g., in AD) irregular spellings force reliance on either the lexical or semantic

route, the former showing relative preservation. In other words, the reader has to 'know' how to say the word, rather than using a phonological decoding strategy to read it successfully out loud. The most widely used test of this sort is the National Adult Reading Test (NART), restandardized in the early 1990s by Nelson and Willison (1991) against the WAIS-R and is due for restandardization. It is used to derive predictions of Full Scale, Verbal or Performance IQ. As such, it can show quite remarkable resilience to the effects of brain damage in individual patients (see Chapter 6 for a more detailed discussion).

Many studies show no differences between groups of dementia patients and controls on this measure (see Morris, 1994 and Chapter 6 of this book). In normative studies NART scores have been shown to account for a high proportion of the variance on the WAIS, better than a combination of the age, gender, years of education and social class (Crawford et al., 1989). In addition, the NART has been shown to be a better predictor of original IQ than the test used originally to ascertain intellectual functioning in earlier life (Crawford et al., 2001). Nevertheless, performance does eventually decline and is seen after longitudinal testing (Fromm et al., 1991) or in moderate dementia, as might be expected (Patterson et al., 1994).

There are a number of alternatives to the NART (2nd edition). These include the Cambridge Contextual Reading Test (Beardsall, 1998; Conway & O'Carroll, 1997) and the Spot-the-Word Test (Baddeley et al., 1992; cf. Beardsall & Huppert, 1997). Additionally, Mockler et al. (in preparation) have developed the Mockler Reading Inventory, which uses words with irregular spellings, but with a wider range of word difficulty, in order to circumvent this difficulty with the NART. The Wechsler Test of Adult Reading (WTAR; Holdnack, 2001), developed in the US but also adapted for UK use, has standardized data on individuals up to 89 years and uses words with irregular pronunciations in order to estimate premorbid ability as well. It has been co-normed with the WAIS-III and WMS-III (Wechsler Memory Scale) and can be used to predict scores on these tests.

In summary, an estimation of premorbid ability provides a useful marker against which to compare current ability and so infer decline. This can be done using a combination of methods, including educational and occupational attainment and tests resistant to cognitive decline, such as vocabulary or reading tests. The most commonly used technique with older adults is still the NART (2nd edition), but this has limitations and recent alternative methods are available.

Intelligence

The most widely used procedure in older adults for testing current IQ is the WAIS and its subsequent versions, including the WAIS-III (Wechsler, 1997). These provide a comprehensive approach, with well-established reliability and validity. The full WAIS-III has the advantage of a range of additional subscales (see Chapter 6 for more detail). However, for obvious reasons, this may be beyond the scope of routine assessment with some older adults with brain damage.

The WAIS-III has also been developed with older adults in mind, with enlarged and clearer stimulus material and normative data that span the 74–89-year age range. In addition, there is less emphasis on speed (e.g., with the inclusion of the Matrix Reasoning Test, a test of visuospatial problem-solving). The US standardization has been supplemented by validation on a UK sample (Wycherley et al., 1999).

Longitudinal intelligence testing is conducted on older adults for the reasons outlined above. A feature of the WAIS is that there are significant practice effects that can in principle lead to an underestimate of decline. Practice effects have been investigated in the WAIS-III, and these appear to be much less of a problem for older adults. For example, whereas IQ is reported as increasing by a mean of 6.3 points in young adults, the increase is only a mean of 3.2 points in 75–89-year-olds (Wechsler, 1997).

In the past, short forms of the WAIS have been useful for older adults and, for example, these have included the form that includes the Vocabulary, Comprehension, Block Design and Object Assembly subtests (Savage et al., 1973). A convenient WAIS-III short form is the Wechsler Abbreviated Scale of Intelligence (WASI; Wechsler, 1999) that uses Similarities, Vocabulary, Block Design and Matrix Reasoning, although these are not exactly the same tests as in the WAIS-III. It incorporates parallel forms, and it also has been validated additionally on a UK normative sample (Mockler & Crawford, unpublished data, in preparation). The WASI can be abbreviated further by just using Vocabulary and Matrix Reasoning, representative tests relating to Verbal and Performance IQ.

Memory Assessment

A common feature of neuropsychological impairment in older adults is memory disturbance. This is partly due to the fact that memory impairment is a primary feature of AD, but it is also common in many other forms of dementia. It is normal for memory to decline in older adults, and one of the purposes of a neuropsychological assessment can be to determine whether the complaints of memory disturbance are clinically significant.

In ascertaining memory loss it is useful to obtain, either informally or through a questionnaire approach, the presenting symptoms of memory loss from both the patient and carer. As well as determining the characteristics of memory difficulties, this can help determine the level of insight of patients into their problems. In AD, insight can vary quite substantially, with anosognosic deficits common (Agnew & Morris, 1998; Hannesdottir & Morris, in press). In addition, the presenting complaints, explored more thoroughly, may give a better idea of the type of memory difficulty experience. For example, in certain instances, a patient may complain of memory impairment, but this can turn out to be problems with word retrieval. In assessing memory, it is appropriate to use basic questions relating to orientation (i.e., the day or week, month, year and location), such as those provided in the WMS. Additionally, engaging patients in conversations about current events where

Table 14.1. A generalized outline of the stages of memory impairment in dementia such as AD

Mild memory impairment
- Lapses in memory are noticed, for example, by failure to carry out errands or conversations with other people; forgetting the details of recent events.
- These problems may be attributed to other factors, such as the effects of stress or depression, or 'normal cognitive ageing'.
- The memory disorder may represent a prodromal period before the onset of AD.
- Complaints of mild memory impairment are not necessarily accompanied by neuropsychological impairment and the patient may be 'worried well'.

Mild or moderate impairment
- The memory impairment becomes more pronounced and more easily noticed by friends and relatives.
- The errors include consistently forgetting important pieces of information, forgetting reasonably familiar people and getting disorientated even in relatively familiar surrounds. The patient becomes unable to keep track of daily events and shows temporal and spatial disorientation.
- The memory impairment may force reliance on a carer, and the person may seek medical help, often prompted by the carer.
- Insight is variable, and frequently the patient may not recognize the true extent of their memory difficulties.

Severe impairment
- The patient is substantially disorientated, and memory impairment can cause safety problems, for example, associated with wandering.
- Severe memory impairment includes forgetting close relatives.
- Marked signs of memory disorder may include paramnesia and confabulation.

it is known that they would have been exposed to information about these (e.g., television news) can help determine everyday memory ability.

In different neuropsychological disorders of old age, including the different types of dementia, the pattern of memory impairment can vary (Morris, 2002). However, a generalized pattern in the development of loss of memory in dementias such as AD can be discerned, as indicated in Table 14.1. At the early stages, the main feature is memory lapses, often initially attributed to absent-mindedness, stress or normal cognitive ageing. Mild memory impairment can represent a prodromal period before the onset of dementia and is the most predictive factor (Fox et al., 1998). Nevertheless, patients can complain of mild memory difficulties yet turn out not to have neuropsychological impairment. As the dementia progresses, the memory impairments become very obvious and there is no difficulty determining their true nature, although it can be useful to ascertain the severity with a view to guiding rehabilitation and management. In the more severe stage, the memory disorder is particularly debilitating and accounts for some of the behavioural problems associated with disorientation.

A range of test batteries can be used to assess memory function in older adults, and some of these are considered in more detail in Chapter 7. The advantage of using a battery is that they are more comprehensive and may cover different facets of memory using tests that have been standardized on the same population. This advantage has to be offset against the length of the overall battery, which may prove too taxing for some older adult patients. Issues to be considered when selecting a battery include whether material is suited to people who may have some sensory loss and whether time limits are imposed on processing information, which may create added pressure for old adults. In the past, memory tests tended not to have good normative data, but this is less often the case now, although care still has to taken in terms of appropriate selection. The Doors and People Test (Baddeley et al., 1994) has user-friendly material that tends to put patients at ease and is potentially one of the more appropriate batteries, with reasonable but not extensive norms for older adults. An alternative, ecologically valid test is the Rivermead Behavioural Memory Test (extended version; Wilson et al., 1999), which has older adult norms and again uses 'friendly' material. The original Warrington Recognition Memory Test has been updated to form the Camden Memory Test (Warrington, 1996). This has shorter verbal and face recognition tests and includes paired associate learning and pictorial memory as well. This battery has good older adult norms, having been developed with this group in mind. It has also been found to produce measurable scores on patients with neurodegenerative disorders, where more demanding tests yield floor effects (Clegg & Warrington, 1994).

The Wechsler series of memory scales—WMS (Wechsler, 1945); WMS-Revised (Wechsler, 1987); WMS-III (Wechsler, 1997)—have been used extensively for older adults. Although the WMS is a very old test, four of the main subtests, Digit Span, Logical Memory, Paired Associate Learning and Visual Reproduction are still very effective as relatively brief and sensitive measures of memory impairment, with individual older adult norms (cf. Spreen & Strauss, 1997). The development of the WMS-R and WMS-III has the advantage of comprehensiveness, but often these batteries are too long for an older adult population. Despite this, the WMS-III has been made more ecologically valid and has substantial USA normative data. Additionally, there are normative data for individual tests, so these in principle can be used separately. A further advantage is that there is a direct comparison with half of the WAIS-III standardization data, so it is possible to explore discrepancies between IQ and memory with greater accuracy. It has also been validated on a UK population (Wycherley et al., 1999).

There are also additional tests that have been developed with older adults in mind. This includes, for example, the Kendrick Object Learning Test, which now forms part of the *KASCA* (p. 305). This test has cards with simple line drawings of objects and can be used with more impaired patients. Another test, the Anomalous Sentence Test (Weeks, 1988), involves repetition of sentences that are grammatically nonsensical (e.g., 'Not in walls to the hunters rain in poetry') and also exceed memory span, so test long-term memory. Individual tests developed for adults in general, but with good older adult norms, can also be used. An example is the Rey Auditory Verbal Learning Test (Mitrushina et al., 1994), which may be used to distinguish between encoding and retrieval processes.

Language Assessment

Language impairment is frequently seen as a neuropsychological disability in older adults, because of the association with stroke, or multi-infarct dementia, and with AD. The characteristics of language breakdown in dementia are dealt with in more detail elsewhere (Morris & McKiernan, 1994; Morris & Worsley, 2002). In AD, it is again useful to think of stages of impairment, as indicated in Table 14.2.

An early sign is word-finding difficulties, which may be elicited in everyday conversation. Lack of ready access to specific words disrupts the crisp flow of language and the person may appear circumlocutious as a result. Nevertheless, difficult word retrieval is a more general feature of cognitive ageing, so should not necessarily be taken as abnormal when a presenting symptom, unless it is more marked. Accompanying word-finding difficulties can be noticeable impairments in comprehending complex verbal material, for example, where grammatical complexity is increased. Again, at a more subtle level, this is also a feature of normal ageing.

At a more advanced level the word-finding difficulties become more obvious and the content of the language becomes more vague and disjointed, complicated by memory impairment and lack of reasoning ability. Allied to this is a deterioration of semantics that results in a general impoverishment of language. There are also positive signs of language disorder, such as paraphasia, where word substitutions may occur, and verbal perseveration. For example, a common feature is ideational perseveration, where the same concept of train or thought reappears inappropriately. Finally, at the later stages, language may be reduced to meaningless phrases or single words and occasionally mutism.

Despite language impairment being a relatively common neuropsychological impairment in older adults, test batteries have not been developed with this age range in mind. Nevertheless, in addition to comprehensive standard batteries (see Chapter 8), brief language batteries are appropriate for use. These include the

Table 14.2. Breakdown of language functioning as AD progresses

Early phase
- Impaired word retrieval manifests as word-finding and confrontation-naming difficulties.
- In conversation the pattern of language is circumlocutionary.
- Comprehension of complex verbal material is impaired.

Middle phase
- Word-finding difficulties are more pronounced and the content of language can become vague and sometimes meaningless.
- The syntax of language output is simplified. Impaired language comprehension is exacerbated by the breakdown of reasoning ability.
- 'Positive' signs of language disorder arise, such as paraphasia and verbal perseveration.

Late phase
- Mutism can occur, but if language is produced this may be limited to the meaningless repetition of words or nonsense sounds.

Schuell Minnesota Aphasia Test (Powell et al., 1980) and the Frenchay Aphasia Screening Test (Enderby et al., 1986), which can still be recommended. In addition, it is possible to test specific areas in a piecemeal fashion, depending on the type of patient and likely deficit.

For testing word retrieval there are two main approaches: word fluency and naming. The former has been tested in a variety of forms, with the most common method being the Controlled Oral Word Association Test (COWAT), which requires the patient to retrieve as many words beginning with a particular letter within a specified time period. Following Crawford et al. (1992), it is possible to predict the score on this test using NART scores. Word fluency is complicated by the executive control needed to set up the retrieval procedures and so is sensitive to prefrontal cortical impairment. It is also complicated by a breakdown in semantics, which may act as an additional factor in word retrieval. Rosen (1980) found that patients with dementia are more reliably differentiated from control subjects when letter cues, rather than category cues (e.g., names of animals), are used as the basis for the verbal fluency task. It should be noted that word fluency is also used to test executive functioning, where the emphasis is on measuring difficulties in setting up the search strategies for retrieval from the lexicon. Thus a deficit in word fluency may indicate a combination of language and executive dysfunction.

The alternative approach, naming, is commonly tested in older adults using either the Boston Naming Test (BNT; Goodglass & Caplan, 2001) or the Graded Naming Test (GNT; McKenna & Warrington, 1983). Both are standardized on older adults (for the BNT, for example, see Whitworth & Larson, 1989; for the GNT, see Warrington, 1997). Data presenting GNT scores across different WAIS-R IQ bands are also presented by Clegg and Warrington (2000) for older adults. The BNT is appropriate for US patients, while the GNT is mainly used for UK patients, although the cultural bias is not sufficient to prevent use with either population.

Executive Functioning

The term 'executive function' has been given to impairments in the sequencing and organization of cognition and behaviour, and tests to measure this encompass those sensitive to frontal lobe damage (see Chapter 9). In older adults, impairments in executive function are common and present a major challenge for neurorehabilitation. For example, a dysexecutive syndrome is a feature of moderate AD and may be seen in other neurodegenerative disorders, including the frontotemporal dementias: diffuse Lewy body disease and motor neurone disease (Morris & Worsley, in press). Despite this, it can be more difficult to assess accurately, partly because executive functioning is known to be sensitive to the effects of normal ageing, with cognitive ageing varying between individuals.

A variety of tests have been used to demonstrate executive dysfunction (e.g., the battery of tests by Becker et al., 1992), incorporating the Wisconsin Card Sorting

Test [WCST], the Stroop Test, Verbal Fluency and Random Generation of Digits). Becker et al.'s study showed a subgroup of AD in which executive dysfunction was more pronounced, but tended to become more generalized as the dementia progressed. A key issue with using executive tests clinically is whether there are adequate norms, given the susceptibility of normal, older adults to do badly on such tests. The WCST (Grant & Berg, 1993), for example, has normative data for people up to 89 years of age. However, this test, which requires subjects to sort cards to a number of changing, undisclosed rules, may be more suitable in the abbreviated version, which is also standardized on older adults (Axelrod & Henry, 1992). The Stroop Test (Trenerry et al., 1989) has normative data for older adults, as does the Trail Making Test and various versions of Verbal Fluency (Spreen & Strauss, 1997). Additionally, the Hayling and Brixton tests (Burgess & Shallice, 1997) have the advantage of relative brevity, with older adult normative data.

A recent development is the Delis–Kaplan Executive Function System (D–KEFS; Delis et al., 2001), which includes a UK adaptation. This includes a range of executive tests designed to be appropriate also for older adults, with normative data up to 89 years. The tests include a card sorting test, trail making, verbal and design fluency, a Stroop test, a version of the Tower of Hanoi, a 20-questions test and a proverbs test. There is also a word context test that measures deductive reasoning and verbal abstract thinking. The D–KEFS has been co-normed with the Wechsler Abbreviated Scale of Intelligence (WASI) to provide information concerning the role of intellectual functioning on executive performance.

Recent attempts to make tests of executive function more 'ecologically' valid have led to the development of such procedures as the Behavioural Assessment of Dysexecutive Syndrome (BADS; Wilson et al., 1996). The normative data for this test go up to 87 years, making this a reasonable procedure to use with older adults. While this is the case, the potential complexity of these types of procedures should be considered, and such tests are obviously not appropriate to use where there is more widespread and substantial cognitive dysfunction, such as in moderate dementia.

Visuospatial Function and Perception

Visuospatial function in older adults is often explored as part of intelligence testing (e.g., using tests of visuo-constructive ability, such as Block Design, or non-verbal reasoning, such as the Matrix Reasoning test). Brief tests of visuospatial function are also incorporated into screening batteries, such as the CAMCOG and the MEAMS. The Visual Object and Space Perception battery (VOSP; Warrington & James, 1991) provides more sensitive tests of visuospatial function, but currently published normative data only include people up to age 69 years. Clegg and Warrington (2000) have however published normative data for the VOSP Animal and Objects Silhouettes tests on older adults ranging in age from 64 to 81 years, providing WAIS-R IQ stratified data as well. For such tests, substantial care should be taken to rule out peripheral sensory impairment as a cause of failure, rather than visuospatial processing impairment *per se*.

More experimentally, tests of visuospatial function have been used in patients with dementia. For example, such tests as the Benton Line Orientation and Face Recognition tests have demonstrated impairments in AD (Eslinger & Benton, 1983), as has figure ground identification (Mendez et al., 1990).

Pure cases of visual agnosia may be less likely in older adults because of more widespread brain damage (e.g., in AD). Nevertheless, object recognition may be tested using the picture recognition tests from the CAMCOG or MEAMS. In these batteries there are also photographs of unusual views of objects that can be used to detect more subtle impairments, which can in principle be followed up using the range of subtests provided by the VOSP.

Computerized Assessment

In recent years, the use of computing technology has had some impact on neuro-psychological assessment of older adults. This is less than might be predicted, given the substantial use and availability of computers in the workplace. The reasons for this are varied, but may reflect the cost of test development and the problem this poses for investing in producing normative data that do not become rapidly outdated as the technology moves on. Another issue with older adults is the extent to which computers are seen as a familiar technology. This is changing, and many older adults are now computer-literate as a matter of course, something that should accelerate during the next decade or so.

In terms of procedures suitable for this population, an early example is the Cognitive Testing Battery (Allen et al., 1993), which includes tests of simple reaction time, visuomotor skill, complex processing and memory. These tests were validated against measures of mental status and good correlations found; hence the computerized version is sensitive to different ability levels. Another example is the Computerized Neuropsychological Evaluation (Ritchie et al., 1993), which uses a touch-sensitive screen and has tests of attention, memory, visuospatial and language function. This battery takes 40 minutes and has been standardized on a large group of older adults.

A relatively old test battery, which is nevertheless updated in term of Windows technology with further modifications, is the Cambridge Automated Neuropsychological Test Battery, designed originally by Evenden et al. (1987). This has a range of specialized tests of memory, attention and planning ability, and uses a touch-sensitive screen. It has the advantage of being standardized on a large sample of older adults (Robbins et al., 1998). The battery has been used extensively either for experimental research or as a research tool for evaluating drug treatment. This test has the potential to be a useful clinical tool, with the proviso that the reliability of some of the executive tests for older adults has been called into question by the finding of low test–retest correlations in some tests (Lowe & Rabbitt, 1998). Nevertheless, this may not be an entirely fair criticism of the battery, since some tests are designed to look at strategy formation and problem-solving, and these may inherently be subject to practice effects. A striking feature of the test is that the paired associate learning test from the memory battery has been shown to be a highly sensitive tool for the detection of AD at the early stages (Swainson et al., 2001).

Development of computerized tests in general is a neglected area, and it is possible that low-cost Windows-based procedures will be developed in the future making full use of the multimedia capabilities of computers.

CONCLUSION

Due to the high incidence of other neurodegenerative or cerebrovascular disorders in older adults, neuropsychological assessment forms a larger part of working with this population as a clinical psychologist. Particular approaches and skills are needed, and clinical neuropsychology with older adults should be considered to some extent a specialist area of work. In essence, there may be great need to adapt the interviewing approach to suit the needs of the individual and tailor the tests to suit a large range of abilities or degree of brain damage; sensory loss is a more prominent problem, and taking into account normal age-related changes in cognition means that tests need to be thoroughly standardized for this population. Finally, a neuropsychological assessment always has to be seen in the wider context of the management of the patient and the questions being asked. In this sense 'a mechanistic approach to assessment is not appropriate', as pointed out by Woods (1999). In this sense, taking the correct approach to the assessment of the older adult requires careful planning and consideration of the patient.

REFERENCES

Agnew, S. K. & Morris, R. G. (1998) The heterogeneity of anosognosia for memory impairment in Alzheimer's disease: A review of the literature and a proposed model. *Aging and Mental Health*, **2**, 7–19.

Allen, C. C., Ellinwood, E. H. & Logue, P. E. (1993) Construct validity of a new computer-assisted cognitive neuromotor assessment battery in normal and inpatient psychiatric samples. *Journal of Clinical Psychology*, **49**, 874–882.

Axelrod, B. N. & Henry, R. R. (1992) Construct validity of a new computer-assisted cognitive neuromotor assessment battery in normal and inpatient psychiatric samples. *Journal of Clinical Psychology*, **49**, 874–882.

Baddeley, A., Emslie, H. & Nimmo-Smith, I. (1992) The Spot-the-Word Test: A robust estimate of verbal intelligence based on lexical decision. *British Journal of Clinical Psychology*, **32**, 55–65.

Baddeley, A. D., Emslie, H. & Nimmo-Smith, I. (1994) *Doors and People*. Thames Valley Test Co., Bury St Edmunds, UK.

Beardsall, L. (1998) Development of the Cambridge Contextual Reading Test for improving the estimation of premorbid intelligence in older persons with dementia. *British Journal of Clinical Psychology*, **37**, 229–240.

Beardsall, L. & Huppert, L. (1997) Short NART, CCRT and Spot-the-Word: Comparisons in older and demented persons. *British Journal of Clinical Psychology*, **36**, 619–622.

Becker, J. T., Bajulaiye, O. & Smith, C. (1992) Longitudinal analysis of a two-component model of the memory deficit in Alzheimer's disease. *Psychological Medicine*, **22**, 437–445.

Burgess, P. & Shallice, T. (1997) *The Hayling and Brixton Tests*. Thames Valley Test Co., Bury St Edmunds, UK.

Clegg, F. & Warrington, E. K. (1994) Four easy tests for older adults. *Memory*, **2**, 167–182.

Clegg, F. & Warrington, E. K. (2000) Psychometric testing of older adults: Provisional normative data for some commonly used tests. *Clinical Neuropsychological Assessment*, **1**, 22–37.

Conway, S. C. & O'Carroll, R. E. (1994) The evaluation of the Cambridge Contextual Reading Test (CCRT) in Alzheimer's disease. *British Journal of Clinical Psychology*, **36**, 623–625.

Crawford, J. R., Stewart, L. E., Cochran, R. H., Foulds, J. A., Besson, J. A. & Parker, D. M. (1989) Estimating premorbid IQ from demographic variables: Regression equations derived from a UK sample. *British Journal of Clinical Psychology*, **28**, 275–278.

Crawford, J. R., Moore, J. W. & Cameron, I. M. (1992) Verbal fluency: A NART-based equation for the estimation of premorbid performance. *British Journal of Clinical Psychology*, **31**, 327–329.

Crawford, J. R., Deary, I. J., Starr, J. M. & Whalley, L. J. (2001) The NART as an index of prior intellectual functioning: A retrospective validity study covering a 66 year interval. *Psychological Medicine*, **31**, 451–458.

Delis, D. C., Kaplan, E. & Kramer, J. H. (2001) *Delis–Kaplan Executive Function System (D-KEFS)*. Psychological Corporation, San Antonio, TX.

Enderby, P. M., Woods, V. A., Wade, D. T. & Langton-Hewer, R. (1986) The Frenchay Aphasia Screening Test: A short simple test for aphasia appropriate for non-specialists. *International Rehabilitation Medicine*, **8**, 166–170.

Eslinger, P. J. & Benton, A. L. (1983) Visuoperceptual performance in aging and dementia: Clinical and theoretical observations. *Journal of Clinical Neuropsychology*, **5**, 213–220.

Evenden, J., Morris, R. G., Sahakian, B. & Robbins, T. W. (1987) *The Cambridge Automated Neuropsychological Test Battery*. Lynxvale Ltd, Cambridge, UK.

Folstein, M. F. & Folstein, S. E. (1988) 'Mini-Mental State': A practical method for grading the cognitive state of patients for the clinician. *Psychopharmacology Bulletin*, **24**, 689–692.

Fox, N. C., Warrington, E. K., Seiffer, A. L., Agnew, S. K. & Rossor, M. N. (1998) Pre-symptomatic cognitive deficits in individuals at risk of familial Alzheimer's disease: A longitudinal perspective study. *Brain*, **131**, 1631–1639.

Fromm, D., Holland, A. L., Nebes, R. L. & Oakley, M. A. (1991) A longitudinal study of work-reading ability in Alzheimer's disease: Evidence from the National Adult Reading Test. *Cortex*, **27**, 367–376.

Golding, E. (1989) *Middlesex Elderly Assessment of Mental State*. Thames Valley Test Co., Bury St Edmunds, UK.

Goodglass, H. & Kaplan, E. (2001) *The Boston Naming Test*. Lippincott Williams and Wilkins, Baltimore.

Grant, D. A. & Berg, E. A. (1993) *The Wisconsin Card Sorting Test*. NFER-Nelson, Windsor, UK.

Hannesdottir, K. & Morris, R. G. (in press) Anosognosia in Alzheimer's disease. In: R. G. Morris & J. Becker (eds) *The Cognitive Neuropsychology of Alzheimer's Disease*. Oxford University Press, Oxford, UK.

Holdnack, J. A. (2001) *The Wechsler Test of Adult Reading*. Psychological Corporation, San Antonio, TX.

Huppert, F. A., Jorm, A. F., Brayne, C., Gill, C., Paykel, E. S. & Beardsall, L. (1996) Psychometric properties of the CAMCOG and its efficacy in the diagnosis of dementia. *Aging, Neuropsychiatry and Cognition*, **3**, 201–214.

Kendrick, D. C. (1985) *Kendrick Cognitive Tests for the Elderly*. NFER-Nelson, Windsor, UK.

Kendrick, D. C. & Watts, G. D. (1999) *The Kendrick Assessment Scales of Cognitive Ageing*. NFER-Nelson, Windsor, UK.

Lowe, C. & Rabbitt, P. (1998) Test/Re-test reliability of CANTAB and ISPOCD neuropsychological batteries: Theoretical and practical issues. *Neuropsychologia*, **39**, 915–923.

McKenna, P. & Warrington, E. K. (1983) *The Graded Naming Test*. Cambridge Cognition Ltd, Cambridge, UK.

Mendez, M. F., Mendez, M. A., Martin, R. N., Smyth, K. A. and Whitehouse, P. J. (1990) Complex visual disturbance in Alzheimer's disease. *Neurology*, **40**, 329–343.

Miller, E. (1977) *Abnormal Ageing*. John Wiley & Sons, Chichester, UK.

Mitrushina, M., Satz, P., Drebing, C. E., Van Gorp, W., Mathews, A., Harker, J. et al. (1994) The differential pattern of memory deficit in normal aging and dementias of different etiology. *Journal of Clinical Psychology*, **50**, 246–252.

Mockler, D. & Crawford, J. Wechsler Abbreviated Scale of Intelligence, UK (WASI-UK): A United Kingdom validation study. In preparation.

Morris, J. C., Heyman, A., Mohs, R. C., Hughes, J. P., van Belle, G., Fillenbaum, G. et al. (1989) A consortium to establish a registry for Alzheimer's disease (CERAD). Part 1: Clinical and neuropsychological assessment. *Neurology*, **39**, 1159–1165.

Morris, R. G. (1994) Recent developments in the neuropsychology of dementia. *International Review of Psychiatry*, **6**, 85–107.

Morris, R. G. & McKiernan, F. (1994) Neuropsychological investigations of dementia. In: A. Burns & R. Levy (eds) *Dementia* (pp. 327–354). Chapman & Hall, London.

Morris, R. G. & Worsley, C. L. (2002) The neuropsychology of Alzheimer's disease. In: V. S. Ramachandran (ed.) *Encyclopedia of the Human Brain* (Vol. 1, pp. 119–129). Academic Press, New York.

Morris, R. G. & Worsley, C. L. (in press) The neuropsychological presentation of Alzheimer's disease and other neurodegenerative disorders. In: P. Halligan, U. Kischka & J. Marshall (eds) *Handbook of Clinical Neuropsychology*. Oxford University Press, Oxford, UK.

Morris, R. G., Worsley, C. L. & Matthew, D. (2000) Neuropsychological assessment in older people: Old principles and new directions. *Advances in Psychiatric Treatment*, **6**, 362–372.

Nelson, H. E. & McKenna, P. (1975) The use of current reading ability in the assessment of dementia. *British Journal of Clinical Psychology*, **14**, 259–267.

Nelson, H. & Willison, J. R. (1991) *National Adult Reading Test (NART): Test Manual* (2nd edn). NFER-Nelson, Windsor, UK.

O'Neill, P. M. & Calhoun, K. S. (1975) Sensory deficits and behavioural deterioration in senescence. *Journal of Abnormal Psychology*, **84**, 579–582.

Patterson, K. E., Graham, N. & Hodges, J. R. (1994) Reading in dementia of the Alzheimer's type: A preserved ability? *Neuropsychology*, **8**, 395–412.

Powell, G. E., Bailey, S. & Clark, E. (1980) A very short version of the Minnesota Aphasia test. *British Journal of Social and Clinical Psychology*, **19**, 189–194.

Ritchie, K., Allard, M., Huppert, F. A., Nargeot, C., Pinek B. & Ledesert, B. (1993) Computerised cognitive examination of the elderly (ECO): The development of a neuropsychological examination for clinic and population use. *International Journal of Geriatric Psychiatry*, **8**, 899–914.

Robbins, T. W., Merle, J., Owen, A. M., Sahakian, B. J., Lawrence, A. D., McInnes, L. & Rabbit, P. M. A. (1998) A study of performance from the CANTAB battery sensitive to frontal lobe dysfunction in a large sample of normal volunteers: Implications for theories of executive functioning and cognitive aging. *Journal of the Cognitive Neuropsychological Society*, **4**, 474–490.

Rosen, W. G. (1980) Verbal fluency in aging and dementia. *Journal of Clinical Neuropsychology*, **2**, 135–146.

Roth, M., Huppert, F. A., Tym, E. & Mountjoy, C. Q. (1988) *CAMDEX—Cambridge Examination of Mental Disorders of the Elderly*. Cambridge University Press, Cambridge, UK.

Roth, M., Huppert, F., Mountjoy, C. Q. & Tym, E. (1999) *CAMDEX-R—The Revised Cambridge Examination for Mental Disorders of the Elderly* (2nd edn). Cambridge University Press, Cambridge, UK.

Savage, R. D., Britton, P. G., Bolton, N. & Hall, E. H. (1973) *Intellectual Functioning in the Aged*. Methuen, London.

Spreen, O. & Strauss, E. (1997) *A Compendium of Neuropsychological Tests. 2nd Edition: Administration Norms and Commentary*. Oxford University Press, New York.

Stoudemire, A., Hill, C. D., Morris, R., Martino-Salzman, D. & Lewison, B. (1993) Long-term affective and cognitive outcome in depressed older adults. *American Journal of Psychiatry*, **150**(6), 896–900.

Swainson, R., Hodges, J. R., Galton, C. J., Semple, J., Michael, A., Dunn, B. D. et al. (2001) Early detection and differential diagnosis of Alzheimer's disease and depression with neuropsychological tasks. *Dementia and Geriatric Cognitive Disorders*, **12**, 265–280.

Trenerry, M. R., Crossen, B., DeBoe, J. & Leber, W. R. (1989) *Stroop Neuropsychological Screening Test*. NFER-Nelson, Windsor, UK.

Unverzagt, F. W., Morgan, O. S., Thesiger, C. H., Eldemire, D. A., Luseko, J., Poluri, S. et al. (1999) Clinical utility of CERAD neuropsychological battery in Jamaicans. *Journal of the International Neuropsychological Society*, **5**, 255–259.

Warrington, E. K. (1984) *Recognition Memory Test Manual*. NFER-Nelson, Windsor, UK.

Warrington, E. K. (1996) *The Camden Memory Test Battery*. Psychology Press, Brighton, UK.

Warrington, E. K. (1997) The graded naming test: A restandardisation. *Neuropsychological Rehabilitation*, **7**, 143–146.

Warrington, E. K. & James, M. (1991) *The Visual Object and Space Perception Battery*. Thames Valley Test Co., Bury St Edmunds, UK.

Wechsler, D. (1945) A standardised memory scale for clinical use. *Journal of Psychology*, **19**, 87–95.

Wechsler, D. (1987) *Wechsler Memory Scale—Revised*. Psychological Corporation, New York.

Wechsler, D. (1997) *The Wechsler Adult Intelligence Scale III*. Psychological Corporation, San Antonio, TX.

Wechsler, D. (1999) *The Wechsler Abbreviated Scale of IQ*. Psychological Corporation, San Antonio, TX.

Weeks, D. (1988) *The Anomalous Sentences Repetition Test*. NFER-Nelson, Windsor, UK.

Whitworth, R. H. & Larson, C. M. (1989) Differential diagnosis and staging of Alzheimer's disease with an aphasia battery. *Neuropsychiatry, Neuropsychology and Behavioral Neurology*, **4**, 255–265.

Wilson, B. A., Cockburn, J. & Baddeley, A. D. (1999) *The Rivermead Behavioural Memory Test [RMBT]: Extended Version*. Thames Valley Test Co., Bury St Edmunds, UK.

Wilson, R. S., Sullivan, M., De Toledo-Morell, L., Stebbins, G. T., Bennett, D. A. & Morrell, F. (1996) Association of memory and cognition in Alzheimer's disease with volumetric estimates of temporal lobe structures. *Neuropsychology*, **10**, 459–463.

Woods, R. T. (1979) Reality orientation and staff attention: A controlled study. *British Journal of Psychiatry*, **134**, 502–507.

Woods, R. T. (1999) Psychological assessment of elderly people. In: R. T. Woods (ed.) *Psychological Problems of Ageing: Assessment, Treatment and Care* (pp. 219–252). John Wiley & Sons, Chichester, UK.

Wycherley, R. J., Benjamin, L., Crawford, J. & Mockler, D. (1999) The Wechsler Adult Intelligence Scale III[UK]. In: *The Wechsler Adult Intelligence Scale—III: Test Manual*. Psychological Corporation, San Antonio, TX.

CHAPTER 15

Neuropsychology and the Law

Graham E. Powell

Psychology Service, London, UK

INTRODUCTION

This chapter is written for neuropsychologists who have no medico-legal experience. It is becoming increasingly inevitable in the UK that neuropsychologists will be required to contribute to the legal process. This could be, for example, to advise on clients' capacity to manage their own affairs, look after their children, instruct their own solicitor, to advise as to whether brain damage was a factor in some criminal act (including issues of differential diagnosis), to advise upon whether neuropsychological deficits arising from brain damage have caused loss of earnings or will cause loss of future earnings, or to advise on whether a neuro-psychological deficit has given rise to a care need or need for treatment. The neuropsychologist has a duty to learn to deal professionally with this interface between neuropsychology and the law, even if there is no intent to develop a medico-legal practice as such. The purpose of this chapter is to introduce in a practical manner the key concepts and skills.

These concepts and skills will differ to some extent from country to country, due to the legal systems being different. This chapter will in terms of legal process deal exclusively with England and Wales (Scotland has yet to adopt, for example, the new rules that apply to civil litigation in the rest of the UK). Those who will be required, for example, to give evidence in the USA will need to read additional material to be found in texts such as Doerr and Carlin (1991), Hall and Sbordone (1993), Hess and Weiner (1999), Melton et al. (1997) or Sweet (1999).

However, across different legal questions and different legal systems, there are core clinical neuropsychological skills. These include the documentation, quantification and causal attribution of deficit as well as discussion of prognosis including treatability and of the everyday meaning of deficit. All of this must be presented within a scientist–practitioner framework in which the neuropsychologist draws upon both personal experience as an expert practitioner and upon an expert knowledge of the background scientific research findings. Indeed, Sweet (1999) sees the demand for clinical neuropsychology input as 'the natural outcome of the success of a strong scientist–practitioner model'. If one is confident in this

Clinical Neuropsychology: A Practical Guide to Assessment and Management for Clinicians.
Edited by L.H. Goldstein and J.E. McNeil. © 2004 John Wiley & Sons, Ltd.

role as a scientist–practitioner, one has the basis for confidence as an expert witness.

The rest of this chapter will set out the professional issues, discuss the nature of the assessment, consider the nature of the report, describe continuing obligations after the report has been submitted and describe the courts and their work. It is therefore broadly a functional and practical analysis. Civil cases will be concentrated upon because this is where neuropsychologists make their primary contribution. However, much of what is said will in broad terms apply to the conduct of the neuropsychologist in criminal settings.

PROFESSIONAL ISSUES

Who Is an Expert?

There is no formal definition of this term, but it implies that the person (a) knows more than a layman, (b) knows more than the court and (c) can supply evidence of this. Therefore, the neuropsychologist can expect to be cross-examined on:

- their formal qualifications;
- membership of professional and learned bodies (which might themselves offer a definition of an expert—for example, the British Psychological Society's Division of Neuropsychology, 2000 states that to give medico-legal evidence on clinical neuropsychological matters, the individual should be a Practitioner Full Member of that division);
- range of experience in the field in general;
- evidence of peer acknowledgement (promotion, awards, fellowships, research and development grants);
- publications or other evidence of scholarship;
- past and current professional practice, in detail;
- continuing professional development;
- membership of approved or accredited lists of expert witnesses, such as that maintained by the Law Society;
- medico-legal experience;
- comments made about them by previous judges in their written, public judgment.

The neuropsychologist will therefore need a detailed CV to supply as requested, as well as a brief CV, often to append to the report. In the CV, reference should be made to previous medico-legal experience, including a breakdown of the percentage of times instruction has been (a) by the claimant, (b) by the defence and (c) on a joint basis. When a lawyer asks for a CV so as to consider issuing instructions, it may also be necessary to provide a copy of a Professional Indemnity Insurance Certificate. Since in theory one could be sued for the full value of the claim should incompetence cause one's instructing side's case to fail, and since claims regularly go well over £1m, it is essential to have this insurance and it must cover medico-legal reporting.

The Rules that Experts Follow

In 1994 Lord Woolf, Master of the Rolls, was appointed by the Lord Chancellor to review current rules, and the result is the Civil Procedure Rules (CPR) 1998. It is CPR Part 35 that primarily deals with experts and applies to all proceedings in the County Courts, the High Court and the Civil Division of the Court of Appeal. A brief summary of some of the rules and Practice Directions (PDs) follows, making it abundantly clear that duty is to the *court*, not to any of the parties:

- It is the duty of any expert to help the court on the matters within his or her expertise (35.3(1)).
- This clearly overrides any obligation to the person from whom he or she has received instructions or by whom he is paid (35.3(2)).
- No party may call an expert or put in evidence an expert's report without the court's permission (35.4(1)).
- The court may limit the amount of the expert's fees and expenses that the party who wishes to rely on the experts may recover from any other party (35.4(4)).
- Expert evidence is to be given in a written report unless the court directs otherwise (35.5(1)).
- An expert's report must (PD1.2):
  1. give details of the expert's qualifications;
  2. give details of any literature or other material that the expert has relied on in making the report;
  3. say who carried out any test or experiment that the expert has used for the report and whether or not the test or experiment has been carried out under the expert's supervision;
  4. give the qualifications of the person who carried out any such test or experiment;
  5. where there is a range of opinion on the matters dealt with in the report (i) summarize the range of opinion and (ii) give reasons for his or her own opinion;
  6. contain a summary of the conclusions reached;
  7. contain a statement that the expert understands his or her duty to the court and has complied with that duty (35.10(2));
  8. contain a statement setting out the substance of all material instructions (whether written or oral). The statement should summarize the facts and instructions given to the expert that are material to the opinions expressed in the report or upon which those opinions are based (35.10(3)).
- An expert's report must be verified by a statement of truth as well as containing the statements required in paragraphs (7) and (8) above.

- The form of the statement of truth was originally as follows (PD1.4): *I believe that the facts I have stated in this report are true and that the opinions I have expressed are correct*. From 25 March 2002 this was amended to: *I confirm that insofar as the facts stated in my report are within my own knowledge I have made clear which they are and I believe them to be true, and that the opinions I have expressed represent my true and complete professional opinion*.
- Attention is drawn to rule 32.14, which sets out the consequences of verifying a document containing a false statement without an honest belief in its truth (i.e., proceedings for contempt of court may be brought against a person if he makes, or causes to be made, a false statement in a document verified by a statement of truth without an honest belief in its truth).
- In addition, an expert's report should comply with the requirements of any approved expert's protocol (PD1.6).
- The court may direct that evidence on a particular issue is to be given by one expert only (35.7(1)).
- Each instructing party may give instructions to the single joint expert (35.8(1)).
- The instructing parties are jointly and severally (i.e., individually) liable for the payment of the single joint expert's fees and expenses (35.8(5)).
- Questions asked for the purpose of clarifying the expert's report should be put, in writing, to the expert not later than 28 days after receipt of the expert's report (35.6).
- Where a party sends a written question or questions direct to an expert, a copy of the questions should, at the same time, be sent to the other party or parties (PD4.2).
- The court may, at any stage, direct a discussion between experts for the purpose of requiring the expert to (35.12.(1)): (a) identify the issues in the proceedings and (b) where possible reach agreement on an issue.
- The court may direct that following a discussion between the experts they must prepare a statement for the court showing (35.12(3)): (a) those issues on which they agree and (b) those issues on which they disagree and a summary of their reasons for disagreeing.

For sight of the full rules, and for a commentary, see a text such as Grainger and Fealy (1999). Various amendments came into force on 25 March 2002. These were quite minor, but importantly include the provision for the expert to file a written request to the court for directions to assist them in carrying out their functions as an expert. Of additional importance is that experts are required to state when an issue falls outside their expertise and to state if they are not able to reach a definite conclusion (e.g., because they do not have sufficient information).

The Role of the Expert in General

The expert has a broader role in the overall legal process than just following the rules. In particular, experts will act as advisers to those instructing them on all matters pertaining to their discipline. This might mean giving an opinion on other reports, commenting on various material, helping to decide what other experts are needed and explaining technical issues. It is important to remember that everything that is written is 'discoverable' (i.e. it may end up in court as part of one's evidence, either submitted by the instructing side or requested by the other side). One cannot say that something is confidential or not to be disclosed without permission. Everything should be written as if it had a statement of truth attached, even routine letters and e-mails.

Nor do the rules explicitly state that it is the responsibility of experts to ensure that their view is as informed as possible. In effect, the expert has to be *proactive*. It is not good enough simply to sit back and base one's view on what solicitors either want to send the expert or what they think the expert needs to see (see Sweet, 1999). The clinical neuropsychologist should therefore be prepared to ask for employment or personnel records, school records and reports, general practitioner and hospital records and any records that seem to be missing. The neuropsychologist should also seek verification as to the status of any unsigned material, seek permission to talk to any relatives or teachers as needed, ask for sight of all other expert reports, suggest further expert assessments and ask for clarification of legal points and concepts.

In providing an opinion the neuropsychologist should be prepared to state that the opinion is subject to sight of document X or material Y or further test Z, otherwise they are open to accusations of jumping to conclusions or of failing to attempt to give the court best advice. Neuropsychologists should then have the mental flexibility to take on board the import of any new material and revise their opinion in a supplementary note.

The rules do not give guidance on professional issues that arise (e.g., when during the course of the examination one obtains clinically relevant material, such as the claimant feeling actively suicidal). Here, neuropsychologists could immediately advise the claimant to go to the GP or treating physician, or they could ask the solicitors to release their report with all haste. They could also ask the solicitor for permission to write a note to the GP advising them of certain points. Another example is when neuropsychologists discover that the claimant was recently tested on a similar battery. They might contact the solicitor immediately, ask if arrangements could be made to share the data already collected and collect more data on a quid pro quo basis. Another example is discovering that the claimant is due for a similar clinical assessment the following week. After the assessment, the neuropsychologist might phone the solicitor and ask permission to release the test results direct to the treating neuropsychologist; there is no need to release the opinion prematurely, the test results would normally be sufficient.

Finally, the neuropsychologist can have a role long before the legal proceedings have formally commenced or a medico-legal report is written. For example, in serious cases the insurance company might ask the neuropsychologist to see someone to advise on his or her ongoing status or the adequacy of current treatment. The neuropsychologist can then attend ward rounds or clinical meetings and feed into the *clinical* process, acting as a source of additional support.

Time and Fees

Given the nature of their work, clinical neuropsychologists spend more time on the assessment than many other professionals (e.g., the neurological examination is much shorter). Neuropsychologists' assessments should not be so short that it does not seem credible that they have given a proper range of tests (and it may be necessary to say how long was spent with the claimant). On the other hand, if the assessment is too long, it will be suggested to the neuropsychologist in cross-examination that the results were influenced by fatigue, by interference between tests and by maximizing the chances of obtaining one or two fluke results. A period of about three hours seems a reasonable allowance for the assessment.

However, the amount of time put into the case will be much more than this (e.g., time arranging/rescheduling appointments, time obtaining notes, reading and annotating notes, telephone calls with claimant and solicitors, scoring the tests, referring to any relevant literature, writing the actual report and proof-reading the final report). It is important to keep a note of all this time and charge for it. This will probably at least double the time spent on just the actual assessment.

Solicitors will normally say that they will pay the neuropsychologist's 'reasonable' fees, but it is becoming more common to actually ask for details of the fee rates. One should therefore be able to state an hourly rate, an estimate of time to be spent on the case and therefore a likely fee for the report, a rate for a half-day court appearance, rate for a full-day court appearance, a differential rate for travelling (if wished), cancellation fees for non-attenders and cancellation fee for cases that settle prior to a hearing (e.g., charge for all time within five working days that cannot be rebooked). It is not recommended to start work on a case until fee levels have been agreed, unless one already has a good working relationship with the solicitor. The solicitor is responsible for paying fees, but, according to the rules, the court has the right to say the neuropsychologist's fees are excessive and to reduce them.

One may be asked to work on a contingency basis (i.e., payment is only made if the case is 'won' by the neuropsychologist's side). This utterly compromises the objectivity of the expert, and I know no neuropsychologist who works on this basis.

It is also possible to be asked to defer payment (i.e., once the case settles or is resolved at trial). Most neuropsychologists decline to do this on the grounds that they might be tempted to offer an opinion more likely to settle the case quickly, in addition to the obvious fact that the case might not be over for years.

Inter- and Intra-professional Issues

Clinical neuropsychology is just one of the professions that will advise the court, and inter-professional disputes do arise. It is important to be able to state in court the nature of a neuropsychologist's profession and its unique contribution, its training, professional accreditation and regulation, the strengths and limitations of neuropsychology and how neuropsychologists are different to a medical doctor/neurologist/speech and language therapist/psychotherapist.

In describing one's own profession and its uniqueness, a proper balance must be struck. One can be confident and enthusiastic, but not to the point of being bombastic and arrogant. Similarly, when criticizing the work or reports of other professions, the criticism should be balanced, reasoned and dispassionate, not a tirade of stereotypic views. One does not have to make all the criticism oneself. The neuropsychologist may provide the barrister with areas to examine, or actual questions to ask.

Having said this, neuropsychology should properly defend its boundaries and not passively accept, for example, misunderstandings by other professions of neuropsychology's role, models or data.

In terms of intra-professional issues, although one's professional colleague is on the 'other side' this does not mean they are an enemy, especially in the new legal climate in which openness and co-operation are encouraged. Therefore, if a colleague holds a different view, it is not one's role to try and make one's view 'win'. To do this would risk breach of duty to the court. Rather, one should carefully consider *how* the difference in views has arisen.

In this manner the strength of one's argument can be compared with the strength of a colleague's argument, and if people both genuinely and in good faith agree to disagree then the court will have to make a decision in the light of *all* the information available to it.

THE ASSESSMENT

Preparation

Prior to the assessment, sufficient material should have been sent to the neuropsychologist to clarify the nature of the key issues and questions. The instructing letter should explain why a clinical neuropsychological assessment is being requested. Typically, within the limits of the individual's competence, the aims of the assessment will be:

- to document the current level of functioning;
- to estimate the likely level of functioning prior to the accident;
- to indicate whether a comparison of these two reveals a deficit;
- to indicate whether there has been a deficit in the past, even if there is no deficit now;
- to indicate when the claimant would have recovered from any such earlier deficit;
- if there is any ongoing deficit, to state the likely course of recovery of function including (a) when recovery will plateau and (b) whether the plateau will be below premorbid levels, leaving a permanent deficit;

- to consider whether treatment or rehabilitation will improve the speed or extent of recovery from deficit and, if so, the nature of such treatment required;
- to state whether the deficit is due to the accident or whether all or part of it predates the accident and is due to unrelated causes (e.g., effects of earlier injuries, pre-existing problems such as dyslexia);
- to consider whether there are psychological (non-organic) factors compounding the level of deficit seen (e.g., depression, post-traumatic stress disorder, motivation);
- to state whether these factors are causally related to the accident and hence also directly attributable to it, or whether they are unrelated;
- to indicate whether these psychological factors can be treated, and, if so, the effect of such treatment upon deficit;
- to indicate whether the person is genuine or whether 'deficits' could be explained by deliberate underperformance (malingering);
- to describe the effect of deficit upon (a) work, (b) relationships, (c) leisure activities; to consider whether the deficit has given rise to a care need (e.g., the need for case management, sleep-in or day-time care/support);
- whether the claimant is capable of managing their own affairs;
- to indicate whether the care need or position regarding capacity will change over time (e.g., with ageing);
- to recommend whether any further reports or specialist investigations are needed.

This is a formidable list (and some questions might well be outside the expertise of any one specific expert, who may have to suggest the instruction of a further professional) and explains just why the clinical neuropsychologist has to examine eventually every source of data to provide a final, rounded opinion. All the material may well not be available at the time of the assessment, and so the opinion may well have to evolve over time as new material is considered.

As for the psychometric assessment itself, the choice of tests is up to the expert, but the expert is liable to cross-examination upon the status of these tests and why they, and not others, were chosen. Therefore one must (a) know one's tests and (b) know why one chooses them. Most clinical neuropsychologists achieve a balance of older, tried-and-trusted tests and newer tests or newer versions of tests.

The use of technicians to collect data is a somewhat vexed question. There is a view that a technician can test blind and hence avoid expectation effects (Doerr & Carlin, 1991), but the psychologist then cannot observe the 'test-taking behaviour'. This is a serious matter because the technician, who is less expert, (a) may miss a crucial observation or aspect of performance and (b) is not able flexibly to select additional tests as he or she proceeds. The rules do allow for technicians (see PD1.2(3) and (4)), but this seems more appropriate for other disciplines (e.g., the neurologist who orders a scan or a hearing test) than for clinical neuropsychologists for whom *behavioural observation* is a legitimate form of data.

The assessment will comprise at least four parts: premorbid IQ, current neuropsychological performance, psychological or clinical state, and interview. There may be a fifth part, the assessment of malingering. These will be considered briefly in turn.

Premorbid Abilities

There are various strategies for estimating premorbid abilities as follows (see also Chapter 6), with a brief note of those medico-legal points that can be made about them:

1. *Assume that the highest subtest score on the WAIS-III (Wechsler Adult Intelligence Scale) represents the original level.* Even normal individuals have a profile of abilities and show quite a wide range of subtest scores (Crawford & Allan, 1996). It makes no sense at all to say that a person's best score is his or her 'real' potential. Anyone using this method may well grossly overestimate IQ loss.

2. *Consider scores on subtests thought to be relatively insensitive to the effects of brain injury.* Vocabulary is highly correlated with IQ and is such a deeply ingrained ability that it is relatively insensitive to the affects of brain injury. Therefore, scores on the Vocabulary subtest can indeed be a guide to premorbid IQ in the absence of dysphasia.

3. *Gauge IQ from educational record.* This is reasonable as long as the person had (a) full access to education and (b) the motivation to take and pass exams. Gauging ability band is made easier now that national statistics on examination pass rates are published annually in the UK and are freely available on the Web. For example, 50% now obtain five or more GCSEs at grades A*–C and only 5.5% fail to get any GCSE passes at all (see http://www.dfes.gov.uk/statistics). Data on estimating IQ and memory ability from educational history are also available from the manual of the Wechsler Test of Adult Reading (WTAR: Holdnack, 2001).

4. *Gauge IQ from occupational record.* Again this is reasonable as a broad approximation, but cultural and sociological constraints on choice of work or progress in work have to be taken into account.

5. *Tests of over-learned skills such as reading.* Reading ability is highly correlated with IQ and is a very over-learned skill, not easily affected by diffuse brain injury. This is the most reliable method, as long as the patient has no history of dyslexia or dysphasia. Tests include the National Adult Reading Test, 2nd edition (Nelson & Willison, 1991), the Spot-the-Word Test (Baddeley et al., 1992) and the WTAR.

6. *Genetic endowment.* If the patient was damaged at birth, then the ability and educational and occupational record of natural parents and siblings may be considered, but account may have to be taken of the fact that previous generations can be disadvantaged in various ways.

Current Neuropsychological Functioning

There is no pro forma for a medico-legal neuropsychological assessment, but, in general, reports are expected to cover certain areas in some detail. These areas are intellect, attention and concentration, speed of processing, memory and executive skills. Reports should also at least consider the following areas and test them more extensively if appropriate: language, constructional/spatial skills, motor skills and sensory deficits. In choosing which tests to give, the neuropsychologist should be prepared to give evidence about the test's reliability, its validity, recent restandardizations, whether it is considered an experimental rather than a proven test, the theories or models on which it is based and their strength, and its ecological validity.

This last point is worth considering because there is a broad trend for tests to be designed to better predict real-life functioning (Powell, 2000; Powell & Wood, 2000). This is being matched in the courts by a demand that clinical neuropsychologists better specify the relevance of their test results to a person's ability to work, run their life, engage in certain leisure activities and so forth. For example, test results are often criticized because:

- data are collected in a quiet, focused environment, whereas real life is noisy and full of distractions;
- cognitive tests are often constructed to measure a pure aspect of processing, whereas real-life tasks are multidimensional;
- we do not have tests that measure some functions, like sense of humour;
- the behaviour of the claimant is constrained by the legal context of the relationship with the examiner, and so is unlike spontaneous behaviour.

It is for these reasons that clinical neuropsychologists do not just consider test results, but *all* sources of data and information, as previously discussed.

A further trend in the medico-legal world is to spend more time on the assessment of executive functions, because of the increasing view that these are especially related to success at return to work, to marital and relationship stability, to care need and to capacity (e.g., see Hall & Sbordone, 1993; Osmon, 1999; Wood & McMillan, 2000). This means that increasingly the neuropsychological assessment will either use a sample of tests from different sources or use one of the newer batteries, such as the Delis–Kaplan Executive Function System (D–KEFS; Delis et al., 2001).

Clinical Status

There are several important reasons that some effort has to be made to describe the clinical or psychological state of the claimant. Test performance might be undermined by overt anxiety, distracting preoccupation, fatigue or depressed mood. When comparing test results obtained at another time or by another psychologist, emotional state at the time of testing might explain differences. Some symptoms may be directly attributable to organic brain damage, such as emotional lability or facile or shallow emotions, and emotional state may relate to whether the time is right for rehabilitation. Emotional state may also suggest the need for psychological treatment or for a further assessment report by a psychiatrist.

A full mental state examination normally cannot be accommodated within a session that is dominated by the cognitive assessment, but screening questionnaires can be given (if necessary, completed outside the session, either before or after it), and mental health will form at least part of the interview.

The Interview

It is not legally possible to insist on interviewing someone who knows the claimant, but this is desirable given the lack of insight shown by some claimants. If a relative cannot attend, it may be possible for them to complete one of the relative questionnaires, or to be interviewed by telephone.

The interview of the claimant fulfils various functions. It allows for a detailed educational and work history to be taken, helping to establish premorbid capacity. It is possible to discuss entries in GP or hospital records to clarify the history (e.g., severity of previous head injuries, degree of emotional vulnerability). It allows the person to mention problems not tapped by the tests. The examiner can explore how some of the deficits observed on tests translate into problems in real life (e.g., at work, in relationships or in self-care). It is a sample of the claimant's behaviour and can suggest problems with, for example, attention, conceptual thinking, insight or anger control. The person's way of life and their typical day can be explored. It affords an opportunity to talk about the future and sense of direction, or alternatively their sense of loss of the changed direction of their life.

It is important during the interview to remember the medico-legal context and pay particular attention to causality, and to keep a written note of anything that is said. The court is entitled to inspect the neuropsychologist's written notes to help validate claims about what was said.

Malingering

DSM-IV (American Psychiatric Association, 1994) indicates that malingering ('the intentional production of false or grossly exaggerated physical or psychological symptoms') should be suspected if any of four criteria are present: (1) medico-legal context of presentation; (2) marked discrepancy between the person's claimed stress or disability and the objective findings; (3) lack of co-operation during the diagnostic evaluation and in complying with the prescribed treatment regime; and (4) the presence of antisocial personality disorder.

Given these broad criteria, every claimant by virtue of being a claimant has to be suspected, but in most cases it will not be an issue, as the prevalence of malingering has been put at 7.5–15% by Trueblood and Schmidt (1993); this is higher than in my own experience in the UK (Powell, 1999), having suspected only 4.1% of head injury cases to be significantly malingering out of a sample of 882, most of the suspected cases having sustained only mild or very mild head injuries.

There is no one test of malingering, but sometimes a pattern gradually builds up that raises the suspicion of conscious exaggeration. Features of test performance that raise the issue include (Powell, 2000):

- a degree of deficit that is disproportionate to the severity of the injury (e.g., see Johnson & Lesniak-Karpiak, 1997);
- bizarre errors not typically seen in patients with genuine deficits;
- patterns of test performance that do not make sense (e.g., doing as badly on easy items as hard items);
- not showing expected patterns (e.g., being as bad on recognition recall as free recall; failing to show any learning whatsoever on auditory–verbal learning tasks; discrepancies between scores on tests measuring similar processes);
- inconsistencies between test performance and behaviour in real life (e.g., unable to repeat short digit strings or short sentences, but in general conversation is able to respond to multi-stage instructions; extreme slowness in answering test questions, but converses and gives the history normally);
- inexplicable claims of remote memory loss even for important life events like weddings (Greiffenstein et al., 1994);
- random responding on forced choice tests (e.g., Warrington, 1984) in the absence of evidence of gross brain damage;
- *below* chance responding on forced choice tests, suggesting the person must know the right answer in order to give the wrong one (Iverson & Franzen, 1996);
- poor performance on tests that look hard but are in fact easy, like the Rey 15- or 16-item test (Paul et al., 1992);
- the absence of any sign of severe anxiety or profoundly low mood such as might cause performance to deteriorate;
- after head injury, the absence of any improvement, or indeed a worsening of performance over time (however, a word of caution here, because a distinctive feature of neuro*behavioural* problems is that they are determined in part by situational and behavioural principles, and so may deteriorate with time—see Powell & Wood, 2000);
- the failure to report deficits for a suspiciously long time following the brain injury, when in retrospect those deficits are claimed to have been severe;
- relative absence of a history of somatization or related disorders.

THE REPORT

The basic structure of a medico-legal report in clinical neuropsychology is as follows.

The Report Is Addressed to the Court

It states who was tested, when the assessment took place, the date of the report itself, the reason for and aims of the assessment, and a summary as needed of the solicitor's letter of instruction. The field of expertise of the report is stated and a brief CV of the expert given (either in the introduction or appended).

Sources of Information

It is necessary to list every document seen as this will enable the reader to know the precise evidence available when the report was written. If a document is unsigned, one should state that it is unsigned. If a document is marked 'draft', it should not be read but sent back, as should a document marked 'not for disclosure'. Remember that once something potentially relevant has been read, one has to admit to having read it or potentially be in contempt of court. Having admitted that one has seen it means the other side can see it too, whether one's instructing solicitor wants to disclose it or not.

Clinical History

There is no one way of setting out the clinical history. Some experts simply refer briefly to previous expert reports and adopt their conclusions. However, this is not a safe thing to do because experts make mistakes, have differing views and select different things from notes and records. Once one has implicitly deferred to their conclusions, it is difficult to challenge them at a later date. It also looks lazy. Rather, as far as possible, it is better to review all the clinical information oneself and draw one's own picture of the clinical history. If the neuropsychologist describes having read something, then cross-examination will have to demonstrate that it was read thoroughly. Omitting important information will make the neuropsychologist's preparation look cursory or biased.

Report of the Assessment and Results

There are several issues to consider here:

- *Should the tests be named?* Some argue that it is the expert's *judgement* that is important, not such details. However, not to name tests can appear evasive and over-controlling and a hindrance to understanding the conclusions and to doing a retest.
- *Should the actual test scores be given?* Again, some argue that to give test scores allows the non-expert to rework the data from an unqualified perspective and offer an alternative view that might confuse the court. However, were an unqualified expert to do this they would be in extreme difficulty under cross-examination. On

balance, the court prefers openness in medico-legal reporting, including test results.

- *Should one give confidence limits based on standard error of measurement?* One needs to be able to explain in lay terms both 'confidence limit' and 'standard error of measurement';
- *Should one give norms?* Citing norms is a minefield as it is always possible to find faults in a normative study and to find studies that give different norms. Personally, I take a generalizability theory perspective (i.e., there is a universe of possible norms, and the expert should know the range of views and data and express an opinion bearing that knowledge in mind).
- *Should one cite references?* Single papers are *never* definitive and may lead to difficulties in cross-examination. It is the neuropsychologist who is the expert and who should be able to draw upon a range of papers to inform their views. If necessary, it is safer and better science to do a mini-review of an area, however time-consuming that might be. If necessary, the solicitor may be able to arrange funding for a researcher to do a literature search, under the supervision of the neuropsychologist.
- *Should the results be put into a standard template?* Using a standard format can make reports look stereotyped and mass-produced, but the whole legal process is structure- and format-driven. Using a standard format actually serves the same function as having a semi-structured interview, reminding the neuropsychologist to cover the whole range of topics and making it less likely that an area will be neglected.

Discussion and Conclusions

The discussion of evidence and drawing of conclusions discriminates between the *scientist* and *pseudo*-scientist (Lees-Haley & Cohen, 1999). Examples of their contrasting styles include:

- describing procedures explicitly versus avoiding disclosure of specific methodology; openly exploring alternatives versus presuming causation and minimizing exploration of alternatives;
- interpreting empirical data with reason and logic versus relying on intuition, experience and speculation;
- making inferences from base rates, law of large numbers and descriptive data versus generalizing from small samples and anecdotes;
- distinguishing between observation and inference versus blurring objective and subjective data;
- attacking the methods of opposing experts versus attacking the person of the opposing expert.

In addition, some common false assumptions made in reports (Long, 1996) include:

- failing to consider information from collateral sources;

- assuming that defective performance means brain damage;
- forgetting the 'psychologist' in neuropsychologist and failing to draw upon advances in our root discipline;
- failing to be flexible in the use or interpretation of tests;
- assuming that cognitive performance is only measured by tests;
- assuming that test data can be interpreted in isolation from context;
- intact performance means no deficits;
- neuropsychology tests are extremely reliable and valid.

Some of the common issues that have to be addressed include:

- *Premorbid status*, both cognitive and psychological, often requiring access to more information, such as school reports and personnel files, bearing in mind that we all tend unwittingly to rewrite history and in the medico-legal context there are obvious pressures to minimize negative features of the history and play up positive ones.
- *The impact of mild head injury*. It is outside the scope of this chapter to review the growing literature on mild head injury, but it is increasingly evident that a percentage of mild head injury patients remain chronically symptomatic even outside the medico-legal context (e.g., Binder, 1997), even if the mechanism is much in dispute (e.g., Bieliauskas, 1999).
- *Confounding factors* affecting test scores. For example, both head injury and depression can cause agitation, loss of interest, indecisiveness, loss of energy, changes in sleep pattern, irritability, concentration difficulty, tiredness or fatigue (see the Beck Depression Inventory; Beck, 1996).
- *Estimation of length of PTA (post-traumatic amnesia)*. Memory has gaps, it is not a videotape to be replayed, but at what point do normal gaps become the patchy memory for events found in PTA? How might stress and even terror have affected memory? To what extent will strong pain relief and sedation have affected recall? These will always be difficult issues, but at least we should stop expecting memory to be 'continuous'; memory can only ever be 'normally' continuous, or, even more accurately, 'normally continuous for the circumstances'.
- *Prognosis*. There is no one prognosis. There is a different prognosis for each neuropsychological function and a different prognosis for the various facets of real life (e.g., work, marriage and leisure activities). The shape and timescale of the recovery curve will depend on moderating variables, such as severity of the injury, mood and treatment effects.
- *Capacity to manage one's own affairs*. The Court of Protection is an office of the Supreme Court and dates back to the Middle Ages when the Crown assumed responsibility for managing the estate of those who were mentally ill or handicapped. The person, to be a 'patient', must (a) have a mental disorder (e.g., neuropsychological deficit) and (b) be incapable of managing and administering their property and affairs by virtue of that disorder (see the British Medical Association and Law Society 1995 guidance on how to gauge capacity). First, the difficulty of the task facing the individual has to be considered: Do they just have routine day-to-day decisions to make or will there be a large sum of money

and/or complex care regime to manage? Second, the degree of support and resources is important: Is there the necessary degree of back-up and advice from other sources? Will they appropriately seek and act upon advice? Third, there is the estimation of degree of vulnerability of the person: Would they make rash and irresponsible decisions? Could they be exploited by others? Could their inability to manage compromise the position of others, like their children? A medical practitioner signs the medical certificate to go to the Official Solicitors, but the psychologist's views will be considered, either by being cited on the form or in oral evidence. In any case it is a *legal* decision as to whether a person is a patient, *not* an expert's decision. Similar considerations pertain to the issue of fitness to plead (i.e., the capacity to give evidence).

AFTER THE REPORT: PREPARATION FOR SETTLEMENT OR JUDGMENT

Once the report has been submitted there will be a process whereby the lawyers on the respective sides see if they can reach an agreement on a figure, a settlement, or whether the issues between the parties are so great that they will have to be decided by a judge hearing the case. There are various ways that the expert's views are developed.

Questions from Instructing Solicitor

The neuropsychologist's solicitor, possibly after taking advice from Counsel, will write seeking clarification of their views. They will also point out any internal contradictions in the report or whether crucial information has been forgotten.

Questions from the Opposing Legal Team

According to the rules, once the neuropsychologist's report has been disclosed, the opposition has 28 days to ask written questions 'for the purpose of clarifying the expert's report'. Note that clarification is the *only* purpose. They should not be sending *new* information to comment upon or be raising *new* issues. If neuropsychologists are in any doubt as to whether the 'questions' put really are covered by CPR 35.6, then they should consult their instructing solicitor, who in any case should have been sent a copy.

Receipt of Further Material

New reports from experts will be sent to the neuropsychologist, commissioned from both sides; medical and other records will also be sent. These should be commented upon in writing, taking care to express one's views as if there were a statement of truth attached and in the light of the fact that these comments might end up disclosed to the court.

Toward the end of the case the neuropsychologist will receive the final witness statements from the claimant and those who know them, and from those who are working with them, like case managers or enablers. They will contain important, up-to-date information, but may read as if they are written by lawyers and often do not put forward a rounded or an unbiased view.

There might be a videotape taken covertly of the claimant to ensure that they present in real life in the same way that they present at medico-legal examination. There are strict rules about how surveillance operatives collect their footage. In examining the tapes it is the case that not all deficits found on tests could in any way be observed on most videos (e.g., memory deficit), but the tapes can still be useful for confirming or contradicting things the neuropsychologist observed or was told (e.g., an inability to walk, being wheelchair-dependent, never going out unaccompanied). Mostly, tapes will confirm an understanding of the case; sometimes they will suggest the person can do somewhat more than one thought and sometimes one will see blatant fraud.

Joint Statements

The rules state that the court can order a discussion between equivalent experts to produce a joint report on areas of agreement and disagreement. Normally, a date is given by which the experts must talk and a date by which the joint statement is produced. The lawyers can raise questions or a draft agenda, but are not bound by it, as a major part of the expert's role is to identify key issues in, say, defining deficit, incapacity or prognosis. The discussion need not be in person; it is normally sufficient to speak on the telephone, and it is usual for one person to be nominated to produce a draft. There are two further rules to know about:

- CPR 35.12(4). The content of the discussion between the experts shall not be referred to at the trial unless the parties agree.
- CPR 35.12(5). When the experts reach agreement on an issue during their discussions, the agreement shall not bind the parties unless the parties expressly agree to be bound by the agreement.

Conference with Counsel

As the case approaches, Counsel will consider if they are for the claimant what claim to put in and if they are for the defence what final offer to make. To help them in this task there is likely to be a conference attended by all experts (e.g., psychologists, psychiatrists, neurologists, employment experts, care experts). This is not necessarily a cosy meeting, because this may be the only chance Counsel has to gauge the neuropsychologist's strength of evidence and how well he or she comes across as a witness. If Counsel can move the expert on key points just in a conference, then his or her evidence may be more vulnerable in the witness box. Therefore, the neuropsychologist can expect to experience a taste of cross-examination by their own side. Needless to say, such conferences require thorough preparation.

The Morning of the Trial

Although in theory it is a 'cards on the table' system, it still seems to be the case that not all the loose ends are tied up by the morning of the trial. Therefore, even at the last moment the neuropsychologist may be commenting on new aspects or even asked to discuss some matters with their opposite number and provide a further joint statement. Therefore, even if the neuropsychologist is not scheduled to give evidence on the first day, they should still arrive at court very thoroughly prepared.

THE COURTS

Types of Court

There are two types of law: criminal and civil. The burden of proof in the criminal court is beyond reasonable doubt, whereas in the civil court it is the balance of probabilities (i.e., 51% to 49%). This reinforces the point that, especially in civil cases, the neuropsychologist need not be 'certain' of their views, but need only have an opinion on likelihood, though it would be prudent for them to know 'how' certain they are.

There are different types of criminal courts. In the *Magistrate*'s Court the solicitors present the case to the magistrate, who can be either a lay person (Justice of the Peace) or a lawyer. The cases will often be minor (e.g., drunk and disorderly), but some will involve a trial (e.g., theft). The sentencing powers of magistrates are limited. In the *Crown* Court barristers will present the case to a high-court judge or 'circuit' judge. There are three levels of the court depending upon how serious the offence is (up to murder), and the Crown Court can act as a court of appeal to the Magistrate's Court. The next level of court is the Appeal Court, the High Court and the Central Criminal Court, at which the most experienced judges sit.

There are also different types of civil court. There are *County* Courts, which are local, and the *High Courts of Justice*, based in London, with three divisions: *Queen's Bench* for damages (hence this is the court with which clinical neuropsychologists will have most dealings); *Chancery* for tax, wills and trusts; and *Family*, for adoption, wardship, divorce and so forth. Permission may be given to take the judgment to the Court of Appeal.

The Layout

All courts have the same basic layout. The judge sits elevated at the bench, the royal coat of arms behind. In front are the court officials (i.e., the clerks and ushers). There will be a witness box to one side of the judge with a copy of the complete papers for the hearing, including one's own reports and letters. It will have a microphone to audiotape the evidence, not to amplify one's voice. To one side of the court there may be a box where the jury sits (juries are primarily confined to criminal cases, but can also be used in civil cases that are, for example, against the police). There may also be an area for the press, a gallery for the public and a secure dock for the accused in a criminal case.

The body of the court itself is divided into two 'camps', because the legal system is adversarial. In criminal cases the defence team will be one side and the prosecution team (the Crown Prosecution Service) on the other. In civil cases there will be a claimant's team and a defence team. In the first row of seats will be the barrister presenting the case. If it is an important case (e.g., one of public interest or of potentially large value), then there may be two barristers, Leading Counsel (Queen's Counsel, QC) and Junior Counsel, who will sit behind. Behind the barristers will sit the solicitors, then come the expert witnesses and interested parties, such as representatives from insurance companies. If there is no public gallery, then the public may take the back rows of seats.

The expert will sit behind the solicitor who has instructed them, within arm's length if possible, so that they can pass written comments forward (e.g., questions that counsel might consider asking or comments on evidence).

The People

Magistrates will be lay persons or solicitors, and judges will vary in experience and background, beginning with Deputy Recorder, rising to High Court Judge through to Law Lord. Magistrates are referred to as 'Your Worship'. In the Crown Court or County Court the judge will be 'Your Honour'. In the High Court, Appeal Court or Central Criminal Court it will be 'My Lord' or 'My Lady' (or His Lordship and Her Ladyship).

The ushers and clerks, as well as supervising the audiotape, will generally take care of the workings of the court room, swearing in the witnesses, making sure they have water, passing documents from Counsel to the judge.

The space between the barrister and the bench is called the bar and is their preserve, hence qualifying is referred to as being 'called to the Bar'. Barristers are self-employed, but work in chambers, co-ordinated by clerks. Distinguished barristers with special expertise rise to the position of Queen's Counsel, referred to as 'taking silk', and they have a somewhat different gown. A Queen's Counsel is normally only instructed in conjunction with Junior Counsel, where 'Junior' simply means not a QC, not that they are either young or inexperienced.

Barristers traditionally are not allowed to meet a client in the absence of the client's solicitor. Solicitors work in firms that are increasingly specialized, especially in personal injury, and are regulated by the Law Society.

There are then three types of witness. An ordinary *witness* is asked to give evidence on what they personally observed (i.e., saw, heard, felt, tasted or smelled, although in personal injury the lay witnesses typically go far beyond this, giving their understanding of situations, making judgements, offering opinions, looking into the future). Then there is a *witness of fact*, who may well be a qualified person, vouching for various facts. For example, a clinical psychologist, as a witness of fact, can confirm that they did see Mr X 10 times, that tests A, B and C were given and that the scores were X, Y and Z, and that normal test procedures were followed. The witness of fact is *not* allowed to give an opinion. Then there is an *expert witness*, who *is* allowed to give an opinion—what they are there for.

Expert witnesses will not only have read all material and submitted one or more reports, but also they are often expected to have observed a claimant in the witness box and to have listened to as many as possible of the lay witnesses, in case anything they see or hear affects their final opinion. They may take into the witness box what is needed for evidence, and anything taken into the witness box is 'discoverable' (i.e. open to inspection). Indeed, the entire work of the expert witness is ultimately discoverable, and so nothing should be thrown away, not even scribbled notes of phone calls.

The Procedures

The neuropsychologist's solicitor will seek from them the dates that they are available to give evidence. Essentially, the only acceptable reason for giving a date as unavailable is being abroad. Attending court takes precedence over all other clinical or personal commitments. If dates from two courts clash, the higher court takes precedence. If both courts are of equal status, the case first issuing a witness summons (subpoena) will take precedence. For this reason, some solicitors will automatically subpoena all their witnesses. The witness summons will state which court (e.g., The High Court of Justice), which division (usually Queen's Bench Division) and which registry (e.g., Cambridge District Registry). It will state the time to arrive and that attendance is daily until no longer required. It will usually tell the expert to bring all notes, records and reports that pertain to the case. The expert may be given a cheque or cash to cover travelling expenses. The expert will be warned that if they do not attend or produce the documents then they may be liable to a fine or imprisonment and be required to pay any costs resulting from their failure to attend or refusal to take an oath or affirm. Typically, the expert will be asked by the solicitor to attend a little earlier than required—first, to make sure of prompt arrival and, second and more importantly, to have any last minute discussion with Counsel.

The usher will open the court doors, and when the judge is ready to enter the court will be instructed to 'rise' and will bow to the judge as they take their seat on the bench. The bow is in fact to the royal coat of arms rather than to the individual judge. The judge will return the bow.

As the trial unfolds, the neuropsychologist may pass observations and comments, clearly written, to the solicitor in front, or to Junior Counsel if the solicitor is absent (making only *important* comments; a snowstorm of notes is overreactive, distracting and can look aggressive). If the solicitor feels it necessary, the note will be passed to Junior Counsel, who will in turn pass it, if appropriate and at an opportune moment, to Leading Counsel. If the number of people present makes it impossible to pass the note forward, it is permitted to stand up and walk to the solicitor with the note, and return to one's seat.

If the expert wishes to leave the Court for any reason, they must inform the solicitor or Counsel in case there is a pressing need to stay, walk to the door and bow directly to the judge before opening the door and leaving. Judges do note who is present in court and who leaves when. A judge might pass comment that witness X diligently and patiently listened to all the evidence before giving their own. Conversely, a judge might point out to witness X that, for example, they did not hear the mother give evidence, in which case, hopefully, they will be able to say that although not personally present they had been briefed as to the content of the evidence. (The expert's instructing solicitor will in fact decide the need to be in court or not, because there are considerations, such as costs.) Similarly, when the expert returns to the court, they should enter, bow to the judge (whether or not they appear to notice) and resume their seat.

When it comes to their own evidence, having been called forward by the barrister, the expert should take the stand and swear the appropriate oath to tell the truth, while holding the appropriate religious text in their right hand. Alternatively, they may 'affirm' if they wish and make a secular oath.

Once evidence has been given, the judge will normally release the witness and they may leave, unless the barrister requires otherwise. Occasionally, it may be made clear that they may have to take the stand again, dependent upon the outcome of some other aspect of the evidence.

The Expert's Oral Evidence

Questioning occurs in a set order. The *examination* is by the neuropsychologist's barrister. It will begin with a statement of the expert's qualifications and then confirm that the appropriate documents in the bundle are the neuropsychologist's and that they represent the neuropsychologist's opinion. The judge will ask if the witness wishes to sit down and gives permission to do so. The barrister then takes the expert through all or part of their report. Questions will then be put to the neuropsychologist that may have arisen out of the evidence of others. Here are some suggestions for giving testimony:

- practise in advance giving a succinct statement of qualifications and relevant experience;
- know your own report thoroughly;
- answer the questions;

- give a definite but reasonable view—nothing is certain but we can be reasonably certain;
- speak in non-technical language and plain English;
- explain clearly any technical terms that have to be used;
- acknowledge vulnerable portions of your evidence or conclusions;
- do not get carried away and end up in an extreme or exaggerated position—the court will be persuaded by the strength of evidence, not by hyperbole;
- present the balance of the evidence openly and do not become an advocate for your side;
- acknowledge the limitations of your expertise and the boundaries of your knowledge and competence;
- if you feel it important, do not hesitate to ask permission to return to a question;
- speak clearly and at a moderate pace, to allow the judge time to keep a written note;

The opposing Counsel will then undertake a *cross-examination* of the neuropsychologist. Not to put too fine a point on it, Counsel will through the questions try 'to demonstrate that the expert witness is stupid, ill-informed, did not have all relevant facts necessary to evaluate the situation, was improperly paid off by the attorney who hired him, and provided an analysis which is illogical and contrary to established scientific principles' (Postol, 1987).

During the cross-examination it is important for the expert not to be overly defensive, to consider genuinely and carefully the importance of new evidence, to consider carefully the strength of counter-arguments and alternative views, to concede points that are right to concede and to defend confidently points that should not be conceded. The expert should not defend the indefensible, but should explain dispassionately and fully any disagreement with Counsel.

The list of questions that might be asked in cross-examination is endless, but a sample of those most commonly asked of neuropsychologists is given in Doerr and Carlin (1991, pp. 229–233); Melton et al. (1997, pp. 532–535) give examples of common strategies used to undermine the strength of a witness. Both texts also set out ways of responding to such questions and strategies.

After the cross-examination, the neuropsychologist's own barrister may, if they wish, undertake a *re-examination*. If the cross-examination has gone badly they will be trying to retrieve the situation and show why the expert's answers are not quite as favourable to the opposition's case as they might at first appear.

Next, the judge will directly ask any questions pertaining to any part of the expert's written or oral evidence, or to any aspect of the case upon which the judge feels the expert may usefully comment.

Finally, both barristers have the opportunity to ask any questions that arise directly from the expert's answers to the judge's questions. The judge will then release the expert from the stand.

Should the expert's evidence run across the adjournment for lunch or continue across consecutive days, they will remain under oath and will not be able to speak to any person about their evidence or the case.

CONCLUSIONS

The key skills in the work of the clinical neuropsychologist as expert witness are the *systematic* collection of solid neuropsychological data, the *focus* on key medico-legal questions, the *proactive gathering* of information, the ability to construct a rational and logical *formulation* of the clinical history and likely future, the ability to present *written evidence* and the ability to give live *oral* evidence. These skills are reflected in the contribution that neuropsychologists make to the legal process, in that neuropsychologists not only describe and quantify deficit but are also theory- and principle-driven and can communicate these explanatory mechanisms to others by way of a formulation that the court recognizes as both scientific and meaningful. As was stated in the beginning, simply be a sound scientist–practitioner and one is most of the way there as an expert witness.

REFERENCES

American Psychiatric Association (1994) *Diagnostic and Statistical Manual of Mental Disorders* (4th edn—DSM-IV). American Psychiatric Association, Washington, DC.

Baddeley, A. D., Emslie, H. & Nimmo-Smith, I. N. (1992) *The Speed and Capacity of Language-processing Test*, Thames Valley Publishing Co., Bury St Edmunds, UK.

Beck, A. T. (1996) *Beck Depression Inventory II*. Psychological Corporation, San Antonio, TX.

Bieliauskas, L. A. (1999) The measurement of personality and emotional functioning. In: J. J. Sweet (ed.) *Forensic Neuropsychology: Fundamentals and Practice* (pp. 121–143). Swets & Zeitlinger, Lisse, The Netherlands.

Binder, L. M. (1997) A review of mild head trauma. Part II: Clinical implications. *Journal of Clinical and Experimental Neuropsychology*, **19**, 432–457.

British Medical Association and Law Society (1995) *Assessment of Mental Capacity: Guidance for Doctors and Lawyers*. British Medical Association, London.

Crawford, J. R. & Allan, K. M. (1996) WAIS-R subtest scatter: Base-rate data from a healthy UK sample. *British Journal of Clinical Psychology*, **35**, 235–247.

Delis, D. C., Kaplan, E. & Kramer, J. H. (2001) *Delis–Kaplan Executive Function System*. Psychological Corporation, San Antonio, TX.

Division of Neuropsychology (2000) *Professional Practice Guidelines*. British Psychological Society, Leicester, UK.

Doerr, H. O. & Carlin, A. S. (eds) (1991) *Forensic Neuropsychology: Legal and Scientific Basis*. The Guilford Press, New York.

Grainger, I. & Fealy M. (1999) *An Introduction to the New Civil Procedures Rules*. Cavendish, London.

Greiffenstein, M. F., Baker, W. J. & Gola, T. (1994) Validation of malingered amnesia measure with a large clinical sample. *Psychological Assessment*, **6**, 218–224.

Hall, H. V. & Sbordone, R. J. (1993) *Disorders of Executive Functions: Civil and Criminal Law Applications*. PMD Publishers Group, Winter Park, FL.

Hess, A. K. & Weiner, I. B. (1999) *The Handbook of Forensic Psychology* (2nd edn). John Wiley & Sons, New York.

Holdnack, J. A. (2001) *Wechsler Test of Adult Reading*. Psychological Corporation, San Antonio, TX.

Iverson, G. L. & Franzen, M. D. (1996) Using multiple objective memory procedures to detect simulated malingering. *Journal of Clinical and Experimental Neuropsychology*, **18**, 38–51.

Johnson, J. L. & Lesniak-Karpiak, K. (1997) The effect of warning on malingering on memory and motor tasks in a college sample. *Archives of Clinical Neuropsychology*, **12**, 231–238.

Lees-Haley, P. R. & Cohen, L. J. (1999) The neuropsychologist as expert witness: Toward credible science in the Courtroom. In: J. J. Sweet (ed.) *Forensic Neuropsychology: Fundamentals and Practice*. Swets & Zeitlinger, Lisse, The Netherlands.

Long, C. J. (1996) Neuropsychological tests: A look at our past and the impact that ecological issues may have on our future. In: R. J. Sbordone and C. J. Long (eds) *Ecological Validity of Neuropsychological Testing*. G R Press/St Lucie Press, Delray Beach, FL.

Melton, G. B., Petrila, J., Poythress, N. G. & Slobogin, C. (1997) *Psychological Evaluations for the Courts: A Handbook for Mental Health Professionals and Lawyers* (2nd edn). Guilford Press, New York.

Nelson, H. E. & Willison, J. (1991) *National Adult Reading Test (NART): Test Manual* (2nd edn). NFER-Nelson, Windsor, UK.

Osmon, D. C. (1999) Complexities in the evaluation of executive functions. In: J. J. Sweet (ed.) *Forensic Neuropsychology: Fundamentals and Practice*. Swets & Zeitlinger, Lisse, The Netherlands.

Paul, D. S., Franzen, M. D., Cohen, S. H. & Fremouw, W. (1992) An investigation into the reliability and validity of two tests used in the detection of malingering. *International Journal of Clinical Neuropsychology*, **14**, 1–9.

Postol, L. P. (1987) A legal primer for expert witnesses. *For the Defense*, **29**, 21–25.

Powell, G. E. (1999) Profile of the suspected malingerer. *Proceedings of the British Psychological Society*, **7**, 135.

Powell, G. E. (2000) Cognitive assessment. In: M. G. Gelder, J. J. Lopez-Ibor & N. C. Anderson (eds) *New Oxford Textbook of Psychiatry*. Oxford University Press, Oxford, UK.

Powell, G. E. & Wood R. Ll. (2000) Assessing the nature and extent of neurobehavioural disability. In: R. Ll. Wood & T. M. McMillan (eds) *Neurobehavioural Disability and Social Handicap*. Psychology Press, London.

Sweet, J. J. (ed.) (1999) *Forensic Neuropsychology: Fundamentals and Practice*. Swets & Zeitlinger, Lisse, The Netherlands.

Trueblood, W. & Schmidt, M. (1993) Malingering and other validity considerations in the neuropsychological evaluation of mild head injury. *Journal of Clinical and Experimental Neuropsychology*, **15**, 578–590.

Warrington, E. K. (1984) *Recognition Memory Test Manual*. NFER-Nelson, Windsor, UK.

Wood, R. Ll. & McMillan, T. M. (eds) (2000) *Neurobehavioural Disability and Social Handicap*. Psychology Press, London.

PART VI

Rehabilitation

CHAPTER 16

Theoretical Approaches to Cognitive Rehabilitation

Barbara A. Wilson

Medical Research Council Cognition and Brain Sciences Unit, Cambridge, UK

INTRODUCTION

In 1993 Caramazza and Hillis wrote a paper entitled 'For a theory of remediation of cognitive deficits'. They said that they were not concerned with the question of whether cognitive models are helpful in rehabilitation, for 'surely they are, it is hard to imagine that efforts at therapeutic intervention would not be facilitated by having the clearest possible idea of what needs to be rehabilitated' (p. 218). Instead they were concerned with the potential role of these models in articulating theoretically informed constraints on cognitive disorders. The belief that detailed assessment informed by theoretical cognitive models can identify 'what needs to be rehabilitated' highlights, perhaps, the major difference between academic neuropsychologists engaged in cognitive rehabilitation and clinical neuropsychologists working at the 'coalface'. For those engaged in the day-to-day practice of helping people with cognitive deficits return to their most appropriate environments (arguably the main purpose of rehabilitation), 'what needs to be rehabilitated' is *not* an impairment identified by a theoretically informed model, but a real-life problem identified by the patient and his or her family. Such problems may well be caused by cognitive deficits, but in most cases we do not try to rehabilitate the deficit so much as the everyday problems seen as important by the patient/family.

Does this mean theoretical models are not important? Of course not. Models of cognitive functioning have proved enormously helpful in identifying cognitive strengths and weaknesses, in explaining phenomena and in making predictions about behaviour. All are important features in designing rehabilitation programmes. Nevertheless, models of cognitive functioning rarely tell us 'what needs to be rehabilitated', but simply what the cognitive constraints are on any programmes we wish to implement.

Take the highly influential working memory model of Baddeley and Hitch (1974). This enables us to understand why someone can have (a) a normal immediate memory with major problems after a delay or distraction, (b) a differ-

Clinical Neuropsychology: A Practical Guide to Assessment and Management for Clinicians.
Edited by L.H. Goldstein and J.E. McNeil. © 2004 John Wiley & Sons, Ltd.

ence between visual and verbal memory and (c) problems with executive function despite a normal phonological loop and visuospatial sketch pad. Once we have established the particular problem of a person (e.g., a deficit in the central executive or an inefficient delayed verbal memory), we are unlikely to set out to 'rehabilitate the central executive or the delayed verbal memory system'. Instead we are more likely to identify the particular problems faced by the individual with these impairments, such as 'problems planning a meal' or 'failure to use a notebook'. These are the kinds of things that 'need to be rehabilitated'.

Models of cognitive functioning are certainly not the only models that influence cognitive rehabilitation. Rehabilitation is one of many fields that needs a broad theoretical base incorporating frameworks, models and methodologies from a number of different fields.

This chapter considers some of the influential models relevant to cognitive rehabilitation together with their strengths and weaknesses and their impact on current clinical practice.

WHAT IS A THEORETICAL MODEL?

A theoretical model is a representation that helps to explain and increase our understanding of related phenomena. Models vary in complexity and detail, ranging from simple analogies to help us explain relatively complex situations, such as the 'faulty switch' analogy to help explain why someone is sometimes able and sometimes unable to carry out a task, through to highly complex computer-based representations to predict the weather. An example more relevant to rehabilitation would be connectionist modelling to explain how a damaged system might learn new skills (see, e.g., Robertson & Murre, 1999).

In rehabilitation, models are useful for facilitating thinking about treatment, explaining treatment to therapists and relatives, and enabling us to conceptualize outcomes. One of the earliest attempts to provide paradigms or models of treatment for people with brain injury was provided by Powell (1981):

1 the non-intervention strategy (letting nature take its course);
2 the prosthetic paradigm whereby patients are helped to make the most effective use of prostheses;
3 practice or stimulation, which is probably the most widely used treatment technique, despite little evidence for its effectiveness;
4 the maximizing paradigm in which therapists tend to maximize the extent, speed and level of learning by such procedures as positive reinforcement and feedback;
5 brain function therapy, or directed stimulation, which aims to focus or direct tasks at certain regions of the brain to increase its activity or re-establish functions in new areas;
6 medical, biochemical and surgical treatments that can sometimes be combined with other therapeutic treatments (Durand, 1982).

Although these paradigms may describe the state of play in rehabilitation they seem to be more a list of headings than theoretical models. Closer to models in the sense of providing theories of treatment are the five models of neuropsychological interventions suggested by Gross and Schutz (1986):

1 the environmental control model;
2 the stimulus–response (S–R) conditioning model;
3 the skill training model;
4 the strategy substitution model;
5 the cognitive cycle model.

Gross and Schutz claim that these models are hierarchical so that patients who cannot learn are treated with environmental control techniques; patients who can learn but cannot generalize need S–R conditioning; patients who can learn and generalize but cannot self-monitor should be given skill training; those who can self-monitor will benefit from strategy substitution; and those who can manage all of the above and are able to set their own goals will be best suited for treatment that is incorporated within the cognitive cycle model.

Although such a hierarchical model has a neatness about it, it is highly unlikely that absolute agreement would be found between therapists who were asked to make decisions about whether a particular patient could learn or generalize. Inability to learn cannot always be recognized with ease. We know that even comatose head-injured patients are capable of some degree of learning (Boyle & Greer, 1983; Shiel et al., 1993). Furthermore, it is possible to teach generalization in many instances (Zarkowska, 1987). Despite these reservations, it can be argued that Gross and Schutz's models are useful in encouraging therapists to think about ways of tackling problems in rehabilitation.

THEORETICAL APPROACHES SPECIFIC TO COGNITIVE REHABILITATION

Sohlberg and Mateer's influential book *An Introduction to Cognitive Rehabilitation* appeared in 1989. The foreword by Gianutsos suggested that cognitive rehabilitation is born of a mixed parentage, including neuropsychology, occupational therapy, speech and language therapy, and special education. Others draw from different fields. In 1987, I argued that three areas from within psychology were important for cognitive rehabilitation: neuropsychology for helping us to understand the organization of the brain, cognitive psychology for providing theoretical models and behavioural psychology for providing a number of treatment strategies that could be modified or adapted to reduce the everyday problems of people with cognitive deficits following damage to the brain (Wilson, 1987a).

McMillan and Greenwood (1993) believed that rehabilitation should draw on clinical neuropsychology, behavioural analysis, cognitive retraining, and group and individual psychotherapy. Diller (1987) also believed that a number of theoretical approaches were important.

This is in contrast to those who believe that only one theoretical approach is necessary—a view more likely to be held by those advocating theoretical models from cognitive neuropsychology as the basis for cognitive rehabilitation. In 1991 Coltheart stated that in order to treat a deficit it is necessary to fully understand its nature, and to do this one has to have in mind how the function is normally achieved. Without this model one cannot determine what kinds of treatment would be appropriate. As stated earlier this approach is limited. People undergoing rehabilitation rarely have isolated deficits, such as difficulty understanding prepositions: they may have emotional, social and behavioural problems together with additional cognitive deficits; and they are more likely to require help with the everyday problems caused by the deficit rather than help with the impairment. However, understanding the deficit in detail (knowing *what* to treat) does not provide information on *how* to treat (see, e.g., Caramazza, 1989). We can conclude from this that theories of cognitive functioning are necessary but not sufficient in cognitive rehabilitation. Until we come up with a grand theory of rehabilitation encompassing cognition, emotion, behaviour, new learning, recovery and all the other factors of importance, no *one* theory is likely to be sufficient. This point is taken up by Sohlberg and Mateer (2001).

The situation is made more complex because some people claim to be following a theoretical approach with little evidence of actually doing so. Gianutsos (1991), for example, said that cognitive rehabilitation is the application of theories of cognitive sciences to traumatic brain injury (TBI) rehabilitation. Apart from the fact that it is not only people with TBI who receive cognitive rehabilitation, there is little evidence she used theories of cognitive neuroscience. Instead she favoured an approach requiring exercise and repeated practise, and clients are engaged for the most part in computerized exercises (Gianutsos, 1981, 1991; Gianutsos and Matheson, 1987; Gianutsos et al., 1985).

Similarly, Sohlberg and Mateer (1989) rightly state that cognitive rehabilitation should be grounded in theory, but Robertson (1991) suggests the authors do not follow their own advice. He concedes that many of the approaches make intuitive sense, but objects to them being called 'theoretical models'. Sohlberg and Mateer (2001) go a long way toward redressing this criticism.

Perhaps the area where theoretical models have been most influential is in the treatment of people with language and reading disorders (see, e.g., Best & Nickels, 2000; Coltheart, 1991; Mitchum & Berndt, 1995; Seron & Deloche, 1989). It was in aphasia therapy that these models first made their appearance. One study (Byng & Coltheart, 1986) describes the treatment of a man with an impairment in mapping meanings on to syntactical structure. This deficit was identified through careful assessment using a model of language. The treatment strategy involved the use of mnemonic cues with colour and spatial coding. The man improved. It could be argued, however, that although the model identified his deficit, it did not dictate (or even hint at) the fact that mnemonics and spatial or colour cues would help remediate the deficit. The treatment strategy would appear to be the result of previous experience, clinical intuition, ingenuity or a combination of these. The model could only determine the man's language strengths and weaknesses, not the method of treatment. Further support for this view comes from another paper published in the same year. Jones (1986) reported a patient with an identical deficit who also improved following treatment. This treatment, too, was said to be determined through use of a theoretical model of language. The treatment, however, was very different from that of Byng and Coltheart (1986). Jones (1986) used a technique of identifying sentence constituents (e.g., actor and verb). In both cases the model highlighted the deficit, but had little impact on the treatment design. Best and Nickels (2000) suggest that it is difficult to predict which therapeutic task or approach is likely to be successful in the remediation of aphasia, and particularly in the rehabilitation of anomia. In reading, for example, it is easier to predict which task or approach to use. Even if it is easier, there are still plenty of examples where theory tells us what is wrong rather than how to treat (Wilson & Patterson, 1990).

Although there is little doubt that theoretical models from cognitive neuro-psychology have been influential in helping us to understand and explain related phenomena and develop assessment procedures (Wilson & Patterson, 1990), the trap waiting for them is rehabilitation irrelevance (Robertson, 1991). Wilson (1997) also argues that other models are required to guide us through the intricate process of rehabilitation.

OTHER MODELS AND THEORETICAL APPROACHES RELEVANT TO COGNITIVE REHABILITATION

Models of assessment

Clinical neuropsychologists are heavily engaged in assessment (i.e., the systematic collection, organization and interpretation of information about a person and his or her situation—Sundberg & Tyler, 1962). Typically, several theoretical models or approaches are used in these assessments. These include (i) the psychometric approach based on statistical analysis, (ii) the localization approach whereby the examiner attempts to assess which parts of the brain are damaged and which are intact, (iii) assessments derived from theoretical models of cognitive functioning (as described above), (iv) definition of a syndrome through exclusion of other explana-tions and (v) ecologically valid assessments. See Wilson (2002a) for a more detailed discussion of these models.

Neuropsychological assessments, however, cannot provide all the information required for cognitive rehabilitation. Although tests enable us to build up a picture of the brain-injured person's strengths and weaknesses, they are unable to pinpoint in sufficient detail the nature of the everyday problems faced by the person and the family. We need to know (i) what problems are causing the greatest difficulty, (ii) what coping strategies are used, (iii) whether the problems are ex-acerbated by anxiety or depression, (iv) if this person can return to work and so forth.

Answers to such questions can be obtained from more functional or behavioural procedures including direct observation, self-report measures (in either natural or simulated settings) or through interviewing techniques. For further discussion of behavioural assessments and a comparison of standardized against functional tests, see Wilson (2002).

Behavioural Theories

Models from learning theory and behavioural psychology have been used in rehabilitation including cognitive rehabilitation for many years. Goodkin (1966) was one of the first to explicitly advocate behavioural techniques with brain-injured adults. Initially applied to motor problems, Goodkin (1969) later applied a behavioural method (operant conditioning) to help a stroke patient with dysphasia improve language skills. It was not until the 1980s, however, that behavioural techniques began, in earnest, to be applied to cognitive problems (Diller, 1980; Ince, 1980; Wilson, 1981a).

Today, behavioural approaches are widely used in rehabilitation to help reduce or compensate for cognitive deficits. Alderman and his colleagues, for example, showed ingenuity in applying strategies from behavioural psychology to patients with both executive problems and behaviour problems (Alderman, 1996; Alderman and Ward, 1991; Alderman et al., 1995).

Behaviour therapy and behaviour modification techniques have been adapted and modified to help people with memory, perceptual, language and reading disorders (Wilson, 1999). These techniques are incorporated into cognitive rehabilitation because they provide a structure, a way of analysing cognitive problems, a means of assessing everyday manifestations of cognitive problems and of evaluating the efficacy of treatment programmes. They also supply us with many strategies, such as shaping, chaining, modelling, desensitization, flooding, extinction, positive reinforcement, response cost and so forth, all of which can be adapted to suit particular rehabilitation purposes.

Critics of this approach (e.g., Prigatano, 1997) may base their criticism on a misunderstanding of the role of behavioural or learning theories in cognitive rehabilitation. Most psychologists in rehabilitation who incorporate principles from learning theory and behavioural psychology do not adhere to rigid behaviourism as advocated by Kazdin (1978) and Skinner (1953). Instead they tend to use such elements as task analysis or anxiety management techniques, modifying these strategies to make them appropriate for the brain-injured client's neurological and neuropsychological status. It is wrong to criticize their use in cognitive rehabilitation as though they were simply a mirror image of Skinner's extreme proposals. Second, behavioural techniques are not used in isolation, but are supplemented by theories, models and technologies from a number of other areas.

Theories of Recovery

Before engaging in cognitive rehabilitation we need to know whether or not our patients are likely to undergo further recovery. If so, then we need to try to determine whether any improvement seen in rehabilitation can be accounted for by the treatment itself or whether natural recovery is responsible or partly responsible (Wilson et al., 2000). Although natural recovery can sometimes be ruled out by ensuring there is a stable baseline prior to treatment (Wilson, 1987b), theories of recovery are helpful in understanding what may be happening to the people we are working with.

The process of recovery is not well understood and probably involves different biological processes (Ponsford, 1995). Changes seen in the first few minutes (e.g., after a mild head injury) presumably reflect the resolution of temporary dysfunction without accompanying structural damage. This is akin to Robertson and Murre's (1999) suggestion that plastic reorganization may occur because of a rapidly occurring alteration in synaptic activity taking place over seconds or minutes. Recovery after several days is more likely to be due to resolution of temporary structural abnormalities, such as oedema or vascular disruption (Jennett, 1990), or to the depression of metabolic enzyme activity (Whyte, 1990). Recovery after months or years is even less well understood. Finger and Stein (1982) suggest several ways this might be achieved including regeneration, diaschisis and plasticity.

According to Robertson and Murre, there are some individuals who show autonomous recovery, others who show very little recovery, even over a period of years, while others show reasonably good recovery provided they receive rehabilitation. They refer to this as a triage of spontaneous recovery, assisted recovery and no recovery. Robertson and Murre believe that the strategy of choice for people in the no recovery group is to teach compensatory approaches; the spontaneous recovery group do not need rehabilitation as they will get better anyway. Consequently, they focus on the assisted recovery group to address issues about brain plasticity. They also believe that the severity of the lesion maps onto this triage, with mild lesions resulting in spontaneous recovery, moderate lesions benefiting from assisted recovery and severe lesions necessitating the compensatory approach.

Although heuristically useful, this idea may be too simplistic. For example, people with mild lesions in the frontal lobes could be more disadvantaged in terms of recovery than people with severe lesions in the left anterior temporal lobe. The former group might have attention, planning and organization problems precluding them from gaining the maximum benefit from the rehabilitation on offer, whereas the latter group with language problems could show considerable plasticity by transferring some of the language functions to the right hemisphere.

Nevertheless, Robertson and Murre (1999) make some interesting arguments and present a model of self-repair in neural networks, based on a connectionist model of recovery of function.

Theories of Emotion

Prigatano (1995, 2000) believes that dealing with the emotional effects of brain injury is essential to rehabilitation success. Social isolation is common after TBI (Talbott, 1989; Wilson, 1991a), so, too, are mood disorders. Kopelman and Crawford (1996) found that 40% of 200 consecutive referrals to a memory clinic were suffering from clinical depression. Evans and Wilson (1992) found anxiety common in people attending a memory group. McKinlay et al. (1981) suggest that depression and anxiety may be expected in about two-thirds of people with TBI.

Gainotti (1993) distinguishes three main factors causing emotional and psychosocial problems after brain injury. First are neurological factors that provoke emotional or behavioural disturbances by disrupting specific neural mechanisms subserving the regulation and control of emotional and social behaviour. The limbic system and the frontal lobes are particularly implicated here. People with brainstem strokes, for example, may show emotionally labile behaviour ranging from tears to laughter in the space of a few moments. Frontal lobe damage may lead to loss of control with anger outbursts. Robinson and Starkstein (1989) suggested that left-hemisphere lesions encroaching on the frontal lobe and related subcortical structures may provoke a psychotic form of depression due to a disruption to the noradrenergic and serotonergic pathways.

Anosognosia, or lack of awareness of one's deficits, is also frequently due to organic impairment. Prigatano and Schacter (1991) provide several theoretical rationales for the existence of anosognosia. Gainotti (1993) also addresses unawareness in some detail. The condition can be due to organic or non-organic causes. The second of Gainotti's three-part classification of emotional and psychosocial disorders are those arising from psychological or psychodynamic factors. These include personal attitudes toward the disability arising from awareness of the disability and implications for the patient's quality of life.

Denial is one of the main mechanisms thought to explain the psychodynamics of the disorder. At some level, patients are aware of their disabilities, but are unable to accept them. Caplan (1987) provides an interesting and readable account of denial. As denial can occur in conditions without any damage to the brain, there must (at least in some cases) be non-organic reasons for its cause (Gainotti, 1993). Another problem for survivors of TBI is post-traumatic stress disorder (PTSD), now recognized as occurring in a substantial percentage of head-injured people (McMillan et al., 1996; Williams et al., 2002). Fear of what might happen in the future, grief at the loss of functioning, panic because one cannot remember where one is or where one should be going, reduced self-esteem because of changes in physical appearance and/or intellectual powers are all common reactions in people surviving damage to the brain.

The third category of emotional and psychosocial disorders include psychosocial factors or the functional effects of the impairment on the network of social relationships and social activities of the patient. This is particularly true of people with TBI. One aspect not covered by Gainotti, but almost certainly of influence in the development of problems, is premorbid personality (Moore & Stambrook, 1995; Williams et al., 1999).

Neurological, physiological and biochemical models, such as those by Robinson and Starkstein (1989), address the issue of why emotional problems may occur after an insult to the brain, but do not offer much help in understanding the psychodynamic and psychosocial causes of emotional and mood disorders. Perhaps the most helpful models here come from cognitive behaviour therapy.

Since Beck's influential book *Cognitive Therapy and Emotional Disorders* appeared in 1976, cognitive behaviour therapy has become one of the most important and best validated psychotherapeutic treatments (Salkovskis, 1996). One of its major strengths has been the development of clinically relevant theories. There are several theories not only for depression and anxiety but also for panic, obsessive–compulsive disorder and phobias (Salkovskis, 1996). Cognitive behaviour therapy is becoming increasingly employed in neurological/neuropsychological rehabilitation centres (Williams et al., 1999).

Analytic psychotherapy is also used in rehabilitation practice. Perhaps the best known proponent of this for the treatment of people surviving brain injury is Prigatano, and those interested in his methods are referred to Prigatano (1999).

The World Health Organization Models

Clinical neurological and neuropsychological rehabilitation has been influenced to a considerable degree over the past 20 years or so by the conceptual frameworks put forward by the World Health Organization (WHO, 1980, 1986). The 1980 framework classified the sequelae of brain injury into impairments, disabilities and handicaps. Impairments can be regarded as damage to physical or mental structures (e.g., hippocampal damage or damage to memory systems); disabilities refer to the particular problems caused by the impairment (e.g., forgetting to use a notebook or getting lost in one's neighbourhood); handicaps can be seen as problems imposed by society because of the disability (e.g., someone in a wheelchair is only handicapped if wheelchair access is unavailable).

To illustrate how this model can be applied to someone with frontal lobe damage, consider the following. A young woman sustained bilateral frontal lobe damage in a road traffic accident. Her physical impairments are the lesions in the frontal lobe; her mental impairments are difficulties with planning and organization and divided attention problems. These are identified on neuropsychological tests. Her disabilities (i.e., how the impairments manifest themselves in everyday life) are (i) she has problems getting started on an activity, (ii) she is easily distracted, (iii) she cannot cope with more than one task at a time and (iv) she perseverates on an incorrect solution. She is handicapped in situations where there is little structure, where the tasks are open-ended and where she has to 'think on her feet'. In a well-structured situation, with prompting to begin a task, where it is clear what constitutes success, where there is little distraction and she does not have to make choices, she is far less handicapped.

Many neuropsychologists are primarily concerned with the identification of impairments (i.e., deficits identified on the basis of neuropsychological tests). Some, however, together with most therapists working in rehabilitation, are more concerned with disabilities and handicaps. It goes without saying that most patients and their families are also more concerned with reducing the everyday problems rather than with poor test performance. The focus of rehabilitation should, for the most part, be on the reduction of these disabilities and handicaps rather than on the reduction of impairments. Given that many programmes still

$P =$ | Participation
Societal circumstances regarding function ... degree of involvement including society's response (may hinder or facilitate).

Our patient is able to participate if provided with adequate structure

$A =$ | Activities and limitations
Our patient's activities are limited because of problems initiating and completing tasks, distractibility, perseverating with incorrect solutions, etc.

$B =$ | Body function and systems
Our patient has frontal lobe damage, poor planning and organizational skills, divided attention deficits, etc.

Figure 16.1. International Classification of Impairments, Disabilities and Handicaps (ICIDH)-2 model

Source: From WHO (2001)

appear to be more concerned with improving test scores than reducing everyday problems (Carney et al., 1999), one can assume that this is done in the hope that by treating the impairments the disabilities will improve. There is no strong evidence that this actually happens. Robertson (1990) and Sloan and Ponsford (1995), for example, found contradictory evidence for attention training programmes. Programmes trying to improve impairments of attention did not, for the most part, lead to improvements in everyday attention (see Chapter 11 of this book). Glisky and Schacter (1986) and Kapur et al. (2002) found no evidence that attempts to improve memory impairments led to change in everyday memory problems.

The 1980 WHO model is now being replaced by another, somewhat similar framework. This classifies the problems resulting from injury or illness into those affecting (i) the body, (ii) activities and (iii) participation. Using our original example of the woman with bilateral lesions to the frontal lobe, the model would look as shown in Figure 16.1.

In practice, the same principles apply as to the 1980 framework (i.e., rehabilitation efforts are directed at reducing limitations and increasing activities and participation). Ways in which this might be achieved have already been discussed to some extent, particularly with regard to specific deficits. The next section considers some theoretical approaches that are more wide-ranging and cover aspects of rehabilitation that are more general.

MORE WIDE-RANGING THEORETICAL APPROACHES

Four models or theoretical frameworks are described that could apply to several rehabilitation problems: either different cognitive problems or cognitive, behavioural, social and emotional problems.

A Framework for Understanding Compensatory Behaviour

Compensation is one of the major tools for enabling people with brain injury to cope in everyday life. Wilson and Watson (1996) described a framework for understanding compensatory behaviour in people with organic memory impairment. Wilson (2000) subsequently used this framework to consider compensation for other cognitive deficits. The framework was developed from one proposed by Bäckman and Dixon (1992) and further modified by Dixon and Bäckman (1999). The framework distinguishes four steps in the evolution of compensatory behaviour: origins, mechanisms, forms and consequences.

Wilson and Watson (1996) considered how Bäckman and Dixon's framework might apply to people with memory impairments consequent upon brain injury. They found much of the framework useful but insufficient to account for all the successes and failures in learning to compensate demonstrated by people with organic memory impairment. For example, Bäckman and Dixon consider severity of impairment affects the extent to which compensation occurs and suggest compensatory behaviour follows a U-shaped curve whereby people with very mild or very severe deficits will not compensate, whereas those with moderate deficits will. They provide examples of normal elderly adults who compensate better than young adults who do not need to compensate and Alzheimer's disease patients who do not have the wherewithal to compensate. Wilson and Watson (1996) regarded this as only partially true and cite the example of severely amnesic people who can compensate despite very severe problems provided they have no or few additional cognitive deficits, particularly no marked executive ones.

Wilson (2000) discusses the use of this framework for understanding compensation in people with language, reading, visuoperceptual and visuospatial deficits. Also considered are factors that predict good use of compensations (Evans et al., in press; Wilson & Watson, 1996). The main predictors appear to be age (younger people compensate better), severity of impairment (very severely impaired people compensate less well), specificity of deficit (those with widespread cognitive impairments appear to compensate less well) and premorbid use of strategies (those using some compensatory aids premorbidly, appear to do better).

This is an area where further work is required. If we can predict, with a reasonable degree of accuracy, who is likely to compensate without too much trouble, we can perhaps target our energies in rehabilitation to help those who are less likely to compensate spontaneously.

Errorless Learning

As the name implies, errorless learning involves learning without errors. Instead of learning by trial and error, errorless learning involves presenting information or demonstrating a task in such a way that mistakes are avoided or significantly reduced. First described by Terrace (1963, 1966) in work with pigeons, it was soon adapted for use with people with developmental learning disabilities (Cullen, 1976; Sidman & Stoddard, 1967; Walsh & Lamberts, 1979). Still widely used for the teaching of cognitive and self-care skills in learning disability, it has only been widely used in cognitive rehabilitation for a few years (but see Wilson, 1981a). This came about because of a second theoretical impetus, namely research into implicit learning (or learning without conscious recollection), from cognitive neuropsychology. In 1994 Baddeley and Wilson considered why certain anomalies occurred in implicit learning. For example, although amnesic patients show learning on fragmented pictures (a perceptual priming task), they sometimes repeat their mistakes. Thus if a fragmented aeroplane is mislabelled in an early trial as a cigar, this error may recur in each subsequent trial. Baddeley and Wilson (1994) believed that (a) implicit memory is poorly equipped for error elimination, yet amnesic patients have to rely on implicit memory given their extremely poor explicit memory skills, and (b) that in trial-and-error learning, incorrect responses were being strengthened or reinforced. In the absence of a memory to benefit from one's mistakes, we needed to strengthen correct rather than incorrect responses. We asked whether amnesic patients learn better if prevented from making mistakes during the learning process? Results from the first experiment (Baddeley and Wilson, 1994) led to an unqualified 'yes' as the answer. All 16 densely amnesic people showed greater learning under an errorless than an errorful condition.

The next step was to see if the principle could be applied to real-life tasks. Wilson et al. (1994) applied errorless learning to real-life problems. They taught (i) a man with amnesia and agnosia to recognize certain objects, (ii) a man with Korsakoff's syndrome to enter a message into an electronic organizer, (iii) names of people to a man with a stroke and (iv) orientation items to a man in post-traumatic amnesia. In each case errorless was compared with errorful learning and found to result in superior learning. Since then, others have used errorless learning to teach people with non-progressive brain damage to use a notebook (Squires et al., 1996), to use a computer (Glisky, 1995) and learn names (Evans et al., 2000). Errorless learning has also been used to help people with Alzheimer's disease relearn names of friends, to use a memory board and other everyday skills (Clare et al., 1999, 2000, 2001).

Baddeley and Wilson (1994) believed that errorless learning was effective because it capitalized on the intact implicit memory skills of amnesic patients. Squires et al. (1997) argued that it capitalized on the residual explicit memory of amnesic patients. Recent work, however, suggests that it may work through both these mechanisms (Page et al., 2001). Thus very severely memory-impaired people with virtually no explicit memory have to rely on implicit memory, whereas those with some, albeit limited, explicit/episodic memory may find that errorless learning benefits both systems.

Errorless learning appears to be superior to trial-and-error learning for people with severe memory deficits. Although used in learning disability to teach a wide range of cognitive and self-care tasks, it is not yet clear whether errorless learning is superior to trial-and-error learning for cognitive problems other than memory. Nor is it clear whether it is the method of choice for motor or other non-cognitive problems. Potentially, this is a powerful treatment method, but further work remains to be carried out.

The SORKC Model (Kanfer & Saslow, 1969)

This well-established model from behavioural psychology is still of value in cognitive rehabilitation because it allows us to incorporate the physical and neurological status of the individual patient along with motivation, emotion and behaviour. SORKC stands for stimulus, organism, response, contingency and consequence.

According to Ciminero (1986), *stimulus* refers to antecedent events or discriminative stimuli that trigger problem behaviour (these events or stimuli can be physical, social or internal). *Organism* refers to a person's biological condition and to individual differences resulting from previous experiences. *Response* refers to the behaviours that are of concern (these can be motor, cognitive or physiological behaviours). *Contingency* refers to schedules of reinforcement in operation. *Consequence* refers to events that follow behaviour (these can be physical, social or self-generated). Wilson (1991b) uses this model to describe the problems and treatment of Jim, a 26-year-old man, who had sustained a severe head injury in a motorcycle accident some five months earlier and who had been in a coma for three weeks. Table 16.1 shows how the SORKC model was used to describe Jim's situation.

The Holistic Model

Ben-Yishay and Prigatano (1990) provide a model of hierarchical stages in the holistic approach through which the patient must work in rehabilitation. These are, in order, engagement, awareness, mastery, control, acceptance and identity. Perhaps the main philosophy of the holistic approach is that it is futile to separate the cognitive, social, emotional and functional aspects of brain injury, given that

Table 16.1. Kanfer and Saslow's (1969) SORKC model as applied to Jim

Copyright © 1991 by the Educational Publishing Foundation, reprinted with permission (from Wilson, 1991b)

Category	Description
Stimulus	Request by occupational therapist for Jim to do some typing; presence of typewriter
Organism	Cognitive impairments resulting from head injury; poor visuospatial and visuoconstruction skill
Response	Leaves seat, swears, throws paper on floor
Contingency	Partial reinforcement: sometimes allowed to leave task, sometimes given attention
Consequence	Escape from task, attention received from occupational therapist and other patients

how we feel affects how we behave and how we think. Holistic programmes, explicitly or implicitly, tend to work through Ben-Yishay and Prigatano's hierarchical stages and are concerned with (i) increasing the individual's awareness of what has happened to him or to her, (ii) increasing acceptance and understanding of what has happened, (iii) providing strategies or exercises to reduce cognitive problems, (iv) develop compensatory skills and (v) provide vocational counselling. All holistic programmes include both group and individual therapy. It can be argued that, like the 'model' of Sohlberg and Mateer (1989) described earlier, the holistic approach is less of a model and more of a series of beliefs, or, as Prigatano (1999) puts it, a series of 'principles'. Nevertheless, the holistic model makes clinical sense and, despite its apparent expense, in the long term it is probably cost-effective (Cope et al., 1991; Mehlbye & Larsen, 1994; Wilson, 1997; Wilson & Evans, 2002).

Despite these positive aspects, it is probably true to say that holistic programmes can be improved. This could be done by incorporating some aspects from learning theory, cognitive psychology and other models referred to above. Through combining a number of different theoretical approaches relevant to cognitive rehabilitation, it might be possible to develop a theoretical model of cognitive rehabilitation that covers all relevant aspects.

TOWARDS AN ALL-ENCOMPASSING THEORY OF COGNITIVE REHABILITATION

In 2002, Wilson published a tentative comprehensive model of cognitive rehabilitation (Wilson, 2002b). This model is reproduced here in Figure 16.2. Figure 16.2 is an attempt to put together many (although not all) of the aspects to take into consideration when undertaking cognitive rehabilitation. The starting point is the person with the cognitive impairments and his or her family. The premorbid personality and lifestyle of the brain-injured person (and other family members) is going to impact on the needs and desires of these people and thus on the rehabilitation

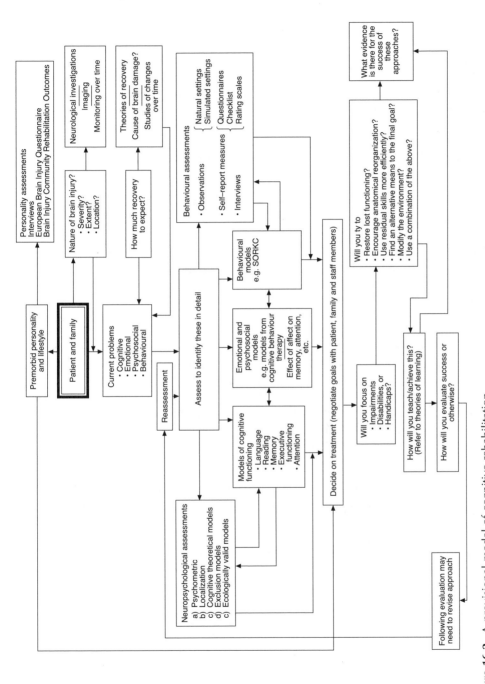

Figure 16.2. A provisional model of cognitive rehabilitation

Reproduced by permission of Psychology Press, Hove, UK (from Wilson, 2002b)

offered. Consequently, it is desirable to carry out an assessment of premorbid personality either through interview or through the administration of one of the measures comparing pre- and post-morbid characteristics. The Brain Injury Community Rehabilitation Outcomes (BICRO; Powell et al., 1998) and the European Brain Injury Questionnaire (EBIQ; Teasdale et al., 1997) both attempt to identify pre- and post-morbid characteristics.

The nature, extent and severity of the brain damage will need to be determined. Much of this information may be obtained from hospital notes and/or the referral forms. Neurological investigations and results from imaging studies may be available and neuropsychological investigations may also add to the picture. It is helpful if people are monitored over time, particularly if a deteriorating condition is suspected. Remember, though, that repeated neuropsychological assessment may not provide reliable information. Improvement in scores may simply reflect a practice effect, whereas no change in scores may mask a deterioration, again because of a practice effect (Wilson et al., 2000).

Further recovery may need to be considered, especially if the person with brain injury is seen in the early days, weeks or months after an insult. Theories of recovery are relevant here. The cause of the brain damage is also relevant. People with TBI, for example, may show recovery for a longer time than, say, someone with encephalitis (Wilson, 1998).

One of the most important tasks in rehabilitation is the identification of current problems. There are several theoretical frameworks one can draw on when determining how to assess these problems. The important point here is that information from standardized tests to help us build up a profile of strengths and weaknesses needs to be complemented by information from functional or behavioural assessments to build up a picture of how the problems affect everyday life.

Cognitive, emotional, psychosocial and behavioural problems will probably need to be evaluated more thoroughly through reference to a more detailed model. Models of language, reading, memory, executive functioning, attention and perception are all available to provide detail about cognitive strengths and deficits. Models from cognitive behaviour therapy, such as the one by Beck (1976, 1996) mentioned earlier, will help explain the emotional and psychosocial problems, while a behavioural model such as the SORKC model (Kanfer & Saslow, 1969) will enable better conceptualization of disruptive or inappropriate behaviours. While this is not an exhaustive list of the type of problems faced by survivors of brain injury, other problems, such as motor or sensory deficits, are more likely to be treated by physiotherapists or other staff. Neuropsychologists, of course, can work together with these others most fruitfully and may need to incorporate models of motor and sensory functioning too.

Having identified the problems, it will be time to decide on rehabilitation strategies. This may well involve the negotiation of suitable goals. Given that one of the main goals of rehabilitation is to enable people to return to their own most appropriate environment, the person with brain injury, family members and rehabilitation staff should all be involved in the negotiating process. Consider whether the main goals are to improve impairments, disabilities or handicaps. Although there may be times or stages in the recovery process where it is appropriate to focus on impairments, the majority of goals for those engaged in cognitive rehabilitation will address disabilities and handicaps.

There is obviously more than one way to try to achieve any goal. Is the method of choice to restore lost functioning, to encourage anatomical reorganization, to help people use their residual skills more efficiently, to find an alternative means to the final goal (functional adaptation), to use environmental modifications to bypass problems or to use a combination of these methods? Whichever method is selected, one should be aware of theories of learning. In Baddeley's words, 'A theory of rehabilitation without a model of learning is a vehicle without an engine' (Baddeley, 1993, p. 235). Evidence for the success of these approaches also needs to be taken into account. The final question is how best to evaluate success or otherwise. Consider Whyte's (1997) view that outcome should be congruent with the level of intervention. If intervening at the impairment level, then outcome measures should be measures of impairment and so forth. As most rehabilitation is concerned with the reduction of disabilities and handicaps, outcome measures should reflect changes in disability and handicap. For example, how well does someone who forgets appointments now remember appointments? There are studies that directly assess such changes. For example, a recent study evaluating the use of a paging system for reducing everyday memory and planning problems (Wilson et al., 2001) measured success in achieving everyday targets before, during and after the provision of a pager. This study demonstrated convincingly that pagers can reduce the everyday problems of people with memory and planning problems following brain injury. The final message of this chapter is that it is possible to marry theory, scientific methodology and clinical relevance.

REFERENCES

Alderman, N. (1996) Central executive deficit and response to operant conditioning methods. *Neuropsychological Rehabilitation*, **6**, 161–186.

Alderman, N. & Ward, A. (1991) Behavioural treatment of the dysexecutive syndrome: Reduction of repetitive speech using response cost and cognitive overlearning. *Neuropsychological Rehabilitation*, **1**, 65–80.

Alderman, N., Fry, R. K. & Youngson, H. A. (1995) Improvement of self-monitoring skills, reduction of behaviour disturbance and the dysexecutive syndrome: Comparison of response cost and a new programme of self-monitoring training. *Neuropsychological Rehabilitation*, **5**, 193–221.

Bäckman, L. & Dixon, R. A. (1992) Psychological compensation: A theoretical framework. *Psychological Bulletin*, **112**, 259–283.

Baddeley, A. D. (1993) A theory of rehabilitation without a model of learning is a vehicle without an engine: A comment on Caramazza and Hillis. *Neuropsychological Rehabilitation*, **3**, 235–244.

Baddeley, A. D. & Hitch, G. (1974) Working memory. In: G. H. Bower (ed.) *The Psychology of Learning and Motivation* (Vol. 8, pp. 47–89). Academic Press, New York.

Baddeley, A. D. & Wilson, B. A. (1994) When implicit learning fails: Amnesia and the problem of error elimination. *Neuropsychologia*, **32**, 53–68.

Beck, A. (1976) *Cognitive Therapy and Emotional Disorders*. International Universities Press, New York.

Beck, A. (1996) Beyond belief: A theory of modes, personality, and psychopathology. In: P. M. Salkovskis (ed.) *Frontiers of Cognitive Therapy* (pp. 1–25). Guilford Press, New York.

Ben-Yishay, Y. & Prigatano, G. P. (1990) Cognitive remediation. In: M. Rosenthal, E. R. Griffith, M. R. Bond & J. D. Miller (eds) *Rehabilitation of the Adult and Child with Traumatic Brain Injury* (2nd edn, pp. 393–409). F. A. Davis, Philadelphia.

Best, W. & Nickels, L. (2000) From theory to therapy in aphasia: Where are we now and where to next? *Neuropsychological Rehabilitation*, **10**, 231–247.

Boyle, M. E. & Greer, R. D. (1983) Operant procedures and the comatose patient. *Journal of Applied Behavior Analysis*, **16**, 3–12.

Byng, S. & Coltheart, M. (1986) Aphasia therapy research: Methodological requirements and illustrative results. In: E. Hjelmquist & L. N. Lilsson (eds) *Communication and Handicap* (pp. 383–398). Lawrence Erlbaum, Hillsdale, NJ.

Caplan, B. (1987) *Rehabilitation Desk Reference*. Aspen, Rockville, MD.

Caramazza, A. (1989) Cognitive neuropsychology and rehabilitation: An unfulfilled promise? In: X. Seron & G. Deloche (eds) *Cognitive Approaches in Neuropsychological Rehabilitation* (pp. 383–398). Lawrence Erlbaum, Hillsdale, NJ.

Caramazza, A. & Hillis, A. E. (1993) For a theory of remediation of cognitive deficits. *Neuropsychological Rehabilitation*, **3**, 217–234.

Carney, N., Chesnut, R. M., Maynard, H., Mann, N. C., Patterson, P. & Helfand, M. (1999) Effects of cognitive rehabilitation on outcomes for persons with traumatic brain injury: A systematic review. *Journal of Head Trauma Rehabilitation*, **14**, 277–307.

Ciminero, A. R. (1986) *Handbook of Behavioral Assessment* (2nd edn). John Wiley & Sons, New York.

Clare, L., Wilson, B. A., Breen, E. K. & Hodges, J. R. (1999) Errorless learning of face–name associations in early Alzheimer's disease. *Neurocase*, **5**, 37–46.

Clare, L., Wilson, B. A., Carter, G., Breen, E. K., Gosses, A. & Hodges, J. R. (2000) Intervening with everyday memory problems in dementia of Alzheimer type: An errorless learning approach. *Journal of Clinical and Experimental Neuropsychology*, **22**, 132–146.

Clare, L., Wilson, B. A., Carter, G., Hodges, J. R. & Adams, M. (2001) Long-term maintenance of treatment gains following a cognitive rehabilitation intervention in early dementia of Alzheimer type: A single case study. *Neuropsychological Rehabilitation*, **11**, 477–494.

Coltheart, M. (1991) Cognitive psychology applied to the treatment of acquired language disorders. In: P. Martin (ed.) *Handbook of Behavior Therapy and Psychological Science: An Integrative Approach* (pp. 216–226). Pergamon Press, New York.

Cope, D. N., Cole, J. R., Hall, K. M. & Barkan, H. (1991) Brain injury: Analysis of outcome in a post-acute rehabilitation system. *Brain Injury*, **5**, 111–139.

Cullen, C. N. (1976) Errorless learning with the retarded. *Nursing Times*, 25 March, 45–47.

Diller, L. (1980) The development of a perceptual remediation program in hemiplegia. In: L. P. Ince (ed.) *Behavior Psychology in Rehabilitation Medicine* (pp. 64–86). Williams & Wilkins, Baltimore.

Diller, L. (1987) Neuropsychological rehabilitation. In: M. J. Meier, A. L. Benton & L. Diller (eds) *Neuropsychological Rehabilitation* (pp. 3–17). Churchill Livingstone, Edinburgh.

Dixon, R. A. & Bäckman, L. (1999) Principles of compensation in cognitive neurorehabilitation. In: D. T. Stuss, G. Winocur & I. H. Robertson (eds) *Cognitive Neurorehabilitation: A Comprehensive Approach* (pp. 59–72). Cambridge University Press, New York.

Durand, V. M. (1982) A behavioral/pharmacological intervention for the treatment of severe self-injurious behavior. *Journal of Autism and Developmental Disorders*, **12**, 243–251.

Evans, J. J. & Wilson, B. A. (1992) A memory group for individuals with brain injury. *Clinical Rehabilitation*, **6**, 75–81.

Evans, J. J., Wilson, B. A., Schuri, U., Andrade, J., Baddeley, A., Bruna, O. et al. (2000) A comparison of 'errorless' and 'trial-and-error' learning methods for teaching individuals with acquired memory deficits. *Neuropsychological Rehabilitation*, **10**, 67–101.

Evans, J. J., Wilson, B. A., Needham, P. & Brentnall, S. (in press) Who makes good use of memory-aids: Results of a survey of 100 people with acquired brain injury. *Journal of the International Neuropsychological Society*.

Finger, S. & Stein, D. G. (1982) *Brain Damage and Recovery: Research and Clinical Perspectives.* Academic Press, New York.

Gainotti, G. (1993) Emotional and psychosocial problems after brain injury. *Neuropsychological Rehabilitation*, **3**, 259–277.

Gianutsos, R. (1981) Training the short- and long-term verbal recall of a post-encephalitis amnesic. *Journal of Clinical Neuropsychology*, **3**, 143–153.

Gianutsos, R. (1991) Cognitive rehabilitation: A neuropsychological specialty comes of age. *Brain Injury*, **5**, 363–368.

Gianutsos, R. & Matheson, P. (1987) The rehabilitation of visual perceptual disorders attributable to brain injury. In: M. Meier, A. Benton & L. Diller (eds) *Neuropsychological Rehabilitation* (pp. 202–241). Churchill Livingstone, London.

Gianutsos, R., Cochran, E. E. & Blouin, M. (1985) *Computer Programs for Cognitive Rehabilitation. Vol. 3: Therapeutic Memory Exercises for Independent Use.* Life Science, Bayport, NY.

Glisky, E. L. (1995) Acquisition and transfer of word processing skill by an amnesic patient. *Neuropsychological Rehabilitation*, **5**, 299–318.

Glisky, E. L. & Schacter, D. L. (1986) Long-term retention of computer learning by patients with memory disorders. *Neuropsychologia*, **26**, 173–178.

Goodkin, R. (1966) Case studies in behavioral research in rehabilitation. *Perceptual and Motor Skills*, **23**, 171–182.

Goodkin, R. (1969) Changes in word production, sentence production and relevance in an aphasic through verbal conditioning. *Behaviour Research and Therapy*, **7**, 93–99.

Gross, Y. & Schutz, L. E. (1986) Intervention models in neuropsychology. In: B. P. Uzzell and Y. Gross (eds) *Clinical Neuropsychology of Intervention* (pp. 179–205). Martinus Nijhoff, Boston.

Ince, L. P. (1980) *Behavior Psychology in Rehabilitation Medicine.* Williams & Wilkins, Baltimore.

Jennett, B. (1990) Scale and scope of the problems. In: M. Rosenthal, E. R. Griffith, M. R. Bond and J. D. Miller (eds) *Rehabilitation of the Adult and Child with Traumatic Brain Injury* (pp. 3–7). F. A. Davis, Philadelphia.

Jones, E. V. (1986) Building the foundations for sentence production in a non-fluent aphasic. *British Journal of Disorders of Communication*, **21**, 63–82.

Kanfer, F. H. & Saslow, G. (1969) Behavioral diagnosis. In: C. Franks (ed.) *Behavior Therapy: Appraisal and Status* (pp. 417–444). McGraw-Hill, New York.

Kapur, N., Glisky, E. L. & Wilson, B. A. (2002) External memory aids and computers in memory rehabilitation. In: A. D. Baddeley, M. D. Kopelman & B. A. Wilson (eds) *Handbook of Memory Disorders* (2nd edn, pp. 757–784). John Wiley & Sons, Chichester, UK.

Kazdin, A. E. (1978) *History of Behavior Modification: Experimental Foundations of Contemporary Research.* University Park Press, Baltimore.

Kopelman, M. & Crawford, S. (1996) Not all memory clinics are dementia clinics. *Neuropsychological Rehabilitation*, **6**, 187–202.

McKinlay, W. W., Brooks, D. N., Bond, M. R., Martinage, D. P. & Marshall, M. M. (1981) The short-term outcome of severe blunt head injury as reported by relatives of the injured persons. *Journal of Neurology, Neurosurgery and Psychiatry*, **44**, 527–533.

McMillan, T. M. & Greenwood, R. J. (1993) Models of rehabilitation programmes for the brain-injured adult. II: Model services and suggestions for change in the UK. *Clinical Rehabilitation*, **7**, 346–355.

McMillan, T. M., Jongen, E. L. & Greenwood, R. J. (1996) Assessment of post-traumatic amnesia after severe closed head injury: Retrospective or prospective? *Journal of Neurology, Neurosurgery and Psychiatry*, **60**, 422–427.

Mehlbye, J. & Larsen, A. (1994) Social and economic consequences of brain damage in Denmark. In: A.-L. Christensen & B. P. Uzzell (eds) *Brain Injury and Neuropsychological Rehabilitation: International Perspectives* (pp. 257–267). Lawrence Erlbaum, Hillside, NJ.

Mitchum, C. C. & Berndt, R. S. (1995) The cognitive neuropsychological approach to treatment of language disorders. *Neuropsychological Rehabilitation*, **5**, 1–16.

Moore, A. D. & Stambrook, M. (1995) Cognitive moderators of outcome following traumatic brain injury: A conceptual model and implications for rehabilitation. *Brain Injury*, **9**, 109–130.

Page, M., Wilson, B. A., Norris, D., Shiel, A. & Carter, G. (2001) Familiarity and recollection in errorless learning. *Journal of the International Neuropsychological Society*, **7**, 413.

Ponsford, J. (1995) Mechanisms, recovery and sequelae of traumatic brain injury: A foundation for the REAL approach. In: J. Ponsford, S. Sloan & P. Snow (eds) *Traumatic Brain Injury: Rehabilitation for Everyday Adaptive Living* (pp. 1–31). Lawrence Erlbaum, Hove, UK.

Powell, G. E. (1981) *Brain Function Therapy*. Gower Press, Aldershot, UK.

Powell, J. H., Beckers, K. & Greenwood, R. (1998) The measurement of progress and outcome in community rehabilitation after brain injury: Towards improved outcome. *Archives of Physical Medicine and Rehabilitation*, **79**, 1213–1225.

Prigatano, G. P. (1995) Personality and social aspects of memory rehabilitation. In: A. D. Baddeley, B. A. Wilson & F. N. Watts (eds) *Handbook of Memory Disorders* (pp. 603–614). John Wiley & Sons, Chichester, UK.

Prigatano, G. P. (1997) Learning from our successes and failures: Reflections and comments on 'Cognitive rehabilitation: How it is and how it might be'. *Journal of the International Neuropsychological Society*, **3**, 497–499.

Prigatano, G. P. (1999) *Principles of Neuropsychological Rehabilitation*. Oxford University Press, New York.

Prigatano, G. P. (2000) Rehabilitation for traumatic brain injury. *The Journal of the American Medical Association*, **284**, 1783.

Prigatano, G. P. & Schacter, D. L. (1991) *Awareness of Deficit after Brain Injury*. Oxford University Press, New York.

Robertson, I. H. (1990) Digit span and unilateral neglect: A puzzling relationship. *Neuropsychologia*, **28**, 217–222.

Robertson, I. H. (1991) Book review. *Neuropsychological Rehabilitation*, **1**, 87–90.

Robertson, I. H. & Murre, J. M. J. (1999) Rehabilitation of brain damage: Brain plasticity and principles of guided recovery. *Psychological Bulletin*, **125**, 544–575.

Robinson, R. G. & Starkstein, S. E. (1989) Mood disorders following stroke: New findings and future directions. *Journal of Geriatric Psychiatry*, **22**, 1–15.

Salkovskis, P. M. (ed.) (1996) *Frontiers of Cognitive Therapy*. Guilford Press, New York.

Seron, X. & Deloche, G. (eds) (1989) *Cognitive Approaches in Neuropsychological Rehabilitation*. Lawrence Erlbaum, Hillsdale, NJ.

Shiel, A., Wilson, B. A., Horn, S., Watson, M. & McLellan, L. (1993) Can patients in coma following traumatic head injury learn simple tasks? *Neuropsychological Rehabilitation*, **3**, 161–175.

Sidman, M. & Stoddard, L. T. (1967) The effectiveness of fading in programming simultaneous form discrimination for retarded children. *Journal of Experimental Analysis of Behavior*, **10**, 3–15.

Skinner, B. F. (1953) *Science and Human Behavior*. Free Press, New York.

Sloan, S. & Ponsford, J. (1995) Managing cognitive problems. In: J. Ponsford, S. Sloan & P. Snow (eds) *Traumatic Brain Injury: Rehabilitation for Everyday Adaptive Living*. Lawrence Erlbaum, Hove, UK.

Sohlberg, M., & Mateer, C. (1989) *An Introduction to Cognitive Rehabilitation: Theory and Practice*. Guilford Press, New York.

Sohlberg, M. M. & Mateer, C. A. (2001) *Cognitive Rehabilitation: An Integrative Neuropsychological Approach*. Guilford Press, New York.

Squires, E. J., Hunkin, N. M. & Parkin, A. J. (1996) Memory notebook training in a case of severe amnesia: Generalising from paired associate learning to real life. *Neuropsychological Rehabilitation*, **6**, 55–65.

Squires, E. J., Hunkin, N. M. & Parkin, A. J. (1997) Errorless learning of novel associations in amnesia. *Neuropsychologia*, **35**, 1103–1111.

Sundberg, N. S. & Tyler, L. E. (1962) *Clinical Psychology*. Appleton-Century-Crofts, New York.

Talbott, R. (1989) The brain injured person and the family. In: R. L. Wood & P. Eames (eds) *Models of Brain Injury Rehabilitation* (pp. 3–16). Chapman & Hall, London.

Teasdale, T. W., Christensen, A.-L., Wilmes, K., Deloche, G., Braga, L., Stachowiak, F. et al. (1997) Subjective experience in brain-injured patients and their close relatives: A European Brain Injury Questionnaire study. *Brain Injury*, **11**, 543–563.

Terrace, H. S. (1963) Discrimination learning with and without 'errors'. *Journal of Experimental Analysis of Behavior*, **6**, 1–27.

Terrace, H. S. (1966) Stimulus control. In: W. K. Honig (ed.) *Operant Behavior: Areas of Research and Application* (pp. 271–344). Appleton-Century-Crofts, New York.

Walsh, B. F. & Lamberts, F. (1979) Errorless discrimination and fading as techniques for teaching sight words to TMR students. *American Journal of Mental Deficiency*, **83**, 473–479.

Whyte, J. (1990) Mechanisms of recovery of function following CNS damage. In: M. Rosenthal, E. R. Griffith, M. R. Bond & J. D. Miller (eds) *Rehabilitation of the Adult and Child with TBI* (2nd edn). F. A. Davis, Philadelphia.

Whyte, J. (1997) Distinctive methodologic challenges. In: M. J. Fuhrer (ed.) *Assessing Medical Rehabilitation Practices: The Promise of Outcomes Research*. Paul H. Brookes, Baltimore.

Williams, W. H., Evans, J. J. & Wilson, B. A. (1999) Outcome measures for survivors of acquired brain injury in day and outpatient neurorehabilitation programmes. *Neuropsychological Rehabilitation*, **9**, 421–436.

Williams, W. H., Evans, J. J., Wilson, B. A. & Needham, P. (2002) Prevalence of Post-traumatic Stress Disorder symptoms after severe traumatic brain injury in a representative community sample. *Brain Injury*, **16**, 673–679.

Wilson, B. A. (1981a) A survey of behavioural treatments carried out at a rehabilitation centre. In: G. Powell (ed.) *Brain Function Therapy* (pp. 256–275). Gower Press, Aldershot, UK.

Wilson, B. A. (1981b) Teaching a patient to remember names after removal of a left temporal lobe tumour. *Behavioural Psychotherapy*, **9**, 338–344.

Wilson, B. A. (1987a) *Rehabilitation of Memory*. Guilford Press, New York.

Wilson, B. A. (1987b) Single-case experimental designs in neuropsychological rehabilitation. *Journal of Clinical and Experimental Neuropsychology*, **9**, 527–544.

Wilson, B. A. (1991a) Long term prognosis of patients with severe memory disorders. *Neuropsychological Rehabilitation*, **1**, 117–134.

Wilson, B. A. (1991b) Theory, assessment and treatment in neuropsychological rehabilitation. *Neuropsychology*, **5**, 281–291.

Wilson, B. A. (1997) Cognitive rehabilitation: How it is and how it might be. *Journal of the International Neuropsychological Society*, **3**, 487–496.

Wilson, B. A. (1998) Recovery of cognitive functions following non-progressive brain injury. *Current Opinion in Neurobiology*, **8**, 281–287.

Wilson, B. A. (1999) *Case Studies in Neuropsychological Rehabilitation*. Oxford University Press, New York.

Wilson, B. A. (2000) Compensating for cognitive deficits following brain injury. *Neuropsychology Review*, **10**, 233–243.

Wilson, B. A. (2002a) Assessment of memory disorders. In: A. D. Baddeley, M. D. Kopelman & B. A. Wilson (eds) *Handbook of Memory Disorders* (2nd edn, pp. 617–636). John Wiley & Sons, Chichester, UK.

Wilson, B. A. (2002b) Towards a comprehensive model of cognitive rehabilitation. *Neuropsychological Rehabilitation*, **12**, 97–110.

Wilson, B. A., and Evans, J. (in press) Does cognitive rehabilitation work? Clinical and economic considerations and outcomes. In: G. Prigatano (ed.) *Clinical Neuropsychology and Cost-outcome Research: An Introduction*. Psychology Press, Hove, UK.

Wilson, B. A. & Patterson, K. E. (1990) Rehabilitation and cognitive neuropsychology: Does cognitive psychology apply? *Journal of Applied Cognitive Psychology*, **4**, 247–260.

Wilson, B. A. & Watson, P. C. (1996) A practical framework for understanding compensatory behaviour in people with organic memory impairment. *Memory*, **4**, 465–486.

Wilson, B. A., Watson, P. C., Baddeley, A. D., Emslie, H. & Evans, J. J. (2000) Improvement or simply practice? The effects of twenty repeated assessments on people with and without brain injury. *Journal of the International Neuropsychological Society*, **6**, 469–479.

Wilson, B. A., Baddeley, A. D., Evans, J. J. & Shiel, A. (1994) Errorless learning in the rehabilitation of memory impaired people. *Neuropsychological Rehabilitation*, **4**, 307–326.

Wilson, B. A., Emslie, H. C., Quirk, K. & Evans, J. J. (2001) Reducing everyday memory and planning problems by means of a paging system: A randomised control crossover study. *Journal of Neurology, Neurosurgery and Psychiatry*, **70**, 477–482.

WHO (1980) *International Classification of Impairments, Disabilities and Handicaps: A Manual of Classification Relating to the Consequences of Disease*. World Health Organization, Geneva.

WHO (1986) *Optimum Care of Disabled People* (Report of a WHO Meeting held in Turku, Finland). World Health Organization, Geneva.

Zarkowska, E. (1987) Discrimination and generalisation. In: W. Yule & J. Carr (eds) *Behaviour Modification for People with Mental Handicaps* (pp. 79–94). Croom Helm, London.

CHAPTER 17

Planning, Delivering and Evaluating Services

Camilla Herbert

Brain Injury Rehabilitation Trust, West Sussex, UK

This chapter will consider the issues relevant to planning and delivering comprehensive services for rehabilitation and long-term care for people with brain injuries. The main focus of the chapter will be acquired brain injury services, but the issues raised are relevant to the broader range of neurological conditions requiring ongoing rehabilitation and support.

INFORMATION TO ASSIST IN PLANNING SERVICES

Epidemiology

The difficulty of obtaining clear and generalizable figures on the incidence and prevalence of brain injuries and other neurodisabilities is well documented. There are few standard methods for the collection of information, and few measures of outcome that cover the broad range of disabilities and handicaps that can arise. Early work by Field (1976) and by Jennett and MacMillan (1981) provide widely quoted figures. Other useful sources include the Medical Disability Society (1988) report, a chapter by Bryden (1988) based on data collected in the Scottish Head Injury Management Study and Johnson and Gleave's (1987) paper based on admissions to Addenbrooke's Hospital in Cambridge.

Figures on levels of disablement are even harder to find. Greenwood and McMillan (1993) estimate the prevalence of significant disablement following brain injury as between 100 and 150 per 100,000 of the population. The Department of Health website's (www.doh.gov.uk) briefing paper on National Service Frameworks states that head injury accounts for 10% of all Accident and Emergency attendances and hospital admission occurs for 300/100,000 population. While most head injuries are minor, 4/100,000 population has handicap or disability six months after a head injury and 0.37/100,000 of the population require long-stay care due to traumatic brain injury. Thornhill et al. (2000) reported high rates of moderate or severe disability at one year post injury in a study of mild,

Clinical Neuropsychology: A Practical Guide to Assessment and Management for Clinicians.
Edited by L.H. Goldstein and J.E. McNeil. © 2004 John Wiley & Sons, Ltd.

moderate and severe head injuries (disability rates of 47%, 45% and 48%, respectively) in Glasgow. This study used self-report measures of disability that may have affected the high rates of symptoms identified. The Glasgow population studied also includes higher rates of alcohol-related incidents and of assaults than have been identified in other similar studies.

Epidemiological data are also difficult to obtain for other conditions. Langton Hewer (1993) gives an overview of the epidemiology of disabling neurological conditions. Annual incidence of stroke is approximately 195/100,000 for a first stroke and 220/100,000 per year for all strokes, representing 550 per health district of 250,000 per year (Oxford Community Stroke Project, 1983). Greenwood and McMillan (1993) report residual neurological signs in about 60% of stroke survivors, but the proportion under 65 with significant disability is unclear. Limited information is available concerning the persisting disablement that occurs after other conditions including subarachnoid haemorrhage, arteriovenous malformations, benign cerebral tumours, encephalitis, anoxic–ischaemic insults, hypoglycaemic damage and carbon monoxide poisoning, but this may be of the order of 4–16 per 100,000. Rates for other disabilities/diagnostic groups are similarly poorly reported. In its briefing paper for the development of National Service Frameworks, the Department of Health website gives incidence and prevalence rates for epilepsy of 50–70/100,000 per year and 500–1,000/100,000, for motor neurone disease of 2/100,000 and 7/100,000, for multiple sclerosis of 4/100,000 and 100/100,000 and for Parkinson's disease the incidence is 1/1,000 in the general population, rising to 1/100 over the age of 65 and 1/50 over the age of 80.

Reports and Recommendations concerning Service Provision

In the UK, as in the USA, there has been an enormous increase during the past 25 years in awareness of the needs of people with brain injury. Whereas in the USA there was a dramatic increase in the 1980s in the number of rehabilitation services, followed by a retraction in the 1990s, in Britain and Europe there have continued to be developments in the provision of services, particularly community-based services. There are a number of reports dating from the late 1980s to the mid-1990s that have considered various aspects of neurological and rehabilitation services, including traumatic brain injury. A list of useful documents is provided in Table 17.1.

A number of published papers have examined service provision and planning for people with brain injury. For example, Murphy et al. (1990) looked at services in North London and surrounding areas and identified significant gaps in provision. Greenwood and McMillan (1993) described current provision, efficacy and good practice in rehabilitation, and Tennant et al. (1995) looked at long-term disability following head injury.

More recently, the UK government has introduced the concept of National Service Frameworks to set standards for clinical services. The National Service Framework for Older Adults has been published and includes specific aims for

Table 17.1. Documents providing useful background information when planning services

Source and title	Date	Content
British Psychological Society: *Services for Young Adult Patients with Acquired Brain Damage*	1989	Epidemiology; problems and prognosis, current services, proposed services, role of clinical psychology
British Psychological Society: *Purchasing Clinical Psychology Services: Services for People With Acquired Neurological Disorders and Their Carers*	1995	Identifies the extent of psychological needs, core psychological services, organization of clinical psychology services, recommended staffing levels and monitoring of services, including quality and audit
Social Services Inspectorate: *A Hidden Disability* (Report of the SSI Traumatic Brain Injury Project)	1997	Recommendations for local authority strategy, policy and provision
British Society of Rehabilitation Medicine: *Rehabilitation after Traumatic Brain Injury*	1998	Reviews resources needed to manage brain injury effectively and provides guidelines for standards of practice. Updates the report of the Medical Disability Society (1988)
Centre for Health Services Studies, University of Warwick: *National Traumatic Brain Injury Study*	1998	Observational study of 10 centres, exploring the relationship between extent of injuries, interventions provided and outcomes at 18 and 36 months
Royal College of Surgeons of England: *Working Party on the Management of Patients with Head Injury*	1999	Detailed recommendations for configuration of acute services, with recognition of the need for appropriate follow-up

the development of stroke services. The document identifies stroke as the single biggest cause of severe disability and the third most common cause of death in the UK. It identifies the need to provide a specialist co-ordinated stroke team within an integrated stroke service, including long-term support for the stroke patient and carer.

Other National Service Frameworks are being developed through a process of consultation, including one for Long-term Neurological Conditions, which is likely to be of considerable relevance to planning brain injury services over the next few years. However, it is unclear at the time of writing whether this document will address the full range of services used by people with neurological problems, particularly the longer term and complex difficulties that people may experience following traumatic brain injury. More details are available on the Department of Health website both about the consultation process and about other existing and proposed Frameworks.

REHABILITATION MODELS

Comprehensive Service Models

In the late 1980s and early 1990s a number of papers outlined comprehensive rehabilitation services, particularly for acquired brain injury (Fussey & Giles, 1988; Oddy et al., 1989; Wade, 1991; Wood & Eames, 1989), and there was broad agreement about the components of an effective service. The various models can be combined to form an outline of a comprehensive service (see Figure 17.1).

It has been recognized for many years that existing services had omissions, gaps and failings, particularly poor communication and follow-up (Greenwood et al., 1994; Murphy et al., 1990). Subsequent working parties and reviews of existing service provision, such as the Social Services Inspectorate's *A Hidden Disability* document (1997), The Royal College of Surgeons report (1999) and the British Society of Rehabilitation Medicine report (1998), have revisited these core areas and reiterated, above all, the need for co-ordinated services.

In America some centres have attempted to provide a comprehensive model of service. Ragnarsson et al. (1993) reported on the development of five 'model' systems of care in the USA, including specialist emergency medical services, acute care within a level 1 trauma center, acute comprehensive rehabilitation services with a complete interdisciplinary team, including vocational and educational preparation, plus long-term interdisciplinary rehabilitation follow-up services and assessment including medical, social, psychological, and vocational scheduled follow-up. Optional components included behaviour modification programmes, rehabilitation services at home, case management and community living options. In addition the services were intended to be accessible, co-ordinated and engaged in clinical research and evaluation. The recommendation in terms of patient volume was that for an annual minimum of 50–80 new patients with moderate or severe traumatic brain injury there must be a service with 10–20 dedicated beds.

There are however significant problems with the concept of an all-encompassing model brain injury service based on one site. Burke (1995) argued that such a system was too big and was not able to meet the whole range of such complex needs. For example, patients with minor brain injuries may not fit easily into services designed for people with severe disability, as they see themselves as different. Conversely, those with very severe injuries requiring slow stream rehabilitation, possibly over two to three years, may not fit into a more acute rehabilitation facility. Severe behaviour disturbance may also not be best managed within the same facility. Children's services are another exception, unless the centre is large enough to have a separate programme for children. They are often better served by a home-based community rehabilitation service, involving families more closely and integrated with educational facilities.

Comprehensive rehabilitation services in the UK have struggled in the era of an internal market in health care, and developments have often been opportunistic, reflecting local conditions and interests rather than levels of need. It is unfortunate that the enormous changes in health and social care provision that have taken

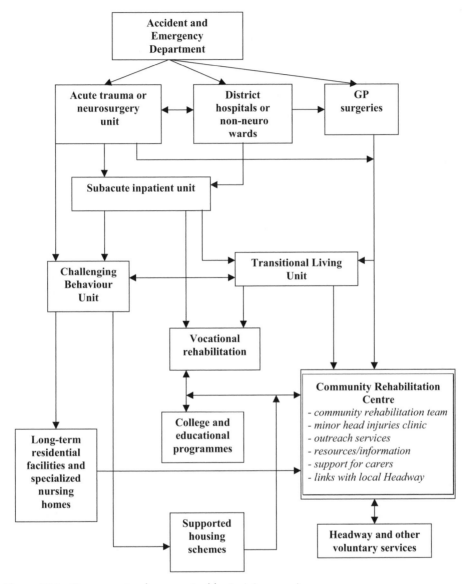

Figure 17.1. Components of an acquired brain injury service

place over the past 10 years have provided few opportunities for collaborative provision between health trusts, or with social services departments. In principle, health needs (e.g., for inpatient or community-based rehabilitation) are met by health authorities, who purchase appropriate treatment either from local services or, if this is not available, from additional specialist provision either in other health regions or in the independent sector. In practice, if local services are not available and if there is not a tradition of using specialist services, professionals and family members often have to make representation on a case-by-case basis to the health authority for funding to be made available for a specialist resource.

Social services departments meet needs for longer term care, where these are not health-related, and meet social and practical support needs. However, there are no standard definitions for both health and social services care needs across the country, which creates inequalities in provision. In addition, although health-related needs continue to be provided free, social services provision is usually means-tested. Users of the service may therefore be required to contribute to the cost of the service provided.

The other and often neglected area of rehabilitation is that of vocational re-habilitation. Resources are usually located within local employment services and job centres and tend to be constrained by the specific schemes or approaches that are available. More flexible packages are often only available to those with access to medico-legal funds. Restrictions on the number of hours of voluntary work that can be carried out each week before benefits entitlements are affected can also create barriers to individual work reintegration programmes.

The concepts of seamless, integrated services involving health, social and vocational support are familiar and supported, but implementation has proved patchy and difficult. More recent developments, including the National Service Frameworks, may provide a more constructive way forward.

Case Management Services

One approach to improving co-ordination of care at least on a case-by-case basis has been the development of case management both within the statutory sector (McMillan et al., 1988) and within the independent sector. Greenwood et al. (1994) identified the limits of case management in the first two years in the absence of adequate service provision. More specifically, they found that, for a given severity of injury, case management increased the chance and range of contact with inpatient and outpatient services, but did not increase the duration of contact. There was no demonstrable improvement in the outcome of the case man-agement group. Case management is not a substitute for adequate service provision.

The National Traumatic Brain Injury Study (1998) reported more positively on the longer term monitoring provided by case managers. Within the statutory services, various terms—including case manager, care co-ordinator and care manager—are used, depending on the agency establishing the post. The roles performed can also vary enormously, including, for example, responsibility for identifying all people with a brain injury in an identified area, or acting as a budget holder with a remit to purchase care for specific clients. An emphasis is usually placed on facilitating communication between agencies, particularly health, social services and education. The variations in the ways of working have usually evolved in response to local pressures and are not necessarily based on a specific model of service provision. This is an area that would benefit from a thorough review and evaluation.

Transitional Living Units

Discharge from acute care or rehabilitation to a more community-based setting is a crucial time where service provision can break down, unless there is a commitment to ensuring continuity. It has been widely recognized that networking, co-ordination, co-operation and collaboration are crucial to a successful transition (Cervelli, 1990). Transitional living units are one way of addressing the problems of community re-entry. Boake (1990) described the model of Transitional Living Centres in America and how they can be integrated with case management, family training, substance abuse issues and other community or longer term problems.

This concept is not as well developed within the UK as it is in the USA. The term is generally used to describe independent living flats or houses where clients are given a greater degree of independence while still receiving considerable levels of therapy and care staff support. This is particularly useful if the client does not have a supportive family network or is unable to return to their pre-injury living arrangements. The complexities of the funding arrangements for rehabilitation can affect the viability and use of such units, unless there are clear agreements and co-operation between health and social care funders.

Challenging Behaviour Services

There are a small number of patients who exhibit behaviour disturbance of such a severity that the rehabilitation services within the acute or subacute sector are unable to manage that individual. Problems can also emerge later in the rehabilitation pathway when the individual leaves the relative structure of the therapy environment and has difficulty coping in the community. The low volume and high cost of providing an appropriate service means that this is unlikely to form a major component of a district-wide service. There are a number of specialist units that have been designed to meet the needs of this challenging group of individuals (e.g., the Kemsley Unit, Northampton; Grafton Manor, Northampton; West Heath, Birmingham; York House, York; Royal Hospital for Neuro-disability, London; Unsted Park, Surrey; Elm Park, Essex), although these are often geographically removed from local services and the total number of beds remains small. Lack of appropriate long-term provision for some of these clients means that beds can remain blocked for extended periods of time.

There is also a general gap in provision for adolescents with traumatic brain injury, but particularly where challenging behaviour is involved. Adolescents have tended to be placed, often inappropriately, either within children's services or adult services. Consideration needs to be given to addressing their particular needs more directly.

Community Rehabilitation Teams

Community teams have been set up in response to the shift toward community care and in recognition of the fact that many people prefer to be treated in their own homes and respond better to care and treatment programmes within the familiar environment. Unfortunately, such teams are sometimes set up without sufficient consideration of the necessary composition of the team or its remit. Ideally, the composition of the team should reflect the nature of the client group and their presenting problems. A team that focuses on the needs of people with multiple sclerosis should differ in skill mix from one that addresses cognitive and behavioural adjustment after brain injury. Where the clients have complex or continuing medical needs it is helpful to have good lines of communication with the acute service, perhaps by having joint clinics with neurologists or rehabilitation consultants.

Experience in mental health settings where multidisciplinary community teams have been common for many years has illustrated some of the pitfalls of inadequately thought through or resourced community teams. The National Traumatic Brain Injury Study report (1998) discussed problems with management and leadership within teams involved in the study. Working together across multidisciplinary areas requires a considerable level of skilled leadership and clear lines of accountability. Such skills are not the province of any one specific discipline and depend more upon the availability of such skills among individual members of staff and the willingness of professional line management to be constructive in identifying how their responsibility to their individual member of staff can complement that individual's role in the functioning of the team.

The National Traumatic Brain Injury Study also highlighted staffing levels as one of the factors affecting the development of services. McMillan and Ledder (2001) surveyed community rehabilitation teams in South-East England and found that most teams focused on physical disability, with stroke and multiple sclerosis being the most common referrals. Only 2 out of 35 teams interviewed specialized in the consequences of cognitive impairment or personality change and less than 3% of people disabled by traumatic brain injury received community rehabilitation. Community teams were described as under-resourced and often professionally isolated. Enderby and Wade (2001) surveyed 98 different community teams and found huge variations in management arrangements, team composition, goals of service and likely lifespan of the service. They concluded that community rehabilitation in the UK is currently characterized by small, often short-term teams with poor identity and that the term 'community rehabilitation' has no clear or consistent meaning.

Evidence for the effectiveness of community teams remains predominantly anecdotal and on a case-by-case basis. An exception is the paper by Powell et al. (2002), which describes a randomized controlled trial of community-based rehabilitation after severe traumatic brain injury and found that the multidisciplinary community team input produced demonstrable gains in terms of practical functioning and independence in a range of activities and in aspects of psychological well-being. These gains were significantly greater for the outreach-treated participants than for those given only written information about alternative resources. Gains were not significant in the areas of increased socialization (where gains made during treatment programmes were not sustained after treatment) or productive employment (where there were limited opportunities available for the individual clients and team members to work with). This highlights the need for specialized, supported employment programmes that can undertake the difficult and time consuming process of job searching and job coaching.

In America, Pace et al. (1999) considered the pros and cons of working within the family home and evaluated both financial and clinical benefits. Effectiveness was measured by percentage of objectives obtained and by family and funder satisfaction ratings. The model, although positively evaluated, was limited by the need to involve a committed family member, who is not available in a significant proportion of cases. Outcome measurement is notoriously difficult in community settings. The general issue of measuring outcome is discussed in more detail later.

Community Rehabilitation Units

Working within the family home is only one model of community-based services, although in the survey by McMillan and Ledder (2001) it was the most common. Some services have used community bases, leisure facilities and other resources on an outreach basis in order to provide a more flexible service. Working within the home itself may not always be appropriate for reasons of space or privacy. While it is likely that the needs of many patients could be met by appropriately resourced community services, such services would be strengthened if they formed part rather than the entirety of rehabilitation provision. Small and under-resourced teams are vulnerable to recruitment and retention problems and difficulties when key personnel are on leave. The concept of a community rehabilitation unit, forming a core facility for the community services, is one way of consolidating resources and expertise, and providing a strong nucleus to the service. Some of the functions of such a unit could include being the central point for referrals, forming the geographical base for one or more community teams, providing links for families and voluntary groups, information resource for professionals, families and clients, and more specific rehabilitation services, such as a minor head injuries clinic (see Figure 17.1).

Vocational Rehabilitation

Studies have looked at return-to-work rates following brain injury and have identified this as a significant problem (Possl et al., 2001; Sander et al., 1996). Cost–benefit analyses have demonstrated the efficacy of regaining and retaining employment both in financial terms and in clinical terms. However, in both the UK and the USA the main difficulty has been identifying who will fund it. Therapists and teams work with individual clients to support them back into existing employment or through employment training schemes, but rarely have the time or opportunities to search for appropriate openings or to provide the longer term support needed to sustain many of these individuals in the workplace. Positive initiatives within the UK have included the collaborative programmes between the brain injury team and the employment services in Aylesbury (Tyerman, 1998) and the developments by Rehab UK, which specializes in centres for vocational rehabilitation. Other services employ vocational trainers or job coaches, although this is more common within the independent sector where the funding issues are different.

Support for Carers

It has been recognized for many years that, following traumatic brain injury, relatives and carers experience high levels of distress that are maintained during the first year post injury (Livingston et al., 1985a, b) and that this distress can continue over many years (Brooks et al., 1987). It has also been found that over time relatives can demonstrate great resilience and, although they remain distressed, they report being able to cope with the difficulties they encounter on a daily basis (Hall et al., 1994). The Social Services Inspectorate report (1997) identified that carers wanted more information and that most local authority practitioners were unable to supply the relevant information. One of the difficulties is that the needs of individuals may change at different rates post injury. Bowen et al. (2001) evaluated the role of support to carers at six months post injury and found a trend that indicated the benefit of early intervention and support to carers. The authors felt that it was probable that some needs would emerge over a longer period of time and affect the level of support required.

Identifying what model of family support should be put in place is not straightforward. While there is clearly an expressed need for information at an early stage, family education programmes do not necessarily meet that need successfully. Herbert (2003) reviewed different models of family support and training, particularly in relation to behavioural changes, and highlighted the problems of providing appropriate support when the needs of different family members vary so greatly and over different timescales. The therapeutic and caring demands placed on relatives can also be enormous and difficult for family members to sustain. For example, Carnevale (1996) described a three-year caregiver training programme for behaviour management in America that was particularly good at addressing behaviours, which included verbal and physical aggression and various forms of disinhibition. However, the programme worked best for those with intact and consistent caregiver systems, who tended to be younger at time of injury and still strongly connected to their family of origin, and although 35 families were involved over the 3-year period only 11 families actually completed the programme.

A community rehabilitation unit has the flexibility to provide an information resource for relatives and form the focus of a range of support services that could meet the differing needs over time. It has the potential to become a central point of contact for referrers and other local services, and as such, if appropriately staffed, could begin to address some of the needs of carers.

Long-term Care and Respite

Although there have been developments at a local level both within the National Health Service and the independent sector in terms of inpatient beds and community teams, there is still a scarcity of available placements in rehabilitation and longer term placements. Some parts of the country are particularly poorly served. For example, in London there are currently no specialist, long-term community placements for people with brain injury. Respite care for families either in their own home or as a short break for the person with the brain injury is an important component of sustaining a long-term package of care, but is extremely difficult to locate.

Supporting people with more severe disabilities within community settings depends too on the willingness of the community to work with difference and diversity. There are many similarities between the movement that resulted in the integration of people with learning disabilities away from institutions to community settings and the greater emphasis now being placed on community services for people with brain injury (Racino & Williams, 1994). DeJong et al. (1990) discuss the contribution that the community could play as a supplement to the resources of the individual and the family and argue that, at least within the American system, public policy could be used to foster greater growth in community involvement.

EVALUATION AND OUTCOME

Unfortunately, evaluation of service models remains rare. The Department of Health's *National Traumatic Brain Injury Study*, established in 1992, had an emphasis on expanding existing community services and was originally designed to develop a range of different service models. Ten of the twelve projects were evaluated over a five-year period by a team from Warwick University. The final report focused on outcomes in general, and the difficulties involved in delivering services, but did not provide clinicians or service planners with the type of evidence that could assist in identifying which models were effective (*National Traumatic Brain Injury Study*, 1998).

Evaluating what works depends on the questions you ask and what you are measuring. There is no simple global measure of outcome that addresses the questions raised in all different settings. A detailed review of outcome measures in brain injury rehabilitation is provided by Fleminger and Powell (1999) as editors of a special issue of the journal *Neuropsychological Rehabilitation*, entitled 'Evaluation of outcomes in brain injury rehabilitation'; this provides an excellent resource for all aspects of outcome research.

QUALITY AND STANDARDS OF CARE

Ensuring quality of care requires investment in training and education of staff and the establishment of standards that can be audited. America has seen the development of CARF (Centre for Accreditation of Rehabilitation Facilities). In the UK, minimum care standards for inpatient units have been published (British Society of Rehabilitation Medicine, 1998; South Thames Brain Injury Rehabilitation

Association, 2000), but as yet there is no consensus about implementing these. There are as yet no published standards for community rehabilitation services although there is work in hand to address this area. Government initiatives to regulate home care services may benefit long-term support packages, if they encourage the accreditation and training of home care workers.

INFORMED CONSENT AND RISK ASSESSMENT

Consideration should be given to the issue of informed consent. It affects services from acute care to long-term community packages, because of the nature of the cognitive deficits experienced by many of the people who sustain brain injuries. This is a difficult and complex issue that needs addressing at a national level and requires new legislation, as the existing and proposed mental health acts do not adequately address the needs of this client group.

Consideration should also be given to risk assessments and risk awareness. Policies should be developed that allow individuals the dignity of taking risks, without placing the carers or professionals involved in a position of negligence (Freeman, 1997). As more clients are living in community settings, the issues of supported packages of care, including the issues of risk management and what constitutes acceptable behaviour, become more common. The view that society takes both at a national or political level and at the local level can have a major impact on the success of projects designed to reintegrate people with disabilities into community settings. There is a widespread ignorance of the type of difficulties with which people with brain injury present, and there can be resistance and objections from local residents. Consultation, education and understanding are key areas in the development of local services.

SERVICE DEVELOPMENT

The enormous variability of the deficits following acquired brain injury, the limitations of the predictive powers of our measures of future needs and the difficulty of evaluating rehabilitation effectiveness because of the role of spontaneous improvement, as well as the lack of specificity of many traditional rehabilitation approaches, have all contributed to the problems of developing appropriate services for people with brain injury. The problems can appear overwhelming.

In terms of service development it is perhaps more constructive to focus on existing services and build on these, while acknowledging the gaps and exclusions as being far from ideal. In reviewing what services are operating, and for whom, it is generally helpful to identify who is excluded and why. In addition to those excluded by age, diagnosis, challenging behaviour, etc., it is necessary to consider whether current and planned services are culturally appropriate for the various groups of users and whether they are accessible (which may include issues such as transport, timing of services and location as well as physical barriers to access). Psychologists have a key role to play in highlighting the range of needs, particularly those involving cognitive, behavioural or emotional deficits, and can be well placed to illustrate the complexities of establishing an appropriate service. For example, running a group to reduce social isolation and build social skills in a group of brain-injured adolescents may be an appropriate intervention, but is likely to require considerable transport costs in order to enable the adolescents to participate in a suitable environment.

When considering a proposal for a new or developing service there are four key questions that can guide the planning process. First, consider *why* the planning is happening. There is a difference between commissioning a national, regional or district strategy compared with reconfiguring or developing a local service. The supportive documentation in terms of the epidemiological information and knowledge of local resources, as well as the level of detail in the proposed models, will inevitably vary and the constraints will be different. Identifying useful research evidence or examples of existing good clinical practice can be used in support of specific service models.

Second, decide *for whom* the service is being planned. Services have traditionally been provided on the basis of age, diagnostic group, level of disability or type of disability. Identifying who is to be the recipient of the service is an important determinant of the model of service, and identifying who is being excluded is also crucial. Services have traditionally evolved rather than developed in a planned way. As a consequence the boundaries of services, their exclusions and acceptance criteria, are often idiosyncratic and reflect local pressures and funding sources. It is common for clients to fall into gaps in service provision where they have multiple diagnoses. Some rehabilitation services, for example, exclude those with previous or current mental health problems, forensic history or learning disability, while the converse also occurs in that someone with a head injury may not receive psychiatric input as they do not meet the criteria for the local mental health service. The clinical rationale for these gaps in service is often weak, as these individuals have multiple and overlapping needs. Closer co-operation between services and sharing of expertise can contribute to a collaborative care plan.

Given that generic community rehabilitation services do not meet the needs of people with more complex problems, it is important to identify clearly what specific needs are being addressed (e.g., for cognitive or behavioural rehabilitation, for physical rehabilitation, or vocational rehabilitation) and to establish acceptance criteria that are inclusive rather than exclusive. Under such a model a young stroke patient seeking to return to work would access the vocational rehabilitation programme, and the person with cognitive deficits secondary to diabetic coma would not be excluded from appropriate rehabilitation because they had not suffered a traumatic injury.

The third question is about *what* is planned and brings together the 'why' and the 'for whom'. Neurorehabilitation can meet physical, cognitive, behavioural, emotional and vocational needs. A comprehensive service will also address care and support for relatives, respite and social rehabilitation. However, planning to reconfigure existing resources within an inpatient service so as to provide an improved follow-up service would be a more specific target than, for example, a requirement to plan a seamless, co-ordinated and 'managed' care pathway for all people with neurological disorders. Decisions about the priorities and which needs will be addressed should be explicit.

Having identified which needs are being addressed, it then becomes relatively easy to address the fourth question, which is *where* the service would best be placed. For some aspects of service, acute and medical care is essential, but for other needs, particularly the longer term rehabilitation needs, an acute care setting is inappropriate and undesirable. Subacute rehabilitation units are a necessary resource for those with more severe disabilities who require longer periods of rehabilitation before they are able to consider returning home, but do not necessarily need to be co-located with an acute service. Transitional living units may be a useful next step for people with continuing difficulties, where it is unclear how much support will be needed in the community, and here proximity either to a subacute unit or to a community rehabilitation unit is essential in order to maintain the intensity of rehabilitation input at this stage. For a small number of people with severe challenging behaviour, a specialist placement in a behavioural unit may be necessary, but, as this is a high-cost service that is not required in significant numbers on a regular basis by any one health district, such provision is probably best purchased on a case-by-case basis from the independent sector. The biggest development in UK services in recent years has been the growth in community services. In the model described above, these are best placed in a community rehabilitation unit, forming the core of the rehabilitation service and linking closely with the other components of the service. There is enormous scope for psychology in promoting effective and collaborative working practices within such a multidisciplinary service.

CONCLUSIONS

Planning brain injury services is a difficult task. Epidemiological information is difficult to obtain and hard to relate to local service needs. Resources and initiatives have tended to build on existing services, which can be a strength, but can also result in existing omissions or exclusions being perpetuated. While there is recognition in many areas of the need for neuropsychological input in a wide range of cases and services, this has not yet been translated consistently into service provision. Differences between various providing agencies coupled with a lack of understanding of the needs in general have contributed to a patchy and unequal service at all levels— between client groups, age groups, types of disability and levels of need—as well as more broadly in terms of inequalities across local and national geographical areas.

The fundamental requirement for such services is that they do need to be planned, taking into account the local context, but with an understanding of the need for multi-agency working. Such an approach cannot be attempted in isolation, and there needs to be a will, both political and societal, to address the needs of the many people who experience some form of neurological disability.

Psychologists have an important role to play in ensuring that this process is informed, open and comprehensive.

REFERENCES

Boake, C. (1990) Transitional living centres in head injury rehabilitation. In: J. S. Kreutzer & P. Wehman (eds) *Community Integration following Traumatic Brain Injury* (pp. 115–124). Edward Arnold, London.

Bowen, A., Tennant, A., Neumann, V. & Chamberlain, M. A. (2001) Neuropsychological rehabilitation for traumatic brain injury: Do carers benefit? *Brain Injury*, **15**, 29–38.

British Psychological Society (1989a) *Services for Young Adult Patients with Acquired Brain Damage.* British Psychological Society, Leicester, UK.

British Psychological Society (1989b) *Psychological and Physical Disability in the National Health Service: Report of the Professional Affairs Board of the British Psychological Society.* British Psychological Society, Leicester, UK.

British Psychological Society (1995) *Purchasing Clinical Psychology Services: Services for People with Acquired Neurological Disorders and Their Carers* (Briefing Paper No. 9, Division of Clinical Psychology). British Psychological Society, Leicester, UK.

British Society of Rehabilitation Medicine (1998) *Rehabilitation after Traumatic Brain Injury* (a Working Party report). British Society of Rehabilitation Medicine, London.

Brooks, N., Campsie, L., Symington, C., Beattie, A. & McKinlay, W. (1987) The effects of severe head injury on patient and relative within seven years of injury. *Journal of Head Trauma Rehabilitation*, **2**, 1–13.

Bryden, J. (1988) How many head-injured? The epidemiology of post head injury disability. In: R. L. Wood and P. Eames (eds) *Models of Brain Injury Rehabilitation* (pp. 17–27). Chapman & Hall, London.

Burke, D. C. (1995) Models of brain injury rehabilitation. *Brain Injury*, **9**, 735–743.

Carnevale, G. J. (1996) Natural-setting behaviour management for individuals with traumatic brain injury: Results of a three-year caregiver training programme. *Journal of Head Trauma Rehabilitation*, **11**, 27–38.

Cervelli, L. (1990) Re-entry into the community and systems of post hospital care. In: M. Rosenthal, E. R. Griffith, M. R. Bond & J. D. Miller (eds) *Rehabilitation of the Adult and Child with Traumatic Brain Injury* (2nd edn, pp. 463–475). F. A. Davis, Philadelphia.

DeJong, G., Batavia, A. I. & Williams, J. M. (1990) Who is responsible for the lifelong well-being of a person with a head injury? *Journal of Head Trauma Rehabilitation*, **5**, 9–22.

Enderby, P. & Wade, D. T. (2001) Community rehabilitation in the United Kingdom. *Clinical Rehabilitation*, **15**, 577–581.

Field, J. H. (1976) *Epidemiology of Head Injuries in England and Wales.* Her Majesty's Stationery Office, London.

Fleminger, S. & Powell, J. (1999) Evaluation of outcomes in brain injury rehabilitation. *Neuropsychological Rehabilitation* (Special issue), **9**, 225–554.

Freeman, E. A. (1997) Community-based rehabilitation of the person with a severe brain injury. *Brain Injury*, **11**, 143–153.

Fussey, I. & Giles, G. M. (1988) The future of brain injury rehabilitation. In: I. Fussey & G. M. Giles (eds) *Rehabilitation of the Severely Brain Injured Adult: A Practical Approach* (pp. 196–200). Croom Helm, London.

Greenwood, R. J. & McMillan, T. M. (1993) Models of rehabilitation programmes for the brain injured adult. I: Current provision, efficacy and good practice. *Clinical Rehabilitation*, **7**, 248–255.

Greenwood, R. J., McMillan, T. M., Brooks, D. N., Dunn, G., Brock, D., Dinsdale, S. et al. (1994) Effects of case management after severe head injury. *British Medical Journal*, **308**, 1199–1205.

Hall, K. M., Karzmark, P., Stevens, M., Englander, J., O'Hare, P. & Wright, J. (1994) Family stressors in traumatic brain injury: A two year follow up. *Archives of Physical Medicine and Rehabilitation*, **75**, 876–884.

Herbert, C. M. (2003) Educating staff and family members in the long term management of behaviour disorders. In: B. A. Wilson, C. M. Herbert & A. S. Shiel (eds) *Behavioural Approaches to Neuropsychological Rehabilitation*. Psychology Press, Hove, UK.

Jennett, B. & MacMillan, R. (1981) Epidemiology of head injuries. *British Medical Journal*, **282**, 101–104.

Johnson, R. & Gleave, J. (1987) Counting the people disabled by head injury. *Injury*, **18**, 7–9.

Langton Hewer, R. (1993) The epidemiology of disabling neurological disorders. In: R. Greenwood, M. P. Barnes, T. M. McMillan & C. D. Ward. (eds) *Neurological Rehabilitation* (pp. 3–12). Churchill-Livingstone, London.

Livingston, M. G., Brooks, D. N. & Bond, M. R. (1985a) Patient outcomes in the year following severe head injury and relatives' psychiatric and social functioning. *Journal of Neurology, Neurosurgery, and Psychiatry*, **48**, 876–881.

Livingston, M. G., Brooks, D. N. & Bond, M. R. (1985b) Three months after severe head injury: Psychiatric and social impact on relatives. *Journal of Neurology, Neurosurgery, and Psychiatry*, **48**, 870–875.

McMillan, T. M. & Ledder, H. (2001) A survey of services provided by community neuro-rehabilitation teams in South East England. *Clinical Rehabilitation*, **15**, 582–588.

McMillan, T. M., Greenwood, R. J., Morris, J. R., Brooks, D. N. & Dunn, G. (1988) An introduction to the concept of head injury case management with respect to the need for service provision. *Clinical Rehabilitation*, **2**, 319–322.

Medical Disability Society (1988) *The Management of Traumatic Brain Injury*. Development Trust for the Young Disabled, London.

Murphy, L. D., McMillan, T. M., Greenwood, R. J., Brooks, D. N., Morris, J. R. & Dunn, G. (1990) Services for severely head-injured patients in North London and environs. *Brain Injury*, **4**, 95–100.

National Traumatic Brain Injury Study (1998) (edited by Stillwell, J., Hawley, C., Stilwell, P. & Davies, C.). Centre for Health Services Studies, University of Warwick, UK.

Oddy, M., Bonham, E., McMillan, T. M., Stroud, A. & Rickard, S. (1989) A comprehensive service for the rehabilitation and long-term care of head injury survivors. *Clinical Rehabilitation*, **3**, 253–259.

Oxford Community Stroke Project (1983) Incidence of stroke in Oxfordshire: First year's experience of a community stroke project. *British Medical Journal*, **287**, 713–717.

Pace, G. M., Schlund, M. W., Hazard-Haupt, T., Christensen, J. R., Lashno, M., McIver, J. et al. (1999) Characteristics and outcome of a home and community-based neurorehabilitation programme. *Brain Injury*, **13**, 535–546.

Possl, J., Jurgensmeyer, S., Karlbauer, F., Wenz, C. & Goldenberg, G. (2001) Stability of employment after brain injury: A 7-year follow up study. *Brain Injury*, **15**, 15–27.

Powell, J., Helsin, J. & Greenwood, R. (2002) Community based rehabilitation after severe traumatic brain injury: A randomized controlled trial. *Journal of Neurology, Neurosurgery and Psychiatry*, **72**, 193–202.

Racino, J. A. & Williams, J. M. (1994) Living in the community: An examination of the philosophical and practical aspects. *Journal of Head Trauma Rehabilitation*, **9**, 35–48.

Ragnarsson, K. T., Thomas, J. P. & Zasler, N. (1993) Model systems of care for individuals with traumatic brain injury. *Journal of Head Trauma Rehabilitation*, **8**, 1–11.

Royal College of Surgeons (1999) *Working Party on the Management of Patients with Head Injury*. The Royal College of Surgeons of England, London.

Sander, A. M., Kreutzer, J. F., Rosenthal, M., Delmonico, R. & Young, M. E. (1996) A multi-centre longitudinal investigation of return to work and community integration following traumatic brain injury. *Journal of Head Trauma Rehabilitation*, **11**, 70–84.

Social Services Inspectorate (1997) *A Hidden Disability* (report of the SSI Traumatic Brain Injury Rehabilitation Project). Department of Health, London.

South Thames Brain Injury Rehabilitation Association (2000) *User's Guide to Minimum Recommended Standards for Post Acute Brain Injury Rehabilitation.* South Thames Brain Injury Rehabilitation Association, London.

Tennant, A., MacDermott, N. & Neary, D. (1995) The long-term outcome of head injury: Implications for service planning. *Brain Injury*, **9**, 595–605.

Thornhill, S., Teasdale, G. M., Murray, G. D., McEwen, J., Roy, C. W. & Penny, K. I. (2000) Disability in young people and adults one year after head injury: Prospective cohort study. *British Medical Journal*, **320**, 631–635.

Tyerman, A. (1998) 'Working out': A Joint DOH/ES Traumatic Brain Injury Vocational Rehabilitation Project report. Unpublished report available from the author.

Wade, D. T. (1991) Policies on the management of patients with head injury: The experience of Oxford region. *Clinical Rehabilitation*, **5**, 141–155.

Wood, R. L. & Eames, P. (1989) *Models of Brain Injury Rehabilitation.* Chapman & Hall, London.

CHAPTER 18

Interventions for Psychological Problems after Brain Injury

Andy Tyerman and **Nigel S. King**

Community Head Injury Service, Aylesbury, UK

INTRODUCTION

People with brain injury have complex psychological needs, reflecting both primary neuropsychological deficits and secondary psychological effects. In neurological rehabilitation the majority of referrals to the clinical neuropsychologist are of those with head injury or stroke. In community disability teams referrals will also include other neurological conditions including cerebral tumour and multiple sclerosis. Neurologically, these client groups contrast in onset, symptom profile and course of disability. Whereas head injury is of immediate onset and stroke sudden, the onset of cerebral tumour is progressive and multiple sclerosis typically episodic and protracted. In terms of the major symptoms, these tend to be physical in the early stages of multiple sclerosis, physical and psychological after stroke and tumour, but predominantly psychological after head injury. Whereas severe head injury, stroke and tumour are usually followed by recovery and adaptation, the course of multiple sclerosis is extremely variable and uncertain (i.e., total remission, relapse/remission or progressive decline).

Secondary psychological impact also tends to differ across neurological conditions. While after head injury the chances of a second injury are low (except in the case of abuse or persistent risk-taking), the person with stroke may be concerned about the chances of a second stroke, the person with a tumour may live in fear of a recurrence and the person with multiple sclerosis may monitor day-to-day symptom fluctuation and exertion in case of provoking a further episode. Thus people with neurological disability face contrasting challenges. Furthermore, onset peaks typically at different stages in the family life cycle: head injury, the teenager or young single adult; multiple sclerosis, the married person with a young family; tumour, those in middle age with older children; and stroke, the older adult, often with grown-up children.

Neuropsychological deficits combined with the psychological impact of neurological disability (and any pre-existing vulnerability factors) can cause a wide range of emotional difficulties. For example, in a recent epidemiological study, the

Clinical Neuropsychology: A Practical Guide to Assessment and Management for Clinicians.
Edited by L.H. Goldstein and J.E. McNeil. © 2004 John Wiley & Sons, Ltd.

frequency of psychiatric disorders among 361 people who reported having incurred a severe head injury associated with a loss of consciousness or confusion was as follows: alcohol abuse/dependence (24.5%); phobic disorder (11.2%); major depression (11.1%); drug abuse/dependence (10.9%); dysthymia (5.5%); obsessive–compulsive disorder (4.7%); schizophrenia (3.4%); panic disorder (3.2%); bipolar disorder (1.6%) (Silver et al., 2001). The incidence was significantly higher (often twofold) compared with those without head injury for all disorders except schizophrenia ('borderline significance') and bipolar disorder. Of those with head injury 32% had at least one psychiatric diagnosis, compared with 20% of those without head injury. Those with head injury were also much more likely to have made a suicide attempt (8.1% compared with 1.9%).

Emotional difficulties may be experienced by some people with brain injury throughout recovery, whereas for others they may surface suddenly and unexpectedly, not infrequently late post onset when services are no longer involved. This emotional impact needs to be addressed both alongside and often well beyond active rehabilitation in order to promote positive adjustment to residual neurological disability. Failure to address emotional needs may impede progress in both rehabilitation and long-term adjustment.

In addressing such needs a wide range of psychological interventions are required. For example, of the first 100 people with head injury seen within our community head injury service in Aylesbury, 36% were provided with some individual psychological treatment for emotional and behavioural difficulties, in addition to individual or group cognitive rehabilitation. This included the following: therapy to promote long-term adjustment (13%); neuropsychological counselling (11%); anxiety management (10%); anger management (11%); intervention for post-traumatic stress disorder (3%); behaviour modification (2%); pain management (2%).

In spite of its central importance, intervention for emotional difficulties after brain injury has to date attracted limited research. Such interventions are sometimes referred to as 'neuropsychotherapy'. Some authors use this term to refer to all psychological aspects of neurological rehabilitation, which we find unhelpful. In this chapter the term 'neuropsychotherapy' is used to refer to the interface between neuropsychological rehabilitation and psychotherapy (i.e., 'the use of neuropsychological knowledge in the psychotherapy of persons with brain disorders' [Judd, 1999] or, conversely, the use of psychotherapeutic approaches in the process of neurological rehabilitation).

This chapter will review the emotional needs of people with neurological disability and related psychological interventions in rehabilitation and long-term adjustment, including the modifications necessary to interventions drawn from a mental health context in order to accommodate neuropsychological constraints.

PSYCHOLOGICAL NEEDS

The psychological needs of people with brain injury relate not only to their neuropsychological deficits but also to the emotional impact of the condition, the wide range of neurological symptoms and their long-term social and family effects.

Neuropsychological Deficits

Most people requiring psychological intervention after neurological illness or injury will have some reduction in cognitive skills, depending on the nature, location and severity of damage. After generalized damage (e.g., head injury and multiple sclerosis) the most common cognitive difficulties are with attention, concentration, memory, speed of information processing and executive functioning (e.g., planning, problem-solving, self-awareness and self-regulation). After more focal damage (e.g., stroke and tumour) specific deficits may also be seen in motor skills, visual perception, spatial judgement, language function, etc. The subjective experience of cognitive impairment can be disturbing and perceptual and spatial deficits can be bewildering and frightening. Loss of the ability to communicate effectively (due to language impairment or severe dysarthria) may be immensely frustrating, as well as socially isolating. Marked impairment of memory disrupts daily living and compromises a sense of continuity, as well as perception of progress in rehabilitation. Disruption to executive function is of particular importance, not only due to its direct effects on independence and self-control but also in the limitations imposed on insight, understanding, use of compensatory strategies and long-term adjustment.

A wide range of behavioural and emotional changes may be experienced as a direct consequence of damage to the brain. These interact with executive dysfunction to result in marked overall change in personality. Common behavioural changes include disinhibition, impulsivity, irritability, intolerance, short temper, aggressive outbursts, lack of initiation and compulsive behaviour. Common emotional changes include agitation, heightened (or flattened) affect, lability, mood swings and depression. (Bi-polar disorders, paranoid or other delusional states are rare but can occur.) Mood swings are particularly common after head injury, depression and emotional lability after stroke, and depression (or sometimes euphoria) after multiple sclerosis. Where such changes are thought to result from disruption in organic and neurochemical processes of mood regulation, anti-depressant and/or mood-stabilizing medication may be required. However, emotional changes after brain injury are commonly an interaction of primary organic and secondary psychological factors. The personal impact of such changes is very variable, depending upon the specific pattern of disability, individual coping and family circumstances.

Personal Impact

A wide range of emotional reactions may be experienced (e.g., confusion, anger, frustration, fear, anxiety, depression and loss of confidence/self-esteem/self-belief) at different stages in the course of recovery and long-term adjustment (Tyerman, 1991).

Early after onset there may be a profound sense of confusion, reflecting an interaction of trauma, cognitive impairment and the bewildering array of symptoms of which the person may be only partially aware. This powerful combination leads some to view the situation as unreal, of not having happened or of themselves as no longer being 'a real person'. As the person becomes aware of what has happened and at least some of the consequences, there may be questions about 'Why me?' This may be tinged with resentment and anger, especially after a head injury for which someone else is held responsible. Stripped of their everyday skills, some experience generalized anxiety, others have specific fears (e.g., of falling for those unsteady on their feet, travel for those injured in a road traffic accident, seizures for those with post-traumatic epilepsy). Miller (1993) also highlights the 'double burden' for those with a malignant cerebral tumour—brain damage plus the trauma/fear of having cancer.

There is for many an enormous frustration with the slow rate and protracted course of recovery. Loss of control over both physical and cognitive skills and behavioural and emotional reactions, combined with an apparent inability to progress as expected, may provoke a profound sense of helplessness. This is particularly so as enormous effort is often invested in rehabilitation. This may be compounded by difficulties in evaluating progress due to lack of insight and/or memory impairment. During the course of recovery there may be increasing doubt and anxiety about the extent of recovery and uncertainties about the future (e.g., Will I ever walk again? Will I be able to drive? Will I be able to return to work? How will I care for the children?).

While for some the emotional impact may be evident early post onset, others may appear surprisingly unconcerned about their predicament during rehabilitation. While this may reflect limited insight into the extent of cognitive and emotional/behavioural changes, often accompanied by unrealistic expectations of a full or near complete recovery, there may also be an element of psychological denial. As such, anxiety, depression and loss of confidence may surface later when the person has developed greater insight and/or struggled to resume former family, work and social roles.

Social and Family Impact

While recovery and adaptation may continue over several years (particularly after head injury), the complex array of neurological disability often has far-reaching vocational, social and family effects (Tyerman, 1995).

There may be a major loss of independence: assistance in daily care for those with severe physical disability; communication aids for those with language impairment or severe dysarthria; guidance and supervision for those with cognitive or personality changes. Others may be independent in daily care but be unable to travel independently, or need help in making decisions or in managing their finances. Return to study or work is often a major challenge. Reduced speed, poor concentration, unreliable memory, headaches and/or fatigue renders many uncompetitive, in addition to any specific restrictions. Parallel restrictions are experienced in leisure activities. Unable to pursue former activities, people with neurological disability often lack the imagination, initiative or confidence to explore alternatives. They may also feel less inclined to pursue an active social life due to lack of confidence, low mood, intolerance to noise or difficulty in contributing to conversations. Friends may feel uneasy about physical disability or struggle to cope with changes in cognition and behaviour: repetitive conversation; irritability and aggression; impulsivity, disinhibition and general loss of refinement in social skills. As such, friendships and social opportunities often decline progressively over subsequent years.

Family functioning is often affected. The person may find that they are unable to fulfil former family roles and, while the family is usually an immense source of strength and comfort, the person may struggle to cope with the demands of family life. Marital and other long-term relationships are particularly vulnerable: some couples adapt positively, some remain close but with less intimacy, but others decide to part.

NEUROPSYCHOLOGICAL ASSESSMENT AND COUNSELLING

Assessment

The psychological effects of brain injury require systematic assessment to clarify needs and plan rehabilitation. In addition to formal cognitive testing, assessment of behaviour and emotional state may be required. This may include family or staff ratings of behaviour early post injury (e.g., using the Agitated Behaviour Scale—Corrigan, 1989 or Neurobehavioural Rating Scale—Levin et al., 1987) and self-rating of emotional state during rehabilitation or long-term adjustment (e.g., using the Hospital Anxiety and Depression Scale—HADS—Zigmond & Snaith, 1983, Beck Depression Inventory—Beck et al., 1961 or Beck Anxiety Inventory—Beck et al., 1988). While such assessments may be sufficient to evaluate psychological problems, it is also important to understand the subjective experience of neurological disability, not just in terms of insight but also in terms of changes in self-concept, expectations of recovery and personal priorities and goals. This allows feedback and rehabilitation goals to be tailored to the perceptions and needs of the individual. It is important also to assess the perceptions and expectations of family members, to whom the person will look for guidance and reassurance, as well as encouragement and support.

As such, within our community head injury service (Tyerman, 1997), initial assessments focus on self and family reports using interview schedules, adapted from Tyerman (1987), available from the authors (i.e., Head Injury Background Interview Schedule, Head Injury Problem Schedule, Head Injury Semantic Differential), along with the HADS. The background interview schedule provides us with a detailed social and clinical history, account of past rehabilitation and current situation and issues. The problem schedule provides a profile of current problems (physical, sensory, cognitive, behavioural, emotional and social), as perceived by the person and a relative. The semantic differential scale provides an assessment of change in self-concept, as viewed by the person and of changes in personality as perceived by family members. The HADS provides a brief screen of anxiety and depression.

Self-ratings may of course be affected by lack of insight and/or denial, and family reports may also underplay the severity of problems early post onset. It is of course essential to obtain full medical details of the brain injury and acute care. However, an understanding of self and family perspectives is fundamental to effective feedback and engagement in rehabilitation. It allows the feedback to take account of self-perceptions and expectations, as well as cognitive constraints and emotional state. In this way the person is more likely to feel understood (not evaluated), more likely to engage positively in rehabilitation and more receptive to psychological intervention.

Feedback

Feedback of complex assessment results to the person (who may lack insight and be defensive) and the family (who may be understandably protective) is a skilled task. This may be provided separately or as part of integrated feedback of rehabilitation team assessments, ideally supported by a summary of strengths and weaknesses written specifically for the client. Where neuropsychological assessment is part of a team assessment, whether fed back separately or jointly, it is vital that inconsistencies across areas of overlap with other professions are addressed prior to feedback. Failure to do so risks adding further to the confusion and anxiety of the patient, as well as undermining the feedback itself (especially where there is lack of insight or denial).

Feedback is viewed productively as the bridge between assessment and intervention. The immediate aim is obviously to feed back assessment results and their implications and provide a rationale for planned intervention. However, feedback also provides an early opportunity to establish a framework of understanding of neurological disability, within which to set current test results and treatment recommendations and on which to build progressively during rehabilitation. A person-centred approach to assessment and feedback may also enable an intrinsically stressful experience to be of immediate therapeutic benefit. Having already investigated self- and family perceptions, a short debrief of the patient on their experience of assessment and any family observations (e.g., about emotional reactions and any subsequent headache, fatigue, irritability, etc.) is recommended prior to discussing results. This helps the feedback to be both anchored in and sensitive to the person's own experience. Where the results of the assessment are both consistent with and start to provide some explanation for the person's own experience, this can provide much needed reassurance for both the person and the family.

Frequent reference to self and family reports, explicit but sensitive handling of any discrepancies in views and ample time to answer questions helps to reduce confusion and misunderstandings. However, assuming that rehabilitation input is ongoing, there is no need to seek to progress too far in promoting insight or raising long-term issues at this early stage. Such issues are best dealt with in carefully graded steps during ongoing 'neuropsychological counselling', within specific psychological treatment, on review or on feedback of reassessment results.

Neuropsychological Counselling

Following assessment and feedback, ongoing neuropsychological counselling can assist the person in understanding and coping with the complex effects of brain injury during the course of recovery. Prigatano (1986) suggests that such psychotherapy after brain injury should attempt to:

1 provide a model or models that help the patient understand what has happened to him or her;
2 help the patient deal with the meaning of the brain injury in his or her own life;
3 help the patient achieve a sense of self-acceptance and forgiveness for himself and herself and others who have caused the accident (*in the case of head injury*);
4 help the patient make realistic commitments to work and interpersonal relations;
5 teach the patient how to behave in different social situations (to improve competence);
6 provide specific behavioural strategies for compensating for neuropsychological deficits;
7 foster a sense of realistic hope.

Neurological disability is for most an unknown entity outside the scope of past experience. As such, a core requirement is education about brain function, neurological illness or injury and its effects. This should be appropriate (i.e., meeting the needs of the recipient), accessible (i.e., in terms of complexity, pace and style) and acceptable (i.e., sensitive to how the information is likely to be received) (Judd, 1999). Education should be incremental, ideally incorporated within neuropsychological counselling and integrated within the overall rehabilitation programme.

At a fundamental level, neuropsychological counselling is likely to involve provision of at least some of the following: general information and explanation; detailed feedback about specific impairments; explanation of treatment rationale; ongoing monitoring of treatment goals; reinforcement of coping strategies; progress review; resettlement planning; and general advice and support. Given the patients' cognitive constraints, it is usually helpful and often necessary to provide visual illustrations (e.g., charts, videotape recordings, etc.) of difficulties and progress alongside verbal explanations. At a deeper level, an experienced practitioner can make use of ongoing monitoring and reassessments/reviews to promote greater insight, more accurate self-appraisal and more realistic expectations of recovery. This may also help the person to review current strengths and weaknesses, thereby facilitating and augmenting the process of resettlement and laying the foundations for positive long-term adjustment.

Some of what may be incorporated within neuropsychological counselling (such as goal setting and monitoring, etc.) should of course be regarded as good clinical practice (King & Tyerman, in press). However, goal setting in the context of lack of insight and unrealistic expectations is a major challenge (Bergquist & Jacket, 1993). The management of reduced self-awareness, a central component of neuro-psychological counselling, is addressed specifically in depth by a number of authors (Judd, 1999; Langer, 1999; Prigatano, 1992). A person-centred approach, either incorporated within or provided alongside the rehabilitation programme, allows for a specific focus on how the person is understanding and coping emotionally with the process of rehabilitation within the context of their particular personal and family circumstances.

In parallel with individual neuropsychological counselling, our experience is that there is much to be gained from specialist group programmes. A number of such psychotherapeutic groups have been reported, some with a broad therapeutic focus (e.g., Ben Yishay & Lakin, 1989; Prigatano, 1986), others addressing specific issues: anger and impulse control (Whitehouse, 1994); frustration and substance abuse (Delmonico et al., 1998); psychosocial issues, self-regulation and anger manage-ment (Langerbahn et al., 1999). Within our community head injury service, we run routinely three related groups: group educational sessions about the nature and effects of brain injury; a cognitive rehabilitation group providing information about the nature of cognitive impairment and relevant coping strategies; and a personal issues group that provides an opportunity to discuss emotional and behavioural changes and their personal, family and social impact. In addition to their educational value, these groups provide valuable peer feedback and support, as well as demonstrating that others share at least some of their difficulties and concerns.

Neuropsychological counselling can therefore serve a vital function in guiding and supporting the person through the process of rehabilitation and resettlement. This function may sometimes be undertaken by other experienced members of the neurorehabilitation team (e.g., through a primary nurse or key worker system), drawing on psychological expertise as appropriate. However, experience suggests that for those with complex cognitive and emotional/behavioural needs, this function is most effectively provided by clinical neuropsychologists. While indi-vidual neuropsychological counselling, ideally combined with a person-focused discussion/support group, will meet many of the emotional needs of persons with brain injury, some will of course require individual psychological therapy.

INDIVIDUAL PSYCHOLOGICAL TREATMENT

The literature on psychological treatment for people with neurological disability is small with virtually no outcome studies to date. Interventions for emotional dis-orders for this population have largely been adapted from the adult mental health field of clinical psychology. A few writers have advocated cognitive behavioural therapy (CBT) as a particularly useful approach, because many of its essential features appear to be adaptable to those with neurological disability. It is structured, educational, focused and collaborative and it involves problem-solving, behavioural training and rehearsal, stress awareness and management, concrete goal setting, the combating of maladaptive thoughts and improving self-awareness (Whitehouse, 1994). In addition, schema-focused CBT potentially provides a framework for exploring and adjusting to a new sense of self.

As previously noted (King & Tyerman, in press), in our experience the most common forms of psychological intervention include the following: (i) cognitive behavioural psychotherapy (CBT) with exposure and/or cognitive restructuring for post-traumatic stress symptoms; (ii) CBT for anger management; (iii) CBT for anxiety and depression; (iv) anxiety management training and CBT for control of anxiety symptoms. Within our community head injury service the parallel use of medication has tended to be where emotional difficulties have a major organic basis and/or where psychological treatment alone is judged to be unlikely to be effective.

Problems do however exist in implementing a cognitive behavioural approach, at least partially, because one of its central techniques—the Socratic dialogue— involves brainstorming ideas, evaluating the usefulness of alternative thoughts and moving from concrete to more abstract ideas. This relies on reasonably well-preserved executive functioning. It is therefore unsurprising that the most common challenges highlighted in the literature relate to reduced awareness, concrete thinking, poor initiation and impulsivity, as well as memory impairment.

Three unique problems are often faced when undertaking psychological treatment after neurological illness or injury. First, there is potentially the lengthy adjustment process that the person experiences in managing a wide range of neurological disabilities, in coping with marked and permanent changes in life circumstances and in adapting to a new sense of self (Butler & Satz, 1988; Prigatano, 1994). Second, the person with neurological disability may be experiencing high anxiety and distress at precisely the same time that their coping resources are greatly reduced (Lewis & Resenberg, 1990). Third, neuropsychological impairments may significantly impede the patient's ability to make use of psychological help.

This section aims to: (1) summarize the main neuropsychological challenges that arise and (2) describe pragmatic modifications suggested to standard therapeutic approaches.

Neuropsychological Challenges

Attention and Concentration

Maintaining emotional and cognitive focus for a therapeutic hour may not be possible, and the ability to switch attention between different ideas and tasks may be difficult. Similarly, mentally 'holding' ideas while temporarily focusing on others may be problematic. Distractibility and tangential speech may also be evident (Carberry & Burd, 1986).

Memory

Remembering what has been discussed in psychotherapy, both within and between sessions, may be impaired (Whitehouse, 1994). As psychotherapy is primarily a verbally based intervention this can pose very significant difficulties. Memory difficulties may also manifest as forgetting to do homework tasks or in having difficulty in acquiring new skills. There is often an assumption in psychological therapies that new skills will be learnt quite quickly over a relatively short number of sessions. This may not be possible. Differential impairments in verbal and visuospatial memory are common when one cerebral hemisphere is more damaged than the other, and this may mean that presenting material in a single modality will be ineffective (Block, 1987).

Executive Functioning

There are four major domains within executive functioning that can impede psychotherapy:

1. Concrete thinking, lack of abstract reasoning, difficulties with cognitive flexibility and problems in switching ideas. All of these can impinge on the person's ability to generalize and think creatively.
2. Difficulties in self-awareness, egocentricity and awareness of others. These may be compounded by, or mistaken for, emotional denial. They may also be related to specific impairments in discriminating emotional states in oneself. All such impairments can impede the ability to think empathically.
3. Impulsivity, disinhibition and specific disorders in emotional regulation (e.g., episodic dyscontrol). These may affect anger control, behavioural regulation and the ability to inhibit self-harm behaviour.
4. Impairments in planning, organizing, thinking ahead and initiating action. These can lead to difficulties throughout a therapeutic encounter, not least in the patient actually attending sessions at the designated time.

Language Functioning

Expressive language difficulties may significantly impair the ability to articulate feeling states and to express emotions more generally. This can lead to frustration in its own right. Slow word finding and problems with sentence construction may mean that less material can be covered in any given session. It may also make it difficult for the therapist to gauge the extent to which any struggles the client has in expressing themselves or any silences in therapy are emotionally or neuropsychologically driven. Receptive language problems with verbal abstraction and symbolic representation may, in addition, make the understanding of therapeutic vocabulary problematic.

Therapeutic Modifications

Many of the challenges noted above are, at least to a mild extent, encountered in patients without brain injury (Carberry & Burd, 1986). Therefore, while some modifications to be discussed are unique to a brain-injured population, many have already been proposed in the adult mental health literature. These, however, will often require a much greater emphasis with patients with neurological impairments.

Attention and Concentration

Reducing the amount of material to be covered in each session and having shorter and more frequent sessions have been suggested as a means of minimizing potential disabilities in this area (Whitehouse, 1994). The pace with which material is presented will consequently be slower, and some have advocated talking more slowly as well (Block, 1987).

Memory

Using notes, audiotapes of sessions, videotapes of sessions and frequent repetition of material, both within and between sessions, may reduce disabilities from memory impairments (Block, 1987; Whitehouse, 1994). Encouraging the patient to repeat key points and the frequent use of 'mini-reviews' to summarize what has been covered in therapy to date may also be useful (Carberry & Burd, 1986). Telephone reminders between sessions for homework tasks (Butler & Satz, 1988) or using family members and caregivers as co-therapists to facilitate between-session learning might be utilized (Benedict et al., 2000). The use of others as co-therapists, however, requires a good deal of reflection, negotiation with the patient and clear understanding of the extent of their role. Using stories, narratives or favourite pieces of music to explore feelings may help therapeutic material be better remembered (Prigatano, 1994). In planning the number of sessions that are likely to be required for therapeutic learning to take place a greater number than usual may be necessary (Whitehouse, 1994).

Where verbal memory is differentially impaired, the use of drawings to express emotions (Prigatano, 1994), the presentation of information in a visual form or encouraging the patient to visualize parts of the session may be useful (Carberry & Burd, 1986). In addition, utilizing *negative automatic imagery* and *adaptive imaginary responses* may be more effective than working with thought-based material (Pickett, 1991). Imagery may have the added advantage of being more emotionally potent due to its ability to 'simplify meaning into sensory experience' in a more direct way. In contrast, relaxation training may be useful in minimizing high general arousal levels, which may impede memory functioning (Miller, 1991).

Executive Functions

Concrete Thinking and Lack of Abstraction

Many clinicians emphasize the need for therapy to be, at least at times, highly task-oriented and functional with the therapist using a direct and concrete style (Becker & Vakil, 1993; Carberry & Burd, 1986; Whitehouse, 1994). A greater behavioural focus may be necessary with a corresponding reduction in cognitive and exploratory techniques. Frequent use of real-life experiments and real-life applications will often be required (Cicerone, 1989). A more directive therapeutic style can be beneficial, and this might actually include supplying the patient with alternatives to maladaptive thoughts when using cognitive techniques. Open-ended questions may have to be limited while graphs, diagrams, brain models, neuroimaging scans and checklists may help make information, ideas and self-monitoring more concrete (Benedict et al., 2000). Role play and therapist modelling should also not be neglected as an additional means of making therapy a less abstract process. Ideas from the learning disability literature suggest that this process may be enhanced by the patient rehearsing skills *in vivo* within sessions. Listing alternative solutions and using written brainstorming techniques to aid cognitive flexibility may be appropriate for those with less severe impairments in this area (Miller, 1991).

Awareness Deficits, Denial and Reduced Empathy

The use of therapeutic humour, exaggeration and fantasy have all been proposed as ways of increasing self-insight (Carberry & Burd, 1986; Miller, 1991; Whitehouse, 1994). Biofeedback may also be a useful way of enhancing clients' awareness of their emotional state (Holland et al., 1999). Lack of awareness can mean that the patient sees no need for therapy. Significant energy is then required in engaging and maintaining a therapeutic alliance (Becker & Vakil, 1993; Miller, 1999). The use of homework assignments as self-monitoring exercises, possibly with the involvement of caregivers to provide specific feedback, can be used. In addition, hand-held counters may be a more powerful means of keeping frequency counts of targeted behaviours and increasing self-awareness. This may also be enhanced by the sensitive use of video feedback of targeted behaviours. This should always be done with adequate time for debriefing, as being confronted with such material may be emotionally threatening. The learning disability literature describes the use of role playing as a means of increasing clients' awareness of negative automatic thoughts when these are inaccessible (Lindsay & Olley, 1998) and empathy may be facilitated through social skills training in active listening and perspective taking skills (Benedict et al., 2000). Using very basic Socratic questions like 'what would your wife feel about that?' or 'what would I, as your therapist, think about that?' may further facilitate empathic thinking (Carberry & Burd, 1986).

It will often be important to gauge the extent to which emotional denial and/or organically driven lack of awareness is operating. Some attempts have been made to guide this difficult judgement (Langer, 1999). Denial has been conceptualized as an attempt to cope with overwhelming emotional material, while organic unawareness has been conceptualized as a failure to recognize the need to cope. Langer suggests that when denial is operating associations and connections related to what is being denied will be systematically avoided and when information is presented that contradicts what is being denied no resolution occurs. He also suggests that denial may be characterized by a restricted range of emotional responses and emotional numbness.

Some clinicians have recommended that when therapeutic challenging or confrontation of sensitive material is required, it is carefully 'titrated' (Langer, 1999). Challenges should be made only when some other form of hope can be introduced and it may be preferable to share partial insights rather than full ones (Miller, 1991, 1999). Such 'titrations' may have to extend over very long periods. For some patients, 'cognitive structures', 'ego strength' and self-esteem will need to be developed before any challenges can occur (Langer, 1999).

Impulsivity and Disinhibition

Clear definition of the therapeutic relationship and the consequent boundaries entailed may need to be made explicit and consistently reinforced when impulsivity and overfamiliarity are a significant problem (Whitehouse, 1994). In addition, where impulse and emotional control are poor the therapist should maximize the client's 'preparedness' prior to presenting any challenging material (Cicerone, 1989; Miller, 1991). Explicitly acknowledging that the patient might disagree with what is about to be said can be a useful technique, as can promoting the client's confidence in their ability to deal with forthcoming material (e.g., 'I'm only going to talk about this because I know you're strong enough to deal with it': Prigatano, 1994). When the client is in an emotionally charged state, comments and interpretations may need to be postponed within the session until the client is calmer (Miller, 1991). Relaxation training might be used as a counter-conditioning method where anger is mediated by high states of general arousal (Uomoto & Brockway, 1992). It may be useful to involve carers in aspects of generalizing therapeutic gains (e.g., getting them to change their style of interaction or their topic of conversation when the client's anger appears to be escalating). In addition, clients may need to be taught behavioural skills so that they themselves can reduce emotional escalation (e.g., using distraction techniques like walking away from a situation or going to listen to some music: Uomoto & Brockway, 1992). Verbal mediation and self-talk might also be emphasized to help clients remind themselves of alternative strategies they can use when emotions become difficult to manage (Cicerone, 1989; Uomoto & Brockway, 1992).

Planning, Organization and Initiation

At times, a therapist will need to act as an 'external executive' or an 'auxiliary ego' to provide clear structure and guidance in therapy (Miller, 1991; Prigatano, 1994). Caregivers may also act in such a way to help structure homework tasks. Encouraging the patient to bring a written agenda to sessions and to regularly summarize what they have learnt or what they want to express in three to four short sentences may also help to impose structure on the therapeutic encounter (Carberry & Burd, 1986). 'Goal ladders' delineating short-term and long-term goals and how these are being worked toward may help the client to organize ideas and priorities, while breaking problems down into their component parts may help in planning therapeutic strategies.

Language

Clear and precise interactions, which consistently relate to real-life situations, can aid receptive language disabilities (Cicerone, 1989). Similarly, using high-frequency words, short sentences and allowing more time for interactions may be of benefit (Block, 1987; Whitehouse, 1994). Restricting the range and number of symbolic interpretations of ideas may also help in simplifying psychotherapy (Miller, 1991).

Using the above techniques, psychological treatments can often be adapted to address specific emotional problems of people with neurological disability during recovery. However, emotional difficulties may still arise or resurface in long-term adjustment.

FACILITATING LONG-TERM ADJUSTMENT

Difficulties in Long-term Adjustment

Given the complexity of neurological disability it is no surprise that some struggle to adjust to their new situation. Those no longer able to function independently and those unable to resume their former work, family and social roles face major challenges. Those with less severe but significant disability may also have to re-evaluate personal aspirations and goals. The process of adjustment will be compounded by executive difficulties (especially lack of awareness and reduced capacity for self-appraisal and problem-solving), as well as any lack of emotional and behavioural control.

In the confusion of the present and the uncertainty about the future there is a tendency for the person with neurological disability to cling to the illusory security of the past. Others may recognize the need for change, but make decisions (such as change of job) that do not take due account of the restrictions arising from their disability, leading to repeated failure, loss of both confidence and self-belief. As previously noted (Carpenter & Tyerman, 1999) commonly observed difficulties in long-term adjustment include the following: preoccupation with lost skills/roles (with a failure to recognize remaining skills and potential); continued striving for unrealistic or even 100% recovery (delaying or limiting positive adjustments); repeated failure and loss of confidence/self-belief (often arising from lack of insight and/or clinging to prior aspirations and standards that can no longer be met); social withdrawal due to fear of loss of emotional and/or behavioural control; strained family relationships (possibly exacerbated by a lack of under-standing of the family impact); and social isolation.

Prigatano (1995) highlights existential questions about the meaning of life that often arise in post-acute rehabilitation (e.g., 'Will I be normal?', 'Is this life worth living after brain injury?'). From a psychotherapeutic perspective Miller (1993) illustrates how many of the problems experienced after brain injury concern funda-mental issues of life and meaning (i.e., death, isolation, meaninglessness and freedom). A crucial issue is how disability impacts upon the person's sense of self or personal identity. Early on in recovery, perceived changes tend to be viewed as temporary with no need to modify personal identity (Tyerman, 1987). However, this will inevitably be challenged by significant long-term disability.

Ellis (1989) suggests that the inability of 'survivors' of brain injury to observe and monitor their behaviour is a prime reason for the disruption of the individual's narrative (i.e., the story one tells oneself and others about one's life and experi-ences). It is suggested that the high level of abstraction needed to observe oneself is 'shattered' and the person is caught up in the ongoing experience of day-to-day life, losing touch with reality because of an inability to grasp the unique differences between events. An understanding of the difference between what a person feels and what he or she observes is considered to be critical for the self-monitoring process. A person's observational level of awareness of his or her own narrative often reflects their degree of functioning (i.e., the more aware of 'self' the person is the better he or she is functioning). As such, Ellis (1989) suggests that 'the primary goal of neuropsychotherapy is to help the brain-injured person form an integrated sense of identity, based in part on post-trauma elements of personality, as well as the person's personality before the trauma'.

Without specialist help, people with neurological disability may flounder: some feel stuck, described by one patient (BJ) as 'stagnating like a septic tank' (Tyerman, 1991); some become emotionally drained by their sustained attempts to find a way forward; and others feel that they are digging themselves into an ever deeper hole. As Burr (1981) observes, they may be grappling with an altered perception of their own worth, their new-found social stigma as a handicapped person, their dependence on others and their lessened sense of freedom of choice. As such, they need help to move from denial to acceptance, from a sense of loss to an appreciation of potential, from dwelling on the past to looking to the future and from seeing themselves as sick to seeing themselves as different. How might such adjustments be facilitated?

Neuropsychotherapeutic Interventions

The challenge of psychological adjustment to neurological disability has been viewed from different therapeutic perspectives, some reaching out from a neuro-psychological context (e.g., Tyerman, 1991), others drawing on psychotherapeutic frameworks (e.g., using Jungian ideas of a hero's journey to help patients to conceptualize the process of exploration, adjustment and redefinition: Prigatano, 1994). While specific approaches vary, a prerequisite for effective 'neuropsychotherapy' is a working understanding of the cognitive, behavioural and emotional constraints experienced by the person with neurological disability and appropriate strategies for managing such difficulties to enable the person to participate effectively in the therapeutic process. As previously discussed, an early requirement of therapy is the establishment of a coherent framework within which the person and therapist can make sense of the situation and work together effectively to find a way of forward.

Ellis (1989) suggests adoption of a model derived from dynamic psychotherapy, as well as an understanding of brain injury and deficits due to trauma. This has three phases: an initial phase of contract setting, building the therapeutic relationship and introducing techniques for communication; a middle phase that seeks to develop and communicate an in-depth understanding of new identity and self-narrative; and a final phase, by which time the therapist should have helped the 'survivor' to use different information-processing aids, support personnel and community services to better enjoy his or her life. Through therapy 'the idealized pre-trauma self' of the brain-injured individual has been allowed to 'die' and the 'survivor' has come to accept some, if not most, of the deficits and the many profound changes that have resulted from the trauma. Part of the primary goal of the treatment has been to help the 'survivor' integrate this acceptance of reality into his or her life in a meaningful way.

While self-awareness is viewed as vital to the process of psychological adjustment, there is also often the need for reconstruction, both of one's self and one's life. Judd (1999) stresses that brain injury is like few other experiences, because the people may be fundamentally changed in their personalities, emotions and abilities. As such there is a need to reconstruct meaning to their lives through interpreting their experiences and to integrate them into a new self-image.

In seeking to facilitate positive long-term adjustment within our community head injury service, a number of therapeutic components have proved of value in individual cases:

1. establishing the person's life history, aspirations and plans prior to injury through in-depth interviewing of the person (and family members as appropriate);
2. reviewing the nature of brain injury and its effects to establish (or reinforce if already established) an appropriate framework of understanding, through revisiting medical records, neuropsychological assessments and subjective/family accounts;
3. tracking the course of recovery (including past assessments and rehabilitation), as experienced subjectively by the person (through interviewing the client and family) and as reported by professionals, in order to place current difficulties in context;
4. explaining about the course of recovery and adjustment after brain injury in general and for the specific person, through use of charting of progress and recovery curves to illustrate contrasting recovery scenarios (e.g., 'high risk',

'expected', 'optimal', 'managed') or through analogies that both have personal meaning and involve various options (e.g., a car journey, mountain walking, sailing voyage);

5. evaluating in-depth changes in skills and life circumstances post injury, through undertaking a life review (and skills reviews if not completed in rehabilitation), charting changes in personal and social circumstances from pre to post injury;

6. exploring changes in self-concept and personal values arising as a result of injury through use of a head injury semantic differential scale, self-descriptions and through repertory grids, incorporating ratings or descriptions pre and post injury;

7. guiding and supporting the person in searching out and evaluating new experiences and redefining themselves and their goals accordingly through structured exercises (including, for example, fixed role therapy from personal construct psychotherapy);

8. establishing a clear and balanced view of how the injury has impacted on the person and then building/reinforcing a constructive image of an informed person seeking to cope positively with the effects of their injury and rebuild their lives;

9. re-evaluating current problems, identifying priorities, formulating/implementing appropriate action plans through guided problem-solving and option appraisal, compensating for the person's cognitive and behavioural/emotional constraints;

10. guiding the person in addressing high priority, achievable goals and in evaluating both the benefits and any costs/risks, with a view to attaining a more positive life position that is sustainable without undue pressure.

Drawing upon the above it has proved possible to achieve therapeutic change for those in difficulty, even many years post injury. This is likely to represent a series of small steps rather than any transformation in self-concept and life circumstances. However, a change in perspective on a particularly frustrating aspect of disability and/or a small positive step forward on one area of life is often sufficient to restore a sense of hope about the future. It has often proved helpful to liken the process of adjustment to a journey of personal discovery. The aim of this journey is to move from a position of denying, feeling controlled by or of battling constantly with one's disability and oneself, to a position whereby the person understands and accommodates their disability sufficiently to deal constructively with their altered circumstances and move forward in their lives. In facilitating this process it is important to take into account the individual's ability to maintain and build on the benefits of therapy. For those with executive difficulties and/or lack of self-confidence/belief, it is usually necessary to build in strategies to help the person to maintain progress. Therapy will often need to be faded out very gradually with provision for follow-up appointments to respond to the difficulties that may still arise.

CONCLUSIONS

In summary, people with brain injury have complex emotional needs. These can be addressed at different stages of recovery and adjustment through a combination of neuropsychological counselling, individual and group psychological treatment and long-term neuropsychotherapy. In our experience such interventions offer a structure within which to assist some people with brain injury to make sense of and accommodate changes in themselves and their lives, to manage specific emotional difficulties, to identify, clarify and prioritize unresolved personal issues, and in finding the strength and direction through which to rebuild their lives within the constraints of neurological disability.

A high priority for the future is for outcome studies to evaluate the effectiveness of such interventions and to identify the salient features of different psycho-therapeutic approaches for particular psychological needs. In the meantime, cross-fertilization of ideas from other fields of clinical psychology may be helpful in the development of psychological therapy for people with neurological disability. For example, the learning disability literature may help inform work with clients with the most severe cognitive impairments; cognitive behavioural therapy for delusional symptoms may help guide means of increasing self awareness; the personality disorder literature may help shape techniques for maintaining thera-peutic boundaries and increasing empathy; and the child literature may pave the way for maximizing the effectiveness of modelling techniques. However, for the time being psychological interventions for people with neurological disability are very much in their infancy with an urgent need for further clinical development and evaluation.

REFERENCES

Beck, A. T., Ward, C. H., Mendelson, M., Mock, J. & Erbaugh, J. (1961) An inventory for measuring depression. *Archives of General Psychiatry*, **4**, 561–571.

Beck, A. T., Epstein, N., Brown, G. & Steer, R. A. (1988) An inventory for measuring clinical anxiety. *Journal of Consulting and Clinical Psychology*, **56**, 893–897.

Becker, H. E. & Vakil, E. (1993) Behavioural psychotherapy of the frontal-lobe-injured patient in an outpatient setting. *Brain Injury*, **7**, 515–523.

Benedict, B. H. B., Shapiro, A., Priore, R., Miller, C., Munschauer, F. & Jacobs, C. (2000) Neuropsychological counselling improves serial behaviour in cognitively-impaired multiple sclerosis patients. *Multiple Sclerosis*, **6**, 391–396.

Ben Yishay, Y. & Lakin, P. (1989) Structured group therapy for brain injury survivors. In: D. W. Ellis & A-L. Christensen (eds) *Neuropsychological Treatment after Brain Injury* (pp. 271–295). Kluwer Academic, Boston.

Bergquist, T. F. & Jacket, M. P. (1993) Awareness and goal setting with the traumatically brain injured. *Brain Injury*, **7**, 275–282.

Block, S. M. (1987) Psychotherapy of the individual with brain injury. *Brain Injury*, **1**, 203–206.

Burr, M. (1981) The rehabilitation and long-term management of the adult patient with head injury. *Australian Family Practitioner*, **10**, 14–16.

Butler, R. W. & Satz, P. (1988) Individual psychotherapy with head-injured adults: Clinical notes for the practitioner. *Professional Psychology: Research and Practice*, **19**, 536–541.

Carberry, H. & Burd, B. (1986) Individual psychotherapy with the brain injured adult. *Cognitive Rehabilitation*, July/August, 22–24.

Carpenter, K. & Tyerman, A. (1999) Working in clinical neuropsychology. In: J. Marzillier & J. Hall (eds) *What is Clinical Psychology?* (3rd edn, pp. 157–183). Oxford University Press, Oxford, UK.

Cicerone, K. D. (1989) Psychotherapeutic interventions with traumatically brain-injured patient. *Rehabilitation Psychology*, **34**, 105–114.

Corrigan, J. D. (1989) Development of a scale for assessment of agitation following traumatic brain injury. *Journal of Clinical and Experimental Neuropsychology*, **11**, 261–277.

Delmonico, R. L., Hanley-Peterson, P. & Englander, J. (1998) Group psychotherapy for persons with traumatic brain injury: Management of frustration and substance abuse. *Journal of Head Trauma Rehabilitation*, **13**, 10–22.

Ellis, D. W. (1989) Neuropsychotherapy. In: D. W. Ellis & A-L. Christensen (eds) *Neuropsychological Treatment after Brain Injury* (pp. 241–269). Kluwer Academic, Boston.

Holland, D., Witty, T., Lawler, J. & Lazzisera, D. (1999) Biofeedback-assisted relaxation training with brain injured patients in acute stages of recovery. *Brain Injury*, **13**, 53–57.

Judd, T. (1999) *Neuropsychotherapy and Community Re-integration. Brain Injury Emotions and Behaviour*. Kluwer Academic/Plenum Publishers, New York.

King, N. & Tyerman, A. (in press) Neuropsychological presentation and treatment of head injury and traumatic brain injury. In: P. Halligan, U. Kischka and J. Marshall (eds) *Handbook of Clinical Neuropsychology*. Oxford University Press, Oxford, UK.

Langer, K. G. (1999) Awareness and denial in psychotherapy. In: K. G. Langer, C. Laatsch & L. Lewis (eds) *Psychotherapeutic Interventions from Adults with Brain Injury or Stroke: A Clinician's Treatment Resource* (pp. 75–96). Psychosocial Press, Madison, CT.

Langerbahn, D. M., Sherr, R. L., Simon, D. & Hanig, B. (1999) Group psychotherapy. In: K. G. Langer, C. Laatsch & L. Lewis (eds) *Psychotherapeutic Interventions from Adults with Brain Injury or Stroke: A Clinician's Treatment Resource* (pp. 167–189). Psychosocial Press, Madison, CT.

Levin, H. S., High, W. M., Goethe, K. E., Sisson, R. A., Overall, J. E., Rhoades, H. M. et al. (1987) The neurobehavioural rating scale: Assessment of the behavioural sequelae of head injury by the clinician. *Journal of Neurology, Neurosurgery and Psychiatry*, **50**, 183–193.

Lewis, L. & Resenberg, S. J. (1990) Psychoanalytic psychotherapy with brain injured adult psychiatric patients. *Journal of Nervous and Mental Disease*, **17**, 69–77.

Lindsay, W. R. & Olley, S. C. M. (1998) Psychological treatment for anxiety and depression for people with learning disabilities. In: W. Fraser, O. Sines & M. Kerr (eds) *Hallas' The Care of People with Intellectual Disabilities* (9th edn). Butterworth Heinemann, Oxford, UK.

Miller, L. (1991) Psychotherapy of the brain-injured patient: Principles and practices. *Cognitive Rehabilitation*, March/April, 24–29.

Miller, L. (1993) *Psychotherapy of the Brain-injured Patient. Reclaiming the Shattered Self*. W. W. Norton, New York.

Miller, L. (1999) A history of psychotherapy with patients with brain injury. In: K. G. Langer, C. Laatsch & L. Lewis (eds) *Psychotherapeutic Interventions for Adults with Brain Injury or Stroke: A Clinician's Treatment Resource* (pp. 27–44). Psychological Press, Madison, CT.

Pickett, E. (1991) Imagery psychotherapy in head trauma rehabilitation. *Brain Injury*, **5**, 33–41.

Prigatano, G. P. (1986) Psychotherapy after brain injury. In: G. P. Prigatano (ed.) *Neuropsychological Rehabilitation after Brain Injury* (pp. 67–95). Johns Hopkins University Press, Baltimore.

Prigatano, G. P. (1992) Neuropsychological rehabilitation and the problem of altered self-awareness. In: N. von Steionbuchel, D. Y. von Cramon & E. Poppel (eds) *Neuropsychological Rehabilitation* (pp. 55–65). Springer-Verlag, New York.

Prigatano, G. P. (1994) Individuality, lesion location and psychotherapy after brain injury. In: A. Christensen & B. P. Uzzell (eds) *Brain Injury and Neuropsychological Rehabilitation: Intervention and Perspectives* (pp. 173–186). Lawrence Erlbaum, Hove, UK.

Prigatano, G. P. (1995) 1994 Sheldon Berrol, MD, Senior Lectureship: The problem of lost normality after brain injury. *Journal of Head Trauma Rehabilitation*, **10**, 87–95.

Silver, J. M., Kramer, R., Greenwald, S. & Weissman, M. (2001) The association between head injuries and psychiatric disorders: Findings from the New Haven NIMH Epidemiologic Catchment Area Study. *Brain Injury*, **15**, 935–945.

Tyerman, A. (1987) Self-concept and psychological change in the rehabilitation of the severely head injured person. Doctoral thesis, University of London.

Tyerman, A. (1991) Counselling in head injury. In: H. Davis & L. Fallowfield (eds) *Counselling and Communication in Health Care* (pp. 115–128). John Wiley & Sons, Chichester, UK.

Tyerman, A. (1995) The social context. In: F. D. Rose & D. A. Johnson (eds) *Brain Injury and After: Towards Improved Outcome* (pp. 97–117). John Wiley & Sons, Chichester, UK.

Tyerman, A. (1997) Head injury: Community rehabilitation. In: C. J. Goodwill, M. A. Chamberlain & C. D. Evans (eds) *Rehabilitation of the Physically Disabled Adult* (2nd edn, pp. 432–443). Stanley Thornes, Cheltenham, UK.

Uomoto, J. M. & Brockway, J. A. (1992) Anger management training for brain injured patients and their family members. *Archives of Physical Medical Rehabilitation*, **73**, 674–679.

Whitehouse, A. M. (1994) Applications of cognitive therapy with survivors of head injury. *Journal of Cognitive Psychotherapy: An International Quarterly*, **8**, 141–160.

Zigmond, A. S. & Snaith, R. P. (1983) The hospital anxiety and depression scale. *Acta Psychiatrica Scandinavica*, **67**, 361–370.

CHAPTER 19

Neurorehabilitation Strategies for People with Neurodegenerative Conditions

Esme Moniz-Cook

Postgraduate Medical Institute of the University of Hull, Kingston-upon-Hull, UK

and

Jennifer Rusted

School of Biological Sciences, Brighton, UK

INTRODUCTION

Neurodegenerative disorders are by definition progressive in nature. Full restoration of function is therefore an unrealistic aim and rehabilitation usually attempts to reduce the rate of decline. Dementia is one of the commonest of the neurodegenerative disorders and will therefore be the focus of this chapter.

The broad goals of rehabilitation in dementia are to prevent 'excess disability' (i.e., disability unrelated to the actual degree of organic brain damage: Sabat, 1994), to promote 'rementia' (i.e., functional improvement in people with dementia: Sixsmith et al., 1993) and to maintain quality of life for both the person with dementia and their family. Cognitive neurorehabilitation is one of a wide range of psychological interventions that have been used with people with dementia and their families to achieve the goals outlined above. There are also a variety of pharmacological approaches to neurorehabilitation in dementia. This chapter will review the current status of cognitive rehabilitation for dementia and the likely impact of pharmacological approaches using 'anti-dementia' drugs.

The application of psychological theory and associated models of assessment, rehabilitation and evaluation of efficacy is an important concern of the clinical neuropsychologist. There are conceptual tensions in dementia that will affect neurorehabilitative practice. For example, much of drug therapy arises from an underlying disease model of dementia, with a focus on neurodegenerative, pathological changes in the brain, and clinically significant outcome is usually measured in terms of the maintenance of cognitive function at or near pretreatment or

Clinical Neuropsychology: A Practical Guide to Assessment and Management for Clinicians.
Edited by L.H. Goldstein and J.E. McNeil. © 2004 John Wiley & Sons, Ltd.

'baseline' levels (Orgogozo, 2000). In comparison, psychological approaches are concerned with models of cognition and neuropsychological functioning, motivation, emotion, coping and behaviour. They may also embrace the 'alternative paradigm to the disease model' (Kitwood, 1996), where the interactions between biology, phenomenology, attitudes, motivation, emotion, self-concept and the social context are incorporated into the programme of rehabilitation. Here, clinical outcomes include the maintenance of cognitive competence, activities of daily living, mood, day-to-day experiences, ability to cope with the disease, the prevention of excess social and psychological disability and the experience of 'burden' and stress in families. Cross-fertilization between the pharmacological and non-pharmacological approaches to rehabilitation and the measurement of clinical outcome is a necessary process for a comprehensive evaluation of the options available to people with dementia and their families.

Much of the research in both cognitive rehabilitation and the anti-dementia drugs has occurred with people with Alzheimer's disease (DAT = dementia Alzheimer type). However, about 40% of people with dementia are thought to have one of the other dementias. In addition, neuropsychological presentations may vary across or within disease type. For example, within DAT, cognitive profiles are not homogeneous (Fleischman & Gabrieli, 1999) and in multi-infarct dementia (MID) performance is usually dependent on the location of vascular damage. Frontal (or frontotemporal) lobe dementia (FLD) can present with different combinations of the range of dysexecutive problems (Mateer, 1999), and particular anatomical lesions (i.e., dorsolateral prefrontal, mesial frontal or orbitofrontal) may be characterized by different behavioural profiles (Campbell et al., 2001). Therefore, even within dementia subtypes, not all patients will have the same neurobehavioural deficits and each area of difficulty may require a different rehabilitative strategy. Neuropsychological practice has much to offer in developing rehabilitation programmes designed to ensure that a person with dementia, irrespective of diagnosis, may be assisted in a meaningful way to achieve the broad goals of rehabilitation that were outlined earlier. The remainder of this chapter explores some of the strategies that have been developed for neurorehabilitation in dementia. The range and scope of cognitive rehabilitation will be considered, and this will be followed by an examination of the impact of pharmacological intervention.

COGNITIVE REHABILITATION

Reality Orientation and Reminiscence Therapy

Historically, the two most common approaches to memory rehabilitation in dementia have been reality orientation (RO) and reminiscence therapy (RT). RO was the first of the psychological therapies that was developed for people with dementia and its primary aim was to improve orientation. Traditional 'classroom' RO usually involved small structured group sessions where a variety of materials were used to enhance general orientation. 'Informal' or continuous RO was developed to emphasize the positive aspects of the person's behaviour, used strengths in order to meet needs in the area of orientation and included environmental adaptation and the use of cues, signposting and memory aids to maintain orientation. RT was originally developed for people without dementia and widened its horizons to access and maintain autobiographical memory in people with dementia (see Schweitzer, 1998). Structured RT group activities used a variety of items and activities to stimulate past, enjoyable, personal memories in people with dementia. Together these two therapies therefore aimed to maintain or improve orientation and autobiographical memory, through continuous presentation and repetition of material. Two recent Cochrane Systematic Reviews on the effectiveness of RO and RT (Spector et al., 2000a, b) concluded that there was some evidence for the efficacy of RO on cognition and behaviour, but that there was insufficient evidence for the efficacy of RT, since only one quasi-experimental study had been documented. One of the more influential studies in the RO Cochrane review was that of Breuil et al. (1994), who used generalized cognitive stimulation within a single-blind randomized controlled design. On the basis of the stronger studies within these two reviews, Spector et al. (2001) developed a 15-session 'evidence-based group intervention' and reported improvements in patient cognition, depression and global functioning (Spector, 2001). This has led to a recent revival of support for broad-based group approaches to improve cognition (Woods, 2002).

Gains in cognitive scores associated with group cognitive stimulation, including the aforementioned attempt to extend the scope of structured group RO, may be of limited value when compared with some of the serious difficulties of mood and behaviour that a patient and family may experience (Bird, 2000). Indeed, the reported benefits often fail to generalize to everyday difficulties experienced by people with dementia (Breuil et al., 1994; Holden & Woods, 1995). A more practical multi-component programme, which included aspects of cognitive rehabilitation, demonstrated positive outcomes on cognition and patient and family experience (Moniz-Cook et al., 1998), but it was unclear which of the components contributed to the outcome and the mechanisms by which success was achieved. Furthermore, even when programmes are focused on one domain (e.g., cognition), 'self-contained therapy programmes', such as generalized cognitive stimulation programmes (see, e.g., Moore et al., 2001; Quayhagen & Quayhagen, 2001), make the dubious assumption that cognitive deficits in people with dementia are homogeneous and may therefore lack theoretical and clinical justification. Tailoring individualized techniques to individual case profiles is one way to reconcile theory, practice and clinically relevant outcomes (Woods & Bird, 1999). Recently, there has been a shift in experimental design toward single case experimental studies (Camp et al., 2000; Clare et al., 1999, 2000, 2001; Moniz-Cook et al., 2003). The practical application of one-to-one approaches, however, will necessarily be limited, given the cost in both human time and resources.

New Learning in Dementia: Strategies for Encoding and Retrieval

There is evidence that people with DAT do have the potential for new learning (Woods, 1996), that implicit memory is less impaired than the more 'effortful' explicit systems and that patients may have greater difficulty in acquisition and encoding, but that once information has been encoded, retrieval is less impaired. Less is known about people with MID, who have more variable cognitive profiles. However, the issue of variability also exists in DAT, where in the early stages the degree of impairment of the explicit memory system is highly variable (Grymonprez et al., 1998), as is the rate of decline (Small & Bäckman, 1998). With respect to other disorders, Lewy body disease (LBD) is associated with severe and fluctuating difficulties with attention and frontal lobe dementia (FLD) is particularly associated with executive dysfunction, while memory itself may be less impaired. Research into cognitive rehabilitation in dementia has concentrated on the effectiveness of approaches that assist both encoding and retrieval of new material.

Strategies to improve encoding and retrieval that have been successful with other populations, were not considered possible for use with people with a dementia (Bäckman, 1996). Reasons for this may be that many of these programmes rely on effortful learning, which is particularly difficult for people with dementia. For example, the least successful of these programmes used internal visual and verbal memory strategies (Bäckman, 1996), such as visualizing a route or working with a verbal mnemonic and these tasks require considerable 'cognitive effort'. An internal strategy (PQRST = preview, question, read, state and test), which is commonly used to learn prose or detail from a newspaper article, has been shown to be superior to simple rehearsal in some brain-injured patients (see Wilson & Moffat, 1992 for a description and Chapter 7 of this book). With the exception of a case study that helped a person with DAT to achieve face–name associations (Hill et al., 1987), the use of internal memory strategies (including PQRST) appear to require too much 'cognitive effort' for the person with dementia. However, used alongside other strategies, such an internal strategy as a visual mnemonic may assist in teaching face–name associations (Clare et al., 1999). Indeed, most learning in people with dementia is enhanced when a number of methods are used simultaneously in training. Methods that are successful include: (a) setting up the task to include another modality, such as motoric cues—acting out a task (Bäckman, 1992; Bird & Kinsella, 1996; Hutton et al., 1996; Martin et al., 1985), olfactory cues (Rusted et al., 1997) or visual associations (Lipinska & Bäckman, 1997); (b) delivering the programme within a meaningful and interesting environmental setting (Moayeri et al., 2000); (c) building retrieval cues into the encoding phase of learning (Bird & Kinsella, 1996); and (d) allowing the person to generate their own retrieval cues (Lipinska et al., 1994).

Some rehabilitative strategies have concentrated particularly on enhancing retrieval, and one commonly used method is the 'spaced retrieval' or 'expanded rehearsal' technique. This strategy involves repeated recall of selected information at gradually increasing time intervals. It has been used in the management of word-finding difficulties (Moffat, 1989) and more extensively by Camp and his colleagues in remembering names of people or objects, locations and prospective tasks. It has also been used in training the use of external memory aids. Spaced retrieval strategies with behavioural problems have been described (see Bird, 2001; Camp et al., 2000, for reviews). These authors offer a theoretical and empirical case for the value of spaced retrieval in achieving outcomes that are clinically relevant, that can extend beyond the training session and that can be used by a variety of therapists and family caregivers. Spaced retrieval reduces cognitive effort, and the act of retrieval may also in itself have a mnemonic effect in enhancing subsequent retrieval success (Bird et al., 1995). It is likely that the training strategy engages implicit memory processes that are relatively spared in the earlier stages of dementia (Camp et al., 1996). However, the technique may employ explicit processing and some expenditure of cognitive effort at least in the initial stages, until retrieval eventually becomes automatic (Bird & Kinsella, 1996). The balance between implicit and explicit processes in new learning and acquisition is likely to be complex and mediated through different anatomical structures (Broks, 2001; Siegel, 1997). Fortunately, application of effective interventions is not dependent on a detailed understanding of this interaction.

Some explicit memory approaches have been carefully designed to reduce errors that may occur at the time of learning a new task or when reinforcing a previously learned task. This process of reducing errors has been described as the 'errorless learning paradigm' (see also Chapters 7 and 16 in this book). It is based on the principle that errors during the learning or relearning phase increase the likelihood of the error itself producing a memory trace and in this sense being 'learned', even if it is subsequently corrected. This reduces the speed of acquisition of the correct response. The paradigm has been used to teach face–name associations to people with DAT and to reduce repetitive questioning with a memory aid (Clare et al., 1999, 2000, 2001). As with the spaced retrieval method, errorless learning is assumed to access implicit memory, but again there is considerable debate as to which aspect of memory function is being facilitated through minimizing errors (Squires et al., 1997).

Implicit Memory Paradigms: Strategies Using Verbal and Procedural Memory

An approach that has been used to enhance verbal skills in amnesic patients is the method of 'vanishing cues', which was designed to take advantage of preserved priming or implicit systems in memory-impaired people (Glisky et al., 1994). It involves partial cueing followed by graded withdrawal of cues over the learning trials; this is sometimes called backward chaining. A related strategy is that of systematically adding cues over learning trials, and this is referred to as forward chaining. Forward and backward chaining have been used in conjunction to teach people with DAT the names and professions of staff (Van der Linden & Juillerat, 1998) and such information as telephone numbers and addresses (see De Vreese et al., 2001). Forward chaining alone was thought to be less effective than backward chaining, as it has the potential to increase errors during the learning phase, but these conclusions are not supported by the data. A combination of backward chaining (vanishing cues), expanded rehearsal (spaced retrieval) and mnemonics was used to teach face–name associations, but, when each was evaluated independently with one participant, forward cueing used on its own was more effective than the use of vanishing cues in isolation (Clare et al., 1999, 2000).

Procedural memory underlies the performance of an instrumental or motor task without 'effortful' or explicit recall of the material. In the case of acquisition of new material, learning rates for motor tasks are thought to be relatively preserved (see Woods, 1996) and, despite global cognitive decline, complex activities and routines can be retrieved accurately in DAT (Rusted & Sheppard, 2002; Rusted et al., 1995). Strategies to enhance procedural memory function involve breaking down the task into components and using prompting (cueing) and fading of prompts to 'reshape' the skills required to complete the target task. The aim is to provide support at the point where the sequence of the task is disrupted and, if necessary, at the point of initiation of the task. Using this method Zanetti et al. (1994, 1997, 2001) have reported improvements in daily living skills for people with mild to moderate DAT. These authors report that following three weeks' training of target skills, the speed of task completion was improved, there was some generalization to other 'untrained' activities, and the effect was maintained at the four-month follow-up. In Sweden, Josephsson et al. (1993) developed individualized programmes to train four patients on an instrumental activity of their choice (such as preparing and consuming a snack) using verbal prompts and cues, acting out and copying by the patient. They reported small successes with three clients, but only one person showed good generalization of skills. The fourth patient was unable to achieve success, probably because her anxiety interfered with the learning process.

Supporting Explicit Memory: Reducing Cognitive Load through the Use of External Memory Aids

Compensatory memory strategies provide support at retrieval and reduce the 'effort' or cognitive 'load' on explicit memory and attention. The development of a 'prosthetic environment' with signs and cues to assist the person (Holden & Woods, 1995) and the current growth of assistive devices or 'smart house technology' on design and architecture in dementia (Franklin, 1996) are examples of broad-based approaches designed to reduce cognitive load and maximize function in people with dementia. The efficacy of these techniques has yet to be established. In so far as they minimize the potential for divided attention during an activity, thereby reducing load on central executive and working memory systems, and limit the distractions of environmental 'noise' (Woods, 1996), they are likely to generate some benefits.

Early single case studies showed that it was possible to teach a person with dementia to use a diary to maintain personal information taught during daily RO (Woods, 1983). Clients could also learn to use a watch and diary or an RO board to enhance prospective memory (Hanley, 1986; Hanley & Lusty, 1984; Kurlychek, 1983). The spaced retrieval technique has also been used successfully for these purposes (Camp et al., 1996). One aspect of Josephsson et al.'s (1993) procedural memory stimulation programme relied on an external aid (a label) to assist patients in locating items required for the routine being trained. In another study, a prosthetic aid (personal memory wallet) was used to improve the quality of conversations, and these improvements were maintained for up to two years (Bourgeois, 1990, 1991, 1992; Bourgeois et al., 1997). The use of a memory aid to improve orientation and reduce repeated questioning with two patients has also been reported (Clare et al., 2000).

The experimental use of an electronic memory aid on the performance of seven ecologically valid prospective memory tasks has been reported recently (Zanetti et al., 2000), and some participants with DAT were included in a randomized controlled trial of a paging system to reduce everyday planning problems (Wilson et al., 2001). In the pager trial the authors attributed lack of success to participants with intellectual deterioration, and it is not clear whether participants with DAT were part of this group.

Neurorehabilitation and Behavioural Problems in Dementia

The successful use of external cues to ameliorate significant behavioural problems (such as overdosing on medication, screaming, resistance or assault during bathing, sexual disinhibition and physical or verbal aggression) in advanced dementia has been described (Bird et al., 1995; Woods & Bird, 1999). Patients with advanced dementia and severe behavioural problems may be taught to associate a cue with adaptive behaviour using the spaced retrieval technique (Bird, 2000; Camp et al., 2000). Bird (2001) reviewed the empirical evidence for the use of cued recall of adaptive behaviour in the management of behavioural disturbance. He concludes that it is possible to utilize the methods of spaced retrieval and fading cues to train people with dementia to associate behaviour with contextual cues and to retain this information over time. Intervening in behavioural problems in DAT is often confounded by the inaccessibility of explicit memory systems. An understanding of the processes by which implicit memory or apraxia can impact on behaviour may provide new routes to intervention for agitation and aggressive behaviour. Evaluation of the interaction of specific perceptual deficits and a person's implicit belief system may also generate strategies for remediation of such particular problems as agitated resistance (Moniz-Cook et al., 2001, 2003). In these reported cases, there is an implied new role for neuropsychological practice in the assessment of specific neuropsychological deficits that may focus a rehabilitation programme, in cases of advanced dementia. These new clinical interventions must be based on an adequate theoretical foundation. For example, Woods (1996) outlines how an understanding of the interacting cognitive subsystems model (Williams, 1994) may assist in developing effective communication and thereby reduce agitation in dementia.

In summary, the emerging research on cognitive rehabilitation suggests that if programmes are well designed and meaningful for patients, their families and staff caregivers, some of the day-to-day problems that are associated with progressive memory loss in DAT can be ameliorated. These strategies, however, are most effective if they are used within the broader framework of the person's own experience and perspective. Factors such as mood, the family and the social context can all influence clinical outcome (Josephsson et al., 1993; Moniz-Cook et al., 1998; Sandman, 1993). Furthermore, Bird (2001) argues that research should be problem-specific rather than attempt to produce generalized cognitive improvement, which he suggests is of little practical value in dementia.

PHARMACOLOGICAL INTERVENTION—THE 'ANTI-DEMENTIA' DRUGS

Consistent with the documented role of the cholinergic system in learning and memory, much of the therapeutic research in the past two decades has been aimed at treatments that may correct the chronic deficiency in cholinergic activity observed in DAT. All currently licensed cholinomimetics are cholinesterase inhibitors (ChEIs). Vitamin E and antioxidant drugs may also be of use for people who cannot tolerate ChEIs. Drugs that are currently under research include anti-inflammatory drugs, oestrogen antagonists and anti-amyloid approaches.

The ChEIs deactivate the enzyme responsible for the breakdown of the neurotransmitter acetylcholine (ACh) from the synaptic cleft, thus prolonging the availability of ACh at the synapse and promoting neuronal communication (i.e., the opportunity for a signal to be transmitted across the synapse). Three of the ChEIs—donepezil (Aricept), rivastigmine (Exelon) and galantamine (Reminyl)—have been licensed for use in the UK and approved by the National Institute for Clinical Excellence (NICE). Physostigmine, one of the earliest ChEIs to be studied, is poorly tolerated and is unlikely to be marketed. Tacrine (Cognex) can have serious hepatotoxic effects and in general is being replaced by its successors: donepezil and rivastigmine. The most recently licensed compound, galantamine (Reminyl), is a ChEI with additional action as an allosteric modulator of nicotinic receptors. It therefore has the benefits of amplifying activity in the ACh neurotransmitter system both pre-and post-synaptically, and there is also a reduced tolerance to the drug over long-term treatment programmes, which alleviates the need for dose adjustments over time (Scott & Goa, 2000). Although relatively recent, trials using galantamine have been probably the most positive of the ChEI research studies.

The potential of the licensed drugs to substantially improve cognition has been the target of considerable scrutiny. Although commonly described as the 'anti-dementia drugs', they do not claim to prevent or cure dementia and most clinical trials have reported decline in cognitive function after acute withdrawal, consistent with the view that the drugs are acting symptomatically to stall the disease temporarily. Indeed, the report by Burns et al. (1999) suggests that after six weeks' washout, all volunteers, independent of treatment group, were at the same point on all scales, implying a more rapid deterioration to baseline for active treatment groups on cessation of drug administration. These drugs can retard disease-related changes on aspects of cognition and neuropsychiatric symptoms over 2.8 years (Doody et al., 2001) and may reduce carer burden (Filit et al., 2000). Most studies also note that cognitive outcome measures return to placebo levels within six weeks of washout, with very few studies reporting any residual effects.

Most recent clinical trials of anti-dementia drugs employ similar methodologies, including randomized double-blind placebo-controlled group designs with chronic administration (in excess of eight weeks) of the drug. They may incorporate an assessment and optimal dose establishment period, following standard practice of physicians administering the drug, and most include an assessment at the end of a 'washout' phase to establish the association between the observed outcome changes and active drug treatment. Most trials last for three to six months in the double-blind phase, but may roll into an open phase with groups of 'responders' continuing to receive the treatment over a period of up to 32 months. Most studies have used a common core of global outcome measures, which allows for comparability across studies. Standard measures of global cognition are the Alzheimer Disease Assessment Scale-Cognitive Section (ADAS-cog; Rosen et al., 1984), which is a clinician-based interview, and the Mini-Mental State Examination (MMSE; Folstein et al., 1975). An ADAS-cog 'improvement' relative to placebo of 3 to 4 points over six months, is seen as a clinically significant effect of treatment (Wilcock, 2000). Usually, reported 'improvements' are associated primarily with stable baselines over time, which contrast with a deteriorating process and impairments relative to baseline for placebo groups. An exhaustive review of the effects of these compounds on global cognition in dementia will not be presented here. Clinical efficacy according to these criteria has been demonstrated in large, multi-site trials with donepezil (Burns et al., 1999), galantamine (Tariot et al., 2000) and rivastigmine (Corey-Bloom et al., 1998). Comparison of the two above-mentioned rivastigmine studies indicates significantly larger treatment effects on the ADAS-cog for one study (Corey-Bloom et al., 1998). The reason for this is not obvious, since performance changes on other measures, such as the Clinician Interview-Based Impression of Change (CIBIC) (see Schneider, 1997) and the MMSE, were comparable in both trials.

As noted previously, for many families cognitive changes may not be the most important outcome. Behavioural and psychological signs and symptoms (BPSD), including neuropsychiatric symptoms, are seen as important predictors of family distress (Donaldson et al., 1997), which in turn can result in the breakdown of care at home for the person with dementia (Jerrom et al., 1993). While drug treatments were designed to target those neurotransmitter systems implicated in cognitive deficits, the aspiration to bring about beneficial effects on processes that determine functional independence of the person with dementia was certainly implied. It is likely that improved basic cognitive skills, such as attention, concentration and processing efficiency, contribute to the successful execution of activities of daily living and to effective interpersonal communication. Few drug studies to date, however, have incorporated adequate measures of functional independence or quality of life, and this omission needs to be addressed (Winbald et al., 2001).

Of the measures currently used, many are global and based on clinical impression (see, for example, the CIBIC or CIBIC-plus; Schneider, 1997). Others have been criticized as insensitive, such as the Interview for Deterioration in Daily Living Activities in Dementia, used by Burns et al. (1999), or lacking psychometric rigour, such as the Patient Deterioration Scale used by Corey-Bloom et al. (1998).

Other measures have shown sensitivity to change, such as the Neuropsychiatric Inventory (Cummings et al., 1994) and the Disability Assessment for Dementia (DAD; Gelinas et al., 1999), which measures instrumental, basic and leisure activities. These may be useful in the monitoring of neurorehabilitative programmes, which include the anti-dementia drugs in clinical practice. Effects of the anti-dementia drugs on caregiver burden are difficult to assess, with the confounding role of caregiver attribution an obvious problem (Filit et al., 2000). In short, the evidence for donepezil, rivastigmine and galantamine suggests more robust treatment-related 'improvements' on cognitive than on activities of daily living and quality-of-life domains. Some trials with galantamine suggest that patients may need less carer involvement in basic activities of daily living (Tariot et al., 2000), but the validity of the measures remain to be established. Gains in all domains appear to be associated with an arrested decline relative to placebo-treated volunteers, rather than a real improvement from baseline. While concepts regarding quality of life remain operationally elusive, pharmacological studies may not in themselves be able to fully embrace this aspect, for either patient or carer.

There is a general consensus among authors that current cholinomimetic treatments appear to provide greatest benefit, both in terms of the size of the improvement and the period over which the improvement can be sustained, when administered to volunteers in the early stages of dementia. The exact operational definition of the 'early stages of dementia' is unclear, but an MMSE score of 18 and above (mild dementia) is often used. In addition, there is some suggestion that apolipoprotein E-4 (APO-E4) genotype may be a modulating factor in treatment with the ChEI tacrine (Farlow et al., 1996) and that men may respond more favourably to treatment than women (MacGowan et al., 1998). The significance of these reported interactions is difficult to interpret since the studies have generally used small numbers of volunteers. In contrast a larger scale trial with galantamine reported no evidence of an interaction between treatment efficacy and APO-E4 genotype (Raskind et al., 2000). Clearly, on a practical level, it is important to continue to work to establish the predictors of positive response to treatments, but, at present, this seems some way off and there are no reliable indicators for use in day-to-day clinical practice.

Since chronic degeneration of cholinergic systems is a primary feature of DAT, these drugs tend to be selectively prescribed to people whose clinical symptoms are consistent with DAT. However, they may also alleviate cognitive deficits in people with vascular dementia (Moretti et al., 2000) and with LBD (McKeith et al., 2000). For people with these types of dementia, the mechanism of action is likely to include more indirect and non-specific effects than in the DAT population.

NEUROREHABILITION IN DEMENTIA—COMBINING COGNITIVE AND DRUG TREATMENTS

Despite the shortcomings of the drugs currently on offer, the notion that there is a 'drug treatment' for dementia may have a profound effect on the person with dementia, the family and the GP. Indeed, the growing demand for evaluation and diagnosis since the licensing of these drugs may reverse the tendency for delayed recognition of dementia in primary care, which has been a major hurdle in the development of early intervention and support programmes (Iliffe, 1997). The expectations of people and their families with regard to the outcome of drug treatments is high, and, while these expectations may not be fully realized, there is now the potential for enhancing the attitudes to rehabilitation in dementia and suppressing the associated nihilism about early detection.

It would appear that the best on offer with currently available drug treatments for dementia is a window of opportunity to arrest the cognitive deficits associated with the disease process, with smaller and less consistent prospects for functional competence and behaviour. Dependence on drug intervention alone is clearly misjudged, and indeed prolonged periods of improved cognition and insight associated with drug therapy may raise ethical considerations (Post & Whitehouse, 1998), especially if this results in increased anxiety and agitation (Whitehouse, 1999). Cognitive rehabilitation techniques clearly warrant consideration in any treatment programme. Direct comparison of ADAS-cog score outcomes suggested that, for small improvements, the cognitive stimulation programme (Spector et al., 2001) was as effective as rivastigmine and, for greater improvements, was more effective than either rivastigmine or donepezil (Spector, 2001). Of perhaps greater interest is the recent memory training trial, which offered a ChEI with and without case-specific cognitive rehabilitation (see De Vreese et al., 2001). This concluded that ChEI use with memory training is superior in arresting decline in cognition and instrumental activities of daily living to ChEI use alone. Within the window of opportunity offered through ChEI use, there may be scope to introduce a programme of non-pharmacological intervention that may ultimately provide better longer term outcomes for the patient and carer. That is, improved alertness, attention and responsiveness might reasonably be expected to enhance the effective implementation of alternative programmes, engaging both client and carer in a positive cycle of effort, motivation and reward. This was reinforced by an evidence-based review on recommendations for treatment in the USA (Doody et al., 2001). The potential of a timely, combined package is obvious, and there is an important role for the clinical neuropsychologist in refining and monitoring case-specific rehabilitation programmes for individual patients and their families.

Transfer of research findings into clinical practice is not without problems. For example, Gifford et al. (1999) found that general physicians often prescribed the anti-dementia drug, tacrine, to people who did not fit the recommended profile for efficacy. They sometimes used inappropriate dosage levels, and the drug was given intermittently to patients by some care home staff. The reverse may also be true for some non-pharmacological intervention, particularly in the area of psychosocial approaches, where much of what is offered by clinicians and support services may not as yet have a strong theoretical or empirical foundation (Robertson et al., 1999). The present review on the theoretical evidence for rehabilitation should go some way to assisting the clinical neuropsychologist in formulating strong neurorehabilitative programmes that take into account models of memory, cognition, emotion and behaviour. Thus the gap between research and what is offered to individuals and their families may be narrowed. The need to focus rehabilitative effort at the symptoms that are the most disabling for the people with dementia, and their families, remains a challenge for both clinicians and researchers.

REFERENCES

Bäckman, L. (1992) Memory training and memory improvement in Alzheimer's disease: Rules and exceptions. *Acta Neurologica Scandinavica*, **139**, 84–89.

Bäckman, L. (1996) Utilizing compensatory task conditions for episodic memory in Alzheimer's disease. *Acta Neurologica Scandinavica*, **165**, 109–113.

Bird, M. (2000) Psychosocial rehabilitation for problems arising from cognitive deficits in dementia. In: R. D. Hill, L. Bäckman & A. S. Neely (eds) *Cognitive Rehabilitation in Old Age* (pp. 249–269). Oxford University Press, Oxford, UK.

Bird, M. (2001) Behavioural difficulties and cued recall of adaptive behaviour in dementia: Experimental and clinical evidence. *Neuropsychological Rehabilitation. Special Issue: Cognitive Rehabilitation in Dementia*, **11**, 357–375.

Bird, M. & Kinsella, G. (1996) Long-term cued recall of tasks in senile dementia. *Psychology and Aging*, **11**, 45–56.

Bird, M., Alexopoulos, P. & Adamowicz, J. (1995) Success and failure in five case studies: Use of cued recall to ameliorate behaviour problems in senile dementia. *International Journal of Geriatric Psychiatry*, **10**, 305–311.

Bourgeois, M. (1990) Enhancing conversation skills in patients with Alzheimer's disease using a prosthetic memory aid. *Journal of Applied Behavior Analysis*, **23**, 29–42.

Bourgeois, M. (1991) Communication treatment for adults with dementia. *Journal of Speech and Hearing Research*, **34**, 831–844.

Bourgeois, M. (1992) Evaluating memory wallets in conversations with persons with dementia. *Journal of Speech and Hearing Research*, **35** (December), 1344–1357.

Bourgeois, M., Burgio, L., Schulz, R., Beach, S. & Palmer, B. (1997) Modifying repetitive verbalisations of community dwelling patients with AD. *Gerontologist*, **37**, 30–39.

Breuil, V., Rotrou, J. de, Forette, F., Tortrat, D., Ganasia-Ganem, A., Frambourt, A. et al. (1994) Cognitive stimulation of patients with dementia: Preliminary results. *International Journal of Geriatric Psychiatry*, **9**, 211–217.

Broks, P. (2001) The sea horse and the almond. *Granta*, autumn, 239–255.

Burns, A., Rosser, M., Hecker, J., Gauthier, S., Petit, H., Moller, H. et al. (1999) The effects of donepezil in Alzheimer's Disease—results from a multinational trial. *Dementia and Geriatric Cognitive Disorders*, **10**, 237–244.

Camp, C., Foss, J. W., O'Hanlon, A. & Stevens, A. (1996) Memory intervention for persons with dementia. *Applied Cognitive Psychology*, **10**, 193–210.

Camp, C., Bird, M. & Cherry, K. (2000) Retrieval strategies as a rehabilitation aid for cognitive loss in pathological aging. In: R. D. Hill, L. Bäckman & A. S. Neely (eds) *Cognitive Rehabilitation in Old Age* (pp. 224–248). Oxford University Press, Oxford, UK.

Campbell, J., Duffy, J. & Salloway, S. (2001) Treatment strategies for patients with dysexecutive syndromes. In: S. P. Salloway, P. F. Malloy & J. D. Duffy (eds) *The Frontal Lobes and Neuropsychiatric Syndrome* (pp. 153–166). American Psychiatric Publishing Inc., Washington.

Clare, L., Wilson, B., Breen, K. & Hodges, J. R. (1999) Errorless learning of face–name associations in early Alzheimer's disease. *Neurocase*, **5**, 37–46.

Clare, L., Wilson, B., Carter, G., Gosses, A., Breen, K. & Hodges, J. R. (2000) Intervening with everyday memory problems in early Alzheimer's disease: An errorless learning approach. *Journal of Clinical and Experimental Neuropsychology*, **22**, 132–146.

Clare, L., Wilson, B., Carter, G., Hodges, J. & Adams, M. (2001) Long-term maintenance of treatment gains following a cognitive rehabilitation intervention in early dementia of

Alzheimer type: A single case study. *Neuropsychological Rehabilitation. Special Issue: Cognitive Rehabilitation in Dementia*, **11**, 477–494.

Corey-Bloom, J., Anand, R. & Veach, J. (1998) A randomised trial evaluating the efficacy and safety of ENA 713 (rivastigmine), a new acetylcholine inhibitor, in patients with mild to moderate severe Alzheimer's Disease. *International Journal of Geriatric Psychopharmacology*, **1**, 55–65.

Cummings, J., Mega, M., Gray, K., Rosenberg-Thompson, S., Carusi, D. & Gornbein, J. (1994) The Neuropsychiatric Inventory: Comprehensive assessment of psychopathology in dementia–NPI. *Neurology*, **44**, 2308–2314.

De Vreese, L., Neri, M., Fioravanti, M., Bellio, L. & Zanetti, O. (2001) Memory rehabilitation in Alzheimer's Disease: A review of progress. *International Journal of Geriatric Psychiatry*, **16**, 794–809.

Donaldson, C., Tarrier, N. & Burns, A. (1997) The impact of dementia on caregivers. *British Journal of Psychiatry*, **170**, 62–68.

Doody, R., Dunn, J., Clark, C., Farlow, M., Foster, N., Liao, T. et al. (2001) Chronic donepezil treatment is associated with slowed cognitive decline in Alzheimer's disease. *Dementia and Geriatric Cognitive Disorders*, **12**, 295–230.

Farlow, M., Lahrii, D., Poirier, J., Davignon, J. & Hui, S. (1996) Apolipoprotein E genotype and gender response to tacrine therapy. *Annals of the New York Academy of Sciences*, **802**, 101–110.

Filit, H., Gutterman, E. & Brooks, R. (2000) Impact of donepezil on caregiving burden for patients with Alzheimer's Disease. *International Psychogeriatric Association*, **12**, 389–401.

Fleischman, D. & Gabrieli, J. (1999) Long term memory in Alzheimer's disease. *Current Opinions in Neurobiology*, **9**, 240–244.

Folstein, M., Folstein, S. & McHugh, P. (1975) Mini Mental State. A practical method of grading the cognitive states of subjects for the clinician. *Journal of Psychiatric Research*, **12**, 189–198.

Franklin, B. (1996) New perspectives on housing and support for older people. In: R. Bland (ed.) *Developing Services for Older People and Their Families* (Research Highlights in Social Work No. 29, pp. 29–43). Jessica Kingsley, London.

Gelinas, I., Gauthier, L., McIntyre, M. & Gauthier, S. (1999) Development of a functional measure for persons with Alzheimer's Disease: The Disability Assessment for Dementia. *American Journal of Occupational Therapy*, **53**, 471–481.

Gifford, D., Lapane, K., Gambassi, G., Landi, F. & Mor, V. (1999) Tacrine use in nursing homes: Implications for prescribing new cholinesterase inhibitors. *Neurology*, **50**, 238–244.

Glisky, E., Schacter, D. & Butters, M. (1994) Domain specific learning and the remediation of memory disorders. In: M. J. Riddoch & G. W. Humphreys (eds) *Cognitive Neuropsychology and Cognitive Rehabilitation* (pp. 527–548). Lawrence Erlbaum, Hove, UK.

Grymonprez, L., Vanberten, M. & Mouly, C. (1998) Follow-up of atypical memory patterns in Alzheimer's Disease. *Neurobiological Aging*, **19**(4), 31.

Hanley, I. (1986) Reality orientation in the care of the elderly patient with dementia—three case studies. In: I. Hanley & M. Gilhooly (eds) *Psychological Therapies for the Elderly* (pp. 65–79). Croom Helm, Beckenham, Kent, UK.

Hanley, I. & Lusty, K. (1984) Memory aids in reality orientation: A single case study. *Behaviour Research and Therapy*, **22**, 709–712.

Hill, R., Evankovich, K., Sheikh, J. & Yesavage, J. (1987) Imagery mnemonic training in a patient with primary degenerative dementia. *Psychology and Aging*, **2**, 204–205.

Holden, U. & Woods, R. (1995) *Positive Approaches to Dementia Care*. Churchill Livingstone, New York.

Hutton, S., Sheppard, L, Rusted, J. & Ratner, H. (1996) Structuring the acquisition and retrieval environment to facilitate learning in individuals with Dementia of the Alzheimer type. *Memory*, **4**, 113–130.

Iliffe, S. (1997) Can delays in the recognition of dementia in primary care be avoided? *Aging and Mental Health*, **1**, 7–10.

Jerrom, B., Mian, I. & Rukanyake, N. (1993) Stress on relative caregivers of dementia sufferers, and predictors of the breakdown of community care. *International Journal of Geriatric Psychiatry*, **8**, 331–337.

Josephsson, S., Bäckman, L., Borell, L., Bernspang, B., Nygard, L. & Ronnberg, L. (1993) Supporting everyday activities in dementia: An intervention study. *International Journal of Geriatric Psychiatry*, **8**, 395–400.

Kitwood, T. (1996) A dialectical framework for dementia. In: R. T. Woods (ed.) *Handbook of the Clinical Psychology of Ageing* (pp. 267–282). John Wiley & Sons, Chichester, UK.

Kurlychek, R. (1983) Use of a digital alarm chronograph as a memory aid in early dementia. *Clinical Gerontologist*, **1**, 93–94.

Lipinska, B. & Bäckman, L. (1997) Encoding-retrieval interactions in mild Alzheimer's disease: The role of access to categorical information. *Brain and Cognition*, **34**, 274–286.

Lipinska, B., Bäckman, L., Mantyla, T. & Viitanen, M. (1994) Effectiveness of self-generated cues in early Alzheimer's disease. *Journal of Clinical and Experimental Neuropsychology*, **16**, 809–819.

MacGowan, S., Wilcock, G. & Scott, M. (1998) Effect of gender and apolipoprotein E genotype on response to anticholinesterase therapy in Alzheimer's disease. *International Journal of Geriatric Psychiatry*, **13**, 625–630.

Martin, A., Browers, P., Cox, C. & Fedio, P. (1985) On the nature of the verbal memory deficits in Alzheimer's disease. *Brain and Language*, **25**, 323–341.

Mateer, C. A. (1999) The rehabilitation of executive disorders. In: D. T. Stuss, G. Winocur & I. Robertson (eds) *Cognitive Neurorehabilitation* (pp. 314–332). Cambridge University Press, Cambridge, UK.

McKeith, I., Del Ser, T., Spano, P., Emre, M., Wesnes, K., Anand, R. et al. (2000) Efficacy of rivastigmine in dementia with Lewy bodies: A randomised, double-blind placebo-controlled international study. *Lancet*, **356**, 2031–2036.

Moayeri, S., Cahill, L., Jin, Y. & Potkin, S. (2000) Relative sparing of emotionally influenced memory in Alzheimer's Disease. *Neuroreport*, **11**, 653–655.

Moffat, N. (1989) Home-based cognitive rehabilitation with the elderly. In: L. W. Poon, D. C. Rubin & B. A. Wilson (eds) *Everyday Cognition in Adulthood and Late Life* (pp. 659–680). Cambridge University Press, Cambridge, UK.

Moniz-Cook, E., Agar, S., Gibson, G., Win, T. & Wang, M. (1998) A preliminary study of the effects of early intervention with people with dementia and their families in a memory clinic. *Aging and Mental Health*, **2**, 199–211.

Moniz-Cook, E., Woods, R. T. & Richards, K. (2001) Functional analysis of challenging behaviour in dementia: The role of superstition. *International Journal of Geriatric Psychiatry*, **16**, 45–56.

Moniz-Cook, E., Stokes, G. & Agar, S. (2003) Difficult behaviour and dementia in nursing homes: Five cases of psychosocial intervention. *International Journal of Clinical Psychology and Psychotherapy*, **10**, 197–208.

Moore, S., Sandman, C., McGrady, K. & Kesslak, P. (2001) Memory training improves cognitive ability in patients with dementia. *Neuropsychological Rehabilitation. Special Issue: Cognitive Rehabilitation in Dementia*, **11**, 245–261.

Moretti, R., Torre, P., Antonello, R. & Cazzato, G. (2000) Rivastigmine in subcortical vascular dementia, a comparison trial on efficacy and tolerability for 12 months follow-up. *European Journal of Neurology*, **8**, 361–365.

Orgogozo, J. (2000) New millennium: New expectations for Alzheimer's disease. *Dementia and Geriatric Cognitive Disorders*, **11**, 1–2.

Post, S. & Whitehouse, P. (1998) Emerging anti-dementia drugs: Preliminary ethical view. *Journal of the American Geriatric Society*, **46**, 784–787.

Quayhagen, M. P. & Quayhagen, M. (2001) Testing of a cognitive stimulation intervention for dementia caregiving dyads. *Neuropsychological Rehabilitation. Special Issue: Cognitive Rehabilitation in Dementia*, **11**, 319–332.

Raskind, M., Peskind, E. & Wessel, T. (2000) Galantamine in Alzheimer's Disease: A 6 month randomised placebo controlled trial with a 6 month extension. *Neurology*, **54**, 2261–2268.

Robertson, I., Stuss, D. & Winocur, G. (1999) Epilogue: The future of cognitive rehabilitation. In: D. Stuss, G. Winocur & I. Robertson (eds) *Cognitive Neurorehabilitation* (pp. 362–366). Cambridge University Press, Cambridge, UK.

Rosen, W., Mohs, R. & Davis, K. (1984) Alzheimer's Disease Assessment Scale—Cognitive and Non-Cognitive Sections (ADAS-Cog, ADAS Non-Cog). *Journal of Psychiatry*, **141**, 1356–1364.

Rusted, J. & Sheppard, L. (2002). Action-based memory in Alzheimer's disease: A longitudinal look at tea-making. *Neurocase*, **8**, 111–126.

Rusted, J., Ratner, H. & Sheppard, L. (1995) When all else fails, we can still make tea: A longitudinal look at activities of daily living in an Alzheimer patient. In: R. Campbell & M. Conway (eds) *Broken Memories* (pp. 397–410). Blackwell, Oxford, UK.

Rusted, J., Marsh, R., Bledski, L. & Sheppard, L. (1997) Alzheimer patients' use of auditory and olfactory cues to aid verbal memory. *Aging and Mental Health*, **1**, 364–371.

Sabat, S. (1994). Excess disability and malignant social psychology: A case study of Alzheimer's disease. *Journal of Community and Applied Social Psychology*, **4**, 157–166.

Sandman, C. (1993) Memory rehabilitation in Alzheimer's Disease: Preliminary findings. *Clinical Gerontologist*, **13**, 19–33.

Schneider, L. (1997) An overview of rating scales used in dementia research. *Alzheimer Insights* (Special Edition), 8–14.

Schweitzer, P. (ed.) (1998) *Reminiscence in Dementia Care*. Age Exchange, London.

Scott, L. & Goa, K. (2000) Galantamine; a review of its use in Alzheimer's disease. *Drug Evaluation*, **60**, 1095–1122.

Siegel, D. (1997) Memory and trauma. In: D. Black, M. Newman, J. Harris-Hendriks & G. Mezey (eds) *Psychological Trauma: A Developmental Approach* (pp. 44–53). Gaskell, Glasgow.

Sixsmith, A., Stilwell, J. & Copeland, J. (1993) 'Rementia': Challenging the limits of dementia care. *International Journal of Geriatric Psychiatry*, **8**, 993–1000.

Small, B. J. & Bäckman, L. (1998) Predictors of longitudinal change in memory, visuospatial and verbal functioning in very old demented adults. *Dementia and Geriatrics Cognitive Disorders*, **9**, 253–256.

Spector, A. (2001) The development and evaluation of an evidence-based psychological therapy programme for people with dementia. Unpublished PhD thesis, University of London.

Spector, A., Orrell, M., Davies, S. & Woods, B. (2000a) Reality Orientation for dementia: A review of the evidence for its effectiveness. *The Cochrane Library* (Issue 2). Update Software, Oxford, UK.

Spector, A., Orrell, M., Davies, S. & Woods, B. (2000b) Reminiscence Therapy for dementia: A review of the evidence for its effectiveness. *The Cochrane Library* (Issue 2). Update Software, Oxford, UK.

Spector, A., Orrell, M., Davies, S. & Woods, B. (2001) Can reality reorientation be rehabilitated? Development and piloting of an evidence-based programme of cognition-based therapy for people with dementia. *Neuropsychological Rehabilitation. Special Issue: Cognitive Rehabilitation in Dementia*, **11**, 377–397.

Squires, E. J., Hunkin, N. M. & Parkin, A. J. (1997) Errorless learning of novel associations in amnesia. *Neuropsychologia*, **35**, 1103–1110.

Tariot, P. N., Solomon, P. R. & Morris, J. C. (2000) A 5 month randomised placebo-controlled trial of galantamine in AD. *Neurology*, **54**, 2269–2276.

Van der Linden, M. & Juillerat, A. (1998) Management of cognitive deficits in patients with Alzheimer's disease. *Reviews Neurologica*, **154**(Second Series), 137–143.

Whitehouse, P. J. (1999) Cholinesterase inhibitors in Alzheimer's disease. *CNS Drugs*, **11**, 167–173.

Wilcock, G. K. (2000) Treatment for Alzheimer's Disease. *International Journal of Geriatric Psychiatry*, **15**, 562–565.

Williams, J. (1994) Interacting cognitive subsystems and unvoiced murmurs: Review of *Affect Cognition and Change* by John Teasdale and Philip Barnard. *Cognition and Emotion*, **8**, 571–574.

Wilson, B. & Moffat, N. (1992) *Clinical Management of Memory Problems* (2nd edn). Chapman & Hall, London.

Wilson, B., Emslie, H. C., Quirk, K. & Evans, J. (2001) Reducing everyday memory and planning problems by means of a paging system: A randomised controlled crossover study. *Journal of Neurology, Neurosurgery and Psychiatry*, **70**, 447–482.

Winbald, B., Brodaty, H., Gauthier, S., Morris, J., Orgogozo, J., Rockwood, K. et al. (2001) Pharmocotherapy of Alzheimer's Disease: Is there a need to redefine treatment success? *International Journal of Geriatric Psychiatry*, **16**, 653–666.

Woods, B. (1996) Cognitive approaches to the management of dementia. In: R. Morris (ed.) *The Neuropsychology of Alzheimer's Disease and Related Dementias: The Cognitive Neuropsychology of Alzheimer's Type Dementia* (pp. 310–326). Oxford University Press, Oxford, UK.

Woods, B. (2002) Editorial: Reality orientation: A welcome return? *Age and Ageing*, **31**, 155–156.

Woods, B. & Bird, M. (1999) Non-pharmacological approaches to treatment. In: G. E. Wilcock, R. S. Bucks & K. Rockwood (eds) *Diagnosis and Management of Dementia: A Manual for Memory Disorder Teams* (pp. 311–331). Oxford University Press, Oxford, UK.

Woods, R. T. (1983) Specificity of learning in reality orientation sessions: A single case study. *Behaviour Research and Therapy*, **21**, 173–175.

Zanetti, O., Magni, E., Binetti, G., Bianchetti, A. & Trabucchi, M. (1994) Is procedural memory stimulation effective in Alzheimer's disease? *International Journal of Geriatric Psychiatry*, **9**, 1006–1007.

Zanetti, O., Binetti, G., Magni, E., Rozzini, L., Bianchetti, A. & Trabucchi, M. (1997) Procedural memory stimulation in Alzheimer's disease: Impact of a training programme. *Acta Neurologica Scandinavica*, **95**, 152–157.

Zanetti, O., Zanieri, G., de Vreese, L. P., Frisoni, G., Binetti, G. & Trabucchi, M. (2000) Utilising a memory aid with Alzheimer's patients. A study of feasibility. Paper presented at the *6th International Stockholm/Springfield Symposium on Advances in Alzheimer's Therapy*, Stockholm, Sweden, September.

Zanetti, O., Zanieri, G., Giovanni, G., de Vreese, L. P., Pezzini, A., Metitieri, T. et al. (2001) Effectiveness of procedural memory stimulation in mild Alzheimer's disease patients: A controlled study. *Neuropsychological Rehabilitation. Special Issue: Cognitive Rehabilitation in Dementia*, **11**, 263–274.

Index

videotapes 64, 218, 335
viruses 39
Visual Analogue Mood Scales (VAMS) 86
visual evoked potentials (VEPs) 65, 235
visual field disorders 229–32, 235–6
visual form agnosia 232
visual information 395–6
Visual Object and Space Perception battery
    (VOSP) 313–14
visual processing 229–32
visually guided action 232
visuoperceptual skills 292–3
visuospatial functions 229–48, 313–14
vocational rehabilitation 372, 375–6
voluntary movement disorders 211–25
VOSP *see* Visual Object and Space
    Perception battery

WAIS-III *see* Wechsler Adult Intelligence
    Scale 3rd edition
WASI *see* Wechsler Abbreviated Scale of
    Intelligence
websites, children's tests 285
Wechsler Abbreviated Scale of Intelligence
    (WASI) 132
Wechsler Adult Intelligence Scale 3rd
    edition (WAIS-III)
    arithmetic subtest 264, 266
    assessments 131–3
    memory disorders 154
    non-spatial attention 244
    older adults 307–8, 310
    test discrepancies 127–8
Wechsler Intelligence Scales for Children 3rd
    edition, processing instrument
    (WISC-III PI) 287–8

Wechsler Intelligence Scales for Children 3rd
    edition (WISC-III) 287–8
Wechsler Memory Scales 3rd edition
    (WMS-III) 149, 151, 154
Wechsler Memory Scales (WMS) 149, 151,
    154, 310
Wechsler Objective Numerical Dimensions
    (WOND) 267
Wernicke's aphasia 169, 174
WHO *see* World Health Organization
Wilson's cognitive rehabilitation model
    358–60
WISC-III PI *see* Wechsler Intelligence Scales
    for Children 3rd edition, processing in-
    strument (WISC-III PI)
WISC-III *see* Wechsler Intelligence Scales
    for Children 3rd edition
withdrawal symptoms 101, 109, 112–13
witnesses 338–41
WMS *see* Wechsler Memory Scales
WMS-III *see* Wechsler Memory Scales 3rd
    edition
WOND *see* Wechsler Objective Numerical
    Dimensions
word deafness 168–9
word list learning tests 151
word-finding difficulties 12, 176, 311
working memory 143, 147–8, 191, 345–6
World Health Organization (WHO) 353–5
writing 179–80, 238, 261
Wundt-Jastrow illusion test 236–7

X-ray computer tomography 66–7

z scores 122, 127, 129